British
Women Poets
of the
Romantic Era

Edited by Paula R. Feldman

British Women Poets of the Romantic Era

AN ANTHOLOGY

The Johns Hopkins University Press

Baltimore & London

This book has been brought to publication with the generous support of the National Endowment for the Humanities

© 1997 The Johns Hopkins University Press
All rights reserved. Published 1997
Printed in the United States of America on acid-free paper

06 05 04 03 02 01 00 99 98 97   5 4 3 2 1

The Johns Hopkins University Press
2715 North Charles Street
Baltimore, Maryland 21218-4319
The Johns Hopkins Press Ltd., London

Library of Congress Cataloging-in-Publication Data will
be found at the end of this book. A catalog record for this
book is available from the British Library.

ISBN 0-8018-5430-X

In Memory of my Grandmothers

Bessie Burka Feldman
and
Clara Ethel Marcus Leon

While lingers in the heart one line,
The nameless poet hath a shrine.

Letitia Elizabeth Landon,
"The Unknown Grave" (1837)

Contents

Acknowledgments

From its very inception, Jeanne West believed in this book, and her encouragement, support, suggestions, and editorial expertise have been invaluable.

My debts to many who have preceded me in considering the lives and works of women poets of the romantic era are apparent in my bibliography and notes. I would like to express my warm thanks most particularly to those scholars who have been of assistance to me not just through their published works but through their conversation and correspondence: Andrew Ashfield, Catherine Burroughs, Nora Crook, Stuart Curran, Roxanne Eberle, Anthony Harding, Kathleen Hickok, Nicholas Jones, Harriet Linkin, William McCarthy, Jeanne Moskal, Judith Pascoe, William Richey, Daniel Robinson, William St. Clair, Barbara Brandon Schnorrenberg, Judith Stanton, and Nanora Sweet. Their generosity and knowledge have made this a better book. Readers Jerome McGann, Anne Mellor, Jeffrey C. Robinson, Jack Stillinger, and Susan Wolfson offered valuable insights and suggestions. Others who have helped me in various ways include Stephen Behrendt, Catherine Castner, Faye Chadwell, Stephanie Dubose, Glen T. Dibert-Himes, Peter Garside, Gerald Graff, Adrian Le Harivel, Ina Rae Hark, Harrison Hayford, Trevor Howard-Hill, Linda Hughes, Martina Kearney, Susan Levin, Martin Levy, Carmel McKenna, Robert Newman, Buford Norman, Faust Pauluzzi, Donald Reiman, Daniel Riess, Ross Roy, and Bob Stuart. For research assistance I am grateful to Kreg Abshire, Dan Albergotti, Brian Cooney, Beth Dethlefson, Beth Diehl, Matthew Hanley, Kathryn Ledbetter, Gary Leising, Price McMurray, Lucy Morrison, Steven Morrison, Malia Myers, Anthony Ouellette, LaDonna Skinner, and Staci Stone.

I owe sincere thanks to my students at the University of South Carolina, who have inspired me with their insights and enthusiasm and whose responses to individual works helped me select poems to include here. I am particularly indebted to Jenny Ariail, Ellen Arnold, Lisa Baghdady, Ralph Edward Ball, Ned Borden, Louise Grant, Amy Hausser, Patrick Kennedy, Peter Larkin, Margaret Loose, Elizabeth Ouzts, Jan van Rosevelt, Thomas Shultz, Lynn Jordan Stidon, Martha Thomas, Mary Sidney Watson, and Carolyn Whetstone.

Financial support from the National Endowment for the Humanities, the University of South Carolina Venture Fund, and the University of South

Carolina English Department helped make this book possible. I have been assisted in my research by the staffs at the British Library, the Houghton Library at Harvard University, the Humanities Research Center at the University of Texas, the Library of Congress, the National Gallery of Ireland, the National Library of Ireland, the National Library of Scotland, the Scottish National Portrait Gallery, the National Portrait Gallery, London, and the Thomas Cooper Library at the University of South Carolina.

I am grateful to The Wordsworth Trust, Grasmere, England, to Rutgers University Press, and to Susan Levin for permission to reprint Dorothy Wordsworth's "An Address to a Child in a High Wind" and "To My Niece Dorothy, a Sleepless Baby"; to the Harry Ransom Humanities Research Center, the University of Texas at Austin, for permission to publish Lady Byron's "To Ada"; and to Oxford University Press for permission to reprint Jane Austen's "Verses to Rhyme with 'Rose'" and "On a Headache." Mary Tighe's sonnet "'Tis past the cruel anguish of suspence" and Maria Edgeworth's "On Chauntry's Statue of Watt in Handsworth Church," "To Mrs. Carr," "Laura Leicester," and "With a Dyed Silk Quilt Sent to Aunt Ruxton" are published courtesy of the National Library of Ireland, Dublin.

Finally, it has been a pleasure to work with the editors and staff at the Johns Hopkins University Press, most especially with Joanne Allen, Douglas Armato, Kimberly Johnson, Barbara Lamb, and Thomas Roche.

Introduction

> The Ladies, I should tell you, have been dealing largely and profitably at
> the shop of the Muses. And the Hon. Mrs. Norton . . . has been proving
> that she has some of the true *ink* in her veins, and has *taken down* several big
> boys in Mr. Colburn's Great Burlington School. Mrs. Hemans, too, has been
> kindly noticed by Mr. Murray, and has accomplished the difficult feat of a
> second edition. Apollo is beginning to discharge his retinue of sprawling
> men-servants, and to have handmaids about his immortal person, to dust his
> rays and polish his bow and fire-irons. If the great He-Creatures intend to
> get into place again, they must take Mrs. Bramble's advice, and "have an eye
> to the maids."
>
> —John Hamilton Reynolds (1832)

Although their influence and even their existence has been largely unac-
knowledged by literary scholars and critics throughout most of the twentieth
century, women poets were, as their contemporary John Hamilton Reynolds
nervously acknowledged, a force to be reckoned with in early-nineteenth-
century Britain.[1] Not only Felicia Hemans and Caroline Norton but Letitia
Elizabeth Landon and Mary Howitt were major players and serious competi-
tors in the literary marketplace of Reynolds's time. Their poetry was reviewed
in the most prestigious journals, respected by discerning readers, reprinted,
imitated, anthologized, sung, memorized for recitation, copied into commonplace books, and bought by the public. Before their time, prominent
writers such as Joanna Baillie, Anna Letitia Barbauld, Hannah More, Mary
Robinson, Anna Seward, Charlotte Smith, Mary Tighe, and others helped to
change the landscape of British poetry both in style and in subject matter.
They were active participants in, and sometimes instigators of, important
literary debates of the age.

There were, of course, many women poets whose books made no splash
at all, but that was true of great numbers of volumes by aspiring male poets

---

1. See "Letters of Edward Herbert, New Series. No. I," *Athenaeum,* 7 January 1832, 6, reprinted in *Selected Prose of John Hamilton Reynolds,* ed. Leonidas M. Jones (Cambridge, Mass.,
1966), 422.

as well. And certainly women who attempted poetry could be patronized, handicapped by their lack of formal education, constrained by needlework, child care, and other household responsibilities, and limited by their socio-economic status. But despite these difficulties and more, a surprising number of women succeeded in becoming an integral and enduring part of the literary scene.

Poetry pervaded everyday life then in a way we can barely begin to comprehend today. It was a major form of expression and entertainment for literate people. Newspapers and periodicals featured it prominently. Friends exchanged poetic gifts, sometimes composed "impromptu" for albums, and sent verse in lieu of thank-you notes and to commemorate births, deaths, and marriages within families. In social circles, poetry was the source of heated discussion, parlor games, and evening readings by the fireside.

This volume reflects not only the prevalence of poetry during the time but also gives a sampling of the varieties of women's poetic enterprises and the many ways in which women participated in this, the most prolific age of verse production. To this end, it chronicles the more obscure, such as Christian Milne, along with the more prominent, such as Charlotte Smith, including works by women in all economic and social strata, from the alehouse keeper Isabel Pagan and the domestic servant Janet Little to the socialite Lady Caroline Lamb. Some of the poets in this volume, such as Ann Radcliffe, Agnes Strickland, and Helen Maria Williams, are generally associated with other genres; however, their poems were well known to their contemporaries.

The strictures of social class, which associated commercial book publication with "being in trade," and the cultural emphasis on female modesty meant that many women who wrote poetry never published or, if they did, were careful to dissociate their names from their works. Yet modern readers forget that in those days poetry sometimes circulated widely in manuscript form; for example, Susanna Blamire's verse became well known through oral transmission and through other unpublished sources. Though it was taught in school, her verse was not printed until 1842, two generations after the poet's death. Writers such as Jane Austen, Lady Byron, Maria Edgeworth, and Dorothy Wordsworth wrote poetry solely for family and close friends. Maria Abdy, Elizabeth Cobbold, and Mary Tighe published only in small private editions.

Certain aristocratic women, such as Lady Anne Lindsay and Carolina, Baroness Nairne, took extreme measures to retain their anonymity and refused to acknowledge their authorship of much admired poems even when pressed to do so by those who had guessed the truth. In both cases, their names were not published with their work until half a century after it first became popular. At the other end of the socioeconomic scale, some poetry came before the public as the result of an act of charity; such was the case with Ann Candler, whose book was produced by subscription with her name appended to aid the solicitation. Even some of the most commercially successful books of poetry, for example, those by Felicia Hemans, Letitia Elizabeth Landon, Mary Robinson, and Charlotte Smith, were motivated by the poets' serious economic need.

But it is not just financial status that separates the poets whose work is contained in this volume. Although they all wrote between the years 1770 and 1840, they wrote in such diverse styles, about such varied experiences and subject matter, expressing such divergent political opinions, that in some cases they have little more in common than their gender. Some were friends who gave one another emotional support. Maria Edgeworth, for example, consoled Anna Letitia Barbauld when *Eighteen Hundred and Eleven* was attacked by the *Quarterly Review.* But others were bitter rivals and even enemies. Anna Seward rarely lost an opportunity to disparage Charlotte Smith, and after a quarrel Hannah More turned on the former object of her patronage and conducted a letter-writing campaign against Ann Yearsley. Some, such as Hannah More and Charlotte Elizabeth Tonna, were conservatives, while others, for instance, Mary Robinson and Helen Maria Williams, were liberals. Mary Hays openly espoused feminist principles; Jane West was outspokenly anti-feminist. Some, such as Elizabeth Cobbold, were married with many children, while others, such as Joanna Baillie, remained contentedly single all their life. Some, such as Letitia Elizabeth Landon, aspired to literary reputation, whereas others, such as Maria Logan, seemed indifferent to public acclaim. Emma Roberts and Anna Maria Jones traveled the world; Jane Taylor and Ann Batten Cristall appear never to have ventured far from their small, circumscribed spaces. Still, however they may have differed, evidence suggests that they read one another's poetry.

The works of the sixty-two poets contained in this volume are presented within the context of their lives, careers, and critical reputations. Certain biographical patterns provide clues about how, within a society that discouraged women's participation in literary culture in subtle and sometimes not so subtle ways, women established themselves as respected poets in London, Edinburgh, or the provinces—a few becoming professional writers and earning a reasonable living. Nearly all women poets came from dissenting households, a religious environment more likely to give them permission to develop and to exercise their talents. Most of them had an educated parent who taught them to read, gave them access to books, and encouraged their writing. Biographical accounts of their childhoods reveal a predictable uniformity—as youngsters they tended to be precocious; they showed an early interest in, and talent for, making verses; they read voraciously; they begged to be allowed to learn more than was customary for girls, and they were often accommodated. A significant number turned to writing professionally only as an economic expedient in a time of financial crisis, using their talent to support their families; Felicia Hemans, Letitia Elizabeth Landon, Mary Russell Mitford, Charlotte Smith, and Ann Yearsley fit this mold. As adults, the most successful found a mentor to guide their continued intellectual development and to introduce them to people who could advance their ambitions. Many were savvy in exploiting family connections or other relationships to gain access to publication.

None, of course, not even the most socially advantaged, had a university education, and many were essentially self-taught. But in certain ways what they felt to be a grave handicap, the lack of a classical education, may have contributed to their originality: since they were not trained in the conventional manner, their work could be more innovative. Contemporary critics often notice their talent or "genius" while deploring the "incorrectness" of their verse.

It is useful to look at women poets together, apart from their male contemporaries, not because of any common ideology (for which one will search in vain) but because their varied perspectives on the world were all shaped by a personal struggle with patriarchal constraints. All of them constructed a poetic self within an environment where artistic expectations were highly gendered. It is revealing to examine their diverse strategies for coming to terms with the tension between their society's concepts of being a writer and a woman, an artist and a daughter, a poet and a mother or a wife. To group them together for reading or study does not mean that we subscribe to the confining essentialist notions of female authorship current during their own era (with which many of them concurred and which many at times even exploited). But it does put us in a better position to see how they departed from gendered expectations, writing, for example, about such "unfeminine" subjects as politics, war, and economics, though sometimes that departure had a disastrous effect on their careers, as in the case of Anna Letitia Barbauld.

To read a volume of poetry by women only allows us to notice and to ponder why it was that women were so drawn to certain motifs and symbols. Birds, for example, permeate verse by women. One may search in vain for the "correspondent breeze," but birds lurk everywhere, not simply as a symbol for ecstatic poetic creation as in John Keats's "Ode to a Nightingale" or Percy Bysshe Shelley's "To a Sky-lark" (though women certainly wrote their share of verse in this popular vein) but also as a perfect metaphor to explore the conflicting desires for freedom and for safety.[2] Birds yearn for release from their caged confinement in the domestic sphere, and birds take refuge in the security of that same cage after escaping from the life-and-death struggles of a vicious natural world. Sometimes, as in Helen Maria Williams's "Elegy on a Young Thrush," birds perish, having mistaken the succor of the hearth for danger. In Mary Howitt's "The Sea-Gull" or Ann Radcliffe's "The Sea-Mew," however, the bird reigns triumphant, enjoying its exhilarating freedom and power of flight. In these poems and others, women debate within and among themselves the virtues of domesticity measured against the excitement of liberty and its attendant danger. But the home itself is far from entirely safe; poetry within this volume explores, too, the disquieting way the secure veneer of the domestic sphere may give way to violence and tragedy (see, for instance, Helen Leigh's "The Revenge"). It unmasks the unnerving ways in which outside events, the home, and the internal world of psychic reality interpenetrate one another, as in, for example, Felicia Hemans's "Arabella Stuart" or Mary Robinson's "The Lady of the Black Tower."

Although the topic is not entirely unknown in the poetry of men, women poets seem to have been particularly drawn to the subject of opium.[3] Intrigued by its power, they celebrate the drug again and again not only for its ability to alleviate physical pain but for its capacity to alter consciousness. In Anna Seward's sonnet "To the Poppy" a woman tormented by love, "Misfortune's Victim," welcomes the kind dreams opium brings, dreams that lull her grief into nothingness. The speaker in Sara Coleridge's "Poppies" marvels that her child, innocent of the "sorrows of the night," little guesses "how good" the poppies are to her for bringing sleep "at midnight's darksome hour." Henrietta O'Neill's "Ode to the Poppy" lauds the "potent charm" of the "soul-soothing plant," which can disarm agonizing pain with its "soft Lethean power." But its power goes even further, for with opium "the mourner bears to live" and "the hopeless die." The speaker hazards that if suicide were not a crime, she would, with the aid of opium, "burst these terrestrial bonds, and other regions try." Maria Logan's remarkable poem "To Opium" celebrates the drug's mood-altering qualities. At opium's command "gay scenes arise / To

2. Poems in this category include, for instance, Elizabeth Bentley's "To a Redbreast," Sara Coleridge's "The Captive Bird with Ardour Sings," Mary Hays's "Ode to Her Bullfinch," Felicia Hemans's "The Wings of the Dove," Mary Robinson's "The Linnet's Petition," Charlotte Smith's Sonnet III, "To a Nightingale," Agnes Strickland's "The Enfranchised; or, The Butterfly's First Flight," Ann Taylor's "The Little Bird's Complaint to His Mistress" and "The Mistress's Reply to Her Little Bird," Helen Maria Williams's "Sonnet to the White-Bird of the Tropic," and Ann Yearsley's "The Captive Linnet."

3. See, for example, Thomas Doubleday's untitled sonnet beginning, "Poppies, that scatter'd o'er this arid plain," published in *Sixty-five Sonnets* (London, 1818).

charm my raptur'd sight," and the drug, she says, revives her poetic powers. In turn, her "Muse / Now pours the grateful strain," proclaiming opium's "peerless worth." Logan, who lived for many years with chronic pain, identifies her own Muse with the poppy flower. The poppy, a weed in English fields, is a "neglected Flow'r." In the same way, her poetic talent is "to all the world unknown," and her "songs are lost in air." But if a respected poet such as Erasmus Darwin should champion the poppy, "Then Fame shall bid each future age, / Admiring, own thy pow'r!"

This volume also contains sonnets, odes, elegies, satires, songs, pastorals, anti-pastorals, love lyrics, epistles, long narrative poems, ballads, riddles, and a portion of an epic.[4] Women tried their hand at every conceivable poetic form, and individual poets, such as Mary Robinson and Ann Yearsley, were remarkably versatile in the number of forms they attempted. Some readers may also be surprised by the range of subject matter in these poems and the variety of tone. Contrary to stereotypical notions of writing by women, many poems in this volume are comic, from Jane Austen's witty "On a Headache" to the gentle, affectionate humor of Susanna Blamire's tour de force, "Stoklewath; or, The Cumbrian Village," to the accomplished parody of Catherine Maria Fanshawe's "Fragment in Imitation of Wordsworth," to the contemptuous comedy of Elizabeth Hands's "A Poem, on the Supposition of an Advertisement Appearing in a Morning Paper." Elizabeth Moody slices her contemporary down to size in her humorous critique "To Dr. Darwin, On Reading His Loves of the Plants." The Countess of Blessington piles up contemporary clichés in "Stock in Trade of Modern Poetesses" to highly comic effect.

Focusing on the poetry of women allows, too, the opportunity to see the extent to which social practices such as training young girls in music and expecting them to perform for small audiences informed their subsequent poetic practice and distinguished it from that of their male counterparts. Many poems in this volume originated as songs, for instance, Lady Anne Lindsay's "Auld Robin Gray," Carolina, Baroness Nairne's "The Laird o' Cockpen," Amelia Opie's "Go, youth Beloved," and Isabel Pagan's "A New Love Song, with the Answer." The traditional female musical "accomplishments" gave women both the opportunity and the incentive to compose verse and to set it to music. In song, moreover, their work became widely known, often long before finding its way into print. "Auld Robin Gray," the single

---

4. Taken from Helen Maria Williams's *Peru.* Other women who wrote epics include Elizabeth Cobbold, Hannah Cowley, Elizabeth Hands, Mary Howitt, and Ann Yearsley. Anna Seward invented a hybrid form that Erasmus Darwin termed the "epic elegy."

most popular contemporary ballad of the English Romantic period, was not only sung throughout Scotland but also carried into England by balladeers and strolling players, translated into French, and sung in Mary Wollstonecraft's *Maria, or the Wrongs of Woman.* In large part, through the works of women, the conversational language of song made its way into the poetic mainstream well before the publication of William Wordsworth and Samuel Taylor Coleridge's *Lyrical Ballads* in 1798.

The prefaces women appended to *their* books of verse were far more apologetic about the deficiencies to be found within than were those of male poets, for women felt profoundly disadvantaged educationally. Even so, certain major works in this volume, among them Anna Letitia Barbauld's *Eighteen Hundred and Eleven,* Charlotte Smith's "Beachy Head," Susanna Blamire's "Stoklewath; or, The Cumbrian Village," Mary Tighe's *Psyche,* and Mary Robinson's "The Camp," are virtuoso performances that can stand unblushingly alongside the most admired works by men of the period. However, with the possible exception of Felicia Hemans, whose collected *Poetical Works* were reprinted by Oxford University Press in 1914 as part of its Standard Authors series, none of the poets in this volume has been considered canonical in the twentieth century.

The fame of many women poets was not short-lived; anthologies from the late nineteenth century attest to the endurance of works not only by Hemans but also by Joanna Baillie, Anna Letitia Barbauld, Susanna Blamire, Ann Grant, Mary Howitt, Letitia Elizabeth Landon, Carolina, Baroness Nairne, Caroline Norton, Amelia Opie, Charlotte Smith, Jane Taylor, and Mary Tighe.[5] As late as 1929 Francis T. Palgrave's *Golden Treasury* still included selections from Anna Letitia Barbauld, Lady Anne Lindsay, Carolina, Baroness Nairne, and Caroline Norton.[6] Even before the present resurgence of interest in nineteenth-century women writers the twentieth century saw printings of books by and about Joanna Baillie, Anna Letitia Barbauld, the Countess of Blessington, Mary Howitt, Letitia Elizabeth Landon, Lady Anne Lindsay,

5. See, for example, the following anthologies: S. O. Beeton, ed., *Beeton's Great Book of Poetry,* 2 vols. (London, 1871); Charles Gibbon, ed., *The Casquet of Literature: being a Selection in Poetry and Prose from the Works of the Most Admired Authors,* 4 vols. (London, 1874–75); James T. Fields and Edwin P. Whipple, eds., *The Family Library of British Poetry from Chaucer to the Present Time* (Boston, 1881); *The Cambridge Book of Poetry and Song* (New York, 1882); Robert Inglis, ed., *Gleanings from the English Poets* (Edinburgh, [c. 1882]); Thomas Young Crowell, ed., *Red Letter Poems by English Men and Women* (New York, 1885); and Andrew Lang, ed., *The Blue Poetry Book,* 2nd ed. (London, 1896).

6. Francis T. Palgrave, ed., *The Golden Treasury, Selected from the Best Songs and Lyrical Poems in the English Language* (London, 1929).

Carolina, Baroness Nairne, Caroline Norton, Amelia Opie, Mary Robinson, Anna Seward, Charlotte Smith, Agnes Strickland, Jane Taylor, Mary Tighe, Helen Maria Williams, and others.

Still, it is clear that World War I and the modernists brought about a profound change in literary taste that left unread most poetry of the romantic era, that written by men as well as that written by women. Decades later, when critics and academics began rediscovering and reviving poetry from this period, they overlooked the works of women. By the 1960s five male poets constituted the "romantic" canon. The women were so effectively "not there" that they were even excluded from consideration as "minor" poets. They appeared in literary history at best as footnotes and at worst solely in familial relation to the "major" male writers.[7] It is no accident that now, at a point in history when women constitute more than half of all students attending college, when publishers recognize as never before the purchasing power of women readers, when women in unprecedented numbers have entered graduate programs in English and joined the faculties of academic institutions, more serious attention is being paid to the literature and the lives of women who wrote poetry during the romantic era. Felicia Hemans said of Mary Tighe, "Her Poetry has always touched me greatly, from a similarity which I imagine I discover between her destiny and my own."[8] Current readers are finding that the poetry written by Tighe and her female contemporaries not only strikes a responsive chord but inspires a rethinking of the meaning of the term *romantic*. To help advance that rethinking, to aid in the process of reassessing and revising traditional narratives about the evolution of ideas, poetic forms, and literary culture of that age, is a major goal of this book.

The plan of this volume was capacious, greedy: to gather together more texts by more women poets of the romantic era than have ever been available in one book in the twentieth century and to accompany those texts with in-depth accounts of the lives and careers of these poets in order to illuminate the peculiar conditions of authorship for women and to place their poetry in its social, historical, and literary context. The poems have a tendency to illuminate one another. In similar fashion, the lives contextualize one another as well as the poetry; conversely, the poetry provides a context for the lives.

---

7. For a discussion of the lack of representation of women writers of the romantic era in the anthologies of the 1960s and 1970s and their recuperation during the 1980s and 1990s, see the introduction to *Romantic Women Writers: Voices and Countervoices*, ed. Paula R. Feldman and Theresa M. Kelley (Hanover, N.H., 1995), 3–4, 269–70.

8. Quoted by Henry Fothergill Chorley in *Memorials of Mrs. Hemans, with Illustrations of her Literary Character from her Private Correspondence*, 2 vols. (London, 1836), 2:176.

This book resists the impulse to narrow the selection of poets to a new canonical few and instead tries to replicate, albeit only in a representative way, the multiplicity of women's poetic voices that the era produced.

The character of modern scholarship and critical debate concerning many of the poets in this volume is just now beginning to take shape. For others it is still unformed. Years hence, will there be a new canon? new canons? no canon? What poets and what works will most engage the scholars, teachers, students, and critics of the future? How will the romantic era be defined? Much remains uncertain. But having more expansive materials close at hand to inform discussion promises at least a brighter climate for debate.

Editorial Note

All poems in this volume were originally penned between the years 1770 and 1840. These boundaries are arbitrary, as any dates purporting to encompass the romantic era must be, and were chosen so as to include such important works as Lady Anne Lindsay's "Auld Robin Gray" and Susanna Blamire's "Stoklewath" from the early 1770s and to reach slightly beyond Queen Victoria's accession to the throne in 1837. However one may define the timespan of the romantic era, the years 1770 to 1840 take in its context.

Whenever possible, the copy text chosen was one published during the poet's lifetime, under her supervision, and before 1840. However, in some cases one or more of these conditions could not be met, for example, in instances of posthumous publication or unpublished texts, such as those by Lady Byron and Maria Edgeworth. The copy text is the earliest known authoritative version except in instances where the poet substantially revised and improved the text (for example, Mary Howitt's "The Voyage with the Nautilus," which she reworked after its first book publication in 1831) or where rarity has made the earliest authoritative version unavailable.

To preserve the historical specificity of the text, the original spelling, capitalization, and punctuation have been retained except that the long s has been modernized, placement of closing quotation marks has been regularized to precede a colon or a semicolon and to follow a comma or a period, and initial words in stanzas in which all the letters were capitalized in the original published version of the poem, now have only the first letter capitalized. In the occasional instances of an obvious typographical error in the copy text the error has been corrected and the editorial intervention noted.

Poets' own notes to texts have been reproduced in full under the assumption that the poet considered these notes a necessary and integral part of her text. The poet's name appears in italics at the end of these notes to differentiate them from editorial notes, which are not signed unless they are appended to an authorial note. Notes to poems are keyed to line numbers where possible and appear at the bottom of the page. Notes to titles, epigraphs, whole stanzas, and to anything that could not be keyed to a line number follow the text of the poem.

Poets appear in the volume in alphabetical order. A chronological listing would have been misleading for long-lived poets such as Joanna Baillie and Anna Letitia Barbauld, who actively published over the course of many years, and for poets such as Catherine Maria Fanshawe, whose work appeared in print decades after it was composed. The texts of each poet are ordered chronologically insofar as the chronology can be determined, generally according to the date of first known publication, which is the date that immediately follows the text. The date of the copy text is given in the "Texts Used" section, following the headnote. Dating of poems is often tentative, however, for many poems first saw publication in periodicals that are now obscure and were frequently published anonymously, under pseudonyms or under different titles, making these early texts difficult to discover.

"Sources for Headnotes," arranged by author, includes only sources not cited in notes to headnotes. The following abbreviations are used in notes to identify frequently cited sources:

Allibone, *Critical Dictionary*	Samuel Austin Allibone. *A Critical Dictionary of English Literature and British and American Authors Living and Deceased from the Earliest Accounts to the Latter Half of the Nineteenth Century.* 3 vols. Philadelphia, 1870–71.
Boyle, *Index*	Andrew Boyle. *An Index to the Annuals,* Vol. 1, *The Authors (1820–1850).* Worcester, 1967.
DLB	*Dictionary of Literary Biography.* Various editors. 167 vols. Detroit, 1978–.
DNB	Leslie Stephen and Sidney Lee, eds. *Dictionary of National Biography.* 22 vols. London, 1917.
Feminist Companion	Virginia Blain, Patricia Clements, and Isobel Grundy, eds. *The Feminist Companion to Literature in English: Women Writers from the Middle Ages to the Present.* New Haven, 1990.
Landry, *Muses of Resistance*	Donna Landry. *The Muses of Resistance: Laboring-Class Women's Poetry in Britain, 1739–1796.* Cambridge, 1990.
Lonsdale, *Eighteenth-Century Women Poets*	Roger Lonsdale, ed. *Eighteenth-Century Women Poets: An Oxford Anthology.* Oxford, 1989.
Mitford, *Recollections*	Mary Russell Mitford, *Recollections of a Literary Life; or, Books, Places, and People.* New York, 1852.
N&Q	*Notes and Queries.* London, 1849–.
Todd, *Dictionary*	Janet Todd, ed. *A Dictionary of British and American Women Writers, 1660–1800.* Totowa, N.J., 1987.

British
Women Poets
of the
Romantic Era

Maria Abdy

(c. 1797–1867)

Maria Abdy, called "Mira" by family and friends, was the daughter of Richard Smith, a solicitor, and Maria Smith, sister of Horace and James Smith, authors of *Rejected Addresses* (1812). A first-born child, she confessed in 1838 in a poem entitled "The Library" that

> Even in childhood's opening day,
>   My shining toys I oft forsook,
> And stole to solitude away
>   To hold sweet converse with a book.[1]

Abdy had a strong interest in science, but she felt frustrated by how few of its mysteries she could comprehend. Science, she observes,

> eludes my eager quest, still soars my grasp above:
> I add from her bright treasury new jewels to my store,
> Yet, miser-like, I murmur that I cannot grasp at more;
> Before me seem exhaustless heaps of mental riches piled,
> Yet still in Learning's highest gifts, I feel myself a child.[2]

In 1821, she married the Reverend John Channing Abdy, curate of St. George the Martyr, Southwark. When his father, the Reverend W. J. Abdy, died in 1823, he applied to the Lord Chancellor to assume his father's position as rector of St. John's, Horsleydown, and, contrary to all expectations, was appointed. The couple had at least one child, a boy, before Maria Abdy was widowed, probably sometime in the 1830s.[3]

For nearly three decades, from the late 1820s to the mid-1850s, Abdy pub-

---

1. *Poetry,* 2nd ser., vol. 2 (London, 1838), 74.
2. "Would I Were a Child," ibid., 85.
3. Arthur H. Beavan sets her marriage date as 1821, the birth of her son as having taken place nine years later, and the date of her widowhood as 1826. Clearly, one or more of these dates must be in error (see Arthur H. Beavan, *James and Horace Smith . . . A Family Narrative Based Upon Hitherto Unpublished Private Diaries, Letters and Other Documents* [London, 1899], 180–82).

lished poems in magazines, periodicals, gift books, and annuals. She is well represented in the *Keepsake* from 1835 onwards, but she also published in *Friendship's Offering,* the *Forget-Me-Not,* the *Book of Beauty,* the *New Year's Gift,* the *New Monthly Magazine,* the *Metropolitan Magazine,* and elsewhere, sometimes signing herself "M.A." She often took as her subjects problems and circumstances of modern life. While much of her work, especially the devotional verse, is pedestrian and ploddingly didactic, she could also be witty, in the manner of the uncles who influenced her, and she was a perceptive observer. Her comic pieces are her most imaginative and successful. "My Very Particular Friend," printed below, became well known. Eventually she collected her poems and published them, titled simply *Poetry,* for private circulation in a series of eight volumes brought out between 1834 and 1862. Abdy died on 19 July 1867.

MAJOR WORK: *Poetry,* 8 vols. (London, 1834–62).

TEXT USED: "My Very Particular Friend" appeared in *The Comic Offering* for 1834, printed in time for the Christmas season of 1833. Both texts printed here are from *Poetry.*

An Original Thought

Does the press wait for copy? I shrink from the task;
One boon from the Genius of fancy I ask;
I want not a subject, I want not a rhyme,
Nor metaphors florid, nor figures sublime;
Additional leisure I sigh not to claim,
And I feel I have *more* than due justice from fame;
I covet what cannot be borrowed or bought,
The gift of a striking Original Thought.

Could Memory desert me, I yet might succeed;
10   Oh! why was I suffered the poets to read?
Would that Campbell and Moore could at once be forgot!
Would my mind were not haunted by Wordsworth and Scott!
When some brilliant idea I have carefully nurst,
I discover that "Shakspeare had thought of it first,"

And my path with such glittering phantoms is fraught
That they really exclude one Original Thought!

The claims of the Annuals I must not neglect,
And two Magazines contributions expect,
Before me the leaves of an Album unclose,
(How I dread its bright pages of azure and rose,)   20
I must write an Address for a Charity soon,
And set some new words to an old German tune;
And how in the world are these works to be wrought,
When I cannot command one Original Thought!

Well, I bow not beneath a peculiar disgrace,
'Tis the fate of our present poetical race,
To live in the sun-shine of summers long o'er,
"Pensioned off," on the wit and the wisdom of yore;
But since Fancy her slights may yet please to repair,
In her lottery still I will venture a share;   30
And perhaps at this moment, the wheel may be fraught
With that capital prize—an Original Thought.

(1834)

My Very Particular Friend

Are you struck with her figure and face?
   How lucky you happened to meet
With none of the gossipping race,
   Who dwell in this horrible street!
They of slanderous hints never tire;
   I love to approve and commend,
And the lady you so much admire,
   Is my *very* particular friend!

How charming she looks—her dark curls
   Really float with a *natural* air;   10
And the beads might be taken for pearls,
   That are twined in that beautiful hair:

Then what tints her fair features o'erspread—
    That she uses *white* paint some pretend;
But, believe me, she only wears *red*
    She's my *very* particular friend!

Then her voice, how divine it appears
    While carolling "Rise gentle moon";
Lord Crotchet last night stopped his ears,
20   And declared that she sung out of tune;
For *my* part, I think that her lay
    Might to Malibran's sweetness pretend;
But people wont mind what *I* say—
    I'm her *very* particular friend!

Then her writings—her exquisite rhyme
    To posterity surely must reach;
(I wonder she finds so much time
    With four little sisters to teach!)
A critic in Blackwood, indeed,
30   Abused the last poem she penned;
The article made my heart bleed—
    She's my *very* particular friend!

Her brother dispatched with a sword,
    His friend in a duel, last June;
And her cousin eloped from her lord,
    With a handsome and whiskered dragoon:
Her father with duns is beset,
    Yet continues to dash and to spend—
She's too good for so worthless a set—
40   She's my *very* particular friend!

All her chance of a portion is lost,
    And I fear she'll be single for life;
Wise people *will* count up the cost
    Of a gay and extravagant wife:
But tis odious to marry for pelf,
    (Though the times are not likely to mend,)
She's a fortune besides in herself—
    She's my *very* particular friend!

That she's somewhat sarcastic and pert,
    It were useless and vain to deny: 50
She's a little too much of a flirt,
    And a slattern when no one is by:
From her servants she constantly parts,
    Before they have reached the year's end;
But her heart is the kindest of hearts—
    She's my *very* particular friend!

Oh! never have pencil or pen,
    A creature more exquisite traced;
That her style does not take with the men,
    Proves a sad want of judgment and taste;   60
And if to the sketch I give now,
    Some *flattering* touches I lend;
Do for partial affection allow—
    She's my *very* particular friend!

                  (1834)

Lucy Aikin

(1781–1864)

Niece of Anna Letitia Barbauld and daughter of Martha Jennings and John Aikin, Lucy Aikin was born in Warrington on 6 November 1781. When she was three years old her family moved to Yarmouth, where her father practiced medicine. Brought up on Barbauld's *Early Lessons* and *Hymns in Prose for Children,* Aikin realized early that words would be her métier. After complaining that her older brother George took half a tart intended for the younger children, she was admonished, "You should be willing to give your brother part of your tart." But she objected to the injustice, and her father, "who," she later recalled, "had listened with great attention to my harangue, exclaimed, 'Why Lucy, you are quite eloquent!' O! never-to-be-forgotten praise! Had I been a boy, it might have made me an orator; as it was, it incited me to exert to the utmost, by tongue and by pen, all the power of words I possessed or could ever acquire—I had learned where my strength lay."[1]

Aikin studied French, Italian, and Latin. Her father was her chief mentor. A close observer of the natural world, he taught his children to know and to love plants, birds, and animals of all kinds. In 1792 the family moved to London, where her father practiced as a physician until his health failed in 1797. Then he took his family to Stoke Newington and devoted the rest of his life, the next quarter-century, to literature. It was during this period that he published, in conjunction with Barbauld, the hugely successful and influential six-volume *Evenings at Home.*

Aikin was seventeen when she first began publishing articles in reviews, magazines, and the *Annual Register.* Believing that "the magic of rhyme is felt in the very cradle," in 1801 she published an anthology, *Poetry for Children, Consisting of Short Pieces to be Committed to Memory,* which included some of her own poems as well as several anonymous contributions by her aunt. It

---

1. Lucy Aikin, *Memoirs, Miscellanies and Letters,* ed. Philip Henery Le Breton (London, 1864), xvii.

went through at least eleven editions and continued to be reprinted as late as 1845. In 1810 Joseph Johnson brought out Aikin's long feminist poem, *Epistles on Women, Exemplifying their Character and Condition in Various Ages and Nations,* documenting not only the history of women's achievements but also their subjugation. It is an ambitious but uneven work, certainly not the equal of Barbauld's tour de force, *Eighteen Hundred and Eleven,* published two years later. However, a comparison of the poems shows the strong intellectual bond that existed between the two women. Aikin's next book was a novel, *Lorimer; a Tale* (1814); but she made her reputation with the two pioneering social histories that followed: *Memoirs of the Court of Queen Elizabeth* (1818), issued in at least six editions during her lifetime, and *Memoirs of the Court of King James the First* (1822), which the *Edinburgh Review* praised as "a work very nearly as entertaining as a novel, and far more instructive than most histories."[2] These innovative works highlight the literary, artistic, and social character of the times rather than the more usual parliamentary or military history.

Aikin lived quietly at Stoke Newington, principally writing and caring for her invalid father until his death in December 1822, when she and her mother moved to Hampstead. In 1823 she published a life of her father *(Memoir of John Aikin, M.D. . . . With a Selection of his Miscellaneous Pieces),* and in 1825 she edited *The Works of Anna Lætitia Barbauld,* including her valuable biography of her aunt, letters, prose pieces, and many poems not published during Barbauld's lifetime. To this day, many of Barbauld's poems can only be dated by the chronological order in which Lucy Aikin placed them in this edition. A short biography of Elizabeth Ogilvy Benger and two more histories followed: *Memoirs of the Court of King Charles the First* (1833) and *The Life of Joseph Addison* (1843), which Thomas Macaulay, writing in the *Edinburgh Review,* thought disappointing.[3] According to Aikin's own account, she knew "almost every literary woman of celebrity."[4] She was an accomplished conversationalist and letter writer. One of her correspondents was fellow Unitarian William Ellery Channing, to whom she wrote for many years (1826–42).[5] Aikin lived the

2. 37 (June 1822): 212–13.

3. Ibid., 78 (July–October 1843). The biography of Benger was published with Benger's *Memoirs of the Life of Anne Boleyn* (London, 1827).

4. Aikin, *Memoirs, Miscellanies and Letters,* 7.

5. Anna Letitia Le Breton published selections from both sides of the correspondence in 1874. She quotes a letter from Channing's nephew and biographer, William Henry Channing, in which he observes that "for many years, indeed, Dr. Channing regarded Miss Aikin as one of his most confidential European friends; and he wrote to her in consequence with the undisguised freedom of familiar intercourse. He valued her letters very highly for the liberal information given in them, as to all movements in the world of letters, of politics and of religion around

last eighteen years of her life with a niece, Anna Letitia Le Breton, first in Wimbledon and then in Hampstead.

At age eighty-four, she died from influenza (29 January 1864); her grave in the old churchyard of Hampstead lies next to that of her lifelong friend Joanna Baillie. In 1864 her nephew, Philip Henery Le Breton, published some of her letters to Channing along with other correspondence, miscellaneous prose pieces, and a memoir, quoting extensively from an autobiography.

MAJOR WORKS: *Epistles on Women, Exemplifying their Character and Condition in Various Ages and Nations. With Miscellaneous Poems* (London, 1810); *Memoirs of the Court of Queen Elizabeth*, 2 vols. (London, 1818); *Memoirs of the Court of King James the First*, 2 vols. (London, 1822); *Memoir of John Aikin, M.D. . . . With a Selection of his Miscellaneous Pieces, Biographical, Moral, and Critical*, 2 vols. (London, 1823); *Memoirs of the Court of King Charles the First*, 2 vols. (London, 1833); *The Life of Joseph Addison*, 2 vols. (London, 1843).

TEXT USED: The text for *Epistles on Women* is from the London edition (1810).

from *Epistles on Women, Exemplifying their Character and Condition in Various Ages and Nations*

from the Introduction

Feeling with gratitude of what her [woman's] heart and mind are capable, the scholars, the sages, and the patriots of coming days will treat her as a sister and a friend. The politic father will not then leave as a "legacy" to his daughters* the injunction to conceal their wit, their learning, and even their good sense, in deference to the *"natural malignity"*† with which most men regard every woman of a sound understanding and cultivated mind; nor will even the reputation of our great Milton himself secure him from the charge of a blasphemous presumption in making his Eve address to Adam the acknowledgement, "God is thy head, thou mine";‡ and in the assertion that

---

her—as to leading persons, new books and rising authors—and as to the tendencies of the times. And so heartily did he enjoy the originality, brightness, spirit, wit and shrewd sagacity with which Miss Aikin's opinions were declared, that, in the hope of inciting her to full response, he seems often to have suggested to her his rising thoughts, as if in half soliloquy" (*Correspondence of William Ellery Channing, D.D., and Lucy Aikin* [Boston, 1874], vii–viii).

the first human pair were formed, "He for God only, she for God in him."§
. . . I have simply endeavoured to point out, that between the two partners
of human life, not only the strongest family likeness, but the most complete
identity of interest subsists: so that it is impossible for man to degrade his
companion without degrading himself, or to elevate her without receiving
a proportional accession of dignity and happiness. This is the chief "moral of
my song";‖ on this point all my examples are brought to bear. I regard it as
the Great Truth to the support of which my pen has devoted itself.

*A reference to John Gregory's *A Father's Legacy to his Daughters* (1774), often
published with Hester Chapone's *Letters on the Improvement of the Mind* (1773).

† Mary Wollstonecraft, in *A Vindication of the Rights of Woman,* quotes Gregory, also
from *A Father's Legacy:* "But if you happen to have any learning, keep it a profound
secret, especially from the men, who generally look with a jealous and malignant eye
on a woman of great parts, and a cultivated understanding."

‡ Aikin slightly misquotes Eve speaking to Adam in Milton, *Paradise Lost* 4.637–
38: "God is thy Law, thou mine: to know no more / Is Woman's happiest knowledge
and her praise." Earlier in the same book, Eve addresses Adam as "my Guide / And
Head" (442–43).

§ Ibid., 4.299.

‖ See Edmund Spenser, *The Faerie Queen,* introduction, line 9.

from *Argument to Epistle I*

Subject proposed—the fame of man extended over every period of life—
that of woman transient as the beauty on which it is founded—Man renders
her a trifler, then despises her, and makes war upon the sex with Juvenal# and
Pope. A more impartial view of the subject to be attempted.

Decimus Junius Juvenalis (A.D. 60?–140?), Roman poet whose satires were widely
admired by eighteenth-century writers.

from *Epistle I*

> E'en while the youth, in love and rapture warm,
> Sighs as he hangs upon her beauteous form,
> Careless and cold he views the beauteous mind,
> For virtue, bliss, eternity designed.
> "Banish, my fair," he cries, "those studious looks;

Oh! what should beauty learn from crabbed books?
Sweetly to speak and sweetly smile be thine;
Beware, nor change that dimple to a line!"

Well pleased she hears, vain triumph lights her eyes;
10   Well pleased, in prattle and in smiles complies;
But eyes, alas! grow dim, and roses fade,
And man contemns the trifler he has made.
The glass reversed by magic power of Spleen,
A wrinkled idiot now the fair is seen;
Then with the sex his headlong rage must cope,
And stab with Juvenal, or sting with Pope.
Be mine, while Truth with calm and artless grace
Lifts her clear mirror to the female face,
With steadier hand the pencil's task to guide,
20   And win a blush from Man's relenting pride.

No Amazon, in frowns and terror drest,
I poise the spear, or nod the threatening crest,
Defy the law, arraign the social plan,
Throw down the gauntlet in the face of man,
And, rashly bold, divided empire claim,
Unborrowed honours, and an equal's name:
No, Heaven forbid! I touch no sacred thing,
But bow to Right Divine in man and king;
Nature endows him with superior force,
30   Superior wisdom then I grant, of course;
For who gainsays the despot in his might,
Or when was ever weakness in the right?
With passive reverence too I hail the law,
Formed to secure the strong, the weak to awe,
Impartial guardian of unerring sway,
Set up by man for woman to obey.
In vain we pout or argue, rail or chide,
He mocks our idle wrath and checks our pride;
Resign we then the club and lion's skin,

13 Spleen] "Passionate, irritable, peevishly angry" *(OED)*.
28 Right Divine] Mary Wollstonecraft, in *A Vindication of the Rights of Woman*, chap. 3, writes: "The *divine right* of husbands, like the divine right of kings, may, it is to be hoped, in this enlightened age, be contested without danger."

And be our sex content to knit and spin;   40
To bow inglorious to a master's rule,
And good and bad obey, and wise and fool;
Here a meek drudge, a listless captive there,
For gold now bartered, now as cheap as air;
Prize of the coward rich or lawless brave,
Scorned and caressed, a plaything and a slave,
Yet taught with spaniel soul to kiss the rod,
And worship man as delegate of God.

from *Epistle II*

What wonder then, the Western wilds among
Where the red Indian's hunter-bow is strung,
(Nature's tough son, whose adamantine frame
No pleasures soften and no tortures tame)
If, fiercely pondering in her gloomy mind
The desperate ills that scowl on womankind,
The maddening mother gripes the infant slave,
And forces back the worthless life she gave?*

"Swift, swift," she cries, "receive thy last release;
Die, little wretch; die once and be at peace!   10
Why shouldst thou live, in toil, and pain, and strife,
To curse the names of mother and of wife?
To see at large thy lordly master roam,
The beasts his portion and the woods his home,
Whilst thou, infirm, the sheltering hut must seek,
Poorly dependent, timorously weak,
There hush thy babe, with patient love carest,
And tearful clasp him to thy milkless breast
Hungry and faint, while feasting on his way
Thy reckless hunter wastes the jocund day?   20
Or, harder task, his rapid courses share,
With patient back the galling burden bear,
While he treads light, and smacks the knotted thong,
And goads with taunts his staggering troop along?
Enough; . . . . 'tis love, dear babe, that stops thy breath;
'Tis mercy lulls thee to the sleep of death:
Ah! would for me, by like indulgent doom,

A mother's hand had raised the early tomb!
O'er these poor bones the moons had rolled in vain,
30   And brought nor stripes nor famine, toil nor pain;
I had not sought in agony the wild,
Nor, wretched, frantic mother! killed my child."
Want hardens man; by fierce extremes the smart
Inflames and chills and indurates his heart,
Arms his relentless hand with brutal force,
And drives o'er female necks his furious course.

* "In all unpolished nations, it is true, the functions in domestic economy which fall naturally to the share of the women, are so many, that they are subjected to hard labour, and must bear more than their full portion of the common burden. But in America their condition is so peculiarly grievous, and their depression so complete, that servitude is a name too mild to describe their wretched state. A wife, amongst most tribes, is no better than a beast of burden, destined to every office of labour and fatigue. While the men loiter out the day in sloth, or spend it in amusement, the women are condemned to incessant toil. Tasks are imposed upon them without pity, and services are received without complacency or gratitude.

"Every circumstance reminds the women of this mortifying inferiority. They must approach their lords with reverence, they must regard them as more exalted beings, and are not permitted to eat in their presence.

"There are many districts in America where this dominion is so grievous, and so sensibly felt, that some women, in a wild emotion of maternal tenderness, have destroyed their female children in their infancy, in order to deliver them from that intolerable bondage to which they knew they were doomed." Robertson's Hist. of America, [3 vols. (Dublin, 1777)], vol. ii, 105.

Hearne describes the women of the Northern tribes which he visited, as wading through the snow encumbered with heavy burdens, while the men, themselves carrying nothing, urged them on with blows and threats. He mentions other particulars, also illustrative of the wretched condition of the American females, too numerous and too horrid for poetical narration.

Certainly Rousseau did not consult the interests of the weaker sex in his preference of savage life to civilized. *Aikin.*

from *Epistle III*

Rise, bright Aspasia, too! thy tainted name
Sails down secure through infamy to fame;
Statesmen and bards and heroes bend the knee,
Nor blushes Socrates to learn of thee.
Thy wives, proud Athens! fettered and debased,
Listlessly duteous, negatively chaste,
O vapid summary of a slavish lot!
They sew and spin, they die and are forgot.
Cease, headlong Muse! resign the dangerous theme,
Perish the glory that defies esteem!   10
Inspire thy trump at Virtue's call alone,
And blush to blazon whom She scorns to own.

from *Argument of Epistle IV*

Man cannot degrade the female sex without degrading the whole race. Ancient Germans—their women free and honoured—hence the valour of the
men, the virtue of both sexes, the success of their resistance to Rome. . . .
Exhortation to Englishmen to look with favour on the mental improvement
of females—to English women to improve and principle their minds, and by
their merit induce the men to treat them as friends.

from *Epistle IV*

Sons of fair Albion, tender, brave, sincere,
(Be this the strain) an earnest suppliant hear!
Feel that when heaven, evolved its perfect plan,
Crowned with its last best gift transported Man,
It formed no creature of ignoble strain,
Of heart unteachable, obtuse of brain;
(Such had not filled the solitary void,
Nor such his soul's new sympathies employed,)
But one all eloquent of eye, of mien;

---

1 Aspasia] Plato describes Aspasia as the preceptress of Socrates and says in his *Menexenus*
that she wrote the celebrated funeral oration of Pericles. She was a brilliant conversationalist
who lived openly with Pericles, a married man. As a result, he endured much ridicule and she
much slander. Pericles successfully defended her against a criminal charge of religious heresy
and corrupting Athenian women.

12 blazon] Proclaim.

10 Intensely human; exquisitely keen
To feel, to know: Be generous then, unbind
Your barbarous shackles, loose the female mind;
Aid its new flights, instruct its wavering wing,
And guide its thirst to Wisdom's purest spring:
Sincere as generous, with fraternal heart
Spurn the dark satirists's unmanly part;
Scorn too the flatterer's, in the medium wise,
Nor feed those follies that yourselves despise.

For you, bright daughters of a land renowned,
20 By Genius blest, by glorious Freedom crowned;
Safe in a polisht privacy, content
To grace, not shun, the lot that Nature lent,
Be yours the joys of home, affection's charms,
And infants clinging with caressing arms:
Yours too the boon, of Taste's whole garden free,
To pluck at will her bright Hesperian tree,
Uncheckt the wreath of each fair Muse assume,
And fill your lap with amaranthine bloom.
Press eager on; of this great art possest,
30 To seize the good, to follow still the best,
Ply the pale lamp, explore the breathing page,
And catch the soul of each immortal age.
Strikes the pure bard his old romantic lyre?
Let high Belphœbe warm, let Amoret sweet inspire:
Does History speak? drink in her loftiest tone,
And be Cornelia's virtues all your own.
Thus self-endowed, thus armed for every state,
Improve, excel, surmount, subdue, your fate!
So shall at length enlightened Man efface

34 Belphœbe warm . . . Amoret sweet] It ought to be remembered for the honour of
Spenser, that no poet has given such pure and perfect, such noble, lovely, and at the same
time various drafts of female characters. His Belphœbe, his Amoret, his Canace, his Britomart
and his Pastora, are a gallery of portraits, all beautiful, but each in a different style from all the
rest. *Aikin.*

36 Cornelia's] Cornelia was the Roman mother of Tiberius and Gaius Gracchus, known
for her purity, excellent character, and intelligence; Plutarch speaks highly of her conduct in
widowhood. Or the reference may be to the daughter of Metellus Scipio, who married Pompeii
after the death of her first husband and whose character and accomplishments were remarkable.
Plutarch says that she was well versed in music, literature, geometry, and philosophy.

That slavish stigma seared on half the race,   40
His rude forefathers' shame; and pleased confess,
'Tis yours to elevate, 'tis yours to bless;
Your interest one with his; your hopes the same;
Fair peace in life, in death undying fame,
And bliss in worlds beyond, the species' general aim.
"Rise," shall he cry, "O Woman, rise! be free!
My life's associate, now partake with me:
Rouse thy keen energies, expand thy soul,
And see, and feel, and comprehend the whole;
My deepest thoughts, intelligent, divide;   50
When right confirm me, and when erring guide;
Soothe all my cares, in all my virtues blend,
And be, my sister, be at length my friend."

(1810)

Jane Austen

(1775–1817)

While acknowledging Jane Austen as "one of the greatest artists . . . that ever lived," George Henry Lewes told Charlotte Brontë that "Miss Austen is not a poetess. . . . [She] has . . . none of the ravishing enthusiasm of poetry." Brontë replied, "Can there be a great artist without poetry?"[1] Certainly many readers consider Austen's novels poetic in their use of language;[2] and her own definition of a novel in *Northanger Abbey*—a "work in which the greatest powers of the mind are displayed, in which the most thorough knowledge of human nature, the happiest delineations of its varieties, the liveliest effusions of wit and humour are conveyed to the world in the best chosen language"—would also seem to many an apt description of poetry.

Born at Steventon, near Basingstoke, in Hampshire, on 16 December 1775, Jane Austen was the seventh of eight children and the youngest daughter of Cassandra Leigh and the Reverend George Austen, rector of Deane and Steventon. Her congenial and cultured family included two female cousins who were novelists, Cassandra Cooke and Cassandra Hawke. At Steventon Rectory, where Jane Austen grew up, her father tutored her and introduced her to the major English authors; he also encouraged her to write. She read Maria Edgeworth, Helen Maria Williams, Samuel Richardson, Samuel Johnson, Jane West, Frances Burney, and many others, and she learned French and some Italian. She enjoyed participating in private theatricals and became well-read in contemporary poetry and fiction. A warm, affectionate person who relished the company of her five brothers, she was especially close to her older sister Cassandra, her chief companion. That relationship was to be the central one in her life.

Her high-spirited juvenilia reveal an appreciation for life's absurdity and

1. Lewes's letter is not extant, but Brontë quoted from it in her reply of 18 January 1848 (see B. C. Southam, ed., *Jane Austen: The Critical Heritage* [London and New York, 1968], 127).

2. See, e.g., George Whalley, "Jane Austen: Poet," in *Jane Austen's Achievement,* ed. Juliet McMaster (London, 1976), 106–33.

show that her skills in parody and burlesque were already well developed. *Love and Friendship,* written when she was fifteen, burlesques Richardson. *A History of England* pokes fun at the writing of history and is authored, she says on the title page, "by a partial, prejudiced, & ignorant Historian." It contains "very few Dates" and takes the side of Mary, Queen of Scots, against Elizabeth I, "that disgrace to humanity, that pest of society."[3] Virginia Woolf later said of Austen's earliest work, "Whatever she writes is finished and turned and set in its relation, not to the parsonage but to the universe. She is impersonal, she is inscrutable."[4]

Austen penned *First Impressions,* later retitled *Pride and Prejudice,* between October 1796 and August 1797. Her father offered it in late October 1797 to the publisher Thomas Cadell, who sent it back unread by return of post. *Susan,* later retitled *Northanger Abbey,* a parody of Ann Radcliffe's *Mysteries of Udolpho,* was complete by 1798. When her father retired in 1801, the family moved to Bath. There she prepared *Northanger Abbey* for the press after it was sold for ten pounds to Crosby & Sons of Bath in 1803. Inexplicably, it was not published. She also began "The Watsons," a novel she left unfinished, perhaps because of her father's death in 1805. After that event she moved with her mother and her sister Cassandra to Southampton. In 1809 they settled in Chawton, near Alton, in a cottage belonging to her brother Edward Knight, where she was to remain for the rest of her life.

In her first year at Chawton, Austen completed a second revision of *Sense and Sensibility,* originally entitled *Elinor and Marianne,* which she had begun in 1795–96 in epistolary form. Published in 1811 by Thomas Egerton in three volumes, it went into a second edition and earned Austen £140. *Pride and Prejudice* (1813) comically portrays the fundamental problems of human conduct and character. In it, Mr. Darcy observes, "The wisest and the best of men, nay, the wisest and best of their actions, may be rendered ridiculous by a person whose first object in life is a joke." Austen's heroine, Elizabeth Bennet, who at this point might be speaking for the author herself, replies, "Certainly, there are such people, but I hope I am not one of them. I hope I never ridicule what is wise and good. Follies and nonsense, whims and inconsistencies do divert me, I own, and I laugh at them whenever I can." *Pride and Prejudice* was well received and went into a second edition in its first year.

The five and one-half years between February 1811 and August 1816 were highly productive; during that time Austen wrote *Mansfield Park* (1814), *Emma* (1816), and *Persuasion* (1818). Like her earlier books, these witty novels, writ-

---

3. *The History of England, from the Reign of Henry the Fourth to the Death of Charles the First,* introduction by A. S. Byatt (Chapel Hill, 1993), 18–19.

4. Ibid., quoted in Byatt's introduction, v.

ten with precision, matchless turns of phrase, and subtle insight into human character, are comedies of manners. Austen's social values are conservative, but her portrayal of domestic life among the provincial gentry is highly critical and ironic. Her heroines are strong women unaided by parents, who are irresponsible, neglectful, or simply absent. The aristocracy is vain, arrogant, and blind to moral worth, and the clergy seem to be more attuned to the size of their income than to any spiritual concerns. Much of Austen's work revolves around the problem of perception, the difficulty of knowing oneself and properly assessing the real merit of others, and the challenge of achieving within oneself a healthy balance between sensibility and rationality. Her narratives emphasize the importance of responsible social behavior, and in each her heroine ultimately succeeds, after much difficulty, in finding a relationship based on love that is mutually supportive and promises fulfillment for both partners. But surrounding that quest are examples of many varieties of disastrous relationships, full of unhappiness and ennui, and many corrupt, vulgar, and misguided characters. Austen's novels all focus on a woman's world-view, and readers are made well aware of her circumscribed space and limited options.

Austen had several opportunities to appear in London society as a literary lion; in each case she refused. Walter Scott was one of her many admirers; his appreciative article on Austen appeared in the March 1816 issue of the *Quarterly Review.* Austen stopped working on *Sandition* in March 1817, debilitated by Addison's disease, which had darkened her last years; the novel remained incomplete. During the last months of her life she wrote letters and light verse. She died on 18 July 1817 in Winchester, where she had gone for medical treatment, and was buried in Winchester Cathedral. In 1809 one of her brothers had bought back the copyright of *Northanger Abbey* from Crosby & Sons, and the book was finally published posthumously in 1818 along with *Persuasion,* an autumnal book that nevertheless seems to take issue with Charlotte Smith's notion that happiness has no second spring. Austen's works appeared anonymously during her lifetime, although her authorship was widely known; it was in the memoir written by her nephew J. E. Austen Leigh, prefixed to these last posthumous works, that her identity was publicly acknowledged for the first time.

Austen admired the poetry of Crabbe and Cowper, but she did not take her own verse seriously, turning it out mostly for her personal enjoyment or for that of her friends. Although she wrote poetry throughout her life, not many examples survive. Charades, *bouts-rimés,* and noun verses were all popular Austen family amusements. "Verses to Rhyme with 'Rose'" appears to have been written as part of a competition between Austen and her mother, her sister Cassandra, and her sister-in-law, Elizabeth Bridges, wife of her brother

Edward. When Lord Brabourne first printed the poem in his 1884 edition of Austen's *Letters,* he noted that it was "enclosed in one of the Letters of 1807" along with three verses by others on the same theme.[5] The manuscript was sold at Sotheby's on 29 October 1962 and is now owned by the Fondation Martin Bodmer, Cologny-Geneva, Switzerland.[6]

The manuscript of "On a Headache" belonged to the family of Charles Austen, and it was purchased in 1926 by John Pierpont Morgan, who presented it to the Bath City Council. It is signed "J. A." and was first published in 1954 in R. W. Chapman's edition of *The Works of Jane Austen.*[7]

MAJOR WORKS: *Sense and Sensibility: A Novel,* 3 vols. (London, 1811); *Pride and Prejudice: A Novel,* 3 vols. (London, 1813); *Mansfield Park: A Novel,* 3 vols. (London, 1814); *Emma: A Novel,* 3 vols. (London: 1816); *Northanger Abbey* and *Persuasion,* 4 vols. (London, 1818).

TEXTS USED: Texts of "Verses to Rhyme with 'Rose'" and "On a Headache" from *The Works of Jane Austen,* ed. R. W. Chapman (London, 1954), vol. 6, *Minor Works.*

Verses to Rhyme with "Rose"

Happy the lab'rer in his Sunday clothes!
In light-drab coat, smart waistcoat, well-darn'd hose,
And hat upon his head, to church he goes;
As oft, with conscious pride, he downward throws
A glance upon the ample cabbage rose
That, stuck in button-hole, regales his nose,
He envies not the gayest London beaux.
In church he takes his seat among the rows,
Pays to the place the reverence he owes,
Likes best the prayers whose meaning least he knows,   10
Lists to the sermon in a softening doze,
And rouses joyous at the welcome close.

(wr. 1807)

5. Jane Austen, *Letters of Jane Austen,* ed. Edward, Lord Brabourne, vol. 2 (London, 1884), 343. The paper is watermarked 1802, and Elizabeth Bridges Austen died in 1808, so the poem was certainly composed between those dates. Its inclusion in a letter of 1807 suggests that year as a likely date of composition. Lord Brabourne also prints the three companion pieces (341–44).

6. David Gilson, "Jane Austen's Verses," *Book Collector* 33, no. 1 (1984): 31.

7. Vol. 6, *Minor Works,* 447–48; Gilson, "Jane Austen's Verses," 32.

On a Headache

When stretch'd on one's bed
With a fierce-throbbing head,
Which precludes alike thought or repose,
How little one cares
For the grandest affairs
That may busy the world as it goes!

How little one feels
For the waltzes and reels
Of our Dance-loving friends at a Ball!
10   How slight one's concern
To conjecture or learn
What their flounces or hearts may befall.

How little one minds
If a company dines
On the best that the Season affords!
How short is one's muse
O'er the Sauces and Stews,
Or the Guests, be they Beggars or Lords.

How little the Bells,
20   Ring they Peels, toll they Knells,
Can attract our attention or Ears!
The Bride may be married,
The Corse may be carried
And touch nor our hopes nor our fears.

Our own bodily pains
Ev'ry faculty chains;
We can feel on no subject beside.
Tis in health and in ease
We the power must seize
30   For our friends and our souls to provide.

(wr. 27 October 1811)

12 flounces] Strips of cloth gathered and sewn along the upper edge onto the skirts of dresses.

Joanna Baillie

(1762–1851)

Walter Scott called Joanna Baillie "the best dramatic writer" in Britain "since the days of Shakespeare and Massinger."[1] Between 1800 and 1826 all of the leading theaters in England, Ireland, Scotland, and the United States produced plays by Baillie, sometimes with great success, with the most widely acclaimed actors playing the leads—among them Edmund Kean, Sarah Siddons, William Charles Macready, Helen Faucit, Ellen Terry, and John Philip Kemble. Her songs in Scots dialect, such as "Woo'd and Married and A,'" "The Maid of Llanwellyn," "Saw Ye Johnny Comin?" and "The Gowan Glitters on the Sward," continue to be sung to this day.

Baillie was born in Bothwell, Lanarkshire, Scotland, on 11 September 1762, the child of Dorothea Hunter and the Reverend James Baillie; her twin sister died within hours of birth. Joanna was a year younger than her brother, Matthew, and two years younger than her sister Agnes, who was her mentor and companion throughout her life. In 1769 her father was appointed minister of the collegiate church at Hamilton, a town of six thousand, to which the family then moved. Baillie's father was an unpleasant man who discouraged the expression of emotion, and his daughter grew up starved for affection. He also proved a neglectful teacher, imparting to Joanna a firm knowledge of ethics and the Bible but little instruction in reading and writing. In fact, she was unable to read well until she was ten years old, when she was sent to a boarding school in Glasgow; there she became a prankster and a leader. She studied history, writing, geography, drawing, music, and mathematics. She often acted out dramatic scenes of her own invention alone on the roof of the house; her classmates helped perform some of these early dramas, while Joanna designed costumes and served as stage manager.

These happy boarding school days came to an end, however, in 1778, when

---

1. Scott to Miss Smith, 4 March 1808, *Familiar Letters of Sir Walter Scott*, vol. 1 (Boston, 1894), 99.

her father died, leaving his family unprovided for. Her mother's brother, William Hunter, a famous London physician, took over support of the family and became the girls' surrogate father. They moved to his estate in Scotland, where Joanna took long walks in the countryside, reading the works of Shakespeare and other writers. When William Hunter died in 1783, Joanna and her mother and sister moved to London to keep house for her brother.

In 1790 Joanna Baillie published, with Joseph Johnson, *Poems; Wherein it is Attempted to Describe Certain Views of Nature and of Rustic Manners.* The book was barely noticed in the reviews. During this time, Baillie probably met a number of writers and artists in the Joseph Johnson circle. When Matthew married Sophia Denman in 1791, Dorothea Baillie and her daughters moved to Hampstead, where they were to spend the rest of their lives.

Hampstead proved a particularly congenial environment for the young poet and budding playwright. In 1798 she published anonymously *A Series of Plays: in Which It is Attempted to Delineate the Stronger Passions of the Mind. Each Passion being the Subject of a Tragedy and a Comedy,* preceded by an eloquent, revolutionary, and immensely influential "Introductory Discourse," from which Wordsworth silently borrowed two years later in his preface to the second edition of his *Lyrical Ballads.* Her aim, as stated in the "Introductory Discourse," was a "series of tragedies, of simpler construction, less embellished with poetical decorations, less constrained by that lofty seriousness which has so generally been considered as necessary for the support of tragick dignity, and in which the chief object should be to delineate the progress of the higher passions in the human breast." She strove, she said, to excite the sympathetic imagination and to foster identification with her characters, for "in examining others we know ourselves." Thus, she preferred to portray the ordinary life of ordinary characters speaking more natural language, for, as she observed, "let one simple trait of the human heart, one expression of passion genuine and true to nature, be introduced [into a work full of poetic diction] and it will stand forth alone in the boldness of reality, whilst the false and unnatural around it, fade away upon every side, like the rising exhalations of the morning." *Basil* and *De Monfort,* two of the three plays contained in this volume, were among the masterpieces of Baillie's dramatic career.

The book created a sensation and was widely and enthusiastically reviewed. Mary Berry stayed up all night reading it and wrote in her diary, "The first question upon everybody's lips is, 'Have you read the series of plays?' Everybody talks in the raptures (I always thought they deserved) of the tragedies and of the introduction as of a new and admirable piece of criticism." [2]

---

2. Mary Berry, *Extracts of the Journals and Correspondence of Miss Berry From the Year 1783 to 1852,* ed. Lady Theresa Lewis, 3 vols. (London, 1865), 2:88.

Baillie guarded the secret of her authorship carefully, sitting demurely silent, for example, while Anna Letitia Barbauld's circle of literary friends discussed the book. Some suspected Walter Scott. Others argued for Ann Radcliffe or Anne Hunter. Hester Lynch Piozzi insisted that the author must be a woman "because both the heroines are *Dames Passées,* and a man has no notion of mentioning a female after she is five and twenty."[3] Mary Berry noted that "no man could or *would* draw such noble, such dignified representations of the female mind as the Countess Albini and Jane de Mountfort [*sic*]. They often make us clever, captivating, heroic, but never rationally superior."[4] The third edition, published in 1800, removed all doubt, bearing the author's name boldly on the title page. In 1836 the *Quarterly Review* recalled "the curiosity excited in the literary circle . . . the incredulity, with which the first rumour that these vigorous and original compositions came from a female hand, was received; and the astonishment, when, after all the ladies who then enjoyed any literary celebrity had been tried and found totally wanting in the splendid faculties developed in those dramas, they were acknowledged by a gentle, quiet and retiring young woman, whose most intimate friends, we believe, had never suspected her extraordinary powers."[5] Another commentator described Baillie as "a small, prim, and Quaker-like looking person, in plain attire, with gentle, unobtrusive manners, and devoid of affectation; rather silent, and more inclined to listen than to talk. There was no tinge of the blue-stocking in her style of conversation, no assumption of conscious importance in her demeanor, and less of literary display than in any author or authoress I had ever been in company with. It was difficult to persuade yourself that the little, insignificant, and rather commonplace-looking individual before you, could have conceived and embodied with such potent energy, the deadly hatred of De Monfort, or the fiery love of Basil."[6]

When *De Monfort* opened at Drury Lane on 29 April 1800, Sarah Siddons and John Philip Kemble played the leads. A critic for the *Dublin University Magazine* noted some years later that "the critics announced the approach of a new era in dramatic literature, and the talents of great actors, then in the zenith, left no doubt that the conceptions of the author would be fully realized. The excitement was great, and the disappointment commensurate. The audience yawned in spite of themselves, in spite of the exquisite poetry, the vigorous passion, and the transcendent acting."[7] The performance was,

---

3. Hester Lynch Thrale Piozzi, *The Intimate Letters of Hester Piozzi and Penelope Pennington, 1788–1821,* ed. O. G. Knapp, 3 vols. (London, 1914), 2:173.

4. Berry, *Extracts of the Journals and Correspondence,* 2:90.

5. *Quarterly Review* 55 (February 1836): 487–513.

6. *Dublin University Magazine* 37 (April 1851): 529.

7. Ibid., 530.

nevertheless, repeated eight times. And the demand for the printed plays continued strong. A revised fourth edition came out in 1802, with a fifth following in 1806. Baillie earned three hundred pounds for a second volume, which appeared in 1802, containing three more plays, including *Ethwald* and *The Election*. Although she was in demand in the world of letters, she spent much of the day caring for her mother, now aged and blind. In 1804 she brought out a volume entitled *Miscellaneous Plays,* which went into a second edition the following year.

In 1808, the year her mother died, she cemented what would become a long and intimate friendship with Walter Scott. She and her sister Agnes were his guests in Edinburgh during March and April of that year. Shortly thereafter, Scott arranged for Baillie's new play, *The Family Legend,* to be produced in Edinburgh, penning the prologue himself. The novelist Henry Mackenzie wrote the epilogue.[8] Baillie was Scott's guest at Abbotsford in 1817; he describes her then as carrying "her literary reputation as freely and easily as the milk-maid in my country does the *leglen,* which she carries on her head, and walks as gracefully with it as a duchess."[9] Admirers of Baillie's works included Maria Edgeworth, Sarah Siddons, William Wordsworth, Anna Jameson, William Ellery Channing, Annabella Milbanke (Lady Byron), Ann Grant of Laggan, Felicia Hemans, Lucy Aikin, Anna Letitia Barbauld, Harriet Martineau, George Ticknor, and Lord Byron, who wrote: "Nothing could do me more honour than the acquaintance of that Lady—who does not possess a more enthusiastic admirer than myself—she is our only dramatist since Otway & Southerne—I don't except Home."[10] However, Francis Jeffrey, editor of the *Edinburgh Review,* took issue with the prevailing opinion of Baillie's *Plays on the Passions* and attacked them in a lead article in July 1803. Even so, he concluded the review by observing that her talents "are superior to those of any of her contemporaries among the English writers of tragedy"; in an 1811 article, he classed her with those he considered the greatest poets of the period—Wordsworth, Southey, and Coleridge.[11]

Longmans is said to have paid Baillie one thousand pounds for her *Met-*

8. John Gibson Lockhart, *Memoirs of the Life of Sir Walter Scott,* 5 vols. (Boston, 1901), 2:152.

9. Ibid., 4:3.

10. Lord Byron to Annabella Milbanke, 6 September 1813, *"Alas! the Love of Women!"* vol. 3 of *Byron's Letters and Journals,* ed. Leslie A. Marchand (Cambridge, Mass., 1974), 109. Later, Byron said in a letter to John Murray, "When Voltaire was asked why no woman has ever written a tolerable tragedy? 'Ah (said the Patriarch) the composition of a tragedy requires *testicles.*'—If this be true Lord knows what Joanna Baillie does—I suppose she borrows them" (2 April 1817, *"So Late into the Night,"* vol. 5 of *Byron's Letters and Journals,* ed. Leslie A. Marchand [London, 1976], 203).

11. *Edinburgh Review* 2 (July 1803): 272, 19 (February 1812): 283.

rical Legends of Exalted Characters (1821), half of which she gave to charity, as was her habit. Her most ambitious act of literary philanthropy was *A Collection of Poems, Chiefly Manuscript, and from Living Authors,* an edited work to benefit a financially troubled friend that appeared in 1823.[12] The subscription list reads like a roster of the British literary world, and the volume includes selections from Hemans, Wordsworth, Barbauld, Scott, Campbell, Crabbe, Lady Dacre, Charles Brinsley Sheridan, Anne Grant of Laggan, Elizabeth Benger, Catherine Fanshawe (anonymously), Margaret Holford, Sir George Beaumont, Robert Southey, Anna Maria Porter, Samuel Rogers, and Baillie herself, who contributed "Address to a Steam-Vessel," printed below.

In 1826 Baillie published two new plays, *The Bride* and *The Martyr.* Though it has often been said that Baillie's work came to be forgotten in the 1830s, her reputation was, in fact, growing in the United States during that period, perhaps in part spurred on by Edmund Kean's Philadelphia and New York productions of *De Monfort* in the early and mid-1820s. Carey and Lea of Philadelphia brought out *The Complete Works of Joanna Baillie* in 1832. In 1836 Longmans published a volume of twelve new plays by Baillie, most written many years earlier. The reviewer for *Fraser's Magazine* wrote,

> Had we heard that a MS. play of Shakespeare's, or an early, but missing, novel of Scott's, had been discovered, and was already in the press, the information could not have been more welcome. . . . It awakened that long dormant eagerness of curiosity with which we used to look forward to the publication of her volumes, in those remote days when Wordsworth was yet unknown, and the first faint beams of the genius of Walter Scott had only shewn themselves in a few and scattered miscellaneous poems. . . . The new work has surpassed all that we had expected, or could have ventured to hope for. . . . To meet with anything in dramatic literature equal to [many of these] we must pass over all that has been written, except by Joanna Baillie herself, during the space of the last two hundred years, and revert to the golden days of Elizabeth and James I.[13]

In 1840 Baillie published a volume of *Fugitive Verses* from earlier years. Though she asked Mary Berry in 1844, "On what spot of the earth lives that bookseller who would now publish at his own risk any part of my works?"[14] she lived to see Longmans bring out a collected edition of her *Dramatic and Poetical Works.* She died shortly afterwards, on 23 February 1851, at the age of

---

12. The friend was Mrs. Stirling, a widowed former schoolmate of Baillie's, who was having difficulty supporting her daughters. See "Unpublished Letters of Joanna Baillie to a Dumfriesshire Laird," ed. Mrs. E. Shirley, *Dumfriesshire and Galloway Natural History and Antiquarian Society: Transactions and Journal of Proceedings* 18 (1934): 10–27.

13. *Fraser's Magazine* 13 (February 1836): 236.

14. Berry, *Extracts of the Journal and Correspondence,* 3:489.

eighty-eight, having retired the day before in her usual state of good health. She was buried in the parish churchyard at Hampstead in the same grave as her sister Agnes, beside her close friend Lucy Aikin. In that same year the poet and critic D. M. Moir reminded his readers that the "new code of poetry" brought out by Wordsworth and Coleridge in the *Lyrical Ballads* did not differ widely from the theories of Joanna Baillie, and for that reason, "it must be admitted, from published proof, that [Baillie] thus forstalled—or at least divided—the claim to originality indoctrinated in the theory and practice of Wordsworth."[15] Despite such harkenings back to the historical record, the Wordsworth myth was even then fast overwhelming the memory of Joanna Baillie's genuinely revolutionary contribution to English letters.

MAJOR WORKS: *Poems; Wherein it is Attempted to Describe Certain Views of Nature and of Rustic Manners* (London, 1790); *A Series of Plays: in Which It is Attempted to Delineate the Stronger Passions of the Mind. Each Passion being the Subject of a Tragedy and a Comedy,* 3 vols. (London, 1798–1812); *Miscellaneous Plays* (London, 1804); *The Family Legend: A Tragedy* (Edinburgh and London, 1810); *Metrical Legends of Exalted Characters* (London, 1821); *Dramas,* 3 vols. (London, 1836); *Fugitive Verses* (London, 1840); *Ahalya Baee: A Poem* (London, 1849); *The Dramatic and Poetical Works of Joanna Baillie,* complete in one volume (London, 1851).

TEXTS USED: "Wind" and "Thunder" first appeared in *Poems; Wherein it is Attempted to Describe Certain Views of Nature and of Rustic Manners.* The text of "Wind" is taken from this book, and "Thunder" is taken from *Fugitive Verses.* "The Kitten" appeared in *The Edinburgh Annual Register* for 1808; my copy text is from *Fugitive Verses.* The text of "Up! Quit Thy Bower!" is taken from "The Beacon" in vol. 3 of *A Series of Plays.* Baillie's version of "Woo'd and Married and A'" was first published in George Thomson's *Original Scottish Airs for the Voice* (London, 1822); my copy text is from *Fugitive Verses.* The text of "Address to a Steam-Vessel" is from *A Collection of Poems, Chiefly Manuscript, and from Living Authors,* ed. Joanna Baillie (London, 1823). "Song" first appeared in *The Bride, A Drama* (London, 1826); my copy text is from *Dramas.* "The Sun Is Down" appeared in "The Phantom: A Musical Drama," in *Dramas,* from which the copy text is taken. The texts of "Lines to a Teapot" and "The Maid of Llanwellyn" both come from *Fugitive Verses.*

15. *Sketches of the Poetical Literature of the Past Half-Century* (Edinburgh and London, 1851), 256.

Wind

Pow'r uncontrollable, who hold'st thy sway
In the unbounded air, whose trackless way
Is in the firmament, unknown of sight,
Who bend'st the sheeted heavens in thy might,
And lift'st the ocean from its lowest bed
To join in middle space the conflict dread;
Who o'er the peopled earth in ruin scours,
And buffets the firm rock that proudly low'rs,
Thy signs are in the heav'ns. The upper clouds
Draw shapeless o'er the sky their misty shrouds;   10
Whilst darker fragments rove in lower bands,
And mournful purple cloaths the distant lands.
In gather'd tribes, upon the hanging peak
The sea-fowl scream, ill-omen'd creatures shriek:
Unwonted sounds groan on the distant wave,
And murmurs deep break from the downward cave.
Unlook'd-for gusts the quiet forests shake,
And speak thy coming—awful Pow'r, awake!

Like burst of mighty waters wakes the blast,
In wide and boundless sweep: thro' regions vast   20
The floods of air in loosen'd fury drive,
And meeting currents strong, and fiercely strive.
First wildly raving on the mountain's brow
'Tis heard afar, till o'er the plains below
With even rushing force it bears along,
And gradual swelling, louder, full, and strong,
Breaks wide in scatter'd bellowing thro' the air.
Now is it hush'd to calm, now rous'd to war,
Whilst in the pauses of the nearer blast,
The farther gusts howl from the distant waste.   30
Now rushing furious by with loosen'd sweep,
Now rolling grandly on, solemn and deep,
Its bursting strength the full embodied sound
In wide and shallow brawlings scatters round;
Then wild in eddies shrill, with rage distraught,
And force exhausted, whistles into naught.

With growing might, arising in its room,
From far, like waves of ocean onward come
Succeeding gusts, and spend their wasteful ire,
40   Then slow, in grumbled mutterings retire:
And solemn stillness overawes the land,
Save where the tempest growls along the distant strand.
But great in doubled strength, afar and wide,
Returning battle wakes on ev'ry side;
And rolling on with full and threat'ning sound,
In wildly mingled fury closes round.
With bellowings loud, and hollow deep'ning swell,
Reiterated hiss, and whistlings shrill,
Fierce wars the varied storm, with fury tore,
50   Till all is overwhelm'd in one tremendous roar.

    The vexed forest, tossing wide,
Uprooted strews its fairest pride;
The lofty pine in twain is broke,
And crushing falls the knotted oak.
The huge rock trembles in its might;
The proud tow'r tumbles from its height;
Uncover'd stands the social home;
High rocks aloft the city dome;
Whilst bursting bar, and flapping gate,
60   And crashing roof, and clatt'ring grate,
And hurling wall, and falling spire,
Mingle in jarring din and ruin dire.
Wild ruin scours the works of men;
Their motly fragments strew the plain.
E'en in the desert's pathless waste,
Uncouth destruction marks the blast:
And hollow caves whose secret pride,
Grotesque and grand, was never ey'd
By mortal man, abide its drift,
70   Of many a goodly pillar reft.
Fierce whirling mounts the desert sand,
And threats aloft the peopl'd land.
The great expanded ocean, heaving wide,
Rolls to the farthest bound its lashing tide;
Whilst in the middle deep afar are seen,

All stately from the sunken gulfs between,
The tow'ring waves, which bend with hoary brow,
Then dash impetuous to the deep below.
With broader sweepy base, in gather'd might
Majestic, swelling to stupendous height,   80
The mountain billow lifts its awful head,
And, curving, breaks aloft with roarings dread.
Sublimer still the mighty waters rise,
And mingle in the strife of nether skies.
All wildness and uproar, above, beneath,
A world immense of danger, dread, and death.

    In dumb despair the sailor stands,
The frantic merchant wrings his hands,
Advent'rous hope clings to the yard,
And sinking wretches shriek unheard: 90
Whilst on the land, the matron ill at rest,
Thinks of the distant main, and heaves her heavy breast.
The peasants leave their ruin'd home,
And o'er the fields distracted roam:
Insensible the 'numbed infant sleeps,
And helpless bending age, weak and unshelter'd weeps.
Low shrinking fear, in place of state,
Skulks in the dwellings of the great.
The rich man marks with careful eye,
Each wasteful gust that whistles by;   100
And ill men scar'd with fancied screams
Sit list'ning to the creaking beams.
At break of ev'ry rising squall
On storm-beat' roof, or ancient wall,
Full many a glance of fearful eye
Is upward cast, till from on high,
From cracking joist, and gaping rent,
And falling fragments warning sent,
Loud wakes around the wild affray,
'Tis all confusion and dismay.   110

    Now powerful but inconstant in its course,
The tempest varies with uncertain force.
Like doleful wailings on the lonely waste,

Solemn and dreary sounds the weaning blast.
Exhausted gusts recoiling growl away,
And, wak'd anew, return with feebler sway;
Save where between the ridgy mountains pent,
The fierce imprison'd current strives for vent,
With hollow howl, and lamentation deep,
120   Then rushes o'er the plain with partial sweep.
A parting gust o'erscours the weary land,
And lowly growls along the distant strand:
Light thro' the wood the shiv'ring branches play,
And on the ocean far it slowly dies away.

(1790)

Thunder

Spirit of strength! to whom in wrath 'tis given,
To mar the earth and shake its vasty dome,
Behold the sombre robes whose gathering folds,
Thy secret majesty conceal. Their skirts
Spread on mid air move slow and silently,
O'er noon-day's beam thy sultry shroud is cast,
Advancing clouds from every point of heaven,
Like hosts of gathering foes in pitchy volumes,
Grandly dilated, clothe the fields of air,
10   And brood aloft o'er the empurpled earth.
Spirit of strength! it is thy awful hour;
The wind of every hill is laid to rest,
And far o'er sea and land deep silence reigns.

Wild creatures of the forest homeward hie,
And in their dens with fear unwonted cower;
Pride in the lordly palace is put down,
While in his humble cot the poor man sits
With all his family round him hushed and still,
In awful expectation. On his way
20   The traveller stands aghast and looks to heaven.
On the horizon's verge thy lightning gleams,

And the first utterance of thy deep voice
Is heard in reverence and holy fear.

From nearer clouds bright burst more vivid gleams,
As instantly in closing darkness lost;
Pale sheeted flashes cross the wide expanse
While over boggy moor or swampy plain,
A streaming cataract of flame appears,
To meet a nether fire from earth cast up,
Commingling terribly; appalling gloom   30
Succeeds, and lo! the rifted centre pours
A general blaze, and from the war of clouds,
Red, writhing falls the embodied bolt of heaven.
Then swells the rolling peal, full, deep'ning, grand,
And in its strength lifts the tremendous roar,
With mingled discord, rattling, hissing, growling;
Crashing like rocky fragments downward hurled,
Like the upbreaking of a ruined world,
In awful majesty the explosion bursts
Wide and astounding o'er the trembling land.   40
Mountain, and cliff, repeat the dread turmoil,
And all to man's distinctive senses known,
Is lost in the immensity of sound.
Peal after peal, succeeds with waning strength,
And hushed and deep each solemn pause between.

Upon the lofty mountain's side
The kindled forest blazes wide;
Huge fragments of the rugged steep
Are tumbled to the lashing deep;
Firm rooted in his cloven rock,   50
Crashing falls the stubborn oak.
The lightning keen in wasteful ire
Darts fiercely on the pointed spire,
Rending in twain the iron-knit stone,
And stately towers to earth are thrown.
No human strength may brave the storm,
Nor shelter skreen the shrinking form,
Nor castle wall its fury stay,
Nor massy gate impede its way:

60   It visits those of low estate,
      It shakes the dwellings of the great,
      It looks athwart the vaulted tomb,
      And glares upon the prison's gloom.
      Then dungeons black in unknown light,
      Flash hideous on the wretches' sight,
      And strangely groans the downward cell,
      Where silence deep is wont to dwell.

         Now eyes, to heaven up-cast, adore,
      Knees bend that never bent before,
70   The stoutest hearts begin to fail,
      And many a manly face is pale;
      Benumbing fear awhile up-binds,
      The palsied action of their minds,
      Till waked to dreadful sense they lift their eyes,
      And round the stricken corse shrill shrieks of horror rise.

         Now rattling hailstones, bounding as they fall
      To earth, spread motley winter o'er the plain,
      Receding peals sound fainter on the ear,
      And roll their distant grumbling far away:
80   The lightning doth in paler flashes gleam,
      And through the rent cloud, silvered with his rays,
      The sun on all this wild affray looks down,
      As, high enthroned above all mortal ken,
      A higher Power beholds the strife of men.

                                                    (1790)

The Kitten

Wanton droll, whose harmless play
Beguiles the rustic's closing day,
When, drawn the evening fire about,
Sit aged crone and thoughtless lout,
And child upon his three-foot stool,
Waiting till his supper cool,
And maid, whose cheek outblooms the rose,
As bright the blazing faggot glows,
Who, bending to the friendly light,
Plies her task with busy slight;   10
Come, shew thy tricks and sportive graces,
Thus circled round with merry faces.

   Backward coiled and crouching low,
With glaring eyeballs watch thy foe,
The housewife's spindle whirling round,
Or thread or straw that on the ground
Its shadow throws, by urchin sly
Held out to lure thy roving eye;
Then stealing onward, fiercely spring
Upon the tempting faithless thing.   20
Now, wheeling round with bootless skill,
Thy bo-peep tail provokes thee still,
As still beyond thy curving side
Its jetty tip is seen to glide;
Till from thy centre starting far,
Thou sidelong veer'st with rump in air
Erected stiff, and gait awry,
Like madam in her tantrums high;
Though ne'er a madam of them all,
Whose silken kirtle sweeps the hall,   30
More varied trick and whim displays
To catch the admiring stranger's gaze.

   Doth power in measured verses dwell,
All thy vagaries wild to tell?
Ah no!—the start, the jet, the bound,

The giddy scamper round and round,
With leap and toss and high curvet,
And many a whirling somerset,
(Permitted by the modern muse
40   Expression technical to use)
These mock the deftest rhymester's skill,
But poor in art though rich in will.

      The featest tumbler, stage bedight,
To thee is but a clumsy wight,
Who every limb and sinew strains
To do what costs thee little pains;
For which, I trow, the gaping crowd
Requite him oft with plaudits loud.

      But, stopped the while thy wanton play,
50   Applauses too thy pains repay:
For then, beneath some urchin's hand
With modest pride thou takest thy stand,
While many a stroke of kindness glides
Along thy back and tabby sides.
Dilated swells thy glossy fur,
And loudly croons thy busy pur,
As, timing well the equal sound,
Thy clutching feet bepat the ground,
And all their harmless claws disclose
60   Like prickles of an early rose,
While softly from thy whiskered cheek
Thy half-closed eyes peer, mild and meek.

      But not alone by cottage fire
Do rustics rude thy feats admire.
The learned sage, whose thoughts explore
The widest range of human lore,
Or with unfettered fancy fly
Through airy heights of poesy,
Pausing smiles with altered air
70   To see thee climb his elbow-chair,
Or, struggling on the mat below,
Hold warfare with his slippered toe.

The widowed dame or lonely maid,
Who, in the still but cheerless shade
Of home unsocial, spends her age
And rarely turns a lettered page,
Upon her hearth for thee lets fall
The rounded cork or paper ball,
Nor chides thee on thy wicked watch,
The ends of ravelled skein to catch,   80
But lets thee have thy wayward will,
Perplexing oft her better skill.

Even he, whose mind of gloomy bent,
In lonely tower or prison pent,
Reviews the coil of former days,
And loathes the world and all its ways,
What time the lamp's unsteady gleam
Hath roused him from his moody dream,
Feels, as thou gambol'st round his seat,
His heart of pride less fiercely beat,   90
And smiles, a link in thee to find,
That joins it still to living kind.

Whence hast thou then, thou witless puss!
The magic power to charm us thus?
Is it that in thy glaring eye
And rapid movements, we descry—
Whilst we at ease, secure from ill,
The chimney corner snugly fill—
A lion darting on his prey,
A tiger at his ruthless play?   100
Or is it that in thee we trace
With all thy varied wanton grace,
An emblem, viewed with kindred eye,
Of tricky, restless infancy?
Ah! many a lightly sportive child,
Who hath like thee our wits beguiled,
To dull and sober manhood grown,
With strange recoil our hearts disown.

And so, poor kit! must thou endure,
110   When thou becomest a cat demure,
Full many a cuff and angry word,
Chased roughly from the tempting board.
But yet, for that thou hast, I ween,
So oft our favoured play-mate been,
Soft be the change which thou shalt prove!
When time hath spoiled thee of our love,
Still be thou deemed by housewife fat
A comely, careful, mousing cat,
Whose dish is, for the public good,
120   Replenished oft with savoury food.
Nor, when thy span of life is past,
Be thou to pond or dung-hill cast,
But, gently borne on goodman's spade,
Beneath the decent sod be laid;
And children shew with glistening eyes
The place where poor old pussy lies.

                            (1808)

Up! Quit Thy Bower!

Up! quit thy bower, late wears the hour;
Long have the rooks caw'd round thy tower;
On flower and tree, loud hums the bee;
The wilding kid sports merrily:
A day so bright, so fresh, so clear,
Shineth when good fortune's near.

Up! Lady fair, and braid thy hair,
And rouze thee in the breezy air;
The lulling stream, that sooth'd thy dream,
10   Is dancing in the sunny beam;
And hours so sweet, so bright, so gay,
Will waft good fortune on its way.

Up! time will tell; the friar's bell
Its service-sound hath chimed well;
The aged crone keeps house alone,
And reapers to the fields are gone;
The active day so boon and bright,
May bring good fortune ere the night.

(1812)

Woo'd and Married and A'

Version Taken from an Old Song of That Name

The bride she is winsome and bonny,
    Her hair it is snooded sae sleek,
And faithfu' and kind is her Johnny,
    Yet fast fa' the tears on her cheek.
New pearlins are cause of her sorrow,
    New pearlins and plenishing too,
The bride that has a' to borrow,
    Has e'en right mickle ado.
        Woo'd and married and a'!
        Woo'd and married and a'!   10
    Is na' she very weel aff
        To be woo'd and married and a'?

Her mither then hastily spak,
    "The lassie is glakit wi' pride;
In my pouch I had never a plack
    On the day when I was a bride.
E'en tak' to your wheel, and be clever,
    And draw out your thread in the sun;

2 snooded] Tied with a ribbon.
5 pearlins] Lace.
6 plenishing] House furnishings.
8 mickle] Much.

11 aff] Off.
14 glakit] Giddy, foolish.
15 plack] Small Scottish coin.

The gear that is gifted, it never
20   Will last like the gear that is won.
                    Woo'd and married and a'!
                    Wi' havins and tocher sae sma'!
              I think ye are very weel aff,
                    To be woo'd and married at a'!"

"Toot, toot!" quo' her grey-headed faither,
        "She's less o' a bride than a bairn,
She's ta'en like a cout frae the heather,
        Wi' sense and discretion to learn.
Half husband, I trow, and half daddy,
30   As humour inconstantly leans,
The chiel maun be patient and steady,
        That yokes wi' a mate in her teens.
                    A kerchief sae douce and sae neat,
                    O'er her locks that the winds used to blaw!
              I'm baith like to laugh and to greet,
                    When I think o' her married at a'!"

Then out spak' the wily bridegroom,
        Weel waled were his wordies, I ween,
"I'm rich, though my coffer be toom,
40   Wi' the blinks o' your bonny blue een.
I'm prouder o' thee by my side,
        Though thy ruffles or ribbons be few,
Than Kate o' the Croft were my bride,
        Wi' purfles and pearlins enow.
                    Dear, and dearest of ony!
                    Ye're woo'd and buikit and a'!
              And do ye think scorn o' your Johnny,
                    And grieve to be married at a'?"

19 gear] Money, booty.	35 greet] Weep.
22 tocher] Dowry.	38 waled] Chosen.
25 quo'] Said.	38 ween] Fear.
26 bairn] Child.	39 toom] Empty.
27 cout] Colt.	40 blinks] Glances.
29 trow] Believe.	40 een] Eyes.
31 chiel maun] Fellow must.	44 purfles] embroidery
33 douce] Sober, grave, unfrivolous.	enow] enough
	45 ony] any
	46 buikit] booked (in the marriage registry)

She turned, and she blushed, and she smiled,
    And she looket sae bashfully down;   50
The pride o' her heart was beguiled,
    And she played wi' the sleeves o' her gown;
She twirled the tag o' her lace,
    And she nippet her boddice sae blue,
Sine blinket sae sweet in his face,
    And aff like a maukin she flew.
        Woo'd and married and a'!
        Wi' Johnny to roose her and a'!
    She thinks hersel very weel aff,
        To be woo'd and married at a'.   60

(1822)

Address to a Steam-Vessel[*]

Freighted with passengers of every sort,
A motley throng, thou leav'st the busy port.
Thy long and ample deck, where scatter'd lie,
Baskets, and cloaks, and shawls of scarlet dye;
Where dogs and children through the crowd are straying,
And, on his bench apart, the fiddler playing,
While matron dames to tressel'd seats repair,—
Seems, on the gleamy waves, a floating fair.

    Its dark form on the sky's pale azure cast,
Towers from this clust'ring group thy pillar'd mast.   10
The dense smoke issuing from its narrow vent
Is to the air in curly volumes sent,
Which, coiling and uncoiling on the wind,
Trails like a writhing serpent far behind.
Beneath, as each merg'd wheel its motion plies,

---

54 nippet] bit
55 Sine blinket] afterwards glanced
56 maukin] hare
58 roose] praise

On either side the white-churn'd waters rise,
And, newly parted from the noisy fray,
Track with light ridgy foam thy recent way,
Then far diverged, in many a welted line
20   Of lustre, on the distant surface shine.

Thou hold'st thy course in independent pride;
No leave ask'st thou of either wind or tide.
To whate'er point the breeze, inconstant, veer,
Still doth thy careless helmsman onward steer;
As if the stroke of some magician's wand
Had lent thee power the ocean to command.
What is this power which thus within thee lurks,
And, all unseen, like a mask'd giant works?
Ev'n that which gentle dames, at morning's tea,
30   From silver urn ascending, daily see
With tressy wreathings playing in the air,
Like the loos'd ringlets of a lady's hair;
Or rising from the enamell'd cup beneath,
With the soft fragrance of an infant's breath:
That which within the peasant's humble cot
Comes from th' uncover'd mouth of sav'ry pot,
As his kind mate prepares his noonday fare,
Which cur, and cat, and rosy urchins share:
That which, all silver'd with the moon's pale beam,
40   Precedes the mighty Geyser's up-cast stream,
What time, with bellowing din exploded forth,
It decks the midnight of the frozen north,
Whilst travellers from their skin-spread couches rise
To gaze upon the sight with wond'ring eyes.

Thou hast to those "in populous city pent"
Glimpses of wild and beauteous nature lent;
A bright remembrance ne'er to be destroyed,
Which proves to them a treasure, long enjoyed,
And for this scope to beings erst confin'd,
50   I fain would hail thee with a grateful mind.
They who had nought of verdant freshness seen

45 "in populous city pent"] *Paradise Lost* 9.445.

But suburb orchards choked with colworts green,
Now, seated at their ease may glide along,
Lochlomond's fair and fairy isles among;
Where bushy promontories fondly peep,
At their own beauty in the nether deep,
O'er drooping birch and berried row'n that lave
Their vagrant branches in the glassy wave:
They, who on higher objects scarce have counted
Than church's spire with gilded vane surmounted,   60
May view, within their near, distinctive ken,
The rocky summits of the lofty Ben;
Or see his purpled shoulders darkly lower
Through the dim drapery of a summer shower.
Where, spread in broad and fair expanse, the Clyde
Mingles his waters with the briny tide,
Along the lesser Cumra's rocky shore,
With moss and crusted lichens flecker'd o'er,
Ev'n he, who hath but warr'd with thieving cat,
Or from his cupboard chaced a hungry rat,   70
The city cobbler, — scares the wild sea-mew
In its mid-flight with loud and shrill halloo;
Or valiantly with fearful threat'ning shakes
His lank and greasy head at Kittywakes.
The eyes that have no fairer outline seen
Than chimney'd walls with slated roofs between,
Which hard and harshly edge the smokey sky,
May Aron's softly-vision'd peaks descry,
Coping with graceful state her steepy sides,

52 colworts] *Colewort* was originally used to describe any cabbage-type plant (genus *Brassica*). Later it came to be used especially for those varieties, such as kale, that do not heart or for others before they heart or are full-grown.

54 Lochlomond's] Loch Lomond is the largest body of inland water in Britain, located north of Glasgow.

62 lofty Ben] Ben Lomond, a mountain to the east of Loch Lomond.

65 the Clyde] The river Clyde rises in the southern uplands of Scotland. In the eighteenth century the Clyde enabled Glasgow to engage in trade with the Americas.

67 the lesser Cumra's] Probably Little Cumbrae, an island in the mouth of the Clyde, offering magnificent views.

74 Kittywakes] The common or vulgar name of a water-bird frequenting that coast. *Baillie.*

78 Aron's] The island of Arran, located just south of Little Cumbrae in the Clyde, is a popular holiday resort famous for its spectacular views, which take in Scotland, Ireland, and England.

80   O'er which the cloud's broad shadow swiftly glides,
        And interlacing slopes that gently merge
        Into the pearly mist of ocean's verge.
        Eyes which admir'd that work of sordid skill,
        The storied structure of a cotton-mill,
        May, wond'ring, now behold the unnumber'd host
        Of marshall'd pillars on fair Ireland's coast,
        Phalanx on phalanx rang'd with sidelong bend,
        Or broken ranks that to the main descend,
        Like Pharaoh's army, on the Red-sea shore,
90   Which deep and deeper went to rise no more.

        Yet ne'ertheless, whate'er we owe to thee,
        Rover at will on river, lake, and sea,
        As profit's bait or pleasure's lure engage,
        Thou offspring of that philosophic sage,
        Watt, who in heraldry of science ranks
        With those to whom men owe high meed of thanks,
        And shall not be forgotten, ev'n when Fame
        Graves on her annals Davy's splendid name!—
        Dearer to fancy, to the eye more fair
100   Are the light skiffs, that to the breezy air,
        Unfurl their swelling sails of snowy hue
        Upon the moving lap of ocean blue:
        As the proud swan on summer lake displays,
        With plumage bright'ning in the morning rays,
        Her fair pavilion of erected wings,—
        They change, and veer, and turn like living things.

        So fairly rigg'd, with shrouding, sails, and mast,
        To brave with manly skill the winter blast
        Of every clime,—in vessels rigg'd like these
        Did great Columbus cross the western seas,

---

84 cotton-mill] The manufacture of cotton fabric started in Belfast after Robert Joy, owner of a paper mill, visited Scotland and learned of modern spinning techniques and technologies. The first cotton mills in Belfast were established in poorhouses and relied on child labor.

95 Watt] James Watt (1736–1819), a Scottish engineer, invented an improved steam engine.

98 Davy's] Sir Humphry Davy (1778–1829), an English chemist, invented a safety lamp for miners, discovered sodium and potassium, and helped to develop the modern scientific method. He was one of the most famous scientists of his time and a popular lecturer.

And to the stinted thoughts of man reveal'd
What yet the course of ages had conceal'd.
In such as these, on high adventure bent,
Round the vast world Magellan's comrades went.
To such as these are hardy seamen found
As with the ties of kindred feeling bound,
Boasting, as cans of cheering grog they sip,
The varied fortunes of "our gallant ship."
The offspring these of bold sagacious man
Ere yet the reign of letter'd lore began.   120

   In very truth, compar'd to these thou art
A daily lab'rer, a mechanic swart,
In working weeds array'd of homely grey,
Opposed to gentle nymph or lady gay,
To whose free robes the graceful right is given
To play and dally with the winds of heaven.
Beholding thee, the great of other days
And modern men with all their alter'd ways,
Across my mind with hasty transit gleam,
Like fleeting shadows of a fev'rish dream: 130
Fitful I gaze with adverse humours teased,
Half sad, half proud, half angry, and half pleased.

                         (1823)

---

* The steam vessel was a relatively recent innovation when Baillie published this poem, and some of the earliest experiments with it were conducted in Scotland, on the bodies of water the poet mentions here. In 1736 Jonathan Hulls obtained a patent in England for a steam vessel, and then the duke of Bridgewater experimented with using steamboats to tow barges. In 1781 the marquis of Jouffroy built a 140-foot steamboat at Lyons and plied the river Saone. In 1788 in Scotland, hundreds of spectators watched a steam vessel built by Taylor and Miller move at the rate of five miles per hour. At the end of 1789 a similar boat built by William Symington for Taylor and Miller, though on a much larger scale, was shown to move at seven miles per hour, which was widely reported in the Edinburgh newspapers. Another boat, the *Charlotte Dundas,* in March 1803 towed two seventy-ton boats against a heavy wind a distance of nineteen miles, to Port Dundas, Glasgow. The *Comet,* with a four-horsepower engine, navigated the Clyde in 1812 and overcame the popular fear that

122 swart] Dark, dusky, swarthy.

the engine might burst. In 1813 three steamers were plying the Clyde between Glasgow and Greenock (part of the voyage described in Baillie's poem). And by 1816, steamboats were to be seen on many rivers throughout Britain.

Song

The gliding fish that takes his play
    In shady nook of streamlet cool,
Thinks not how waters pass away,
    And summer dries the pool.

The bird beneath his leafy dome,
    Who trills his carol, loud and clear,
Thinks not how soon his verdant home
    The lightning's breath may sear.

Shall I within my bridegroom's bower,
10   With braids of budding roses twined,
Look forward to a coming hour
    When he may prove unkind?

The bee reigns in his waxen cell,
    The chieftain in his stately hold,
To-morrow's earthquake, — who can tell?
    May both in ruin fold.

                            (1826)

The Sun Is Down

The sun is down, and time gone by,
The stars are twinkling in the sky,
Nor torch nor taper longer may
Eke out a blythe but stinted day;
The hours have pass'd with stealthy flight,
We needs must part: good night, good night!

The bride unto her bower is sent,
And ribald song and jesting spent;
The lover's whisper'd words and few
Have bade the bashful maid adieu;   10
The dancing floor is silent quite,
No foot bounds there: good night, good night!

The lady in her curtain'd bed,
The herdsman in his wattled shed,
The clansmen in the heather'd hall,
Sweet sleep be with you, one and all!
We part in hopes of days as bright
As this gone by: good night, good night!

Sweet sleep be with us, one and all!
And if upon its stillness fall   20
The visions of a busy brain,
We'll have our pleasure o'er again,
To warm the heart, to charm the sight,
Gay dreams to all! good night, good night!

                              (1836)

Lines to a Teapot

On thy carved sides, where many a vivid dye
In easy progress leads the wandering eye,
A distant nation's manners we behold,
To the quick fancy whimsically told.

  The small-eyed beauty with her Mandarin,
Who o'er the rail of garden arbour lean,
In listless ease; and rocks of arid brown,
On whose sharp crags, in gay profusion blown,
The ample loose-leaved rose appears to grace
The skilful culture of the wonderous place;   10
The little verdant plat, where with his mate
The golden pheasant holds his gorgeous state,
With gaily crested pate and twisted neck,

Turned jantily his glossy wings to peck;
The smooth-streaked water of a paly gray,
O'er which the checkered bridge lends ready way,
While, by its margin moored, the little boat
Doth with its oars and netted awning float:
A scene in short all soft delights to take in,
20   A paradise for grave Grandee of Pekin.
With straight small spout, that from thy body fair,
Diverges with a smart vivacious air,
And round, arched handle with gold tracery bound,
And dome-shaped lid with bud or button crowned,
Thou standest complete, fair subject of my rhymes,
A goodly vessel of the olden times.

But far less pleasure yields this fair display
Than that enjoyed upon thy natal day,
When round the potter's wheel, their chins upraising,
30   An urchin group in silent wonder gazing,
Stood and beheld, as, touched with magic skill,
The whirling clay swift fashioned to his will, —
Saw mazy motion stopped, and then the toy
Complete before their eyes, and grinned for joy;
Clapping their naked sides with blythe halloo,
And curtailed words of praise, like *ting, tung, too!*
The brown-skinned artist, with his unclothed waist
And girded loins, who, slow and patient, traced,
Beneath his humble shed, this fair array
40   Of pictured forms upon thy surface gay,
I will not stop in fancy's sight to place,
But speed me on my way with quickened pace.
Packed in a chest with others of thy kind,
The sport of waves and every shifting wind,
The Ocean thou hast crossed, and thou mayest claim
The passing of the Line to swell thy fame,
With as good observation of the thing
As some of those who in a hammock swing.

46 the Line] The equator.

And now thou'rt seen in Britain's polished land,
Held up to public view in waving hand 50
Of boastful auctioneer, whilst dames of pride
In morning farthingals, scarce two yards wide,
With collared lap-dogs snarling in their arms,
Contend in rival keenness for thy charms.
And certes well they might, for there they found thee
With all thy train of vassal cups around thee,
A prize which thoughts by day, and dreams by night,
Could dwell on for a week with fresh delight.

Our pleased imagination now pourtrays
The glory of thy high official days, 60
When thou on board of rich japan wert set,
Round whose supporting table gaily met
At close of eve, the young, the learned, the fair,
And even philosophy and wit were there.
Midst basons, cream-pots, cups and saucers small,
Thou stood'st the ruling chieftain of them all;
And even the kettle of Potosi's ore,
Whose ample cell supplied thy liquid store,
Beneath whose base the sapphire flame was burning,
Above whose lid the wreathy smoke was turning, 70
Though richly chased and burnished it might be,
Was yet, confessed, subordinate to thee.
But O! when beauty's hand thy weight sustained,
The climax of thy glory was attained!
Back from her elevated elbow fell
Its three-tired ruffle, and displayed the swell
And gentle rounding of her lily arm,
The eyes of wistful sage or beau to charm—
A sight at other times but dimly seen
Through veiling folds of point or colberteen. 80
With pleasing toil, red glowed her dimpled cheek,

---

52 farthingals] Hooped petticoats.

67 Potosi's ore] Potosi is the name of both a city and a region in south-central Bolivia; during the sixteenth and seventeenth centuries the region was one of the world's leading sources of silver.

80 colberteen] An open lace with a square ground, worn in the seventeenth and eighteenth centuries.

Bright glanced her eyes beneath her forehead sleek,
And as she poured the beverage, through the room
Was spread its fleeting, delicate perfume.
Then did bright wit and cheerful fancy play
With all the passing topics of the day.
So delicate, so varied and so free
Was the heart's pastime, then inspired by thee,
That goblet, bowl or flask could boast no power
90   Of high excitement, in their reigning hour,
Compared to thine;—red wildfire of the fen,
To summer moonshine of some fairy glen.

But now the honours of thy course are past,
For what of earthly happiness may last!
Although in modern drawing-room, a board
May fragrant tea from menial hands afford,
Which, poured in dull obscurity hath been,
From pot of vulgar ware, in nook unseen,
And pass in hasty rounds our eyes before,
100   Thou in thy graceful state art seen no more.
And what the changeful fleeting crowd, who sip
The unhonoured beverage with contemptuous lip,
Enjoy amidst the tangled, giddy maze,
Their languid eye—their listless air betrays.
What though at times we see a youthful fair
By white clothed board her watery drug prepare,
At further corner of a noisy room,
Where only casual stragglers deign to come,
Like tavern's busy bar-maid; still I say,
110   The honours of thy course are passed away.

Again hath auctioneer thy value praised,
Again have rival bidders on thee gazed,
But not the gay, the young, the fair, I trow!
No; sober connoisseurs, with wrinkled brow
And spectacles on nose, thy parts inspect,
And by grave rules approve thee or reject.
For all the bliss which china charms afford,
My lady now has ceded to her lord.

And wisely too does she forego the prize,
Since modern pin-money will scarce suffice   120
For all the trimmings, flounces, beads and lace,
The thousand needful things that needs must grace
Her daily changed attire. — And now on shelf
Of china closet placed, a cheerless elf,
Like moody statesman in his rural den,
From power dismissed — like prosperous citizen,
From shop or change set free — untoward bliss!
Thou rest'st in most ignoble uselessness.

(1840)

The Maid of Llanwellyn*

Song, Written for a Welch Melody

I've no sheep on the mountain, nor boat on the lake,
Nor coin in my coffer to keep me awake,
Nor corn in my garner, nor fruit on my tree,
Yet the Maid of Llanwellyn smiles sweetly on me.

Softly tapping at eve to her window I came,
And loud bayed the watch-dog, loud scolded the dame;
For shame, silly Lightfoot! what is it to thee,
Though the Maid of Llanwellyn smiles sweetly on me?

The farmer rides proudly to market or fair,
The clerk at the alehouse still claims the great chair,   10
But, of all our proud fellows, the proudest I'll be,
While the Maid of Llanwellyn smiles sweetly on me.

---

120 pin-money] An allowance allotted to a woman for her personal expenses, such as clothing and incidentals. The term came to mean a trivial sum of money.
3 garner] Storehouse for grain.

For blythe as the urchin at holyday play,
And meek as a matron in mantle of gray,
And trim as a lady of gentle degree,
Is the Maid of Llanwellyn, who smiles upon me.

(1840)

---

*The names of many Welsh towns begin with *Llan,* but the name Llanwellyn does not correspond to any locale on a modern map. It may be a fictional place, or perhaps it existed as a small crossroads.

Anna Letitia Barbauld

(1743–1825)

William Wordsworth is reported to have said of the ending of Anna Letitia Barbauld's poem "Life," a staple in anthologies throughout the nineteenth century, "I am not in the habit of grudging people their good things, but I wish I had written those lines."[1] And Frances Burney reputedly recited the last stanza nightly before bed. As poet, educator, essayist, and critic, she was widely acknowledged to be one of the literary giants of her time. Born on 20 June 1743 in Kibworth Harcourt, a village in Leicestershire, she was the eldest child and only daughter of Jane Jennings and John Aikin, a dissenting clergyman and teacher. Shortly after his marriage, John Aikin had given up his pulpit for health reasons. Instead he taught school and instructed Anna Letitia and her brother, John, four years her junior. She would learn French, Italian, and, despite her father's misgivings, Latin and Greek. Her mother was a cultivated, strict, neat, and punctual woman with polished manners; she and her daughter never had a congenial relationship, and Anna Letitia struggled against the tight rein her puritanical parents imposed. Because she was brought up isolated from playmates, her childhood was largely an unhappy one, and even in adulthood she never seemed entirely at ease socially. Thin, with a healthy, fair, complexion, regular features, and dark blue eyes, she was considered beautiful and became known for her wit and imagination.

In 1758, when she was fifteen, her father became a tutor at the newly founded Warrington Academy in Lancashire, a center for dissenting thought. The fifteen years she spent in Lancashire were the happiest of her life. The scientist and theologian Joseph Priestley was one of her father's colleagues and became Anna Letitia's close, lifelong friend. Josiah Wedgwood was a regular visitor. Her brother John, Priestley, and the intellectually stimulating environment of Warrington encouraged her to write. As a result, in 1773 she published with Joseph Johnson a slender book entitled simply *Poems*, in-

1. Henry Crabb Robinson, *Henry Crabb Robinson on Books and Their Writers*, ed. Edith J. Morley, 3 vols. (London, 1938), 1:8, 2:651.

cluding "An Address to the Deity" and "The Mouse's Petition" (both printed below). It contained verse epistles, hymns, fables, odes, and songs on many subjects, and it went through four editions within the year. Critics were as enthusiastic as general readers. The February 1773 *Monthly Review* noted, "We very seldom have an opportunity of bestowing praise with so much justice, and so much pleasure." Mary Scott wrote in the *Female Advocate* the following year:

> Fir'd with the Music, Aikin, of thy lays,
> To thee the Muse a joyful tribute pays;
> Transported dwells on that harmonious line,
> Where taste, and spirit, wit, and learning shine;
> Where Fancy's hand her richest colourings lends,
> And ev'ry shade in just proportion blends.
> How fair, how beauteous to our gazing eyes
> Thy vivid intellectual paintings rise!
> We feel thy feelings, glow with all thy fires,
> Adopt thy thoughts, and pant with thy desires.
> Proceed, bright maid! and may thy polish'd page
> Refine the manners of a trifling age.

That same year, Barbauld collaborated with her brother to publish with Joseph Johnson *Miscellaneous Pieces in Prose, by J. and A. L. Aikin,* containing "On Romances," the essay of which Samuel Johnson observed: "The imitators of my style have not hit it. Miss Aikin has done it the best; for she has imitated the sentiment as well as the diction."[2]

In May 1774 Anna Letitia Aikin married Rochemont Barbauld, a clergyman of French descent, formerly a pupil at Warrington and six years her junior. Shortly after their marriage the couple moved to Palgrave, in Suffolk, where he became minister of a dissenting congregation and opened a boys' boarding school. The poet kept all of the accounts and taught a class of little boys history, geography, drama, speech, English grammar, and composition. She was dismayed to find no suitable books for young children. As she put it, "A grave remark or a connected story, however simple, is above his capacity, and *nonsense* is always below, for folly is worse than ignorance. Another defect is the want of *good paper,* a *clear and large type,* and large spaces. Those only who have actually taught young children can be sensible how necessary these assistances are."[3] To answer this need for her students, as well as for her brother's child, Charles Rochemont Aikin, whom she had adopted when

---

2. James Boswell, *Boswell's Life of Johnson,* ed. George Birkbeck Hill, 6 vols. (Oxford, 1887), 3:172.

3. Barbauld, from her introduction to *Lessons for Children in Four Parts* (Philadelphia, 1818), iii.

he was not quite two, she wrote four volumes entitled *Lessons for Children* (1778–79) for those aged two to four years. In 1781 she published, with Joseph Johnson, *Hymns in Prose for Children;* it went through twenty-eight editions by 1836. It continued to be reprinted throughout the nineteenth century and was translated into French, German, Italian, Spanish, and Hungarian. Countless British children were brought up on the *Hymns,* and modern commentators have noted their influence on William Blake's *Songs of Innocence* (1789) and *Songs of Experience* (1794). However, Samuel Johnson and Charles James Fox thought she wasted her talents writing books for children. Johnson reputedly told James Boswell: "Miss [Aikin] was an instance of early cultivation, but in what did it terminate? In marrying a little Presbyterian parson, who keeps an infant boarding-school, so that all her employment now is 'To suckle fools, and chronicle small-beer.'" [4] Perhaps she had Johnson in mind when she wrote in the preface to *Lessons,* "The task is humble, but not mean, for to lay the first stone of a noble building and to plant the first idea in a human mind can be no dishonor to any hand." She and her husband spent their vacations in London, where she met many literary people belonging to the Joseph Johnson and Elizabeth Montagu circles, including Frances Burney, Hester Chapone, and Hannah More.

The Barbaulds gave up their school in 1785 and left that autumn for Switzerland and France. In June 1786 they returned to London, where they stayed until early 1787. Then they settled in Hampstead, where they took a few pupils and Rochemont Barbauld performed clerical duties at a small chapel. Dismayed at her diminished literary productivity, Anna Letitia's brother John urged her in a sonnet to "Seize, seize the lyre! resume the lofty strain!" She then began to publish political pamphlets opposing the war with France. Her verse *Epistle to William Wilberforce* (1791) attacked the slave trade. In Hampstead she became a close friend of her neighbors Agnes and Joanna Baillie and collaborated with her brother on *Evenings at Home; or, The Juvenile Budget Opened: Consisting of a Variety of Miscellaneous Pieces for the Instruction and Amusement of Young Persons,* published in six volumes between 1792 and 1796. Fourteen of the ninety-nine pieces were hers. [5] She also worked as an editor and literary critic, penning an introduction to Mark Akenside's *Pleasures of*

4. Boswell, *Boswell's Life of Johnson,* 2:408. She said of Johnson that he was "far from a great character, he was continually sinning against his conscience, and then afraid of going to Hell for it. A Christian, and a man of the town; a philosopher, and a bigot; acknowledging life to be miserable, and making it more miserable through fear of death" (Anna Letitia Le Breton, *Memoir of Mrs. Barbauld, Including Letters and Notices of her Family and Friends* [London, 1874], 56).

5. Though the pieces were not signed, Lucy Aikin identifies those written by Barbauld in *The Works of Anna Lætitia Barbauld, with a Memoir,* ed. Lucy Aikin, 2 vols. (London, 1825), 1:xxxvi–xxxvii.

the Imagination (1794) and writing a preface to a volume of William Collins's *Poetical Works* (1797). After 1796, when her brother became literary editor, she also contributed poetry to the *Monthly Magazine,* where "Washing-Day" (printed below) was first published in December 1797. Her literary associates came to include Walter Scott, William Wordsworth, Samuel Rogers, and Samuel Taylor Coleridge, who recorded her famous objection to "The Rime of the Ancient Mariner" as improbable and lacking a moral. Though Barbauld and Coleridge admired each other's work, the relationship grew cool around 1804, when he took offense at reviews of his work that he sometimes incorrectly attributed to her.

John Aikin moved from London to Stoke Newington because of his health in 1798. The two siblings had always been close and found the separation difficult; in 1802 Barbauld convinced her husband to leave Hampstead for Stoke Newington, where she lived for the rest of her life. In 1804 Maria Edgeworth invited her to visit Ireland to help her start a periodical featuring literature by women. Barbauld cordially agreed to contribute and even offered to recruit other authors but declined to help found the magazine, observing that "there is no bond of union among literary women, any more than among literary men; different sentiments and different connections separate them much more than the joint interest of their sex would unite them."[6] During her early years in Stoke Newington she edited Samuel Richardson's letters in six volumes (1804), prefacing them with a critical biography of the author. She also edited selected essays from the *Spectator,* the *Tatler,* the *Guardian,* and the *Freeholder* in three volumes (1804); some regard the preliminary essay she contributed to these volumes as her most successful piece of literary criticism.

Rochemont Barbauld suffered from mental illness, which gradually became more serious; he was subject to depression, irritability, and rages. After the couple's move to Stoke Newington, his rages became increasingly violent, but despite the danger, the poet would not allow him to be institutionalized or restrained. When Rochemont angrily pursued her with a knife, forcing her to flee for her life to her brother's home, she finally agreed to have her husband sent to London to live with an attendant next-door to their adopted son, Charles. On 11 November 1808, however, Rochemont bribed his way out of the house and drowned himself in the New River. Barbauld wrote a touching memoir of her husband, published in the *Monthly Repository of Theology and General Literature.* Lucy Aikin wrote that Barbauld's "spirits were deeply wounded, both by the severe trials through which she had passed, and by the mournful void" brought on by her husband's death.[7]

6. Le Breton, *Memoir of Mrs. Barbauld,* 86–87.
7. Aikin, *Works of Anna Lætitia Barbauld,* 1:xliv.

Barbauld threw herself into editorial work, publishing in 1810 *The British Novelists* in fifty volumes, which included a long prefatory essay entitled "Origin and Progress of Novel Writing," as well as a critical introduction to each novel. The next year she published *The Female Speaker; or, Miscellaneous Pieces in Prose and Verse, Selected from the Best Writers, and Adapted to the Use of Young Women.* Her poetic tour de force, *Eighteen Hundred and Eleven, a Poem,* came out in 1812. A prophetic work, it anticipates Eliot's *The Wasteland* by more than a century. But it provoked rage and indignation from most of Barbauld's contemporary critics, who accused her of being, among other things, a traitor to her country. According to Henry Crabb Robinson, even William Godwin "was full of . . . censure of Mrs. Barbauld's new poem . . . which he called cowardly, time-serving, Presbyterian, besides a string of epithets which meant only that he found the work wretched."[8] John Wilson Croker's critique in the June 1812 *Quarterly Review* was particularly harsh. "We had hoped, indeed," he said, "that the empire might have been saved without the intervention of a lady-author," and he warned her "to desist from satire, which indeed is satire on herself alone," entreating her not to "put herself to the trouble of writing any more party pamphlets in verse."[9] Maria Edgeworth wrote to her friend, "I cannot describe to you the indignation, or rather the disgust, that we felt at the manner in which you are treated in the Quarterly Review, so ungentlemanlike, so unjust, so insolent a review I never read. . . . But it is not their criticism on your poem which incenses me, it is the odious tone in which they dare to speak of the most respectable and elegant female writer that England can boast. The public, the *public* will do you justice!"[10] Despite the support of friends, Barbauld took Croker's advice to heart and put aside plans to issue a complete edition of her poetry. Though she continued to write criticism for the *Monthly Review* until at least 1815, she never published another volume of poetry. Thus it was that at the height of her powers Barbauld was effectively silenced as a poet.

At the age of eighty Barbauld wrote to Edgeworth, "I only find that many things I knew I have forgotten, many things I *thought* I knew, I find I knew nothing about; some things, I know, I have found not worth knowing, and some things I would give—Oh! what would one not give to know, are beyond the reach of human ken."[11] Her conversation and her mind were sharp to the last. She died on 9 March 1825, at the age of eighty-one. Her niece and literary companion, Lucy Aikin, brought out in the same year a two-volume

8. Crabb Robinson, *On Books and Their Writers,* 1:63.
9. 7:309, 313.
10. Le Breton, *Memoir of Mrs. Barbauld,* 157.
11. Ibid., 185.

edition of Barbauld's collected *Works,* containing shorter prose pieces and poetry, including some previously unpublished, with copies of correspondence and a memoir. A large collection of Barbauld's papers and manuscripts was destroyed in the bombing of London in World War II. What remains is now scattered.[12]

MAJOR WORKS: *Poems* (London, 1773); *Hymns in Prose for Children* (London, 1781); *Lessons for Children,* 4 vols. (London, 1787–88); *An Address to the Opposers of the Repeal of the Corporation and Test Acts* (London, 1790); *Epistle to William Wilberforce, Esq. on the Rejection of the Bill for Abolishing the Slave Trade* (London, 1791); [with John Aikin], *Evenings at Home; or, The Juvenile Budget Opened: Consisting of a Variety of Miscellaneous Pieces for the Instruction and Amusement of Young Persons,* 6 vols. (London, 1792–96); *Eighteen Hundred and Eleven, a Poem* (London, 1812); *The Works of Anna Lætitia Barbauld, with a Memoir,* ed. Lucy Aikin, 2 vols. (London, 1825); *The Poems of Anna Letitia Barbauld,* ed. William McCarthy and Elizabeth Kraft (Athens, Ga., 1994).

TEXTS USED: Texts of "The Mouse's Petition" and "A Summer Evening's Meditation" from the second edition of *Poems.* Texts of "An Inventory of the Furniture in Dr. Priestley's Study," "Tomorrow," "Inscription for an Ice-House," "To the Poor," "Washing-Day," "Life," "The Baby-House," and "Riddle" from *The Works of Anna Lætitia Barbauld.* Text of "Eighteen Hundred and Eleven" from *Eighteen-Hundred and Eleven, a Poem.* I am indebted to William McCarthy for his advice about several of Barbauld's poems.

Notes on Barbauld's poetry are mostly drawn from McCarthy and Kraft, *The Poems of Anna Letitia Barbauld.*

The Mouse's Petition[*]
Found in the Trap where he had
been confin'd all Night

Parcere subjectis, & debellare superbos.
—Virgil[†]

Oh! hear a pensive captive's prayer,
For liberty that sighs;
And never let thine heart be shut
Against the prisoner's cries.

12. A full inventory of manuscripts appears in *The Poems of Anna Letitia Barbauld,* ed. William McCarthy and Elizabeth Kraft (Athens, Ga., 1994), 365–68.

For here forlorn and sad I sit,
Within the wiry grate;
And tremble at th' approaching morn,
Which brings impending fate.

If e'er thy breast with freedom glow'd,
And spurn'd a tyrant's chain,   10
Let not thy strong oppressive force
A free-born mouse detain.

Oh! do not stain with guiltless blood
Thy hospitable hearth;
Nor triumph that thy wiles betray'd
A prize so little worth.

The scatter'd gleanings of a feast
My scanty meals supply;
But if thine unrelenting heart
That slender boon deny,   20

The chearful light, the vital air,
Are blessings widely given;
Let nature's commoners enjoy
The common gifts of heaven.

The well taught philosophic mind
To all compassion gives;
Casts round the world an equal eye,
And feels for all that lives.

If mind, as ancient sages taught,
A never dying flame,   30
Still shifts thro' matter's varying forms,
In every form the same,

Beware, lest in the worm you crush
A brother's soul you find;
And tremble lest thy luckless hand
Dislodge a kindred mind.

21 The cheerful light, the vital air,] See line 17 of Helen Maria Williams's "Elegy on a Young Thrush."

Or, if this transient gleam of day
Be *all* of life we share,
Let pity plead within thy breast
40   That little *all* to spare.

So may thy hospitable board
With health and peace be crown'd;
And every charm of heartfelt ease
Beneath thy roof be found.

So when unseen destruction lurks,
Which men like mice may share,
May some kind angel clear thy path,
And break the hidden snare.

                    (wr. 1771; pub. 1773)

---

*To Doctor Priestley. *Barbauld.* [Joseph Priestley (1733–1804), a theologian and scientist, best remembered as the discoverer of oxygen, was, at the time of this poem's composition, studying the nature of gases; Barbauld was visiting him at Leeds. According to a contemporary, William Turner, "In the course of these investigations, the suffocating nature of various gases required to be determined, and no more easy or unexceptionable way of making such experiments could be devised, than the reserving of these little victims of domestic economy, which were thus at least as easily and as speedily put out of existence, as by any of the more usual modes. It happened that a captive was brought in after supper, too late for any experiment to be made with it that night, and the servant was desired to set it by till next morning. Next morning it was brought in after breakfast, with its petition twisted among the wires of its cage. It scarcely need be added, that the petition was successful" ("Mrs. Barbauld," *Newcastle Magazine,* n.s., 4 [1825]: 184). *Ed.*]

† "To spare the humbled, and to tame in war the proud!" (*Aeneid,* 6.853).

An Inventory of the Furniture
in Dr. Priestley's Study

A map of every country known,
With not a foot of land his own.
A list of folks that kicked a dust
On this poor globe, from Ptol. the First;
He hopes, — indeed it is but fair, —
Some day to get a corner there.
A group of all the British kings,
Fair emblem! on a packthread swings.
The Fathers, ranged in goodly row,
A decent, venerable show,   10
Writ a great while ago, they tell us,
And many an inch o'ertop their fellows.
A Juvenal to hunt for mottos;
And Ovid's tales of nymphs and grottos.
The meek-robed lawyers, all in white;
Pure as the lamb, — at least, to sight.
A shelf of bottles, jar and phial,
By which the rogues he can defy all, —
All filled with lightning keen and genuine,
And many a little imp he'll pen you in;   20
Which, like Le Sage's sprite, let out,
Among the neighbours makes a rout;
Brings down the lightning on their houses,
And kills their geese, and frights their spouses.
A rare thermometer, by which
He settles, to the nicest pitch,
The just degrees of heat, to raise
Sermons, or politics, or plays.
Papers and books, a strange mixed olio,

9 The Fathers] The works of the church fathers.

13 Juvenal] The Roman poet's works would have supplied quotations for Priestley's writings.

15 The meek-robed lawyers, all in white] Law books would have been bound in vellum.

17-19 A shelf of bottles . . . All filled with lightning] Leyden jars, in which electricity was stored. When the electricity was discharged, the spark resembled lightning.

21 LeSage's] Alain René Lesage (1668–1747), author of *Le Diable Boiteux* (1707), in which a student releases from a laboratory vial a spirit who wreaks havoc on the neighborhood.

30   From shilling touch to pompous folio;
        Answer, remark, reply, rejoinder,
        Fresh from the mint, all stamped and coined here;
        Like new-made glass, set by to cool,
        Before it bears the workman's tool.
        A blotted proof-sheet, wet from Bowling.
        —"How can a man his anger hold in?"—
        Forgotten rimes, and college themes,
        Worm-eaten plans, and embryo schemes;—
        A mass of heterogeneous matter,
40   A chaos dark, nor land nor water;—
        New books, like new-born infants, stand,
        Waiting the printer's clothing hand;—
        Others, a motley ragged brood,
        Their limbs unfashioned all, and rude,
        Like Cadmus' half-formed men appear;
        One rears a helm, one lifts a spear,
        And feet were lopped and fingers torn
        Before their fellow limbs were born;
        A leg began to kick and sprawl
50   Before the head was seen at all,
        Which quiet as a mushroom lay
        Till crumbling hillocks gave it way;
        And all, like controversial writing,
        Were born with teeth, and sprung up fighting.

        "But what is this," I hear you cry,
        "Which saucily provokes my eye?"—
        A thing unknown, without a name,
        Born of the air and doomed to flame.
                              (wr. 1771; pub. 1825)

    45 Cadmus'] An allusion to Ovid's *Metamorphoses,* 3.88–123, in which Cadmus plants the
    teeth of a dragon. Armed men spring up, feet first, and kill one another.

A Summer Evening's Meditation

One sun by day, by night ten thousand shine.
—Young*

'Tis past! The sultry tyrant of the south
Has spent his short-liv'd rage; more grateful hours
Move silent on; the skies no more repel
The dazzled sight, but with mild maiden beams
Of temper'd light, invite the cherish'd eye
To wander o'er their sphere; where hung aloft
DIAN's bright crescent, like a silver bow
New strung in heaven, lifts high its beamy horns
Impatient for the night, and seems to push
Her brother down the sky. Fair VENUS shines   10
Even in the eye of day; with sweetest beam
Propitious shines, and shakes a trembling flood
Of soften'd radiance from her dewy locks.
The shadows spread apace; while meeken'd Eve,
Her cheek yet warm with blushes, slow retires
Thro' the Hesperian gardens of the west,
And shuts the gates of day. 'Tis now the hour
When Contemplation, from her sunless haunts,
The cool damp grotto, or the lonely depth
Of unpierc'd woods, where wrapt in solid shade   20
She mused away the gaudy hours of noon,
And fed on thoughts unripen'd by the sun,
Moves forward; and with radiant finger points
To yon blue concave swell'd by breath divine,
Where, one by one, the living eyes of heaven
Awake, quick kindling o'er the face of ether
One boundless blaze; ten thousand trembling fires,
And dancing lustres, where th' unsteady eye
Restless, and dazzled wanders unconfin'd
O'er all this field of glories: spacious field!   30
And worthy of the master: he, whose hand
With hieroglyphics older than the Nile,
Inscrib'd the mystic tablet; hung on high
To public gaze, and said, adore, O man!

The finger of thy GOD. From what pure wells
Of milky light, what soft o'erflowing urn,
Are all these lamps so fill'd? these friendly lamps,
For ever streaming o'er the azure deep
To point our path, and light us to our home.
40   How soft they slide along their lucid spheres!
And silent as the foot of time, fulfil
Their destin'd courses: Nature's self is hush'd,
And, but a scatter'd leaf, which rustles thro'
The thick-wove foliage, not a sound is heard
To break the midnight air; tho' the rais'd ear,
Intensely listening, drinks in every breath.
How deep the silence, yet how loud the praise!
But are they silent all? or is there not
A tongue in every star that talks with man,
50   And wooes him to be wise; nor wooes in vain:
This dead of midnight is the noon of thought,
And wisdom mounts her zenith with the stars.
At this still hour the self-collected soul
Turns inward, and beholds a stranger there
Of high descent, and more than mortal rank;
An embryo GOD; a spark of fire divine,
Which must burn on for ages, when the sun,
(Fair transitory creature of a day!)
Has clos'd his golden eye, and wrapt in shades
60   Forgets his wonted journey thro' the east.

        Ye citadels of light, and seats of GODS!
Perhaps my future home, from whence the soul
Revolving periods past, may oft look back
With recollected tenderness, on all
The various busy scenes she left below,
Its deep laid projects and its strange events,
As on some fond and doating tale that sooth'd
Her infant hours; O be it lawful now
To tread the hallow'd circle of your courts,
70   And with mute wonder and delighted awe
Approach your burning confines. Seiz'd in thought
On fancy's wild and roving wing I sail,
From the green borders of the peopled earth,

And the pale moon, her duteous fair attendant;
From solitary Mars; from the vast orb
Of Jupiter, whose huge gigantic bulk
Dances in ether like the lightest leaf;
To the dim verge, the suburbs of the system,
Where chearless Saturn 'midst her watry moons
Girt with a lucid zone, majestic sits   80
In gloomy grandeur; like an exil'd queen
Amongst her weeping handmaids: fearless thence
I launch into the trackless deeps of space,
Where, burning round, ten thousand suns appear,
Of elder beam; which ask no leave to shine
Of our terrestrial star, nor borrow light
From the proud regent of our scanty day;
Sons of the morning, first born of creation,
And only less than him who marks their track,
And guides their fiery wheels. Here must I stop,   90
Or is there aught beyond? What hand unseen
Impels me onward thro' the glowing orbs
Of habitable nature; far remote,
To the dread confines of eternal night,
To solitudes of vast unpeopled space,
The desarts of creation, wide and wild;
Where embryo systems and unkindled suns
Sleep in the womb of chaos; fancy droops,
And thought astonish'd stops her bold career.
But oh thou mighty mind! whose powerful word   100
Said, thus let all things be, and thus they were,
Where shall I seek thy presence? how unblam'd
Invoke thy dread perfection?
Have the broad eye-lids of the morn beheld thee?
Or does the beamy shoulder of Orion
Support thy throne? O look with pity down
On erring guilty man; not in thy names
Of terror clad; not with those thunders arm'd
That conscious Sinai felt, when fear appall'd
The scatter'd tribes; thou hast a gentler voice,   110

108–9 those thunders arm'd / That conscious Sinai felt] In *Exodus* 19, God delivers the Ten
Commandments in a cloud of "thunders and lightnings."

That whispers comfort to the swelling heart,
Abash'd, yet longing to behold her Maker.

But now my soul unus'd to stretch her powers
In flight so daring, drops her weary wing,
And seeks again the known accustom'd spot,
Drest up with sun, and shade, and lawns, and streams,
A mansion fair and spacious for its guest,
And full replete with wonders. Let me here
Content and grateful, wait th' appointed time
120 And ripen for the skies: the hour will come
When all these splendours bursting on my sight
Shall stand unveil'd, and to my ravish'd sense
Unlock the glories of the world unknown.

                                        (1773)

* Edward Young, *Night Thoughts,* 7.746.

Tomorrow

See where the falling day
In silence steals away
Behind the western hills withdrawn:
Her fires are quenched, her beauty fled,
While blushes all her face o'erspread,
As conscious she had ill fulfilled
The promise of the dawn.

Another morning soon shall rise,
Another day salute our eyes,
10 As smiling and as fair as she,
And make as many promises:
But do not thou
The tale believe,
They're sisters all,
And all deceive.

                    (wr. 1780; pub. 1802)

Inscription for an Ice-House

Stranger, approach! within this iron door
Thrice locked and bolted, this rude arch beneath
That vaults with ponderous stone the cell; confined
By man, the great magician, who controuls
Fire, earth and air, and genii of the storm,
And bends the most remote and opposite things
To do him service and perform his will, —
A giant sits; stern Winter; here he piles,
While summer glows around, and southern gales
Dissolve the fainting world, his treasured snows   10
Within the rugged cave. — Stranger, approach!
He will not cramp thy limbs with sudden age,
Not wither with his touch the coyest flower
That decks thy scented hair. Indignant here,
Like fettered Sampson when his might was spent
In puny feats to glad the festive halls
Of Gaza's wealthy sons; or he who sat
Midst laughing girls submiss, and patient twirled
The slender spindle in his sinewy grasp;
The rugged power, fair Pleasure's minister,   20
Exerts his art to deck the genial board;
Congeals the melting peach, the nectarine smooth,
Burnished and glowing from the sunny wall:
Darts sudden frost into the crimson veins
Of the moist berry; moulds the sugared hail:
Cools with his icy breath our flowing cups;
Or gives to the fresh dairy's nectared bowls
A quicker zest. Sullen he plies his task,
And on his shaking fingers counts the weeks
Of lingering Summer, mindful of his hour   30
To rush in whirlwinds forth, and rule the year.

(wr. c. 1793; pub. 1825)

15 fettered Sampson] In *Judges* 16, Sampson is bound and his hair, the source of his strength, is cut. Barbauld may have been thinking of Milton's treatment of the story in *Samson Agonistes*.

18–19 Midst laughing girls . . . twirled the slender spindle] An allusion to "Deianira to Hercules," related by Ovid in *Heroides*: "Ah, how often, while with dour finger you twisted the thread, have your too strong hands crushed the spindle!" (lines 113, 115) (McCarthy and Kraft, *The Poems of Anna Letitia Barbauld*, 293–94).

To the Poor

Child of distress, who meet'st the bitter scorn
Of fellow-men to happier prospects born,
Doomed Art and Nature's various stores to see
Flow in full cups of joy—and not for thee;
Who seest the rich, to heaven and fate resigned,
Bear *thy* afflictions with a patient mind;
Whose bursting heart disdains unjust controul,
Who feel'st oppression's iron in thy soul,
Who dragg'st the load of faint and feeble years,
10   Whose bread is anguish, and whose water tears;
Bear, bear thy wrongs—fulfill thy destined hour,
Bend thy meek neck beneath the foot of Power;
But when thou feel'st the great deliverer nigh,
And thy freed spirit mounting seeks the sky,
Let no vain fears thy parting hour molest,
No whispered terrors shake thy quiet breast:
Think not their threats can work thy future woe,
Nor deem the Lord above like lords below;—
Safe in the bosom of that love repose
20   By whom the sun gives light, the ocean flows;
Prepare to meet a Father undismayed,
Nor fear the God whom priests and kings have made.*

                                        (wr. 1795; pub. 1825)

---

*These lines, written in 1795, were described by Mrs. B., on sending them to a friend, as "inspired by indignation on hearing sermons in which the poor are addressed in a manner which evidently shows the design of making religion an engine of government." *Lucy Aikin.*

Washing-Day

> . . . and their voice,
> Turning again towards childish treble, pipes
> And whistles in its sound.————*

The Muses are turned gossips; they have lost
The buskined step, and clear high-sounding phrase,
Language of gods. Come then, domestic Muse,
In slipshod measure loosely prattling on
Of farm or orchard, pleasant curds and cream,
Or drowning flies, or shoe lost in the mire
By little whimpering boy, with rueful face;
Come, Muse, and sing the dreaded Washing-Day.
Ye who beneath the yoke of wedlock bend,
With bowed soul, full well ye ken the day   10
Which week, smooth sliding after week, brings on
Too soon;—for to that day nor peace belongs
Nor comfort;—ere the first gray streak of dawn,
The red-armed washers come and chase repose.
Nor pleasant smile, nor quaint device of mirth,
E'er visited that day: the very cat,
From the wet kitchen scared and reeking hearth,
Visits the parlour,—an unwonted guest.
The silent breakfast-meal is soon dispatched;
Uninterrupted, save by anxious looks   20
Cast at the lowering sky, if sky should lower.
From that last evil, O preserve us, heavens!
For should the skies pour down, adieu to all
Remains of quiet: then expect to hear
Of sad disasters,—dirt and gravel stains
Hard to efface, and loaded lines at once
Snapped short,—and linen-horse by dog thrown down,
And all the petty miseries of life.
Saints have been calm while stretched upon the rack,
And Guatimozin smiled on burning coals;   30

2 buskined] Tragic.

30 Guatimozin] Or Guauhtemoc (1497–1522), nephew and son-in-law of Montezuma and successor to Quetlavaca as emperor of Mexico from 1520 to 1521. William Robertson's *History*

But never yet did housewife notable
Greet with a smile a rainy washing-day.
—But grant the welkin fair, require not thou
Who call'st thyself perchance the master there,
Or study swept, or nicely dusted coat,
Or usual 'tendance;—ask not, indiscreet,
Thy stockings mended, though the yawning rents
Gape wide as Erebus; nor hope to find
Some snug recess impervious: shouldst thou try
40   The 'customed garden walks, thine eye shall rue
The budding fragrance of thy tender shrubs,
Myrtle or rose, all crushed beneath the weight
Of coarse checked apron,—with impatient hand
Twitched off when showers impend: or crossing lines
Shall mar thy musings, as the wet cold sheet
Flaps in thy face abrupt. Woe to the friend
Whose evil stars have urged him forth to claim
On such a day the hospitable rites!
Looks, blank at best, and stinted courtesy,
50   Shall he receive. Vainly he feeds his hopes
With dinner of roast chicken, savoury pie,
Or tart or pudding:—pudding he nor tart
That day shall eat; nor, though the husband try,
Mending what can't be helped, to kindle mirth
From cheer deficient, shall his consort's brow
Clear up propitious:—the unlucky guest
In silence dines, and early slinks away.
I well remember, when a child, the awe
This day struck into me; for then the maids,
60   I scarce knew why, looked cross, and drove me from them:
Nor soft caress could I obtain, nor hope
Usual indulgencies; jelly or creams,
Relic of costly suppers, and set by
For me their petted one; or buttered toast,
When butter was forbid; or thrilling tale
Of ghost or witch, or murder—so I went
And sheltered me beside the parlour fire:

---

of America, 3 vols. (Dublin, 1777) describes how Guatimozin defended his country against the
Spaniards and how Cortés tortured him.

There my dear grandmother, eldest of forms,
Tended the little ones, and watched from harm,
Anxiously fond, though oft her spectacles   70
With elfin cunning hid, and oft the pins
Drawn from her ravelled stocking, might have soured
One less indulgent.—
At intervals my mother's voice was heard,
Urging dispatch: briskly the work went on,
All hands employed to wash, to rinse, to wring,
To fold, and starch, and clap, and iron, and plait.
Then would I sit me down, and ponder much
Why washings were. Sometimes through hollow bowl
Of pipe amused we blew, and sent aloft   80
The floating bubbles; little dreaming then
To see, Mongolfier, thy silken ball
Ride buoyant through the clouds—so near approach
The sports of children and the toils of men.
Earth, air, and sky, and ocean, hath its bubbles,
And verse is one of them—this most of all.

                                              (1797)

* Shakespeare, *As You Like It,* 2.7.161–63.

77 clap] "To slap or strike with a flat surface, so as to smooth or flatten" *(OED).*
77 plait] "To fold . . . flat, to double" *(OED).*
82 Mongolfier] John Michel Montgolfier (1740–1810) and Jacques Etienne Montgolfier (1745–1799) launched the first hot-air balloon in Annonay, France, in the summer of 1783. Joseph Priestley's experiments with oxygen in 1774 helped make this event possible.
85 Earth . . . hath its bubbles] See *Macbeth* 1.3.79: "The earth hath bubbles, as the water has."

Eighteen Hundred and Eleven, a Poem[*]

Still the loud death drum, thundering from afar,
O'er the vext nations pours the storm of war:
To the stern call still Britain bends her ear,
Feeds the fierce strife, the alternate hope and fear;
Bravely, though vainly, dares to strive with Fate,
And seeks by turns to prop each sinking state.
Colossal power with overwhelming force
Bears down each fort of Freedom in its course;
Prostrate she lies beneath the Despot's sway,
10   While the hushed nations curse him—and obey.

Bounteous in vain, with frantic man at strife,
Glad Nature pours the means—the joys of life;
In vain with orange blossoms scents the gale,
The hills with olives clothes, with corn the vale;
Man calls to Famine, nor invokes in vain,
Disease and Rapine follow in her train;
The tramp of marching hosts disturbs the plough,
The sword, not sickle, reaps the harvest now,
And where the Soldier gleans the scant supply,
20   The helpless Peasant but retires to die;
No laws his hut from licensed outrage shield,
And war's least horror is the ensanguined field.

Fruitful in vain, the matron counts with pride
The blooming youths that grace her honoured side;
No son returns to press her widow'd hand,
Her fallen blossoms strew a foreign strand.
—Fruitful in vain, she boasts her virgin race,
Whom cultured arts adorn and gentlest grace;
Defrauded of its homage, Beauty mourns,
30   And the rose withers on its virgin thorns.
Frequent, some stream obscure, some uncouth name
By deeds of blood is lifted into fame;
Oft o'er the daily page some soft one bends
To learn the fate of husband, brothers, friends,

Or the spread map with anxious eye explores,
Its dotted boundaries and penciled shores,
Asks *where* the spot that wrecked her bliss is found,
And learns its name but to detest the sound.

And think'st thou, Britain, still to sit at ease,
An island Queen amidst thy subject seas,   40
While the vext billows, in their distant roar,
But soothe thy slumbers, and but kiss thy shore?
To sport in wars, while danger keeps aloof,
Thy grassy turf unbruised by hostile hoof?
So sing thy flatterers; but, Britain, know,
Thou who hast shared the guilt must share the woe.
Nor distant is the hour; low murmurs spread,
And whispered fears, creating what they dread;
Ruin, as with an earthquake shock, is here,
There, the heart-witherings of unuttered fear,   50
And that sad death, whence most affection bleeds,
Which sickness, only of the soul, precedes.
Thy baseless wealth dissolves in air away,
Like mists that melt before the morning ray:
No more on crowded mart or busy street
Friends, meeting friends, with cheerful hurry greet;
Sad, on the ground thy princely merchants bend
Their altered looks, and evil days portend,
And fold their arms, and watch with anxious breast
The tempest blackening in the distant West.   60

Yes, thou must droop; thy Midas dream is o'er;
The golden tide of Commerce leaves thy shore,
Leaves thee to prove the alternate ills that haunt
Enfeebling Luxury and ghastly Want;
Leaves thee, perhaps, to visit distant lands,
And deal the gifts of Heaven with equal hands.

Yet, O my Country, name beloved, revered,
By every tie that binds the soul endeared,
Whose image to my infant senses came
Mixt with Religion's light and Freedom's holy flame!   70

If prayers may not avert, if 'tis thy fate
To rank amongst the names that once were great,
Not like the dim cold Crescent shalt thou fade,
Thy debt to Science and the Muse unpaid;
Thine are the laws surrounding states revere,
Thine the full harvest of the mental year,
Thine the bright stars in Glory's sky that shine,
And arts that make it life to live are thine.
If westward streams the light that leaves the shores,
80   Still from thy lamp the streaming radiance pours.
Wide spreads thy race from Ganges to the pole,
O'er half the western world thy accents roll:
Nations beyond the Apalachian hills
Thy hand has planted and thy spirit fills:
Soon as their gradual progress shall impart
The finer sense of morals and of art,
Thy stores of knowledge the new states shall know,
And think thy thoughts, and with thy fancy glow;
Thy Lockes, thy Paleys shall instruct their youth,
90   Thy leading star direct their search for truth;
Beneath the spreading Platan's tent-like shade,
Or by Missouri's rushing waters laid,
"Old father Thames" shall be the Poet's theme,
Of Hagley's woods the enamoured virgin dream,
And Milton's tones the raptured ear enthrall,
Mixt with the roaring of Niagara's fall;
In Thomson's glass the ingenuous youth shall learn
A fairer face of Nature to discern;
Nor of the Bards that swept the British lyre
100   Shall fade one laurel, or one note expire.
Then, loved Joanna, to admiring eyes
Thy storied groups in scenic pomp shall rise;

73 Crescent] The Ottoman Empire.

89 Thy Lockes, thy Paleys] John Locke (1632–1704), author of *Essay concerning Human Understanding* (1690), and William Paley (1743–1805), author of *The Principles of Moral and Political Philosophy* (1785).

94 Hagley's woods] The estate of Lord Lyttelton in Worcestershire (McCarthy and Kraft, *The Poems of Anna Letitia Barbauld,* 313).

97 Thomson's glass] James Thomson's poem *The Seasons* (1730) (ibid., 313).

101 Joanna] Joanna Baillie (1762–1851), playwright and poet.

Their high soul'd strains and Shakespear's noble rage
Shall with alternate passion shake the stage.
Some youthful Basil from thy moral lay
With stricter hand his fond desires shall sway;
Some Ethwald, as the fleeting shadows pass,
Start at his likeness in the mystic glass;
The tragic Muse resume her just controul,
With pity and with terror purge the soul,   110
While wide o'er transatlantic realms thy name
Shall live in light, and gather *all* its fame.

Where wanders Fancy down the lapse of years
Shedding o'er imaged woes untimely tears?
Fond moody Power! as hopes—as fears prevail,
She longs, or dreads, to lift the awful veil,
On visions of delight now loves to dwell,
Now hears the shriek of woe or Freedom's knell:
Perhaps, she says, long ages past away,
And set in western waves our closing day,   120
Night, Gothic night, again may shade the plains
Where Power is seated, and where Science reigns;
England, the seat of arts, be only known
By the grey ruin and the mouldering stone;
That Time may tear the garland from her brow,
And Europe sit in dust, as Asia now.

Yet then the ingenuous youth whom Fancy fires
With pictured glories of illustrious sires,
With duteous zeal their pilgrimage shall take
From the blue mountains, or Ontario's lake,   130
With fond adoring steps to press the sod
By statesmen, sages, poets, heroes trod;
On Isis' banks to draw inspiring air,
From Runnymede to send the patriot's prayer;
In pensive thought, where Cam's slow waters wind,
To meet those shades that ruled the realms of mind;

133 On Isis' banks] The Thames River is called the Isis in Oxford.
134 Runnymede] The site where King John signed the Magna Carta.
135 where Cam's slow waters wind] The river Cam flows past Cambridge University.

In silent halls to sculptured marbles bow,
And hang fresh wreaths round Newton's awful brow.
Oft shall they seek some peasant's homely shed,
140 Who toils, unconscious of the mighty dead,
To ask where Avon's winding waters stray,
And thence a knot of wild flowers bear away;
Anxious inquire where Clarkson, friend of man,
Or all-accomplished Jones his race began;
If of the modest mansion aught remains
Where Heaven and Nature prompted Cowper's strains;
Where Roscoe, to whose patriot breast belong
The Roman virtue and the Tuscan song,
Led Ceres to the black and barren moor
150 Where Ceres never gained a wreath before:
With curious search their pilgrim steps shall rove
By many a ruined tower and proud alcove,
Shall listen for those strains that soothed of yore
Thy rock, stern Skiddaw, and thy fall, Lodore;
Feast with Dun Edin's classic brow their sight,
And visit "Melross by the pale moonlight."

But who their mingled feelings shall pursue
When London's faded glories rise to view?

138 Newton's] Isaac Newton (1642–1727), founder of the modern science of optics, who first demonstrated the principle of universal gravitation.

141 Avon's winding waters] The Avon River flows through Stratford-upon-Avon, birthplace of William Shakespeare.

143 Clarkson] Thomas Clarkson (1760–1846), the abolitionist.

144 Jones] Sir William Jones (1746–94), linguist; husband of poet Anna Maria Jones.

146 Cowper's] William Cowper (1731–1800), one of the most admired poets of the late eighteenth century.

147–50 Where Roscoe . . . a wreath before:] The Historian of the age of Leo has brought into cultivation the extensive tract of Chatmoss. *Barbauld*. [William Roscoe (1753–1831), poet, agriculturalist, and friend of Barbauld who, like her, opposed the war, demonstrated at Chat Moss, in Lancashire, that high-quality crops could be cultivated on moorland (McCarthy and Kraft, *The Poems of Anna Letitia Barbauld*, 314). *Ed*.]

154 Thy rock, stern Skiddaw, and thy fall, Lodore] A mountain and a waterfall, respectively, in the Lake District.

155 Dun Edin's classic brow] Perched above the city of Dun Edin, or Edinburgh, is Arthur's Seat, an ancient volcanic peak.

156 "Melross by the pale moonlight"] See Walter Scott, *The Lay of the Last Minstrel* (1805), 2.i.

The mighty city, which by every road,
In floods of people poured itself abroad; 160
Ungirt by walls, irregularly great,
No jealous drawbridge, and no closing gate;
Whose merchants (such the state which commerce brings)
Sent forth their mandates to dependent kings;
Streets, where the turban'd Moslem, bearded Jew,
And wooly Afric, met the brown Hindu;
Where through each vein spontaneous plenty flowed,
Where Wealth enjoyed, and Charity bestowed.
Pensive and thoughtful shall the wanderers greet
Each splendid square, and still, untrodden street; 170
Or of some crumbling turret, mined by time,
The broken stair with perilous step shall climb,
Thence stretch their view the wide horizon round,
By scattered hamlets trace its ancient bound,
And, choked no more with fleets, fair Thames survey
Through reeds and sedge pursue his idle way.

With throbbing bosoms shall the wanderers tread
The hallowed mansions of the silent dead,
Shall enter the long isle and vaulted dome
Where Genius and where Valour find a home; 180
Awe-struck, midst chill sepulchral marbles breathe,
Where all above is still, as all beneath;
Bend at each antique shrine, and frequent turn
To clasp with fond delight some sculptured urn,
The ponderous mass of Johnson's form to greet,
Or breathe the prayer at Howard's sainted feet.

Perhaps some Briton, in whose musing mind
Those ages live which Time has cast behind,
To every spot shall lead his wondering guests
On whose known site the beam of glory rests: 190

185–86 Johnson's form . . . Howard's sainted feet.] Marble statues of Samuel Johnson (1708–84), poet, essayist, and author of the pioneering work *A Dictionary of the English Language* (1755), and John Howard (1726–90), prison reformer, whom Barbauld elsewhere describes as "the martyr of humanity," stand in the nave of St. Paul's Cathedral (McCarthy and Kraft, *The Poems of Anna Letitia Barbauld*, 208, 315).

Here Chatham's eloquence in thunder broke,
Here Fox persuaded, or here Garrick spoke;
Shall boast how Nelson, fame and death in view,
To wonted victory led his ardent crew,
In England's name enforced, with loftiest tone,
Their duty,—and too well fulfilled his own:
How gallant Moore, as ebbing life dissolved,
But hoped his country had his fame absolved.
Or call up sages whose capacious mind

200   Left in its course a track of light behind;
Point where mute crowds on Davy's lips reposed,
And Nature's coyest secrets were disclosed;
Join with their Franklin, Priestley's injured name,
Whom, then, each continent shall proudly claim.

Oft shall the strangers turn their eager feet
The rich remains of ancient art to greet,
The pictured walls with critic eye explore,
And Reynolds be what Raphael was before.
On spoils from every clime their eyes shall gaze,

210   Egyptian granites and the Etruscan vase;
And when midst fallen London, they survey
The stone where Alexander's ashes lay,
Shall own with humbled pride the lesson just
By Time's slow finger written in the dust.

---

191 Chatham's] William Pitt, first earl of Chatham (1708–78), prime minister during the Seven Years' War.

192 Fox persuaded . . . Garrick spoke] Charles James Fox (1749–1806), who advocated parliamentary reform, and David Garrick (1717–79), the famed actor, producer, and playwright.

197 Moore] General Sir John Moore (1761–1809) led a heroic 125-mile retreat from Napoleon's forces at Madrid and was fatally wounded after evacuating his troops.

201 Davy's] Sir Humphrey Davy (1778–1829), English chemist.

203 Franklin, Priestley's] Benjamin Franklin (1706–90), American writer, inventor, diplomat, and philosopher, was a friend of Joseph Priestley's.

208 Reynolds] Sir Joshua Reynolds (1723–92), the most admired British portrait painter of the eighteenth century.

210 Egyptian granites and the Etruscan vase] An allusion to the contents of the British Museum.

212 The stone where Alexander's ashes lay] A granite sarcophagus at the British Museum was thought to be that of Alexander the Great (McCarthy and Kraft, *The Poems of Anna Letitia Barbauld*, 315).

There walks a Spirit o'er the peopled earth,
Secret his progress is, unknown his birth;
Moody and viewless as the changing wind,
No force arrests his foot, no chains can bind;
Where'er he turns, the human brute awakes,
And, roused to better life, his sordid hut forsakes: 220
He thinks, he reasons, glows with purer fires,
Feels finer wants, and burns with new desires:
Obedient Nature follows where he leads;
The steaming marsh is changed to fruitful meads;
The beasts retire from man's asserted reign,
And prove his kingdom was not given in vain.
Then from its bed is drawn the ponderous ore,
Then Commerce pours her gifts on every shore,
Then Babel's towers and terraced gardens rise,
And pointed obelisks invade the skies;   230
The prince commands, in Tyrian purple drest,
And Egypt's virgins weave the linen vest.
Then spans the graceful arch the roaring tide,
And stricter bounds the cultured fields divide.
Then kindles Fancy, then expands the heart,
Then blow the flowers of Genius and of Art;
Saints, heroes, sages, who the land adorn,
Seem rather to descend than to be born;
Whilst History, midst the rolls consigned to fame,
With pen of adamant inscribes their name.   240

The Genius now forsakes the favoured shore,
And hates, capricious, what he loved before;
Then empires fall to dust, then arts decay,
And wasted realms enfeebled despots sway;
Even Nature's changed; without his fostering smile
Ophir no gold, no plenty yields the Nile;
The thirsty sand absorbs the useless rill,
And spotted plagues from putrid fens distill.
In desert solitudes then Tadmor sleeps,
Stern Marius then o'er fallen Carthage weeps;   250

249 Tadmor] Biblical name for Palmyra (ibid., 316).
250 Stern Marius then o'er fallen Carthage weeps] Plutarch (*Lives* 9.577) tells of the stern

Then with enthusiast love the pilgrim roves
To seek his footsteps in forsaken groves,
Explores the fractured arch, the ruined tower,
Those limbs disjointed of gigantic power;
Still at each step he dreads the adder's sting,
The Arab's javelin, or the tiger's spring;
With doubtful caution treads the echoing ground,
And asks where Troy or Babylon is found.

And now the vagrant Power no more detains
260   The vale of Tempe, or Ausonian plains;
Northward he throws the animating ray,
O'er Celtic nations bursts the mental day:
And, as some playful child the mirror turns,
Now here now there the moving lustre burns;
Now o'er his changeful fancy more prevail
Batavia's dykes than Arno's purple vale,
And stinted suns, and rivers bound with frost,
Than Enna's plains or Baia's viny coast;
Venice the Adriatic weds in vain,
270   And Death sits brooding o'er Campania's plain;
O'er Baltic shores and through Hercynian groves,
Stirring the soul, the mighty impulse moves;
Art plies his tools, and Commerce spreads her sail,
And wealth is wafted in each shifting gale.
The sons of Odin tread on Persian looms,
And Odin's daughters breathe distilled perfumes;
Loud minstrel Bards, in Gothic halls, rehearse

Caius Marius (born c. 157 B.C.), who told an official barring him from returning to Africa to tell the governor "that thou hast seen Marius a fugitive, seated amid the ruins of Carthage" (McCarthy and Kraft, *The Poems of Anna Letitia Barbauld,* 316).

    260 The vale of Tempe, or Ausonian plains] Classical Greece and Rome; the vale of Tempe is in Thessaly, and *Ausonian* is Virgilian for "Italian" (McCarthy and Kraft, *The Poems of Anna Letitia Barbauld,* 316).

    266 Batavia's dykes than Arno's purple vale] Holland was called the Batavian Republic during Napoleon's occupation. The Arno River is in Italy.

    268 Than Enna's plains or Baia's viny coast] Baia was a resort town on the Bay of Naples. Enna was a valley in Sicily, according to classical mythology (ibid., 316, 244).

    271 Hercynian groves] Germany's Black Forest (ibid., 316).

    275 Odin] Norse god of war, poetry, knowledge, and wisdom.

The Runic rhyme, and "build the lofty verse":
The Muse, whose liquid notes were wont to swell
To the soft breathings of the 'Æolian shell,   280
Submits, reluctant, to the harsher tone,
And scarce believes the altered voice her own.
And now, where Caesar saw with proud disdain
The wattled hut and skin of azure stain,
Corinthian columns rear their graceful forms,
And light varandas brave the wintry storms,
While British tongues the fading fame prolong
Of Tully's eloquence and Maro's song.
Where once Bonduca whirled the scythed car,
And the fierce matrons raised the shriek of war,   290
Light forms beneath transparent muslins float,
And tutored voices swell the artful note.
Light-leaved acacias and the shady plane
And spreading cedar grace the woodland reign;
While crystal walls the tenderer plants confine,
The fragrant orange and the nectared pine;
The Syrian grape there hangs her rich festoons,
Nor asks for purer air, or brighter noons:
Science and Art urge on the useful toil,
New mould a climate and create the soil,   300
Subdue the rigour of the northern Bear,
O'er polar climes shed aromatic air,
On yielding Nature urge their new demands,
And ask not gifts but tribute at her hands.

London exults: — on London Art bestows
Her summer ices and her winter rose;
Gems of the East her mural crown adorn,
And Plenty at her feet pours forth her horn;
While even the exiles her just laws disclaim,

---

278 "build the lofty verse"] See Milton, *Lycidas* line 11: "build the lofty rhyme."
288 Tully's eloquence and Maro's song] Cicero Marcus Tullius (106–43 B.C.), Roman statesman, orator, and prolific author, and Publius Vergilius Maro (70–19 B.C.), Roman poet.
289 Bonduca] Boadicea, legendary queen of the Britons (McCarthy and Kraft, *The Poems of
Anna Letitia Barbauld,* 316).
301 the northern Bear] The North Star, part of the constellation Ursa Minor.

310   People a continent, and build a name:
        August she sits, and with extended hands
        Holds forth the book of life to distant lands.

        But fairest flowers expand but to decay;
        The worm is in thy core, thy glories pass away;
        Arts, arms and wealth destroy the fruits they bring;
        Commerce, like beauty, knows no second spring.
        Crime walks thy streets, Fraud earns her unblest bread,
        O'er want and woe thy gorgeous robe is spread,
        And angel charities in vain oppose:
320   With grandeur's growth the mass of misery grows.
        For see,—to other climes the Genius soars,
        He turns from Europe's desolated shores;
        And lo, even now, midst mountains wrapt in storm,
        On Andes' heights he shrouds his awful form;
        On Chimborazo's summits treads sublime,
        Measuring in lofty thought the march of Time;
        Sudden he calls:—" 'Tis now the hour!" he cries,
        Spreads his broad hand, and bids the nations rise.
        La Plata hears amidst her torrents' roar;
330   Potosi hears it, as she digs the ore:
        Ardent, the Genius fans the noble strife,
        And pours through feeble souls a higher life,
        Shouts to the mingled tribes from sea to sea,
        And swears—Thy world, Columbus, shall be free.

                                                        (1812)

* Barbauld completed work on the poem in early December 1811, and it was published by 5 February 1812. Anne Grant's *Eighteen Hundred and Thirteen* (1814) was written as a counterstatement (McCarthy and Kraft, *The Poems of Anna Letitia Barbauld*,
309, 311).

325 Chimborazo's] Mountain in Ecuador.
329 La Plata] City in Argentina, about thirty-five miles southeast of Buenos Aires.
330 Potosi] City in south-central Bolivia.

Life

Animula, vagula, blandula.*

Life! I know not what thou art,
But know that thou and I must part;
And when, or how, or where we met,
I own to me's a secret yet.
But this I know, when thou art fled,
Where'er they lay these limbs, this head,
No clod so valueless shall be,
As all that then remains of me.
O whither, whither dost thou fly,
Where bend unseen thy trackless course,   10
    And in this strange divorce,
Ah tell where I must seek this compound I?

To the vast ocean of empyreal flame,
    From whence thy essence came,
    Dost thou thy flight pursue, when freed
    From matter's base encumbering weed?
      Or dost thou, hid from sight,
      Wait, like some spell-bound knight,
Through blank oblivious years the' appointed hour,
To break thy trance and reassume thy power?   20
Yet canst thou without thought or feeling be?
O say what art thou, when no more thou'rt thee?

    Life! we've been long together,
    Through pleasant and through cloudy weather;
      'Tis hard to part when friends are dear;
      Perhaps 't will cost a sigh, a tear;
      Then steal away, give little warning,
        Choose thine own time;
Say not Good night, but in some brighter clime
      Bid me Good morning.   30

        (wr. 1812; pub. 1825)

---

* Alexander Pope translated this line from a Latin poem attributed to the emperor Hadrian (A.D. 76–138) as follows: "Ah fleeting Spirit! wand'ring Fire."

The Baby-House

Dear Agatha, I give you joy,
And much admire your pretty toy,
A mansion in itself complete
And fitted to give guests a treat;
With couch and table, chest and chair,
The bed or supper to prepare;
We almost wish to change ourselves
To fairy forms of tripping elves,
To press the velvet couch and eat
From tiny cups the sugared meat.

I much suspect that many a sprite
Inhabits it at dead of night;
That, as they dance, the listening ear
The pat of fairy feet might hear;
That, just as you have said your prayers,
They hurry-scurry down the stairs:
And you'll do well to try to find
Tester or ring they've left behind.

But think not, Agatha, you own
That toy, a Baby-house, alone;
For many a sumptuous one is found
To press an ampler space of ground.
The broad-based Pyramid that stands
Casting its shade in distant lands,
Which asked some mighty nation's toil
With mountain-weight to press the soil,
And there has raised its head sublime
Through æras of uncounted time,—
Its use if asked, 'tis only said,
A Baby-house to lodge the dead.
Nor less beneath more genial skies
The domes of pomp and folly rise,
Whose sun through diamond windows streams,
While gems and gold reflect his beams;
Where tapestry clothes the storied wall,
And fountains spout and waters fall;

The peasant faints beneath his load,
Nor tastes the grain his hands have sowed,
While scarce a nation's wealth avails
To raise thy Baby-house, Versailles.   40
And Baby-houses oft appear
On British ground, of prince or peer;
Awhile their stately heads they raise,
The' admiring traveller stops to gaze;
He looks again—where are they now?
Gone to the hammer or the plough:
Then trees, the pride of ages, fall,
And naked stands the pictured wall;
And treasured coins from distant lands
Must feel the touch of sordid hands;   50
And gems, of classic stores the boast,
Fall to the cry of—Who bids most?
Then do not, Agatha, repine
That cheaper Baby-house is thine.
                              (wr. c. 1818; pub. 1825)

Riddle

From rosy bowers we issue forth,
From east to west, from south to north,
Unseen, unfelt, by night, by day,
Abroad we take our airy way:
We foster love and kindle strife,
The bitter and the sweet of life:
Piercing and sharp, we wound like steel;
Now, smooth as oil, those wounds we heal:
Not strings of pearl are valued more,
Or gems enchased in golden ore;   10
Yet thousands of us every day,
Worthless and vile, are thrown away.
Ye wise, secure with bars of brass
The double doors through which we pass;
For, once escaped, back to our cell
No human art can us compel.
                              (1825)

Mrs. E.-G. Bayfield

(fl. 1803–1816)

Little is currently known about the woman who published under the name "Mrs. E.-G. Bayfield" and who may have been born Laura Cooper. Subscribers to her *Fugitive Poems* (1805) included Elizabeth Inchbald, Jane Porter, William Jerningham, and Elizabeth Cobbold, as well as many officers of the Twenty-third Regiment. The volume opens with a poetic "Address to the Subscribers" by her friend Mary Cockle, who confides that the poet has known "sorrow's darkest hour" in her roles as wife and mother and that she patiently awaits the return of her husband, an army officer stationed overseas. Bayfield had at least three children, but, according to Cockle, "o'er the blossoms of maternal love / Th'ungenial gale of chill misfortune blows." This may refer to economic hardship brought on by the absence of Bayfield's husband or perhaps to the illness or death of some of her children.

In her dedication, Bayfield declares that "the qualities of a parasite were never those in which I have been accustomed to excel" but thanks her subscribers for their compassion. Though she describes her poems as products of her "infant muse," the *Annual Review* declared that the subscribers to *Fugitive Poems* had "no reason to blush at this extension of their patronage" and that the poems "do credit to the feelings of the author as a mother and a wife."[1] Longmans paid six guineas for the book.

In 1806 Bayfield published a selection from one of her favorite authors, Johann Georg Zimmermann, entitled *Gleanings from Zimmermann on Solitude; to Which are Added, Occasional Observations, and an Ode to Retirement,* dedicated to the Duchess of York and to the women of Great Britain.[2] Also attributed to Bayfield are nine anonymous novels dating from 1803 to 1814. She was apparently still living in 1816, but her later life is obscure.

---

1. *Annual Review* 4 (1805): 565.
2. See the review in ibid., 5 (1806): 593;. The book was also reviewed in the *Eclectic Review* (2 [December 1806]: 1038–39) and in the *Monthly Mirror* (22 [October 1806]: 253–54).

MAJOR WORKS: *Fugitive Poems* (London, 1805); *Gleanings from Zimmermann on Solitude; to Which are Added, Occasional Observations, and an Ode to Retirement* (London, 1806); and the following anonymous novels attributed to her, all probably published in London: *Light and Shade* (1803), by the author of *Federetta; The Aunt and the Niece* (1804); *Eversfield Abbey* (1806); *Love as It May Be, and Friendship as It Ought to Be,* later retitled *A Winter at Bath* (1807); *The Corinna of England, and a Heroine in the Shade* (1808); *The Banks of the Wye* (1809); *The Woman of Colour, A Tale* (1809); *Black Rock House, or Dear Bought Experience* (1810); and *The Splendour of Adversity, a Domestic Story* (1814).

TEXT USED: Text of "The Danger of Discontent" from *Fugitive Poems.*

The Danger of Discontent

Mary exclaims—"Mama's severe,
"And papa's conduct quite austere:
"When to some darling wish inclin'd,
"Or on some plan I fix my mind;
"With grave advice I'm thwarted."—

"Oh, soon may that holiday period come
When I shall be blest with my husband and home;
When no cross papa nor mama more shall teaze,
And I live with the *man of my heart,* quite at ease."

The wishes of Mary were not long suspended,   10
But tho' soon completed, her case was not mended;
For tho' much she respected her conjugal vows,
They were held very light by her profligate spouse
And poor simple Mary was pained to discover
The wonderful diff'rence 'twixt husband and *lover;*
Of late he's so rude and tyrannical grown,
That no longer she boasts of a *home of her own;*
Tho' her pride scarce permits the plain truth to appear,
Yet it speaks in the sigh and the silent-shed tear.
In those hours of dejection, her mem'ry portrays   20
The *now* cherish'd delights of her happier days,
And mama's grave advice, which of late could not move,
Now appears in the garb of affection and love.

"Dear parents," she mentally cries, "oh! forgive
The ingrate, who would not your maxims receive;
Fain, fain would she now to your mansion repair,
And, press'd to your bosoms, forget ev'ry care—
But wishes are vain—and your child must remain,
While her aching heart whispers she forg'd her own chain.
30   Then this truth let us own, which experience will prove—
No affection's so binding as filial love;
And no keener anguish can sorrow impart,
Than that which is caus'd by the *man of your heart.*"

(1805)

Elizabeth Bentley

(1767–1839)

Born in Norwich in November 1767, Elizabeth Bentley was the only child of Mary Lawrence, a cooper's child, and Daniel Bentley, an educated journeyman shoemaker, who taught his daughter reading and spelling. According to the poet's own account, she enjoyed "such books as were in the house; which were chiefly a spelling-book, fable-book, dictionary, and books of arithmetic; and . . . such little pamphlets as I could borrow of my neighbours." Around 1777 Elizabeth's father was partially paralyzed by a stroke. Unable now to pursue his craft, he became a peddler and taught Elizabeth writing. In late 1782 he took the job of bookkeeper for the London Coach, but several months later, in January 1783, he died of a second stroke. Elizabeth was fifteen. She recalled that two years after her father's death she developed "an inclination for writing verses, which I had no thought nor desire of being seen." But her mother showed them to acquaintances, who offered encouragement. Bentley then invested in a secondhand grammar book, from which, she said, she "attained the art of expressing myself correctly in my native language."[1] She read Goldsmith, Collins, Pope, Gray, Thomson, Shakespeare, and Milton.[2]

In 1791, when Elizabeth was twenty-four, the Reverend John Walker, of Norwich, sponsored a subscription to publish her *Genuine Poetical Compositions, on Various Subjects*. Dedicated to William Drake Jr., M.P., it included a brief autobiographical account and a portrait of the poet, a plainly dressed, plump young woman with a serious, determined gaze. William Cowper, Amelia Alderson (Opie), Eliza Knipe (later Elizabeth Cobbold), Thomas Bowdler, Elizabeth Carter, Hester Chapone, Sir William Jones, and other literary figures were among the book's nearly two thousand subscribers. A

1. Elizabeth Bentley to the Reverend Mr. Walker, 23 July 1790, in the preface to *Genuine Poetical Compositions, on Various Subjects* (Norwich, 1791).

2. See "Lines, Addressed as a Tribute of Gratitude to the Subscribers in General," ibid., 67–69.

second edition was promised, though whether it actually appeared is unclear. Among the most accomplished works in the book is the long poem "On the Abolition of the African Slave-Trade. July, 1789," which asserts,

> Too long the vile reproach has stain'd our land,
> Of arming Cruelty's despotic hand
> With legal pow'r

Her argument rehearses many of the typical anti-slavery arguments of the time but is most forceful in its condemnation of the violent severing of domestic and emotional bonds:

> To break the dearest, tend'rest ties of life,
> Rend from the husband's arms the much-lov'd wife!
>
> . . . .
>
> More cruel yet to seize the infant train,
> Regardless of the poignant, deep-felt pain,
>
> . . . .
>
> The grief that must the father's heart o'erflow!
> The mother's frantic ecstacy of woe!

Reversing stereotypical tropes, she labels as savage those Britains who fail to feel for the plight of the enslaved and who condone the violation of domestic values; she argues, too, for the rational faculties and capacity for feeling of African peoples. Citing the African Ignatius Sancho, "Whose genius claim'd him an exalted place / Amongst the sons of learning, wit and fame," she argues as well for the intellectual and creative potential of those forced into servitude. The book is dominated, though, by fairly conventional odes to abstract entities. Still, reviews were favorable. The *Gentleman's Magazine* called the book "an extraordinary performance" and said the poems showed "strong marks of a polished and superior mind." The *Monthly Review* called the poems "elegant and harmonious," and the *New Annual Register* observed, "Her imagination is strong and lively; her language, in general, correct and elegant, and her numbers harmonious." The *Critical Review* said, "In several of these poems . . . we trace the marks of original genius" and praised Bentley's "strong and lively imagination."[3]

The proceeds from the book purchased an annuity for Bentley and her mother, who together opened a school, charging twopence a week per child. Bentley's verse appeared frequently in the *Norfolk Chronicle,* and she also brought out a small collection of children's poetry, which sold for a shil-

---

3. *Gentleman's Magazine* 62 (1791): 747; *Monthly Review,* n.s., 6 (1791): 285 (the review appears to have been written by sister poet Elizabeth Moody); *New Annual Register* 12 (1791): 270; *Critical Review,* n.s., 3 (1791): 94.

ling. In 1805, after the battle of Trafalgar, Bentley's *Ode on the Glorious Victory over the French and Spanish Fleets, on the 21st of October, 1805, and the Death of Lord Nelson* appeared in a four-page pamphlet. The June 1821 issue of the *Gentleman's Magazine* contains another of her poems, "Lines to the Memory of W. Stevenson, Esq. F. S. A. Who died May 13, 1821."[4]

In that same year she published, again by subscription, *Poems; being the Genuine Compositions of Elizabeth Bentley, of Norwich.* This book includes elegiac, devotional, and nationalistic poetry, along with poems on the seasons and the natural world. Another volume, *Miscellaneous Poems; being the Genuine Compositions of Elizabeth Bentley, of Norwich,* was published by subscription in 1835. Little is known about Bentley's later life except that the Royal Literary Fund came to her aid in 1829 as it had in 1799. She died in 1839.

MAJOR WORKS: *Genuine Poetical Compositions, on Various Subjects* (Norwich, 1791); *Ode on the Glorious Victory over the French and Spanish Fleets, on the 21st of October, 1805, and the Death of Lord Nelson* (Norwich, [1805?]); *Poems; being the Genuine Compositions of Elizabeth Bentley, of Norwich* (Norwich, London, and Cambridge, 1821); *Miscellaneous Poems; being the Genuine Compositions of Elizabeth Bentley, of Norwich* (Norwich, 1835).

TEXT USED: Text of "To a Redbreast" from *Poems; being the Genuine Compositions of Elizabeth Bentley, of Norwich.*

To a Redbreast, That Flew into the House, and Suffered Itself to be Taken by the Hand of the Authoress

> Fear not, sweet Bird! thy flutt'ring cease,
>   Nor deem thy freedom fled:
> Soon shalt thou feel thy glad release;
>   No evil need'st thou dread.
>
> The hand that grasps thy downy plumes,
>   Its prize shall soon forego;
> No heart thy life to thraldom dooms,
>   Nor triumphs in thy woe.

4. *Gentleman's Magazine*, 2nd ser., 91 (June 1821): 548.

Go, guiltless captive, sport in air,
    New plume thy ruffled wing;
To yonder waving spray repair,
    Thy sprightly warblings sing.

In search of spotless pleasures rove,
    Go seek thy anxious mate,
And mid thy brethren of the grove,
    Th'eventful tale relate.

Go, say what fears thy breast alarm'd,
    Lest Cruelty's fell knife,
Th'unfeeling hand of Sport had arm'd,
    To end thy hapless life.

How sudden Anguish fix'd her wound;
    How thy swoln bosom beat,
Lest some sad prison's wiry bound
    Should all thy joys defeat.

Thy glad escape delighted tell,
    And grant my only boon;
Oft near the cottage where I dwell
    Thy grateful carols tune.

When chilly snow conceals the land,
    And storms pervade the skies,
And surly Winter's icy hand
    Th'accustom'd food denies,

With cautious, timid glance no more
    Athwart the threshold steal,
But fearless pass the op'ning door,
    And pick thy plenteous meal.

O come, and Nature's bounty share,
    A free and welcome guest;
No ruthless grasp, nor tangling snare,
    Shall e'er thy steps molest.

(1821)

Matilda Betham

(1776–1852)

Eldest of the fourteen children of Mary Damant of Eye, in Suffolk, and the Reverend William Betham of Stonham, Aspall, Suffolk, Mary Matilda Betham was an accomplished poet, scholar, and painter of miniatures. Her father, headmaster of a secondary school, antiquary, and author of two books of genealogy, had a large personal library; there Matilda, as she was called, read widely, chiefly in history, but she was given an education in sewing to prevent a "too strict application to books."[1] She learned French on visits to London, and in 1796, in Cambridge, she took lessons from Agostino Isola, Italian instructor to Thomas Gray and William Wordsworth. In 1797 she published *Elegies, and Other Smaller Poems* with the publishers Jermyn & Forster in Ipswich and with Longmans in London. It was widely and enthusiastically reviewed.

This early success encouraged Betham, around the turn of the century, to settle in London, hoping to earn a living with her pen. She was the close friend of Robert Southey and Charles and Mary Lamb and knew John Opie, Frances Holcroft, Hannah More, Anna Letitia Barbauld, Germaine de Staël, and Samuel Taylor Coleridge. To supplement her literary income, Betham gave readings from Shakespeare and taught herself to paint miniatures, eventually exhibiting her portraits at the Royal Academy. In 1804 she published *A Biographical Dictionary of the Celebrated Women of Every Age and Country,* a volume of early feminist scholarship representing more than six years' research. She also seems to have been writing a novel during this period, though the book has not been traced and may never have been published. In 1808 her volume of *Poems* was noticed in such important publications as the *Critical Review,* the *Monthly Review,* and the *Annual Review.*

Robert Southey, Charles Lamb, and Samuel Taylor Coleridge were all admirers of Betham's poetry. On 9 September 1802 Coleridge wrote "To Matilda Betham, from a Stranger," observing:

---

1. M. Betham-Edwards, *Six Life Studies of Famous Women* (London, 1880), 235.

> And now the fair, wild offspring of thy genius,
> Those wanderers, whom thy fancy had sent forth
> To seek their fortune in this motley world,
> Have found a little home within *my* heart[2]

Coleridge visited an exhibition of Betham's paintings in 1808 and asked her to design a seal for him. She painted his portrait in 1811. According to contemporary accounts, Betham was an excellent conversationalist.

In the spring of 1814 Betham asked Robert Southey to recommend a literary project that might prove lucrative. He suggested several possibilities, including translating a popular tale into verse. The result was her *Lay of Marie* (1816), based upon the story of the poet Marie de France. It portrays a woman composing and singing her own life story, a commentary on the woman writer. Charles Lamb proofread the poem in press and made some substantive, though not always helpful, changes. In one letter he remarks, "You will find one line I have ventured to alter. . . . You had made hope & yoke rhime, which is intolerable." The poem not only attracted little critical attention but sold poorly, plunging its author into debt which, according to the Lambs, "led to little accidents unbecoming a woman and a poetess to suffer."[3]

Betham's last book of poetry was *Vignettes: In Verse* (1818). She suffered a mental breakdown sometime between 1818 and 1820, and her family subsequently had her institutionalized. After her release she apparently abandoned both painting and publishing as careers; she left London, but how she occupied herself during the 1820s is unclear. During the 1830s she was living at Islington with her elderly parents and, judging from an 1833 letter of Charles Lamb to Betham's sister, may not have been comfortable financially.[4] Betham returned to London in her old age. Even then she could be found at literary gatherings

> her face beaming with animation and intelligence, . . . usually surrounded by a
> little court. "I would rather talk to Matilda Betham than to the most beautiful
> young woman in the world," said one of her youthful admirers of the other sex,
> in her old age; and those who listened to her bright sallies, her piquant stories,
> her apt quotations, forgot that she was no longer the Matilda of former days.[5]

She continued her literary friendships with the Lambs, Robert Southey, and others. In her early seventies she wrote of herself in a notebook:

---

2. *The Complete Poetical Works of Samuel Taylor Coleridge,* ed. Ernest Hartley Coleridge (Oxford, 1912), 375.

3. Charles Lamb, *The Letters of Charles Lamb,* ed. James Fagan, vol. 4 (Boston, 1905), 84–85.

4. Quoted in Betham-Edwards, *Life Studies,* 295.

5. As recalled by Amelia B. Edwards and quoted in ibid., 299–300.

> Though Age advances, strength decays,
> Enjoyments come a thousand ways —
> The bending trunk of Life's old tree
> Still blossoms forth abundantly![6]

In old age Charles Lamb told her, "Did I not love your verses, have I ever failed to see that you had the most feminine soul of all our poet- or prose-esses?"[7]

MAJOR WORKS: *Elegies, and Other Smaller Poems* (Ipswich and London, [1797]); *A Biographical Dictionary of the Celebrated Women of Every Age and Country,* (London, 1804); *Poems* (London, 1808); *The Lay of Marie: A Poem* (London, 1816); *Vignettes: In Verse* (London, 1818).

TEXTS USED: Texts of "To Miss Rouse Boughton, Now the Right Hon. Lady St. John," "Sonnet," "To a Llangollen Rose," "Fragment," and "The Daughter" from *Poems.* Texts of "II ('Lucy, I think not of thy beauty')" and "VII ('Come, Magdalen, and bind my hair')" from *Vignettes: in Verse.*

To Miss Rouse Boughton,*
Now the Right Hon. Lady St. John,
Aberystwith, July 5th 1799

> Louisa, while thy pliant fingers trace
>   The solemn beauties of the prospect round,
> Or, on thy instrument, with touching grace,
>   Awaken all the witcheries of sound:
>
> Mild, as thy manners, do the colours rise,
>   As soft and unobtrusive meet the view;
> And, when the varied notes the ear surprize,
>   We own the harmony as strictly true.
>
> Be thine the praise, alas! a gift how rare!
> Artless, and unpretending, to excel!   10

---

6. Quoted in Ernest Betham, ed., *A House of Letters. Being excerpts from the Correspondence of Miss Charlotte Jerningham . . . and Others, with Matilda Betham, etc.* (London, 1905), 245.

7. Ibid., 232–33.

Forget the envied charm of being fair,
  To learn the noblest science,—acting well!
And let no world the seal of truth displace,
Or spoil the heart's accordance with the face!
                              (1808)

*Relative of Sir Charles William Rouse-Boughton. Betham knew the Rouse-Boughton family through her work as a painter of miniature portraits.

Sonnet

Urge me no more! nor think, because I seem
Tame and unsorrowing in the world's rude strife,
That anguish and resentment have not life
Within the heart that ye so quiet deem:
In this forc'd stillness only, I sustain
My thought and feeling, wearied out with pain!
Floating as 'twere upon some wild abyss,
Whence, silent Patience, bending o'er the brink,
Would rescue them with strong and steady hand,
10   And join again, by that connecting link,
Which now is broken:—O respect her care!
Respect her in this fearful self-command!
No moment teems with greater woe than this,
Should she but pause, or falter in despair!
                              (1808)

To a Llangollen Rose, The Day after
It Had Been Given by Miss Ponsonby*

Soft blushing flow'r, my bosom grieves,
To view thy sadly drooping leaves:
For, while their tender tints decay,
The rose of Fancy fades away!
As pilgrims, who, with zealous care,
Some little treasur'd relic bear,
To re-assure the doubtful mind,
When pausing memory looks behind;
I, from a more enlighten'd shrine,
Had made this sweet memento mine:
But, lo! its fainting head reclines;
It folds the pallid leaf, and pines,
As mourning the unhappy doom,
Which tears it from so sweet a home!
(wr. 1799; pub. 1808)

* Sarah Ponsonby lived with Lady Eleanor Butler in the vale of Llangollen in
Wales. Their life embodied a rural ideal, and tourists made pilgrimages to their home.

Fragment

A Pilgrim weary, toil-subdued,
I reach'd a country, strange and rude,
And trembled, lest approaching eve
My hope of shelter might deceive;
When I espied a hunter train,
Prowling at leisure o'er the plain,
And hasten'd on to ask relief,
Of the ill-omened, haughty chief.
His eye was artful, keen, and bold,
His smile malevolently cold,
And had not all my fire been fled,
And every earthly passion dead,

His pity to contempt allied,
Had rous'd my anger and my pride;
But as it was, I bent my way,
Where his secluded mansion lay,
Which rose before my eyes at length,
A fortress of determin'd strength,
And layers of every colour'd moss
20   The lofty turrets did emboss,
As tho' the hand of father Time,
Prepar'd a sacrifice sublime,—
Giving his daily rites away,
To aggrandize some future day.
Here as I roam'd the walls along,
I heard a plaintive broken song;
And ere I to the portal drew,
An open window caught my view,
Where a fair dame appear'd in sight,
30   Array'd in robes of purest white.
Long snowy folds confin'd her hair,
And left a polish'd forehead bare.
O'er her meek eyes, of deepest blue,
The sable lash long shadows threw;
Her cheek was delicately pale,
And seem'd to tell a piteous tale,
But o'er her looks such patience stole,
Such saint-like tenderness of soul,
That never did my eyes behold,
40   A beauty of a lovelier mold.

        The lady sigh'd, and closely prest
A sleeping infant to her breast;
Shook off sweet tears of love, and smil'd,
Kissing the fingers of the child,
Which round her own unconscious clung,
Then fondly gaz'd, and softly sung:

        Once like that sea, which ebbs and flows,
        My bosom never knew repose,
        And heavily each morn arose.

I bore with anger and disdain,   50
I had no power to break my chain,
No one to whom I dar'd complain.

And when some bird has caught my eye,
Or distant sail been flitting by,
I wish'd I could as freely fly.

But I can now contented be,
Can tell, dear babe, my griefs to thee,
And feel more brave, and breathe more free.

And when thy father frowns severe,
Although my spirit faints with fear,   60
I feel I have a comfort near.

And when he harshly speaks to me,
If thou art smiling on my knee,
He softens as he looks on thee.

To soothe him in an evil hour
The bud has balm, oh! may the flower
Possess the same prevailing power!

Nor forc'd to leave thy native land,
To pledge a cold, unwilling hand,
May'st thou receive the hard command.   70

My mother had not half the zeal,
The aching fondness which I feel,
She had no broken heart to heal!

And I was friendless when she died,
Who could my little failings chide,
And for an hour her fondness hide.

But I can see no prospect ope,
Can give no fairy vision scope,
If thou art not the spring of hope.

80   I cannot thy affection draw,
                     By childhood's first admiring awe;
                     Be tender pity then thy law!

                     This heart would bleed at every vein,
                     I could not even life sustain,
                     If ever thou should'st give me pain.

                     O! soul of sweetness! can it be,
                     That thou could'st prove unkind to me!
                     That I should fear this blow from thee!

                     Alas! e'en then I would not blame,
90   My love to thee should be the same,
                     And judge from whence unkindness came!

Her words grew indistinct and slow,
Her voice more tremulous and low,
When suddenly the song was o'er,
A whisper even heard no more —
She had discern'd my nearer tread;
Appear'd to feel alarm, and fled.

     *   *   *   *   *   *

                                      (1808)

The Daughter

"Come, mournful lute! dear echo of my woe!
   No stranger's tread in this lone spot I fear,
Sweeter thy notes in such wild places flow,
   And, what is more, my Henry cannot hear!

He will not know my pain and my despair,
   When that dread scene arises on my view,
Where my poor father would not hear my pray'r,
   Or grant his only child a last adieu!

He will not know that still the hour I mourn,
    When death all hopes of pardon snatch'd away;   10
That still this heart by sad remembrance torn,
    Repeats the dreadful mandate of that day.

Luckless for him has been my constant love,
    Luckless the destiny I bade him brave,
For since a parent did our vows reprove,
    Sorrow was all the gift my fondness gave.

Then, though I knew my father's stern command,
    The short-liv'd conflict of affection o'er,
I offer'd to the youth my dowerless hand,
    And fondly reason'd thus on being poor,   20

"Can pomp or splendour elevate the soul,
    Brighten the lustre that illumes the eye!
Make the rough stream of life more smoothly roll,
    Suppress the tear, or waft away the sigh!

Can happiness a purer joy receive,
    In the proud mansions of the rich and great?
Or, tell me, can the wounded bosom heave
    With blunted anguish under robes of state!

No! Henry, no! Alas! too well you know,
    The misery of an affected smile,   30
The pain of clearing the thought-clouded brow,
    To covet for yourself the hateful toil!

And since my choice, and reason both approve,
    Since I have known you many a circling year,
And time has well assur'd me of your love,
    Tell me, my Henry, what have I to fear?

My father, though by world prudence led,
    Will pardon when our happiness is told."
Alas! no curses fell upon my head,
    But never did he more his child behold.   40

He would not, dying, hear my ardent prayer!
    But cruel! said, I leave her all my store;
She wrung my doating heart with deep despair,
    And even now perhaps desires no more.

This is the stroke which all my peace destroys,
    The dagger which no art can draw away,
The thought which every faculty employs,
    Withers my bloom, and makes my strength decay.

His death, his sorrows are the heavy curse
50   That hang above my poor, distracted head!
His dying words have scatter'd vain remorse,
    For vain, though bitter, are the tears I shed.

And yet my father to my soul was dear,
    But tender pity was on Henry's side;
I painted him relenting, not severe,
    Nor fancied I could be an orphan bride.

Ah me! excuses will not cure my pain!
    At least, forgetfulness can little plead.
A widow'd parent!—I deserv'd disdain,
60   'Tis fit these eyes should weep, this heart should bleed!

But yet assist me heaven! to hide my grief,
    My waning health from love's suspicious eyes!
This malady admits of no relief,
    And nought augments the pain, but Henry's sighs.

Perhaps e'en now he wonders at my stay,
    Sees the white fogs of evening rise around,
Comes out to seek me in my devious way,
    But turns not to this unfrequented ground.

Alas! my love, thy anxious care is vain!
70   Nothing can stop yon wand'rer of the sky;
Nothing can long this fleeting life retain!
    For oh! I feel that I must shortly die.

But cease my lute, this low, desponding strain,
   It floats too long upon the heavy air;
Henry may pass and know that I complain.
   One moment's peace to him is worth my care."

She said, and toward the cheerless mansion flew,
   Her slender, sylph-like form array'd in white,
Not clearly seen amidst surrounding dew,
   Seem'd like a spirit ling'ring in its flight.   80

Poor Henry, who had watch'd her in the shade,
   In aching silence list'ning to her song,
At distance follow'd slowly through the glade,
   Pausing forgetful as he pass'd along.

                (1808)

II

Lucy, I think not of thy beauty,
   I praise not each peculiar grace;
To see thee in the path of duty,
   And with that happy, smiling face,
Conveys more pleasure to thy friend,
Than any outward charm could lend.

I see thy graceful babes caress thee,
   I mark thy wise, maternal care,
And sadly do the words impress me,
   The magic words—that thou art fair.   10
I wonder that a tongue is found
To utter the unfeeling sound!

For, art thou not above such praises?
   And is this all that they can see?
Poor is the joy such flattery raises,
   And, oh! how much unworthy thee!
Unworthy one whose heart can feel
The voice of truth, the warmth of zeal!

O Lucy, thou art snatch'd from folly,
   Become too tender to be vain,
The world, it makes me melancholy,
   The world would lure thee back again!
And it would cost me many sighs,
To see it win so bright a prize!

Though passing apprehensions move me,
   I know thou hast a noble heart;
But, Lucy, I so truly love thee,
   So much admire thee as thou art,
That, but the shadow of a fear,
Wakes in my breast a pang sincere.
                        (1818)

VII

Come, Magdalen, and bind my hair,
   And put me on my sad array;
I to my father's house repair,
   And hear his final doom today.

But wrap me in that cypress veil;
   At first his eye I would not brave,
'Till he shall bid the mourner hail,
   And knows I come from Edwin's grave.

I, late his boast, his heir, his pride,
   Must like a guilty vassal kneel;
I, who was gallant Edwin's bride,
   Must to my widow'd state appeal!

Closely within my heart must keep
   His praise for whom that heart is riv'n,
And let each fond resentment sleep,
   For I must die or be forgiven.
                        (1818)

Susanna Blamire

(1747–1794)

Susanna Blamire was born in Cumberland, England, at Cardew Hall, six miles from Carlisle, near the Scottish border, on 12 January 1747, the youngest child of Isabella Simpson of Thackwood and William Blamire, a yeoman farmer. When Blamire was barely seven, her mother died. Her father remarried a year later, and Blamire's wealthy widowed aunt, Mary Stevenson Simpson (1702–85), asked to raise Susanna and her two older brothers and sister. The children were sent to live with her at Thackwood, a substantial manor house just outside the village of Stokedalewath, eight miles south of Carlisle. When she was only eleven, Blamire's father died, and Mary Simpson became the children's legal guardian. Aunt Mary had a relish for reading, which was quickly passed on to her adoring niece. For a short time Blamire attended a village school at Raughton-Head, about a mile away, where she learned the rudiments of reading, writing, and arithmetic. She may subsequently have had tutors from the nearby school at Sebergham, but virtually nothing is known about any later education. Internal evidence in her poetry suggests that she knew the works of Milton, Collins, Gray, Prior, and Ramsay but not those of Burns. Her brother Richmond, who became a London bookseller and publisher, with offices on Craven Street, in the Strand, kept the family stocked with books and with news of the city. Her brother William became a naval surgeon; on visits home, he regaled them with tales of sea voyages as well as troubling stories of war.

At an early age Blamire showed a talent for verse, sometimes entertaining her family with rhymes, but these were usually tossed in the fire, considered merely amusements of the moment. Even as a youngster, though, Blamire envisioned a larger audience. She would sometimes pin scraps of verse to the boughs of trees, where they could be seen by passersby on the public road. Her Aunt Mary and her brother William actively discouraged her from writing poetry. But even so, she was in the habit of taking her guitar, her

favorite musical instrument, into the woods to play and to compose songs.[1]
She was so fond of dancing that, meeting an itinerant musician on the road,
she was likely to dismount her horse and ask him to play while she danced
in the grass. "Miss Sukey," as her neighbors called her, was in their parlance
"a bonny and varra lish [lively] young lass."[2] She enjoyed people and, like her
mother, earned a reputation for her knowledge of herbal remedies. Patrick
Maxwell describes her at this period as "somewhat above the middle size, and
a countenance—though slightly marked with the smallpox—beaming with
good nature; her dark eyes sparkled with animation, and won every heart at
the first introduction."[3]

While visiting her Aunt Fell and her curate husband in Chillingham, in
the Border Country, Blamire met the family of the earl of Tankersville. She
charmed them so much that they asked her to visit and then asked her to
extend her stay. She regaled them with her songs, eventually confessing her
authorship. The old earl urged her to compose more in the Cumberland dialect, and she obliged him. But she was to become a victim of her own success,
for Lord Ossulston, the earl's heir, soon fell in love with her, and she with
him. The elder Tankersvilles did not consider a yeoman's daughter to be an
appropriate match and quickly sent the young man abroad. In "Stoklewath,"
Blamire dramatizes this experience in the account of Anna and William and,
to a lesser degree, in the story of Ethelinde and the Hermit; in both tales, parents intervene to separate young lovers. "What Ails This Heart o' Mine" gives
expression to feelings of loss similar to those Blamire probably experienced
on this painful occasion.

In 1767, when Blamire was twenty, her sister Sarah married Colonel
Graham of the Forty-second Regiment, located in the mid-Highlands of
Scotland. Blamire lived with them at Gartmore for the next six years. During
that time she so enthusiastically embraced Scotland and the Scottish manners, language, legends, and music that she began writing songs in Scots
dialect.[4] Her in-laws seem to have encouraged her poetic composition and
may well have been a literary family. The Grahams took Blamire, who had
never traveled further than Carlisle for the winter, to visit Ireland and Lon-

---

1. She also played the flageolet, a small wind instrument similar to a recorder (Henry
Lonsdale, *The Worthies of Cumberland* [London, 1873], 59).

2. Patrick Maxwell, "Memoir of Miss Susanna Blamire," in *The Poetical Works of Miss Susanna
Blamire, "The Muse of Cumberland,"* comp. Henry Lonsdale, M.D. (Edinburgh, 1842), xxiii.

3. Ibid.

4. Henry Lonsdale dubbed her "The Muse of Cumberland" and took Sarah Tytler and J. L.
Watson to task for including Blamire, an Englishwoman, in their *Songstresses of Scotland* (2 vols.
[London, 1871]); he apparently forgot that Blamire's mother was Scottish (see Lonsdale, *Worthies
of Cumberland*).

don, where she studied music. In Carlisle she met the poet Catherine Gilpin, of Scaleby Castle. The two became close friends, collaborating on the composition of the popular song "The Cumberland Scold" and eventually wintering together at 14 Finkle Street, Carlisle, with trips to Gilsland Spa in summer. In 1786 Blamire's brother William married the well-educated Jane Christian, of Ewanrigg Hall, Cumberland. Jane became Blamire's mentor, a relationship Blamire celebrates in "The Bower of Elegance, Addressed to a Very Accomplished Woman."

Blamire's health was never robust. She suffered from dyspepsia and complained of rheumatism in her middle twenties. By the time she was thirty-seven, she had asthmalike symptoms and probably heart disease. She was bedridden the last several months of her life and died on 5 April 1794, at forty-eight. Her brother William was one of her attending physicians. As she wished, she was buried at Raughton Head Chapel, in Carlisle, near her Aunt Mary Simpson, who had died nine years earlier. In her will she left most of her property to her sister, Sarah, and asked that she "will not suffer her grief to become excessive for the loss of one whose every hour she was the means of rendering easy, happy, and delightful."[5] Nevertheless, Sarah's grief was so profound that she was unable ever to approach her sister's grave.[6] Despite Blamire's desire for a small private funeral, eighty or ninety mourners appeared, most uninvited.

Two of her most famous songs, "The Nabob" and "The Old Chelsea Pensioners," are based upon real incidents. And there are strong autobiographical elements in her tour de force, "Stoklewath; or, The Cumbrian Village," named for the village nearest Thackwood, where she and Sarah returned to live after the death of Colonel Graham in 1773. Blamire portrays the family at this period in one of the poem's closing passages: two sisters, "one fam'd for goodness, and one fam'd for joke," take their evening stroll with their brother. "Stoklewath" has been compared to Goldsmith's *The Deserted Village,* but it was influenced more by Thompson's *The Seasons.* Despite its neoclassical verse form, it is a thoroughly original work, affectionately celebrating village life and simple domestic activities long before William Wordsworth's championing of these values; but the poem also shows, with rich detail, striking natural imagery and wry humor, the essential ephemerality of human life and memory. Stories within stories undermine the traditional pastoral ideal by juxtaposing personal conflict against the wars of nations and showing love bringing sorrow, alienation, and tragedy. The poem subtly critiques British colonialism and not so subtly rebukes England for its victimization of sol-

---

5. Quoted in Lonsdale, *Worthies of Cumberland,* 106–7.
6. Sarah Graham died four years later, in 1798, and is buried beside her sister.

diers and insensitivity to the poor. It rejects materialism and embraces the notion that all human hearts are the same—even in those meeting as enemies on the field of battle. She paints in shocking detail the enormous human price of warfare. Blamire's language, in this and other poems, is simple and often affecting. Her shorter lyrics, especially, show idiomatic ease and grace.

Most of Blamire's poems were written on the backs of letters, on receipts, or on any scrap of paper that might have been handy; the only exceptions are "Stoklewath" and a few songs found in fair copy.[7] The earliest dated surviving Blamire poem, "Written in a Churchyard, on Seeing a Number of Cattle Grazing in It," which shows the influence of Gray's "Elegy in a Country Churchyard," was written when she was nineteen. "Stoklewath" was composed sometime after 1773, probably around 1780.[8] Very few of Blamire's poems found their way into print during her lifetime, so most are difficult to date. Nonetheless, they were extremely popular, sung as songs and circulated in manuscript and in commonplace books. A few were published anonymously as single sheets in the 1780s and then were reprinted in collections such as *Calliope, or the Musical Miscellany* (1788).[9] But most remained unpublished at her death. Robert Anderson printed at least five of her songs in his *Cumberland Ballads* (Wigton, 1808) but only acknowledged her authorship for one of them. "What Ails This Heart o' Mine?" appeared in volume 6 of *The Scots Musical Museum,* published in June 1803. "The Chelsea Pensioners" was published in *The Caledonian Musical Repository* (1806). Many of her songs, but especially "The Nabob," "What Ails This Heart o' Mine," and "The Chelsea Pensioners,"[10] continued to be sung in the Carlisle region for decades after her death.

7. Henry Lonsdale, who examined her manuscripts, noted ruefully that her whist copybook seemed to have received more care than her poetry manuscripts (Lonsdale, *Worthies of Cumberland,* 102).

8. It includes a description of a milkmaid singing "Auld Robin Gray," having learned it at the last fair (see line 80). Thus, it could not have been written before 1772, when Lady Ann Lindsay composed the song. (Lady Ann told Sir Walter Scott that her song "was born soon after the close of the year 1771" [letter of July 1823, quoted in Scott's introduction to *Auld Robin Gray; A Ballad,* ed. Walter Scott (Edinburgh, 1825)].) Patrick Maxwell dates "Stoklewath" 1771 (in *Poetical Works,* xxxvi), but this is clearly incorrect. In the description of her family at the poem's close, Blamire's brother-in-law, Colonel Graham, is absent. He did not die until 1773, and it was not until then that Blamire and Sarah Graham returned to Thackwood.

9. "The Siller Croun" was published in sheet form about 1780 and appeared in Johnson's *Scots Musical Museum,* 3:249, published in Edinburgh in 1790. Patrick Maxwell says it first appeared in a single sheet copy published by Napier, an Edinburgh musician (*Poetical Works,* xli, 204). It also appeared in an early collection entitled *The National Minstrel* edited by D. Weir, who attributed it to Blamire. "The Waefu' Heart" was published in London in 1788 (*Poetical Works,* 206).

10. Sometimes titled "The Veterans" or "The Days o' Langsyne."

Blamire's poetry was rescued from almost certain oblivion by the combined efforts of Julia Thompson and Henry Lonsdale, of Carlisle, and Patrick Maxwell, of Edinburgh. Thompson preserved fourteen of Blamire's poems in her commonplace book and taught them to her pupils. In the late 1820s, Maxwell decided to collect Blamire's poetry, and in 1829 he sought out and interviewed Robert Anderson, who possessed a memoir of Blamire. He located Julia Thompson in 1833, and she allowed him to borrow her commonplace book, containing eleven poems he had never seen. Henry Lonsdale, one of Thompson's pupils, met Jane Christian Blamire, niece of the poet, in 1839; she entrusted a cache of Blamire manuscripts to Lonsdale, who, in turn, having met Patrick Maxwell in Edinburgh in 1836 and having learned of his project, passed them on, with his notes on Blamire's life. In 1842, nearly half a century after the poet's death, Maxwell published a collected edition of Blamire's works, some in standard English, others in Scots and in Cumbrian dialect, including ballads, epistles, elegies, and other lyrics— eighty-five poems in all—with notes and a biographical memoir. *Chambers' Edinburgh Journal,* reviewing the volume in 1842, stated that her songs thrilled "a sympathetic string deep in the reader's bosom. It may, indeed, be confidently predicted of several of these lyrics, that they will live with the best productions of their age, and longer than many that were at first allowed to rank more highly."[11]

MAJOR WORK: *The Poetical Works of Miss Susanna Blamire, "The Muse of Cumberland,"* comp. Henry Lonsdale, M.D., with a preface, memoir, and notes by Patrick Maxwell (Edinburgh, 1842).

TEXTS USED: All texts taken from *The Poetical Works of Miss Susanna Blamire, "The Muse of Cumberland."*

---

11. Three decades later, Lonsdale published *Worthies of Cumberland,* with an expanded biography of the poet.

The Nabob

Air—Traveller's Return

When silent time, wi' lightly foot,
    Had trod on thirty years,
I sought again my native land
    Wi' mony hopes and fears:
Wha kens gin the dear friends I left
    May still continue mine?
Or gin I e'er again shall taste
    The joys I left langsyne?

As I drew near my ancient pile,
10   My heart beat a' the way;
Ilk place I pass'd seem'd yet to speak
    O' some dear former day;
Those days that follow'd me afar,
    Those happy days o' mine,
Whilk made me think the present joys
    A' naething to langsyne!

The ivy'd tower now met my eye,
    Where minstrels used to blaw;
Nae friend stepp'd forth wi' open hand,
20   Nae weel-kenn'd face I saw;
Till Donald totter'd to the door,
    Wham I left in his prime,
And grat to see the lad return
    He bore about langsyne.

I ran to ilka dear friend's room,
    As if to find them there,

---

5 gin] If.
8 langsyne] Long ago.
11 Ilk] Each.
15 Whilk] Which.

20 weel-kenn'd] Well-known.
23 grat] Wept.
25 ilka] Every.

I knew where ilk ane used to sit,
    And hang o'er mony a chair;
Till soft remembrance threw a veil
    Across these een o' mine,   30
I clos'd the door, and sobb'd aloud,
    To think on auld langsyne!

Some pensy chiels, a new sprung race,
    Wad next their welcome pay,
Wha shudder'd at my Gothic wa's,
    And wish'd my groves away:
"Cut, cut," they cried, "those aged elms,
    Lay low yon mournfu' pine":
Na! na! our fathers' names grow there,
    Memorials o' langsyne.   40

To wean me frae these waefu' thoughts,
    They took me to the town;
But sair on ilka weel-kenn'd face
    I miss'd the youthfu' bloom.
At balls they pointed to a nymph
    Wham a' declar'd divine;
But sure her mother's blushing cheeks
    Were fairer far langsyne!

In vain I sought in music's sound
    To find that magic art,   50
Which oft in Scotland's ancient lays
    Has thrill'd through a' my heart:
The sang had mony an artfu' turn;
    My ear confess'd 'twas fine;
But miss'd the simple melody
    I listen'd to langsyne.

Ye sons to comrades o' my youth,
    Forgie an auld man's spleen,

27 ilk ane] Each one.
33 pensy chiels] Conceited young men.
43 sair] Sore.

Wha 'midst your gayest scenes still mourns
    The days he ance has seen:
When time has past, and seasons fled,
    Your hearts will feel like mine;
And aye the sang will maist delight
    That minds ye o' langsyne!

                    (wr. 1788; pub. 1842)

60 *(line 60 marker)*

The Siller Croun

And ye shall walk in silk attire,
    And siller hae to spare,
Gin ye'll consent to be his bride,
    Nor think o' Donald mair.
O wha wad buy a silken goun
    Wi' a poor broken heart!
Or what's to me a siller croun,
    Gin frae my love I part!

The mind wha's every wish is pure
    Far dearer is to me;
And ere I'm forc'd to break my faith
    I'll lay me doun an' dee!
For I hae pledg'd my virgin troth
    Brave Donald's fate to share;
And he has gi'en to me his heart,
    Wi' a' its virtues rare.

His gentle manners wan my heart,
    He gratefu' took the gift;
Could I but think to seek it back
    It wad be waur than theft!

2 siller] Silver money.
3 Gin] If.
7 siller croun] Silver crown.
20 waur] Worse.

For langest life can ne'er repay
   The love he bears to me;
And ere I'm forc'd to break my troth
   I'll lay me doun an' dee.

(1790)

What Ails This Heart o' Mine?

Air—Sir James Baird

What ails this heart o' mine?
   What ails this watery ee?
What gars me a' turn cauld as death
   When I take leave o' thee?
When thou art far awa
   Thou'lt dearer grow to me;
But change o' place and change o' folk
   May gar thy fancy jee.

When I gae out at een,
   Or walk at morning air,   10
Ilk rustling bush will seem to say
   I us'd to meet thee there.
Then I'll sit down and cry,
   And live aneath the tree,
And when a leaf fa's i' my lap
   I'll ca't a word frae thee.

I'll hie me to the bower
   That thou wi' roses tied,
And where wi' mony a blushing bud
   I strove mysell to hide.   20

3 gars] Makes.
8 gar thy fancy jee] Make your fancy change.
11 Ilk] Each.

I'll doat on ilka spot
    Where I hae been wi thee;
And ca' to mind some kindly word
    By ilka burn and tree!

Wi' sic thoughts i' my mind,
    Time through the world may gae,
And find my heart in twenty years
    The same as 'tis to-day.
'Tis thoughts that bind the soul,
30   And keep friends i' the ee;
And gin I think I see thee aye,
    What can part thee and me!
           (wr. bef. 1794; pub. 1803)

The Chelsea Pensioners[*]

Air — The Days o' Langsyne

When war had broke in on the peace of auld men,
And frae Chelsea to arms they were summon'd again;
Twa vet'rans grown gray, wi' their muskets sair soil'd,
Wi' a sigh were relating how hard they had toil'd;
The drum it was beating, to fight they incline,
But aye they look back to the days o' langsyne.

Oh! Davy, man, weel thou remembers the time,
When twa brisk young callans, and baith i' our prime,
The Duke bade us conquer, and show'd us the way,
10   And mony a braw chiel we laid low on that day;

---

24 ilka burn] Every stream.   6 langsyne] Long ago.
25 sic] Such.   8 callans] Boys.
3 sair] Sorely.   10 braw chiel] Fine young man.

Yet I'd venture, fu' cheerfu', this auld trunk o' mine,
Could William but lead, and I fight, as langsyne.

But garrison duty is a' we can do,
Tho' our arms are worn weak yet our hearts are still true;
We carena for dangers by land or by sea,
For Time is turn'd coward and no thee and me;
And tho' at the change we should sadly repine,
Youth winna return, nor the strength o' langsyne.

When after our conquests, it joys me to mind
How thy Janet caress'd thee and my Meg was kind;   20
They follow'd our fortunes, tho' never so hard,
And we cared na for plunder wi' sic a reward;
E'en now they're resolv'd baith their hames to resign,
And will follow us yet for the sake o' langsyne.

(wr. bef. 1794; pub. 1806)

* The title refers to the more than five hundred inhabitants of the Royal Hospital
in Chelsea, a home for old soldiers founded by Charles II, designed by Christopher
Wren, and completed in 1692.

Barley Broth

Air — Crowdy

If tempers were put up to seale,
  Our Jwohn's wad bear a duced preyce;
He vow'd 'twas barley i' the broth, —
  Upon my word, says I, it's reyce.

"I mek nea faut," our Jwohnny says,
  "The broth is guid and varra neyce;
I only say — it's barley broth."
  Tou says what's wrang, says I, it's reyce.

22 sic] Such.

"Did ever mortal hear the leyke!
    As if I hadn't sense to tell!
Tou may think reyce the better thing,
    But barley broth dis just as well."

"And sae it mud, if it was there;
    The deil a grain is i' the pot;
But tou mun ayways threep yen down,—
    I've drawn the deevil of a lot!"

"And what's the lot that I have drawn?
    Pervarsion is a woman's neame!
Sae fares-te-weel! I'll sarve my king,
    And never, never mair come heame."

Now Jenny frets frae mworn to neet;
    The Sunday cap's nae langer neyce;
She aye puts barley i' the broth,
    And hates the varra neame o' reyce.

Thus treyfles vex, and treyfles please,
    And treyfles mek the sum o' leyfe;
And treyfles mek a bonny lass
    A wretched or a happy weyfe!
          (wr. bef. 1794; pub. 1842)

10

20

13 mud] Must.
14 deil] Devil.
15 tou mun ayways threep yen down] You must always throw one down.
19 sarve my king] Join the army.

Stoklewath;* or, The Cumbrian Village

From where dark clouds of curling smoke arise,
And the tall column mounts into the skies;
Where the grim arches of the forge appear,
Whose fluted pillars prop the thickening air;
Where domes of peers and humble roofs are found
Alike to spread their mingled vapours round;
From denser air and busy towns I run,
To catch a glimpse of the unclouded sun;
Foe to the toils which wealth and pomp create,
And all the hard-wrought tinsel of the great.   10

    Aurora now had left her crimson bed,
And the sky glowed with pure reflected red;
The moving stars withdrew their timorous light,
As her gilt chariot burst upon the sight;
The glittering pearls that gentle Eve had born,
Were all adorning the sweet brow of Morn;
And every shrub, and every opening flower,
Unlock'd some jewel for the rising hour.
Meanwhile unseen the fragrant zephyr flew,
And gather'd essence from the balmy dew;   20
I wander'd on, till Fancy bade me stay,
And spend with Health and her one holiday.

    Where the clear stream its useful tenor holds,
And the shorn flocks come whiten'd from the folds;
Where on each side the cottages are seen,
Which orchards shelter, and which poplars screen;
There many an apple, in autumnal pride,
Glows with red cheek, and blushes side by side;
Which with nice care is lock'd in oaken chest,
Till Christmas comes, and tarts draw out the feast.   30
Nor does the garden useful herbs deny,
Fenc'd round with thorns that point their spears on high;

---

5 peers] The nobility in Britain—dukes, marquises, earls, viscounts, and barons.
10 tinsel] Silk or wool interwoven with gold or silver thread.

There the thyme blows, from which brown bees distil
The sweets that all their waxen storehouse fill.
The parsley next extends its useful row,
And marjorum sweet is ever taught to grow;
Next balm, and sage, and hyssop, physic yield,
With cordial mint, the doctor of the field.
There spreading cabbage all their strength produce,
40   And take firm root to stand for winter's use.
Carrots and turnips Sunday-feasts supply,
Till blest potatoes meet the thankful eye.
There the tall pea in stately grandeur stalks,
And humbler bean midst her own fragrance walks.
The ripening currant many a warbler brings,
'Mongst whom the blackbird spreads his sooty wings.
But O! forbear with lure or artful snare
To trap this sweetest songster of the air,
Nor quench in darkness his quick visual ray,
50   Shut out from liberty and glorious day.
Enough, enough! while to the cage confin'd,
Through all the house his wilding wood-notes wind;
Let him at least the gift of light retain,
Nor hear his whistling pipe with conscious pain!
And, look, where ornament her care bestows!
Above the lily nods the blushing rose,
The fringing poppy and the peony vie
Which shall look gayest in the village eye.
Nor think not these unmeet for Sunday's pride,
60   When with a woolen thread the nosegay's tied!
There southernwood, and thyme, like broom, behold
Spreading their shade o'er the dark marigold.
Sweetwilliam next, in wig of early pride,
Smiles on himself as if his bob he eyed;
The rose and lily round the posy stray,
And in the church waft faintness far away,
When tir'd with walking many a sultry morn
Through new cut hay, or fields of standing corn;
E'en while at prayers a sudden chillness steals,
70   And all the heart the creeping sickness feels;

64 bob] Short for *periwig,* a wig whose bottom locks are turned up into bobs or short curls.

No salts are there,—yet thyme and mint renew
The wasting sense, and cheer from pew to pew.

But now the sun sends forth his scorching rays,
And the hot cattle startling cease to graze;
While to the pool, or darkest shade they hie,
And with the scourging tail whip off th' offending fly.

Along the path that winds around the hill
You lose the milkmaid—though you hear her still.
At the last fair she caught yon thrilling lay,
And now the woods repeat "Auld Robin Gray." 80
The waving pail swims lightly on her head,
For equal steps to measur'd music tread.

Adown the stream where woods begin to throw
Their verdant arms around the rocks below,
A rustic bridge across the tide is thrown,
Where briars and woodbine hide the hoary stone,
A simple arch salutes th' admiring eye,
And the mill's clack the tumbling waves supply.
But lest society some loss should share,
And nearest neighbours lack their neighbour's fare, 90
The tottering step-stones cross the stream are laid,
O'er which trips lightly many a busy maid,
And many a matron, when one failing cow
Bids no big cheese within the cheese-vat grow,
Their wealthier neighbour then, her bowls to swell,
Will gladly take what they as gladly sell.

The morning toils are now completely o'er,
The bowls well scalded, and well swept the floor.
The daughter at the needle plies the seam,
While the good mother hastens to the stream: 100
There the long webs, that wintry moons began,
Lie stretch'd and beaming in the summer's sun;

71 salts] Smelling salts.
88 clack] Clapper of a mill, an instrument that, by striking the hopper, causes the corn to be shaken into the millstones.

And lest he scorch them in his fervid hours,
She scoops along the nice conducted showers;
Till like the snow, that tips the mountain's height,
The brown's dull shade gives place to purest white;
While her sweet child knee-deep is wading seen,
Picking bright stones, or tumbling on the green.

But now the sun's bright whirling wheels appear
110   On the broad front of noon, in full career,
A sign more welcome hangs not in the air,
For now the sister's call the brothers hear;
Dinner's the word, and every cave around
Devours the voice, and feasts upon the sound.
'Tis dinner, father! all the brothers cry,
Throw down the spade, and heave the pickaxe by;
'Tis dinner, father! home they panting go,
While the tired parent still pants on more slow.
Now the fried rasher meets them on the way,
120   And savoury pancakes welcome steams convey.
Their pace they mend, till at the pump they stand,
Deluge the face, and purify the hand,
And then to dinner. There the women wait,
And the tired father fills his chair of state;
Smoking potatoes meet their thankful eyes,
And Hunger wafts the grateful sacrifice;
To her libations of sweet milk are pour'd,
And Peace and Plenty watch around the board.

Now, till the sun has somewhat sunk in height,
130   Yet long before he dips his wheels in night,
The nut-brown labourers their senses steep
In the soft dews of renovating sleep;
The worthy sire to the soft bed repairs,
The sons beneath the shade forget their cares.
The clock strikes two, it beats upon the ear,
And soon the parent's anxious voice they hear;
Come, come, my lads, you must not sleep all day!
They rub their eyes, start up, then stalk away.

119 rasher] Thin slice of bacon or ham.

But let me not at twelve forget to eye
The learned school-dame's jumping, shrill-ton'd fry.   140
Some near at home to dinner dancing run,
Eager for play when the repast is done;
Others more distant, bring their satchel'd fare
Safely infolded by a mother's care.
On a wood trencher stands the tower-like pie,
While bread and cheese form battlements on high;
A crust for 'tween-meals in a corner stows,
And guarded butter oaten-cakes enclose;
And shining tin-flasks of new milk, which seem
Best to demand the name of good thick cream!   150

The dinner done; the happy train so gay,
In various groups disperse to various play;
Some to the hounded-hare the sinews strain,
And fleet as greyhounds scour along the plain.
At last the hare through all her windings caught
Gets leave to breathe, and breath brings change of thought;
For races some, but more for foot-ball cry,
Mark out their ground, and toss the globe on high;
The well fought field deals many a galling stroke,
And many a chief's o'erthrown, and many a shin is broke.   160

These active feats, while manly imps essay,
The gentler sex choose out a gentler play;
They form a smiling circle on the green,
Where chuckstones, dolls, and totums, all are seen;
A nest of linnets, a few happy elves,
Run home to see if yet they pick themselves,
Though but an hour ago their throats they cramm'd,
And chirp'd, and cheep'd, and well the mother shamm'd.

Escap'd in happy hour from rod-taught lore,
Their books forgot, nor work remember'd more;   170
All share the joy, but one imprison'd slave,

---

164 chuckstones, dolls, and totums] Chuckstones are marbles or small, rounded quartz
pebbles used in the game of check-stone, also called chuckie-stanes, chucks, and taw *(OED)*.
Totums are little children, tots.

Who from offended worth no boon would save.
The dame he said was like a clocking hen,
Who ne'er would let them out when it did rain;
And if again his hands she dar'd to switch,
He'd call her to her face a wrinkl'd witch.
This told a wheedler, much dislik'd by all,
Whom in abhorrence they tale-pyet call,
Who for a raisin or a fig would tell
180   Faults of a brother he lov'd ne'er so well;
Th' offender's soul no threaten'd pain unbends,
Nor with the dame will his proud heart be friends,
He loves her not; for this the hour of play,
And much-wished dinner, both are snatch'd away.
And now the dame in neat white mob is seen,
Her russet gown, silk kerchief, apron clean,
At the school door her tremulous voice is heard,
And the blithe game's unwillingly deferr'd.

From noon till morn rests female toil; save come
190   The evening hours when lowing cows draw home.
Now the good neighbour walks her friend to see,
And knit an hour, and drink a dish of tea.
She comes unlook'd for, — wheat-bread is to seek,
The baker has none, got no yeast last week;
And little Peggy thinks herself ill sped,
Though she has got a great piece gingerbread.
Home she returns, but disappointment's trace
Darkens her eye, and lengthens all her face;
She whispers lowly in her sister's ear,
200   Scarce can restrain the glistening, swelling tear.
The mother marks, and to the milk-house goes,
Blythe Peggy smiles, she well the errand knows;
There from the bowl where cream so coolly swims,
The future butter generously skims,
And, flour commixing, forms a rural bread
That for the wheaten loaf oft stands in stead;

177 wheedler] One who entices or persuades by coaxing, cajolery, or flattery.
178 tale-pyet] Tale-piet, a chattering magpie.
185 mob] Cap.

Cup after cup sends steaming circles round,
And oft the weak tea's in the full pot drown'd;
It matters not, for while their news they tell
The mind's content, and all things move on well.   210

   The sun has now his saffron robe put on,
Stept from his chariot that with rubies shone,
The glittering monarch gains the western gate,
And for a moment shines in regal state;
His streaming mantle floats along the sky,
While he glides softly from the gazing eye;
From saffron tinge to yellow soon it flew,
Sea-green the next, and then to darkest blue.

   Now different cares employ the village train,
The rich in cattle press the milky vein;   220
When, lo! a voice sends direful notes around,
And sharp vexation mingles in the sound;
'Tis little Peggy, she the pail would fill,
And on old Hawky try her early skill.
She strok'd and clapp'd her, but she'd not allow;
The well known hand best pleased the knowing cow;
Tho' cabbage leaves before her band was cast,
Hawky refus'd the coaxing rich repast;
And when the little hand unapt she found,
She kick'd, and whelm'd her on the slippery ground.   230

   Along yon hedge now mouldering and decay'd,
In gather'd heaps you see the fragments laid;
Piled up with care to swell the nightly blaze,
And in the widow's hut a fire to raise.
See where she comes with her blue apron full,
Crown'd with some scatter'd locks of dingy wool.
In years she seems, and on her well patch'd clothes
Want much has added to her other woes.
There is a poor-house; but some little pride
Forbids her there her humbled head to hide;   240
O'er former scenes of better days she runs,
And every thing like degradation shuns!

Now hooded Eve slow gliding comes in view,
Busied in threading pearls of diamond dew;
Waking the flowers that early close the eye,
And giving drops to those that else would die.
And what is man but such a tender flower,
That buds, blooms, fades, and dies within the hour?

Where round yon cottage the rosemary grows,
250   And turncap lilies flaunt beside the rose,
Two aged females turn the weary wheel,
And, as they turn, their slumbering thoughts reveal:
"How long is't, think ye, since th' old style was lost?
Poor England may remember't to her cost!
E'er since that time the weather has grown cold,
(For Jane forgets that she is now grown old).
I knew when I liv'd servant at Woodmile,
So scorching hot the weather was in April,
The cows would startle, and by ten o'clock
260   My master us'd his horses to unyoke;
'Tis not so now; the sun has lost its power;
The very apples now-a-days are sour!
Could not the Parson tell the reason why
There are such changes both in earth and sky?"

" 'Tis not these only," Margaret replied,
"For many a change besides have I espied.
Look at the girls!—they all dress now-a-days
Like them fine folk who act them nonsense plays!
No more the decent mob surrounds the face,
270   Border'd with edging, or bit good bone-lace;
Gauze flappets soon—that will not last a day—
We'll see them flaunting whilst they're making hay!
All things are chang'd, the world's turned upside down,
And every servant wears a cotton gown,
Bit flimsy things, that have no strength to wear,
And will like any blotting-paper tear!

253 th' old style] Reference to the calendar used prior to the Gregorian, or New Style, calendar. In 1752 George Parker (1697–1764), the earl of Macclesfield, changed the calendar by
removing fourteen days from the Julian calendar.
271 Gauze flappets] Finery for gentlewomen.

I made my Nelly a half-worsted gown,
She slighting told me 't would not do in town!
This pride! this pride! it sure must have a fall,
And bring some heavy judgment on us all!   280
They're grown so bold too, and their lads allow,
When courting them, to skulk behind a cow,
Till all's in bed. My John, when courting me,
Us'd after supper to come manfully;
For oft he us'd to say he knew no place
Where honesty need fear to show its face.
No more it need! My master us'd to cry,—
He fear'd but two things—to turn thief, and lie."

    The leading crow her colony brings home,
And two by two they seek their leafy dome.   290
Of all the branches that invite to rest,
Each loves the one that hangs above its nest;
What though of rudest architecture made,
Nor thorns surrounding nor with clay inlaid,
Yet 'tis the spot where infant days began,
That thus attaches both the crow and man!
Now on the green the youth their gambols keep,
Stretching their sinews in the bounding leap;
Others the wrestler's glory would maintain,
Twist the strong nerve and fill the swelling vein;   300
One youth his pipe blows from the rocky hill,
Seated like Pan above the clacking mill;
Another strikes the violin's cheerful string,
Light to the dance the bounding virgins spring;
'Tis most part nature, yet some art is found
When one—two—three lies heavy on the ground;
For 'tis not airy feet which seem to fly,
Then come descended quivering from the sky,
Nor form that every Grace was known to bend,
Nor foot that every feathered Hour would lend,   310
Has any merit here;—but feet of sound,
Which tabour-like re-echo on the ground;
Or as the drum a certain sound repeats,

302 Pan] Greek god of pastures and flocks.

Flutters now low, and then in thunder beats;
From Nature and from Art how wide the sphere!
Courts unimprov'd would be what you see here.

Now Eve had sprinkled every flower with dew,
And her gauze hood was wet and dripping through;
A light grey cloak to the warm fleece allied,
320   Her chilly fingers close and closer tied,
That, with a fur-lined cap, the ears' delight,
Was given her by her elder sister Night.

From walks retired, that shun the inquiring view,
A faithful couple to the shades withdrew.
The maid had every blush that bloom can give,
Where youth fresh glowing bids the blossom live,
And the fair cheek, with lilies all bespread,
Shades the full rose, and hides its bolder red,
Pure as the drop that in the early morn
330   Hangs with such sweetness smiling on the thorn,
Artless as youth before the cranky wile
Shadows the frown, or plays within the smile;
She moves, the wonder of the rural plain,
And many a sigh steals to her ear in vain.

A youth there was like her, of better mould,
Whose soul deem'd lightly of the weight of gold.
Around his birth some favouring fortune shone,
Which some call merit, though no way their own;
The Church was laid out as his rising line,
340   Himself delighting in the text divine;
That text, at home by country masters taught,
Might stint the learning but keep back the fault,
For sure great knowledge we should all despise,
Unless the man be virtuous as he's wise.

The mother's eye had long o'er all her son
With many a fear, and much observance run,
Seen where beneath the elms a path was worn,—
Mark'd him at pensive eve, and laughing morn
Still seek the shade,—now with sad step, and slow,

With folded arms, and head declining low;   350
Then livelier thoughts awake a quicker pace,
And hope breaks out and glows along his face.
Thus to the partner of her thirty years
She soft began:—Thou calmer of my fears,
Oft has thy firmer mind my sorrows stilled,
As from thy lips thy better sense distilled,
Hast thou observ'd our dearest hope of late?
Whose spirits flag with some uncommon weight,—
Some secret anguish sickens o'er his soul,
And silent night has seen the torrent roll,   360
The wandering stream has from his eyelids crept,
And his moist pillow shewn he has not slept.
My life, rejoin'd the father, in thy mind
The mist of tenderness the optics blind,
Imagin'd ills from feeling ever flow,
All things look big when seen through clouds of woe;
I've mark'd no difference save what study brings,
They all turn grave who search the source of things.
This not believing, ceas'd she to reply,
But still sent forth her keen inquiring eye,   370
Mark'd when sweet Anna's name breath'd in the sound,
How quick his eye sprung from the thoughtful ground;
And when just praise the beauteous maid would grace,
Joy smooth'd his brow, and blushes dyed his face.
This wak'd suspicion—rumour told the whole,
And now she knew what sicken'd o'er his soul.

   The father skill'd in all the ways of man,
Thus, to his mate affectionate, began:
In all distempers of the feverish mind,
The greatest good from change of scene we find.   380
Tho' one dear object, touchstone of our woe,
Seems to go with us wheresoe'er we go,
Yet gay variety divides the view,—
Spite of ourselves we gaze at what is new;
Back-turning thought will far-past scenes survey,
That fainter grow, worn out by length of way;
A softer mist o'er every object spreads,
Figures grow dim, and towers scarce shew their heads:

Back-turning thought strains his sunk hollow eye,
390 But scenes retire, and dearest objects fly;
He lags no more—by soft degrees is stole
The keenest anguish that inwraps the soul.
To college, then, our sorrowing son shall go,
New loves, or friends, shall wear out all his woe;
Ideas changing as new views arise
Let in new light, and almost change the eyes;
Objects adored, that matchless seem'd before,
Excite no wonder, and delight no more.
The mother sigh'd, the starting tear withheld,
400 To her fond partner ever fond to yield;
Nor ever felt she what is call'd command,
His wish grew hers in magic quickness bland.

And now Pretence had whisper'd to the maid
Thro' all the wood her new wash'd flock had stray'd;
The youth too sought the shade in hopes to clear
Her pearl-set eye that hung with many a tear.
Far from the uproar of the loud cascade,
Where the slow stream crept softly to the shade,
Beneath a rock with venturous trees o'erhung,
410 That seem by some enchantment to have sprung,
For the scant soil nor moss nor grass bestows,
But yawning cliffs the sinewy roots expose;
There on her cheek the roses felt the dew,
Which drop by drop extracts their softest hue:
"Why weeps my Anna? Sure she knows this heart,
And knows in absence we but seem to part;
Though mountains rise, and the slow weary day
Draws out the journey a long length of way,
Yet trust me, Anna, still my soul shall be
420 Chain'd to thy soul, and never part from thee!"
Sweet Anna shook her head—sad sighs oppose
The labouring words that to the threshold rose;
The lip kept moving, but no accent fell,
Yet the round tear perhaps can speak as well.
"O cease, my Anna, or declare thy fears,
I cannot, cannot bear these softening tears!
What have I done to tempt thy generous mind

To form a thought that I can grow unkind?"
"Nothing"—she sobb'd,—"but—but it cannot be—
But every eye must take delight in thee!   430
Some maid whom education softens o'er,
To whose rich mind each day keeps adding more;
Whose winning manners mixed with every grace,
Invite the eye, and keep it from the face,—
And, when she speaks, Persuasion's lyre is strung,
And the sweet words come warbling from her tongue;
If such a one thy heart in fetters hold,—
For I have not one fear from sordid gold,
I shall not blame my William,—still may he
Taste every bless, whate'er becomes of me."   440
"Dearest of women," William thus rejoined,
"How can such fears e'er cloud so bright a mind!
In finer arts I know some may excel,
Some have more grace, and some few speak as well
Yet the sweet accent will but thrill my ear,
Trust me, my Anna, 't will not reach me here.
This heart is thine, and every faithful chord
Will only vibrate to thy well known word:
From infant years thy growing worth I've known,
Our wish the same, and our delights but one;   450
Believest thou this? The winged hours shall press
One after one, to crown my happiness;
The day shall come when I shall claim my own,
And freely to the world my love make known."
So saying, to their homes they separate go,
He more at ease—she something less in woe.

In this gay village hangs a wonderous sign,
The Hounds and Hare are the immense design.
There hunters crack their whips, and seem to bound
O'er every hedge, nor touch the mimic ground;   460
The huntsman winds his horn, his big cheeks swell,
And whippers-in make lagging terriers yell;
The sportive scene tempts many a wight to stay,
As to the school he drags th' unwilling way.

461 winds] Blows.

Around the front inviting benches wait,
Conscious of many a glass and sage debate;
The great man of the village cracks his joke,
Reads o'er the news and whiffs the curling smoke;
Tells tales of old, and nods, and heaves the can,
470   Makes fixed decrees, and seems much more than man.
"Come, Jack, sit down. Thy father, man, and me,
Broke many a glass, and many a freak had we.
'Twas when he sought thy mother, at Carel Fair
(I mind the corn was very bad that year)
We met thy mother and my wife i' the street,
And took them into Beck's to get a treat;
Blind Joseph played, and I took out thy mother,
Thy father, he was shy, he got another;
And when I took her back, as you may see,
480   I whipp'd her blushing on thy father's knee.
Then in came Robin Bell, who lik'd her too,
And bit his lip, and turn'd both red and blue,
Teas'd her to dance, as you may see, and then
Kept her himself, nor brought her back again.
I fir'd at this, while up thy father rose,
Gave him a kick, and tweak'd him by the nose.
They stripped to fight, as you may see, and I
In seeing fair play got a blacken'd eye;
I durst not shew my face at home next day,
490   But bade my mother say I went away,
But kept my bed, i'fegs, as you may see;
Who is it now fights for their lasses? eh!"
The blacksmith laugh'd, the cobbler gave a smile,
And the pleas'd tailor scratch'd his head the while.

But hark! what sounds of mingl'd joy and woe
From yon poor cottage bursting seem to flow.
'Tis honest Sarah. Sixpence-Harry's come,
And, after all his toils, got safely home.

472 freak] Prank, caper.
491 i'fegs] Oath meaning "in faith" or "by my faith."

"Welcome, old soldier, welcome from the wars!
Honour the man, my lads, seam'd o'er with scars! 500
Come give's thy hand, and bring the t'other can,
And tell us all thou'st done, and seen, my man."
Now expectation stares in every eye,
The jaw falls down, and every soul draws nigh,
With ear turn'd up, and head held all awry.
"Why, sir, the papers tell you all that's done,
What battle's lost, and what is hardly won.
But when the eye looks into private woes,
And sees the grief that from one battle flows,
Small cause of triumph can the bravest feel, 510
For never yet were brave hearts made of steel.
It happen'd once, in storming of a town,
When our bold men had push'd the ramparts down,
We found them starving, the last loaf was gone,
Beef was exhausted, and they flour had none;
Their springs we drain, to ditches yet they fly—
The stagnant ditch lent treacherous supply;
For soon the putrid source their blood distains,
And the quick fever hastens through their veins.
In the same room the dying and the dead— 520
Nay, sometimes, even in the self-same bed,—
You saw the mother with her children lie,
None but the father left to close the sunken eye.

In a dark corner, once myself I found
A youth whose blood was pouring through the wound;
No sister's hand, no tender mother's eye
To stanch that wound was fondly watching by;
Famine had done her work, and low were laid
The loving mother and the blooming maid.
He rais'd his eyes, and bade me strike the blow, 530
I've nought to lose, he cried, so fear no foe;
No foe is near, I softly made reply,

499 the wars] References to the European phases of the French and Indian War, the Seven
Years' War (1756–63), King William's War (1689–97), Queen Anne's War (1702–13), and King
George's War (1744–48).

A soldier, friend, would save and not destroy.
A drop of cordial in my flask I found;
(And I myself am sovereign for a wound;
I'll bleed you all, lads! if you should be ill,
And in the toothache I've no little skill.
Our drummer too, poor man, dealt much in horns,
And I've his very knack of cutting corns.)
540   Well; as I dress'd the youth, I found 'twas he
That oft had charm'd the sentinels and me;
From post to post like lightning he would fly,
And pour down thunder from his red-hot sky;
We prais'd him for't,—so I my captain told,
For well I knew he lik'd the foe that's bold;
So then the surgeon took him in his charge,
And the captain made him prisoner at large."
"Was he a Spanishman, or Frenchman, whether?
But it's no matter; they're all rogues together!"
550   "You're much mistaken: Goodness I have found
Spring[s] like the grass that clothes the common ground;
Some more, some less, you know, grows every where;
Some soils are fertile, and some are but bare.
Nay, 'mongst the Indians I've found kindly cheer,
And as much pity as I could do here!
Once in the woods I stray'd a length of way,
And thought I'd known the path that homeward lay;
We'd gone to forage, but I lost the rest,
Which, till quite out of hearing, never guess'd.
560   I hollow'd loud, some voices made reply,
But not my comrades; not one friend was nigh.
Some men appear'd, their faces painted o'er,
The wampum-belt, and tomahawk they bore;
Their ears were hung with beads, that largely spread
A breadth of wing, and cover'd half the head.
I kiss'd the ground; one older than the rest
Stepp'd forth, and laid his hand upon my breast,

---

563 wampum-belt] Wampum are beads made from the ends of shells rubbed, polished, and threaded on strings; used by native Americans as jewelry or money as well as for symbolic purposes.

Then seiz'd my arms, and sign'd that I should go,
And learn with them to bend the sturdy bow:
I bow'd and follow'd; sadly did I mourn,   570
And never more expected to return."
Here Sarah sobb'd, and stepp'd behind the door,
And with her tears bedew'd the dusty floor.
"We travell'd on some days through woods alone,
At length we reach'd their happy silent home.
A few green acres the whole plot compose,
Which woods surround, and fencing rocks enclose,
Skirting whose banks, a river fond of play
Sometimes stood still, and sometimes ran away;
The branching deer would drink the dimpl'd tide,   580
And crop the wild herbs on its flowery side, —
Around the silent hut would sometimes stray,
Then, at the sight of man, bound swift away;
But all in vain; the hunter's flying dart
Springs from the bow, and quivers in the heart.
A mother and four daughters here we found,
With shells encircled, and with feathers crown'd,
Bright pebbles shone amidst the plaited hair,
While lesser shells surround the moon-like ear.
With screams at sight of me away they flew   590
(For fear or pleasure springs from what is new);
Then, to their brothers, screaming still they ran,
Thinking my clothes and me the self-same man;
When bolder grown, they ventur'd something near,
Light touch'd my coat, but started back with fear.
When time and use had chas'd their fears away,
And I had learned some few short words to say,
They oft would tell me, would I but allow
The rampant lion to o'erhang my brow,
And on my cheek the spotted leopard wear,   600
Stretch out my ears, and let my arms go bare."
"O mercy on us!" cried the listeners round,
Their gaping wonder bursting into sound.
"Tho' different in their manners, yet their heart
Was equal mine in every better part.
Brave to a fault, if courage fault can be;

Kind to their fellows, doubly kind to me.
Some little arts my travell'd judgment taught,
Which, tho' a prize to them, seem'd greater than they ought.

610   "Needless with bows for me the woods to roam,
I therefore tried to do some good at home.
The birds, or deer, or boars, were all their food,
Save the swift salmon of the silver flood;
And when long storms the winter-stores would drain,
Hunger might ask the stinted meal in vain.
Some goats I saw that brows'd the rocks among,
And oft I thought to trap their playful young;
But not till first a fencing hedge surrounds
Their future fields, and the enclosure bounds;
620   For many a father owns a hatchet here,
Which falls descending to his wealthy heir.
The playful kid we from the pitfall bring,
O'erspread with earth, and many a tempting thing;
Light lay the branches o'er the treacherous deep,
And favourite herbs among the long grass creep.
The little prisoner soon is taught to stand,
And crop the food from the betrayer's hand.
A winter-store now rose up to their view,
And in another field the clover grew;
630   But, without scythes or hooks, how could we lay
The ridgy swathe and turn it into hay;
At last, of stone we form'd a sort of spade,
Broad at the end, and sharp, for cutting made;
We push'd along, the tender grass gave way,
And soon the sun turn'd every pile to hay.
It was not long before the flocks increased,
And I first gave the unknown milky feast.
Some clay I found, and useful bowls I made,
Tho', I must own, I marr'd the potter's trade;
640   Yet use is every thing—they did the same
As if from China the rude vessels came.
The curdling cheese I taught them next to press;
And twirl'd on strings the roasting meat to dress.
In all the woods the Indian corn was found,
Whose grains I scatter'd in the faithful ground;

The willing soil leaves little here to do,
Or asks the furrows of the searching plough;
Yet something like one with delight I made,
For tedious are the labours of the spade,
The coulter and the sock were pointed stone,   650
The eager brothers drew the traces on,
I stalk'd behind, and threw the faithful grain,
And wooden harrows closed the earth again:
Soon sprung the seed, and soon 'twas in the ear,
Nor wait the golden sheaves the falling year;
In this vast clime two harvests load the field,
And fifty crops th' exhaustless soil can yield.

    "Some bricks I burnt, and now a house arose,
Finer than aught the Indian chieftain knows;
A wicker door, with clay-like plaster lin'd,   660
Serv'd to exclude the piercing wintry wind;
A horn-glaz'd window gave a scanty light,
But lamps cheer'd up the gloom of lengthen'd night;
The cotton shrub through all the woods had run,
And plenteous wicks our rocks and spindles spun.
Around their fields the yam I taught to grow,
With all the fruits they either love or know.
The bed I rais'd from the damp earth, and now
Some little comfort walk'd our dwelling through.
My fame was spread: the neighbouring Indians came,   670
View'd all our works, and strove to do the same.
The wampum-belt my growing fame records,
That tells great actions without help of words.
I gain'd much honour, and each friend would bring
'Mong various presents many a high-priz'd thing.
And when, with many a prayer, I ask once more
To seek my friends, and wander to the shore,
They all consent,—but drop a sorrowing tear,
While many a friend his load of skins would bear.
Riches were mine; but fate will'd it not so,—   680
They grew the treasure of the Spanish foe;

650 The coulter and the sock] The iron blade fixed in front of the plowshare together with
the plowshare.

My Indian friends threw down their fleecy load,
And, like the bounding elk, leap'd back into the wood.

"What though a prisoner! countrymen I found,
Heard my own tongue, and bless'd the cheerful sound;
It seem'd to me as if my home was there,
And every dearest friend would soon appear.
At length a cartel gave us back to share
The wounds and dangers of a bloody war.
690   Peace dawn'd at last, and now the sails were spread,
Some climb the ship unhurt, some few half dead.
Not this afflicts the gallant soldier's mind,
What is't to him tho' limbs are left behind!
Chelsea a crutch and bench will yet supply,
And be the veteran's dear lost limb and eye!

"When English ground first struck the sailor's view,
Huzza! for England, roar'd the jovial crew.
The waving crutch leaped up in every hand,
While one poor leg was left alone to stand;
700   The very name another limb bestows,
And through the artery the blood now flows.
We reach'd the shore, and kiss'd the much-lov'd ground,
And fondly fancied friends would crowd around;
But few with wretchedness acquaintance claim,
And little pride is every where the same.

"In coming down, the seeing eye of day
Darken'd around me, and I lost my way.
Where'er a light shot glimmering through the trees,
I thither urg'd my weary trembling knees,
710   Tapp'd at the door, and begg'd, in piteous tone,
They'd let a wandering soldier find his home;
They barr'd the door, and bade me beg elsewhere,
They'd no spare beds for vagabonds to share.
This was the tale where'er I made a halt,
And greater houses grew upon the fault;

688 cartel] Written agreement for the exchange or ransom of prisoners.
694 Chelsea] The Royal Hospital, a home for old soldiers.

The dog was loos'd to keep me far at bay,
And saucy footmen bade me walk away,
Or else a constable should find a home
For wandering captains from the wars new come.
Alas! thought I, is this the soldier's praise   720
For loss of health, of limb, and length of days?
And is this England?—England, my delight!
For whom I thought it glory but to fight—
That has no covert for the soldier's night!
I turn'd half fainting, led through all the gloom
By the faint glimmerings of the clouded moon.
One path I kept, that seem'd at times to end,
And oft refus'd the guiding clew to lend;
The thread unhop'd as oft again I found,
Till it forsook the open fields around;   730
By slow degrees, to towering woods it crept,
As if beneath their shade it nightly slept.
I here had halted, lest some beasts of prey,
In midnight theft, had pac'd the treacherous way,
But that a twinkling light sometimes appear'd,
Sometimes grew dim, and sometimes brightly clear'd;
This could not be the lure of beasts of prey;
They know no art of imitating day,
Much pleas'd I thought. The mazy path yet led
Through shrubby copse, by taller trees o'erspread;   740
A wimpling rill ran on, and wreath'd its way
Through tufts of flowers, that made its borders gay;
And now a rock the parting leaves unfold,
On which a withering oak had long grown old,
The curling ivy oft attempts to hide
Its sad decay, with robes of verdant pride,
Yet through her leafy garb the eye can peer,
And see it buys the youthful dress too dear.
A hollow cavern now methought I spied,
Where clustering grapes came wandering down its side, 750
Between whose leaves a ray of light would dart,
That both rejoic'd and terrified my heart.
I ventur'd in,—my breath I scarcely drew,
Nought save a taper met my wondering view;
An inner cavern beamed with fuller light,

And gave a holy hermit to my sight;
Himself and Piety seem'd but the same,
And Wisdom for grey hairs another name;
Some traces yet of sorrow might be found,
760   That o'er his features walk'd their pensive round;
Devotion seem'd to bid them not to stray,
But human feelings gave the wanderers way.
His eye he rais'd from the instructive page,
An eye more sunk by wearing grief than age;
Surprise a moment o'er his features spread,
And gave them back their once accustom'd red."
"Welcome my son—a hermit's welcome share,
And let the welcome mend the scanty fare.
A soldier's toils the softest couch requires,
770   The strengthening food, and renovating fires;
Not such the hermit's needy cell bestows,
Pamper'd alone by luxury of woes,
The falling tears bedew the crusty bread,
And the moss pillow props the weary head;
The limpid brook the heats of thirst allay,
And gather'd fruits the toilsome search repay;
When hunger calls, these are a feastful store,
And languid Sorrow asks for nothing more;
Sufficient that her eye unseen can weep,
780   Stream while awake, and flow yet more in sleep.
'Tis now twelve years since Solitude first drew
Her closing curtain round my opening view,
Since first I left my once delightful home,
Along with Grief and Solitude to roam."

Much I express'd my wonder, how a mind
So stor'd as his could herd from all mankind.
"You speak," he said, "like one whose soul is free,
Slave to no wish, nor chain'd to misery.
When ceaseless anguish clouds the summer's sky,
790   And fairest prospects tarnish in the eye;
When cheerful scenes spread every lure in vain,
And sweet Society but adds to pain;
When weeping Memory incessant brings
The sad reversion of all former things,

And show-like Fancy all her colouring lends,
To gild those views that opened with our friends:
When joyful days through the whole year would run,
And Mirth set out and travel with the sun;
When Youth and Pleasure hand in hand would stray,
And every month was little less than May;   800
When changing Fortune shifts th' incessant scene,
And only points to where our joys have been,
Is it a wonder from the world we run,
And all its fleeting empty pageants shun?

"There is a something in a well known view,
That seems to shew our long past pleasure through;
Sure in the eye a fairy land is found,
When former scenes bring former friends around.
Let but the woods, the rocks, the streams appear,
And every friend you see and think you hear;   810
Their words, their dress, their every look, you find
Swell to the sight, and burst upon the mind;
Though many a spring has lent the blossom gay,
And many an autumn blown the leaf away,
Unchang'd the lasting images remain,
Of which Remembrance ever holds the chain.
E'en the mind's eye a glassy mirror shews,
And far too deeply her bold pencil draws;
The life-like pictures rise before the sight,
Glow through the day, and sparkle through the night.   820
Ah! sure e'en now my Ethelind appears,
Though dimly seen through this sad vale of tears.
That winning form, where elegance has wove
The thousand softnesses of gentlest love;
That meaning eye, that artless blushing cheek,
Which leaves so little for the tongue to speak;
The nameless graces of her polish'd mind;
That laughing wit, and serious sense refined;
That altogether which no art can reach,
And which 'tis nature's very rare to teach;   830
That nameless something which pervades the soul,
Wins not by halves, but captivates the whole;
Yet, if one feature shone before the rest,

'Twas surely Pity by Religion drest.
Have I not seen the softly stealing tear,
Hung in her eye, like gem in Ethiop's ear!
Whilst the dark orb the glittering diamond shed,
From her fair cheek the frighten'd roses fled,
Asham'd that, such a gem so sweetly clear,
840　　Aught, save the lily, should presume to wear.

"Sure there's a pleasure in recounting woes!
And some relief in every tear that flows!
Else why call back those days for ever flown,
And with them every joy this heart can own?
Pleasure and pain is the sad mixture still,
Taste but the good, and you must taste the ill;
Dear Recollection is a sorceress fair
That brings up pleasures livelier than they were;
Delighted Fancy dwells upon the view,
850　　Compares old scenes with what she meets with new;
The present hour grows dull, her charms decay,
And, one by one, drop silently away.
Neglect succeeds—Neglect, the worst of foes,
That married love or single friendship knows,
Whose torpid soul congeal'd in stupor lies,
Nor sees one charm, nor hears the smothering sighs;
Sees not the hourly load of comforts brought
By fond affection, watching every thought,
Nor the heart beating with the wish to please,—
860　　Cold, cold Neglect, nor hears, nor feels, nor sees!

"Thus, in the present hour too, oft slides by
The many a charm that might detain the eye;
But just as if from woes we could not part,
We veil the sight, and close shut up the heart;
So I myself would ne'er forget the day
When Ethelinda vowed her heart away.
Our births were equal, but exalted views
For the fair daughter bade the sire refuse.
O'er seas I roam, in quest of much-priz'd wealth,
870　　Though, after all, the greatest good is health!
Where'er I roam'd, my Ethelind was there,

My soul's companion join'd me every where;
Whatever scenes entrapped my travelling eye,
My fancied Ethelind stood smiling by,
Her just opinion met my listening ear,
And her remarks on men, and climes, I hear.
This was not absence, or it was a dream,
Which, though unreal, yet would real seem.
Each day the tongue-like pen some story told,
Of growing love, or less increasing gold;   880
Yet fortune frown'd not; and, in lengthening time,
One day I saw that mark'd her to be mine.
Hail! heaven-taught letters, that through years convey
The deathless thought, as if just breath'd to-day!
That gives the converse of an absent friend,
And, for a moment, makes that absence end;
For, while the eager eyes the lines run o'er,
Distance steps back, and drags the chain no more;
For one short moment the dear friends we see
Close by our side, just as they used to be.   890
Such sweet delusions are not form'd to last,
And Fancy's visions far too soon are past.
No such delights my heart-wrote lines attend,
They met the hand of a deceitful friend;
Her brother, anxious for a lord's success,
Thought it no sin to blast my happiness,
Kept up my letters, and base stories told,
That I had sold myself to age, and gold.
Her good opinion baffled long the tale,
And love for long kept down the struggling scale.   900
But when, from year to year, Hope pointed on,
And the last hope with the last year was gone,
She tried to think I must be base, and strove
To scorn the man who could give up her love;
Yet her soft heart no other flame confessed,
It lodged the tenant of her faithful breast.

"Home I return'd, much wearied out with woes,
And every fear that fretful silence knows.
Fear for her death was far my greatest dread;
How could I bear to think her with the dead!   910

Did she but live, methought my griefs might end,
When the warm lover cool'd into the friend.
I reach'd my home, and quick inquiries made,
Found her unmarried—found she was not dead.
And now, to know the cause of all my woe,
With hope and fear, and joy, and grief, I go;
A thousand fears would stop me in my way,
A thousand hopes forbid one moment's stay.
As nigh the house with anxious step I drew,
920   Fond recollections crowded all the view;
I felt a tear creep round and round my eye,
That shame of man, and yet I know not why.
While at the door her faithful maid I saw,
The short quick breath I scarce had power to draw;
Where—is—your la—my lips no more would move."
"She's in the arbour, sir, you us'd to love."
"Something like hope a cordial drop bestow'd,
The heart grew warm, and the pale cheek now glow'd.
Near to the arbour silently I drew,
930   And trembling look'd the leafy lattice through;
The sprightly air which once lit up her face,
To pensive softness long had given place;
Its gentle charms around her features crowd,
And tenderest feeling her fine figure bow'd;
More dear she seem'd, more interesting far,
Than when her eye was call'd the evening star;
On her fair hand she lean'd her drooping head,
And many a tear bedew'd the page she read;
'Twas Milton's Paradise—the book I knew,
940   Once my own profile on the leaf I drew,
And wrote beneath this truth-dictated line—
'With thee conversing I forget all time';
Her eye I saw ran every feature o'er,
And scann'd the line where truth seem'd writ no more;
She shook her head, its meaning well I knew:
" 'Twas even thus, ye once lov'd lines adieu";

939 Milton's Paradise] Milton's *Paradise Lost* (1663).
942 With thee conversing I forget all time] From *Paradise Lost* 4.639.

The book she shut—so softly was it clos'd,
As if life's joys alone were there repos'd.

"I walk'd around, the crimping grass would say,—
Some heavy foot has brush'd our dews away;   950
She started up, and, shaking off the tear,
Strove hard to make the pearl-set eye more clear;
But when my form the parting leaves betray'd,
And fuller light around my features play'd,
She grows a statue, wrought by Michael's art,
A marble figure, with a human heart,
More pale, more cold, than Medici can seem,
Or all the forms that from the quarry teem.
I bow'd, but spoke not, injur'd as I thought,
And wishing much to show the sense I ought;   960
I durst not trust th' impatient tongue to move,
For, ah! I felt it would but talk of love.
I silent stand." "What art thou, vision, say,
Why dost thou cross a wretched wanderer's way?
Sure 'tis the whimsy of a feverish mind
That fancies forms none but itself can find!"
"I bow'd again." "Oh! speak if thou art he
That once was dear—so very dear to me?"
"Yes, Ethelind, most sure—too sure I'm he
That once was dear, so very dear to thee;   970
Why has thy heart its fondness all forborne
To swell my sails, and ask my quick return?"
"A married man!—she sharply made reply,"
With much resentment sparkling in her eye,—
"A married man has every right to hear
What thoughts pursue us through the changing year!
Yes, I will tell you: happy was the day
In which you gave your heart and hand away.
I gave not mine, yet free from every vow
That would have tied me to a wretch like you.   980
I feel as blissful in my single state,

955 Michael's art] Michelangelo (1475–1564), the Italian Renaissance sculptor, painter, architect, and poet.

As you, no doubt, feel in your wealthy mate!"
She rose to go: "My Ethelind, forbear!
Some cruel monster has abus'd your ear;
Your faithful lover see before you stand,
Your faithful lover dares to claim your hand;
No other vows that plighted faith could stain,
No other loves melt o'er this heart again!
Let easy fortune nameless comforts spread,
990   And slope for life the soft descending tread.
No needful cares, to study how the year
Shall rule its squares, and run its circles clear;
The generous hand no close restraint shall know,
But opening bounty from the fingers flow.
The saddest sight the pitying eyes receive,
Is to see wretchedness with nought to give;
The heart-wrung tear, though e'er so fully shed,
Brings no warm clothing, and affords no bread.
On you shall pleasure wait with ready call,
1000   Speed to the play, or hasten to the ball;
Where safest ease her flowery carpet throws,
And gilded domes their rainbow-lights dispose;
Where splendour turns e'en common things to show,
And plain good comforts ornamental grow.
'Midst scenes like these would Ethelinda blaze,
While wreathing diamonds lend their mingling rays;
Wealth is her own, for it is mine to give,
As it is hers, to bid me how to live.
But should domestic peace her soul allure,
1010   For splendour but hides grief, it cannot cure,—
If in sweet converse hours should steal away,
While we still wander at the close of day;
If every wish preventing love should see,
And all the world we to ourselves should be,
I only wait the soft assenting smile,
To be whate'er her heart would ask the while;
O yes, dear friend! I yet can read the line,
'With thee conversing I forget all time';
Domestic peace has every charm for me,
1020   How doubly charming when enjoy'd with thee!

"Now honour pleaded that my fame should bleed,
And life is rul'd by her detested creed;
This idol, honour, at whose shrine appears
The heart-broke friend, dissolv'd in endless tears.
He, fiery youth, impatient of control,
And the grey veteran sorry from his soul,
Th' injuring and the injur'd both repair,
And both expect her laurel wreath to wear;
It matters not where right or wrong began,
The man who fights must be an honest man,   1030
Though every baseness that the heart can know
Should damp his soul, and keep his sword in awe;
Sole proof of excellence such warriors give—
Wretches who die, because they dare not live!
The guilty breast is ever up in arms,
And the least look the conscious soul alarms!
Should your quick eye the shuffling card detect,
Or should the gamester think you but suspect,
His injur'd honour dares you to the fight,
And all the world admits the challenge right!   1040
Not to accept it blasts a virtuous fame,
And links your memory with eternal shame;
It matters not though pure your life appears
On the long record of revolving years;
Though heaven you fear, and heaven's forbidding law,
That stamps him criminal who dares to draw,
Yet man, vain man, breaks through the laws of heaven,
Dies by the sword, and hopes to be forgiven;
For what we duels from high fashion call,
Is Suicide, or Murder, after all!   1050

    "Sometimes the heart almost approves the deed,
When barbarous wounds make reputation bleed;
Of all the crimes of any shape or dye,
That looks the blackest in true feeling's eye,
If a dear sister's purity we feel,
Nature cries out—where is th' avenging steel?
Avenging steel! how impotent the word,
And all the threats and cures that tend the sword!

"Sweet Reputation, like a lily fair,
1060 Scents every breath that winnows through the air;
The colouring sunbeam on its whiteness plays,
And dances round and round with gilding rays;
Anon dark clouds these gilding rays withhold,
And the leaf shrivels with the sudden cold;
A blighting vapour sails along the skies,
And the meek lily droops its head, and dies:
Nor can a sword, or the depending pen,
Clear the lost female character again;
The vindication better never hear,—
1070 That fame is safest that has nought to clear;
And female fame is such a tender flower,
It cannot even bear a pitying shower;
Courage in man is something near as nice,
Which life must buy, and wear at any price.

"Much 'gainst my conscience, and against heaven's law,
My destin'd brother to account I draw;
Against his life I meant no hand to rear,—
I meant but with the world to settle clear;
A self-defence, e'en in th' appointed field,
1080 Was all the sword I ever thought to wield.
Hard was the onset; in the fatal strife
His hand I saw aim'd only at my life;
I wav'd its point, still hoping to disarm,
And guard both lives secure from every harm.
I parried long; he made a lounging stroke,
And my sad weapon in his bosom broke."
" 'Tis past he said—much injur'd man, adieu!
I've done you wrong—but you'll forgive it now."
"In that sad moment every pang I found
1090 That darts through father's, brother's, sister's, wound!
In what new lights I then saw Honour's creed,
How sunk in sin seem'd the detested deed;
The world's applause was stripped of all its charms,
And the whole Conscience met the Man in arms,
Guilt, sorrow, pity warr'd within the breast,
With sad remorse, that never can have rest.
My weeping Ethelind now, too, I saw,

Lost in the floods of never ending woe!
For, ah! what woes can ever hope an end
That mourn a brother slaughter'd by a friend!   1100
Then from his breast some brief, brief lines he drew,—
The blots were many, though the words were few":
"Fly me, for ever, it is time we part,
You've kill'd a brother, and you've broke a heart."
"Tortur'd in soul from place to place I flew,
But swift-wing'd thought as swiftly would pursue;
Unless from memory our thoughts can run,
How vain to journey round and round the sun.
At last this solitude my sorrow sought,
For cities leave no bar for entering thought;   1110
I here have liv'd, in hopes the time will come,
That makes my cell my wish'd-for silent tomb."
"His tears fresh flow'd, and mine ran down my cheek,
Our griefs were such as neither tongue could speak;
At last we parted—he to endless woe,
While happy I to wife and children go."

　　Now scolding Nancy to the ale-house flies—
"What are you doing—hearing Harry's lies!
Thomas, get in, and do not sit to drink,
There's work enough at home, if you would think!"   1120

　　And now the sisters take their evening walk;
One fam'd for goodness, and one fam'd for joke,
For physic, too, some little is renown'd,
With every salve that loves to heal the wound;
The pulse she feels with true mysterious air,
While Mrs Graham of strengthening broths takes care.
That sickness must be hopeless of all end,
Which her good home-made wine no way can mend;
The brother then his skill of medicine tries,
And rarely in his hands the lingering patient dies.   1130

　　Now the white owl flits o'er the dusky ground,
Foreruns the night, and makes his trumpet sound.
The winds are lull'd asleep, and now you hear
The murmuring stream hum slumber in your ear.

Sweet Row, flow on, and be thy little vale
The future glory of the happy tale;
Long be thy banks bespread as they are now
With nibbling sheep, or richer feeding cow;
With rock, and scar, and cottage on the hill,
1140   With curling smoke, and busy useful mill;
Long may yon trees afford their leafy screen,
And long from winter save the fading green;
In every season in their speckled pride,
Safe may the trout through all thy windings glide;
Safe may the fowl adown thy waters swim,
Bathe the webb'd foot, or o'er thy mirror skim,
Nor yet the schoolboy cast the deadly stone,
And take that life, no frailer than his own;
For peace and plenty, and the cheerful tale,
1150   For happy wives, for mirth, and honest ale,
For maidens fair, and swains of matchless truth,
And all the openness of artless youth,
Whene'er a Cumbrian Village shall be fam'd,
Let Stoklewath be not the last that's nam'd!
                              (wr. aft. 1773; pub. 1842)

* The provincial pronunciation of Stokdalewath. *Patrick Maxwell.*

Countess of Blessington

(1790–1849)

Editor, poet, novelist, and society hostess, the countess of Blessington was born on 1 September 1790, the third child and second daughter of Ellen Sheehy and Edmund Power of Knockbrit in Tipperary, Ireland, a country gentleman fallen on hard times. An alcoholic given to violent rages, Power was abusive both to his wife, who suffered from severe depression, and to his children. Despite her unhappy home, Margaret, as she was christened, amused herself by improvising stories for her siblings. Her mother's friend Anne Dwyer taught her to read and gave her the rudiments of an education. Despite Margaret's pleas, her parents married her, for financial reasons, when she was only thirteen to Captain Maurice St. Leger Farmer of the Forty-seventh Regiment, a man she loathed. Violent and sadistic, he not only beat her but locked her up when he went away, sometimes leaving her without food for long stretches of time. Some believed him insane, including several in his own family, who warned Margaret's father before the wedding. Margaret lived with Farmer for three months; when he was ordered to rejoin his regiment, she refused to follow and returned in early 1804 to her parents' house, where her unsympathetic father treated her as an interloper. When her husband was discharged from the service for drawing a sword on his superior, he left for India; Margaret again refused to join him.

By 1807 she had escaped the miseries of her father's house by going to live in rural Hampshire, England, with Captain Thomas Jenkins of the 11th Light Dragoons. He was a kindly man, and these were happy years, spent reading and entertaining. After five years, at the behest of Charles John Gardiner, the second viscount Mountjoy, she parted amicably from Jenkins and went to live in Manchester Square, London. A widower seven years her senior who had a yearly income of thirty thousand pounds, Gardiner had been educated at Eton and at Christ Church, Oxford. He was elected representative peer for Ireland in 1809 and became earl of Blessington in 1816. In October 1817 Margaret's estranged husband, Maurice Farmer, intoxicated while visiting friends in the King's Bench Prison, fell to his death from a window. She and Lord Blessington were thus able to marry on 16 February 1818; Margaret Power Farmer then became known as Marguerite, countess of Blessington.

Her marriage thrust Lady Blessington into the brilliant society and splendor of the fashionable life of London. The couple lived in a luxurious mansion at 11 St. James's Square; for the next three years it would be a social and literary center and the rendezvous of London celebrities. Lord Blessington had a refined taste for literature and the arts and was especially fond of drama. Seldom attending Parliament, and still more seldom speaking, he supported the cause of the Roman Catholics. Sydney Morgan, in her novel *Florence Macarthy,* caricatures him as the stage-struck and flamboyantly dressed "Lord Rosbrin." Lady Blessington published four essays anonymously in early 1822 as *The Magic Lantern, or Sketches of Scenes in the Metropolis,* and she published a book entitled *Sketches and Fragments* later that same year.

Beneath their veneer of wealth, Lord and Lady Blessington were in financial trouble as a result of extravagant spending. As did many who wished to live more cheaply, in August 1822 they set out for the Continent, with Marguerite's younger sister, Mary Ann Power, in tow. The entourage traveled first to Paris, then to Switzerland and the south of France, where they were joined by their friend Alfred, Count d'Orsay, a handsome young Frenchman. Hoping to see Lord Byron, they arrived in Genoa, Italy, at the end of March 1823. One week later Lady Blessington met the poet. The close friendship that developed between them was one of the high points of her life and would provide the material for one of her most well-known literary works, *Conversations of Lord Byron* (1832). Byron wrote a *jeu d'esprit* and a poem to her. In early June 1823 the Blessingtons left Genoa for Naples, via Lucca, Florence, and Rome. They made their home in Naples for nearly three years, sailing on the Bay of Naples in the *Bolivar,* Byron's former yacht. In February 1826 they left Naples and traveled throughout Italy, returning to Paris in June 1828. In Florence and Venice they had spent time with Walter Savage Landor, who became one of Lady Blessington's closest friends. In Naples, early in their Italian tour, Count D'Orsay married Lord Blessington's fifteen-year-old daughter, Lady Harriet Gardiner, after Lord Blessington offered him a large part of his fortune in return. On 23 May 1829 Lord Blessington died suddenly at the age of forty-six.

Lady Blessington remained in Paris during the revolution of 1830 and left shortly afterwards for London, where she faced slanderous published accounts of a ménage à trois involving her, Count D'Orsay, and her stepdaughter. Her husband had left her an income of two thousand pounds a year, along with considerable debts. The mansion in St. James's Square was too expensive to maintain, so in late 1831 she rented a home in Seamore Place, Mayfair, where she lived from 1832 to 1836, before moving to the more spacious and elegant Gore House, Kensington, her residence until 1849. According to her first biographer, R. R. Madden, "The salons of Lady Blessington were opened nightly to men of genius and learning, and persons of celebrity of all climes, to travelers of every European city of distinction. Her abode became a centre of attraction for the beau monde of the intellectual classes, a place of reunion for remarkable persons of talent or eminence of some sort or another, and certainly the most agreeable resort of men of literature, art, science, of strangers of distinction, travelers, and public characters of various pursuits, the most agreeable that ever existed in this country."[1] In his diary entry for 27 February 1835, Benjamin Robert Haydon wrote, "Went to Lady Blessington's in the evening; . . . Every body goes to Lady Blessington. She has the first news of every thing, and every body seems delighted to tell her. . . . She is the center of more talent & gaiety than any other Woman of Fashion in London."[2] An extraordinary conversationalist—expressive, uninhibited, and known for her memorable quips—she could distill in short, witty sentences the essence and value of an entire book. Her influence and power became considerable.

Lady Blessington turned to writing to make up the difference between her income of two thousand pounds and the four thousand pounds she spent yearly to support herself and at least seven family members. (Count D'Orsay's young wife left him in the autumn of 1831, but he remained a fixture in Lady Blessington's household, taking a small house nearby to quiet the gossip. Even so, proper ladies refused to be seen with Lady Blessington after dark.) She wrote furiously. *Conversations of Lord Byron,* her best-known work today, appeared in serialized form in the *New Monthly Magazine* beginning in July 1832 and running intermittently for a year and a half. It caused an instant sensation, encouraging her in her new profession and leading to a close friendship with the editor of the magazine, the novelist Edward Bulwer, later Sir Edward Bulwer-Lytton, who introduced her to young Isaac D'Israeli, also to become a good friend. Her first novel, *Grace Cassidy; or, the Repealers,* a well-received *roman à clef* for which she received four hundred pounds from Richard Bentley, came out in 1833. In early 1834, *Conversations of Lord Byron* was published in book form. Despite accusations that she was not the real author and that the conversations were not genuine, it sold well. Another

1. *The Literary Life and Correspondence of the Countess of Blessington,* ed. R. R. Madden, 2 vols. (New York, 1855), 1:143.

2. *Diary of Benjamin Robert Haydon,* ed. Willard Bissell Pope, vol. 4 (Cambridge, 1963), 270–71.

novel, *The Two Friends,* describing life in Paris as she knew it, came out in January 1835. She edited two literary gift books, Charles Heath's *Book of Beauty* (beginning in 1833 for the 1834 volume) and the *Keepsake* (beginning in 1838 for the 1839 volume), work that necessarily brought her into contact with almost every other author of any stature in Britain. She filled in the gaps in each literary annual with her own poetry or prose. The financial rewards were great. According to William Jerdan, "As an author and editor of 'Heath's Annual' for some years, Lady Blessington received . . . an amount somewhere midway between £2000 and £3000 per annum, and her title, as well as talents, had considerable influence in 'ruling high prices.'"[3] As a woman editor, unable to meet with contributors, publishers, and artists in a business office, as her male counterparts did, she compensated by entertaining them in her home.

In addition to her editing, in 1836 she brought out *The Confessions of an Elderly Gentleman,* and the following year, *The Victims of Society. The Confessions of an Elderly Lady* appeared in 1838, the same year a publisher in Philadelphia brought out a two-volume collected *Works.* The following year she published *The Governess, Desultory Thoughts and Reflections* and two volumes of *The Idler in Italy,* a highly successful travel book based on observations taken from her own diaries; a third volume followed the next year. *The Belle of a Season,* a long poem, came out in 1840, and the following year she published *The Idler in France,* based on her travel diaries. *The Lottery of Life and Other Tales* appeared in 1842, and *Strathern; or, Life at Home and Abroad: A Story of the Present Day* came out in 1845, having first been serialized in the Sunday *Times.* Two more novels followed: *Memoirs of a Femme de Chambre* (1846) and *Marmaduke Herbert; or, the Fatal Error* (1847). Eventually, however, her life was made miserable by deadlines, contentions with publishers, a heavy correspondence with contributors and artists, and a diminishing income. When Charles Heath died insolvent in 1848, he owed Lady Blessington nearly seven hundred pounds. By this time the heyday of literary gift books and annuals was over. Her novels were commanding less in the marketplace as well. A potato blight in 1845 seriously diminished her income from Lord Blessington's estate, and that income had disappeared by 1848.

In the spring of 1849 the contents of Lady Blessington's home had to be sold to satisfy her creditors. Worn down by anxiety, embarrassments, and demands she could not meet, she nevertheless refused all offers of help from friends. She left for Paris in mid-April 1849, taking an apartment in the Rue du Cerq, close to the Champs Élysées; just six weeks later, on 4 June 1849,

3. *The Autobiography of William Jerdan,* vol. 4 (London, 1853), 320.

only two months short of her sixtieth birthday, she suffered what was probably a heart attack and died without regaining consciousness. The inscription on her monument reads, in part, "Men, famous for art and science / In distant lands, / Sought her friendship: / And the historians and scholars, the poets, and wits, and painters, / Of her own country, / Found an unfailing welcome / In her ever hospitable home." An obituary published in the *Athenaeum* for 9 June 1849 noted, "It would not be difficult to point out ladies of celebrity as bas bleus of far superior abilities as authoresses, of imaginations with richer stores of wit and poetry, of more erudition, and better cultivated talents; but we shall find none who, for an equal length of time, maintained an influence of fascination in literary and fashionable society over the highest intellects, and exercised dominion over the feelings as well as over the faculties of those who frequented her abode." Lady Blessington's final novel, *Country Quarters*, appeared posthumously in 1850.

MAJOR WORKS: *The Magic Lantern; or Sketches of Scenes in the Metropolis* (London, 1822); *Sketches and Fragments* (London, 1822); *Journal of a Tour through the Netherlands to Paris, in 1821* (London, 1822); *Rambles in Waltham Forest. A Stranger's Contribution to the Triennial Sale for the Benefit of the Wanstead Lying-in Charity* (London, 1827); *Grace Cassidy; or, the Repealers. A Novel*, 3 vols. (London, 1833); *Conversations of Lord Byron with the Countess of Blessington* (London, 1834); *The Two Friends; a Novel*, 3 vols. (London, 1835); *The Confessions of an Elderly Gentleman* (London, 1836); *Gems of Beauty Displayed in a Series of Twelve . . . Engravings . . . with Fanciful Illustrations, in Verse* (London and New York, 1836); *The Victims of Society*, 3 vols. (London, 1837); *The Confessions of an Elderly Lady* (London, 1838); *The Governess*, 3 vols. (London, 1839); *Desultory Thoughts and Reflections* (London, 1839); *The Idler in Italy*, 3 vols. (London, 1839–40); *The Belle of a Season* (London, 1840); *The Idler in France*, 2 vols. (London, 1841); *The Lottery of Life and Other Tales*, 3 vols. (London, 1842); *Meredyth*, 3 vols. (London, 1843); *Strathern; or, Life at Home and Abroad: A Story of the Present Day*, 4 vols. (London, 1845); *Memoirs of a Femme de Chambre. A Novel*, 3 vols. (London, 1846); *Lionel Deerhurst, or Fashionable Life under the Regency* (London, 1846); *Marmaduke Herbert; or, The Fatal Error. A Novel, Founded on Fact* (London, 1847); *Country Quarters*, 3 vols. (London, 1850).

EDITED WORKS: *The Book of Beauty* (1834–49); *Keepsake* (1839–49).

TEXT USED: Text of "Stock in Trade of Modern Poetesses" from the *Keepsake* for 1833.

Stock in Trade of Modern Poetesses

Lonely shades, and murm'ring founts;
Limpid streams, and azure mounts;
Rocks and caverns, ocean's roar;
Waves whose surges lash the shore;
Moons, that silver radiance shed,
When the vulgar are "a-bed";
Stars and planets shining high,
Make one feel 'twere bliss to die;
Twilight's soft mysterious light;
10   Suns whose rays are "all" too bright;
Wither'd hopes, and faded flowers,
Beauties pining in their bowers;
Broken harps, and untuned lyres;
Lutes neglected, unquench'd fires;
Vultures pecking at the heart,
Leaving owners scarce a part;
Doves that, frighted from the breast,
Seek in vain some sweeter rest;
Feather'd songsters of the grove,
20   Warbling notes of joy and love;
Hearts a prey to dark despair,
Why, or how, we hardly care;
Pale disease feeds on the cheek,
Health how feeble—head how weak—
Bursting tear and endless sigh—
Query, can she tell us why?
Pallid nymphs with fronts of snow,
Ebon locks with graceful flow;
Lips of rose leaves' tender dyes,
30   Eyes that mock cerulean skies;
And a foot too which may pass
Over, yet not bend, the grass.—
Next a hero, with an air—
Half a brigand—half corsair;

30 cerulean] Blue, cloudless.
34 corsair] Privateer, pirate.

Dark, mysterious in his life,
Dreadful in the battle's strife;
Vice and virtue in his breast,
War for empire—banish rest—
Raving still of glory—fame—
While dishonour marks his name;   40
Loving one, and only one—
Though he has that one undone;
A Macedoine of good and evil,
One part hero—three parts devil:
Quite an Admirable Crichton
Is the hero all now write on.—
This now is all the stock in trade,
With which a modern poem's made.

(1833)

---

43 Macedoine] Medley or mixture of unrelated things.

45 Crichton] James Crichton (1560–82), called "the Admirable Crichton," a famous Scottish scholar and adventurer.

Mary Ann Browne

(1812–1844)

Although Mary Ann Browne was sometimes said to be the sister of Felicia Hemans, in fact they were not related. Born in 1812 in Maidenhead, England, Browne said that she "could not recollect when she was not clothing her thoughts in verse."[1] By the time she was eighteen she had three major books of poetry to her credit. Only fifteen when Hatchard & Son, the London publisher, brought out her first volume, *Mont Blanc, and Other Poems* (1827), she moved to the more prestigious firm of Longmans for the publication of *Ada, and Other Poems* (1828). Dedicated to her father, it was praised in *Blackwood's* and went through at least three editions in its first year.

Repentance: and Other Poems followed the next year and appears to have been virtually ignored. As a result, Browne's health and spirits suffered. Even so, she commanded a strong presence in the literary annuals—the *Winter's Wreath*, the *Literary Souvenir*, the *Gem*, the *Iris*, and the *New Year's Gift*. She changed to the publishing house of Hamilton, Adams, for subsequent volumes of poetry, which came out somewhat more slowly than before—*The Coronal: Original Poems, Sacred and Miscellaneous* in 1833, *The Birth-Day Gift* in 1834, *Ignatia and Other Poems* in 1838, and *Sacred Poetry* in 1840.

On a visit to Ireland in 1839 Browne befriended the editor of the *Dublin University Magazine*, who gave her encouragement and published her poems. In 1842, aged thirty, she married a Scotsman, James Gray, a nephew of the poet James Hogg, and settled in Cork. During this period, Browne contributed many poems to the *Forget-Me-Not* and *Friendship's Offering*. The marriage was happy, though brief; Browne died in 1844. The same year, Longmans published her last volume, *Sketches from the Antique: and Other Poems*.

Sarah J. Hale, in her *Woman's Record*, said of Browne, "Her style is modelled on the manner of the old bards; and though her poetry never reaches the height she evidently sought to attain, it is excellent for its pure taste and

---

1. *Feminist Companion*, 455.

just sentiment; while a few instances of bold imagination show vividly the ardour of a fancy, which prudence and delicacy always controlled."[2] Mary Russell Mitford, who met Browne when she was only fourteen and knew her throughout the succeeding years, observed, "Of all poetesses, George Sand herself not excepted, she seems to me to touch with the sweetest, the firmest, the most delicate hand, the difficult chords of female passion."[3]

MAJOR WORKS: *Mont Blanc, and Other Poems* (London, 1827); *Ada, and Other Poems* (London, 1828); *Repentance; and Other Poems* (London, 1829); *The Coronal; Original Poems, Sacred and Miscellaneous* (London, 1833); *The Birth-Day Gift* (London and Liverpool, 1834); *Ignatia and Other Poems* (London, 1838); *Sacred Poetry* (London, 1840); *Sketches from the Antique: and Other Poems* (London, 1844).

TEXTS USED: Texts of "A World without Water" and "The Song of the Elements" from the *Winter's Wreath* (London, 1832); texts of "The Wild Horse" and "To a Wild Bee" from *The Coronal*.

A World without Water

> Yesternight I prayed aloud,
>   In anguish and in agony;
> Upstarting from the fiendish crowd
>   Of shapes and thoughts that tortured me.
>   —Coleridge*

I had a dream in the dead of night;
    A dream of agony;
I thought the world stood in affright,
Beneath the hot and parching light
    Of an unclouded sky:
I thought there had fallen no cooling rain
For months upon the feverish plain,
    And that all the springs were dry:

2. Sarah J. Hale, *Woman's Record; or, Sketches of all Distinguished Women, from the Creation to A.D. 1868. Arranged in Four Eras. With Selections from Authoresses of Each Era,* 3rd ed., rev. (New York, 1870), 228.
3. Mitford, *Recollections,* 223.

And I was standing on a hill,
   And looking all around:
I know not how it was; but still
   Strength in my limbs was found,
As if with a spell of threefold life,
   My destinies were bound.

Beneath me was a far-spread heath,
   Where once had risen a spring.
Looking as bright as a silver wreath
   In its graceful wandering:
But now the sultry glance of the sun,
   And the glare of the dark blue sky,
Had checked its course,—no more to run
   In light waves wandering by.

And farther on was a stately wood,
   With its tall trees rising high.
But now like autumn wrecks they stood
   Beneath a summer sky:
And every leaf, though dead, did keep
   Its station in mockery;
For there was not one breath to sweep
   The leaves from each perishing tree;
And there they hung dead, motionless;
   They hung there day by day,
As though Death were too busy with other things
   To sweep their corpses away.

Oh, terrible it was to think
   Of human creatures then!
How they did seek in vain to drink
   In every vale and glen;
And how the scorched foot did shrink
   As it touched the slippery plain:
And some had gathered beneath the trees
   In hope of finding shade;
But alas! there was not a single breeze
   Astir in any glade!

The cities were forsaken,
    For their marble wells were spent;
And their walls gave back the scorching glare
    Of that hot firmament:
But the corses of those who died were strewn
    In the street, as dead leaves lay,   50
And dry they withered—and withered alone,
    They felt no foul decay!

Night came. The fiery Sun sank down,
    And the people's hope grew strong:
It was a night without a moon,
It was a night in the depth of June,
    And there swept a wind along;
'Twas *almost cool:* and then they thought
Some blessed dew it would have brought.

Vain was the hope!—there was no cloud   60
    In the clear dark blue Heaven;
But, bright and beautiful, the crowd
    Of stars looked through the even.
And women sat them down to weep
    Over their hopeless pain:
And men had visions dark and deep,
    Clouding the dizzy brain:
And children sobbed themselves to sleep,
    And never woke again.

The morning rose—not as it comes   70
    Softly 'midst rose and dew—
Not with those cool and fresh perfumes
    That the weariest heart renew,
—But the Sun sprang up, as if eager to see
    What next his power could do!

A mother held her child to her breast
    And kissed it tenderly,
And then she saw her infant smile;
    What could that soft smile be?

80   A tear had sprung with a sudden start,
      To her hot feverish eye;
    It had fallen upon that faint child's lip
      That was so parched and dry.

I looked upon the mighty Sea;
      Oh, what a sight it was!
All its waves were gone save two or three,
      That lay like burning glass,
Within the caves of those deep rocks
      Where no human foot could pass.

90   And in the very midst, a ship
      Lay in the slime and sand;
With all its sailors perishing
      Even in sight of land;
Oh! water had been a welcome sight
      To that pale dying band!

Oh, what a sight was the bed of the Sea!
      The bed where he had slept,
Or tossed and tumbled restlessly,
      And all his treasures kept
100   For ages: he was gone; and all
      His rocky pillows shewn,
With their clustering shells, and sea-weed pall,
      And the rich gems round them thrown.

And the monsters of the deep lay dead,
      With many a human form.
That there had found a quiet bed
      Away from the raging storm;
And the fishes, sodden in the sun,
      Were strewn by thousands round;
110   And a myriad things, long lost and won,
      Were there, unsought for, found.

I turned away from earth and sea,
      And looked on the burning sky,

But no drop fell, like an angel's tear—
    The founts of Heaven were dry:
The birds had perished every one;
    Not a cloud was in the air,
And desolate seemed the very Sun,
    He looked so lonely there!

And I began to feel the pang—   120
    The agony of thirst;
I had a scorching swelling pain,
    As if my heart would burst.
My tongue seemed parched; I tried to speak—
    The spell that instant broke;
And, starting at my own wild shriek,
    In mercy I awoke.

                (1832)

* Samuel Taylor Coleridge, "The Pains of Sleep," lines 14–17.

The Song of the Elements

FIRST VOICE. — EARTH

I sit amidst the universe,
    As I've sate for ages gone,
And though God hath bound me with a curse,
    I am bathed in the light of the sun;
And I bear within my bosom the pride
    Of many a kingly throne,—
There the diamond and ruby are scattered wide,
    And the changeless rocks are my zone;
And the mighty forest springs from my breast,
    And the mountain doth upward dart,   10
And though the clouds are on its crest,
    Its root is in my heart.
I am the mother of all things
    That have filled me since life began;

The nursing mother of founts and springs,
　　The own true mother of man:
His limbs are formed from my finest clay,
　　And let him die by earth or sea,
He must perish and pass away,
20　　And come again to me.
Oh, man is strong in his power and might,
　　But I, his mother am more strong;
He is mine by a parent's right—
　　Sisters! take up the song!

ALL THE ELEMENTS

We four dwell all apart, yet, still
　　We are bound by a viewless chain,
The thrones, that God hath given, we fill
　　Each with a separate reign.
Contending oft, like the kings of earth,
30　　Triumphant for an hour;
Yet the fallen rising again, in the birth,
　　Of its own unvanquished power.

SECOND VOICE. — AIR

I lap the earth as with a robe,
　　And I bind it like a rim,
And the clouds that shadow o'er the globe
　　Upon my bosom swim.
And in the summer eve I play
　　O'er earth like a sportive child;
And in the winter night I sway
40　　The world, with a tempest wild:
I dash on the rocks the helpless seas,
　　Like wine from a reveller's cup,
And the proud earth cannot hold her trees,
　　If I will to root them up.
And then I come in the autumn morn,
　　With a fresh and stirring voice,
And I shake in the valley the golden corn,
　　And the dying flowers rejoice:
I creep into the withering rose,
50　　And lull it as if to sleep,

Then up I start from that false repose,
　　And its leaves to the cold earth sweep.
Man must breathe me, or he dies
　　The minion of my power,
I have supplied with the breath of sighs
　　His heart from his earliest hour:
And, like an unseen enemy,
　　I battle with the strong;
Such might as this is claimed by me,—
　　Sisters! take up the song!　　　　　　　　　　60

All the Elements
We four dwell all apart, yet, still
　　We are bound by a viewless chain;
The thrones that God hath given we fill,
　　Each with a separate reign.
Contending oft like the kings of earth,
　　Triumphant for an hour,
Yet the fallen rising again, in the birth
　　Of its own unvanquished power.

Third Voice. — Fire
I live in the light of the blazing sun,
　　And in the shining stars;　　　　　　　　　　70
And restless o'er the world I run,
　　And nought my glory mars.
Silently, creep I thro' the earth,
　　'Midst many a precious stone,
And till the volcano gives me birth,
　　My being is unknown;
And in the tempest's glooming cloud,
　　I hide my burning wing,
And wait till the wind gives summons loud,
　　And then from my tent I spring!—　　　　　　80
Like a conqueror from the ambush I come,
　　With a fatal glittering spear,
And with a quick and sudden doom,
　　Earth's mightiest things I sear.
I can strike man dead, if 'tis my will,
　　As a leaf falls from the tree,

'Tis I who makes his heart's pulse thrill,
    He lives not without me.
Oh, man is a wondrous creature! our aid
90   Must make him stand or fall,
A thing of elements, and made
    Dependant on them all!
He prides himself in the pomp and power,
    That do to us belong;—
We laugh at him in his proudest hour;
    Sisters! take up the song!

ALL THE ELEMENTS

We four dwell all apart, yet, still
    We are bound by a viewless chain;
The thrones that God has given we fill,
100   Each with a separate reign;
Contending oft like the kings of earth,
    Triumphant for an hour;
Yet the fallen rising again, in the birth
    Of its own unvanquished power.

FOURTH VOICE. — WATER

I burst from the earth, but for my birth
    I claim God's will alone,
Who made me queen of a realm serene,
    And placed me on my throne;
My throne of sunken rocks and caves,
110   Where the crimson coral dwells,
Where I may let my weary waves
    Sleep on the pearly shells;
And in vast rocks sometimes I'm pent,
    Like a soul for some dark crime:
Till the prison at last is broken and rent,
    And comes my rejoicing time.
And I float sometimes in a quiet river,
    Under the cloud's passing shade,
And its broad breast doth in sunlight quiver,
120   In loveliness arrayed;
And, down in my depths, I let the light
    Of the quiet blue sky dwell,

And the images of stars at night
 Are seen in my lovely cell.
Sometimes in the north I lie,
 Congealed, like a mighty isle,
Cold and unmoved 'neath the wintry sky,
 Unwon by the light's faint smile.
And then at last there shines a day
 Sunnily on my home,   130
And the icy bars to my path give way,
 And thundering out I come!
And rush upon the fated bark,
 With my waves in unprisoned glee,
And we whirl it down to the caverns dark,
 That are treasure rooms for me!
In the desert vast, where the caravan
 Is drooping for lack of shade,
Oh, how lordly, haughty man,
 Is my dependant made! —   140
As much as when in his fragile ship
 My waves did round him throng.
He dies if I do not bathe his lip.
 Sisters! take up the song!

ALL THE ELEMENTS
We four dwell all apart, yet, still
 We are bound by a viewless chain;
The thrones that God hath given we fill,
 Each with a separate reign;
Contending oft like the kings of earth,
 Triumphant for an hour,   150
Yet the fallen rising again, in the birth
 Of its own unvanquished power.
     (1832)

The Wild Horse

Broad are the palms, whose boughs
Shut out the sunshine from the little pool
    Which lies, while noontide glows
Fierce in the Arabian heaven, serene and cool.
    The reed, whose graceful stem
Riseth beside it, arrow-like and tall,
    Mirrored in that pure gem,
Looks moveless as the few strong beams that fall
    Upon the waters calm;
10 Yet here at even-tide the winds shall rise,
    Bringing the wild flower's balm,
And singing low their vesper melodies.

    But it is noon—high noon,
And a sound cometh up the forest glade,
    Breaking the dreamy tune
By the small insects 'neath the leaflets made:
    Nearer and nearer now,
And lo! with measured step of matchless force,
    The white star on his brow,
20 He comes to rest him here, the desert Horse!
    He stoops, and the long mane
Falls like a veil over the glossy neck,
    That never curved to rein,
That no gay bells or silver trappings deck;

    And through that falling shroud
The dark eye looks, with clear and steady gaze,
    As if the steed were proud
Of the reflection of its freeborn rays,
    Down in the water still
30 That bubbles with his breath, as from the lake
    He drinks the draught so chill,
So sweet, the thirst of summer days to slake;
    His head is raised again,
And yet he pauses for one downward look,
    Then onward to the plain,
Fitter for him than the secluded nook!

Fitter in sooth for him!
His is the daring heart, the gallant front,
      The strong and nervous limb,
All made to bear the summer's fiercest brunt.   40
      Fitter for him the free!
Lo the earth scattereth from his bounding hoof,
      As on he goes in glee;
The plain his palace, and the sky his roof.
      He lifts his head on high,
And tosses back the forelock, that his gaze
      May be upon the sky,
In the unclouded glory of its blaze.

      He stops, and then doth start,
Even as he will; he owns no master's yoke—   50
      His is the mighty heart
That never could be bowed, although it broke.
      Oh never curb was made,
That might subdue the pulses of that steed;
      Oh never hand was laid
Upon that neck, by nature's charter freed!
      Better that he should lie
Beneath these cloudless heavens, a worthless corse,
      Than bow in slavery,
The beautiful, the brave, the noble horse!   60
      Better that he should fall
And perish, in the desert of his birth,
      Than live to know the thrall
Of human tyranny is on the earth.

                                        (1833)

To a Wild Bee

Roamer of the mountain!
    Wanderer of the plain!
Lingerer by the fountain,
    Where thou dost sustain
A part in Nature's rich, and wild and
        varied strain!

Fairy of the summer!
    I love to watch thy flight,
When first thou art a comer,
10   On wings so gauzy light,
Flitting in wildering maze before my
        dazzled sight.

Thou hummest o'er the heather
    Upon the breezy hill;
And in sultry weather,
    When every wind is still,
Float'st through the waveless air unto the
        singing rill.

On the moorland mosses,
20   Thou sip'st the fragrant thyme;
And the tufted bosses
    Of greenest grass doth climb,
With struggling feet, to rest thy wings in
        noontide's prime.

In the lily's blossom,
    An ivory palace tower, —
In the roses bosom,
    Safe from the sudden shower,
Thou shelterest, heeding not how thunder
30   clouds may lower.

21 bosses] Seats of straw, hassocks.
27 In the roses bosom] This clearly should read, "In the rose's bosom."

Thou lov'st the cool green places
    Where the dew lies late,
Where the twilight's traces
        Are, near her palace gate, —
Her palace midst the trees, wherein she
        keeps her state.

Thou lov'st the sunny Hours,
        When upwards thou dost spring,
With the dew from chaste, cool flowers
        And mosses on thy wing, —   40
The sweet enslaving dew, that doth so closely
        cling.

Thou lov'st the sunset's glowing,
        When, with thy mimic toil,
Half weary, thou art going
        Laden with thy sweet spoil,
Unto thy quiet home, wherein is no
        turmoil.

Oh vagrant, happy rover!
        Gatherer of treasures rare!   50
Never did truest lover
        A heart so happy bear,
As thou, who woo'st all flowers, without a
        fear or care.

I would that I might ever
        Have thee before mine eyes!
Surely I should endeavour
        To learn to be as wise,
And all the simple gifts of holiest nature
        prize.   60

But even now, unsteady!
        Thou tak'st again thy flight,
Thy little wings already
        Are quivering in the light,
Thy hum is faintlier heard, thou darted
        from my sight!

I would, when death hath stilled me,
　　And checked this restless heart,
When his icy hand has chilled me,
70　　　And I must needs depart,
I would I might be laid where thou, wild
　　　wanderer, art!

And then the winds should whisper,
　　And the willow branches wave;
And the cricket, merry lisper,
　　And the throstle, minstrel brave,
And thou, thou murmuring bee! should
　　　chorus o'er my grave.
　　　　　　　　(1833)

76 throstle] Thrush, especially the song thrush, or mavis, *Turdus musicus.*

Lady Byron

(*née* Anne Isabella Milbanke)
(1792–1860)

The courtship, married life, and subsequent divorce of Anne Isabella "Annabella" Milbanke and George Gordon, the sixth Lord Byron, has been exhaustively chronicled, as has the life of their only child—Ada, countess of Lovelace. What has not been so well recounted is that Lady Byron was a poet as well as a wife. At thirteen she told her mother, "I composed a few lines last night in Blank verse, imitating Young's most melancholy stile. I am doubtful whether I have succeeded, as I cannot say I was in a very gloomy humour. The subject I chose was a lamentation for a deceased friend."[1] She was always a voracious reader of poetry and plays, including works by her father's favorites, Shakespeare, Otway, Dryden, and Darwin, as well as those by Cowper, Beaumont and Fletcher, Jonson, Massinger, Hartley, and Henrietta O'Neill. She and her mother were patrons of Joseph Blacket, the cobbler poet, with whom Milbanke exchanged verses in 1809, a year before Blacket's death at twenty-three.[2]

Milbanke attended Thomas Campbell's weekly lectures on poetry at the Royal Institution in the spring of 1812. At about this time, she first saw Byron at a morning party at Lady Caroline Lamb's, just after *Childe Harold's Pilgrimage,* cantos 1 and 2, had earned him overnight fame.[3] In their first conversation, on 13 April, they talked about Blacket. Lady Caroline subsequently sent Byron some of Annabella Milbanke's poetry, to which he responded,

> I have read over the few poems of Miss Milbank with attention.—They display fancy, feeling, & a little practice would very soon induce facility of expression.—Though I have an abhorrence of Blank verse, I like the lines on Dermody so much that I wish they were in rhyme.—The lines in the cave at

1. Letter dated 26 October 1805, quoted in Malcolm Elwin, *Lord Byron's Wife* (New York, 1962), 79.
2. Ibid., 80–84.
3. The party took place on 25 March 1812 (ibid., 105).

Seaham have a turn of thought which I cannot sufficiently commend & here I am at least candid as my own opinions differ upon such subjects.—The first stanza is very good indeed, & the others with a few slight alterations might be rendered equally excellent.—The last are smooth & pretty.—But these are all, has she no others?—She certainly is a very extraordinary girl, who would imagine so much strength & variety of thought under that placid counte- nance? . . . I have no hesitation in saying that she has talents, which were it proper or requisite to indulge, would have led to distinction.—A friend of mine (fifty years old & an author but not *Rogers*) has just been here, as there is no name to the M.S.S. I shewed them to him, & he was much more en- thusiastic in his praises than I have been.—He thinks them beautiful; I shall content myself with observing that they are better much better than anything of Miss M's protegee Blacket. You will say as much of this to Miss M. as you think proper.—I say all this very sincerely, I have no desire to be better ac- quainted with Miss Milbank, she is too good for a fallen spirit to know or wish to know, & I should like her more if she were less perfect.[4]

On 30 November 1813 Byron described Milbanke in his journal as "a poet- ess—a mathematician—a metaphysician, and yet, withal, very kind, gener- ous, and gentle, with very little pretension. Any other head would be turned with half her acquisitions, and a tenth of her advantages."[5] Nearly a year later, in a letter of October 1814, shortly before her marriage, Milbanke implicitly acknowledged the dual dimensions of her literary status: "I could never have married *to please* my friends. . . . I have become so *notorious* by the reflected light of fame,—and I amuse myself with thinking how many *good sort of people* will pity me—'Poor thing!—Well, I did not think she would have been dazzled at last by Talent—But they say she had always a little romantic turn for poetry herself':—So they will conclude it to be an alliance of the *Muses*."[6] Shortly after the marriage, John Murray, Byron's publisher, wrote to James Hogg, "Could you not write a poetical epistle, a lively one, to Lady Byron— she is a good mathematician, writes poetry, understands French, Italian, Latin and Greek—and tell her that as she has prevented Lord B. from fulfilling his promise to you, she is bound to insist upon its execution, and to add a poem of her own to it by way of interest."[7] Lady Byron continued to write verse during her marriage. One poem, dated 15 December 1815, five days

4. Lord Byron to Lady Caroline Lamb, 1 May 1812, in *"Famous in my Time,"* vol. 2 of *Byron's Letters and Journals,* ed. Leslie A. Marchand (Cambridge, Mass., 1973), 175–76.

5. *"Alas! The Love of Women!"* vol. 3 of *Byron's Letters and Journals,* ed. Leslie A. Marchand (Cambridge, Mass., 1974), 227.

6. Quoted by permission of the Harry Ransom Humanities Research Center, University of Texas at Austin (shelfmark Byron, GGNB, Misc I, Letters).

7. Samuel Smiles, *A Publisher and his Friends: Memoir and Correspondence of the Late John Murray,* 2 vols. (London and New York, 1891), 1:347.

after Ada's birth, bears the telling title "On a Mother Being Told She Was an Unnatural One." In another of the same period, entitled "A Contemplation of the Future," she writes:

> No, no—it will not break—this heart
>   Will labour still to beat;
> Tho' now as free from pause or start
>   As in its winding-sheet
> The heavy pulse moves changeless on,
> The ebb and flow of Hope are gone.[8]

The influence of Byron's sensibility is evident in a fragment dated 1 March 1816:

> And heart-wrung I could almost hate
>   The thing I may not love,
> And ask, while shuddering o'er its fate,
>   If pity dwelt above.[9]

After their separation, and, indeed, until the end of her life, Lady Byron's poetry reflected her continuing preoccupation with what became the central event in her life, her break with Lord Byron. She replied to his poem "Fare Thee Well," which he wrote during their separation and sent to her on 20 March 1816, with her own twenty-three-stanza poem dated 29 April 1816, "On the Words 'Fare Thee Well, by Thee Forsaken.'" A love poem alleging that the separation had been caused by treachery, it imagines his penitent return to her, closing with the following stanzas:

> But it must come—thine hour of tears,
>   When self-adoring pride shall bow—
> And thou shalt own my "blighted years,"
>   The fate that thou inflictest—*thou!*
>
> *Thy* virtue—but from ruin still
>   Shall rise a wan and drooping peace,
> With pardon for unmeasured ill,
>   And Pity's tears—if Love's must cease![10]

Richard Edwards not only pirated Byron's poem but published her answer as *Lady Byron's Responsive "Fare Thee Well"*; it was popular enough to enjoy a

---

8. Quoted in Ethel Colburn Mayne, *The Life and Letters of Anne Isabella Lady Noel Byron, from Unpublished Papers in the Possession of the Late Ralph, Earl of Lovelace* (New York, 1929), 233. Elwin, in *Lord Byron's Wife*, quotes from other poems of this period: "A Sister's Sentiments," which he believes was written about September 1815 (381), and one beginning "Can this mean peace? the calmness of the good?" (401).

9. Quoted in Mayne, *Life and Letters*, 233.

10. Quoted in Elwin, *Lord Byron's Wife*, 470. See also Mayne, *Life and Letters*, 234.

third edition and also became a favorite in the handwritten album books of the period.[11]

Lady Byron sent Theresa Villiers the poem entitled "To Ada" on the child's first birthday, adding, "It has occurred to me that [these lines] might be misunderstood, as if they expressed a wish that she were with her father, such as he is; when on the contrary, I consider her as *fatherless*."[12]

Though controversy surrounded Lady Byron throughout her life, it did not prevent her from maintaining a wide circle of literary friends. She was close to Sarah Siddons,[13] corresponded with William Frend from the time she was fourteen until his death, thirty-five years later, and knew Lady Ann Lindsay, Anna Jameson, Caroline Norton, Maria Edgeworth, Harriet Martineau, Joanna Baillie, Amelia Opie, Charles Babbage, the duchess of Devonshire, and Harriet Beecher Stowe, who published a vindication of her in 1870. Most of Lady Byron's poems remain unpublished to the present day, though some enjoyed wide private circulation. The Harry Ransom Humanities Research Center at the University of Texas at Austin owns a dozen manuscript poems in the hand of Lady Byron.[14]

TEXT USED: "To Ada," manuscript dated 10 December 1816 in Augusta Leigh's commonplace book, Harry Ransom Humanities Research Center, University of Texas at Austin, shelfmark Leigh AMR MISC B.

11. Samuel C. Chew, *Byron in England: His Fame and After-Fame* (London, 1924), 21–22. Plummer and Brewis published in the same year *A Reply to Fare Thee Well!!! Lines Addressed to Lord Byron. Also "To a Sleeping Infant,"* by the Same. R. S. Kirby brought out another edition in 1816.

12. Quoted in Mayne, *Life and Letters,* 262. Mayne also publishes poems entitled "Lines Supposed to be Spoken at the Grave of Dermody" (12), "On Seaham—1817" (272), "Ada's Guitar—1832" (334), "The Byromania" (44), and several untitled poems (96, 124, 173, 192–93, 278–79, 311).

13. Milbanke told Byron on 16 October 1814 that "since I was twelve years old she [Siddons] has loved me with maternal anxiety" (quoted in Mayne, 464).

14. These poems include "To Ada," "To the Widow," "On Reading Lines to ———'s Memory," "To Mrs. Henry Siddons," "To Georgiana," "Sounds from the Shore," "Sonnet on Reuben's Picture," "The Minister," "In Answer to Some Lines by ———," "As One in Suffering All Who Suffers Nothing," one beginning "I look'd on those ruins with youthful eyes," and another beginning "Oh no! 'tis not the stranger's hand," apparently titled in a copy in the Lovelace Papers "Ada's Guitar—1832" (Mayne, 334; Harry Ransom Humanities Research Center, University of Texas at Austin [shelfmarks Byron, GGNB, Misc I; Byron, GGNB, Misc IX; Byron Letters IIIB; Byron, GGNB, Misc IX]). Augusta Leigh's commonplace book also contains poems by Lady Byron, including "To Ada," and is shelfmarked Leigh AMR, Misc B.

To Ada

Thine is the smile and thine the bloom
    When Hope might image ripened Charms
But mine is fraught with memory's gloom
    Thou art not in a Father's arms!

And *there* I could have loved thee most
    And *there* have felt thou wert so dear
That though my worldly all were lost,
    My heart had found a world more near!*

What art thou now? a monument
    That rose to weep o'er buried Love—   10
A fond & filial mourner sent,
    To dream of ties restored above—

Thou Dove! who may'st not find a rest[†]
    Save in one frail and shattered bark!
A lonely Mother's bleeding breast—
    May Heaven provide a surer ark!

To bear thee over Sorrow's waves
    Which deluge all of realms below
Till thou the child of Him who saves
    A holier Ararat shall know!   20

Nor deem me heedless—if for thee[‡]
    No earthly wish now claims a part
Too dear such wish—too vain to me—
    Thou art not near a Father's heart!
              (wr. 10 December 1816)

16 ark] See Gen. 6–9.
20 Ararat] According to Gen. 8:4, the place where Noah's ark came to rest after the Flood.

* In the copy in the Lovelace Papers this line reads, "I still had felt my life is *here!*" (Mayne, *Life and Letters,* 262).

† In the copy of this poem in the Lovelace Papers this line reads, "Thou fatherless—who mayst not rest." The third line of this stanza reads, "A lonely Mother's offered breast—" (ibid.).

‡ In the copy in the Lovelace Papers this line reads, "Nor think me frozen, if for thee" (ibid., 263).

Dorothea Primrose Campbell

(1793–1863)

Born and raised in what was then the remote coastal town of Lerwick, in the Shetland Islands, to the north of Scotland, Dorothea Primrose Campbell was the oldest child of Elizabeth ("Betty") and Duncan Campbell, a surgeon. Her family was impoverished first by the debts of her grandfather and then by the death of her father. In desperation, she took her poems to a bookseller and printer in Inverness, J. Young. In his preface to her volume, dated 15 April 1811, he explained,

> These Poems are the productions of a young female who had not attained her seventeenth year when they were put to the Press; and were undoubtedly writ-ten without any view to publication, until the distresses of a numerous family, of which she is the eldest, induced the Authoress to offer the greater part of them to the Publisher for any trifle he might think proper to give for them. Struck with the beauty and simplicity which, in his opinion, they appeared to possess, and feeling for the helpless situation of one who seemed so uncon-scious of their value, he could not in justice take advantage of that which was so much in his power. He therefore proposed to Publish them by Subscription for the sole benefit of the Authoress; and trusting to a liberal and humane circle of friends by whom he has been powerfully aided, he has the happiness to state that the means which they have afforded have conferred advantages on the Authoress which she could not otherways have enjoyed; . . .

Campbell dedicated the volume to Jane, duchess of Gordon. Young cited the poet's "extreme timidity and inexperience" to explain why he, and not Campbell, had penned the preface. But the poems themselves show a good deal of familiarity with the dreary and sometimes treacherous ways of the world. In her poetic universe, lovers are often faithless, children drown, husbands die in battle, the innocent suffer, siblings betray each other, and ordinary people go mad. Even so, true love can triumph, though usually only in an idyllic afterlife; justice can prevail, with the faithless or cruel punished, sometimes through supernatural forces; and a neglected orphan can be saved, in a fairy-tale-like narrative. Several of the poems are explicitly anti-war, and others urge social consciousness upon the wealthy. Campbell valorizes the working-class life and condemns the materialistic values of the rich. In "Lubin to Silvia" she suggests that women diminish themselves by becoming beautiful ornaments, urging, "Turn from thy treach'rous glass, dear maid! / And view thy much neglected mind."

In 1812 Campbell opened a school at Lerwick. When Walter Scott, a distant relative, visited the Northern Isles in 1814, she met him, and in 1816, when her book was reprinted with some additions, she dedicated it to Scott. But because of the financial difficulties of the publisher, Baldwin, Cradock and Joy, she did not profit from this second edition. Plagued by illness, poverty, and her mother's addiction to opium, she managed to keep going. Scott probably sent her money, but he told William Erskine in 1821, "I have a long miserable letter from the miserable Miss Campbell. I enclose a part of it, and the rest relating to circumstances which seem confidential. I suspect she is very imprudent."[1] Campbell published a novel, *Harley Radington,* in 1821, but A. K. Newman, the publisher, paid her only in copies. Newman promised money for a second tale, but it appears not to have been published and is now untraced. After this period, Campbell seems to have given up writing for publication. In 1842 she moved to England to work as a governess, but this job evaporated when her employer fell on hard times. The Royal Literary Fund paid her thirty pounds in 1844. She died in 1863 in Kentish Town, London, at an asylum for aged governesses.

MAJOR WORKS: *Poems* (Inverness, 1811), republished with additions and revisions as *Poems by Miss D. P. Campbell of Zetland* (London, 1816); *Harley Radington; a Tale,* 2 vols. (London, 1821).

TEXT USED: Text of "The Shetland Fisherman" from *Poems* (1811).

1. The letter is dated 27 September 1821 from Abbotsford in *The Letters of Sir Walter Scott,* ed. Herbert J. C. Grierson, vol. 7 (London, 1934), 12 and n. Scott's great-grandmother was from the clan Campbell.

The Shetland Fisherman

O, fair arose the summer dawn,
　　No sullen mist was seen to lour,
Night's dreary shadows were withdrawn,
　　And Morning brought her golden hour.

Soft was the air, and breathing balm,
　　The sea-fowl clamour'd on the shore,
The sky serene, the ocean calm,
　　And hushed the breakers' deafening roar.

And, slowly in the glittering east,
　　The sun now raised his orient head,　　　　　　　10
His beamy glories, round him cast,
　　On rock and steep their radiance shed.

A trembling stream of glory lay
　　Across the ocean's rippling bed,
And quick his bright beams sipp'd away
　　The dew-drops from each grassy blade.

The soaring lark soon mock'd the eye,
　　But still was heard his matin song,
The sea-gull floats with ominous cry,
　　The hungry raven flits along.　　　　　　　　　　20

And heard was many a female voice,
　　That echoed o'er the rocky shore;
And lisping children gay rejoice,
　　And listen for the distant oar.

At length the six-oar'd boat appears,
　　Slow moving o'er the unruffled tide;
Their long, long stay, with artless tears,
　　Their little prattlers fondly chide.

"How could thee stay so long at sea?
　　High blew the wind, and Mammy wept,
Tom could not sleep, but thought on thee,
　　Tho' sweetly little Mary slept."

Anxious the wife her husband views,
　　Who weary drags his limbs along;
Hey Kate! he gayly cries, what news?
　　Then carols blithe his morning song,

"How couldst thou, William, stay so long
　　Upon the dark and stormy sea;
Where tempests sweep, and dangers throng,
　　So far from thy dear babes and me?

O! dark and dismal was the night,
　　And fearful was the tempest's roar;—
And many a sheeted ghost, or sprite,
　　Shriek'd wildly on the sea-beat shore.

I listen'd fearful to the wind,
　　And heard a groan in every blast!
A thousand fears disturb'd my mind,
　　E'en when the tempest's rage was past."

["]But we've successful been, dear Kate,
　　Behold, my lass, that plenteous load!—
To-day, I mean, to dine in state!
　　On haddock, turbot, ling, and cod."

The hardy swain, with raptur'd eyes,
　　Kisses his rose-lipp'd babes and Kate,
Then to his humble home he hies,
　　And blesses Heaven with heart elate.

Tho' coarse his fare, yet sweet to toil
　　The morsel seems, to hunger sweet!
The scanty produce of the soil,
　　By Kate prepared both clean and neat.

30

40

50

60

Then on his straw bed careless thrown,
   He sinks into the arms of sleep;
Leaves it to paltry Wealth to groan,
   And pamper'd Luxury to weep.

                 (1811)

Ann Candler

(1740–1814)

But for the intervention of another woman poet, Ann Candler probably would have died in a workhouse near Ipswich. Her life began more auspiciously than it threatened to end. She was born on 18 November 1740 in Yoxford, Suffolk, to a working-class family; her father, William More, was a glove maker. When she was ten the family moved to Ipswich, where her mother died the following year.

Ann Candler's undoing was her marriage at age twenty-two to an alcoholic with little sense of responsibility to his growing family. The couple settled in Sproughton, three miles from Ipswich. After a year her husband joined the militia, and Candler saw him for only twenty-eight days each summer. Even so, she became pregnant regularly. She bore seven children in the first fifteen years of her marriage — three sons and four daughters, though one of the boys died in infancy. In 1777 her husband enlisted in the line, plunging Candler and her six children into abject poverty. Unable to care for the children during an illness that lasted nearly three months, she agreed to send four of them to the Tattingstone workhouse. In 1780 she was able to visit her husband briefly in London, but soon thereafter she took refuge in the workhouse, where she gave birth to twin sons on 20 March 1781. One of her poems concerns their death a few weeks later.

Her husband returned in 1783, having been discharged from the military, and she left Tattingstone to join him. But soon they both became ill and ended up in the workhouse together. He stayed six months before leaving once more, and Candler never saw him again. In a long, autobiographical letter dated 1801 Candler wrote, "All I can urge to extenuate, or palliate my folly is, that he was my husband, and the father of my children, and that my affection for him was unbounded."[1] Candler may have been the classic

---

1. Quoted in "Memoirs of the Life of Ann Candler" (unsigned), in *Poetical Attempts, by Ann Candler, a Suffolk Cottager, with a Short Narrative of her Life,* ed. [Elizabeth Cobbold] (Ipswich, 1803), 10.

codependent, but she was not the typical pauper. From the workhouse, she published poems in the *Ipswich Journal,* including "On the Death of a Most Benevolent Gentleman" (1785), "To the Inhabitants of Yoxford" (1787), and two songs written for a woman who had befriended her, one of which was called "An Invitation to Spring" (1789).

It is not clear when Ann Candler came to the attention of the poet and wealthy philanthropist Elizabeth Cobbold, but it could not have been before 1790, when Cobbold herself moved to Ipswich, and was probably much later. Cobbold may have seen one of Candler's religious poems printed in the *Ipswich Journal* in the 1790s, among them a paraphrase of the fifth chapter of the second book of Kings, "History of Joseph, in an Address to a Young Man," and "Life of Elijah the Prophet." Or Candler may herself have applied to Cobbold, whose third book, *The Mince Pye,* was causing a stir in 1800. At any rate, by that year there was a plan to relieve Candler's situation by publishing by subscription a collection of her poems. Cobbold corrected, arranged, and introduced the modestly titled *Poetical Attempts, by Ann Candler, a Suffolk Cottager, with a Short Narrative of her Life* and presumably recommended copies to her affluent friends. More than five hundred copies sold, and by 24 May 1802, after surviving more than twenty years in the workhouse, Candler was able to move to a furnished room at Copdock, near Sproughton, close to her married daughter.

The slim, sixty-eight-page octavo volume, including nearly twenty pages of autobiography, was published in 1803 and sold in Ipswich and London. Because she knew the character of the workhouse from the inside rather than from the outside, Candler's seems a more authentic voice of protest against workhouse conditions than that of Wordsworth in *The Old Cumberland Beggar* (lines 177–83). And, as Donna Landry points out, the irony is that Candler "is as much a 'lone recluse' as any Wordsworthian solitary although she lives confined among many, in enforced sociality."[2] Candler's poems and her autobiography evoke the pathos of life in the euphemistically named "houses of industry." Still, as Landry notes, Candler's snobbery blunts her social protest. She reserves her greatest rancor not for the social system that established and maintains the workhouses or for the callous rich and powerful who do nothing to ameliorate the suffering these institutions shelter but for her fellow inhabitants, to whom she feels superior by reason of education and sensibility. Candler died more than a decade after leaving the workhouse, on 6 September 1814, at Holton, Suffolk; she was seventy-four.

2. Landry, *Muses of Resistance,* 278.

MAJOR WORKS: *Poetical Attempts, by Ann Candler, a Suffolk Cottager, with a Short Narrative of her Life,* ed. [Elizabeth Cobbold] (Ipswich, 1803).

TEXT USED: Text of "Reflections on My Own Situation" from *Poetical Attempts*.

Reflections on My Own Situation, Written in T-tt-ngst-ne House of Industry, February 1802

How many years are past and gone,
   How alter'd I appear,
How many strange events have known,
   Since first I enter'd here!

Within these dreary walls confin'd,
   A lone recluse, I live,
And, with the dregs of human kind,
   A niggard alms receive.

Uncultivated, void of sense,
10   Unsocial, insincere,
Their rude behavior gives offence,
   Their language wounds the ear.

Disgusting objects swarm around,
   Throughout confusions reign;
Where feuds and discontent abound,
   Remonstrance proves in vain.

No sympathising friend I find,
   Unknown is friendship here;
Not one to soothe, or calm the mind,
20   When overwhelm'd with care:

Peace, peace, my heart, thy duty calls,
   With cautious steps proceed:
Beyond these melancholy walls,
   I've found a friend indeed!

I gaze on numbers in distress,
   Compare their state with mine:
Can I reflect, and not confess
   A providence divine?

And I might bend beneath the rod,
   And equal want deplore,   30
But that a good and gracious God
   Is pleas'd to give me more:

My gen'rous friends, with feeling heart,
   Remove the pondrous weight,
And those impending ills avert
   Which want and woes create.

Yet what am I, that I should be
   Thus honor'd and carest?
And why such favors heap'd on me,
   And with such friendship blest?   40

Absorb'd in thought I often sate
   Within my lonely cell,
And mark'd the strange mysterious fate
   That seem'd to guide me still.

When keenest sorrow urg'd her claim,
   When evils threaten'd dread,
Some unexpected blessing came,
   And rais'd my drooping head.

In youth strange fairy tales I've read,
   Of magic skill and pow'r,   50
And mortals, in their sleep, convey'd
   To some enchanted tow'r.

In this obscure and lone retreat,
   Conceal'd from vulgar eyes,
Two rival genii us'd to meet
   And counterplots devise.

The evil genius, prone to ill,
 Mischievous schemes invents,
Pursues the fated mortal still,
60   And ev'ry woe augments.

Insulted with indignant scorn,
 Aw'd by tyrannic sway,
A prey to grief each rising morn,
 And cheerless all the day.

But fate and fortune in their scenes
 A pleasing change decree:
The friendly genius intervenes,
 And sets the captive free.

Content and freedom thus regain'd,
70   Depriv'd of both before;
So great the blessing, when obtain'd,
 What can he wish for more?

The tales these eastern writers feign
 Like facts to me appear;
The fabled suff'rings they contain,
 I find no fictions here.

And since, in those romantic lays,
 My miseries combine,
To bless my lengthen'd wane of days,
80   Their bright reverse be mine.

Look down, O God! in me behold
 How helpless mortals are,
Nor leave me friendless, poor, and old,
 But guide me with thy care.

       (1803)

---

73 these eastern writers] A reference to fantastic tales of the mysterious Orient, such as
William Beckford's *Vathek, An Arabian Tale* (1786) or Voltaire's *Memnon, Histoire Orientale* (1747),
republished in 1748 under the title *Zadig.*

Elizabeth Cobbold

(*née* Eliza Knipe)

(1767–1824)

❧❧❧❧❧❧❧❧❧❧❧❧❧❧❧

Born in Watling Street, London, in 1767, Elizabeth, or Eliza, Knipe lived in Liverpool, Manchester, and Ipswich, traveling to London frequently. She was sixteen when she published her first book, *Poems on Various Subjects* (1783). Her next volume, *Six Narrative Poems* (1787), was dedicated to her friend Sir Joshua Reynolds and was favorably received. In November 1790 she ignored gossip and married William Clarke, a man twice her age who was Ipswich's comptroller of the customs. He died in 1791, only six months after their marriage. The same year she published in Liverpool a two-volume novel, *The Sword; or, Father Bertrand's History of his own Times; from the Original Manuscript* (1791).

Shortly thereafter, in 1792, she married the wealthy brewer John Cobbold, a widower with fourteen children. They made their home on his estate at the Cliff Brewery, near Ipswich, overlooking the banks of the Orwell River, and soon had seven children of their own, six sons and a daughter. With so many children now under foot, Cobbold's writing took a back seat to domestic duties. In her "Letter to D. G. Esq.—on a Visit at Em——y" she describes the regimen of her daily life:

> Forgive me for so long delaying to write,
> 'Twas not that I wanted the will to indite,
> I had not the pow'r, for my time was bestow'd
> On employments at home, or engagements abroad.
> A botanist one day, or grave antiquarian;
> Next morning a sempstress, or abecedarian,
> Now making a frock, and now marring a picture,
> Next conning a sage philosophical lecture;
> At night at the play, or assisting to kill
> The time of the idlers with whist or quadrille;
> In cares, or amusements still taking a part,
> Though science and friendship are nearest my heart.[1]

1. *Poems by Mrs. Elizabeth Cobbold with a Memoir of the Author*, [ed. Laetitia Jermyn] (Ipswich, 1825), 155–56.

Cobbold spoke French, Italian, and German; was knowledgeable in botany, entomology, geology, mineralogy, and conchology; had a strong interest in music and painting, both in oils and watercolors; and was a frequent contributor to periodicals and scientific works related to natural history. She supplied Sir James Smith, president of the Linnaean Society, with information on the habits of many plants for his *Flora Anglica*. The naturalist Sowerby recognized her contributions to mineral conchology by naming a fossil shell after her *(Nucula cobboldiae)*. Cobbold tried her hand at epigram, song, ode, sonnet, elegy, ballad, opera, tragedy, and even epic. In 1800 she published a burlesque poem, *The Mince Pye; an Heroic Epistle: Humbly Addressed to the Sovereign Dainty of a British Feast. By Caroline Petty Pasty.* The *British Critic* described it as "a playful, good humoured, and facetious trifle, ridiculing the splendid and truly magnificent publication of the *Soverign* by Mr. [Charles Small] Pybus. It is dedicated to the veritable *Soverign* of a British table, namely, a Plum-Pudding. . . . Mr. Pybus's Poem was adorned with a superb engraving of the Imperial Crown of Russia [Emperor Paul]; to this Poem a Mince-Pye is prefixed."[2] The frontispiece is Cobbold's own sketch of Hannah Glass, a famous cookbook writer.

Some called Cobbold "a petticoated pedant," but she ignored them, good-humoredly acknowledging that by twenty-nine she had become "a fat unfashionable dame" and confessing that she had no "taste for dress, or shape to shew it."[3] Her drawing room, however, was filled with furnishings of her own making, and her conversation was said to rival her literary talents. The Gothic novelist Clara Reeve was one of her friends. Beginning in 1809, Cobbold became a regular contributor to Raw's *Ladies' Fashionable Repository*. She was also a philanthropist and patron of the theater. In 1803, to relieve the suffering of an impoverished fellow poet, she corrected, arranged, and introduced *Poetical Attempts, by Ann Candler, a Suffolk Cottager, with a Short Narrative of her Life*. One of Cobbold's best-known and most often reprinted poems, "The Nurse and the Newspaper," was performed in 1805 as the epilogue for a play given to benefit a local maternity hospital. Spoken by the captain of the Royal Engineers dressed as a nurse, it provoked the hoped-for hilarity. In 1812 Cobbold founded the Society for Clothing the Infant Poor, an organization that provided warm clothing to more than two thousand infants in its first dozen years.

Cobbold's biographer, Laetitia Jermyn, recalls that at one gathering a female acquaintance "thought proper, with much tartness and personality,"

2. 17 (February 1801): 188–89.
3. "A Character of the Author by Herself," *Poems by Mrs. Elizabeth Cobbold*, 37.

to censure the idea of women as poets and "thanked God she could not write poetry!" in answer to which Cobbold "observed, that it was the first time she had ever heard any one thank God for their *ignorance.*"[4] For nearly twenty years Cobbold held an annual party on the night before Valentine's Day. She designed valentines for all eighty guests, writing the verses and drawing the illustrations herself. In 1813 and 1814, in response to the urging of friends, she printed the verses for private circulation in a book entitled *Cliff Valentines*. In 1815 she donated the profits from her "Ode to the Victory of Waterloo" to the Waterloo subscription. She died on 17 October 1824 at the age of fifty-seven. The next year Jermyn prefixed a memoir to a selection of Cobbold's poems and drawings. Years later, her son Richard (1797–1877) included her as a character in his novel *The History of Margaret Catchpole: A Suffolk Girl* (1847).

MAJOR WORKS: *Poems on Various Subjects* [by Eliza Knipe] (Manchester, 1783); *Six Narrative Poems* [by Eliza Knipe] (London, 1787); *The Sword; or, Father Bertrand's History of his own Times; from the Original Manuscript* (1791); *The Mince Pye; an Heroic Epistle: Humbly Addressed to the Sovereign Dainty of a British Feast. By Carolina Petty Pasty* (London, 1800); *Cliff Valentines, 1813* (Ipswich, [1813]); *Cliff Valentines, 1814* (Ipswich, [1814]); *Ode on the Victory of Waterloo* (Ipswich, 1815); *Poems by Mrs. Elizabeth Cobbold with a Memoir of the Author,* [ed. Laetitia Jermyn] (Ipswich, 1825).

TEXTS USED: Texts of "On the Lake of Windermere" and "Keswick" from *Poems on Various Subjects.* Text of "The Nurse and the Newspaper" from *The Lady's Monthly Museum, or Polite Repository of Amusement and Instruction; being an Assemblage of Whatever Can Tend to Please the Fancy, Interest the Mind, or Exalt the Character of the British Fair* (London), November 1805, 354–55.

4. "Memoir of Mrs. Elizabeth Cobbold," ibid., 17.

On the Lake of Windermere

Haste, airy Fancy! and assist my song;
To thee each thought poetic must belong:
Whilst led by thee I tune the soften'd lay,
Windermere, pleas'd, shall own thy magic sway.
That beauteous lake! whose charming prospects shew,
In varied lights, as thou dost bid them glow.
And lo! attentive to her suppliant's pray'r,
The goddess, swiftly, cleaves the ambient air:
Drawn by six harness'd griffins, see! she rides;
10   Di'monds and sapphires deck her chariot sides;
The laughing loves around her person play,
And spread their plumage to the sunny ray:
The goddess' self, in painted vest array'd,
Has, o'er her head, Thaumantia's bow display'd,
Whose changing shades, presented to the sight,
Display rich scenes of variegated light.
Here, the full purple tinct imperial glows;
There, blooming lustre emulates the rose;
The edges glist'ning with the hue of day,
20   In golden beams reluctant melt away:
With hair loose floating, and disorder'd mein,
Swift from her car steps the fantastic queen:
Her right hand holds a book, whose leaves close seal'd,
Were ne'er, save to the eye of thought, reveal'd:
Her left an ebon wand, whose magic power
Varies the face of Nature ev'ry hour;
Transports the lively soul to realms unknown,
Or wafts th' ideas o'er each distant zone.
Blest with imagination's subtle fire!
30   I feel the goddess all my soul inspire:
I range, with her, o'er each Arcadian scene,
The waving wood, and primrose-dimpled green:

---

4 Windermere] The largest lake in England. Located in the Lake District, it contains many islands and is known for its beauty.

14 Thaumantia's] Iris, daughter of Thaumas and Electra, sister of the Harpies. Iris was originally the personification of the rainbow.

25 ebon] Ebony.

But all ideal beauties disappear,
When, once, compar'd with lovely Windermere.
Here, bounteous Nature holds her rural court,
Where the delighted Graces all resort.
Forgive, Oh Muse! if I attempt to paint
Those prospects, where the boldest tincts prove faint.
First, from Lowe Wood, across the watry plain
Cast your pleas'd eye, and view the wide domain   40
Where all the fairest of the Naiads reign:
Mark the rich lustre of each golden ray,
When, on the curling waves, the sun beams play.
The cooling zephyrs now their wings expand,
We hoist our sails, and leave the lessening land:
See, o'er the gentle flood the vessel dance,
As swift she cleaves the liquid wide expanse:
Wantonly gay, her milk-white sides she laves,
And gladly kisses the translucent waves:
As now, more distant from Lowe Wood she flies,   50
What pleasing prospects strike our ravish'd eyes!
The White House peeping thro' the tufted grove,
The rising mount, and bowling-green alcove;
While, in perspective, distant hills arise,
Whose airy summits seem to touch the skies.
Now, Bowness comes in sight, turn round and say,
If with indiff'rence, you can well survey
The scene, where Nature's greatest charms unite,
To form such mingled hues of shade and light,
That e'en the pencil of a Claude must fail—   60
How little, here, would all his art avail!
The dark slope interspers'd with broken rocks,
The verdant meadows, and the fleecy flocks;
The isle where winter hardly dares appear,
But spring eternal blossoms thro' the year:
The bold rotunda, full before us plac'd,
By situation, more than stile, is grac'd;
And while the scenes a double beauty wear,
We bless the Architect who rais'd it there.

56 Bowness] The ward of Windermere, on the east side of Lake Windermere.

60 Claude] Claude Gellée (1600–1682), a renowned French landscape painter who was popular in seventeenth- and eighteenth-century England.

70   How pleasant, on the surface of the lake,
        With hook and line, the scaly fry to take!
        Dear sport! congenial to the pensive mind,
        To soft ideas, and a soul refin'd:
        Where, gazing on the wonders of the deep,
        We lull each wild, tumultuous, thought to sleep.
        Reader, forgive, if fancy tir'd, omits
        Some striking beauties, and the less forgets;
        Benevolence will surely intervene,
        And overlook the errors of eighteen.

                                    (1783)

Keswick

        Lo! how the orient morning sweetly lights
        The western side of Keswick's beauteous vale;
        And gilds, with yellow beams, the mountain tops;
        While on the east, the brown projecting rocks
        Cast a dark shade; majestically grand!
        Purpling the dale beneath; thro' which, the lake
        Spontaneous rolls along his silver tide.
        Where shall the eye find rest, in this wide scene
        Of beauteous horror? where th' o'erhanging cliff
10   Threatens with ruin, all who are so bold,
        To pass beneath his darkly, low'ring brow.
        Here, mountains pil'd on mountains, meet the view,
        Upon whose cloud-envelop'd heights, the bird,
        Sacred to mighty Jove, her aery builds.
        The roaring water, down the rocky steep,
        Rushes impetuous, with resistless force;
        Now dashing on the broken crags, it foams
        And rages with redoubled violence:
        Now, falling in wide sheets from rock to rock,
20   'Till tumbling down some rugged precipice,

2 Keswick's] Town on the river Greta at the outlet of Derwent Water, in Cumberland, in the Lake District. S. T. Coleridge, Sara Coleridge, and Robert Southey all lived in Keswick for many years.

It gains the bottom of the dale below;
Then joins the shining flood, and gently flows.
Behold the surface of the chrystal lake,
Studded with islands of perpetual green;
Within whose shady woods, the feather'd choir
Chant their sweet songs, nor dread the arts of man.
The halcyon here, recluse, sequester'd bird,
Spreads her bright plumage to the view of Heav'n:
Here, living groves of the Dodonean tree,
Shade above shade, climb the adjacent hills;   30
Upon whole sides, the yellow waving corn,
A noble contrast forms to the dark oaks,
And charms the sight with golden brilliancy.
All round this lovely scene, the mountains raise
Their spiry heads above the swelling clouds
That rest upon their shoulders, and, sometimes,
Driv'n by the winds with rudest violence,
Against their fellow clouds with fury dash.
Here, the god Æolus his empire holds,
In hollow caves, and here he reigns supreme: 40
Oft times his blust'ring subjects issue forth
With deaf'ning roar, from some wide cavern's mouth,
And make mock thunder echo thro' the rocks:
Inflated by their breath, the turbid lake
Swells high in heaving waves, and boldly threats
The banks which stop its furious mad career—
Horror magnificent! how shall I paint
The majesty and grandeur of the scene?
My pen's unequal to the task—I stop.

(1783)

27 halcyon] Bird anciently fabled to breed about the time of the winter solstice in a nest
floating on the sea, charming the wind and waves, so that the sea was then especially calm. It
is usually identified with a species of kingfisher.

29 Dodonean] A reference to Dodona in ancient Epirus, where a famed oracle of Zeus
lived in a grove of oaks. The priests of Dodona interpreted the rustling of the oak trees as the
messages of the gods.

39 Æolus] God of the winds in classical Greek mythology.

The Nurse and the Newspaper;
An Occasional Epilogue to a Play Represented for the Benefit of the Ipswich Lying-in Charity

The Scene draws, and discovers an old Nurse rocking a Cradle; a Table near her, with Bottles, Baskets, and a Newspaper upon it.

Hush! pretty darling, hush!—Bye, bye, bye, bye,
There's a good child. So now it does not cry.
What, shall I sing a song, or story try at,
To keep this little helpless bantling quiet?
It will not, on an honest Nurse's conscience,
Be the first baby that was lull'd with nonsense.

Young Master sleeps; his caps are neatly laid,
His victuals ready, and the caudle made.
What shall I do the minutes to amuse?
10   Why, though no *Scholard,* I can read the News:—
But can I understand it?—No; I fear
There's nothing in *my way* to study there.

Well, let me see:
      (Putting on her Spectacles, and taking up the Paper.)
      Dear! dear! who could have thought it?
What's here?—All News, as pat as if I'd bought it.
"Labour!" "Deliv'rance!" now, by my discretion,
In ev'ry line a touch at my profession!
      (Reads.)
"We hear, from Boulogne, that the num'rous fry
"Of rafts, sloops, brigs, and gun-boats, are *laid by:*
20   "The troops, that late were *groaning* for invasion,
"Are *crying out* upon a new occasion:
"And they who Britain's valour dar'd disparage,
"Find all their boastings end in—*a miscarriage.*"
Why aye, that's right! but England, free and hearty,

8 caudle] Thin gruel that can be mixed with wine or ale, sweetened, or spiced.
18 Boulogne] Major port city on the English Channel in northwestern France. In 1803 Napoleon ordered the massing there of an army to invade England; however, it never crossed the Channel.

Laugh'd always at their threats, and Bonaparte.
    (Reads.)
"Now, *big* with just revenge, the *teeming* North
"Collects her forces, *brings* her myriads *forth;*
"She finds that France in lawless sway *increases;*
"That Italy is *falling all to pieces:*
"Such *times give birth* to more than common zeal,   30
"And Austria *labours* for the public weal,
"To fix a lasting peace on balanc'd pow'r,
And bless all Europe with a *happy hour.*"

My stars! how joyous folks will drink and sing!
I'll take a thimble-full to—"Bless the King!"
    (Reads.)
"Vain are the plots the foe to Freedom *bred;*
"His projects *prettily are brought to bed:*
"Soon may the hour be *pregnant* with his doom,
"And the Usurper find *his time is come.*"
Lord! Lord! I think the World is *lying-in!*   40
What's next?—O! here advertisements begin;
So, to proceed with decent regularity—
    (Reads.)
"The annual Meeting of the Ipswich Charity
"Maintain'd by mod'rate weekly contribution"—

Aye, this I know: a glorious Institution!
That soothes the hour with pain and grief opprest,
And makes, by timely aid, the cottage blest.
What honest heart but would rejoice to say,
This charity is *in a thriving way?*
Still rich in kind protectors, may it flourish,   50
And Britain's hardier sons and daughters nourish.
I'm sure I wish it well, and so for certain,
Do all our worthy friends behind the curtain.
    (To the Audience.)
Then, since 'tis your applause our *pangs* beguiles,
Since our delights are *cradled* in your smiles,
Assist our *labours, hush to rest* our errors,
And give us *safe deliv'ry* from our terrors.
        (1805)

Sara Coleridge
(1802–1852)

꧁ ꧂

Poet, editor, translator, author of children's literature and fairy tales, Sara Coleridge, born on 22 December 1802 in Keswick, in the Lake District, was the only daughter and youngest child of Sara Fricker and Samuel Taylor Coleridge. Because her parents were estranged for almost all of her childhood, she never lived with her father for much more than a few weeks at a time, and he sometimes allowed years to elapse between letters. While he lived in London, she lived with her mother in Greta Hall, in Keswick, the home of her uncle, Robert Southey. She would later admit that she had known both William Wordsworth and Southey better than she had known her father.

Although her father was hardly an attentive parent, Sara did impress him; after his final visit to Keswick, in February 1812, he wrote of her: "Little Sara [then nine years old] . . . reads French tolerably & Italian fluently, and I was astonished at her acquaintance with her native Language. The word 'hostile' occurring in what she read to me, I asked her what 'hostile' meant? And she answered at once—Why! inimical: only that inimical is more often used for things and measures, and not, as hostile is, to persons & nations. . . . [S]he is such a sweet-tempered, meek, blue-eyed Fairy, & so affectionate, trustworthy, & really serviceable!"[1] Before long, she was also learning Latin and Spanish (she would later learn Greek and German), continuing her voracious reading in the Southeys' extensive library, and becoming a talented musician. John Murray published her first book when she was nineteen, a three-volume translation from the Latin of Martin Dobrizhoffer's *An Account of the Abiphones, an Equestrian People of Paraguay*. Most of the money Murray gave her for the project went to help send her brother Derwent to Cambridge University.

At the end of 1822, Sara's mother took her to London, where she spent three weeks of an eight-month trip in Highgate, getting to know her father.

1. *Collected Letters of Samuel Taylor Coleridge,* ed. Earl Leslie Griggs, 6 vols. (Oxford, 1956–71), 3:375.

It was the first time she had seen him in a decade. On this same trip, in January 1823, she met her first cousin Henry Nelson Coleridge. Four years older than Sara and a graduate of King's College, Cambridge, he had just begun reading for the law. Before she left London the two had become secretly engaged. The engagement was to last six and a half years, while he established himself in his profession; in the meantime, she translated for John Murray the memoirs of Chevalier Bayard from the sixteenth-century French.

It was probably in this period, during a bout with depression, that she first began experimenting with opium as a sedative for sleep; she was certainly using it by October 1825. A month later she told her brother Derwent, "It has done me much good & no harm — and I might exclaim with Mrs O'Neil, 'Hail lovely blossom that can'st ease the wretched victims of disease.'"[2]

When Sara and Henry married, on 3 September 1829, they moved to 21 Downshire Place, Hampstead, not far from her father's home at the Grove. Despite precarious health, including several serious physical and mental breakdowns, she would spend nearly all of the next decade pregnant, depending upon opium increasingly heavily. Her son Herbert was born in October 1830 and her daughter Edith in July 1832. In January 1834, after giving birth to twins who lived only a few days, she was overcome by severe depression; by the spring her opium use had become so heavy that she could not break herself of the habit. Even so, intellectual and literary pursuits became her haven, and she became increasingly interested in literary controversies, theological debates, and the works of women writers. She would eventually include in her circle of friends Joanna Baillie, Maria Jane Jewsbury, Harriet Martineau, Elizabeth Barrett Browning, Anna Jameson, William Gladstone, Thomas Carlyle, Thomas Macaulay, and Henry Crabb Robinson.

In the spring and summer of 1834 Sara Coleridge began writing short poems for the instruction of her children; they were published by J. W. Parker the following September as *Pretty Lessons in Verse for Good Children*. The book sold well, going through five editions in five years. "Poppies," printed below, appeared in that volume, a decision the poet came to regret because of family sensitivities on the subject. In July of that year her father died, and his death, ironically, gave her new purpose as a writer and editor. She assisted her husband, his literary executor, in his edition of Coleridge's *Table Talk* (1835), edited her father's *Literary Remains* (4 vols., 1836–39) and became the driving but invisible force behind his eventual canonization. She began editing his *Aids to Reflection* and transcribing his marginalia.

2. Quoted in Bradford Keyes Mudge, *Sara Coleridge, A Victorian Daughter: Her Life and Essays* (New Haven, 1989), 37. See also Henrietta O'Neill's "Ode to the Poppy" in this volume.

Meanwhile, she was working through her complex feelings about being a mother in the process of drafting her own imaginative work, *Phantasmion,* from which most of the poems below are taken. The setting is inspired by the wild and beautiful scenery of her childhood in the Lake District. Her protagonist is Phantasmion, the young prince of Palmland, told in a garden of his mother's death; shortly thereafter he witnesses the death of a companion and then loses his father. A fairy, Potentilla, queen of the insects, grants his requests for wings and suction feet; the tale relates his adventures as he pursues Iarine, beautiful daughter of the king of Rockland. Phantasmion's complex world is filled with good, evil, and capricious spirits who intervene in the military conflicts and love relationships of mortals. The tale treats love, ambition, hatred, fallibility, and madness in a lush and vivid prose style filled with sensuous images of the exotic and fantastic. Poems record the innermost feelings of the characters. In a letter to her husband of 29 September 1837 Coleridge admits that her chief aim in *Phantasmion* was not a moral but consisted "in cultivating the imagination, and innocently gratifying the curiosity of the reader, by exhibiting the general and abstract beauty of things through the vehicle of a story, which, as it treats of human hopes, and fears, and passions, and interests, and of those changeful events and varying circumstances to which human life is liable, may lend an animation to the accompanying descriptions, and in return receive a lustre from them."[3] She expresses a similar view in a verse written in her own copy of *Phantasmion:*

> Go, little book, and sing of love and beauty,
> To tempt the worldling into fairy-land;
> Tell him that airy dreams are sacred duty,
> Bring better wealth than aught his toils command,—
> Toils fraught with mickle harm.
> But if thou meet some spirit high and tender,
> On blessed works and noblest love intent.
> Tell him that airy dreams of nature's splendor,
> With graver thoughts and hallowed musings blent,
> Prove no too earthly charm.[4]

The book was published anonymously in June 1837 to mostly positive notices. The *Quarterly Review* observed that "'Phantasmion' is not a poem, but it is poetry from beginning to end, and 'has many poems within it. It is one of a race that has particularly suffered under the assaults of political economy

---

3. Quoted in *Memoir and Letters of Sara Coleridge,* ed. [Edith Coleridge], 2 vols. (London, 1873), 1:191.
4. Written about 1845 and quoted in ibid., 1:175.

and useful knowledge;—a Fairy Tale, the last, we suppose, that will ever be written in England, and unique in its kind. It is neither German nor French. It is what it is—pure as crystal in diction, tinted like an opal with the hues of an everspringing sunlit fancy."[5] But as Sara Coleridge noted, "In these days . . . to print a Fairy Tale is the very way to be *not read,* but shoved aside with contempt. I wish, however, I were only as sure that *my* fairy-tale is worth printing, as I am that works of this class are wholesome food, by way of variety, for the childish mind."[6]

Sara Coleridge continued to write reviews (published anonymously in the *Quarterly Review*), essays, and poetry, but her major project for the rest of her life was editing her father's works and remaking his image—from that of the dissolute, self-indulgent, plagiarizing poet into the respected philosopher and Victorian sage. She painstakingly assembled a fragmentary and miscellaneous corpus into what Leslie Stephen called the "centre of intellectual life in England." Virginia Woolf said that Sara Coleridge "found her father [by editing his works] as she had not found him in the flesh; and she found that he was herself."[7] Coleridge included with each new work she edited a substantial introduction or appendix defending, explaining, or qualifying her father's theories. An early biographer, Henry Reed, justly observed that she "expended in the desultory form of notes, and appendices, and prefaces, an amount of original thought and an affluence of learning, which, differently and more prominently presented, would have made her famous."[8]

Henry Coleridge's death on 25 January 1843 made Sara's income from writing even more necessary. Within the next few years she would complete what are now considered her two most significant editing projects—the 1847 edition of the *Biographia Literaria* and the 1850 edition of *Essays on His Own Times.* According to Norman Fruman, even though modern editors acknowledge a debt to Sara Coleridge, her "intelligence, energy, learning, and above all her willingness to lay damaging materials clearly before the reader, have . . . never received anything like the praise they deserve."[9] Her edition of the *Biographia* included a 180-page defense of her father's literary accomplishments and character, persuasively depicting him as a philosopher hero and forever altering the terms of Coleridge criticism and discourse. In her 75-page introduction to her three-volume collection of her father's political

5. September 1840, 132.

6. Coleridge to Arabella Brooke, 29 July 1837, quoted in Coleridge, *Memoir and Letters,* 1:175.

7. "Sara Coleridge," in *Death of the Moth and Other Essays,* by Virginia Woolf (New York, 1970), 111–18; Woolf's essay first appeared in the *New Statesman and Nation,* 26 October 1940.

8. Henry Reed, "The Daughter of Coleridge," *Literary World,* January 1853.

9. *SiR* 24 (1985): 141–42.

writings and periodical publications, *Essays on His Own Times,* she underlined his altruism, his practical thought, and his serious moral and political philosophy. It was while working on this essay that she confided to a friend that her father seemed "ever at my ear, in his books, more especially his marginalia—speaking not personally to me, and yet in a way so natural to my feelings, that *finds* me so fully, and awakens such a strong echo in my mind and heart, that I seem more intimate with him now than I ever was in life." [10] Yet late in her life she had misgivings about having chosen to devote her talents mainly to editing her father's works. She observed, "It is something to myself to feel that I am putting in order a literary house that otherwise would be open to censure. . . . But when there is not mere carelessness but a positive coldness in regard to what I have done, I do sometimes feel as if I had been wasting myself a good deal—at least as far as worldly advantage is concerned." [11] But she persisted. Her last major editorial project was a collection of her father's poetry, which she aptly described as "sensuous and impassioned," a description as true of her own best poetry as it was of his.

Sara Coleridge died of untreated breast cancer on 3 May 1852 at home at 10 Chester Place, Regent's Park, and was buried in the old Highgate churchyard beside her parents, her husband, and her son. She is said to have left thousands of pages of unpublished manuscripts—essays, letters, journals, poems, and long theological dialogues. In the family tradition, her daughter Edith published her mother's memoir and letters, which twentieth-century scholars have read mostly as an addendum to Samuel Taylor Coleridge's life.

MAJOR WORKS: *Phantasmion* (London, 1837; reprint, London, 1874); *Pretty Lessons in Verse for Good Children* (London, 1834).

EDITED WORKS: Editions of Samuel Taylor Coleridge's work, including, most importantly, *Biographia Literaria,* 2 vols. (London, 1847), and *Essays on His Own Times,* 3 vols. (London, 1850).

TEXTS USED: Text of "Poppies" from *Pretty Lessons in Verse for Good Children.* Texts of "I Was a Brook," "Blest Is the Tarn," "Milk-White Doe," "I Tremble When with Look Benign," and "The Captive Bird with Ardour Sings" from *Phantasmion.*

10. Coleridge to E. Quillinan, 1850, *Memoir and Letters,* 2:315.
11. Sara Coleridge to Henry Crabb Robinson, 28 October 1848, quoted in Henry Crabb Robinson, *Diary, Reminiscences, and Correspondences of Henry Crabb Robinson,* ed. Thomas Sadler (New York, 1967).

Poppies

The poppies blooming all around
    My Herbert loves to see;
Some pearly white, some dark as night,
    Some red as cramasie:

He loves their colours fresh and fine,
    As fair as fair may be;
But little does my darling know
    How good they are to me.

He views their clust'ring petals gay,
    And shakes their nut-brown seeds;   10
But they to him are nothing more
    Than other brilliant weeds.

O! how shouldst thou, with beaming brow,
    With eye and cheek so bright,
Know aught of that gay blossom's power,
    Or sorrows of the night?

When poor Mama long restless lies,
    She drinks the poppy's juice;
That liquor soon can close her eyes,
    And slumber soft produce: 20

O then my sweet, my happy boy
    Will thank the Poppy-flower,
Which brings the sleep to dear Mama,
    At midnight's darksome hour.

(1834)

2 Herbert] Coleridge's son.
4 cramasie] Crimson cloth.

I Was a Brook

I was a brook in straitest channel pent,
Forcing 'mid rocks and stones my toilsome way,
A scanty brook in wandering well nigh spent;
But now with thee, rich stream, conjoin'd I stray,
Through golden meads the river sweeps along,
Murmuring its deep full joy in gentlest undersong.

I crept through desert moor and gloomy glade,
My waters ever vex'd, yet sad and slow,
My waters ever steep'd in baleful shade:
10   But, whilst with thee, rich stream, conjoin'd I flow,
E'en in swift course the river seems to rest,
Blue sky, bright bloom, and verdure imag'd on its breast.

And, whilst with thee I roam through regions bright,
Beneath kind love's serene and gladsome sky,
A thousand happy things that seek the light,
Till now in darkest shadow forc'd to lie,
Up through the illumin'd waters nimbly run,
To shew their forms and hues in the all revealing sun.

                                             (1837)

Blest Is the Tarn

Blest is the tarn which towering cliffs o'ershade,
Which, cradled deep within the mountain's breast,
Nor voices loud, nor dashing oars invade:
Yet e'en the tarn enjoys no perfect rest,
For oft the angry skies her peace molest,
With them she frowns, gives back the lightning's glare,
Then rages wildly in the troubled air.

1 tarn] Small mountain lake.

This calmer lake, which potent spells protect,
Lies dimly slumbering through the fires of day,
And when yon skies, with chaste resplendence deck'd,   10
Shine forth in all their stateliest array,
O then she wakes to glitter bright as they,
And view the face of heaven's benignant queen
Still looking down on hers with smile serene!

What cruel cares the maiden's heart assail,
Who loves, but fears no deep felt love to gain,
Or, having gain'd it, fears that love will fail!
My power can soothe to rest her wakeful pain,
Till none but calm delicious dreams remain,
And, while sweet tears her easy pillow steep,   20
She yields that dream of bliss to ever welcome sleep.

(1837)

Milk-White Doe, 'Tis But the Breeze

Milk-white doe, 'tis but the breeze
Rustling in the alder trees;
Slumber thou while honey-bees
          Lull thee with their humming;
Though the ringdove's plaintive moan
Seems to tell of pleasure flown,
On thy couch with blossoms sown,
          Fear no peril coming.

Thou amid the lilies laid,
Seem'st in lily vest array'd,   10
Fann'd by gales which they have made
          Sweet with their perfuming;
Primrose tufts impearl'd with dew;
Bells which heav'n has steep'd in blue
Lend the breeze their odours too,
          All around thee blooming.

None shall come to scare thy dreams,
Save perchance the playful gleams;
Wake to quaff the cooling streams
          Of the sunlit river;
20   Thou across the faithless tide
Needest not for safety glide,
Nor thy panting bosom hide
          Where the grasses shiver.

When the joyous months are past,
Roses pine in autumn's blast,
When the violets breathe their last,
          All that's sweet is flying:
Then the sylvan deer must fly,
30   'Mid the scatter'd blossoms lie,
Fall with falling leaves and die
          When the flow'rs are dying.

              (1837)

I Tremble When with Look Benign

I tremble when with look benign
Thou tak'st my offer'd hand in thine,
Lest passion-breathing words of mine
          The charm should break:
And friendly smiles be forced to fly,
Like soft reflections of the sky,
Which, when rude gales are sweeping by,
          Desert the lake.

Of late I saw thee in a dream,
10   The day-star pour'd his hottest beam,
And thou, a cool refreshing stream,
          Didst brightly run:
The trees where thou wert pleased to flow,
Swell'd out their flowers, a glorious show,
While I, too distant doom'd to grow,
          Pined in the sun.

By no life-giving moisture fed,
A wasted tree, I bow'd my head,
My sallow leaves and blossoms shed
        On earth's green breast: 20
And silent pray'd the slumbering wind,
The lake, thy tarrying place, might find,
And waft my leaves, with breathings kind,
        There, there, to rest.

          (1837)

The Captive Bird with Ardour Sings

The captive bird with ardour sings,
Where no fond mate rewards the strain,
Yet, sure, to chant some solace brings,
        Although he chants in vain:
But I my thoughts in bondage keep,
Lest he should hear who ne'er will heed,
And none shall see the tears I weep,
        With whom 'twere vain to plead.

No glossy breast, no quivering plume,
Like fan unfurl'd to tempt the eye,   10
Reminds the prisoner of his doom,
        Apart, yet all too nigh:
O would that in some shrouded place
I too were prisoned fancy free,
And ne'er had seen that beaming face,
        Which ne'er will beam on me!

When kindred birds fleet o'er the wave,
From yellow woods to green ones fly,
The captive hears the wild winds rave
        Beneath a wint'ry sky!   20
And, when my loved one hence shall fleet,
Bleak, bleak will yonder heav'n appear,
The flowers will droop, no longer sweet,
        And every leaf be sere.

          (1837)

Hannah Cowley

(1743–1809)

~~~~~~

Hannah Cowley was born on 14 March 1743 in Tiverton, Devonshire, but little is known of her early life except that her father was the classical scholar and bookseller Philip Parkhouse. At about the age of twenty-five, when she married Thomas Cowley, she moved with him to London, where he was a Stamp Office clerk, newspaper writer, and editor of the *Gazetteer*. According to one of her contemporaries, "The lady herself paid no great deference to the opinion of her husband. Indeed, she was a being of a superior cast; and, though they passed their time happily enough together, thanks to her discreet and compliant spirit, there did not seem to be any thing congenial in their dispositions. She was lively, open, and engaging; he was sententious, close, and repulsive."[1] The couple had four children, the eldest of whom died early; in 1783 Thomas Cowley left for India with the East India Company, never to return to England. From that time forward, Hannah Cowley lived essentially as a single mother, writing to supplement her family's income.

Cowley's writing career began with a chance remark. While attending a play, she observed, "Why I could write as well myself." Her husband laughed. In reply, the next morning she began composing the first act of a comedy. A couple of weeks later she sent a draft of *The Runaway* to David Garrick, who was encouraging and suggested revisions. On 15 February 1776 he opened the play at the Theatre Royal in Drury Lane, and it had a successful run of seventeen performances. One of the villains is the learned Lady Dinah, but the play also features Bella, a witty and independent heroine whose type would become a staple in Cowley's dramas. The *Critical Review* marveled at the "untutored genius" of the work, which was extraordinarily successful and established Cowley's reputation as a dramatist. The play was frequently revived.

According to an early biographer, "She was accustomed to say that [in

1. *Antijacobin Review* 46 (February 1814): 135.

composing her works] she always succeeded best when she did not herself know what she was going to do, and suffered the events, and even the plot, to grow under her pen. It is this that has so often given an air of real nature to her works."[2] Cowley's next produced play, *Who's the Dupe?*, a farce targeting pedantry and vulgarity, premiered on 10 April 1779. In her prologue to the 1813 edition she explained that just as learned male authors have satirized female faults and ridiculed their "whims and vanity," so, as a woman, she felt called upon to subject to their due share of laughter learned men "whose sarcastic pen" has spared neither "Matron Maid or Bride." Her witty heroine cleverly foils her father's plans to marry her to an Oxford pedant by outfoxing both the father and the pedant; in the end she marries the man she loves, while her father never understands that he has been duped. This play was to become one of Cowley's most popular, with a total of 126 performances recorded in 1779 and 1780 alone.

George Colman the elder produced Cowley's tragedy in blank verse, *Albina*, which opened at the Haymarket on 31 July 1779; but despite its spectacular mad scenes, it was not as enthusiastically received as her previous plays and closed after a nine-day run. When she saw Hannah More's *The Fatal Falsehood*, Cowley publicly accused More of having plagiarized the plot from her *Albina*. The disagreement was so unpleasant that More never staged another play; and it was nine years before Cowley hazarded another production, a tragedy, *The Fate of Sparta*, with Sarah Siddons playing the female lead, Chelonice, a woman torn between her husband and her father. Arthur Murphy, writing in the *Monthly Review*, contended that "the general character of Mrs. Cowley's style may be given in her own language: 'Words, whose sounds vibrate on the ear, / But cannot raise ideas in the mind.'"[3] The *English Review* damned it even more harshly, but it had a good run.[4]

The Belle's Stratagem, a comedy of manners centering on courtship and marriage in which the heroine cleverly demonstrates that an English woman can be as appealing to a fashionable man of the world as a Continental woman, opened on 22 February 1780 and was eventually to become one of Covent Garden's standard repertory pieces. It played for 28 nights in its first season and had been acted on the London stage 118 times by 1800. In 1782 the *Critical Review* called *The Belle's Stratagem* the "best dramatic production of a female pen . . . since the days of Centilivre, to whom Mrs. Cowley is at least equal in fable and character, and far superior in easy dialogue and purity

---

2. Quoted in ibid., 137, from the memoir to *The Works of Mrs. Cowley, Dramas and Poems*, 3 vols. (London, 1813).

3. 78 (May 1788): 404–5.

4. 11 (1788): 250–53.

of diction."[5] But her next three productions were failures and survive only in manuscript.

Cowley's comedy of manners *Which is the Man?*, set in London, opened on 9 February 1782 and was more successful. One of the play's characters is Lady Bell Bloomer, who "is mistress of her whole situation, and cannot be surprised." By this time Cowley had established the nature of her unconventional heroines, who are generally the leading characters. Her plays stress the importance of women's minds and the need to treat women as responsible human beings. Cowley's typical heroines tend to be spirited, witty, and resourceful women capable of outfoxing men and foiling their designs. They have respect for their own integrity as well as inner strength, which helps them to resist victimization at the hands of fathers or husbands; frequently they help each other.

In 1780 Cowley published *The Maid of Arragon*, a long poem in blank verse whose action takes place in Spain during the occupation by the Moors. Cowley dedicated the poem, whose subject is filial affection, to her father. Although Cowley intended to extend the poem to two books, she completed and published only one.

Susanna Centlivre's *A Bold Stroke for a Wife* suggested the title of Cowley's next play, *A Bold Stroke for a Husband*, produced on 25 February 1783, but the two plays bear few other resemblances. Departing from the typical formula for English comedy of romantic intrigue, she made women rather than men the main intriguers. With resourcefulness and, of course, bold strokes, the two heroines, one involved in a serious plot and another in a comic plot, rescue themselves from the unhappy situations the men close to them have created. The play ran successfully for eighteen nights and was revived during the next three seasons.

More Ways Than One, a poetic comedy, opened at Covent Garden on 6 December 1783, dedicated to Cowley's husband, who had left England that year for India. The two heroines, Arabella and Miss Archer, together foil the plot of Arabella's guardian and the old man he has chosen to be her husband; both men treat Arabella as merely a piece of property at the center of their financial negotiations, but Arabella ends up with the man she loves. The play received mixed reviews, though it played for eighteen performances.

A School for Greybeards (produced on 25 November 1786), inspired by Aphra Behn's *The Lucky Chance* (1686), continues the satire of old men who covet beautiful young women who do not love them and condemns arranged marriages without love. The opening-night audience found the play indecent,

5. 53 (1782): 314.

and it ran for only nine performances. In her preface to the printed version, Cowley notes ruefully that a woman playwright can portray vulgar characters, but only if they speak with politeness and elegance.

In 1786 Cowley published *The Scottish Village, or Pitcairne Green*, a long narrative poetic romance that portrays the vices and virtues of civilized life through the eyes of a philosopher. But her greatest poetic notoriety would come the following year, when she replied to a poem she had read in the *World* for 29 June 1787 entitled "Adieu and Recall to Love," signed "Della Crusca," pseudonym of Robert Merry. "I read the beautiful lines and without rising from the table at which I was sitting answered them," recalled Cowley, whose reply, "The Pen," published two weeks later in the *World*, was signed "Anna Matilda."[6] Thus began a two-year poetic correspondence, attracting widespread public attention, in which the principals, though expressing ardent enthusiasm for each other in print, were kept ignorant of each other's identities by the editors of the *World*. Eventually John Bell published Cowley's contributions in *The Poetry of Anna Matilda* (1788), and some selections were printed in *The Poetry of the World* (1788) and *The British Album* (1790). Finally, on 31 March 1789, the platonic "lovers" met and found each other disappointing. By the next day Cowley's identity was public knowledge. Merry said farewell to her in "The Interview," published on 16 June, and three days later Cowley returned the favor in "To Della Crusca, who said, 'When I am dead, write my Elegy,'" a poem that imagines his death. Although William Gifford in *The Baviad* (1791) and *The Maeviad* (1795) ridiculed what became known as the "Della Cruscan" style of poetry practiced in this correspondence by Merry and Cowley, it was widely imitated.

Cowley visited France in 1788 to oversee the education of her daughters and absorbed many of the ideals of the coming revolution. She contributed "Edwina, the Huntress," a poetic tale set in the Lake District, to William Hutchinson's *History of Cumberland* (1794). In 1790 her seventeen-year-old daughter died, and in 1796 another daughter married in Calcutta. In June of the following year her husband died while journeying to visit this daughter.

A Day in Turkey: or, The Russian Slaves (produced by Covent Garden on 3 December 1791) is unlike any of Cowley's other works, featuring dancing, song, and extraordinary stage effects. This comic opera appealed to the popular taste for melodrama, spectacle, and exotic setting. As in all of Cowley's comedies, there are serious elements. For example, one of the heroines, Paulina, courageously protests the slavery in the seraglio, and in later

6. W. N. Hargreaves-Mawdsley, *The English Della Cruscans and Their Time, 1783–1828* (The Hague, 1967), 161.

revisions Cowley highlights the degradation of women whose minds are ignored and whose bodies are exploited as sex objects. The play ran for fourteen performances despite mixed reviews, some of which criticized her for celebrating the ideals of the French Revolution.

The Town Before You (produced on 6 December 1794) is a comedy of manners full of intrigue. It was Cowley's theatrical swan song and ran for ten performances. A contemporary remarked that "those around Mrs. Cowley perceived, with surprize, that she never seemed to hold literature in much esteem. Her conversation was never literary. She was no storer up of her letters. She disliked literary correspondence. . . . It was still more extraordinary, that she never attended the first representation of her own pieces; and was never known to read a play or a poem written by another person. Travels were her favourite works."[7] A reviewer for the *European Magazine* recounted that "many were the instances in which she was known to compose quicker than a careful amanuensis could copy."[8] Contemporaries described Cowley as indifferent to fame and highly domestic.

Cowley's last major work was *The Siege of Acre. An Epic Poem* (1801), celebrating the recent defense of Acre by British troops led by Sir Sidney Smith against Napoleonic forces. Into the historic narrative, taken from Smith's letters and French accounts, Cowley incorporated two imaginary domestic episodes, one depicting a bride who follows her lover to war and another portraying two daughters who attempt to restrain their soldier father from a dangerous military mission. Set among the Christians of Syria, the poem includes affecting portrayals of the painful consequences of war. It was published in the *Annual Register* in four books in 1799 and was reprinted in six books in 1801 by the Oriental Press in London. In her preface Cowley explains, "With trembling inquietude I venture to place in the hands of the Public, a Poem, on one of the most important passages of a War which has stretched its hideous form over two thirds of the globe. The subject forced itself to my pen—I could not resist it; and could I have communicated to my pen the glow with which the Siege impressed my imagination, I should have less to fear for the reception of the Poem." Elizabeth Moody criticized her in the *Monthly Review* for having chosen a theme that was not dignified enough for an epic nor worthy of such length and for having written a poem whose style was not sufficiently polished. The reviewer from the *Gentleman's Magazine* was of another mind, praising the vigor of the poem's language, the harmony of its versification, its "masterly" characterization, and its origi-

7. *Antijacobin Review* 46 (February 1814): 138.
8. 66 (September 1814): 232.

nality. The reviewer remarks that "an Epic Poem by a lady is a new epoch in the literary world; the first, as far as we know, in any country. . . . Whilst we do not withhold our assent to Mrs. Cowley's superiority in all the walks of the Drama, we did not expect to find the nerve and strength of wing necessary to such an undertaking. . . . This work does honour not only to female genius but to the art itself. . . . We were a little surprised at some *military* reflections, and at the clearness with which a female mind comprehends the relationship between our modern implements of war and those used by the conquerors of Persia and Babylon."[9]

In 1801 Cowley left London for her birthplace, Tiverton, in Devon, a place she had memorialized in "The Scottish Village" and at the end of her "Fireside Tour." There she continued to write poetry and to revise her plays. She died on 11 March 1809, at the age of sixty-seven. In 1813 a three-volume edition of her works appeared, including eleven of her thirteen plays in their revised states,[10] a memoir, and nearly a full volume of her poems, some of which had never before been published. Cowley was always more popular with the public than with the critics, who found her writing both too romantic and not sufficiently polished. Still, the critic for the *Antijacobin Review* recognized "the fertility of her invention, and her knowledge of human life," and the critic for the *Literary Panorama* maintained that "the vivacity of her characters insured success."[11] While her posthumous reputation rested principally on her comedies, one contemporary critic observed that her poems contain "sensibility always awake, description always vivid, a loftiness of mind, and a sweetness of measure, that will also assist in preventing her name from dying with her!"[12]

MAJOR WORKS: *The Runaway, A Comedy: As it is Acted at the Theatre-Royal in Drury-Lane* (London, 1776); *Albina, Countess Raimond; A Tragedy, As it is Performed at the Theatre-Royal in the Haymarket* (London, 1779); *Who's the Dupe? A Farce* (London, 1779); *The Maid of Arragon; A Tale. Part I* (London, 1780); *The Belle's Stratagem: A Comedy, of Five Acts: as it is Now Performing at the Theatre in Smock-Alley* (Dublin, 1781); *Which is the Man? A Comedy, As Acted at the Theatre-Royal in Covent-Garden* (London, 1783); *A Bold Stroke for a Husband, A Comedy* (Dublin, 1783); *More Ways Than One, A Comedy, As Acted at the Theatre Royal in Covent Garden* (London, 1784); *A School for Greybeards; or, The Mourning Bride: A Comedy, In Five Acts. As Performed at the Theatre Royal, Drury-Lane* (London, 1786); *The Scottish Village: or, Pitcairne Green. A Poem* (London, 1786); *The Fate of Sparta; or, The Rival Kings. A Tragedy. As It is Acted at the Theatre-Royal,*

9. 71 (September 1801): 817–19.
10. Only *The School for Eloquence* and *The World as It Goes* are missing.
11. *Antijacobin Review* 46 (February 1814): 136; *Literary Panorama* 15 (July 1814): 889.
12. *European Magazine* 66 (September 1814): 234.

in Drury-Lane (London, 1788); *The Poetry of Anna Matilda* (London, 1788); *A Day in Turkey; or, The Russian Slaves. A Comedy, As Acted at the Theatre Royal, in Covent Garden* (London, 1792); *The Town Before You, A Comedy, As Acted at the Theatre-Royal, Covent-Garden* (London, 1795); *The Siege of Acre. An Epic Poem. In Six Books* (London, 1801); *The Works of Mrs. Cowley, Dramas and Poems,* 3 vols. (London, 1813).

TEXTS USED: Text of "Monologue" from *The Maid of Arragon; A Tale.* Text of "Invocation" from *The Poetry of Anna Matilda.*

Monologue

O CHATTERTON! for thee the pensive song I raise,
Thou object of my wonder, pity, envy, praise!
Bright star of Genius!—torn from life and fame,
My tears, my verse, shall consecrate thy name!
Ye Muses! who around his natal bed
Triumphant sung, and all your influence shed;
APOLLO! thou who rapt his infant breast,
And, in his dædal numbers, shone confest,
Ah! why, in vain, such mighty gifts bestow
10   —Why give fresh tortures to the Child of Woe?
Why thus, with barb'rous care, illume his mind,
Adding new sense to all the ills behind?

    Thou haggard! Poverty! whose *cheerless* eye
Transforms young rapture to the pond'rous sigh;
In whose drear cave no Muse e'er struck the lyre,
Nor Bard e'er *madden'd* with poetic fire;
Why all thy spells for CHATTERTON combine?
His thought *creative,* why must thou confine?
Subdu'd by thee, his pen no more obeys,
20   No longer gives the song of ancient days;
Nor paints in glowing tints from distant skies,

---

1 Chatterton] Thomas Chatterton (1752–70), laboring-class poet and playwright who left his native Bristol to make his living as a writer in London. After only four months he had published poems and essays in eleven of the leading periodicals. Still, he never earned enough to eat daily, and on the edge of starvation he committed suicide.

Nor bids *wild scen'ry* rush upon our eyes —
Check'd in her flight, his rapid genius cowers,
Drops her sad plumes, and yields to thee her powers.

    Behold him, Muses! see your fav'rite son
The prey of WANT, ere manhood is begun!
The bosom *ye* have fill'd, with anguish torn —
The mind *you* cherish'd, drooping and forlorn!

    And now *Despair* her sable form extends,
Creeps to his couch, and o'er his pillow bends.   30
Ah, see! a deadly bowl the fiend conceal'd,
Which to his eye with caution is reveal'd —
Seize it, APOLLO! — seize the liquid snare!
Dash it to earth, or dissipate in air!
Stay, hapless Youth! refrain — abhor the draught,
With pangs, with racks, with deep repentance fraught!
Oh, hold! the cup with woe ETERNAL flows,
More — *more* than *Death* the pois'nous juice bestows!
In vain! — he drinks — and now the searching fires
Rush thro' his veins, and writhing he expires!   40
No sorrowing *friend,* no *sister, parent,* nigh,
To sooth his pangs, or catch his parting sigh;
Alone, *unknown,* the Muses' darling dies,
And with the vulgar dead unnoted lies!
Bright star of Genius! — torn from life and fame,
My tears, my verse, shall consecrate thy name!
                        (1780)

Invocation

Written on a very hot day, in August 1783

Cooling zephyrs haste away,
Round my humid temples play;
Groves and grots in pity leave,
On my fainting bosom breathe!
Skim, as you pass, your silken wings
O'er gurgling founts, and glassy springs.
Oh! come from Greenland's icy plains,
Where silver Winter constant reigns;
Or from the Arctic, higher fly
10   Thro' the chill Norwegian sky——
Turn not to Gallia's sunny vales,
Nor mix with yours Italia's gales,
Strait o'er the northern ocean sweep,
Where pearls the frozen Naïads weep;
But on high Grampia's fleecy top,
Where kids, the gelid herbage crop,
There zephyr touch!—then, with new wing
Fresh from its chilly caverns spring.
Oh! linger not, midst England's fields,
20   Nor taste the sweets the garden yields;
Heed not our meadows' gaudy charms,
But dart, with vigour, to my arms!

(1788)

15 Grampia's] The chief mountain chain in Scotland, forming the boundary between the Highlands and Lowlands.

Ann Batten Cristall

(c. 1768–after 1816)

Close friend of Mary Wollstonecraft and her sister Everina, Ann Batten Cristall published *Poetical Sketches* in 1795. Subscribers to this volume, brought out by Joseph Johnson, included not only both Wollstonecrafts but also Anna Letitia Barbauld, John Aiken, Amelia Alderson (later Opie), William Frend, Samuel Rogers, Anna Maria Porter, Mary Hays, John Wolcot (Peter Pindar), and George Dyer. Cristall herself subscribed to Sarah Spence's *Poems* that same year. It is not unlikely that she knew William Blake, given their mutual connection to the Joseph Johnson circle and the fact that her sister Elizabeth was an engraver and her brother Joshua a painter. She probably knew William Godwin as well, through Mary Wollstonecraft. George Dyer urged Mary Hays to collaborate on a novel with Cristall, who he thought might write the poetic interludes. Dyer described Cristall as having "a very fine talent for poetry: one or two of her songs are, I think, as beautiful as any I know."[1]

In the introduction to *Poetical Sketches* Cristall's modesty far exceeds what was customary:

> These light effusions of a youthful imagination, written at various times for the entertainment of my idle hours, I now present to such Readers whose minds are not too seriously engaged; and should they afford any degree of amusement, my most sanguine expectations will be answered. . . . Most of my days have been passed in solitude, and the little knowledge I have acquired cannot boast the authority of much experience; my opinions, therefore, would carry little weight. . . . From among my juvenile productions I have principally selected for this volume some poetical tales and unconnected sketches, which a love for the beauties of nature inspired. The versification is wild, and still incorrect, though I have taken much pains to reduce it to some degree of order; they were written without the knowledge of any rules; of which their irregularity is the natural consequence. . . . I can only add, that what I have written is genuine, and that I am but little indebted either to ancient or modern poets.

1. Quoted in *The Love-Letters of Mary Hays (1779–1780)*, ed. A. F. Wedd (London, 1925), 238.

Seeming almost to have regretted her decision to allow her poems to be published, she confesses: "Those who have ever felt the warm influence of the Muse, must know that her inspirations are flattering and seductive; that she often raises the heart with vanity and then overwhelms it with fears: such will readily believe, that with a fluctuating mind, and a trembling heart, I address the public, without any pretence for being treated with particular indulgence. — A strong motive first influenced me to this attempt, before I had sufficiently considered its boldness; and having once adventured, I found it too late to recede."

Most reviewers faulted Cristall for technical imperfections but praised her for her "genius, and warmth of imagination."[2] The *Critical Review* found in her book "much simplicity of design, and genuine original painting," as well as "animated . . . just and beautiful description." William Enfield, writing for the *Monthly Review,* commented on her "vigour of fancy." The *New Annual Register* cited the usual technical faults but added that "the beauties, however, greatly preponderate, and discover marks of genius, sentiment, and pathos, which give fair promise of future excellence."[3] In a letter to Joseph Cottle dated 13 March 1797, Robert Southey remarked, "But Miss Christal, — have you seen her poems? — a fine, artless, sensible girl! . . . Her heart is alive, she loves poetry, she loves retirement, she loves the country: her verses are very incorrect, and the literary circles say she has no genius; but she has genius, Joseph Cottle, or there is no truth in physiognomy."[4]

The little we know about Cristall's family and early life is largely due to the modest fame later enjoyed by her younger brother Joshua (1767–1847), who is considered one of the founders of the English school of watercolorists. Their father was Joseph Alexander Cristall, a Scottish sea captain, and their mother was Ann Batten from Penzance, the well-educated daughter of a merchant with a modest independent income. They were married in April 1767. At one time her father owned his own ship, and he subsequently went into the sail-, mast-, and block-making business, with yards at Penzance, Fowey, and, later, Rotherhithe. When Ann was young the family moved to London and later to Blackheath. Educated partly by their mother, Ann and her brother Joshua "studied together as children, and hand in hand did they daily walk to London and back for their schooling when the family lived at Rotherhithe."[5] Family life, however, appears to have been stormy. Her father is described as a man "of an extremely jealous disposition, and his time ashore was usually a

2. See, e.g., *British Critic* 5 (1795): 423–24.

3. *Critical Review,* n.s., 13 (1795): 287, 289; *Monthly Review,* n.s., 20 (1795): 99; *New Annual Register* 16 (1795): 278.

4. Quoted in Roger Lonsdale, *Eighteenth Century Women Poets* (Oxford, 1989), 485.

5. Ibid., 484.

period of trouble and discomfort in the family."[6] Cristall's poetry hints at violence. Mary Wollstonecraft was aware of some difficulty, writing to Joshua, "I have seldom seen your sister since you left town. I fear her situation is very uncomfortable. I wish she could obtain a little more strength of mind. If I were to give a short definition of virtue, I should call it fortitude."[7] Wollstonecraft told Joshua, "I know that you earnestly wish to be the friend and protector of your amiable sister and hope no inconsiderate act or thoughtless mode of conduct will add to her cares—for her comfort very much depends on you."[8]

Cristall seems to have dropped out of literary circles shortly after the publication of her book and to have published little else. Apparently, she became a teacher, did not marry, and was still alive as late as 1816, when the *Biographical Dictionary of Living Authors* listed her under "Cristall."[9] Her later life is unknown.

MAJOR WORK: *Poetical Sketches* (London, 1795).

TEXTS USED: Texts of all poems from *Poetical Sketches*.

Written in Devonshire, near the Dart

Hail, Devon! in thy bosom let me rest,
And pour forth music from my raptur'd breast:
    I'll stray thy meadow'd hills
      And plains along,
      And loudly sing the widely-varied song,
Tracing thy rivers, and thy bubbling rills.

Oft, rising from the sea, the tempest lours,
    And buoy'd on winds the clouds majestic sail,
Which scattering burst in wide and frequent showers,
    Swelling the streams which glide thro' every vale;   10

6. Ibid.
7. Quoted in ibid.
8. *Collected Letters of Mary Wollstonecraft,* ed. Ralph M. Wardle (Ithaca, 1979), 188.
9. [John Watkins and Frederic Shoberl], eds., *A Biographical Dictionary of the Living Authors of Great Britain and Ireland; comprising Literary Memoirs and Anecdotes of their Lives; and a Chronological Register of their Publications, etc.* (London, 1816).

Yet are the marshy plains bedeck'd with flowers,
  And balmy sweets are borne on every gale.

Where Dart romantic winds its mazy course,
  And mossy rocks adhere to woody hills,
  From whence each creeping rill its store distils,
And wandering waters join with rapid force;
  There Nature's hand has wildly strewn her flowers,
And varying prospects strike the roving eyes;
Rough-hanging woods o'er cultur'd hills arise;
20 Thick ivy spreads around huge antic towers,
    And fruitful groves
Scatter their blossoms fast as falling showers,
Perfuming ev'ry stream which o'er the landscape pours.

Along the grassy banks how sweet to stray,
  When the mild eve smiles in the glowing west,
And lengthen'd shades proclaim departing day,
And fainting sun-beams in the waters play,
  When every bird seeks its accustom'd rest!
  How grand, to see the burning orb descend,
30 And the grave sky wrapp'd in its nightly robes,
Whether resplendent with the starry globes,
Or silver'd by the mildly-solemn moon,
When nightingales their lonely songs resume,
  And folly's sons their babbling noise suspend!

Or when the darkening clouds fly o'er the sea,
  And early morning beams a chearful ray,
Waking melodious songsters from each tree;
How sweet beneath each dewy hill
  Amid the pleasing shades to stray,
40 Where nectar'd flowers their sweets distil,
  Whose watery pearls reflect the day!
To scent the jonquil's rich perfume,
  To pluck the hawthorn's tender briars,
As wild beneath each flowery hedge
Fair strawberries with violets bloom,
  And every joy of spring conspires!

Nature's wild songsters from each bush and tree
    Invite the early walk, and breathe delight;
What bosom heaves not with warm sympathy
    When the gay lark salutes the new-born light?   50
Hark! where the shrill-ton'd thrush,
    Sweet whistling, carols the wild harmony!
The linnet warbles, and from yonder bush
    The robin pours soft strains of melody!

Hail, Devon! while through thy lov'd woods I stray,
O! let me loudly pour the grateful lay!
    Tell each luxuriant bank where violets grow,
Each mazy vale, where fragrant woodbines wind,
    How much of their bewitching charms they owe
To the sweet peace which fills my happy mind.   60
Ah! where again will it such pleasures find?
O, lov'd society! the heartfelt lay
    Is all the humble Muse can now bestow;
Thy praises still I sing, as on I stray,
    Writ in my heart amid each strain they flow.
                    (1795)

To a Lady, on the Rise of Morn

Rise, blossom of the spring,
    The dews of morn
    Still linger on the barren thorn;
Arise, and sing!

O! join my rapt'rous song!
    And o'er the wild bleak hills
And unfledg'd fields along
    Pursue the trickling rills:
      O, rise!
Cloath'd with that modest grace   10
That veils the glowing beauties of thine face,
      And downward points the radiance of thine eyes.

I wait thee on the thawing mountains,
Where spring dissolves the lingering fountains;
O! trace with me the opening flowers;
Brave the sharp breeze, damp dews, and vernal showers.
Wild various Nature strews her charms,
And storms surround her mildest calms;
  O! to her frowns let us superior be,
20 Taste each delight, and hail the coming spring,
  Singing the heavenly song of liberty!

          (1795)

Songs of Arla (from "The Enthusiast")

Song I

Wild wing my notes, fierce passions urge the strain;
  Strong flame the fires that kindle in my soul;
I strike the wiery harp, nor will refrain;
Mad is despair, and scorns each feeble rein,
  Feelings like mine no virtue can control.
Stifled, th'inflated heart with pain respires,
  My crimson veins with struggling blood are press'd,
My cheeks are flush'd with passion's transient fires;
My brain with agonies distracted flies,
10 Till the fierce streams burst from my burning eyes,
  And drowning torrents cool my panting breast.

Song II

With awe my soul the wreck of Nature views,
  The storm amid the echoing mountain hears;
  The sighs of Autumn, mingling with my tears,
Mourn the sad ravages which time pursues.
Hear the wild roar of the tempestuous blast,
  Whirling the forest leaves to distant air!
See blooming flowers in scatter'd fragments cast,
  While torrents pouring thunder on the ear!

The sun's bright beam in dreary winter lost,
Not joyless is, as me, on passion's tempest tost.   10

My youthful charms fade 'neath my burning eyes,
The soul-entrancing morn of pleasure flies;
    A raging sorrow sweeps without control
Those germs of genius which alone inspire:
    The sensual passions which consum'd my soul,
Burn my distemper'd bosom with their fire.
    Long lightnings glance still from my streaming eyes,
Though vain around the fiery circles roll;
Virtue and pleasure vanish from my soul;
    The transient shadow of my glory flies.   20

Song III

Impassion'd strains my trembling lips rehearse,
    Echoing my soul the numbers pierce the skies,
      I seem (delusions thus my mind impair)
    To catch the potent fires of EDRAN's eyes:
On loftiest pinions then, more noble verse
    Bursts into sound, and floats upon the air,
    Till memory bursts on my deluded heart,
      Mingling discordant strains of deep despair.
Distracting thoughts upon my spirit pour,
    No longer in delusive dreams I rest,   10
Such passions mingle with each bitter shower!
    A father's image meets my troubled breast;
    Ah! wandering heart! how bitterly distress'd!
Consuming flames will soon thy strength o'erpower,
    And thou abandon'd die, with guilt oppress'd.
                    (1795)

Verses Written in the Spring

From yon fair hill, whose woody crest
The mantling hand of spring has dress'd,
Where gales imbibe the May-perfume,
And strew the blushing almond's bloom,
I view the verdant plains below,
And lucid streams which gently flow,
The opening foliage, drench'd with showers,
Weep o'er the odorous vernal flowers;
And while before my temper'd eye
From glancing clouds swift shadows fly,
While nature seems serene and bless'd,
And inward concord tunes my breast,
I sigh for those by fortune cross'd,
Whose souls to Nature's charms are lost.

Whether by love of wealth betray'd,
Absorb'd in all the arts of trade,
Or deep engross'd in mighty schemes,
Toss'd in ambition's empty dreams,
Or proud amid the learned schools,
Stiffen'd by dull pedantic rules,
Or those who ne'er from forms depart,
The slaves of fashion and of art.

O! lost to bliss! the pregnant air,
The rising sun, the ripening year,
The embrios that on every bush
'Midst the wild notes of songsters blush;
The violet's scent, the varying hues
Which morn's light ray strikes 'mid the dews,
To them are lost—involv'd in care,
They cannot feel, they cannot share.

I grieve, when round I cast my eyes,
And feel a thousand pleasures rise,
That this fair earth, by Heaven bestow'd,

(Which human fury stains with blood)
Should teem with joys which reach the heart,
And man be thus absorb'd in art.

(1795)

A Song of Arla
Written during her Enthusiasm

Flush'd, from my restless pillow I arose,
To calm my thoughts, sad stranger to repose;
Wandering through woods, by night's dread shadows gloom'd,
At every glade I pensive rear'd my eyes,
And view'd the fleecy clouds fleet o'er the skies,
Which gathering thick a thousand forms assum'd.
Sudden, while yet I gaz'd, the heavens grew bright;
The graceful star of night
Shot, 'midst the dark assembled host of clouds,
A pure resplendent light.   10

The parting vapours floating on the air
Seem'd spirits teeming with immortal fire,
Bright emanations of th' Eternal Sire
Unto my soul reveal'd by ardent prayer.

Clear, by the moon, a numerous host I view,
Circling its orb, the unclad spirits wing,
On music's pinions mystic flights pursue,
Glide through the air, and heavenly numbers sing;
While from on high
Descend long beams of light;   20
A thousand visions crowd upon my sight;
I seem to mount, and, borne along the sky,
Rapt'rous I sing, in frenzied ecstasy:

---

34 (Which human fury stains with blood)] A reference to the French Revolution, specifically
to the Reign of Terror.

"Whither flies my soul, amid the lunar night?
"Glory rushes on my sight!
"Seraphic music fills my ear,
"Visionary forms appear
"In solemn grandeur dight!
"Drawn by silver rays
30   "Round the all-attracting orb,
"While Night her sable wings displays,
"Which every vivid beam absorb.
"Amid the sacred host I fly,
"Fraught with solemn harmony.
"Mingling with the lunar beams,
"From every eye immortal genius gleams;
"The soul of sound
"Pervades the shadowy space around:
"From each wild harp a nightly spirit springs,
40   "And peals of heavenly music sings;
"Grand clouds of darkness, hurried by the wind,
"Bearing th' emanations of the mind:
"The touch most fine,
"The gleam most magic;
"The voice most rapt'rously divine,
"Strains most wild and energetic!
"All, all combine,
"They gather, stream;
"The sounds encrease, they join,
50   "While still we fly the circle round,
"We dart along, wake every sound,
"And amidst harmony, and light, and darkness, shine."

Now op'd the starry regions on my sight,
And 'thwart dark space shot radiant streams of light;
Th' aereal forms in mists dissolving rise,
Yet still I hear the grand concordant song,
Echo'd by all the offspring of the skies,
Who each in their eternal language sung,
While all around brake forth ethereal rays:
From high I heard a new and awful sound,
60   Swelling with voice divine the song of praise.

My feeble sense no longer bears the light,
Oppos'd my eye-lids close,
The heavenly forms I lose
Amid th' all-piercing light.
My ears resound no more, my pulses cease,
And for a while my soul was hushed to peace.

Till, waking in the fields, with chill'd affright,
I feel a shivering being wandering in the night.

(1795)

An Ode

Almighty Power! who rul'st this world of storms!
    Eternal Spirit of Infinity!
Whose wisdom Nature's boundless space informs,
    O! look with mercy on man's misery;
Who, tost on all the elements by turns,
With languor droops, or with fierce passion burns.

Submissive to life's casualties I sing;
    Though short our mortal day, and stor'd with pains,
And strongly Nature's truths conviction bring,
    That no firm happiness this world contains: 10
Yet hope, sweet hope, supports the pious breast,
Whose boundless views no earthly griefs arrest.

What dire disorder ravages the world!
    Beasts, birds, fish, insects, war with cruel strife!
Created matter in contention whirl'd
    Spreads desolation as it bursts to life!
And men, who mental light from heaven enjoy,
Pierce the fraternal breast, and impiously destroy.

Unknown, and nothing in the scale of things,
    Yet would I wisdom's ways aloud rehearse,   20

Touch'd by humanity, strike loud the strings,
        And pour a strain of more inspired verse;
But reason, truth, and harmony are vain,
No power man's boundless passions can restrain.

Stupendous Nature! rugged, beauteous, wild!
        Impress'd with awe, thy wondrous book I read:
Beyond this stormy tract, some realm more mild,
        My spirit tells me, is for man decreed;
Where, unallay'd, bliss reigns without excess:
30   Thus hope excentric points to happiness!

                                        (1795)

Song on Leaving the Country
Early in the Spring

While joy re-animates the fields,
And spring her odorous treasures yields;
While love inspires the happy grove,
        And music breaks from every spray;
I leave the sweet retreat I love
        Ere bloss'ming hawthorn greets the May;
Sad destiny! O! let me plaintive pour
O'er the unopen'd bud an unrefreshing shower.

To yonder hills, which bound the sight,
10   Where blushing eve dissolves in night,
To the wild heath, o'er which the gale
        Bleak wafts each sweet perfume of spring,
And to the weed-grown briary vale
        Sorrowing the parting lay I sing;
"Sweet flowers of spring, enlivening day,
"Nature's unfolding charms fleet fast away."

At morn I've view'd the glimmering light
Break from the east, and chase the night;

Then stray'd amid the frosty dews,
     While soaring larks shrill chanting rise,   20
And mark'd the thousand varying hues
     That streak the glowing morning skies.
"Sweet air of spring, enlivening day,
"Nature's unfolding charms fleet fast away."

No daisied lawns shall greet my eye,
Reluctant from their sweets I fly;
No more, wild wandering o'er the plains,
     I share each innocent delight;
The tinkling flocks, the woodland strains,
     The rural dance no more invite.   30
Sad destiny. O! let me plaintive pour
O'er the unopen'd bud an unrefreshing shower.

             (1795)

Catherine Ann Dorset

(1750?–1817?)

Charlotte Smith's younger sister, Catherine Ann, was born shortly before the death of their mother, Ann Towers Turner, and, like Smith, was raised by her maternal aunt, Lucy Towers, amid every material advantage. Their father, a member of the landed gentry with holdings in Surrey and Sussex, was also a poet; a man of wit and fashion, he was cultured and intellectual and had a love of nature and poetry that he passed on to his daughters. About 1770 Catherine Ann married an army captain, Michael Dorset. Smith was responsible for her sister's first appearing in print: she inserted anonymously at least eleven of Catherine Ann's poems in her own *Conversations Introducing Poetry: Chiefly on Subjects of Natural History. For the Use of Children and Young Persons* (1804).[1] When Dorset was widowed around 1805, she sold her interest in the family estate, Bignor Park, and turned to writing as an occupation.

In 1807 Dorset brought out anonymously a comic, narrative poem for children, *The Peacock "At Home": A Sequel to the Butterfly's Ball*, illustrated by William Mulready, in John Harris's Cabinet Series. Gently satirizing the social foibles of the aristocracy and the upper middle class, it teaches children in an enjoyable way about birds and alludes in its conclusion to Dorset's own aspirations as an author:

> Then long live the Peacock, in splendour unmatch'd,
> Whose Ball shall be talk'd of by birds yet unhatch'd;
> His fame let the Trumpeter loudly proclaim,
> And the Goose lend her quill to transmit it to fame!

William Roscoe's *The Butterfly's Ball and the Grasshopper's Feast* and Dorset's sequel, both brought out by the same publisher, so captured the popular

---

1. These poems include "The Mimosa," "To the Lady-Bird," "The Humble Bee," "The Doormouse Just Taken," "The Squirrel," "The Hot-House Rose," "The Glow-Worm," "The Captive Fly," "The Nautilus," "The Humming-Bird" and "The Blighted Rose" (retitled "The Cankered Rose"). All were reprinted by Dorset under her own name in *The Peacock "At Home"; and Other Poems* (London, 1809).

imagination that together they reportedly sold forty thousand copies in the first year. The *British Critic* believed *The Peacock "At Home"* to be superior to Roscoe's poem; it admired Dorset's knowledge of natural history as well as her "playful wit conducted by genius, judgment, and taste" and maintained that " 'The Peacock at Home,' for neat and natural humour, just appropriation of character and action to the birds introduced, variety of plan, and felicity of execution, cannot well be surpassed." The *Monthly Review* said that the poem had been "deservedly applauded" not only for the knowledge of birds it imparted and its ability to educate its young audience but also for its amusing critique of human behavior.[2]

In 1807 Harris also published anonymously Dorset's *The Lion's Masquerade. A Sequel to the Peacock at Home,* of which the *Antijacobin Review* noted, "The King of beasts has here found a poet worthy to record his royal amusements. These are no puerile strains; and, though not above the capacity of children . . . they exhibit such *humour* and *point* as will render them amusing to readers of riper years and maturer understanding."[3] William Godwin's Juvenile Library brought out *Think before You Speak: Or, the Three Wishes. A Tale,* which Dorset translated from the French, in 1809. That same year Dorset allowed her name to be attached to an expanded edition of *The Peacock "At Home,"* brought out by John Murray in London and Harris in Edinburgh, which included twenty additional short poems for children. By 1812 *The Peacock "At Home"* had gone through twenty-six editions, and it was still being reprinted and illustrated as late as 1883.

MAJOR WORKS: *The Peacock "At Home": A Sequel to the Butterfly's Ball* (London, 1807); *The Lion's Masquerade. A Sequel to the Peacock at Home* (London, 1807); *The Lioness's Rout; being a Sequel to the Butterfly's Ball, the Grasshopper's Feast, and the Peacock "At Home"* (London, [1808]); *Think before You Speak: Or, the Three Wishes. A Tale* (London, 1809); *The Peacock At Home; and Other Poems* (London, 1809); *The Peacock Abroad; or Visits Returned* (Greenwich, 1812); *The Peacock, and Parrot, on their Tour to Discover the Author of "The Peacock at Home"* (London, 1816).

TEXTS USED: Text of "The Humble Bee" from Charlotte Smith's *Conversations Introducing Poetry: Chiefly on Subjects of Natural History. For the Use of Children and Young Persons,* 2 vols. (London, 1804); in her 1809 volume, *The Peacock at Home and Other Poems,* Dorset acknowledges that the poem is hers rather than her sister's. Text of "To the Lady-Bird" from *The Peacock at Home; and Other Poems.*

2. *British Critic* 30 (November 1807): 554–56; *Monthly Review* 54 (December 1807): 446–47.
3. 29 (January 1808): 75.

The Humble Bee

Good morrow, gentle humble bee,
You are abroad betimes, I see,
And sportive fly from tree to tree,
                    To take the air;

And visit each gay flower that blows;
While every bell and bud that glows,
Quite from the daisy to the rose,
                    Your visits share.

Saluting now the pied carnation,
Now on the aster taking station,
Murmuring your ardent admiration;
                    Then off you frisk,

Where poppies hang their heavy heads,
Or where the gorgeous sun-flower spreads
For you her luscious golden beds,
                    On her broad disk.

To live on pleasure's painted wing,
To feed on all the sweets of Spring,
Must be a mighty pleasant thing,
                    If it would last.

But you, no doubt, have wisely thought,
These joys may be too dearly bought,
And will not unprepar'd be caught
                    When Summer's past.

---

9 carnation] *Dianthus caryophyllus.* [This and the following botanical notes are from the original publication of the poem in Charlotte Smith's *Conversations Introducing Poetry* (1804). It is unclear whether the notes are Smith's or Dorset's. *Ed.*]

10 aster] *Aster chinensis.*

13 poppies] Poppy, *Papaver somniferum.*

14 sun-flower] Sun-flower, *Helianthus anorenus.*

For soon will fly the laughing hours,
And this delightful waste of flowers
Will shrink before the wintry showers
              And winds so keen.

Alas! who then will lend you aid,
If your dry cell be yet unmade,   30
Nor store of wax and honey laid
              In magazine?

Then, Lady Buzz, you will repent,
That hours for useful labour meant
Were so unprofitably spent,
              And idly lost.

By cold and hunger keen oppress'd,
Say, will your yellow velvet vest,
Or the fur tippet on your breast,
              Shield you from frost?   40

Ah! haste your winter stock to save,
That snug within your Christmas cave,
When snows fall fast and tempests rave,
              You may remain.

And the hard season braving there,
On Spring's warm gales you will repair,
Elate thro' crystal fields of air,
              To bliss again!
                    (1804)

To the Lady-Bird

Oh! Lady-bird, Lady-bird, why dost thou roam
So far from thy comrades, so distant from home?
Why dost thou, who canst revel all day in the air,
Who the sweets of the grove and the garden canst share;
In the fold of a leaf, who canst form thee a bower,
And a palace enjoy in the tube of a flower;
Ah, why, simple Lady-bird, why dost thou venture,
The dwellings of man so familiar to enter?
Too soon you may find, that your trust is misplac'd,
10   When by some cruel child you are wantonly chas'd,
And your bright scarlet coat, so bespotted with black,
May be torn by his barbarous hands from your back;
And your smooth jetty corselet be pierc'd with a pin,
That the urchin may see you in agonies spin;
For his bosom is shut against pity's appeals,
He has never been taught that a Lady-bird feels.
Ah, then you'll regret you were tempted to rove,
From the tall climbing hop, or the hazle's thick grove,
And will fondly remember each arbour and tree,
20   Where lately you wander'd contented and free;
Then fly, simple Lady-bird! — fly away home,
No more from your nest, and your children to roam.

(1804)

Maria Edgeworth

(1768–1849)

In his 1829 preface to *Waverley,* Walter Scott acknowledges his considerable debt to the artistry of Maria Edgeworth, author of the innovative novel *Castle Rackrent* (1800): "Without being so presumptuous as to hope to emulate the rich humour, pathetic tenderness, and admirable tact which pervade the works of my accomplished friend, I felt that something might be attempted for my own country, of the same kind with that which Miss Edgeworth so fortunately achieved for Ireland." Lord Byron recalled in 1813, "I had been the lion of 1812: Miss Edgeworth and Madame de Staël . . . were the exhibitions of the succeeding year."[1] Author of *Belinda, Leonora, Patronage,* and other novels and tales, Edgeworth was one of the most respected educational writers and novelists of the age. Moreover, her tales for children, informed by Enlightenment educational theory and shaped by her role as surrogate mother to her many younger siblings, were popular and influential.

Born at Black Bourton, Oxfordshire, on 1 January 1768, Maria was the second surviving child and eldest daughter of Anna Maria Elers and Richard Lovell Edgeworth, an Anglo-Irish landowner, educational theorist, scientist, and author. Maria Edgeworth's mother died in childbirth in 1773, and Maria grew up adoring and emulating her father, who married four times altogether, eventually producing twenty-two children, eighteen of whom survived infancy.[2] His second wife, Honora Sneyd, was the foster sister of Anna Seward. Maria Edgeworth grew up on Anna Letitia Barbauld's *Lessons for Children* and attended boarding schools in England, where she received conventional instruction. Although she was sometimes considered "naughty," her childhood was a relatively happy one.

In 1782 her nonconformist father, who adhered to the ideas of the English

---

1. Byron's "Ravenna Journal," 19 January 1821, in *"Born for Opposition,"* vol. 8 of *Byron's Letters and Journals* (London, 1978), 29.

2. The last of Maria Edgeworth's siblings was born in 1812. She was older than her father's fourth wife.

provincial Enlightenment and was the friend of Erasmus Darwin, Joseph Priestley, Thomas Day, James Watt, and Josiah Wedgwood, returned with his family to his estate at Edgeworthstown, County Longford, Ireland, to take part in Irish reform. Maria, who was fifteen, became her father's intellectual companion, amanuensis, domestic helper, and assistant in running the estate. Her first literary work was a translation he requested of Madame de Genlis's *Adèle et Théodore.* When her father returned to London in 1791, she remained in Ireland, where she forged a deep and lasting friendship with his sister, Margaret Ruxton.

Edgeworth eventually joined her father and stepmother in England, but she disliked fashionable London society. The family returned to Ireland in 1793. In 1795 Edgeworth published *Letters for Literary Ladies* with Joseph Johnson, publisher of Erasmus Darwin, Anna Letitia Barbauld, Joseph Priestley, and others, who was to bring out all of her work until his death two decades later. The book argues for the intellectual capacities and rights of women but advocates that they remain in the domestic sphere rather than enter the political realm. The following year she brought out her hugely successful volume *The Parent's Assistant,* which comprised stories and a play for children in the tradition of Mary Wollstonecraft, Sarah Trimmer, Madame de Genlis, and Thomas Day, espousing Edgeworth family progressive educational theory.

Edgeworth became her father's assistant in literary as well as in business matters, co-authoring several books with him, including *Practical Education* (1798), which outlines the theories behind the stories in *The Parent's Assistant. Practical Education* applies Enlightenment principles to early childhood education, drawing examples from the Edgeworth family; it was immediately recognized as an important book. These ideas are further illustrated in Maria Edgeworth's *Early Lessons* (1801), for children. In 1799 she and her father proposed to Anna Letitia Barbauld that they start a liberal journal for women, to be called the *Feminead,* but Barbauld rejected the idea, believing that ideological differences between women authors would keep the journal from succeeding. Maria Edgeworth's innovative first novel, *Castle Rackrent,* published in January 1800, was written without her father's guidance and published anonymously. Considered a landmark in the history of the novel for its technique, it is a portrait, both comic and critical, of Irish provincial life, with a humorously unreliable narrator using everyday speech. It depicts a series of irresponsible landlords, a metaphor for British oversight of Ireland, and the inevitability of capitalist forces' undermining the power of an already grossly corrupt and irresponsible aristocracy. This book was to have a profound influence on Walter Scott, James Fenimore Cooper, and Ivan Sergeevich Turgenev. Her next book, *Belinda* (1801), is a novel of manners with an independent heroine who is both feminine and rational.

It critiques fashionable society and the ideology of sensibility as it portrays Belinda making her way for the first time in the adult world and choosing between three suitors. Edgeworth collaborated with her father to pen the *Essay on Irish Bulls* (1802), a complex and highly ironic text ostensibly about "Irish bulls," a type of contradiction or paradox, but, more importantly, a defense of Irish speech patterns and culture.

In the fall of 1802 Edgeworth took a tour through the Midlands of England with her family, continuing on to Paris, where she and her father were feted for their educational works and met intellectuals and writers, including Madame de Genlis. With much pain, in December she declined a proposal of marriage from a Swedish courtier and intellectual, Abraham Niclas Clewberg-Edelcrantz, though her father urged her to accept. Before returning home they visited Glasgow and Edinburgh, where Maria met the novelist Elizabeth Hamilton and leaders of the Scottish Enlightenment.

Her *Popular Tales* (1804) are a critique of Hannah More's "Cheap Repository" tracts, which advocate patience, uncomplaining suffering, subordination, and a religious faith that looks to an afterlife for its reward. Edgeworth focuses instead on the virtues of toleration, self-discipline, self-improvement, and the support of the family. Unbeknownst to her father, in 1805 Edgeworth published *The Modern Griselda,* a satire on women who aspire to high society and reject domestic roles. She elaborates in *Léonora* (1806), an epistolary, satirical novel with a bright, virtuous, domestic heroine at its center. In 1809 the Edgeworths brought out *Essays on Professional Education,* concerned with moral and intellectual instruction and advocating professions independent of the patronage system. Maria Edgeworth's *Tales of Fashionable Life* (1809, 1812), including "Ennui" and "The Absentee," set the social criticisms of the *Essays* in fictional form, using realistic detail and dialect. These tales attack middle-class aspirations for "fashionable" society and advocate reform, principally through the professionalization of the gentry. In 1811 she wrote notes and a preface for Mary Leadbeater's *Cottage Dialogues Among the Irish Peasantry.*

Although by this time Edgeworth had become one of the most widely read and respected authors in Britain, she repeatedly rejected invitations to leave Ireland to be lionized. But in the spring of 1813 she did make a long trip to England with her family. She saw William Roscoe in Liverpool, and in London she met Mary Berry, Thomas Malthus, Lord Byron, Thomas Moore, and Jane Marcet, a scientist with whom she corresponded for some years afterwards. While Edgeworth was well liked, her father was considered overbearing. On this trip Edgeworth also saw Etienne Dumont, a Swiss intellectual with whom she had been exchanging letters for years and whom she considered marrying.

Patronage (1814) contrasts the lives of two families belonging to the landed gentry, the Falconers and the Percys. The Falconers ultimately fail because of their reliance on the patronage system and blind chance; the Percys prosper by cultivating self-discipline, independence, and professional knowledge. Caroline Percy is Edgeworth's model woman, who looks for an intellectual equal in a husband and marries Count Altenberg, an idealized version of Edgeworth's own unsuccessful Swedish suitor, Edelcrantz. Edgeworth earned the enormous sum of twenty-one hundred pounds for this reformist novel.

Edgeworth published her *Continuation of Early Lessons* in 1814 and wrote the preface and final chapter, "On Parody," for her father's *Readings on Poetry* (1816). Her memoir of the novelist Elizabeth Hamilton appeared in the September 1816 issue of the *Monthly Magazine,* and in 1817 she published *Comic Dramas in Three Acts. Harrington* (1817) is a novel inspired by a correspondence with Rachel Mordecai, an American Jew who wrote to Edgeworth to object to her stereotyping of Jewish characters. *Harrington* contains several examples of admirable Jewish characters, including the virtuous, cultivated, and wealthy Montenero, an intellectual, Israel Lyons, and an honorable peddler. The hero of the novel, the young professional Harrington, overcomes his fear of Jews and eventually falls in love with and marries Berenice, whom he believes to be Jewish but who is revealed in the end to be Christian. The novel also includes some of Edgeworth's earlier themes—the superiority of reason over prejudice or custom, the potential of the middle class to become cultured and public-spirited, and the need for the working classes to be treated more fairly.

Ormond, a novel published with *Harrington,* has an Irish protagonist modeled on Henry Fielding's Tom Jones who has adventures in England, Ireland, and France. He rejects French court culture and fashionable coquettes and marries a virtuous and sensible Englishwoman, symbolically carrying out a "union" of English and Irish gentry. Eighteen seventeen was a difficult year for Edgeworth, for in June her father died; she completed and published his *Memoirs* in 1820. She journeyed to England several times in the early 1820s, and in 1823, on a visit to Scotland, met Walter Scott. The two became fast friends, and he and John Gibson Lockhart, his son-in-law, visited her at Edgeworthstown in 1825. At about this time Edgeworth took over control of the Edgeworth estate, which was being mismanaged, from her brother Lovell; she continued to manage the estate until 1839. Her last novel, *Helen* (1834), which took five years to write, is a critique of the silver-fork novels then in vogue; it portrays a strong bond between two women and asserts the primacy of the domestic sphere over all others. Elizabeth Gaskell admired this book and imitated it in *Wives and Daughters.*

Maria Edgeworth died at Edgeworthstown on 22 May 1849 after a brief illness. She had been the most commercially successful novelist before Walter

Scott eclipsed all others with *Waverley* (1814). According to her own calculations, Edgeworth earned more than eleven thousand pounds from writing during her lifetime.

Edgeworth's favorite poets included Pope, Barbauld, and Scott, whose *Lay of the Last Minstrel* is said to have aided her recovery after a serious illness. In her preface to *Readings on Poetry,* for children, she complained that "an unconscionable quantity of what we may be permitted to call common place *poetry,* is by many parents forced upon the youthful memory."[3] Instead of rote memorization, the standard practice at the time, she championed teaching children to understand the meaning of poetic language, exposing them to the best poetry, and encouraging them to form their own judgments about it. In her chapter "On Parody," she observes that "it would be more satisfactory to us, to hear young persons make one observation of their own, it would be more satisfaction to us, to see the pleasure lighten in their eyes, on the discovery of an allusion, an imitation, a parody, on the perception of any beauty of poetry discerned *for* themselves, and *by* themselves, than it could possibly give us to know that every word in this book, that all the criticisms of Warton, or Johnson, or of all the best criticks that ever wrote, were merely impressed on the memory of the pupil."

Although writing poetry seems to have been an integral part of Edgeworth's everyday life, she never published a line of it. Family albums, however, contain not only transcripts in her hand of verse by her father but also signed poetry of her own composition, along with poems by other members of the household.[4] Maria Edgeworth's verse seems to have been produced solely for the entertainment of her family, for the private communication of feeling to family members or friends, or for special occasions. None of her writing, whether prose or poetry, was penned in private; she was almost always surrounded by children or subject to other frequent interruptions.

MAJOR WORKS: *Letters for Literary Ladies, to Which is Added An Essay on the Noble Science of Self-Justification* (London, 1795); *The Parent's Assistant; or, Stories for Children,* 3 vols. (London, 1796); *Castle Rackrent: an Hibernian Tale. Taken from the Facts, and from the Manners of the Irish Squires, Before the Year 1782* (London, 1800); *Belinda,* 3 vols. (London, 1801); *Early Lessons,* 10 pts. in 5 vols. (London, 1801–2); *Moral Tales for Young People,* 5 vols. (London, 1801); *Popular Tales,* 3 vols. (London, 1804); *The Modern Griselda: A Tale* (London, 1805); *Leonora,* 2 vols. (London, 1806); *Tales of Fashionable Life,* 6 vols.

3. P. xx of the edition published in Boston in 1816. This book was co-authored with her father, but Maria Edgeworth penned the preface and the chapter entitled "On Parody."

4. See David C. Sutton, ed., *Location Register of English Literary Manuscripts and Letters: Eighteenth and Nineteenth Centuries,* 2 vols. (London, 1995), 760–61, for an inventory of Maria Edgeworth's unpublished verse.

(London, 1809 [vols. 1–3], 1812 [vols. 4–6]); *Continuation of Early Lessons,* 2 vols. (London, 1814); *Patronage,* 4 vols. (London, 1814); *Comic Dramas, in Three Acts* (London, 1817); *Harrington, a Tale; and Ormond, a Tale,* 3 vols. (London, 1817); *Rosamond: A Sequel to Early Lessons,* 2 vols. (London, 1821); *Frank: a Sequel to Frank in Early Lessons,* 3 vols. (London, 1822); *Harry and Lucy Concluded: Being the Last Part of Early Lessons,* 4 vols. (London, 1825); *Helen: a Tale,* 3 vols. (London, 1834).

WITH RICHARD LOVELL EDGEWORTH: *Practical Education,* 2 vols. (London, 1798); *Essay on Irish Bulls* (London, 1802); *Readings on Poetry* (London, 1816); *Memoirs of Richard Lovell Edgeworth, Esq.,* 2 vols. (London, 1820).

TEXTS USED: Text of "On Chauntry's Statue of Watt in Handsworth Church" from an Edgeworth family commonplace book in the National Library of Ireland, MS 23,445; texts of "To Mrs. Carr Accepting From Her as a Keepsake a Lamp Which She Had Used for Twenty Years in Her Children's Room & Which She Lately Lent to Me during My Sister's Illness at Frognel 1 May 1819," "Laura Leicester, Supposed to Exclaim at the Sight of a Colourbox and Portfolio Sent to her by Mrs. and Miss Sneyd Jan 7 1819," and "With a Dyed Silk Quilt Sent to Aunt Ruxton to be Thrown over When She Lies on the Sofa" from another Edgeworth family commonplace book in the National Library of Ireland, MS 23,447, acc. 3744. Each poem was signed by Maria Edgeworth.

On Chauntry's Statue of Watt
in Handsworth Church[*]

He thinks, he lives, he breathes celestial breath,
'Tis but the trance of thought—it is not death,
—One moment more & he will move, will rise
There is within him that which never dies:
Immortal as th' immortal soul is he
That body incorrupt shall ever be:
The perishable body gone, the flesh the bone
Of Watt—th' immortal genius lives in Chauntrys stone.

(wr. 1831)

[*]James Watt (1736–1819), a Scottish inventor responsible for an improved steam engine, was a friend of the Edgeworth family. He had a house in Handsworth and was

buried in a vault in the Handsworth parish church beneath a chapel built expressly to house the life-size marble statue of him by the noted sculptor Sir Francis Chantrey (1781–1841).

To Mrs. Carr, Accepting from Her As a Keepsake a Lamp Which She Had Used for Twenty Years in Her Children's Room & Which She Lately Lent to Me during My Sister's Illness at Frognel 1 May 1819*

Lamp! never doomd to waste the midnight oil
In Fashion's revels—Fashion's ceaseless toil
Thy happier lot—with steady ray serene
To mark the bliss of life's domestic scene
When soft with cautious step, & noiseless tread
The mother sought her sleeping darlings' bed
With breath suppressed lowbending stood to view
Their arms entwined their cheeks of rosy hue
Your friendly flame assisted her to trace
The father's likeness in the infant face: 10
And oft you saw the child in slumber blest
Feel the soft kiss & turn to be carest,
While still in sleep the ready smile would play
Then sweet in circling dimples, melt away—
No torch triumphant nor the festal blaze
Of full illumination's proudest rays
Had e'er the power such pleasure to impart
As thou, dear Lamp! to the fond Mother's heart
In sickness, doubly dear thy faithful light
Watched the lone hours of suffering's lengthy Night   20
In forms grotesque thy flut'ring shadows thrown
Amused the feverish eye with wonders all thy own
Unwearied still thy paly circlet burned
Till the grey morning's rising sun returned:
Dear humble Lamp! I love, I prize thee more
Than ever magic lamp was prized of yore
For thine is fond Association's art
To call up images that touch the heart;

Full to my mind you bring affection's face,
30   And every kind & every winning grace
That soothed the anxious, blest the happy hour
With Friendship—Wisdom—wit's united power
Dear keepsake Lamp! your constant flame shall shine
Soon at my much loved home for me & mine
While grateful friends exulting in the sight
Eye the safe shade & bless the useless Light!

                                        (wr. 1819)

*Francis Morton Carr, who lived on Frognel Lane, was a neighbor of Joanna
Baillie in Hampstead.

Laura Leicester, Supposed to Exclaim
at the Sight of a Colourbox and Portfolio Sent
to Her by Mrs. and Miss Sneyd Jan. 7 1819

Chalks! dear Mamma! red green & blue
For me!—and a portfolio too!
Paper! oh give me in a minute
I'll draw the world and all that's in it
I'll draw a house—I'll draw a town
I'll draw a bird—I'll draw a flower!
Each flower that buds each flower that blows
Carnation—Honeysuckle Rose
All things that creep all things that fly
10   I have you all within my eye
I'll paint the Parrot's crimson beak
I'll paint the Linnet's yellow streak
I'll paint the caterpillar's rings
Stay Butterfly—I'll paint your wings
I'll paint the Sun in all his Glory
I'll paint the blindmen in the story
Or beggarman with legs uneven
Or puppet show—with puppets seven
I'll draw in *miniature*—in small

Man—woman *child* I'll have ye all! 20
I know an eye that's bright and witty
I know a nose that's very pretty
Turn Sophy—turn my dear, this way
No—leave her for another day
I'll draw poor Puss—she takes it ill!
I'll draw Mamma—for she'll sit still
But ma'am today I'm not quite steady
Besides you know we've nothing ready
Tomorrow then we will begin
And *then*—what praises I shall win! 30
I'll draw at once like Emma Sneyd
You smile! but Ma'am I will indeed
I'll work so hard!—I'll never play
Begin I will this very day
   Begin! my child—that's wondrous easy
And ma'am I'll *finish* too—to please ye
                    (wr. 1819)

With a Dyed Silk Quilt Sent to Aunt Ruxton to Be Thrown over When She Lies on the Sofa*

Go wretched dyed resuscitated thing
Round my dear Aunt your dingy covering fling
Warm on her feet—& light upon her breast
Hung round her shoulders soothe her soft to rest
Henceforth poor quilted one, nor Lyrian dye
Nor persic loom far famed, with thee shall vie
While rival cachmeres jealous boast their art
Close & more she'll fold you to her heart
While fondly murmuring betwixt sleep & wake
She owns she loves you *"for Maria's sake"* 10
Ay! & will love you ever o'er and o'er

6 persic] Persian.
7 cachmeres] Cashmeres.

The older, still she loves her friend the more
Loves with a love that youthful love defies
So warm—so well bred—& *I* think so wise

(wr. 1821)

---

* Margaret Edgeworth Ruxton, sister of Richard Lovell Edgeworth, was for half a century, until her death in 1830, a major influence on Maria Edgeworth's life.

Susan Evance

(fl. 1808–1818)

Susan Evance's contemporary reviewers seem to have known as little about her as we do. James Clarke edited *Poems by Miss S. E., Selected from her Earliest Productions, to Those of the Present Year,* which included poems, many of them sonnets, composed between 1803 and 1808, published in London by Longmans in 1808. The critic for the *Anti-Jacobin Review* complained that "we are not told what is her age, her studies, or her education, or any thing respecting her."[1] Her poems suggest that she had a brother in the navy as well as sisters. Commentators assumed that she was young, and the unimpressed critic for the *Eclectic Review* supposed that she was a disciple of Robert Merry and the Della Cruscans.[2] Still, most notices for the book were favorable. The *British Critic* called her poems "remarkable for their elegance and sensibility," thought they showed "some of the best qualities of poetical excellence," and worried that real misfortune might have inspired their melancholy.[3] The more skeptical *Monthly Review* observed, "When fictitious wretchedness gives way to more rational considerations, she pleases by her power of imagery, her justness of reflection, and her elegance of thought."[4] And her unaffected style won praise from the *Poetical Register.*[5]

Elizabeth Hill included work by Evance in her anthology *A Sequel to the Poetical Monitor* (London, 1815) along with selections from Charlotte Smith, Amelia Opie, Elizabeth Moody, Hannah More, Anna Letitia Barbauld, and others. In 1818 Evance published *A Poem Occasioned by the Cessation of Public Mourning for . . . the Princess Charlotte; together with Sonnets and Other Productions,* printed by Suttaby, Evance, and Fox, a firm with which she may have

1. 33 (July 1809): 296.
2. 5 (April 1809): 381–82.
3. 33 (May 1809): 516–17.
4. 60 (October 1809): 216.
    5. 7 (1808): 564. The *Critical Review,* 3rd ser., 16 (1809): 329–31, thought her sonnets resembled and were "equal to those of [William Lisles] Bowles," a much-admired sonneteer.

had some family connection. But this book received little notice and seems to have been her last. Her poems do not appear in the literary gift books or annuals of the 1820s. Perhaps she died young or renounced poetry for domestic duties.

MAJOR WORKS: *Poems . . . Selected from her Earliest Productions, to Those of the Present Year,* [ed. James Clarke] (London, 1808); *A Poem Occasioned by the Cessation of Public Mourning for Her Royal Highness the Princess Charlotte; together with Sonnets and Other Productions* (London, 1818).

TEXTS USED: All texts from *Poems . . . Selected from her Earliest Productions, to Those of the Present Year.*

Sonnet to Melancholy

When wintry tempests agitate the deep,
　　On some lone rock I love to sit reclin'd;
And view the sea-birds on wild pinions sweep,
　　And hear the roaring of the stormy wind,
That, rushing thro' the caves with hollow sound,
　　Seems like the voices of those viewless forms
Which hover wrapp'd in gloomy mist around,
　　Directing in their course the rolling storms.
Then, Melancholy! thy sweet power I feel,
10　　　For there thine influence reigns o'er all the scene;
Then o'er my heart thy "mystic transports" steal,
　　And from each trifling thought my bosom wean.
My raptur'd spirit soars on wing sublime
Beyond the narrow bounds of space or time!
　　　　　　　　　　　　(wr. 1803; pub. 1808)

Sonnet Written in a Ruinous Abbey

As 'mid these mouldering walls I pensive stray,
  With moss and ivy rudely overgrown,
I love to watch the last pale glimpse of day,
  And hear the rising winds of evening moan.

How loud the gust comes sweeping o'er the vale!
  Now faintly murmurs midst those distant trees;
The owl begins her melancholy wail,
  Filling with shrieks the pauses of the breeze.

Fancy, thy wildest dreams engage my mind—
  I gaze on forms which not to earth belong;   10
I see them riding on the passing wind,
  And hear their sadly-sweet, expressive song.
Wrap'd in the dear tho' visionary sound,
In spells of rapture all my soul is bound!
                              (wr. 1803; pub. 1808)

Sonnet to a Violet

Spring's sweet attendant! modest simple flower,
  Whose soft retiring charms the woods adorn,
How often have I wander'd at that hour,
  When first appear the rosy tints of morn,
To the wild brook—there, upon mossy ground,
  Thy velvet form all beautiful to view;
To catch thy breath that steals delicious round,
  And mark thy pensive smile thro' tears of dew:
But then I sigh that other Vi'lets bloom,
  Unseen, in wilds where foot-step never trod,   10
Find unadmir'd, unnotic'd, there a tomb,
  And mingle silent with the grassy sod;
Ah, so the scatter'd flowers of genius rise;
  These bloom to charm—that, hid—neglected dies.
                              (wr. 1803; pub. 1808)

Sonnet to the Clouds

O ye who ride upon the wand'ring gale,
  And silently, yet swiftly pass away—
  I love to view you, when the glimmering ray
Of early morning tints your forms so pale,
Or when meek twilight gleams above the steep,
  As in fantastic changeful shapes ye fly
  Far in the west,—when smiles the summer sky,
Or when rough wintry winds with fury sweep
Along the hill your darkly-frowning forms,
10   All desolate and gloomy as my heart.
  Ah! could I but from this sad earth depart
And wander careless as the roving storms
Amidst your shadowy scenes—borne by the wind,
Far I would fly, and leave my woes behind!

                        (wr. 1804; pub. 1808)

Written during a Storm of Wind

Cease your desolating sound,
  O ye furious winds! forbear—
Every gust that swells around
  Chills my shuddering heart with fear.

Ah! the thoughtless time is past
  When I mark'd the rapid flight
Of each wildly rushing blast,
  With romantic gay delight.

When in sportive frolic dance,
10   With the gale I skimm'd the plain,
Or would breathlessly advance,
  Laughing at its fury vain.

Often too, in graver mood,
   I have heard the tempest roll,
While a joy sublimely rude
   Has possess'd and charm'd my soul.

But I cannot listen now
   To the wild, the dreadful sound;
Sad I see the forest bow,
   Mournful mark its groans around.   20

Fanciful I seem to hear
   Ocean roaring in the storm:
And behold the bark appear,
   Which contains a Brother's form.

Hope had pictur'd scenes of joy
   When he reach'd his native shore—
Should the tempest these destroy!
   —Winds, in pity blow no more.
           (wr. 1807; pub. 1808)

Catherine Maria Fanshawe

(1765–1834)

Catherine Maria Fanshawe grew up in genteel and cultured circumstances in and around London. She was born in Shabden, in Chipstead, Surrey, on 6 July 1765, to Penelope Dredge of Reading and John Fanshawe, a Surrey squire employed by George III.[1] Her two brothers died young, leaving the poet and her two sisters, Penelope and Elizabeth Christiana, to inherit the family fortune. Catherine Maria traveled to Italy many times in pursuit of health and suffered from some sort of physical disability.

All three sisters were artists, part of a small literary, artistic, and scientific coterie, and lived together throughout their lives at 15 Berkeley Square, London, and at Midhurst House, Richmond. Some of their contemporaries found their manners too "cold and formal";[2] but Mary Russell Mitford found Catherine Maria "dazzling," while John Gibson Lockhart, Scott's biographer, said she was "a woman of rare wit and genius, in whose society Scott greatly delighted."[3] Fanshawe corresponded with Anne Grant of Laggan, was a friend of Mary Berry (who laid "half her formality . . . upon the family to which she belongs")[4] and of Joanna Baillie, who published several of her poems in the collection she edited in 1823.

Fanshawe's drawings and etchings were admired for their variety as well as for their virtuosity.[5] She was, moreover, an accomplished letter writer and reader of Shakespeare as well as a poet. Mitford ranked her literary talent on

---

1. He was the first clerk of the board of green cloth.

2. See Mary Somerville, *Personal Recollections, from Early Life to Old Age, of Mary Somerville* (Boston, 1876), 222.

3. Mitford, *Recollections,* 158; John Gibson Lockhart, *Memoirs of the Life of Sir Walter Scott,* 5 vols. (Boston, 1901), 4:124–25.

4. Mary Berry, *Extracts of the Journals and Correspondence of Miss Berry from the Year 1783 to 1852,* ed. Lady Theresa Lewis, 3 vols. (London, 1865), 2:451.

5. Fanshawe illustrated Shakespeare's "Seven Ages of Man" in large watercolors. Her sketchbooks include English landscapes, portraits, and scenery from her Italian travels (*DNB;* Mitford, *Recollections,* 157–58).

a par with that of Scott, Wordsworth, Edgeworth, and Siddons. What distinguished Fanshawe from the others, Mitford thought, was that she abstained from being a published author, while she threw out "here and there such choice . . . bits as prove that nothing but disinclination to enter the arena debar[red] her from winning the prize."[6]

When Fanshawe is remembered today, it is usually in a footnote, for a popular poem widely, though mistakenly, attributed to Lord Byron—"A Riddle," retitled in many sources "Enigma" or "Riddle on the Letter H."[7] Inspired by a conversation on the misuse of the letter *H* at a houseparty at Deepdene, Surrey, Fanshawe composed the poem late one night and read it to the assembled guests at breakfast the next morning. James Smith altered the first line to read " 'Twas whispered in heaven, 'twas muttered in hell."[8]

Fanshawe was accomplished enough at parody to fool the experts. In his note to "Fragment in Imitation of Wordsworth," William Harness records that "when the . . . lines were read to a distinguished friend and admirer of Wordsworth, she thought them beautiful, and wondered he had never shown them to her."[9] Many of Fanshawe's occasional verses have perished. But their character—their spontaneity and wit—survive in some fragments, such as Fanshawe's skillful parody of Pope's "Here shall the spring its earliest sweets bestow, / Here the first roses of the year shall blow." On the occasion of the first opening of Regent's Park in London, Fanshawe altered a word in one line and a letter in the next to observe, "Here shall the spring its earliest coughs bestow, / Here the first noses of the year shall blow."

Fanshawe died at Putney Heath on 17 April 1834, after a long and painful illness. The Reverend William Harness, to whom she left her etchings and literary manuscripts, had the *Memorials of Miss C. W. Fanshawe* printed in 1865 for private circulation; it contained many of her poems, her description of a dinner party at the home of Sir Humphrey Davy, attended by Lord Byron and

---

6. Mitford, *Recollections*, 157–58.

7. The misattribution occurs especially in the album books and in pirated editions of Byron's works. See, e.g., *The Miscellaneous Poems of Lord Byron, Consisting of Hours of Idleness, English Bards, Curse of Minerva, &c. &c.* (London, 1828); see also Samuel C. Chew, *Byron in England: His Fame and After-Fame* (London, 1924), 183. I am grateful to William St. Clair for showing me many examples of this interesting misattribution in his collection of album books and Byron pirates.

8. The popular consciousness so insisted on the alteration that it is not uncommon to find, as in my copy of Baillie's *Collection of Poems, Chiefly Manuscript* (1823), that a former owner has drawn through Fanshawe's first line to "correct" it to Smith's version. The *DNB* refers to Smith's line as the "accepted" reading.

9. *The Literary Remains of Catherine Maria Fanshawe, with Notes by the Late Reverend William Harness* (London, 1876), 71.

Germaine de Staël, and nine photographs of Fanshawe's etchings. Pickering reissued the book in 1876, after Harness's death, in an edition of 250, without the illustrations. How it was that Fanshawe, who, as Mitford believed, had "powers to command the most brilliant literary success," could have been content to stay on the sidelines, offering "a warm and unenvying sympathy in the success of others,"[10] remains, like her most famous poem, an enigma.

MAJOR WORKS: *Memorials of Miss C. W. Fanshawe,* ed. W. Harness (n.p., [1865]); *The Literary Remains of Catherine Maria Fanshawe, with Notes by the Late Reverend William Harness* (London, 1876).

TEXTS USED: Text of "A Riddle" from *A Collection of Poems, Chiefly Manuscript, from Living Authors,* ed. Joanna Baillie (London, 1823). Text of "Fragment in Imitation of Wordsworth" from *The Literary Remains of Catherine Maria Fanshawe.*

A Riddle

'Twas in heaven pronounced, and 'twas muttered in hell,
And echo caught faintly the sound as it fell:
On the confines of earth 'twas permitted to rest,
And the depths of the ocean its presence confest;
'Twill be found in the sphere when 'tis riven asunder,
Be seen in the lightning, and heard in the thunder.
'Twas allotted to man with his earliest breath,
Attends at his birth, and awaits him in death,
Presides o'er his happiness, honor, and health,
Is the prop of his house, and the end of his wealth.
In the heaps of the miser 'tis hoarded with care,
But is sure to be lost on his prodigal heir.
It begins every hope, every wish it must bound,
With the husbandman toils, and with monarchy is crown'd.
Without it the soldier, the seaman may roam,
But wo to the wretch who expels it from home!
In the whispers of conscience its voice will be found,
Nor e'en in the whirlwind of passion be drown'd.

10

10. Mitford, *Recollections,* 158.

'Twill not soften the heart; but though deaf be the ear,
It will make it acutely and instantly hear.   20
Yet in shade let it rest like a delicate flower,
Ah breathe on it softly—it dies in an hour.

(1823)

Fragment in Imitation of Wordsworth

There is a river clear and fair,
   'Tis neither broad nor narrow;
It winds a little here and there—
It winds about like any hare;
And then it takes as straight a course
As on the turnpike road a horse,
   Or through the air an arrow.

The trees that grow upon the shore,
Have grown a hundred years or more;
   So long there is no knowing.   10
Old Daniel Dobson does not know
When first those trees began to grow;
But still they grew, and grew, and grew,
As if they'd nothing else to do,
   But ever to be growing.

The impulses of air and sky
Have reared their stately stems so high,
   And clothed their boughs with green;
Their leaves the dews of evening quaff,—
   And when the wind blows loud and keen,   20
I've seen the jolly timbers laugh,
   And shake their sides with merry glee—
   Wagging their heads in mockery.

Fix'd are their feet in solid earth,
   Where winds can never blow;
But visitings of deeper birth
   Have reached their roots below.

For they have gained the river's brink,
And of the living waters drink.

30 There's little Will, a five years' child—
  He is my youngest boy;
To look on eyes so fair and wild,
  It is a very joy:—
He hath conversed with sun and shower,
And dwelt with every idle flower,
  As fresh and gay as them.
He loiters with the briar rose,—
The blue belles are his play-fellows,
  That dance upon their slender stem.

40 And I have said, my little Will,
Why should not he continue still
  A thing of Nature's rearing?
A thing beyond the world's control—
A living vegetable soul,—
  No human sorrow fearing.

It were a blessed sight to see
That child become a willow tree,
  His brother trees among.
He'd be four time[s] as tall as me,
50 And live three times as long.

      (wr. bef. 1834; pub. 1876)

Anne Grant

(Mrs. Grant of Laggan)
(1755–1838)

The poet and nonfiction writer who would do more than any other writer, with the exception of Walter Scott, to dispel the general prejudice against the Scottish Highlanders was born Anne Macvicar on 21 February 1755 in Glasgow. Her mother was a descendant of an ancient family, the Stewarts of Invernahayle, and her father, Duncan Macvicar, was an officer in a Highland regiment. In 1757 Anne's father left to join his company in America, where the French and Indian War was then raging. The next year Anne crossed the Atlantic with her mother, and the two settled temporarily in Albany, New York, before taking the perilous journey up the Mohawk River in 1760 to Oswego to join her father, who fought at Ticonderoga. Her mother taught her to read, and she studied the Old Testament as a storybook. Because of his religious beliefs her father discouraged literary pursuits, and her mother insisted that she occupy her time with needlework. In 1762, peace having been declared between Britain and France, her father's regiment returned to Albany. There Anne discovered Milton's *Paradise Lost* and spent two winters with the distinguished Catalina Schuyler, who introduced her to the works of Shakespeare, Pope, Addison, and others. Later she recalled, "Whatever culture my mind has received I owe to her."[1] In 1765 her father retired from the army on half-pay, and the British government granted him and his fellow officers two thousand acres apiece. Captain Macvicar took his own allotment in Vermont and bought cheaply the surrounding plots of other officers returning to England, planning to settle with his family on the resulting large estate. But, dogged by ill-health, in 1768 he returned with his family to Scotland. Fourteen-year-old Anne arrived in Glasgow without any of the fashionable feminine "accomplishments" but with a love and understanding of nature, a familiarity with books, and extraordinary travel experience. The

1. Anne Grant, *Letters from the Mountains,* 2 vols., 6th ed. (London, 1845), 1:110.

estate in Vermont was subsequently confiscated during the American Revolution, thus ending what Anne Grant later facetiously termed "The History of an Heiress."

In 1773 the family moved to Fort Augustus, in Inverness, on the banks of Loch Ness, where Anne's father had been made barrack master. In May of 1779 she married the Reverend James Grant, former chaplain at the fort, who had become pastor to the parish of Laggan, a remote village fifty miles from both Perth and Inverness. Superintendence of their farm, which made them self-sustaining, as well as care of the twelve children eventually born to the couple all devolved upon her. Highlanders were not accepting of outsiders, so Anne Grant won her neighbors over by adopting Highland customs, learning the native Gaelic, and teaching it to her children in their infancy. She enjoyed her surroundings and the poetic beauty of the Gaelic language so much that she began translating Gaelic verse. While she was generally happy in Laggan, the years there were saddened by the deaths of four of her children.

In 1801 Anne's husband died, and she found that she had been left in debt with eight children to support and only a small pension due to her as the widow of a military chaplain. Friends decided to gather the poems she had written for their entertainment and publish them by subscription. With the active patronage of the duchess of Gordon, *Poems on Various Subjects* (1803) garnered three thousand subscribers. Among the thirty-two poems were translations of Gaelic songs, including Grant's words to "Oh Where, Tell Me Where, Is Your Highland Laddie Gone?" which her first stanza answers, "He's gone with streaming banners, where noble deeds are done, / And my sad heart will tremble, till he come safely home." The *New Annual Register* praised the book for "evincing a very creditable portion of poetic animation, a refined taste, and a feeling heart."[2] The *Anti-Jacobin Review* criticized her sometimes unhappy word choice, faulty grammar, and the lack of unity of the central work, "The Highlanders," but also noted that "in liveliness of fancy, and in richness of imagery, as well as of expression [the poems] frequently abound. They display, too, very considerable stores of acquired knowledge, with great acuteness of observation."[3] The *Monthly Magazine* contended that "there is a strain of simplicity and unaffected feeling in these poems which will give them a permanent interest."[4]

Grant's daughter Mary's illness in 1802 took her to Bristol Hotwells, and in June 1803 she reluctantly left Laggan for Woodend, near Stirling. When her son Duncan received a commission in the East India Company, she was

2. 24 (1803): 328.
3. 16 (October 1803): 116–117.
4. Suppl., 16 (15 January 1804): 632.

faced with how to raise money to outfit him. Her friends suggested that she publish a selection of her letters. Accordingly, in January 1805 she went to London, where she met Joanna Baillie and Catherine Maria Fanshawe and took her manuscript to Longman and Rees. Within a few days, *Letters from the Mountains* was accepted; though personal material had been edited out, with its lively descriptions of rural Scottish scenery, legends, and manners, the book became the rage in the summer of 1806, making her a celebrity and bringing her a tidy profit. The second edition paid her an additional three hundred pounds. But she was not allowed for long to enjoy her triumph: in April 1807 her daughter Charlotte died at the age of seventeen, and in July of that same year her twenty-year-old daughter Catherine died.

Perhaps to distract herself, Grant set down her recollections of her early mentor, Catalina Schuyler, and of life in Albany, New York, before the Revolution. Published in 1808 as *Memoirs of an American Lady,* the book sold well in both Britain and America, though it did not enjoy the same vogue in Britain as *Letters from the Mountains.* Also in 1808 she published *The Highlanders, and Other Poems,* whose title poem sought to detail for a largely ignorant English reading public the Scottish highland way of life. The *New Annual Register* said, "There is much smoothness and elegance, and some beautiful and appropriate descriptions in these poems; but it is to her prose, and not to her poetry, that this lady must chiefly look for success."[5] The *Edinburgh Review* deemed her poetry "really not very good" and called "The Highlanders" "heavy and uninteresting."[6] But the *Eclectic Review* observed of Grant that "her imagination is always animated and not infrequently sublime; and her sentiments alternate between a gaiety which will exhilarate, and a pensiveness which will soften, every reader of sensibility."[7]

In the spring of 1809 Grant met Walter Scott in Edinburgh, where she moved with her family in March 1810 and started a small school. Her promotion of the Highlands and of the Gaelic language made her a celebrity in the Scottish literary capital; she was known, too, for her wit and conversation, so that despite her Tory leanings, her home became a gathering place for writers of all political persuasions, including Frances Jeffrey, John Wilson (Christopher North), Henry Mackenzie, Felicia Hemans, Robert Southey, Joanna Baillie, Thomas Campbell, Walter Scott, George Ticknor, James Hogg, and Robert Owen. Before the secret was well known, many suspected Grant of being the author of the Waverley novels.

Capitalizing on the interest in Scottish rural life, Grant published in 1811

5. 29 (1808): 406.
6. 18 (August 1811): 481.
7. 4 (November 1808): 1034.

her *Essays on the Superstition of the Highlands of Scotland, with Translations from the Gaelic,* and in 1814 she published a long poem, *Eighteen Hundred and Thirteen,* which the *Universal Magazine* panned with the observation, "The events of the last year deserved to be recorded in language that may never perish; but we are afraid Mrs. Grant's well meant effort will hardly survive the present year."[8] The *British Critic* was appreciative, however, noting, "There is easy and graceful flow throughout the whole, and in many parts a neatness and point, which remind us strongly of Pope.[9] In 1821 the Highland Society of London awarded her their gold medal for the best "Essay on the Past and Present State of the Highlands of Scotland." Grant was permanently disabled by a fall in 1820, but in 1825 Sir Walter Scott, Francis Jeffrey, Henry Mackenzie, and others successfully petitioned King George IV to give her a small pension on the civil establishment of Scotland. Her later life was darkened by the successive deaths of all of her remaining children except her youngest son, John-Peter Grant, who in 1844 published her autobiography and letters— an important record of literary life and society in Edinburgh. She died of influenza on 7 November 1838 at the age of eighty-four and was buried in the New Cemetery of Edinburgh's St. Cuthbert's Church. Walter Scott had said of her, "Her literary works although composed amidst misfortune and privation, are written at once with simplicity and force, and uniformly bear the stamp of a virtuous and courageous mind."[10]

MAJOR WORKS: *Poems on Various Subjects* (Edinburgh, London, Glasgow, Perth, Aberdeen, Elgin, and Inverness, 1803); *Letters from the Mountains, being a Selection from the Author's Correspondence with her Intimate Friends from 1773 to 1804,* 3 vols. (London, 1806); *The Highlanders, and Other Poems* (London, 1808); *Memoirs of an American Lady, with Sketches of Manners and Scenery in America as They Existed Previous to the Revolution* (London, 1808); *Essays on the Superstitions of the Highlanders of Scotland* (London, 1811); *Eighteen Hundred and Thirteen: A Poem, in Two Parts* (Edinburgh and London, 1814); *Memoir and Correspondence of Mrs. Grant of Laggan,* ed. J. P. Grant, 3 vols. (London, 1844).

TEXT USED: Text from *Poems on Various Subjects.*

8. 1 (August 1814): 127.

9. N.s., 2 (September 1814): 324–26.

10. Quoted in James Grant Wilson, *The Poets and Poetry of Scotland; from the Earliest to the Present Time,* 2 vols. (London, 1876), 1:340.

Postscript

Jean, fetch that heap of tangled yarn,
And bring those stockings here to darn,
And get from Anne the dairy keys,
That I may go and count my cheese:
To every useful occupation,
Befitting of my place and station,
I'll henceforth dedicate my time,
And if again I write in rhyme,
'Twill be a shrewd severe lampoon
On country wives who fly to town,   10
And leave their dairy and relations,
To curl their hair, and follow fashions:
Or else an acrimonious satire
On matrons, who in spite of Nature,
With common useful duties quarrel,
To plant in vain the barren laurel!

(1803)

Elizabeth Hands
(fl. 1789)

Nothing is known about the childhood of Elizabeth Hands, not even her surname before her marriage to a blacksmith near Rugby by 1785. She had been a domestic servant in the household of the Huddesfords of Allesley, near Coventry, but whether she continued in service after her marriage is unclear. She had at least one daughter.

Jopson's Coventry Mercury published Hands's poems under the pseudonym Daphne. These poems impressed Thomas James, the headmaster at Rugby School, and by 1788 masters at the school were seeking subscribers for her book. *The Death of Amnon. A Poem. With an Appendix: Containing Pastorals, and other Poetical Pieces* appeared in Coventry, printed for the author, in 1789. The volume contains a 28-page introduction and 127 pages of poems; the list of more than a thousand subscribers includes Anna Seward, Thomas Warton, and Edmund Burke.

In the dedication, to the aristocratic dramatist Bertie Greatherd (1759–1826), Hands describes herself as "born in obscurity, and never emerging beyond the lower stations in life." Internal evidence in the poems suggests that she had read Pope, Young, Swift, Prior, Milton, Shakespeare, and Butler. The title poem is an ambitious epic in five cantos written in blank verse. It retells the Old Testament story from 2 Samuel of the incestuous rape of Tamar, daughter of King David, by her brother Amnon and the revenge murder of Amnon by his brother Absalom. Shorter poems include mock heroic verse, counter-georgics, pastorals, anti-pastorals, parody, self-parody, and satire, in which Hands anticipates the scornful reception of her work by "polite" society. Some of the lyrics feature a young woman named Daphne, Hands's earlier pseudonyn, suggesting some personal identification with her character's feelings when she is rejected by a lover, experiences romantic desire, is courted, and eventually marries.

Hands's poetry mocks English literary tradition and calls into question social stratification. Other subjects include female friendship, childbirth, and equality between men and women. Her poems are written in colloquial language, some irreverently comic, and can be deceptively simple. She portrays her working-class figures with dignity and questions many of the standard middle- and upper-class conceptions of the laboring class. Her working poor are independent and capable of finding conjugal happiness without the blessing of institutionalized religion. They also harbor resentments against class oppression. Hands's poetry expresses a nostalgia for simple village life, which was rapidly disappearing. And some of her work contains an absurdist element. But there are self-contradictions as well. For example, as Donna Landry points out, "her emphasis on sexual morality and respectability can be seen to be at odds with her criticisms of increasingly formalized, legally regulated, and property-conscious marriages among the rural poor." Landry describes Hands as an "agile ventriloquist of the masculine canon" but notes that she altered the traditional pastoral by replacing the shepherd with a central dominating female figure who could speak her mind. "Hands's rustic nymphs have the upper hand with their lovers. . . . Female, not male, desire is the motor of these pastorals. These shepherdesses are usually so pleased with themselves that they can desire, mourn, or dismiss their suitors with equal spirit. Hands's pastorals testify to her skill in producing comic pleasure and irreverent reversals of generic expectation."[1]

As Hands anticipated, critical reception of her volume was mixed. Apparently oblivious to the irony, the *Monthly Review* quoted as its own response to her book the satirical last nineteen lines of Hands's "A Poem, on the Supposition of the Book Having Been Published and Read," with its "genteel" dismissal of Hands's work delivered by the pompous rector, who is then unceremoniously interrupted. The review closes with the observation, "Whatever may be thought of the *character* of this poetry, we cannot but form the most favourable conclusions with respect to *that* of the writer, — forming, as we do, our judgment from the uncommonly numerous list of subscribers: among whom are many names of persons of rank, and consideration. There could be no motive for extraordinary patronage, but a benevolent regard to merit — of some kind."[2]

The *Analytical Review* was equally condescending but more harsh: "As there is a respectable number of subscribers prefixed to this volume, we may be excused, if we do not lend a hand to support an humble muse, whose chief merit is a *desire* to please; — but, if we cannot praise the attempt of a servant-maid of low degree, to catch a poetical wreath, even after making due

1. See Landry, *Muses of Resistance*, 193, 197, 198.
2. N.s., 3 (1790): 345–46.

allowance for her situation, we will let her sing-song die in peace."[3] The
Gentleman's Magazine, however, praised "The Death of Amnon" and noted,
"If here and there an unequal line has insinuated itself into the five cantos of
this heroic poem . . . we must pardon the inexperienced Muse, and consider
it as more than compensated by the sentiments conveyed in the whole."[4]
Modern readers, however, may find the shorter lyrics more appealing.

What became of Hands after the publication of this one book of verse—
how she lived, whether she wrote more poetry, and when she died—remains
a mystery.

MAJOR WORK: The Death of Amnon. A Poem. With an Appendix: Containing Pastorals,
and Other Poetical Pieces (Coventry, 1789).

TEXTS USED: All texts from The Death of Amnon. A Poem.

A Poem, on the Supposition of an Advertisement Appearing in a Morning Paper, of the Publication of a Volume of Poems, by a Servant Maid

> The tea-kettle bubbled, the tea things were set,
> The candles were lighted, the ladies were met;
> The how d'ye's were over, and entering bustle,
> The company seated, and silks ceas'd to rustle:
> The great Mrs. Consequence open'd her fan;
> And thus the discourse in an instant began:
> (All affected reserve, and formality scorning,)
> I suppose you all saw in the paper this morning,
> A Volume of Poems advertis'd—'tis said
> They're produc'd by the pen of a poor Servant Maid.
> A servant write verses! says Madame Du Bloom;
> Pray what is the subject?—a Mop, or a Broom?
> He, he, he,—says Miss Flounce; I suppose we shall see
> An Ode on a Dishclout—what else can it be?
> Says Miss Coquettilla, what ladies so tart?

10

3. 6 (1790): 96.
4. 60, pt. 1 (1790): 540.

Perhaps Tom the Footman has fired her heart;
And she'll tell us how charming he looks in new clothes,
And how nimble his hand moves in brushing the shoes;
Or how the last time that he went to May-Fair,
He bought her some sweethearts of ginger-bread ware.   20
For my part I think, says old lady Marr-joy,
A servant might find herself other employ:
Was she mine I'd employ her as long as 'twas light,
And send her to bed without candle at night.
Why so? says Miss Rhymer, displeas'd; I protest
'Tis pity a genius should be so deprest!
What ideas can such low-bred creatures conceive,
Says Mrs. Noworthy, and laught in her sleeve.
Says old Miss Prudella, if servants can tell
How to write to their mothers, to say they are well,   30
And read of a Sunday the Duty of Man;
Which is more I believe than one half of them can;
I think 'tis much *properer* they should rest there,
Than be reaching at things so much out of their sphere.
Says old Mrs. Candour, I've now got a maid
That's the plague of my life—a young gossipping jade;
There's no end of the people that after her come,
And whenever I'm out, she is never at home;
I'd rather ten times she would sit down and write,
Than gossip all over the town ev'ry night.   40
Some whimsical trollop most like, says Miss Prim,
Has been scribbling of nonsense, just out of a whim,
And conscious it neither is witty or pretty,
Conceals her true name, and ascribes it to Betty.
I once had a servant myself, says Miss Pines,
That wrote on a Wedding, some very good lines:
Says Mrs. Domestic, and when they were done,
I can't see for my part, what use they were *on;*
Had she wrote a receipt, to've instructed you how
To warm a cold breast of veal, like a ragou,   50
Or to make a cowslip wine, that would pass for Champaign;
It might have been useful, again and again.
On the sofa was old lady Pedigree plac'd,
She own'd that for poetry she had no taste,
That the study of heraldry was more in fashion,

And boasted she knew all the crests in the nation.
Says Mrs. Routella,—Tom, take out the urn,
And stir up the fire, you see it don't burn.
The tea things remov'd, and the tea-table gone,
60   The card-tables brought, and the cards laid thereon,
The ladies ambitious for each other's crown,
Like courtiers contending for honours sat down.

(1789)

A Poem, on the Supposition of the Book Having Been Published and Read

The dinner was over, the table-cloth gone,
The bottles of wine and the glasses brought on,
The gentlemen fill'd up the sparkling glasses,
To drink to their king, to their country and lasses:
The ladies a glass or two only required,
To th'drawing-room then in due order retir'd;
The gentlemen likewise that chose to drink tea;
And, after discussing the news of the day,
What wife was suspected, what daughter elop'd,
10   What thief was detected, what 'twas to be hop'd,
The rascals would all be convicted, and rop'd;
What chambermaid kiss'd when her lady was out;
Who won, and who lost, the last night at the rout;
What lord gone to France, and what tradesman unpaid,
And who and who danc'd at the last masquerade;
What banker stopt payment with evil intention,
And twenty more things much too tedious to mention.
Miss Rhymer says, Mrs. Routella, ma'am, pray
Have you seen the new book (that we talk'd of that day,
20   At your house you remember) of Poems, 'twas said
Produc'd by the pen of a poor Servant Maid?
The company silent, the answer expected;
Says Mrs. Routella, when she'd recollected;
Why, ma'am, I have bought it for Charlotte; the child
Is so fond of a book, I'm afraid it is spoil'd:

I thought to have read it myself, but forgat it;
In short, I have never had time to look at it.
Perhaps I may look it o'er some other day;
Is there any thing in it worth reading, I pray?
For your nice attention, there's nothing can 'scape.   30
She answer'd,—There's one piece, whose subject's a Rape.
A Rape! interrupted the Captain Bonair,
A delicate theme for a female I swear;
Then smerk'd at the ladies, they simper'd all round,
Touch'd their lips with their fans,—Mrs. Consequence frown'd.
The simper subsided, for she with her nods,
Awes these lower assemblies, as Jove awes the gods.
She smil'd on Miss Rhymer, and bad her proceed—
Says she, there are various subjects indeed:
With some little pleasure I read all the rest,   40
But the Murder of Amnon's the longest and best.
Of Amnon, of Amnon, Miss Rhymer, who's he?
His name, says Miss Gaiety's quite new to me:—
'Tis a Scripture tale, ma'am,—he's the son of King David,
Says a Reverend old Rector: quoth madam, I have it;
A Scripture tale?—ay—I remember it—true;
Pray is it i' th'old Testament or the new?
If I thought I could readily find it, I'd borrow
My house-keeper's Bible, and read it to-morrow.
'Tis in Samuel, ma'am, says the Rector:—Miss Gaiety   50
Bow'd, and the Reverend blush'd for the laity.
You've read it, I find, says Miss Harriot Anderson,
Pray, sir, is it any thing like Sir Charles Grandison?
How you talk, says Miss Belle, how should such a girl write
A novel, or any thing else that's polite?
You'll know better in time, Miss:—She was but fifteen:
Her mama was confus'd—with a little chagrin,
Says,—Where's your attention, child? did not you hear
Miss Rhymer say, that it was poems, my dear?

41 Amnon's] In the Bible, Amnon was the eldest son of David and Ahinoam and half-brother of Absalom. Amnon's rape of Tamar, daughter of David and Maacah and full sister of Absalom, was avenged by Absalom's murder of Amnon. This murder resulted in a rift between David and Absalom. Hands's poem appeared in a book entitled *The Death of Amnon.*

53 Sir Charles Grandison] Title and the central character of an epistolary novel by Samuel Richardson. Sir Charles is a paragon of all virtues.

60   Says Sir Timothy Turtle, my daughters ne'er look
           In anything else but a cookery book:
           The properest study for women design'd;
           Says Mrs. Domestic, I'm quite of your mind.
           Your haricoes, ma'am, are the best I e'er eat,
           Says the Knight, may I venture to beg a receipt.
           'Tis much at your service, says madam, and bow'd,
           Then flutter'd her fan, of the compliment proud.
           Says Lady Jane Rational, the bill of fare
           Is th'utmost extent of my cookery care:
70   Most servants can cook for the palate I find,
           But very few of them can cook for the mind.
           Who, says Lady Pedigree, can this girl be;
           Perhaps she's descended of some family:—
           Of family, doubtless, says Captain Bonair,
           She's descended from Adam, I'd venture to swear.
           Her Ladyship drew herself up in her chair,
           And twitching her fan-sticks, affected a sneer.
           I know something of her, says Mrs. Devoir,
           She liv'd with my friend, Jacky Faddle, Esq.
80   'Tis sometime ago though; her mistress said then,
           The girl was excessively fond of a pen;
           I saw her, but never convers'd with her—*though*
           One can't make acquaintance with servants, you know.
           'Tis pity the girl was not bred in high life,
           Says Mr. Fribbello;—yes,—then, says his wife,
           She doubtless might have wrote something worth notice:
           'Tis pity, says one,—says another, and so 'tis.
           O law! says young Seagram, I've seen the book, now
           I remember, there's something about a mad cow.
90   A mad cow!—ha, ha, ha, ha, return'd half the room;
           What can y'expect better, says Madam Du Bloom?
           They look at each other,—a general pause—
           And Miss Coquettella adjusted her gauze.
           The Rector reclin'd himself back in his chair,
           And open'd his snuff-box with indolent air;
           This book, says he, (snift, snift) has in the beginning,
           (The ladies give audience to hear his opinion)

---

64 haricoes] Ragout (originally of mutton) or a green bean or kidney bean.

Some pieces, I think, that are pretty correct;
A stile elevated you cannot expect:
To some of her equals they may be a treasure,   100
And country lasses may read 'em with pleasure.
That Amnon, you can't call it poetry neither,
There's no flights of fancy, or imagery either;
You may stile it prosaic, blank-verse at the best;
Some pointed reflections, indeed are exprest;
The narrative lines are exceedingly poor:
Her Jonadab in a ——— the drawing room door
Was open'd, the gentlemen came from below,
And gave the discourse a definitive blow.

(1789)

Written, Originally Extempore, on Seeing a Mad Heifer Run through the Village Where the Author Lives

When summer smil'd, and birds on ev'ry spray,
In joyous warblings tun'd their vocal lay,
Nature on all sides shew'd a lovely scene,
And people's minds were, like the air, serene;
Sudden from th'herd we saw an heifer stray,
And to our peaceful village bend her way.
She spurns the ground with madness as she flies,
And clouds of dust, like autumn mists, arise;
Then bellows loud: the villagers alarm'd,
Come rushing forth, with various weapons arm'd: 10
Some run with pieces of old broken rakes,
And some from hedges pluck the rotten stakes;
Here one in haste, with hand-staff of his flail,
And there another comes with half a rail:
Whips, without lashes, sturdy plough-boys bring,
While clods of dirt and pebbles others fling:
Voices tumultuous rend the listening ear;

107 Jonadab] Son of Shimeah, David's brother, and cousin of Amnon. He provided Amnon with the plan that led to Tamar's rape.

Stop her—one cries; another—turn her there:
But furiously she rushes by them all,
20   And some huzza, and some to cursing fall:
A mother snatch'd her infant off the road,
Close to the spot of ground where next she trod;
Camilla walking, trembled and turn'd pale;
See o'er her gentle heart what fears prevail!
At last the beast, unable to withstand
Such force united, leapt into a pond:
The water quickly cool'd her madden'd rage;
No more she'll fright our village, I presage.

(1789)

A Song

Ye swains cease to flatter, our hearts to obtain,
If your persons plead not, what your tongues say is vain;
Though fickle you call us, believe me you're wrong,
We're fixt as a rock, as a rock too are strong.

Though sometimes, when suddenly struck with your charms,
We melt into softness, and sink in your arms,
Or breathe a soft sigh, when you from us depart;
That shakes not the purpose that's firm in the heart.

Too vainly ye boast we are easily won;
10   If on you, as on all, we should smile like the sun,
You laugh in your sleeves, when you from us retire,
And think that we love, when we only admire.

We are not so easily led by the nose,
Though with coxcombs we chatter, and flirt with the beaux;
Yet seldom or never our hearts they command,
Though sometimes through pity we give them our hand.

23 Camilla] In Greek legend, a virgin warrior queen of the Volscian. In the *Aeneid* she is
killed by the Trojans.

A tony, a coxcomb, a beau, or a clown,
Well season'd with money, may sometimes go down;
But these in our hearts we can never revere;
The worthy man only can hold a place there.   20

(1789)

On a Wedding

Hark! hark! how the bells ring, how happy the day,
   Now Thirsis makes Daphne his bride;
See cheerful birds chirping on ev'ry green spray,
   And summer shines forth in its pride.

The lads and the lasses, so jocund and gay,
   Their happiness hail with a song;
And Thirsis enchantingly pipes to their lay,
   Inspiring with mirth all the throng.

The bride and the bride-groom then join in the dance
   And smiling trip nimbly around;   10
The sprightly gay bride's-maids as nimbly advance,
   And answer their smiles with a bound.

With all marriage articles pen'd on the heart,
   The parties so sweetly agreed;
They needed no lawyer, with quibbling art,
   Or parchment to draw up a deed.

For Love, the first blessing of blessings below,
   That Heaven to mortals can give,
Was all the kind shepherdess had to bestow,
   And all that she wish'd to receive.   20

(1789)

17 tony] Slang term for a fool or simpleton.
  2 Thirsis] A conventional name in pastoral poetry, found in Virgil's seventh eclogue, Milton's
L'Allegro, and elsewhere.
  2 Daphne] In Greek mythology, Daphne was beloved by Apollo.

The Widower's Courtship

Roger a doleful widower,
    Full eighteen weeks had been,
When he, to meet the milk-maid Nell,
    Came smiling o'er the green.

Blithe as a lad of seventeen,
    He thus accosted Nell;
Give me your pail, I'll carry it
    For you, if you think well.

Says Nell, indeed my milking-pail
10   You shall not touch, I vow;
I've carried it myself before,
    And I can carry it now.

So side by side they walk'd a-while,
    Then he at last did say;
My inclination is to come
    And see you, if I may.

Nell understood his meaning well,
    And briskly answer'd she;
You may see me at any time,
20   If you look where I be.

Says he, but hear me yet a-while,
    I've something more to tell;
I gladly wou'd a sweetheart be
    Unto you, Mistress Nell.

A sweetheart I don't want, says Nell,
    Kind Sir, and if you do,
Another you may seek, for I
    Am not the lass for you.

When she had made him this reply,
   He'd nothing more to say   30
But—Nelly, a good night to you,
   And homeward went his way.

(1789)

Mary Hays

(1760–1843)

~~~~~~

Friend and disciple of Mary Wollstonecraft and William Godwin, Mary Hays
was born in Southwark, London, into a family of middle-class radical dis-
senters. Soon after her father's death in 1777, Hays fell in love with her
neighbor and mentor, John Eccles, and he with her; but in 1780, after over-
coming his family's objections and shortly before they were to be married,
he died of a fever.[1] To assuage her grief, she turned to intensive reading of
novels, poetry, history, philosophy, and theology.

In 1788 Hays heard a sermon given by the rational dissenter Robert Robinson and began a correspondence that eventually led to his becoming her close
friend and adviser; he not only gave her recommendations for reading but
drew her out of her unhappy isolation and into a nonconformist circle that
included his disciples, George Dyer and William Frend. Although she had
published poetry and some fiction, she attracted considerable attention with
her first book, *Cursory Remarks on an Enquiry into the Expediency and Propriety
of Public or Social Worship* (1792), a response to Gilbert Wakefield's attack on
dissenting public worship and a defense of nonconformist practices, which
she published under the pseudonym Eusebia just after Robinson's death.

Hays had written but not yet published her *Appeal to the Men of Great Britain in Behalf of Women* when she read Mary Wollstonecraft's *Vindication of the
Rights of Woman* (1792). She wrote appreciatively to Wollstonecraft, and the
two met at the home of the radical publisher Joseph Johnson. Soon after a
breakfast together, Hays wrote, "This lady appears to me to possess the sort
of genius which Lavater calls the one to ten million. Her conversation, like
her writings, is brilliant, forcible, instructive and entertaining. She is the
true disciple of her own system, and commands at once fear and reverence,
admiration and esteem."[2] At about this time, Hays became acquainted with

1. Her love letters were published in London in 1925 by her great-great-niece A. F. Wedd
as *The Love-Letters of Mary Hays (1779–1780)*.
2. Ibid., 5.

other members of Joseph Johnson's circle of artists, philosophers, and writers, including Thomas Payne, William Blake, William Godwin, and Thomas Holcroft.

In 1793, having benefited from Wollstonecraft's suggestions, Hays published *Letters and Essays, Moral and Miscellaneous,* discussing materialism, Unitarianism, republicanism, and feminism. The *English Review* savaged it. Even so, in 1795 Hays decided to make writing her career and left her widowed mother's home to embark on an independent life at 30 Kirby Street, Hatton Garden. During this period she wrote for the *Critical Review,* began a study of mathematics, and penned sermons to be delivered by Dr. Disney of Essex Street Chapel. She also fell in love with William Frend, only to be painfully disappointed when he made clear that the feeling was not mutual.

William Godwin became her mentor at about this time and suggested that she try her hand at fiction. The result was *Memoirs of Emma Courtney,* published by Godwin's friend George Robinson in November 1796. An autobiographical, feminist novel, it shocked contemporary audiences with its honest portrayal of female sexual desire. Hays's friendship with Godwin and her unrequited love affair with Frend figure prominently in the plot, and because the real-life identities of the characters are only thinly disguised, the book was the subject of much talk. An epistolary novel, it quotes real letters to Hays from Godwin, called "Mr. Francis" in the story; William Frend appears as Augustus Harley. The *Monthly Review* said that Hays displayed "great intellectual powers," the *European Magazine* called it "a work of extraordinary merit, from the perusal of which much moral benefit, if properly understood, may flow," while the *Anti-Jacobin Review,* predictably, ridiculed it.[3] Hays was also writing for the *Monthly Magazine* in 1796 and 1797, at one point defending Godwin, at another joining in the debate concerning women's education, arguing for women's intellectual equality.

When Mary Wollstonecraft returned from two years on the Continent, Hays renewed their friendship and reintroduced Wollstonecraft to Godwin. The romance that then ensued between her two friends irrevocably altered both of their lives. Ironically, Hays's radical ideas were being attacked by Elizabeth Hamilton, Richard Polwhele, S. T. Coleridge, the *Anti-Jacobin,* and others at about the same time that she was urging her even more radical friends, Wollstonecraft and Godwin, to do the conventional thing and marry. Hays was with Wollstonecraft during her last illness and wrote some of the letters announcing her death.

By 1799, when Joseph Johnson brought out Hays's second novel, the *Vic-*

---

3. *Monthly Review,* n.s., 22 (1797): 449; *European Magazine* 31 (1797): 34; *Anti-Jacobin Review* 3 (May 1799): 54–58.

tim of Prejudice, written, she said, "to delineate the mischiefs that have ensued from the too great stress laid on the reputation for chastity in woman," her feminist and Jacobin stance had become intensely unpopular, and the book met with ridicule and anger. In his *Reminiscences,* Robinson describes Hays at this time as "a very zealous political and moral reformer," who professed Mary Wollstonecraft's opinions "with more zeal than discretion. This brought her into disrepute with the rigid, and her character suffered, but most undeservedly. Whatever her principles might have been, her conduct was rigidly correct."[4] Coleridge was not so kind. He told Southey, "Of Miss Hayes' intellect I do not think so highly as you, or rather, to speak sincerely, I think not *contemptuously* but certainly *despectively* thereof. Yet I think you likely in this case to have judged better than I; for to hear a thing, ugly and petticoated, ex-syllogize a God with cold-blooded precision, and attempt to run religion through the body with an icicle, an icicle from a Scotch Hog-trough! *I* do not endure it; my eye beholds phantoms, and 'nothing is but what is not.' "[5]

Despite Coleridge's opinion, Hays and Southey remained good friends for many years, and in 1814 there was a plan for Hays to live with Southey's family in Keswick. The same cannot be said for her friendship with Godwin, which cooled in 1800, possibly because of his remarriage. Later, when Charles Lloyd, who had ridiculed her in his novel *Edmund Oliver* (1798), sent the rumour abroad that Hays, in the manner of Emma Courtney, had offered herself to him, she became the talk of London and retreated from public view. Elizabeth Hamilton satirized her in *Memoirs of Modern Philosophers* (1800) as Bridgetina Botherim. Hays published *Female Biography; or, Memoirs of Illustrious and Celebrated Women of all Ages and Countries* in six volumes in 1803. This record of women's achievement in Greece, Rome, Britain, and Europe was popular in both England and America and is the work for which Hays was remembered in the latter part of the nineteenth century. By 1814 she was living in Hot Wells, Clifton, had become an admirer of Maria Edgeworth and Hannah More, and was writing evangelical tracts for the poor, such as *Family Annals, or, the Sisters* (1817). She was eighty-three when she died in 1843.

MAJOR WORKS: *Cursory Remarks on an Enquiry into the Expediency and Propriety of Public or Social Worship* (London, 1792); *Appeal to the Men of Great Britain in Behalf of Women; Letters and Essays, Moral and Miscellaneous* (London, 1793); *Memoirs of Emma Courtney,* 2 vols. (London, 1796); *The Victim of Prejudice,* 2 vols. (London, 1799); *Female Biog-*

4. *Henry Crabb Robinson on Books and Their Writers,* ed. Edith J. Morley, 3 vols. (London, 1938), 1:5.

5. *Letters of Samuel Taylor Coleridge,* ed. Ernest Hartley Coleridge, 2 vols. (Boston, 1895), 1:323.

raphy; or, *Memoirs of Illustrious and Celebrated Women of all Ages and Countries*, 6 vols. (London, 1803); *Family Annals, or, the Sisters* (London, 1817).

TEXTS USED: Text of "Invocation to the Nightingale" from *The Lady's Poetical Magazine, or, Beauties of British Poetry*, ed. [James Harrison], 4 vols. (London, 1781–82), 2:464–65. Text of "Ode to Her Bullfinch" from *Universal Magazine* 77 (December 1785): 329.

Invocation to the Nightingale

Wand'ring o'er the dewy meadow,
　　Oft at ev'ning hour I go;
Fondly courting Philomela's
　　Sympathetick plaints of woe.

Sometimes, hush'd in still attention,
　　Leaning pensive o'er a stile,
Fancy bids her sound delusive
　　Lull the yielding sense awhile.

Soft the visionary musick,
　　Rising floats upon the gale:　　　　　　　　　　10
Now it sinks in strains more languid,
　　Dying o'er the distant vale.

Starting from the dream of fancy,
　　Nought my list'ning ear invades,
Save the hum of falling waters,
　　Save the rustling aspin-shade.

"Little songstress, soothe my sorrows,
　　"Wrap my soul in softest airs;
"Such as erst, in Lydian measures,
　　"Charm'd the Grecian hero's cares.　　　　　　20

3 Philomela] In classical mythology, the nightingale.

"But, if forc'd by cruel rusticks
  "To lament thy ruin'd care;
"Breathe thy saddest strains of anguish,
  "Strains that melodize despair.

"Deeply vers'd in Sorrow's lessons,
  "Best my heart thy griefs can know;
"Pity dwells within the bosom
  "Soften'd by an equal woe.

"While thy melancholy plainings
30   "All my hapless fate renew,
"Heart-felt sighs shall load the zephyrs,
  "Tears increase the falling dew.

"Cease to shun me, lovely mourner;
  "Sweetly breathe the melting strain:
"Oft thou deign'st to charm the rustick,
  "Roving thoughtless o'er the plain.

"Yet, to him, thy softest trillings
  "Can no sympathy impart;
"Wouldst thou seek for kindred feelings,
40   "See them trembling in my heart!"

Vain, alas! my Invocation,
  Vain the pleadings of the muse!
Wrapp'd in silent shades, the charmer
  Doth her tuneful lay refuse.

Clouds obscure deform the æther,
  Rising damps involve the plain;
Pensively I hasten homeward,
  To avoid the coming rain.*

(1781)

---

* When Hays republished this poem in *Letters and Essays, Moral, and Miscellaneous* (London, 1793), she added to the title the subtitle "Written near the New Forest in Hampshire" and revised the last stanza to read: "Homeward as I hopeless wander, /

Faintly sighs the evening breeze; / Shadowy beams the moon's pale lustre, / Glittering through the waving trees."

Ode to Her Bullfinch

Little wanton flutt'rer, say
Whither wou'dst thou wing thy way?
Why those airy circles make,
All untry'd the thorny brake?
Various dangers lurking lie
In the guise of liberty;
See the wily fowler laid
Close beneath the hawthorn shade;
Mark his tyrannous intent,
Full on schemes of murder bent;   10
For within that rugged breast
Meek-ey'd Pity ne'er wou'd rest,
Nor the softer powers of Love
E'er that stoick heart could move,
Little trembler, hither fly,
In my bosom safely lie;
Sympathy and tenderness
Doth that bosom still possess;
There thy glossy plumes unfold
Plumes of azure and of gold;   20
While secure from every harm,
Pining want and rude alarm,
A willing captive still remain,
Nor with thy liberty to gain.

Whisp'ring Nature prompts to fly,
Seeking sweet society;
Or the gentler voice of Love
Bids thee range the mazy grove;
Ah! thy fond intent forbear,
Transient joys which end in care;   30
All a parent's anxious woe

Soon thy downy breast would know,
Lest the school-boy's truant eye
Shou'd thy tender young descry;
Lest the ruder vernal storm
Shou'd thy little nest deform,
Hither then, thou wanton, fly,
Bless thy soft captivity;
And lull with notes of soothing sound
40   The pangs which do my bosom wound.

(1785)

Felicia Hemans

(1793–1835)

꒰꒷꒦꒷꒦꒷꒦꒷꒦꒷꒦꒷꒦꒷꒦꒷꒦꒷꒦꒷꒦꒷꒦꒷꒦꒷꒷꒰

Felicia Hemans was one of the most widely read and influential poets of the nineteenth century. Her work, as popular in America as in Britain, was admired by Percy Bysshe Shelley, William Wordsworth, Lady Morgan, Matthew Arnold, William Michael Rossetti, Marian Evans (George Eliot), Elizabeth Barrett, and countless other writers and literary critics of discerning taste. It continued to be widely anthologized, set to music, quoted, illustrated by artists, ensconced in tooled leather bindings, and made the subject of school recitations well into the twentieth century. Oxford University Press published a volume of her collected works in 1914.

Felicia Dorothea Browne was born at 118 Duke Street, Liverpool, on 25 September 1793, to Felicity Dorothea Wagner, daughter of the imperial and Tuscan consul at Liverpool, and George Browne, an Irish merchant. As a child she was an avid reader in the family's extensive library. When she was seven, her father suffered a financial setback and, for economy's sake, the family left Liverpool, at that time a bustling trade center, for an old, spacious mansion called Gwrych near Abergele, North Wales, poised among rocky hills overlooking the sea. The sights and sounds of this lonely and beautiful landscape appear frequently in Hemans's poetry. Although she visited London while still a child, in the winters of 1804 and 1805, she did not enjoy it and never returned. Her mother taught her English grammar, French, drawing, and music; a local clergyman taught her Latin, ruing "that she was not a man to have borne away the highest honors at college!"[1] She taught herself Spanish, Italian, Portuguese, and German.

At the age of fourteen Hemans published by subscription with the London firm of Cadell and Davies a handsome quarto volume simply titled *Poems*. One of the 978 subscribers was handsome Captain Alfred Hemans of the

---

1. Henry Fothergill Chorley, *Memorials of Mrs. Hemans, with Illustrations of her Literary Character from her Private Correspondence,* 2 vols. (London, 1836), 1:17.

Fourth Regiment. *England and Spain; or, Valour and Patriotism,* also an apprentice book, came out the same year and expresses her enthusiasm for the Peninsular Campaign, in which two of her brothers served as members of the Twenty-third Royal Welsh Fusiliers. Percy Bysshe Shelley, having heard of Felicia Browne from his cousin, Thomas Medwin, a subscriber to *Poems,* wrote to her hoping to initiate a friendship, but she rebuffed him. In 1809 her family moved to Bronwylfa, near St. Asaph in Flintshire, in the valley of the Clwyd. Before leaving for the front in Spain, Captain Hemans declared his love; despite her family's disapproval of the match, the couple married after his return three years later, on 30 July 1812, shortly before the publication of *The Domestic Affections, and Other Poems,* a book ignored by the reviewers. Captain Hemans was appointed adjutant to the Northamptonshire Local Militia, and the couple moved to Daventry, where their first son, Arthur, was born.

Soon afterwards, however, the Northamptonshire Militia disbanded and the young family went to live with her mother in Bronwylfa. Three more sons followed in quick succession. Shortly before Hemans gave birth to their fifth son in September 1818, her husband left her. Although the two exchanged letters and consulted about their children, they seem to have come to a mutual agreement to live apart. Her failed marriage remained throughout her life a source of such intense embarrassment that she would never speak of it. During the six years of her married life she produced not only five children but three major books. Byron told John Murray that he considered Hemans's *Restoration of the Works of Art to Italy* (1816) "a good poem— very," but he condemned her *Modern Greece* (1817) as "Good for nothing— written by some one who had never been there."[2]

Still, Hemans garnered increasing recognition. She sent Walter Scott a poem inspired by *Waverley,* and he published it in the *Edinburgh Annual Register* for 1815. In 1819 "The Meeting of Wallace and Bruce on the Banks of the Carron" won a prize of fifty pounds and was published in the September issue of *Blackwood's Magazine.*[3] One of her rivals in the competition—James Hogg, "the Ettrick Shepherd"—admitted that her entry was "greatly superior

---

2. See Byron to Murray, 30 September 1816 and 4 September 1817, in *"So late into the night,"* vol. 5 of *Byron's Letters and Journals,* ed. Leslie A. Marchand (London, 1976), 108, 262. She owned a small lock of Byron's hair, which she wore in her favorite brooch until she was disillusioned by reviews of Thomas Moore's *Life of Byron* (1830) and called the poet "the wreck of what might have been" ([Harriett Hughes], "Memoir of the Life and Writings of Mrs. Hemans," in *The Works of Mrs. Hemans; with a Memoir of her Life, by her Sister,* [ed. Harriett Hughes], 7 vols. [Edinburgh and London, 1839], 1:227).

3. Her stanzas on the "Death of the Princess Charlotte" had appeared in *Blackwood's* the previous April.

both in elegance of thought and composition. Had I been constituted the judge myself, I would have given hers the preference by many degrees."[4] The *Quarterly Review* for October 1820 published an appreciative four-year retrospective review of Hemans's work by William Gifford, and in June 1821 she won the fifty-guinea prize of the Royal Society of Literature for the best poem on Dartmoor. In the same year, she composed her *Welsh Melodies,* recreations of Welsh history and translations of Welsh poems set to music. They remained popular as songs for more than a hundred years.

Most of her whimsical poems were never published, though the "Mineralogist" poems reproduced below survive to show her comic side. A writer for the *Edinburgh Monthly Review,* reviewing Hemans's *Tales, and Historic Scenes* (1819), thought her poetry possessed "an exquisite airiness and spirit, with an imagery which quite sparkles," and admired her "vivacity and fertility of imagination" as well as her "sublime eloquence."[5] In the spring of 1820 Hemans met Bishop Reginald Heber, who became her mentor and encouraged her to write plays. Hemans's own favorite playwrights were Coleridge, whose "Remorse" she admired, and Joanna Baillie, whose "Ethwald" and "The Family Legend" were early favorites. She particularly liked Baillie's heroines, about whom she said, "Nothing in all her writings delights me so much as her general idea of what is beautiful in the female character. There is so much gentle fortitude, and deep self-devoting affection in the women whom she portrays, and they are so perfectly different from the pretty 'un-idea'd girls,' who seem to form the *beau idéal* of our whole sex in the works of some modern poets."[6] Later, in 1827, the two poets corresponded and became close friends. John Murray published *The Siege of Valencia; A Dramatic Poem. The Last Constantine: with Other Poems* in the summer of 1823; it contains "The Voice of Spring," a poem set to music and sung by wandering minstrels. Hemans's five-act tragedy, *The Vespers of Palermo,* was produced at Heber's urging at Covent Garden on 12 December 1823, with Charles Kemble playing the tortured hero, Procida. Based on a historical incident, the play contained two strong female heroes and concerns itself with the struggle for freedom in a plot mixing love and violence. It closed after only one night; however, at Joanna Baillie's urging, Walter Scott persuaded Sarah Siddons to stage it in Edinburgh the following April, where, with an epilogue by Scott delivered by Siddons, it played successfully.

In 1823 Hemans began contributing to the *New Monthly Magazine,* edited by Thomas Campbell, where her "Lays of Many Lands" first appeared, and in

4. Quoted in Peter W. Trinder, *Mrs. Hemans* (Cardiff, 1984), 19.
5. 2 (August 1819): 207.
6. [Hughes], "Memoir," 69.

1827 she became a regular contributor to *Blackwood's Edinburgh Magazine*. In 1825 she brought out *The Forest Sanctuary; and Other Poems,* the title work of which she considered one of her best. Written in the laundry, the only quiet place in the house, its stanza is a variation of Spenser's. A Spanish hero flees religious persecution during the sixteenth century and finds refuge with his child in a North American forest. Marian Evans called the book "exquisite."[7]

Professor Andrews Norton of Harvard University, who with the critic Andrew Peabody ranked Hemans's work above that of Milton and Homer, asked permission to superintend the publication of a complete edition of her works in Boston, and in 1826 the publishing firm of Hilliard, Gray, Little, and Wilkins brought out *The League of the Alps, The Siege of Valencia, The Vespers of Palermo, and Other Poems.* It was in this book that "Casabianca" first appeared. For the next hundred years, school children would be asked to recite this poem, which actually is a critique of the obedience to patriarchal authority that it seems most to extoll. "The Landing of the Pilgrim Fathers" was also a favorite of her American audience, with whom her poetry became so popular that scores of imitators sprang up. *Hymns on the Works of Nature, for the Use of Children* followed in 1827, appearing first in America and only six years later in Britain. Norton reprinted *The Forest Sanctuary* in 1827 and *Records of Woman* in 1828.

When her eldest brother married in the spring of 1825, Hemans moved with her sons, her mother, and her unmarried sister, Harriett (who would later write an early biography of the poet), to a house called Rhyllon, a quarter-mile away just across the River Clwyd. The next three years would be the happiest of her life, but the breakup of this household inspired many of the poems in her most successful book, *Records of Woman,* published in May 1828 by William Blackwood and dedicated to Joanna Baillie. Hemans noted, "I have put my heart and individual feelings into it more than any thing else I have written."[8] The book was deeply colored by the death on 11 January 1827 of her mother and the impending marriage of her sister Harriett. Written mostly at Rhyllon, with her children at play around her, the poems document the courage, nobility, and tragedy of women's lives; embedded in their painful situations lies a critique of the domestic ideal and of patriarchal values. Like most contemporary commentators, unaware of its subtle subversiveness, Francis Jeffrey wrote an appreciative, long review of this book and *The Forest Sanctuary* (1826) for the October 1829 *Edinburgh Review.* Maria Jane Jewsbury,

7. Marian Evans, *The George Eliot Letters,* ed. Gordon S. Haight, 6 vols. (New Haven, 1954), 1:72.

8. Letter of 23 March 1828 to Mary Russell Mitford, quoted in Chorley, *Memorials of Mrs. Hemans,* 1:130.

who spent the summer and fall of 1828 near Hemans at St. Asaph, later depicted the poet during this period and her effect upon her in the character of Egeria in *The Three Histories:* "She did not dazzle—she subdued me. Other women might be more commanding, more versatile, more acute; but I never saw one so exquisitely feminine. She was lovely without being beautiful; her movements were features." Jewsbury dedicated her *Lays of Leisure Hours* to Hemans and encouraged her to read William Wordsworth's poetry.

In the autumn of 1828, William E. West painted Hemans's portrait at the request of Alaric Watts, editor of the *Literary Souvenir,* who was putting together a gallery of the living British poets. West stayed at Rhyllon and produced three portraits altogether, one of which was exhibited at Somerset House, home of the Royal Academy of Arts.[9] Not long after West's stay, Hemans left Wales for Wavertree, a town outside Liverpool, where she had friends and where she hoped to find better schools for her sons. "I am now," she wrote, "for the first time in my life, holding the reins of government, independent, managing a household myself; and I never liked anything less than *'ce triste empire de soi-même.'*"[10] She grew depressed and ill; the whole household, including the poet, contracted whooping cough. Even so, it was during her three years at Wavertree that she got to know Henry Fothergill Chorley, Caroline Hamilton, and Rose D'Aguilar Lawrence, all of whom would write early biographies of her, and was visited by Mary Howitt and Andrews Norton from America. In addition, Hemans's proximity to Liverpool and her growing reputation caused her to be besieged by admirers and autograph seekers from England and America.

In the summer of 1829, on a trip to Scotland, she visited Walter Scott. Scott had once told Joanna Baillie that Hemans "is somewhat too poetical for my taste—too many flowers I mean, and too little fruit—but that may be the cynical criticism of an elderly gentleman";[11] he liked Hemans personally, however, and invited her to be his houseguest at Abbotsford. Hemans considered this visit to be one of the high points of her life. Scott told her at parting, "There are some whom we meet, and should like ever

9. One portrait, judged by her family to be the best likeness, inspired Hemans's poem "To My Own Portrait" and was given to her sister, Harriett Hughes, who used it for the frontispiece to the seven-volume 1839 edition of Hemans's *Works;* the third portrait went to Professor Andrews Norton in Boston. The portrait for Watts, which Hughes considered to be an unsatisfactory likeness, was later acquired by Fisher, proprietor of *Fisher's Drawing-Room Scrap-Book;* engravings from it appeared in that annual as well as in *The Christian Keepsake.*

10. Letter of 10 November 1828 to Mary Russell Mitford, quoted in [Hughes], "Memoir," 156.

11. Letter of 11 July 1823, quoted in John Gibson Lockhart, *Memoirs of the Life of Sir Walter Scott,* 5 vols. (Boston, 1901), 4:126.

after to claim as kith and kin; and *you* are one of those."[12] On the same trip she stopped at Edinburgh, met Ann Grant of Laggan, dined with Francis Jeffrey, visited Henry Mackenzie, and sat for a bust by Angus Fletcher. In June 1830 she was William Wordsworth's guest for more than two weeks at Rydal Mount; she then moved nearby to a cottage called Dove Nest on the banks of Lake Windermere, where she stayed until mid-August. She and Wordsworth found each other charming and became good friends, though the women in the household were far less enthusiastic. Later Hemans dedicated *Scenes and Hymns of Life* (1834) to William Wordsworth. She published *Songs of the Affections* early in the summer of 1830; most had already appeared separately in *Blackwood's Magazine*. After sending her two oldest boys to join their father in Italy, in April 1831 she left Wavertree for Dublin, by way of Bronwylfa. From Dublin, she went to visit a brother in Kilkenny, making a pilgrimage to Mary Tighe's grave in Woodstock along the way.

Hemans took a house in Upper Pembroke Street in Dublin and began, in the autumn of 1831, to compose melodies for her poems, including her influential *Hymns for Childhood* and *National Lyrics, and Songs for Music*.[13] Many of her poems would eventually be set to music by others. In 1834 she contracted scarlet fever, followed by a cold that turned to ague. Despite declining strength and health, she composed "Thoughts during Sickness," a series of seven sonnets. Eventually she lost the use of her limbs and barely had the energy to read. Suffering from fever and delirium, on Sunday, 26 April 1835, she dictated the "Sabbath Sonnet," her last poem. She died at 20 Dawson Street, Dublin, on 16 May, at the age of forty-one and was buried nearby within the vaults of St. Anne's Church. Her brothers erected a tablet in the cathedral of St. Asaph, which reads, in part, "in memory of Felicia Hemans, whose character is best pourtrayed in her writings." She once remarked that "it has ever been one of my regrets that the constant necessity of providing sums of money to meet the exigencies of the boys' education, has obliged me to waste my mind in what I consider mere desultory effusions. . . . My wish ever was to concentrate all my mental energy in the production of some more noble and complete work: something of pure and holy excellence, (if there be not too much presumption in the thought,) which might permanently take its place as the work of a British poetess."[14] Nevertheless, at her death many of her poems had already acquired the stature of standard English lyrics—"The

---

12. Hemans, journal entry, July 1829, quoted in [Hughes], "Memoir," 191.

13. By the summer of 1832 she had moved to 36 Stephen's Green in order to avoid the street noise of her former home, and by the spring of 1833 she had moved again, to 20 Dawson Street.

14. Quoted in [Hughes], "Memoir," 296–97.

Stately Homes of England," "The Better Land," "The Graves of a Household," "The Treasures of the Deep," and "Casabianca" foremost among them.

Many poetic tributes were written to Hemans, even during her lifetime; she preferred the one written by Catherine Grace Godwin above the rest. Many were later to eulogize her, including Wordsworth in his "Epitaphs" (16, "Ex tempore Effusion Upon the Death of James Hogg"), Letitia Elizabeth Landon in "Stanzas on the Death of Mrs. Hemans," Maria Abdy in "Lines Written on the Death of Mrs. Hemans," and Lydia Sigourney in "Monody on Mrs. Hemans." Although she once assured a correspondent that "I utterly disclaim all wish for the post of 'Speaker to the Feminine Literary House of Commons,'" in her own way she was just that—in her identification with and portrayal of the plights of other women and their struggle to surmount or to simply endure the constraints on their lives. Her popularity throughout the nineteenth century owed much to the clarity of her language, the passion of her lyricism, and her implicit critique of patriarchal authority.

MAJOR WORKS: *England and Spain; or, Valour and Patriotism* (London, 1808); *Poems* (Liverpool and London, 1808); *The Domestic Affections, and Other Poems* (London, 1812); *The Restoration of the Works of Art to Italy: A Poem* (Oxford and London, 1816); *Modern Greece. A Poem* (London, 1817); *Translations from Camoens, and Other Poets, with Original Poetry* (Oxford and London, 1818); *Tales, and Historic Scenes, in Verse* (London, 1819); *Wallace's Invocation to Bruce; A Poem* (Edinburgh and London, 1819); *The Sceptic; a Poem* (London, 1820); *Stanzas to the Memory of the Late King* (London, 1820); *Dartmoor; a Poem: Which Obtained the Prize of Fifty Guineas Proposed by the Royal Society of Literature* (London, 1821); *The Siege of Valencia; A Dramatic Poem. The Last Constantine: With Other Poems* (London, 1823); *The Vespers of Palermo; a Tragedy, in Five Acts* (London, 1823); *The Forest Sanctuary; and Other Poems* (London, 1825); *The League of the Alps, The Siege of Valencia, The Vespers of Palermo, and Other Poems,* [ed. Andrews Norton] (Boston, 1826); *Hymns on the Works of Nature, for the Use of Children,* [ed. Andrews Norton] (Boston, 1827), republished as *Hymns for Childhood* (Dublin, 1834); *Records of Woman: With Other Poems* (Edinburgh and London, 1828); *Songs of the Affections, with Other Poems* (Edinburgh and London, 1830); *National Lyrics, and Songs for Music* (Dublin and London, 1834); *Scenes and Hymns of Life, with Other Religious Poems* (Edinburgh and London, 1834); *Poetical Remains of the Late Mrs. Hemans,* [ed. D. M. Moir] (Edinburgh and London, 1836); *The Works of Mrs. Hemans; with a Memoir of her Life, by her Sister,* [ed. Harriett Hughes], 7 vols. (Edinburgh and London, 1839).

TEXTS USED: Texts of "Epitaph on Mr. W——, a Celebrated Mineralogist," "Epitaph on the Hammer of the Aforesaid Mineralogist," "Troubadour Song," and "I Dream of All Things Free" from *The Works of Mrs. Hemans.* "The Voice of Spring" from *The Siege of Valencia; A Dramatic Poem. The Last Constantine: with Other Poems.* "The Messenger

Bird" and "Bring Flowers" from *The Forest Sanctuary; and Other Poems.* "The Graves of a Household," "The Landing of the Pilgrim Fathers in New England," "A Monarch's Death-Bed," "Gertrude, or Fidelity till Death," "The Image in Lava," "Indian Woman's Death-Song," and "Arabella Stuart" from *Records of Woman: with Other Poems.* "Casabianca," "The Wings of the Dove," and "The Dreamer" from the second edition of *The Forest Sanctuary; and Other Poems* (London and Edinburgh, 1829). "The Coronation of Inez de Castro" and "The Return" from *Songs of the Affections, with Other Poems.* "The Painter's Last Work—A Scene" from *Blackwood's Edinburgh Magazine* for February 1832.

Epitaph on Mr. W——, a Celebrated Mineralogist*

Stop, passenger! a wondrous tale to list—
Here lies a famous Mineralogist.
Famous indeed! such traces of his power,
He's left from Penmaenbach to Penmaenmawr,
Such caves, and chasms, and fissures in the rocks,
His works resemble those of earthquake shocks;
And future ages very much may wonder
What mighty giant rent the hills asunder,
Or whether Lucifer himself had ne'er
10   Gone with his crew to play at foot-ball there.

His fossils, flints, and spars, of every hue,
With him, good reader, here lie buried too—
Sweet specimens! which, toiling to obtain,
He split huge cliffs, like so much wood, in twain.
We knew, so great the fuss he made about them,
Alive or dead, he ne'er would rest without them,
So, to secure soft slumber to his bones,
We paved his grave with all his favorite stones.
His much-loved hammer's resting by his side;
20   Each hand contains a shell-fish petrified:
His mouth a piece of pudding-stone incloses,
And at his feet a lump of coal reposes:
Sure he was born beneath some lucky planet—
His very coffin-plate is made of granite.

Weep not, good reader! he is truly blest
Amidst chalcedony and quartz to rest:
Weep not for him! but envied be his doom,
Whose tomb, though small, for all he loved had room:
And, O ye rocks!—schist, gneiss, whate'er ye be,
Ye varied strata!—names too hard for me—   30
Sing, "Oh, be joyful!" for your direst foe,
By death's fell hammer, is at length laid low.
Ne'er on your spoils again shall W—— riot.
Clear up your cloudy brows, and rest in quiet—
He sleeps—no longer planning hostile actions,
As cold as any of his petrifactions;
Enshrined in specimens of every hue,
Too tranquil e'en to dream, ye rocks, of you.

                                   (wr. 1816; pub. 1836)

* The mineralogist was C. Pleydell N. Wilton, whose autograph copy of the poem was entitled "Epitaph on Mr Wilton, a Celebrated Mineralogist." His copy concludes with the note, "This gentleman unfortunately fell off a rock, whilst in the act of exclaiming *"Ocular demonstration."* According to Wilton, the event occurred "during one of those 'mountain rambles' so delightfully enlivened by the wit & good humour of Mrs. Hemans, in the neighborhood of Dyganwy. . . . . [The lines] were addressed & presented to him at the hands of Mrs. Hemans, on the morning of his starting for St. John's College Cambridge, and of leaving the town of Aberconway in North Wales, where, in the Harp Inn, in company with six other fellow students of that University, he had been reading mathematics during the summer vacation of the year 1816" (National Library of Scotland, MS 4090 Blackwood, folios 193–94; quoted by permission of the Trustees of the National Library of Scotland). Wilton later became an assistant chaplain in New South Wales and incumbent of the Cathedral of Christ Church, Newcastle.

29 schist, gneiss] Types of rock.

Epitaph on the Hammer
of the Aforesaid Mineralogist*

Here in the dust, its strange adventures o'er,
A hammer rests, that ne'er knew rest before.
Released from toil, it slumbers by the side
Of one who oft its temper sorely tried;
No day e'er passed, but in some desperate strife
He risked the faithful hammer's limbs and life:
Now laying siege to some old limestone wall,
Some rock now battering, proof to cannon-ball;
Now scaling heights like Alps or Pyrenees,
10   Perhaps a flint, perhaps a slate to seize;
But, if a piece of copper met his eyes,
He'd mount a precipice that touch'd the skies,
And bring down lumps so precious, and so many,
I'm sure they almost would have made — a penny!
Think, when such deeds as these were daily done,
What fearful risks this hammer must have run.
And, to say truth, its praise deserves to shine
In lays more lofty and more famed than mine:
Oh! that in strains which ne'er should be forgot,
20   Its deeds were blazon'd forth by Walter Scott!
Then should its name with his be closely link'd,
And live till every mineral were extinct.
Rise, epic bards! be yours the ample field —
Bid W——'s hammer match Achilles' shield:
As for *my* muse, the chaos of her brain,
I search for specimens of wit in vain;
Then let me cease ignoble rhymes to stammer,
And seek some theme less arduous than the hammer;
Rememb'ring well, "what perils do environ"
30   Woman or "man that meddles with cold iron."
                                    (wr. 1816; pub. 1839)

*According to Wilton, this poem and the previous one "were composed by
Mrs. Hemans when on a visit, . . . at Rose Hill, the residence of the then incumbent
of Conway. . . . [While walking in the mountains,] Wilton discovered on the Druid

The Voice of Spring

I come, I come! ye have call'd me long,
I come o'er the mountains with light and song!
Ye may trace my step o'er the wakening earth,
By the winds which tell of the violet's birth,
By the primrose-stars in the shadowy grass,
By the green leaves, opening as I pass.

I have breathed on the south, and the chesnut flowers
By thousands have burst from the forest-bowers,
And the ancient graves, and the fallen fanes,
Are veil'd with wreaths on Italian plains;   10
—But it is not for me, in my hour of bloom,
To speak of the ruin or the tomb!

I have look'd o'er the hills of the stormy north,
And the larch has hung all his tassels forth,
The fisher is out on the sunny sea,
And the rein-deer bounds o'er the pastures free,
And the pine has a fringe of softer green,
And the moss looks bright, where my foot hath been.

I have sent through the wood-paths a glowing sigh,
And call'd out each voice of the deep blue sky;   20
From the night-bird's lay through the starry time,
In the groves of the soft Hesperian clime,
To the swan's wild note, by the Iceland lakes,
When the dark fir-branch into verdure breaks.

From the streams and founts I have loosed the chain,
They are sweeping on to the silvery main,

9 fanes] Banners, flags fallen in battle.

They are flashing down from the mountain brows,
They are flinging spray o'er the forest-boughs,
They are bursting fresh from their sparry caves,
30   And the earth resounds with the joy of waves!

Come forth, O ye children of gladness, come!
Where the violets lie may be now your home.
Ye of the rose lip and dew-bright eye,
And the bounding footstep, to meet me fly!
With the lyre, and the wreath, and the joyous lay,
Come forth to the sunshine, I may not stay.

Away from the dwellings of care-worn men,
The waters are sparkling in grove and glen!
Away from the chamber and sullen hearth,
40   The young leaves are dancing in breezy mirth!
Their light stems thrill to the wild-wood strains,
And youth is abroad in my green domains.

But ye!—ye are changed since ye met me last!
There is something bright from your features pass'd!
There is that come over your brow and eye,
Which speaks of a world where the flowers must die!
—Ye smile! but your smile hath a dimness yet—
Oh! what have ye look'd on since last we met?

Ye are changed, ye are changed!—and I see not here
50   All whom I saw in the vanish'd year!
There were graceful heads, with their ringlets bright,
Which toss'd in the breeze with a play of light,
There were eyes, in whose glistening laughter lay
No faint remembrance of dull decay!

There were steps that flew o'er the cowslip's head,
As if for a banquet all earth were spread;
There were voices that rung through the sapphire sky,
And had not a sound of mortality!
Are they gone? is their mirth from the mountains pass'd?
60   —Ye have look'd on death since ye met me last!

I know whence the shadow comes o'er you now,
Ye have strewn the dust on the sunny brow!
Ye have given the lovely to earth's embrace,
She hath taken the fairest of beauty's race,
With their laughing eyes and their festal crown,
They are gone from amongst you in silence down!

They are gone from amongst you, the young and fair,
Ye have lost the gleam of their shining hair!
—But I know of a land where there falls no blight,
I shall find them there, with their eyes of light!   70
Where Death midst the blooms of the morn may dwell,
I tarry no longer—farewell, farewell!

The summer is coming, on soft winds borne,
Ye may press the grape, ye may bind the corn!
For me, I depart to a brighter shore,
Ye are mark'd by care, ye are mine no more.
I go where the lovèd who have left you dwell,
And the flowers are not death's—fare ye well, farewell!

(1823)

The Messenger Bird

*Some of the native Brazilians pay great veneration to a certain bird that sings mournfully in the night-time. They say it is a messenger which their deceased friends and relations have sent, and that it brings them news from the other world. — See Picart's Ceremonies and Religious Customs.**

Thou art come from the spirits' land, thou bird!
    Thou art come from the spirits' land!
Through the dark pine-grove let thy voice be heard,
    And tell of the shadowy band!

We know that the bowers are green and fair
    In the light of that summer shore,
And we know that the friends we have lost are there,
    They are there—and they weep no more!

And we know they have quench'd their fever's thirst
10   From the Fountain of Youth ere now,[†]
For *there* must the stream in its freshness burst,
                Which none may find below!

And we know that they will not be lur'd to earth
                From the land of deathless flowers,
By the feast, or the dance, or the song of mirth,
                Though their hearts were once with ours;

Though they sat with us by the night-fire's blaze,
                And bent with us the bow,
And heard the tales of our fathers' days,
20   Which are told to others now!

But tell us, thou bird of the solemn strain!
                Can those who have lov'd forget?
We call—and they answer not again—
                —Do they love—do they love us yet?

Doth the warrior think of his brother *there,*
                And the father of his child?
And the chief, of those that were wont to share
                His wandering through the wild?

We call them far through the silent night,
30   And they speak not from cave or hill;
We know, thou bird! that their land is bright,
                But say, do they love there still?

                                        (1824)

---

[*] Bernard Picard (1673–1733) was a French artist known for his book illustrations. His illustrations for *The Ceremonies and Religious Customs of the Various Nations of the Known World* are among his best-known works.

[†] An expedition was actually undertaken by Juan Ponce de Leon, in the 16th century, with the view of discovering a wonderful fountain, believed by the natives of Puerto Rico to spring in one of the Lucayo Isles, and to possess the virtue of restoring youth to all who bathed in its waters.—See [William] Robertson's History of America [3 vols. (Dublin, 1777)]. *Hemans.*

Bring Flowers

Bring flowers, young flowers, for the festal board,
To wreathe the cup ere the wine is poured;
Bring flowers! they are springing in wood and vale,
Their breath floats out on the southern gale,
And the touch of the sunbeam hath waked the rose,
To deck the hall where the bright wine flows.

Bring flowers to strew in the conqueror's path—
He hath shaken thrones with his stormy wrath!
He comes with the spoils of nations back,
The vines lie crush'd in his chariot's track,   10
The turf looks red where he won the day—
Bring flowers to die in the conqueror's way!

Bring flowers to the captive's lonely cell,
They have tales of the joyous woods to tell;
Of the free blue streams, and the glowing sky,
And the bright world shut from his languid eye;
They will bear him a thought of the sunny hours,
And a dream of his youth—bring him flowers, wild flowers!

Bring flowers, fresh flowers, for the bride to wear!
They were born to blush in her shining hair.   20
She is leaving the home of her childhood's mirth,
She hath bid farewell to her father's hearth,
Her place is now by another's side—
Bring flowers for the locks of the fair young bride!

Bring flowers, pale flowers, o'er the bier to shed,
A crown for the brow of the early dead!
For this through its leaves hath the white-rose burst,
For this in the woods was the violet nurs'd.
Though they smile in vain for what once was ours,
They are love's last gift—bring ye flowers, pale flowers!   30

Bring flowers to the shrine where we kneel in prayer,
They are nature's offering, their place is *there!*

They speak of hope to the fainting heart,
With a voice of promise they come and part,
They sleep in dust through the wintry hours,
They break forth in glory—bring flowers, bright flowers!

(1824)

Troubadour Song

The warrior cross'd the ocean's foam
    For the stormy fields of war;
The maid was left in a smiling home
    And a sunny land afar.

His voice was heard where javelin showers
    Pour'd on the steel-clad line;
Her step was 'midst the summer flowers,
    Her seat beneath the vine.

His shield was cleft, his lance was riven,
10   And the red blood stain'd his crest;
While she—the gentlest wind of heaven,
    Might scarcely fan her breast.

Yet a thousand arrows pass'd him by,
    And again he cross'd the seas;
But she had died as roses die
    That perish with a breeze.

As roses die, when the blast is come
    For all things bright and fair—
There was death within the smiling home—
20   How had death found her there?

(1824)

The Graves of a Household

They grew in beauty, side by side,
    They fill'd one home with glee;—
Their graves are sever'd, far and wide,
    By mount, and stream, and sea.

The same fond mother bent at night
    O'er each fair sleeping brow;
She had each folded flower in sight,—
    Where are those dreamers now?

One, midst the forests of the west,
    By a dark stream is laid—
The Indian knows his place of rest,
    Far in the cedar shade.

The sea, the blue lone sea, hath one,
    He lies where pearls lie deep;
He was the lov'd of all, yet none
    O'er his low bed may weep.

One sleeps where southern vines are drest
    Above the noble slain:
He wrapt his colours round his breast,
    On a blood-red field of Spain.

And one—o'er *her* the myrtle showers
    Its leaves, by soft winds fann'd;
She faded midst Italian flowers,—
    The last of that bright band.

And parted thus they rest, who play'd
    Beneath the same green tree;
Whose voices mingled as they pray'd
    Around one parent knee!

10

20

They that with smiles lit up the hall,
    And cheer'd with song the hearth,— ˙
30 Alas! for love, if *thou* wert all,
    And nought beyond, oh, earth!

                  (1825)

The Landing of the Pilgrim Fathers in New England

Look now abroad—another race has fill'd
  Those populous borders—wide the wood recedes,
And towns shoot up, and fertile realms are till'd;
  The land is full of harvests and green meads.
          —Bryant*

The breaking waves dash'd high
    On a stern and rock-bound coast,
And the woods against a stormy sky
    Their giant branches toss'd;

And the heavy night hung dark,
    The hills and waters o'er,
When a band of exiles moor'd their bark
    On the wild New-England shore.

Not as the conqueror comes,
    They, the true-hearted came;
10 Not with the roll of the stirring drums,
    And the trumpet that sings of fame:

Not as the flying come,
    In silence and in fear;—
They shook the depths of the desert gloom
    With their hymns of lofty cheer.

Amidst the storm they sang,
   And the stars heard and the sea!
And the sounding aisles of the dim woods rang
   To the anthem of the free.   20

The ocean-eagle soar'd
   From his nest by the white wave's foam,
And the rocking pines of the forest roar'd—
   This was their welcome home!

There were men with hoary hair,
   Amidst that pilgrim band;—
Why had *they* come to wither there,
   Away from their childhood's land?

There was woman's fearless eye,
   Lit by her deep love's truth;   30
There was manhood's brow serenely high,
   And the fiery heart of youth.

What sought they thus afar?
   Bright jewels of the mine?
The wealth of seas, the spoils of war?—
   They sought a faith's pure shrine!

Aye, call it holy ground,
   The soil where first they trod!
They have left unstain'd what there they found—
   Freedom to worship God.   40

                (1825)

---

* William Cullen Bryant, "The Ages," st. 32, lines 1–4.

A Monarch's Death-Bed

*The Emperor Albert of Hapsburgh, who was assassinated by his nephew,
afterwards called John the Parricide, was left to die by the way-side, and
only supported in his last moments by a female peasant, who happened to
be passing.*

A monarch on his death-bed lay—
   Did censers waft perfume,
And soft lamps pour their silvery ray,
   Thro' his proud chamber's gloom?
He lay upon a greensward bed,
   Beneath a darkening sky—
A lone tree waving o'er his head,
   A swift stream rolling by.

Had he then fall'n as warriors fall,
10   Where spear strikes fire with spear?
Was there a banner for his pall,
   A buckler for his bier?
Not so;—nor cloven shields nor helms
   Had strewn the bloody sod,
Where he, the helpless lord of realms,
   Yielded his soul to God.

Were there not friends with words of cheer,
   And princely vassals nigh?
And priests, the crucifix to rear
20   Before the glazing eye?
A peasant girl that royal head
   Upon her bosom laid,
And, shrinking not for woman's dread,
   The face of death survey'd.

Alone she sat:—from hill and wood
   Red sank the mournful sun;
Fast gush'd the fount of noble blood,
   Treason its worst had done!

With her long hair she vainly press'd
  The wounds to staunch their tide—   30
Unknown, on that meek humble breast,
  Imperial Albert died!

(1826)

Gertrude, or Fidelity till Death

The Baron Von Der Wart,[*] *accused, though it is believed unjustly, as an accomplice in the assassination of the Emperor Albert, was bound alive on the wheel, and attended by his wife Gertrude, throughout his last agonizing hours, with the most heroic devotedness. Her own sufferings, with those of her unfortunate husband, are most affectingly described in a letter which she afterwards addressed to a female friend, and which was published some years ago, at Haarlem, in a book entitled* Gertrude Von Der Wart, or Fidelity unto Death.

      Dark lowers our fate,
And terrible the storm that gathers o'er us;
But nothing, till that latest agony
Which severs thee from nature, shall unloose
This fix'd and sacred hold. In thy dark prison-house,
In the terrific face of armed law,
Yea, on the scaffold, if it needs must be,
I never will forsake thee.
                —Joanna Baillie[†]

Her hands were clasp'd, her dark eyes rais'd,
  The breeze threw back her hair;
Up to the fearful wheel she gaz'd—
  All that she lov'd was there.
The night was round her clear and cold,
  The holy heaven above,
Its pale stars watching to behold
  The might of earthly love.

"And bid me not depart," she cried,
    "My Rudolph, say not so!
This is no time to quit thy side,
    Peace, peace! I cannot go.
Hath the world aught for *me* to fear,
    When death is on thy brow?
The world! what means it?—*Mine* is *here*—
    I will not leave thee now.

"I have been with thee in thine hour
    Of glory and of bliss;
Doubt not its memory's living power
    To strengthen me thro' *this!*
And thou, mine honour'd love and true,
    Bear on, bear nobly on!
We have the blessed heaven in view,
    Whose rest shall soon be won."

And were not these high words to flow
    From woman's breaking heart?
Thro' all that night of bitterest wo
    She bore her lofty part;
But oh! with such a glazing eye,
    With such a curdling cheek—
Love, love! of mortal agony,
    Thou, only *thou* shouldst speak!

The wind rose high,—but with it rose
    Her voice, that he might hear:
Perchance that dark hour brought repose
    To happy bosoms near;
While she sat striving with despair
    Beside his tortured form,
And pouring her deep soul in prayer
    Forth on the rushing storm.

She wiped the death-damps from his brow,
    With her pale hands and soft,
Whose touch upon the lute-chords low,
    Had still'd his heart so oft.

She spread her mantle o'er his breast,
    She bath'd his lips with dew,
And on his cheek such kisses press'd
    As hope and joy ne'er knew.

Oh! lovely are ye, Love and Faith,
    Enduring to the last!   50
She had her meed—one smile in death—
    And his worn spirit pass'd.
While ev'n as o'er a martyr's grave
    She knelt on that sad spot,
And, weeping, bless'd the God who gave
    Strength to forsake it not!

                        (1826)

*One of four conspirators who murdered the emperor Albert, king of the Romans, in 1308, Von Der Wart was the only one of the four to be captured. The plot on Albert's life was the result of growing dissatisfaction in Swabia and the Swiss cantons with Albert's rule and the increasing scope of his dominion.
† From *De Monfort: A Tragedy* (5.2.65–72).

Casabianca*

The boy stood on the burning deck
    Whence all but he had fled;
The flame that lit the battle's wreck,
    Shone round him o'er the dead.

Yet beautiful and bright he stood,
    As born to rule the storm;
A creature of heroic blood,
    A proud, though child-like form.

The flames rolled on—he would not go,
    Without his Father's word;   10
That Father, faint in death below,
    His voice no longer heard.

He called aloud:—"Say, Father, say
　　If yet my task is done?"
He knew not that the chieftain lay
　　Unconscious of his son.

"Speak, Father!" once again he cried,
　　"If I may yet be gone!
And"—but the booming shots replied,
20　　And fast the flames rolled on.

Upon his brow he felt their breath,
　　And in his waving hair,
And looked from that lone post of death,
　　In still, yet brave despair.

And shouted but once more aloud,
　　"My Father! must I stay?"
While o'er him fast, through sail and shroud,
　　The wreathing fires made way.

They wrapt the ship in splendour wild,
30　　They caught the flag on high,
And streamed above the gallant child,
　　Like banners in the sky.

There came a burst of thunder sound—
　　The boy—oh! where was he?
Ask of the winds that far around
　　With fragments strewed the sea!—

With mast, and helm, and pennon fair,
　　That well had borne their part—
But the noblest thing which perished there
40　　Was that young faithful heart!

　　　　　　　　　　　(1826)

---

* Young Casabianca, a boy about thirteen years old, son to the Admiral of the Orient, remained at his post (in the Battle of the Nile) after the ship had taken fire, and

all the guns had been abandoned; and perished in the explosion of the vessel, when the flames had reached the powder. *Hemans.* [The Battle of the Nile, between British and French forces, took place in 1798. Napoleon Bonaparte had invaded Egypt in July to try to damage British trade, but British Admiral Horatio Nelson found the French fleet anchored in Abukir Bay, east of Alexandria, and destroyed it on 1–2 August. Louis de Casabianca, commander of the French ship *Orient,* and his ten-year-old son, Giacomo, were among those killed by British forces. *Ed.*]

The Wings of the Dove

Oh! that I had the wings of a dove, that I might flee away and be at rest.*

    Oh! for thy wings, thou dove!
Now sailing by with sunshine on thy breast;
    That, borne like thee above,
I too might flee away, and be at rest!

    Where wilt thou fold those plumes,
Bird of the forest-shadows, holiest bird?
    In what rich leafy glooms,
By the sweet voice of hidden waters stirr'd?

    Over what blessed home,
What roof with dark, deep, summer foliage crown'd,   10
    O! fair as ocean's foam!
Shall thy bright bosom shed a gleam around?

    Or seek'st thou some old shrine
Of nymph or saint, no more by votary wooed,
    Though still, as if divine,
Breathing a spirit o'er the solitude?

    Yet wherefore ask thy way?
Blest, ever blest, whate'er its aim, thou art!
    Unto the greenwood spray,
Bearing no dark remembrance at thy heart!   20

No echoes that will blend
A sadness with the whispers of the grove;
    No memory of a friend
Far off, or dead, or chang'd to thee, thou dove!

    Oh! to some cool recess
Take, take me with thee in the summer wind,
    Leaving the weariness
And all the fever of this life behind:

    The aching and the void
30 Within the heart whereunto none reply,
    The young bright hopes destroyed—
Bird! bear me with thee through the sunny sky!

    Wild wish, and longing vain,
And brief upspringing to be glad and free!
    Go to thy woodland reign!
My soul is bound and held—I may not flee.

    For even by all the fears
And thoughts that haunt my dreams—untold, unknown,
    And burning woman's tears,
40 Poured from mine eyes in silence alone;

    Had I thy wings, thou dove!
High midst the gorgeous Isles of Cloud to soar,
    Soon the strong chords of love
Would draw me earthwards—homewards—yet once more.

                                                (1827)

*Psalms 55:6.

The Image in Lava[*]

Thou thing of years departed!
    What ages have gone by,
Since here the mournful seal was set
    By love and agony!

Temple and tower have moulder'd,
    Empires from earth have passed, —
And woman's heart hath left a trace
    Those glories to outlast!

And childhood's fragile image
    Thus fearfully enshrin'd,   10
Survives the proud memorials rear'd
    By conquerors of mankind.

Babe! wert thou brightly slumbering
    Upon thy mother's breast,
When suddenly the fiery tomb
    Shut round each gentle guest?

A strange dark fate o'ertook you,
    Fair babe and loving heart!
One moment of a thousand pangs —
    Yet better than to part!   20

Haply of that fond bosom,
    On ashes here impress'd,
Thou wert the only treasure, child!
    Whereon a hope might rest.

Perchance all vainly lavish'd,
    Its other love had been,
And where it trusted, nought remain'd
    But thorns on which to lean.

Far better then to perish,
   Thy form within its clasp,
Than live and lose thee, precious one!
   From that impassion'd grasp.

Oh! I could pass all relics
   Left by the pomps of old,
To gaze on this rude monument,
   Cast in affection's mould.

Love, human love! what art thou?
   Thy print upon the dust
Outlives the cities of renown
   Wherein the mighty trust!

Immortal, oh! immortal
   Thou art, whose earthly glow
Hath given these ashes holiness—
   It must, it *must* be so!

              (1827)

*The impression of a woman's form, with an infant clasped to the bosom, found at the uncovering of Herculaneum. *Hemans.* [Herculaneum, an ancient city in Italy near Naples, was destroyed, along with Stabiae and Pompeii, when Mount Vesuvius erupted in A.D. 79. Excavation of Herculaneum began in the eighteenth century, and much was found perfectly preserved under more than fifty feet of volcanic material. Plaster casts were made of some of the human forms whose images the lava preserved. *Ed.*]

The Coronation of Inez de Castro*

Tableau, où l'Amour fait alliance avec la Tombe;
union redoutable de la mort et de la vie!
—Madame de Staël†

There was music on the midnight;—
    From a royal fane it roll'd,
And a mighty bell, each pause between,
    Sternly and slowly toll'd.
Strange was their mingling in the sky,
    It hush'd the listener's breath;
For the music spoke of triumph high,
    The lonely bell, of death.

There was hurrying through the midnight—
    A sound of many feet;   10
But they fell with a muffled fearfulness,
    Along the shadowy street:
And softer, fainter, grew their tread,
    As it near'd the minster-gate,
Whence a broad and solemn light was shed
    From a scene of royal state.

Full glow'd the strong red radiance,
    In the centre of the nave,
Where the folds of a purple canopy
    Swept down in many a wave;   20
Loading the marble pavement old
    With a weight of gorgeous gloom,
For something lay 'midst their fretted gold,
    Like a shadow of the tomb.

And within that rich pavilion,
    High on a glittering throne,
A woman's form sat silently,
    'Midst the glare of light alone.
Her jewell'd robes fell strangely still—
    The drapery on her breast   30
Seem'd with no pulse beneath to thrill,
    So stonelike was its rest!

But a peal of lordly music
　　Shook e'en the dust below,
When the burning gold of the diadem
　　Was set on her pallid brow!
Then died away that haughty sound,
　　And from the encircling band
Stept Prince and Chief, 'midst the hush profound,
40　　With homage to her hand.

Why pass'd a faint, cold shuddering
　　Over each martial frame,
As one by one, to touch that hand,
　　Noble and leader came?
Was not the settled aspect fair?
　　Did not a queenly grace,
Under the parted ebon hair,
　　Sit on the pale still face?

Death! Death! canst *thou* be lovely
50　　Unto the eye of Life?
Is not each pulse of the quick high breast
　　With thy cold mien at strife?
—It was a strange and fearful sight,
　　The crown upon that head,
The glorious robes, and the blaze of light,
　　All gather'd round the Dead!

And beside her stood in silence
　　One with a brow as pale,
And white lips rigidly compress'd,
60　　Lest the strong heart should fail:
King Pedro, with a jealous eye,
　　Watching the homage done,
By the land's flower and chivalry,
　　To her, his martyr'd one.

But on the face he look'd not,
　　Which once his star had been;
To every form his glance was turn'd,
　　Save of the breathless queen:

Though something, won from the grave's embrace,
    Of her beauty still was there,   70
Its hues were all of that shadowy place,
    It was not for *him* to bear.

Alas! the crown, the sceptre,
    The treasures of the earth,
And the priceless love that pour'd those gifts,
    Alike of wasted worth!
The rites are closed:—bear back the Dead
    Unto the chamber deep!
Lay down again the royal head,
    Dust with the dust to sleep!   80

There is music on the midnight—
    A requiem sad and slow,
As the mourners through the sounding aisle
    In dark procession go;
And the ring of state, and the starry crown,
    And all the rich array,
Are borne to the house of silence down,
    With her, that queen of clay!

And tearlessly and firmly
    King Pedro led the train,—   90
But his face was wrapt in his folding robe,
    When they lower'd the dust again.
'Tis hush'd at last the tomb above,
    Hymns die, and steps depart:
Who call'd thee strong as Death, O Love?
    Mightier thou wast and art.

                    (1828)

---

* Inez de Castro (d. 1355) was mistress of Pedro I of Portugal. She was murdered according to the wishes of Alfonso IV, Pedro's father. After Pedro's accession (1357), he had her body placed in a spectacular mausoleum and according to legend, he had the corpse crowned and forced courtiers to kiss the hand of the dead queen.

† "Scene, where Love allies with the Grave, a terrible marriage of death and life!" (imperfectly drawn from Germaine de Staël's *D'Allemagne* [1810]).

Indian Woman's Death-Song

An Indian woman, driven to despair by her husband's desertion of her for another wife, entered a canoe with her children, and rowed it down the Mississippi towards a cataract. Her voice was heard from the shore singing a mournful death-song, until overpowered by the sound of the waters in which she perished. The tale is related in Long's Expedition* to the source of St. Peter's River.

Non! je ne puis vivre avec un coeur brisé. Il faut que je retrouve la joie, et que je m'unisse aux esprits libres de l'air.
— *Bride of Messina,* Translated by Madame de Staël†

Let not my child be a girl, for very sad is the life of a woman.
— *The Prairie*‡

Down a broad river of the Western wilds,
Piercing thick forest glooms, a light canoe
Swept with the current: fearful was the speed
Of the frail bark, as by a tempest's wing
Borne leaf-like on to where the mist of spray
Rose with the cataract's thunder. — Yet within,
Proudly, and dauntlessly, and all alone,
Save that a babe lay sleeping at her breast,
A woman stood: upon her Indian brow
Sat a strange gladness, and her dark hair wav'd
As if triumphantly. She press'd her child,
In its bright slumber, to her beating heart,
And lifted her sweet voice, that rose awhile
Above the sound of waters, high and clear,
Wafting a wild proud strain, her song of death.

Roll swiftly to the Spirit's land, thou mighty stream and free!
Father of ancient waters, roll! and bear our lives with thee!
The weary bird that storms have toss'd, would seek the
    sunshine's calm,
And the deer that hath the arrow's hurt, flies to the woods of
    balm.

10

17 Father of ancient waters] "Father of Waters," the Indian name for the Mississippi. *Hemans.*

Roll on!—my warrior's eye hath look'd upon another's face,   20
And mine hath faded from his soul, as fades a moonbeam's
    trace;
My shadow comes not o'er his path, my whisper to his
    dream,
He flings away the broken reed—roll swifter yet, thou
    stream!

The voice that spoke of other days is hush'd within *his* breast,
But *mine* its lonely music haunts, and will not let me rest;
It sings a low and mournful song of gladness that is gone,
I cannot live without that light—Father of waves! roll on!

Will he not miss the bounding step that met him from the
    chase?
The heart of love that made his home an ever sunny place?
The hand that spread the hunter's board, and deck'd his
    couch of yore?—   30
He will not!—roll, dark foaming stream, on to the better
    shore!

Some blessed fount amidst the woods of that bright land
    must flow,
Whose waters from my soul may lave the memory of
    this wo;
Some gentle wind must whisper there, whose breath may
    waft away
The burden of the heavy night, the sadness of the day.

And thou, my babe! tho' born, like me, for woman's weary
    lot,
Smile!—to that wasting of the heart, my own! I leave thee
    not;
Too bright a thing art *thou* to pine in aching love away,
Thy mother bears thee far, young Fawn! from sorrow and
    decay.

She bears thee to the glorious bowers where none are heard
    to weep,   40
And where th' unkind one hath no power again to trouble
    sleep;

And where the soul shall find its youth, as wakening from a
　　dream,—
One moment, and that realm is ours—On, on, dark rolling
　　stream!

　　　　　　　　　　　　　　　　　　　　　　　(1828)

* *Narrative of an Expedition to the source of St. Peter's River,* a play written by William
Hypolitus Keating (1799–1840) based on the notes of Stephen H. Long, commander
of the expedition; the play was first performed in 1823 by order of John Calhoun,
then U.S. secretary of war, and published the following year in Philadelphia.

† "No. I cannot go on living with a broken heart. I must find joy again and unite
myself with the free spirits of the air." Translated from the original German, from
Schiller's tragedy *Braut von Messina, Die, oder, Die feindlichen Bruder,* first performed
and published in 1803.

‡ Hemans slightly misquotes this passage from chap. 26 of James Fenimore Cooper's novel *The Prairie* (1827). The original reads, "Let him not be a girl, for very sad is
the life of a woman."

Arabella Stuart*

And is not love in vain,
Torture enough without a living tomb?
　　—Byron†

Fermossi al fin il cor che balzò tanto.
　　—Pindemonte‡

I

'Twas but a dream!—I saw the stag leap free,
　　Under the boughs where early birds were singing,
I stood o'ershadow'd by the greenwood tree,
　　And heard, it seemed, a sudden bugle ringing
Far thro' a royal forest: then the fawn
Shot, like a gleam of light, from grassy lawn
To secret covert; and the smooth turf shook,
And lilies quiver'd by the glade's lone brook,
And young leaves trembled, as, in fleet career,
A princely band, with horn, and hound, and spear,

10

Like a rich masque swept forth. I saw the dance
Of their white plumes, that bore a silvery glance
Into the deep wood's heart; and all pass'd by,
Save one—I met the smile of *one* clear eye,
Flashing out joy to mine.—Yes, *thou* wert there.
Seymour! a soft wind blew the clustering hair
Back from thy gallant brow, as thou didst rein
Thy courser, turning from that gorgeous train,
And fling, methought, thy hunting-spear away,
And, lightly graceful in thy green array,   20
Bound to my side; and we, that met and parted,
   Ever in dread of some dark watchful power,
Won back to childhood's trust, and, fearless-hearted,
   Blent the glad fulness of our thoughts that hour,
Ev'n like the mingling of sweet streams, beneath
Dim woven leaves, and midst the floating breath
Of hidden forest flowers.

II

'Tis past!—I wake,
   A captive, and alone, and far from thee,   30
My love and friend! Yet fostering, for thy sake,
   A quenchless hope of happiness to be;
And feeling still my woman's spirit strong,
In the deep faith which lifts from earthly wrong,
A heavenward glance. I know, I know our love
Shall yet call gentle angels from above,
By its undying fervour; and prevail,
Sending a breath, as of the spring's first gale,
Thro' hearts now cold; and, raising its bright face,
With a free gush of sunny tears, erase
The characters of anguish; in this trust,   40
I bear, I strive, I bow not to the dust,
That I may bring thee back no faded form,
No bosom chill'd and blighted by the storm,
But all my youth's first treasures, when we meet,
Making past sorrow, by communion, sweet.

III

And thou too art in bonds!—yet droop thou not,
Oh! my belov'd!—there is *one* hopeless lot,
But one, and that not ours. Beside the dead
There sits the grief that mantles up its head,
50   Loathing the laughter and proud pomp of light,
When darkness, from the vainly-doting sight,
Covers its beautiful! If thou wert gone
   To the grave's bosom, with thy radiant brow,—
If thy deep-thrilling voice, with that low tone
   Of earnest tenderness, which now, ev'n now,
Seems floating thro' my soul, were music taken
For ever from this world,—oh! thus forsaken,
Could I bear on?—thou liv'st, thou liv'st, thou'rt mine!
With this glad thought I make my heart a shrine,
60   And by the lamp which quenchless there shall burn,
Sit, a lone watcher for the day's return.

IV

And lo! the joy that cometh with the morning,
   Brightly victorious o'er the hours of care!
I have not watch'd in vain, serenely scorning
   The wild and busy whispers of despair!
Thou hast sent tidings, as of heaven.—I wait
   The hour, the sign, for blessed flight to thee.
Oh! for the skylark's wing that seeks its mate
   As a star shoots!—but on the breezy sea
70   We shall meet soon.—To think of such an hour!
   Will not my heart, o'erburden'd by its bliss,
Faint and give way within me, as a flower
   Borne down and perishing by noontide's kiss?
Yet shall I *fear* that lot?—the perfect rest,
The full deep joy of dying on thy breast,
After long-suffering won? So rich a close
Too seldom crowns with peace affection's woes.

---

52 Covers its beautiful!] "Wheresoever you are, or in what state soever you be, it sufficeth me you are mine. *Rachael wept, and would not be comforted, because her children were no more.* And that, indeed, is the remediless sorrow, and none else!"—From a letter of Arabella Stuart's to her husband.—See [Isaac D'Israeli's] Curiosities of Literature. *Hemans.*

V

Sunset!—I tell each moment—from the skies
  The last red splendour floats along my wall,
Like a king's banner!—Now it melts, it dies!   80
  I see one star—I hear—'twas not the call,
Th' expected voice; my quick heart throbb'd too soon.
I must keep vigil till yon rising moon
Shower down less golden light. Beneath her beam
Thro' my lone lattice pour'd, I sit and dream
Of summer-lands afar, where holy love,
Under the vine, or in the citron-grove,
May breathe from terror.
              Now the night grows deep,
And silent as its clouds, and full of sleep.   90
I hear my veins beat.—Hark! a bell's slow chime.
My heart strikes with it.—Yet again—'tis time!
A step!—a voice!—or but a rising breeze?
Hark!—haste!—I come, to meet thee on the seas.

*   *   *   *   *   *   *   *   *

VI

Now never more, oh! never, in the worth
Of its pure cause, let sorrowing love on earth
Trust fondly—never more!—the hope is crush'd
That lit my life, the voice within me hush'd
That spoke sweet oracles; and I return   100
To lay my youth, as in a burial-urn,
Where sunshine may not find it.—All is lost!
No tempest met our barks—no billow toss'd;
Yet were they sever'd, ev'n as we must be,
That so have lov'd, so striven our hearts to free
From their close-coiling fate! In vain—in vain!
The dark lines meet, and clasp themselves again,
And press out life.—Upon the deck I stood,
And a white sail came gliding o'er the flood,
Like some proud bird of ocean; then mine eye   110
Strained out, one moment earlier to descry
The form it ached for, and the bark's career
Seem'd slow to that fond yearning: it drew near,
Fraught with our foes!—What boots it to recall

The strife, the tears? Once more a prison-wall
Shuts the green hills and woodlands from my sight,
And joyous glance of waters to the light,
And thee, my Seymour, thee!

    I will not sink!
120 Thou, *thou* hast rent the heavy chain that bound thee;
 And this shall be my strength—the joy to think
  That thou mayst wander with heaven's breath around thee,
And all the laughing sky! This thought shall yet
Shine o'er my heart, a radiant amulet,
Guarding it from despair. Thy bonds are broken,
And unto me, I know, thy true love's token
Shall one day be deliverance, tho' the years
Lie dim between, o'erhung with mists of tears.

VII

My friend, my friend! where art thou? Day by day,
130 Gliding, like some dark mournful stream, away,
My silent youth flows from me. Spring, the while,
 Comes and rains beauty on the kindling boughs
Round hall and hamlet; Summer, with her smile,
 Fills the green forest;—young hearts breathe their vows;
Brothers long parted meet; fair children rise
Round the glad board; Hope laughs from loving eyes:
All this is in the world!—These joys lie sown,
The dew of every path—On *one* alone
Their freshness may not fall—the stricken deer,
140 Dying of thirst with all the waters near.

VIII

Ye are from dingle and fresh glade, ye flowers!
 By some kind hand to cheer my dungeon sent;
O'er you the oak shed down the summer showers,
 And the lark's nest was where your bright cups bent,
Quivering to breeze and rain-drop, like the sheen
Of twilight stars. On you Heaven's eye hath been,
Thro' the leaves, pouring its dark sultry blue
Into your glowing hearts; the bee to you
Hath murmur'd, and the rill.—My soul grows faint

With passionate yearning, as its quick dreams paint 150
Your haunts by dell and stream,—the green, the free,
The full of all sweet sound,—the shut from me!

IX

There went a swift bird singing past my cell—
    O Love and Freedom! ye are lovely things!
With you the peasant on the hills may dwell,
    And by the streams; but I—the blood of kings,
A proud, unmingling river, thro' my veins
Flows in lone brightness,—and its gifts are chains!
Kings!—I had silent visions of deep bliss,
Leaving their thrones far distant, and for this 160
I am cast under their triumphal car,
An insect to be crush'd.—Oh! Heaven is far,—
Earth pitiless!

Dost thou forget me, Seymour? I am prov'd
So long, so sternly! Seymour, my belov'd!
There are such tales of holy marvels done
By strong affection, of deliverance won
Thro' its prevailing power! Are these things told
Till the young weep with rapture, and the old
Wonder, yet dare not doubt,—and thou, oh! thou, 170
    Dost thou forget me in my hope's decay?—
Thou canst not!—thro' the silent night, ev'n now,
    I, that need prayer so much, awake and pray
Still first for thee.—Oh! gentle, gentle friend!
How shall I bear this anguish to the end?

Aid!—comes there yet no aid?—the voice of blood
Passes Heaven's gate, ev'n ere the crimson flood
Sinks thro' the greensward!—is there not a cry
From the wrung heart, of power, thro' agony,
To pierce the clouds? Hear, Mercy! hear me! None 180
That bleed and weep beneath the smiling sun,
Have heavier cause!—yet hear!—my soul grows dark—
Who hears the last shriek from the sinking bark,
On the mid seas, and with the storm alone,
And bearing to th' abyss, unseen, unknown,

Its freight of human hearts?—th' o'ermastering wave!
Who shall tell how it rush'd—and none to save?

Thou hast forsaken me! I feel, I know,
There would be rescue if this were not so.
190   Thou'rt at the chase, thou'rt at the festive board,
Thou'rt where the red wine free and high is pour'd,
Thou'rt where the dancers meet!—a magic glass
Is set within my soul, and proud shapes pass,
Flushing it o'er with pomp from bower and hall;—
I see one shadow, stateliest there of all,—

Thine!—What dost *thou* amidst the bright and fair,
Whispering light words, and mocking my despair?
It is not well of thee!—my love was more
Than fiery song may breathe, deep thought explore,
200   And there thou smilest, while my heart is dying,
With all its blighted hopes around it lying;
Ev'n thou, on whom they hung their last green leaf—
Yet smile, smile on! too bright art thou for grief!

Death!—what, is death a lock'd and treasur'd thing,
Guarded by swords of fire? a hidden spring,
A fabled fruit, that I should thus endure,
As if the world within me held no cure?
Wherefore not spread free wings—Heaven, Heaven! controul
These thoughts—they rush—I look into my soul
210   As down a gulph, and tremble at th' array
Of fierce forms crowding it! Give strength to pray,
So shall their dark host pass.
             The storm is still'd.
  Father in Heaven! Thou, only thou, canst sound
The heart's great deep, with floods of anguish fill'd,
  For human line too fearfully profound.
Therefore, forgive, my Father! if Thy child,
Rock'd on its heaving darkness, hath grown wild
And sinn'd in her despair! It well may be,

205 Guarded by swords of fire?] "And if you remember of old, *I dare die.*———Consider
what the world would conceive, if I should be violently enforced to do it." *Fragments of her
Letters.* Hemans.

That Thou wouldst lead my spirit back to Thee,   220
By the crush'd hope too long on this world pour'd,
The stricken love which hath perchance ador'd
A mortal in Thy place! Now let me strive
With Thy strong arm no more! Forgive, forgive!
Take me to peace!

        And peace at last is nigh.
   A sign is on my brow, a token sent
Th' o'erwearied dust, from home: no breeze flits by,
    But calls me with a strange sweet whisper, blent
Of many mysteries.   230
        Hark! the warning tone
Deepens—its word is *Death*. Alone, alone,
And sad in youth, but chasten'd, I depart,
Bowing to heaven. Yet, yet my woman's heart
Shall wake a spirit and a power to bless,
Ev'n in this hour's o'ershadowing fearfulness,
Thee, its first love!—oh! tender still, and true!
Be it forgotten if mine anguish threw
Drops from its bitter fountain on thy name,
Tho' but a moment.   240

    Now, with fainting frame,
With soul just lingering on the flight begun,
To bind for thee its last dim thoughts in one,
I bless thee! Peace be on thy noble head,
Years of bright fame, when I am with the dead!
I bid this prayer survive me, and retain
Its might, again to bless thee, and again!
Thou hast been gather'd into my dark fate
Too much; too long, for my sake, desolate
Hath been thine exiled youth; but now take back,   250
From dying hands, thy freedom, and re-track
(After a few kind tears for her whose days
Went out in dreams of thee) the sunny ways
Of hope, and find thou happiness! Yet send,
Ev'n then, in silent hours a thought, dear friend!
Down to my voiceless chamber; for thy love
Hath been to me all gifts of earth above,

Tho' bought with burning tears! It is the sting
Of death to leave that vainly-precious thing
260   In this cold world! What were it then, if thou,
With thy fond eyes, wert gazing on me now?
Too keen a pang!—Farewell! and yet once more,
Farewell!—the passion of long years I pour
Into that word: thou hear'st not,—but the wo
And fervour of its tones may one day flow
To thy heart's holy place; there let them dwell—
We shall o'ersweep the grave to meet—Farewell!

(1828)

* "The Lady Arabella," as she has been frequently entitled, was descended from Margaret, eldest daughter of Henry VII, and consequently allied by birth to Elizabeth, as well as James I. This affinity to the throne proved the misfortune of her life, as the jealousies which it constantly excited in her royal relatives, who were anxious to prevent her marrying, shut her out from the enjoyment of that domestic happiness which her heart appears to have so fervently desired. By a secret, but early discovered union with William Seymour, son of Lord Beauchamp, she alarmed the cabinet of James, and the wedded lovers were immediately placed in separate confinement. From this they found means to concert a romantic plan of escape; and having won over a female attendant, by whose assistance she was disguised in male attire, Arabella, though faint from recent sickness and suffering, stole out in the night, and at last reached an appointed spot, where a boat and servants were in waiting. She embarked; and, at break of day, a French vessel, engaged to receive her, was discovered and gained. As Seymour, however, had not yet arrived, she was desirous that the vessel should lie at anchor for him; but this wish was overruled by her companions, who, contrary to her entreaties, hoisted sail, "which," says D'Israeli, "occasioned so fatal a termination to this romantic adventure. Seymour, indeed, had escaped from the Tower;—he reached the wharf, and found his confidential man waiting with a boat, and arrived at Lee. The time passed; the waves were rising; Arabella was not there; but in the distance he descried a vessel. Hiring a fisherman to take him on board, he discovered, to his grief, on hailing it, that it was not the French ship charged with his Arabella; in despair and confusion he found another ship from Newcastle, which for a large sum altered its course, and landed him in Flanders."—Arabella, meantime, whilst imploring her attendants to linger, and earnestly looking out for the expected boat of her husband, was overtaken in Calais Roads by a vessel in the King's service, and brought back to a captivity, under the suffering of which her mind and constitution gradually sank.—"What passed in that dreadful imprisonment, cannot perhaps be recovered for authentic history,—but enough is known; that her mind grew impaired, that she finally lost her reason, and, if the duration of her imprisonment

was short, that it was only terminated by her death. Some effusions, often begun and never ended, written and erased, incoherent and rational, yet remain among her papers." — *D'Israeli's Curiosities of Literature.*

The following poem, meant as some record of her fate, and the imagined fluctuations of her thoughts and feelings, is supposed to commence during the time of her first imprisonment, whilst her mind was yet buoyed up by the consciousness of Seymour's affection, and the cherished hope of eventual deliverance. *Hemans.*

†From *The Prophecy of Dante,* canto 3, line 148. The full passage reads, "Perhaps he'll *love,* — and is not love in vain / Torture enough without a living tomb?"

‡"The heart that beat so strongly stopped at last." From Ippolito Pindemonte (1753–1828), author of *Field Poems* (1788), *Field Prose* (1784), and a well-regarded translation of the *Odyssey.*

The Dreamer

There is no such thing as *forgetting* possible to the mind; a thousand accidents may, and will, interpose a veil between our present consciousness, and the secret inscription on the mind; but alike, whether veiled or unveiled, the inscription remains forever.
— *English Opium Eater* *

Thou hast been call'd, O, Sleep! the friend of wo,
But 'tis the *happy* who have call'd thee so.
— Southey †

Peace to thy dreams! — thou art slumbering now,
The moonlight's calm is upon thy brow;
All the deep love that o'erflows thy breast
Lies 'midst the hush of thy heart at rest,
Like the scent of a flower in its folded bell,
When eve thro' the woodlands hath sigh'd farewell.

Peace! — the sad memories that through the day,
With a weight on thy lonely bosom lay,
The sudden thoughts of the changed and dead,
That bow'd thee, as winds bow the willow's head,   10
The yearnings for faces and voices gone —
All are forgotten! — Sleep on, sleep on!

Are they forgotten?—It is not so!
Slumber divides not the heart from its wo.
E'en now o'er thine aspect swift changes pass,
Like lights and shades over wavy grass:
Tremblest thou, Dreamer?—O love and grief!
Ye have storms that shake e'en the clos'd-up leaf!

20

On thy parted lips there's a quivering thrill,
As on a lyre ere its chords are still;
On the long silk lashes that fringe thine eye,
There's a large tear gathering heavily;
A rain from the clouds of thy spirit press'd—
Sorrowful Dreamer! this is not rest!

It is Thought at work amidst buried hours,
It is Love keeping vigil o'er perish'd flowers.—
Oh! we bear within us mysterious things,
Of Memory and Anguish, unfathom'd springs,
And Passion, those gulfs of the heart to fill,

30

With bitter waves, which it ne'er may still.

Well might we pause ere we gave them away,
Flinging the peace of our couch away!
Well might we look on our souls in fear,
They find no fount of oblivion here!
They forget not, the mantle of sleep beneath—
How know we if under the wings of death?

(1829)

---

*Thomas De Quincey (1785–1859), *Confessions of an English Opium-Eater* (1821).
†Robert Southey, *The Curse of Kehama* (1810) 15.12.10–11.

The Return

"Hast thou come with the heart of thy childhood back?
 The free, the pure, the kind?"
—So murmur'd the trees in my homeward track,
 As they play'd to the mountain-wind.

"Hath thy soul been true to its early love?"
 Whisper'd my native streams;
"Hath the spirit nursed amidst hill and grove,
 Still revered its first high dreams?"

"Hast thou borne in thy bosom the holy prayer
 Of the child in his parent-halls?"   10
—Thus breathed a voice on the thrilling air,
 From the old ancestral walls.

"Hast thou kept thy faith with the faithful dead,
 Whose place of rest is nigh?
With the father's blessing o'er thee shed,
 With the mother's trusting eye?"

—Then my tears gush'd forth in sudden rain,
 As I answer'd—"O, ye shades!
I bring not my childhood's heart again
 To the freedom of your glades.   20

"I have turn'd from my first pure love aside,
 O bright and happy streams!
Light after light, in my soul have died
 The day-spring's glorious dreams.

"And the holy prayer from my thoughts hath pass'd—
 The prayer at my mother's knee;
Darken'd and troubled I come at last,
 Home of my boyish glee!

"But I bear from my childhood a gift of tears,
　　To soften and atone;
And oh! ye scenes of those blessed years
　　They shall make me again your own."

(1829)

30

The Painter's Last Work—A Scene*

Clasp me a little longer on the brink
Of life, while I can feel thy dear caress;
And when this heart hath ceased to beat, oh! think,
And let it mitigate thy woe's excess,
That thou hast been to me all tenderness,
And friend to more than human friendship just.
　　　—Gertrude of Wyoming†

Scene—A Room in an Italian Cottage. The Lattice opening upon a Landscape at sunset.

Francesco—Teresa

TERESA

The fever's hue hath left thy cheek, beloved!
Thine eyes, that make the day-spring in my heart,
Are clear and still once more. Wilt thou look forth?
Now, while the sunset with low-streaming light—
The light thou lov'st—hath made the chestnut-stems
All burning bronze, the lake one sea of gold!
Wilt thou be raised upon thy couch, to meet
The rich air fill'd with wandering scents and sounds?
Or shall I lay thy dear, dear head once more
On this true bosom, lulling thee to rest
With vesper hymns?

FRANCESCO
　　　No, gentlest love! not now:
My soul is wakeful—lingering to look forth,
Not on the sun, but thee! Doth the light sleep

10

So gently on the lake? and are the stems
Of our own chestnuts by that alchymy
So richly changed?—and is the orange-scent
Floating around?—But I have said farewell,
Farewell to earth, Teresa! not to thee,
Nor yet to our deep love, nor yet awhile   20
Unto the spirit of mine art, which flows
Back on my soul in mastery!—one last work!
And I will shrine my wealth of glowing thoughts,
Clinging affection and undying hope,
All that is in me for eternity,
All, all, in that memorial.

                    TERESA
                    Oh! what dream
Is this, mine own Francesco? Waste thou not
Thy scarce-returning strength; keep thy rich thoughts
For happier days! they will not melt away   30
Like passing music from the lute;—dear friend!
Dearest of friends! thou canst win back at will
The glorious visions.

                    FRANCESCO
                    Yes! the unseen land
Of glorious visions hath sent forth a voice
To call me hence. Oh! be thou not deceived!
Bind to thy heart no *earthly* hope, Teresa!
I must, *must* leave thee! Yet be strong, my love,
As thou hast still been gentle!

                    TERESA
                    Oh, Francesco!   40
What will this dim world be to me, Francesco,
When wanting thy bright soul, the life of all—
My only sunshine!—How can I bear on?
How can we part? We that have loved so well,
With clasping spirits link'd so long by grief—
By tears—by prayer?

FRANCESCO
Ev'n *therefore* we can part,
With an immortal trust, that such high love
Is not of things to perish.
                    Let me leave
50 One record still, to prove it strong as death,
Ev'n in Death's hour of triumph. Once again,
Stand with thy meek hands folded on thy breast,
And eyes half veil'd, in thine own soul absorb'd,
As in thy watchings, ere I sink to sleep;
And I will give the bending flower-like grace
Of that soft form, and the still sweetness throned
On that pale brow, and in that quivering smile
Of voiceless love, a life that shall outlast
60 Their delicate earthly being. There—thy head
Bow'd down with beauty, and with tenderness,
And lowly thought—even thus—my own Teresa!
Oh! the quick glancing radiance, and bright bloom
That once around thee hung, have melted now
Into more solemn light—but holier far,
And dearer, and yet lovelier in mine eyes,
Than all that summer flush! For by my couch,
In patient and serene devotedness,
Thou hast made those rich hues and sunny smiles,
70 Thine offering unto me. Oh! I may give
Those pensive lips, that clear Madonna brow,
And the sweet earnestness of that dark eye,
Unto the canvass—I may catch the flow
Of all those drooping locks, and glorify
With a soft halo which is imaged thus—
But how much rests unbreathed! My faithful one!
What thou hast been to me! This bitter world,
This cold unanswering world, that hath no voice
To greet the heavenly spirit—that drives back
80 All Birds of Eden, which would sojourn here
A little while—how have I turn'd away
From its keen soulless air, and in *thy* heart,
Found ever the sweet fountain of response,
To quench my thirst for home!

The dear work grows
Beneath my hand—the last! Each faintest line
With treasured memories fraught. Oh! weep thou not
Too long, too bitterly, when I depart!
Surely a bright home waits us both—for I,
In all my dreams, have turn'd me not from God;   90
And Thou—oh! best and purest! stand thou there—
There, in thy hallow'd beauty, shadowing forth
The loveliness of love!

                                   (1832)

* Suggested by the closing scene in the life of the painter Blake; as beautifully
related by Allan Cunningham. *Hemans.* [Cunningham's account appeared in his *Lives
of the Most Eminent British Painters, Sculptors and Architects,* 6 vols. (London, 1830),
2:140–79. *Ed.*]

† Pt. 3, st. 29, lines 1–6. By Thomas Campbell (1777–1814), the poem was first published in 1809. It concerns the death of Gertrude Waldegrave and her father during
the destruction of the settlement at Wyoming, Pennsylvania, by Indians in 1778.

I Dream of All Things Free

I dream of all things free!
    Of a gallant, gallant bark,
That sweeps through storm and sea,
    Like an arrow to its mark!
Of a stag that o'er the hills
    Goes bounding in his glee;
Of a thousand flashing rills—
    Of all things glad and free.

I dream of some proud bird,
    A bright-eyed mountain king!   10
In my visions I have heard
    The rushing of his wing.
I follow some wild river,
    On whose breast no sail may be;

Dark woods around it shiver—
—I dream of all things free!

Of a happy forest child,
    With the fawns and flowers at play;
Of an Indian 'midst the wild,
    With the stars to guide his way:
Of a chief his warriors leading,
    Of an archer's greenwood tree:—
My heart in chains is bleeding,
    And I dream of all things free!

(1833)

Mary Howitt

(1799–1888)

~~~~~~

Mary Howitt, remembered today for writing some of the most popular ballads of her time, for introducing humor into children's poetry, and for being the first English translator of Hans Christian Anderson and Fredrika Bremer, was born in Coleford, Gloucestershire, on 12 March 1799. Called "Polly" as a child, she was the second daughter of Ann Wood and Samuel Botham, an iron worker turned land surveyor. Her parents were both devout members of the Society of Friends, and the household was a constricted world of isolation and quiet, so much so that the children had unusual difficulty learning to speak. Her father forbade secular literature on religious grounds, but he read frequently from the Bible, and in his absence Mary's mother, who possessed a strong narrative gift, told stories and recited a large repertoire of poetry from memory. A nurse sang ballads that shaped Mary's sensibilities. Although fiction, music, dancing, and theater all were off-limits, Mary compensated by creating battle scenes out of the damp spots on the wall of the Friends' meeting house and imagining heads of animals and people in the grain of the wood seats. After attending a school for girls at Uttoxeter, in 1809 Mary enrolled at a Friends' school in Croydon, where a copy of Barbauld's *Hymns in Prose* was confiscated from her. In 1812 she began attending Hannah Kilham's Friends' school in Sheffield, where her interest in writers and authorship was awakened. Here she and her older sister, Anna, who would remain best friends throughout life, together wrote several prose tales and an epic. Mary became an insatiable reader, clandestinely devouring the *Spectator,* the *Gentleman's Magazine,* old English poetry and drama, Shakespeare, and the latest books of poetry, including Moore and Byron, which she copied into her album and learned by heart. When she was seventeen she stood under an apple tree by her house and prayed that one day she would become a famous writer.

In 1817 Mary met William Howitt, seven years her senior. They studied botany together, and he introduced her to the *Edinburgh Review,* the novels of Scott, the engravings of Thomas Bewick, and the poetry of Wordsworth, Coleridge, Crabbe, and Shelley. They became engaged early in 1819 and were married in a Quaker ceremony at Uttoxeter on 16 April 1821. Their marriage would endure for over half a century and would be cited by Margaret Fuller in *Woman in the Nineteenth Century* as a prime example of the union of intellectual companionship. William had been apprenticed to a builder but vowed he would one day write books. He bought a chemist's shop in Hanley, which he operated for seven months. In April 1822, only a few months after Mary had given birth to a stillborn child, the couple sailed to Dunbarton and embarked on a five-hundred-mile walking tour of Scotland, visiting Abbotsford, the home of Sir Walter Scott, along the way. They published an account of this trip, "A Scottish Ramble in the Spring of 1822 by Wilfred and Wilfreda Wender," the first of many collaborative writing projects, two years later in the Staffordshire *Mercury*. At trip's end, they joined William's brothers Godfrey and Richard in Nottingham, a center of religious dissent and radical politics and the prosperous core of the weaving trade; there William and Richard opened another chemist's shop. Mary and William published their first joint book, *The Forest Minstrel, and Other Poems,* with Baldwin, Cradock and Joy in April 1823. It received good reviews, but its sales were not significant.

In January 1824, having already lost three infants, Mary gave birth to a frail baby girl, Anna Mary, but almost died herself from puerperal fever. Only four of her ten children would survive to adulthood, and Mary was to outlive all but Alfred William (b. 1830) and Margaret Anastasia (b. 1839). Throughout her childbearing years Mary was a productive writer. She and William began contributing to the literary gift books and annuals as well as to periodicals such as *Time's Telescope* and Hone's *Table Book*. In 1827 they brought out another collaborative effort, *The Desolation of Eyam, and Other Poems,* inspired by the heroic story of the vicar of Eyam during the plague years. The book got a mixed response. The *Eclectic Review* denounced it as "anti-Quakerish, atheistical, and licentious in style and sentiment," but the *Noctes Ambrosianae* was full of praise, calling Mary's language "chaste and simple—her feelings tender and pure—and her observation of nature accurate and intense."[1] Gradually, the couple began to gather around them an intellectual and artistic circle, getting to know William Wordsworth, William Hone, James Montgomery, and their neighbor Ann Taylor Gilbert.

In December 1829 the Howitts traveled to London, where they visited

1. *Eclectic Review* 34 (November 1828): 675; *Noctes Ambrosianae,* published serially, reprinted in 5 vols. (New York, 1863), quotation on 3:171.

Zillah Watts, editor of the *New Year's Gift,* and her husband, Alaric A. Watts, editor of the *Literary Souvenir,* as well as Anna Maria and Samuel Carter Hall, editors of the *Amulet* and the *Juvenile Forget-Me-Not.* They met, too, the painter John Martin, Bryan Waller Procter, Allan Cunningham, Barbara Hofland, and Letitia Elizabeth Landon (L.E.L.). Friendship with the Halls, the Wattses, and other editors helped the Howitts make the transition from pharmacy to authorship as their principal source of family income. During the 1830s, 1840s, and 1850s, Mary and William produced an astonishing number of works, as they struggled to support themselves as writers—publishing each year from one to four books, writing not only poetry but also reviews, fictional tales, and periodical articles. They also worked for humanitarian and political causes, kept up an active social calendar, took long walking tours, and conducted a heavy correspondence. Mary came to correspond with some of the leading women authors of her time, including Maria Jane Jewsbury, Joanna Baillie, Mary Russell Mitford, Letitia Elizabeth Landon, Anna Jameson, Caroline Bowles, Anna Maria Hall, Elizabeth Gaskell, and Felicia Hemans. Hemans had initiated the correspondence after reading the passage in "The Record of Poetry," from *The Desolation of Eyam,* praising her work. The two poets met in Liverpool in 1828 at the home of William Chorley, editor of the *Winter's Wreath,* a literary annual to which both women contributed.

Mary's *Sketches of Natural History* (1834) contained what is today her best-known poem, "The Spider and the Fly. An Apologue. A New Version of an Old Story." This book provided, according to Alexander H. Japp, "one of the first effective popularizations of science" in English[2] and helped to cultivate the fanciful in literature for children. Her book of dramatic sketches, *The Seven Temptations,* influenced by Joanna Baillie, was published the same year; although it was damned by the critics, she always considered it her most original and best work. In 1836 the Howitts visited Edinburgh, where they began a long friendship with David Macbeth Moir (Delta). He later said of Mary's ballads, "She has few contemporary rivals, whether we regard her pictures of stern wild solitary nature, or of all that is placid, gentle, and benignant in the supernatural."[3] They also met Robert Chambers, to whose mass-circulation weekly, *Chambers' Edinburgh Journal,* Mary would contribute regularly and anonymously, and William Tait, for whose *Tait's Edinburgh Magazine* both Howitts would write. In a typical year, Mary contributed poems

---

2. Quoted in Alfred H. Miles, *The Poets and the Poetry of the Century,* vol. 7, *Joanna Baillie to Mathilde Blind* (London, [1894]), 83.

3. *Sketches of the Poetical Literature of the Past Half-Century* (Edinburgh, 1851), 273.

and tales to annuals and wrote ballads for the *Monthly Repository* and the Edinburgh journals. She planned her writing so that her periodical publications
could be gathered together into books to bring in additional income. She
was resourceful, too, in developing writing projects. When her sister Emma
sent a journal of her children's life in Cincinnati, Mary published it under
the title *Our Cousins in Ohio* and wrote a companion volume, *Children's Year,*
about two of her own children. Not infrequently she would first contribute
a poem to a magazine, then sell it to a literary annual, and later include it
in a book of poems most of which had been previously published. She also
recycled her work from one book to the next, in some instances publishing
a poem many times, often revising it with each new appearance. This system
enabled her to make a substantial contribution to her family's income. In
1836, for example, Richard Bentley paid her £150 for a three-volume novel
entitled *Wood Leighton;* combined with the £50 she earned for other writings
that year, that added up to a respectable living. Allan Cunningham wrote
that "Mary Howitt has shown herself mistress of every string of the minstrel's
lyre, save that which sounds of broil and bloodshed. There is more of the old
ballad simplicity than can be found in the strains of any living poet besides."[4]
Letitia Elizabeth Landon described her in her novel *Romance and Reality* as
one who "gave me more the idea of a poet than most of our modern votaries
of the lute. . . . She is as creative in her imaginary poems, as she is touching
and true in her simple ones." *Birds and Flowers and Other Country Things* (1838)
contained some of Mary Howitt's most successful lyrics; it was followed the
next year by *Hymns and Fireside Verses* (1839), dedicated to Caroline Bowles.
Queen Victoria presented a copy of the latter to at least one of her ministers.

After fourteen years in Nottingham, in 1836 the Howitts went to live in
Surrey, near London, where they could be closer to the center of British
publishing. Mary took over from Landon the editorship of the *Drawing-Room
Scrap-Book,* for which she provided all the copy in 1840 and 1841. The publisher Thomas Tegg, having seen one of Mary's short stories, commissioned
her to write thirteen tales for children in a series called Tales for the People
and Their Children, paying her one thousand pounds in installments. Several of the books came out each year in the early 1840s and went through
many editions. One of them, *Little Coin, Much Care; or, How Poor Men Live,
A Tale* (1842) inspired Elizabeth Gaskell as she wrote *Mary Barton.* Another,
Autobiography of a Child, tells the story of her own childhood.

By this time both Mary and William Howitt had become well-known and
well-respected writers in England as well as in America, where Thomas Cow-

4. Quoted in "William and Mary Howitt," *Leisure Hour* 26 (15 September 1877): 586.

perthwait, a Philadelphia publisher, bound Mary's *Poetical Works* with that of Keats. In America, by the mid-1840s she was the most highly respected of living foreign poets.[5] In the American annuals, she is among the three British authors appearing most frequently. Howitt developed many American friendships. Through William Lloyd Garrison, she met Frederick Douglass, to whom she sent books and for whom she became active in 1847 and 1848 in raising a subscription. Margaret Fuller, who visited the Howitts in the summer of 1846, recalled that "in Mary Howitt, I found the same engaging traits of character we are led to expect from her books for children."[6] *Godey's Lady's Book* included Mary Howitt among the "Illustrious Women of Our Time." In 1840 the Howitts went to live in Germany, settling in Heidelberg. They visited Munich, Prague, Berlin, Vienna, and Dresden, not returning to London until April 1843, when they settled at The Grange, Upper Clapton.

Mary Howitt had a facility for learning languages, which served her well as a writer. When she discovered the work of the Swedish feminist novelist Fredrika Bremer, she read all she could of her work in German translations, then began learning Swedish. Working from the German and in concert with William, she translated into English Bremer's popular novel *The Neighbours*. Beginning in 1843, they translated Bremer's fiction directly from the Swedish, eventually translating nineteen books in all. Later, Mary Howitt learned Danish so that she could translate the works of Hans Christian Andersen. In March 1844 the Howitts suffered a devastating blow when their ten-year-old son Claude died from the aftereffects of a fall. That summer the family moved to The Elms, Lower Clapton, where for the first time in her life Mary had a study of her own.

In the 1840s the Howitts were active in politics, supporting anti–corn law legislation, the peace movement, women's economic rights, the movement for national compulsory education, Irish relief, Catholic emancipation, the anti-enclosure act, the extension of suffrage, and the revision of the poor laws. As humanitarians, they opposed capital punishment, slavery, child labor, and cruelty to animals. They shared a bond of political liberalism with friends such as Leigh Hunt, Lucretia Mott, and Richard Hengist Horne. The Howitt circle also came to include Charles Kean, Charles Dickens, Charles and Mary Cowden Clarke, Alfred Tennyson, the Rossettis, and other Pre-Raphaelites. Mary could be outspoken about her opinions. In March 1854 seventeen-year-old Anne Thackeray was shocked when Mary "announced her opinion that women should sit in Parliament." For many years Mary wrote ballads and

5. Carl R. Woodring, *Victorian Samplers: William and Mary Howitt* (Lawrence, Kans., 1952), i.

6. R. W. Emerson, W. H. Channing, and J. F. Clarke, *Memoirs of Margaret Fuller Ossoli*, 2 vols. (New York, 1869), 2:183.

translations for Dickens's *Household Words.* In 1846 William became an editor and part owner of the *People's Journal,* and in January 1847 William and Mary founded the weekly *Howitt's Journal* to advocate democratic causes. It began with a circulation of thirty thousand and cost one shilling. Elizabeth Gaskell contributed "Libbie Marsh's Three Eras"—her literary debut—and later two more short stories.[7] *Howitt's Journal* gave *Jane Eyre* a positive review. As early as February 1830, Mary had praised William Blake's engravings, and the Howitts reprinted his design "Death's Door" on the front page of the 20 November issue of *Howitt's Journal.* After eighteen months, however, the weekly ceased publication; it had never made a profit and had led the Howitts into bankruptcy. They moved to more modest quarters at 28 Upper Avenue Road, St. John's Wood, near Regent's Park.

Mary's *Poems and Ballads* (1847) enjoyed great popularity, and she worked with William in 1851 to construct the first English history of Scandinavian literature. In June 1852 William sailed with his two sons to Australia to prospect for gold, returning two and a half years later with no fortune but with rich material for books. By the late fifties William and Mary were making annual trips to the Continent. In March 1867 they moved to The Orchard, Claygate, near Esher, where they became active in the Royal Society for the Prevention of Cruelty to Animals; in a dozen books Mary urged children to be kind to animals. Her world was shaken in 1863 when their son Charlton drowned in Lake Brunner, New Zealand, but the couple achieved a financial security they had never before had in 1865 when William was awarded a civil list pension of £140 per year. They left for Switzerland and Italy in 1870, intending to return in a year. But instead, because they could live more cheaply abroad, they made their home in Rome, where they knew Joseph Severn and Louisa May Alcott. William died of bronchitis on 3 March 1879 at the age of eighty-seven and was buried in the Protestant cemetery in Rome, near the graves of Percy Bysshe Shelley and John Keats. Shortly thereafter the queen awarded Mary a civil list pension of £100 a year "in consideration of literary services."

Two years later Mary moved with her daughter Margaret to a villa near Meran. She and William had resigned from the Society of Friends in 1847 and had allied themselves with Unitarianism. Later they subscribed to spiritualism, frequently holding seances at their home. Now, influenced by Margaret's adopted faith, in 1882 Mary converted to Roman Catholicism. In early January 1888 she had an audience with Pope Leo XIII. Weeks later, on 30 January,

7. She published under the pseudonym Cotton Mather Mills. The Howitts also encouraged Gaskell to write; they read her first novel, *Mary Barton,* in manuscript and helped her publish it.

at the age of nearly eighty-nine, she died of bronchitis in Rome; by special dispensation, she was buried beside William in the Protestant cemetery. She had authored, co-authored, edited, or translated well over one hundred books.

MAJOR WORKS: *The Seven Temptations* (London, 1834); *Sketches of Natural History* (London, 1834); *Tales in Prose* (London, [1836]); *Tales in Verse* (London, [1836]); *Wood Leighton; or, A Year in the Country*, 3 vols. (London, 1836); *Birds and Flowers and Other Country Things* (London, 1838); *Hymns and Fireside Verses* (London, 1839); *Hope On, Hope Ever! A Tale* (London, 1840); *Sowing and Reaping; or, What Will Come of It?* (London, 1840); *Strive and Thrive, a Tale* (London, 1840); *Fireside Verses* (London, [1845]); *My Own Story; or, The Autobiography of a Child* (London, 1845); *Ballads, and Other Poems* (London, 1847); *Our Cousins in Ohio* (London, 1849); *Marion's Pilgrimage, a Fire-side Story, and Other Poems* (London, [1859]); *The Poet's Children* (London, [1863]); *Birds and Their Nests* (London, [1872]).

WITH WILLIAM HOWITT: *The Forest Minstrel, and Other Poems* (London, 1823); *The Desolation of Eyam: The Emigrant, a Tale of the American Woods: And Other Poems* (London, Edinburgh, and Dublin, 1827); *Howitt's Journal of Literature and Popular Programs*, 1847–48.

TEXTS USED: Texts of "The Countess Lamberti" and "The Fairies of the Caldon Low" from *Ballads, and Other Poems.* "The Spider and the Fly" appeared in 1829 in the *New Year's Gift;* this copy-text is from *Sketches of Natural History* (1834). "The Voyage with the Nautilus" appeared in *The Gem* for 1831; this copy-text is the revised text printed in *Ballads, and Other Poems.* Text of "Tibbie Inglis; or, The Scholar's Wooing" from the *Forget-Me-Not* for 1834. Texts of "The Nettle-King" and "The Broom-Flower" from *Sketches of Natural History.* "A Swinging Song" appeared in the *New Year's Gift* for 1836 and in *Tales in Verse;* this text is taken from *Tales in Verse for Young People* (1865). Text of "The Sea-Gull" from *Birds and Flowers, and Other Country Things.* Text of "Old Christmas" from *Hymns and Fireside Verses.*

The Countess Lamberti

She still was young; but guilt and tears
Had done on her the work of years.
In a lone house of penitence
　　She dwelt; and, saving unto one,
A sorrowing woman meek and kind,
　　Words spake she unto none.

It was about the close of May,
　　When they two sate apart
In the warm light of parting day,
　　　　That she unsealed her burdened heart.

"They married me when I was young,
　　A very child in years;
They married me at the dagger's point,
　　Amid my prayers and tears.

"To Count Lamberti I was wed,
　　He to the pope was brother,
They made me pledge my faith to him
　　The while I loved another:
Ay, while I loved to such excess,
　　My love than madness scarce was less!

"I would have died for him, and he
　　Loved me with equal warmth and truth.
Lamberti's age was thrice mine own,
　　And he had long outlived his youth.

"His brow was scarred by many wounds;
　　His eye was stern, and cold, and grave;
He was a soldier from his youth,
　　And all confessed him brave;
He had been much in foreign lands,
　　And once among the Moors a slave.

"I thought of him like Charlemagne,
 Or any knight of old:
When I was a child upon the knee
 His deeds to me they told.

"I knew the songs they made of him,
 I sang them when a child:
Giuseppe sang them too with me,
 He loved all tales of peril wild.

"I tell thee, he was stern and grey;
 His years were thrice mine own.   40
That I was to Giuseppe pledged,
 To all my kin was known.

"My heart was to Giuseppe vowed;
 Love was our childhood's lot;
I loved him ever; never knew
 The time I loved him not.

"He was an orphan, and the last
 Of a long line of pride:
My father took him for his son;
 He was to us allied.   50

"And he within our house was bred,
From the same books in youth we read,
Our teachers were the same; and he
Was as a brother unto me;
 A brother!—no, I never knew
How warm a brother's love might be;
 But dearer every year he grew.

"Love was our earliest, only life;
 Twin forms that had one heart
Were we, and for each other lived,   60
 And never thought to part.

"My father had him trained for war;
 He went to Naples, where he fought:

And then the Count Lamberti came,
　　And me in marriage sought;
He from my father asked my hand,
　　And I knew nought of what they planned.

"I was no party in the thing.
　　Why he was ever at my side
70　　I knew not; nor why, when we rode,
　　My father bade me with him ride.

"No, no! And when Lamberti spoke
　　Of love, I misbelieving heard;
And strangely gazed into his face,
　　Appalled at every word.

"It seemed to me as if there fell
From some old saint a tone of hell;
As if the hero heart of pride,
Which my Giusepp' had sanctified
80　　Among the heroes of old time,
Before me blackened stood with crime.

"That night my father sought my room,
　　And, furious betwixt rage and pride,
He bade me on an early day
　　Prepare to be Lamberti's bride.

"I thought my father too was mad,
　　Yet silently I let him speak;
I had no power for word or sign,
　　I felt the blood forsake my cheek.

90　　"And my heart beat with desperate pain,
　　The sting of rage was at its core;
There was a tumult in my brain,
　　And I fell senseless on the floor.

"At length, upon my knees, I prayed
　　My father to regard the vow

Which to Giuseppe I had made.
   Oh Heaven! his furious brow,
His curling lip of sneering scorn,
   Like fiends they haunt me now.

"Ay, spite my vows, they made me wed,   100
   Young as I was in years;
At the dagger's point they married me,
   Amid my prayers and tears.

"Our palace was at Tivoli,
   An ancient place of Roman pride,
Girt round with a sepulchral wood,
Wherein a ruined temple stood;
   And there, whilst I was yet a bride,
   I saw Giuseppe at my side.

"My own Giuseppe! He had come   110
   From Naples with a noble train;
He came to claim me for his wife:
   Would God we ne'er had met again!

"Lamberti's speech still harsher grew,
   And darker still his spirit's gloom;
At length, all suddenly, one day
   He hurried me to Rome.

"I had a dream, three times it came:
   I saw as plainly as by day
A horrid thing, the bloody place   120
   Where young Giuseppe lay.

"I saw them in that ancient wood,
   I heard him wildly call on God;
I saw him stabbed; I saw him dead
   Upon the bloody sod.

"I knew the murderers, they were two;
   I saw them with my sleeping eye;

I knew their voices stern and grim;
I saw them plainly murder him
    In the old wood at Tivoli.
130
Three times the dream was sent to me,
    It could not be a lie.

"I knew it could not be a lie;
    I knew his precious blood was spilt;
I saw the murderer day by day
    Dwell calmly in his guilt.

"No wonder that a frenzy came;
    At midnight from my bed I leapt,
I snatched a dagger in my rage,
140
    I stabbed him as he slept.

"I say, I stabbed him as he slept.
    It was a horrid deed of blood;
But then I knew that he had slain
    Giuseppe in the wood.

"I told my father of my dream;
    I watched him every word I spake;
He tried to laugh my dream to scorn,
    And yet I saw his body quake.

"They fetched Giuseppe from the wood,
150
    And a great funeral feast they had;
They buried Count Lamberti too,
    And said that I was mad.

"I was not mad, and yet I bore
    A curse that was no less;
And many, many years went on
    Of gloomy wretchedness.

"I saw my father, how he grew
    An old man ere his prime;
I knew the secret penance-pain
160
    He bore for that accursëd crime.

"I too, there is a weight of sin
　　Upon my soul,—it will not hence:
'Tis therefore that my life is given
　　To one long penitence."

　　　　　　　　　　(1829)

The Spider and the Fly.
An Apologue. A New Version of an Old Story

"Will you walk into my parlour?" said the Spider to the Fly,
" 'Tis the prettiest little parlour that ever you did spy;
The way into my parlour is up a winding stair,
And I've many curious things to shew when you are there."
"Oh no, no," said the little Fly, "to ask me is in vain,
For who goes up your winding stair can ne'er come down again."

"I'm sure you must be weary, dear, with soaring up so high;
Will you rest upon my little bed?" said the Spider to the Fly.
"There are pretty curtains drawn around; the sheets are fine and thin,
And if you like to rest awhile, I'll snugly tuck you in!"　　　　10
"Oh no, no," said the little Fly, "for I've often heard it said,
They never, never wake again, who sleep upon your bed!"

Said the cunning Spider to the Fly, "Dear friend what can I do,
To prove the warm affection I've always felt for you?
I have within my pantry, good store of all that's nice;
I'm sure you're very welcome—will you please to take a slice?"
"Oh no, no," said the little Fly, "kind sir, that cannot be,
I've heard what's in your pantry, and I do not wish to see!"

"Sweet creature!" said the Spider, "you're witty and you're wise,
How handsome are your gauzy wings, how brilliant are your eyes!　　20
I've a little looking-glass upon my parlour shelf,
If you'll step in one moment, dear, you shall behold yourself."
"I thank you, gentle sir," she said, "for what you're pleased to say,
And bidding you good morning now, I'll call another day."

The Spider turned him round about, and went into his den,
For well he knew the silly Fly would soon come back again:
So he wove a subtle web, in a little corner sly,
And set his table ready, to dine upon the Fly.
Then he came out to his door again, and merrily did sing,
30   "Come hither, hither, pretty Fly, with the pearl and silver wing;
Your robes are green and purple—there's a crest upon your head;
Your eyes are like the diamond bright, but mine are dull as lead!"

Alas, alas! how very soon this silly little Fly,
Hearing his wily, flattering words, came slowly flitting by;
With buzzing wings she hung aloft, then near and nearer drew,
Thinking only of her brilliant eyes, and green and purple hue—
Thinking only of her crested head—poor foolish thing! At last,
Up jumped the cunning Spider, and fiercely held her fast.
He dragged her up his winding stair, into his dismal den,
40   Within his little parlour—but she ne'er came out again!

And now dear little children, who may this story read,
To idle, silly flattering words, I pray you ne'er give heed:
Unto an evil counsellor, close heart and ear and eye,
And take a lesson from this tale, of the Spider and the Fly.

                                                          (1829)

The Voyage with the Nautilus

I made myself a little boat,
    As trim as trim could be;
I made it of a great pearl shell
    Found in the Indian Sea.

I made my masts of wild sea-rush
    That grew on a secret shore,
And the scarlet plume of the halcyon
    Was the pleasant flag I bore.

---

7 halcyon] Kingfisher; in ancient legends, a bird that breeds in a nest floating on the sea and
charms the waves and winds into calm.

For my sails I took the butterfly's wings;
    For my ropes the spider's line; 10
And that mariner old, the Nautilus,
    To steer me over the brine.

For he had sailed six thousand years,
    And knew each isle and bay;
And I thought that we, in my little boat,
    Could merrily steer away.

The stores I took were plentiful:
    The dew as it sweetly fell;
And the honey that was hoarded up
    In the wild bee's summer cell. 20

"Now steer away, thou helmsman good,
    Over the waters free;
To the charmèd Isle of the Seven Kings,
    That lies in the midmost sea."

He spread the sail, he took the helm;
    And, long ere ever I wist,
We had sailed a league, we had reached the isle
    That lay in the golden mist.

The charmèd Isle of the Seven Kings,
    'Tis a place of wondrous spell; 30
And all that happed unto me there
    In a printed book I'll tell.

Said I, one day, to the Nautilus,
    As we stood on the strand,
"Unmoor my ship, thou helmsman good,
    And steer me back to land;

"For my mother, I know, is sick at heart,
    And longs my face to see.

---

11 Nautilus] Marine animal with an unusual, chambered shell found in tropical waters of
the western Pacific and Indian Oceans.

What ails thee now, thou Nautilus?
    Art slow to sail with me?
Up! do my will; the wind is fresh,
    So set the vessel free."

He turned the helm; away we sailed
    Towards the setting sun:
The flying-fish were swift of wing,
    But we outsped each one.

And on we went for seven days,
    Seven days without a night;
We followed the sun still on and on,
    In the glow of his setting light.

Down and down went the setting sun,
    And down and down went we;
'Twas a splendid sail for seven days
    On a smooth descending sea.

On a smooth, descending sea we sailed,
    Nor breeze the water curled:
My brain grew sick, for I saw we sailed
    On the down-hill of the world.

"Good friend," said I to the Nautilus,
    "Can this the right course be?
And shall we come again to land?"
    But answer none made he;
And I saw a laugh in his fishy eye,
    As he turned it up to me.

So on we went; but soon I heard
    A sound as when winds blow,
And waters wild are tumbled down
    Into a gulf below.

And on and on flew the little bark,
    As a fiend her course did urge;
And I saw, in a moment, we must hang
    Upon the ocean's verge.

I snatched down the sails, I snapped the ropes,
    I broke the masts in twain;
But on flew the bark and 'gainst the rocks,
    Like a living thing did strain.

"Thou'st steered us wrong, thou helmsman vile!"
    Said I to the Nautilus bold;
"We shall down the gulf; we're dead men both!
    Dost know the course we hold?"   80

I seized the helm with a sudden jerk,
    And we wheeled round like a bird;
But I saw the Gulf of Eternity,
    And the tideless waves I heard.

"Good master," said the Nautilus,
    "I thought you might desire
To have some wondrous thing to tell
    Beside your mother's fire.

"What's sailing on a summer sea?
    As well sail on a pool;   90
Oh, but I know a thousand things
    That are wild and beautiful!

"And if you wish to see them now,
    You've but to say the word."
"Have done!" said I to the Nautilus,
    "Or I'll throw thee overboard.

"Have done!" said I, "thou mariner old,
    And steer me back to land."
No other word spake the Nautilus,
    But took the helm in hand.   100

I looked up to the lady moon,
    She was like a glow-worm's spark;
And never a star shone down to us
    Through the sky so high and dark.

We had no mast, we had no ropes,
 And every sail was rent;
And the stores I brought from the charmëd isle
 In the seven days' sail were spent.

But the Nautilus was a patient thing,
110 And steered with all his might
On the up-hill sea; and he never slept,
 But kept the course aright.

And for thrice seven nights we sailed and sailed;
 At length I saw the bay
Where I built my ship, and my mother's house
 'Mid the green hills where it lay.

"Farewell!" said I to the Nautilus,
 And leaped upon the shore;
"Thou art a skilful mariner,
120 But I'll sail with thee no more!"

           (1831)

Tibbie Inglis, or The Scholar's Wooing

Bonny Tibbie Inglis!
 Through sun and stormy weather,
She kept upon the broomy hills
 Her father's flock together.

Sixteen summers had she seen —
 A rosebud just unsealing —
Without sorrow, without fear,
 In her mountain sheiling.

She was made for happy thoughts,
10 For playful wit and laughter,
Singing on the hills alone,
 With Echo singing after.

She had hair as deeply black
    As the cloud of thunder;
She had brows so beautiful,
    And dark eyes sparkling under.

Bright and witty shepherd-girl!
    Beside a mountain-water
I found her, whom a king himself
    Would proudly call his daughter.   20

She was sitting 'mong the crags,
    Wild, and mossed, and hoary,
Reading in an ancient book
    Some old martyr-story.

Tears were starting to her eyes,
    Solemn thought was o'er her;
When she saw in that lone place
    A stranger stand before her,

Crimson was her sunny cheek,
    And her lips seemed moving   30
With the beatings of her heart—
    How could I help loving!

Among the crags I sat me down,
    Upon the mountain hoary,
And made her read again to me
    That old, pathetic story.

And then she sang me mountain-songs,
    Till all the air was ringing
With her clear and warbling voice,
    As when the lark is singing.   40

And when the eve came on at length,
    Among the blooming heather,
We herded on the mountain's side
    Her father's flock together.

And near unto her father's house
  I said "Good night" with sorrow,
And only wished that I might say
  "We'll meet again to-morrow."

I watched her tripping to her home;
50   I saw her meet her mother:
"Among a thousand maids," I cried,
  "There is not such another!"

I wandered to my scholar's home—
  Silent it looked and dreary;
I took my books, but could not read—
  Methought that I was weary.

I laid me down upon my bed,
  My heart with sadness laden;
I dreamt but of the mountains wild,
60   And of the mountain-maiden.

I saw her in her ancient book
  The pages turning slowly;
I saw her lovely crimson cheek,
  And dark eye drooping lowly.

The dream was like the day's delight,
  A life of pain's o'erpayment:
I rose, and with unwonted care
  Put on my sabbath-raiment.

To none I told my secret thought,
70   Not even to my mother,
Nor to the friend who from my youth
  Was dear as is a brother.

I gat me to the hills again,
  Where the little flock was feeding,
And there young Tibbie Inglis sate,
  But not the old book reading.

She sate as if absorbing thought
  With a heavy spell had bound her,
As silent as the mossy crags
  Upon the mountains round her.   80

I thought not of my sabbath-dress,
  I thought not of my learning;
I thought but of the gentle maid,
  Who, I believed, was mourning.

Bonny Tibbie Inglis!
  How her beauty brightened,
Looking at me half abashed
  With eyes that flashed and lightened!

There was no sorrow then I saw,
  There was no thought of sadness.   90
Oh, Life! what after-joy hast thou
  Like Love's first certain gladness!

I sate me down among the crags,
  Upon the mountain hoary;
But read not then the ancient book—
  Love was our pleasant story.

And then she sang me songs again,
  Old songs of love and sorrow,
For our sufficient happiness
  Great charm from woe could borrow.   100

And many hours we talked in joy,
  Yet too much blessed for laughter:—
I was a happy man that day—
  And happy ever after!
          (1834)

The Nettle-King

There was a Nettle both great and strong;
And the threads of his poison flowers were long;
He rose up in strength and height also,
And he said, "I'll be king of the plants below!"
It was a wood both drear and dank,
There grew the Nettle so broad and rank;
And an Owl sate up in an old ash tree
That was wasting away so silently;
And a Raven was perched above his head,
10 And they both of them heard what the Nettle-king said;
And there was a toad that sate below,
Chewing his venom sedate and slow,
And he heard the words of the Nettle also.

The Nettle he throve, and the Nettle he grew,
And the strength of the earth around him he drew:
There was a pale Stellaria meek,
But as he grew strong, so she grew weak;
There was a Campion, crimson-eyed,
But as he grew up, the campion died;
20 And the blue Veronica, shut from light,
Faded away in a sickly white;
For upon his leaves a dew there hung,
That fell like a blight from a serpent's tongue,
And there was not a flower about the spot,
Herb-Robert, Harebell, nor Forget-me-not.
Yet up grew the Nettle like water-sedge,
Higher and higher above the hedge;
The stuff of his leaves was strong and stout,
And the points of his stinging-flowers stood out;
30 And the Child that went in the wood to play,
From the great King-nettle would shrink away!

"Now," says the Nettle, "there's none like me;
"I am as great as a plant can be!
"I have crushed each weak and tender root,

"With the mighty power of my kingly foot;
"I have spread out my arms so strong and wide,
"And opened my way on every side;
"I have drawn from the earth its virtues fine,
"To strengthen for me each poison-spine;
"Both morn and night my leaves I've spread,   40
"And upon the falling dews have fed,
"Till I am as great as a forest-tree;
"The great wide world is the place for me!"
Said the Nettle-king in his bravery.

Just then came up a Woodman stout,
In the thick of the wood he was peering about.
The Nettle looked up, the Nettle looked down,
And graciously smiled on the simple clown:
"Thou knowest me well, Sir Clown," said he,
"And 'tis meet that thou reverence one like me!"   50
Nothing at all the man replied,
But he lifted a scythe that was at his side,
And he cut the Nettle up by the root,
And trampled it under his heavy foot;
And he saw where the Toad in its shadow lay,
But he said not a word, and went his way.

(1834)

The Broom-Flower

O the Broom, the yellow Broom,
    The ancient poet sung it,
And dear it is on summer days
    To lie at rest among it.

I know the realms where people say
    The flowers have not their fellow;
I know where they shine out like suns,
    The crimson and the yellow.

I know where ladies live enchained
    In luxury's silken fetters,
And flowers as bright as glittering gems
    Are used for written letters.

But ne'er was flower so fair as this
    In modern days or olden;
It groweth on its nodding stem
    Like to a garland golden.

And all about my mother's door
    Shine out its glittering bushes,
And down the glen, where clear as light
    The mountain-water gushes.

Take all the rest,—but give me this,
    And the bird that nestles in it;
I love it, for it loves the broom,
    The green and yellow linnet.

Well, call the rose the queen of flowers,
    And boast of that of Sharon,
Of lilies like to marble cups,
    And the golden rod of Aaron.

I care not how these flowers may be
    Beloved of man and woman;
The Broom it is the flower for me
    That groweth on the common.

Oh the Broom, the yellow Broom,
    The ancient poet sung it,
And dear it is on summer days
    To lie at rest among it!

                 (1834)

A Swinging Song

Merry it is on a summer's day,
All through the meadows to wend away;
To watch the brooks glide fast or slow,
And the little fish twinkle down below;
To hear the lark in the blue sky sing,
Oh, sure enough, 'tis a merry thing—
But 'tis merrier far to swing—to swing!

Merry it is on a winter's night,
To listen to tales of elf and sprite,
Of caves and castles so dim and old—   10
The dismallest tales that ever were told;
And then to laugh, and then to sing—
You may take my word is a merry thing—
But 'tis merrier far to swing—to swing!

Down with the hoop upon the green;
Down with the ringing tambourine;—
Little heed we for this or for that;
Off with the bonnet, off with the hat!
Away we go like birds on the wing!
Higher yet! higher yet! "Now for the King!"   20
This is the way we swing—we swing!

Scarcely the bough bends, Claude is so light—
Mount up behind him—there, that is right!
Down bends the branch now!—swing him away;
Higher yet—higher yet—higher I say!
Oh, what a joy it is! Now let us sing
"A pear for the Queen—an apple for the King!"
And shake the old tree as we swing—we swing!
(1836)

22 Claude] One of the poet's sons.

The Sea-Gull

Oh, the white Sea-gull, the wild Sea-gull,
 A joyful bird is he,
As he lies like a cradled thing at rest
 In the arms of a sunny sea!
The little waves rock to and fro,
 And the white Gull lies asleep,
As the fisher's bark, with breeze and tide,
 Goes merrily over the deep.
The ship, with her fair sails set, goes by,
10   And her people stand to note,
How the Sea-gull sits on the rocking waves,
 As if in an anchored boat.
The sea is fresh, the sea is fair,
 And the sky calm overhead,
And the Sea-gull lies on the deep, deep sea,
 Like a king in his royal bed!
Oh, the white Sea-gull, the bold Sea-gull,
 A joyful bird is he,
Throned like a king, in calm repose
20   On the breast of the heaving sea!
The waves leap up, the wild wind blows,
 And the gulls together crowd,
And wheel about, and madly scream
 To the deep sea roaring loud; —
And let the sea roar ever so loud,
 And the winds pipe ever so high,
With a wilder joy the bold sea-gull
 Sends forth a wilder cry, —

For the Sea-gull he is a daring bird,
30   And he loves with the storm to sail;
To ride in the strength of the billowy sea,
 And to breast the driving gale!
The little boat she is tossed about,
 Like a sea-weed to and fro;
The tall ship reels like a drunken man,
 As the gusty tempests blow.

But the Sea-gull laughs at the fear of man,
　And sails in a wild delight
On the torn-up breast of the night-black sea,
　Like a foam cloud, calm and white.　　　　　　　　40
The waves may rage and the winds may roar,
　But he fears not wreck nor need,
For he rides the sea, in its stormy strength,
　As a strong man rides his steed.

Oh the white Sea-gull, the bold sea-gull!
　He makes on the shore his nest,
And he tries what the inland fields may be;
　But he loveth the sea the best!
And away from land a thousand leagues,
　He goes 'mid surging foam;　　　　　　　　　　50
What matter to him is land or shore,
　For the sea is his truest home!
And away to the north 'mid ice-rocks stern,
　And amid the frozen snow,
To a sea that is lone and desolate,
　Will the wanton sea-gull go.
For he careth not for the winter wild,
　Nor those desert-regions chill;
In the midst of the cold, as on calm, blue seas,
　The sea-gull hath his will!　　　　　　　　　　60
And the dead whale lies on the northern shores,
　And the seal, and the sea-horse grim,
And the death of the great sea-creatures makes
　A full, merry feast for him!
Oh the wild sea-gull, the bold sea-gull!
　As he screams in his wheeling flight:
As he sits on the waves in storm or calm,
　All cometh to him aright!
All cometh to him as he liketh best;
　Nor any his will gainsay;　　　　　　　　　　70
And he rides on the waves like a bold, young king,
　That was crowned but yesterday!

　　　　　　　　　　　　　(1838)

Old Christmas

Now he who knows old Christmas,
    He knows a carle of worth;
For he is as good a fellow,
    As any upon the earth!

He comes warm cloked and coated,
    And buttoned up to the chin,
And soon as he comes a-nigh the door,
    We open and let him in.

We know that he will not fail us,
10   So we sweep the hearth up clean;
We set him the old armed chair,
    And a cushion whereon to lean.

And with sprigs of holly and ivy
    We make the house look gay,
Just out of an old regard to him, —
    For it was his ancient way.

We broach the strong ale barrel,
    And bring out wine and meat;
And thus have all things ready,
20   Our dear old friend to greet.

And soon as the time wears round,
    The good old carle we see,
Coming a-near; — for a creditor
    Less punctual is than he!

He comes with a cordial voice
    That does one good to hear;
He shakes one heartily by the hand,
    As he hath done many a year.

2 carle] A man of the common people.

And after the little children
   He asks in a cheerful tone,   30
Jack, Kate, and little Annie,—
   He remembers them every one!

What a fine old fellow he is!
   With his faculties all as clear,
And his heart as warm and light
   As a man's in his fortieth year!

What a fine old fellow, in troth!
   Not one of your griping elves,
Who, with plenty of money to spare,
   Think only about themselves!   40

Not he! for he loveth the children;
   And holiday begs for all;
And comes with his pockets full of gifts,
   For the great ones and the small!

With a present for every servant;—
   For in giving he doth not tire;—
From the red-faced, jovial butler,
   To the girl by the kitchen-fire.

And he tells us witty old stories;
   And singeth with might and main;   50
And we talk of the old man's visit
   Till the day that he comes again!

Oh he is a kind, old fellow
   For though that beef be dear,
He giveth the parish paupers
   A good dinner once a year!

And all the workhouse children
   He sets them down in a row,
And giveth them rare plum-pudding,
   And two-pence a-piece also.   60

Oh, could you have seen those paupers,
   Have heard those children young,
You would wish with them that Christmas
   Came often and tarried long!

He must be a rich old fellow,—
   What money he gives away!
There is not a lord in England
   Could equal him any day!

Good luck unto old Christmas,
70   And long life, let us sing,
For he doth more good unto the poor
   Than many a crownèd king!

              (1839)

The Fairies of the Caldon Low.
A Midsummer Legend

"And where have you been, my Mary,
   And where have you been from me?"
"I've been at the top of the Caldon Low,
   The midsummer-night to see!"

"And what did you see, my Mary,
   All up on the Caldon Low?"
"I saw the glad sunshine come down,
   And I saw the merry winds blow."

"And what did you hear, my Mary,
10   All up on the Caldon Hill?"
"I heard the drops of the water made,
   And the ears of the green corn fill."

"O! tell me all, my Mary,
   All, all that ever you know;

For you must have seen the fairies,
    Last night, on the Caldon Low."

"Then take me on your knee, mother;
    And listen, mother of mine.
A hundred fairies danced last night,
    And the harpers they were nine.   20

"And their harp-strings rung so merrily
    To their dancing feet so small;
But oh! the words of their talking
    Was merrier far than all."

"And what were the words, my Mary,
    That then you heard them say?"
"I'll tell you all, my mother;
    But let me have my way.

"Some of them played with the water,
    And rolled it down the hill;   30
'And this,' they said, 'shall speedily turn
    The poor old miller's mill:

" 'For there has been no water
    Ever since the first of May;
And a busy man will the miller be
    At dawning of the day.

" 'Oh! the miller, how he will laugh
    When he sees the mill-dam rise!
The jolly old miller, how he will laugh
    Till the tears fill both his eyes!'   40

"And some they seized the little winds
    That sounded over the hill;
And each put a horn unto his mouth,
    And blew both loud and shrill:

" 'And there,' they said, 'the merry winds go
    Away from every horn;

And they shall clear the mildew dank
    From the blind, old widow's corn.

" 'Oh! the poor, blind widow,
50   Though she has been blind so long,
She'll be blithe enough when the mildew's gone,
    And the corn stands tall and strong.'

"And some they brought the brown lint-seed,
    And flung it down from the Low;
'And this,' they said, 'by the sunrise,
    In the weaver's croft shall grow.

" 'Oh! the poor, lame weaver,
    How will he laugh outright,
When he sees his dwindling flax-field
60   All full of flowers by night!'

"And then outspoke a brownie,
    With a long beard on his chin;
'I have spun up all the tow,' said he,
    'And I want some more to spin.

" 'I've spun a piece of hempen cloth,
    And I want to spin another;
A little sheet for Mary's bed,
    And an apron for her mother.'

"With that I could not help but laugh,
70   And I laughed out loud and free;
And then on the top of the Caldon Low
    There was no one left but me.

"And all on the top of the Caldon Low
    The mists were cold and grey,
And nothing I saw but the mossy stones
    That round about me lay.

    61 brownie] "A benevolent spirit or goblin, of shaggy appearance, supposed to haunt old houses, esp. farm houses in Scotland, and sometimes to perform useful household work while the family were asleep" *(OED)*.

"But, coming down from the hill-top,
    I heard afar below,
How busy the jolly miller was,
    And how the wheel did go.   80

"And I peeped into the widow's field,
    And, sure enough, were seen
The yellow ears of the mildewed corn,
    All standing stout and green.

"And down by the weaver's croft I stole,
    To see if the flax were sprung;
But I met the weaver at his gate,
    With the good news on his tongue.

"Now this is all I heard, mother,
    And all that I did see;   90
So, pr'ythee, make my bed, mother,
    For I'm tired as I can be."
                                (1839)

Anna Maria Jones

(1748–1829)

Born on 5 December 1748, Anna Maria Jones was the second child and eldest of five daughters of Anna Maria Mordaunt and Jonathan Shipley, the dean of Winchester and bishop of St. Asaph. Her father was a man with literary interests, and he taught his daughter both classical and modern languages. At the age of thirty-five she married Sir William Jones, an Oxford-educated scholar, author, and philologist, remembered today as a pioneer in comparative linguistics and the first to perceive the common ancestry of the Indo-European languages. He had already published a Persian grammar, a history of Persian literature, and translations of Persian and Arabic poetry and was also well versed in chemistry, mathematics, botany, law, and music. Anna Maria had known him for some years before he proposed in October 1782; they were married the following April. A friend of Benjamin Franklin's, he was an enlightened partner who valued not only Anna Maria's excellent linguistic abilities but also her "Good sense, and good temper, agreeable manners, . . . feeling heart, [and] domestick affections," as well as her "knowledge of the world and contempt of what is wrong in it."[1] He had recently been knighted and appointed judge of the British Supreme Court at Fort William in Bengal.

Shortly after the wedding, the couple sailed for India by way of Madeira and Cape Verde, arriving in Calcutta in September. They spent their evenings reading aloud in the original languages from Ariosto, Tasso, Metastasio, Dante, Boccaccio, Petrarch, and others. An acute observer, Anna Maria enjoyed botanical research, recording what she discovered in sketches and watercolors. She also drew and painted local fauna, which her husband described in Latin. While he presided over the court, she wrote letters and poems. Each autumn they escaped Calcutta for a rural retreat on the Ganges, where they had a dairy and kept flocks and herds (including pet sheep and a

---

1. Sir William Jones to Viscount Althorp, 27 October 1782, *The Letters of Sir William Jones,* ed. G. H. Cannon, 2 vols. (Oxford, 1970), 2:586.

tiger cub) and where they were "literally lulled to sleep by Persian nightingales."[2] Anna Maria saw much of India during her ten years' residence, once taking a perilous trip up the Ganges through the jungle to Benares.

But the climate of India, according to Sir William, was "such as we had no idea of in England, excessive heat at noon, and an incessant high wind from morning to night."[3] Anna Maria's health suffered, especially during the warmest season, and she was frequently ill with digestive disorders, colds, fevers, rheumatism, and, on at least one occasion, dysentery, for which she took laudanum. Finally, the physicians told her that for the sake of her health she would have to leave India. She promised in October 1791 to return to Europe, but she could not bring herself to leave until more than two years later, in December 1793. Just before her departure, she published in Calcutta a volume entitled *The Poems of Anna Maria Jones.* Her husband stayed behind to complete his work, intending to return to England the following year. But he became ill only months later and died on 27 April 1794 at the age of forty-seven. According to her sister Elizabeth, "Anna . . . reproached herself severely for having left Jones, though he had been well then and she would have sacrificed her own life by remaining."[4]

After her return to England, Anna Maria Jones lived at Worting House, near Basingstoke, with long stays in London, and in 1806 she adopted her sister's children. She edited her husband's voluminous writings, published in 1799 by G. G. & J. Robinson as *The Works of Sir William Jones,* and gathered the necessary letters and papers for a memoir, written by her husband's friend John Shore, Lord Teignmouth, and published in 1804. Anna Maria Jones died on 7 July 1829. Her manuscript journals and letters from India were destroyed in 1857. A pen-and-ink sketch of her from the mid-1780s is in William Jones's notebook in the Osborne Collection at Yale, reproduced in Garland Cannon's edition of the *Letters of Sir William Jones* (1970). Some of her sketches are preserved in the Royal Asiatic Society in London, and four of her letters are in the British Library.

MAJOR WORKS: *The Poems of Anna Maria Jones* (Calcutta, 1793).

TEXT USED: Text of "Sonnet to the Moon" from *The Poems of Anna Maria Jones.*

---

2. *Memoirs of the Life, Writings, and Correspondence of Sir William Jones,* ed. Lord Teignmouth, 2 vols. (London, 1835), 2:27.

3. Ibid.

4. Elizabeth Shipley to Sarah Ponsonby, 26 January 1795, quoted in *The Hanwood Papers of the Ladies of Langollen & Caroline Hamilton,* ed. Mrs. G. H. Bell (London, 1930), 274.

Sonnet to the Moon

Thou lovely Sorc'ress of the witching Night,
  Whose paly Charms thro' sombre Regions glide;
Lur'd by the Softness of thy silver Light,
  The Muse pathetic glows with conscious Pride.

On the gem'd Margin of the lustrous Flood,
  Whose ripling Waters glide so sweetly by;
Oft have I list'ning to its Murmurs stood,
  Trac'd thy pure Ray, and wing'd a lonely Sigh!

For *Thou,* chaste *Cynthia,* o'er my gentle Soul,
10   Shed'st the mild Beam of Contemplation's Sway;
Thy fascinating Spell with proud Controul
  Sweeps the full Cadence of my trembling Lay:
Then gleam, bright Orb, from Midnight's velvet Vest,
And dart thy pearly Lustre o'er my pensive Breast.

                                                    (1793)

9 Cynthia] A name for Artemis or Diana and used poetically in reference to the moon.

Lady Caroline Lamb

(1785–1828)

The poet and novelist Lady Caroline Lamb was born on 13 November 1785, the only daughter of Frederick Ponsonby, third earl of Bessborough, and Lady Henrietta Frances Spencer, daughter of John, first earl of Spencer. When she was four she went with her mother to live in Italy, where she was raised mostly by servants. On her return to England at age nine, her mother found her unmanageable, so she was sent to live with her cousins at Devonshire House.

Lady Caroline later recalled, "My mother, having boys, wished ardently for a girl; and I, who evidently ought to have been a soldier, was found a naughty girl—forward, talking like Richard the Third. I was a trouble, not a pleasure, all my childhood, for which reason . . . I was ordered by the late Dr. Warre neither to learn anything nor see any one, for fear the violent passions and strange whims they found in me should lead to madness. . . . the end was, that until fifteen I learned nothing."[1] Her education was so neglected that when she was ten she was still unable to write or spell.

On 3 June 1805, at the age of nineteen, Lady Caroline married the handsome, twenty-six-year-old William Lamb, afterwards Lord Melbourne, whom she had known all her life. He had been educated at Eton and Cambridge and had been admitted to the bar. She considered him the cleverest person she had ever met and the most daring in his opinions. It was a love match, but tempestuous from the beginning, with frequent quarrels and reconciliations.

Lady Caroline's contemporaries describe her as bright, generous, impulsive, vain, excitable, full of originality, and having great powers of conversation. According to the *Literary Gazette,* her manners "had a fascination which it is difficult for any who never encountered their effect to conceive."[2] But despite her advantages in life, she was not happy and indulged what her friend

1. Sydney, Lady Morgan, *Lady Morgan's Memoirs: Autobiography, Diaries and Correspondence,* 2nd ed., rev., 2 vols. (London, 1863), 2:211.

2. 1828, 108.

Lady Morgan called a "restless craving after excitement—after the something unattained and unattainable. . . . Sometimes she sought this in the exercise of her pencil and her pen; sometimes in the more dangerous exercise of her affections and her imagination."[3]

In the spring of 1812 Lady Caroline met Lord Byron, shortly thereafter confiding in her journal the famous observation that he was "mad—bad—and dangerous to know."[4] For the next several months Byron was frequently at her home, Melbourne House, a center of fashionable social life. He confessed that he found her "the cleverest most agreeable, absurd, amiable, perplexing, dangerous fascinating little being," but he also said that she had "a total want of common conduct" and dubbed her heart "a little volcano."[5] Nevertheless, he sent her passionate love letters, and she became equally taken with him. On 9 August she sent him as a keepsake a lock of her pubic hair, signing herself "Your Wild Antelope."

To separate her from Byron, in late August her family took her on a trip to Ireland; in early November Byron sent her a cruel letter breaking off the affair, using the seal of his new paramour, Lady Oxford. Lady Caroline fell ill, but she was to have her revenge. In early 1816 she wrote *Glenarvon,* a melodramatic, gothic *roman à clef* featuring Byron caricatured as the villain-hero and reprinting the text of his farewell letter. The author herself appeared as Calantha, the heroine, and there were cutting portraits of many of her friends, acquaintances, and family members, including her husband and such literary figures as Samuel Rogers. The book had been written, she said, "unknown to all (save a governess . . .), in the middle of the night,"[6] and it was published by Henry Colburn in three volumes in May, within weeks of Byron's departure from England. Although Lady Caroline was not named as the author, her identity was easily guessed. The novel created a sensation and was wildly popular, both with the aristocracy, whom it critiqued but who enjoyed reading about each other, and with the middle class, curious to know how the bluebloods lived. It went through three editions in the first few weeks and was quickly translated into Italian. Although probably secretly flattered, Byron, who had been sent a copy by Germaine de Staël, remarked, "If the authoress had written the *truth* . . . the romance would not only have been more *romantic,* but more entertaining. As for the likeness, the

3. *Lady Morgan's Memoirs,* 1:441.

4. Recorded in ibid., 2:200.

5. Lord Byron to Lady Caroline Lamb, [April 1812?], in *"Famous in my Time,"* vol. 2 of *Byron's Letters and Journals,* ed. Leslie A. Marchand (Cambridge, Mass., 1973), 170–71.

6. *Lady Morgan's Memoirs,* 2:202.

picture can't be good—I did not sit long enough."[7] Lady Caroline's husband, however, along with all of his family, was humiliated and asked for a separation; in the end, though, he could not go through with it. Still, the novel made her a pariah among London's fashionable set.

A New Canto (1819), an anonymous poem satirizing Byron's *Don Juan,* attributed in many sources to Lady Caroline, is probably not her work. In response to the advice of the Italian author, Ugo Foscolo, who advised her to "write a book which will offend nobody; women cannot afford to shock," she penned her second novel, *Graham Hamilton,* which she sent to Colburn in 1820 "with an earnest injunction neither to name the author nor to publish it at that time." Colburn finally brought it out in two volumes in 1822. A more mature work of fiction, it paints a fond picture of her aunt, Georgiana, duchess of Devonshire, who had died in 1806. While it did not shock, it also did not sell.

Ada Reis; a Tale, which appeared anonymously in three volumes in March 1823, draws on Lady Caroline's memories of her privileged but emotionally destitute childhood in Naples. Although it was artistically more successful than her previous novels, it was a commercial failure. She also contributed poems to several literary annuals, including *Friendship's Offering,* the *Bijou,* and the *Keepsake.* Several of her poems were set to music by Isaac Nathan and others. Her literary friends came to include the young William Godwin, the poet Elizabeth Benger, and Bulwer Lytton while he was still at Cambridge. Lady Morgan became her confidante and comforter.

Lady Caroline was deeply affected when, in July 1824, she accidentally encountered Byron's funeral procession. The following year, she and her husband separated. He had won a Whig seat in Parliament in the early years of their marriage and was made Irish secretary in 1827; he would go on to inherit his father's title and become home secretary in 1830 and prime minister from 1835 to 1841. But Lady Caroline would not live to see his rise to fame. She spent the remainder of her life at Brocket, their country estate, with her father-in-law and her retarded son, the only one of her three children to survive. She died at Melbourne House, Whitehall, on 26 January 1828 at the age of forty-two. Several literary characters were modeled after her, including Mrs. Felix Lorraine in Benjamin Disraeli's *Vivian Grey,* Lady Monteagle in his *Venetia,* and Lady Bellenden in Catherine Grace Gore's *Greville; or, A Season in Paris.* Lady Morgan said of her, "She was eloquent, most eloquent, full of ideas, and of graceful gracious expression; but her subject was always

7. "*So late into the night,*" vol. 5 of *Byron's Letters and Journals,* ed. Leslie A. Marchand (London, 1976), 131.

herself. She confounded her dearest friends and direst foes, for her feelings were all impulses, worked on by a powerful imagination."[8]

MAJOR WORKS: *Glenarvon,* 3 vols. (London, 1816); *Graham Hamilton,* 2 vols. (London, 1822); *Ada Reis, a Tale,* 3 vols. (London, 1823); *Fugitive Pieces and Reminiscences of Lord Byron . . . also Some Original Poetry, Letters, and Recollections of Lady Caroline Lamb,* ed. I. Nathan (London, 1829).

TEXT USED: "Invocation to Sleep" from the *Keepsake* for 1830.

Invocation to Sleep

Oh balm of nature to the mind opprest,
Descend and calm the tumults of my breast;
Bind with Oblivion's veil these wakeful eyes,
And still the varying passions as they rise;
While airy dreams, in Fancy's fictious light,
Sport in the gloomy darkness of the night;
And a bright Angel, borne on silver wings,
To heaven's high arch his song of triumph sings:
Oh, sleep! descend, and, on thy downy breast,
10   Lull, with thy poppy wreath, my soul to rest!

(1830)

8. *Lady Morgan's Memoirs,* 2:254–55.

Letitia Elizabeth Landon

(1802–1838)

Letitia Elizabeth Landon was born on 14 August 1802 at No. 25 Hans Place, Chelsea, the eldest child of Catherine Jane Bishop and John Landon. At age six she became a day student at a school run by the future Countess St. Quentin, a poet. Caroline Lamb and Mary Russell Mitford both had studied there. The young Letitia Landon acquired from her schoolmistress a love of poetry and from her French instructor, Count St. Quentin, a flawless French accent.

When Letitia was seven years old her family moved to Trevor Park, East Barnet, where Elizabeth Landon, a cousin, taught Letitia history, geography, grammar, and literature. Novels were forbidden, but Letitia read them clandestinely. She also read history and travel literature and had a tutor for French and music. Her favorite author was Walter Scott, and one of her favorite works was Homer's *Odyssey*. In later life she recalled, "I cannot remember the time when composition in some shape or other was not a habit. I used to invent long stories, which I was only too glad if I could get my mother to hear. These soon took a metrical form; and I used to walk about the grounds, and lie awake half the night, reciting my verses aloud."[1]

In 1814, when Letitia was thirteen, the hitherto affluent family suffered severe financial difficulties, bringing about a move to Lewis Place, Fulham, and then, after a year, to Old Brompton. Her days of formal schooling were over, but she continued her writing and voracious reading. One day her mother asked William Jerdan, a neighbor and editor of the *Literary Gazette*, to read some of Letitia's work. Jerdan, suspecting that the elder Landon was the author, offered comments and suggestions. Not long afterwards, he accepted one of Letitia's short pieces, "Rome," for the 11 March 1818 issue of the *Gazette*. She signed it "L." The following issue contained her poem "The

---

1. Quoted in Samuel Carter Hall, *A Book of Memories of Great Men and Women of the Age, from Personal Acquaintance*, 2nd ed. (London, 1877), 269.

Michaelmas Daisy." Soon Landon's poetry began to appear often in the pages of the *Gazette,* and she began to think about using her writing to help support her family.

By 1820 Landon was working on a long poem, "The Fate of Adelaide." Sarah Siddons, the distinguished actress and a friend of Landon's grand-mother's, helped Landon in August 1821 to publish *The Fate of Adelaide, a Swiss Romantic Tale; and Other Poems.* Dedicated to Siddons, the book sold well, but its publisher, John Warren, failed, and Landon earned no money for her work. By this time, however, Jerdan had become her mentor. Beginning in the summer of 1821, under the initials "L.E.L.," she published a series of "Poetical Sketches" that Jerdan had commissioned from her. Within months her poems became the rage. In 1831 Edward Bulwer-Lytton, writing for the *New Monthly Magazine,* recalled that at college "there was always in the reading-room of the Union a rush every Saturday afternoon for the 'Literary Gazette,' and an impatient anxiety to hasten at once to the corner of the sheet which contained the three magical letters 'L.E.L.' And all of us praised the verse, and all of us guessed at the author. We soon learned it was a female, and our admiration was doubled, and our conjectures tripled. Was she young? Was she pretty? And . . . was she rich?"[2] When Jerdan revealed that the author was a "young lady yet in her teens," scores of young men promptly fell in love with her. The Quaker poet Bernard Barton in February 1822 published an admiring apostrophe to L.E.L., closing with the lines,

> I know not who, or what, thou art,
>   Nor do I seek to know thee,
> While Thou, performing thus thy part,
>   Such banquets canst bestow me.
> Then be, as long as thou shalt list,
>   My viewless, nameless melodist.[3]

Landon's initials became her name. But her literary popularity had so far been of little value financially, so in July 1824, under the title *The Improvisatrice; and Other Poems,* she published with Hurst and Robinson a collection of her "Poetical Sketches" from the *Literary Gazette.* The manuscript had been rejected by Murray, Longmans, and Colburn, as well as by several other publishers, but the volume turned out to be a smashing success, going through six editions the first year and earning L.E.L. three hundred pounds. *The Gentleman's Magazine* declared, "We have seldom seen a voice more conspicuous for vivid imagination, felicity of diction, vigorous condensation of language, and

2. Laman Blanchard, *Life and Literary Remains of L.E.L.,* 2 vols. (Philadelphia, 1841), 1:32.
3. *London Literary Gazette,* 9 February 1822, 89.

passion-intensity of sentiment." And the *Ladies' Monthly Museum* observed, "The authoress displays a cultivated genius, which will enable her to attain a distinguished place among the British votaries of the Muses."[4] Landon's poetic reputation was now established.

Landon's good business sense led her to capitalize on her new-found fame, and she quickly brought out another volume, entitled *The Troubadour; Catalogue of Pictures, and Historical Sketches,* in July 1825. It earned her six hundred pounds. In December 1826 she published a sequel entitled *The Golden Violet, with its Tales of Romance and Chivalry; and Other Poems,* which contained "Erinna," a poem whose object she said was to "trace the progress of a mind highly-gifted, well-rewarded, but finding the fame it won a sting and a sorrow, and finally sinking beneath the shadows of success." Though expensive, this volume also sold well. Critics complained that her poetry was monotonous, so in her next book, published in October 1829, *The Venetian Bracelet, The Lost Pleiad, a History of the Lyre, and Other Poems,* she sought a remedy in greater social consciousness, a deeper psychological perspective, and a stronger sense of the dramatic. She portrayed love as linked to misery and death and life itself as a mockery. Increasingly, Landon came to know the liabilities of being a woman with literary talent. She told a friend, "Did we not know this world to be but a place of trial—our bitter probation for another and for a better—how strange in its severity would seem the lot of genius in a woman. The keen feeling—the generous enthusiasm—the lofty aspiration—and the delicate perception—are given but to make the possessor unfitted for her actual position."[5]

After the death of her father, Landon's family depended upon her as its sole financial support. She continued to write regularly for the *Literary Gazette,* not only signed poetry but unsigned critical reviews. She had been contributing in a major way to most of the literary gift books and annuals, almost since their inception, but in 1831 she took over the editorship of *Fisher's Drawing-Room Scrap-Book,* a handsome annual published in quarto containing more than thirty poems to illustrate an equal number of fine, steel-plate engravings. She continued as editor, contributing all of the verse not otherwise ascribed, until her departure from England in 1838. Her early biographer, Laman Blanchard, says that Landon wrote so quickly that "it would take her just as long to copy, as to compose" her poems.[6]

4. *Gentleman's Magazine* 94 (July 1824): 61–63; and *Ladies' Monthly Museum,* n.s., 20 (1824): 106.

5. Quoted in Blanchard, *Life and Literary Remains,* 1:215.

6. Ibid., 40.

In 1832, in addition to contributing to the annuals and to the *New Monthly Magazine* and editing the *Drawing-Room Scrap-Book,* she wrote all of the copy for *The Easter Gift, a Religious Offering* for 1833 and for Heath's *Book of Beauty* for 1833. Her female literary friends came to include Emma Roberts, Maria Jane Jewsbury, Mary Russell Mitford, Agnes Strickland, Jane Porter, and Anna Maria Hall. Hall encouraged her to write a novel, and *Romance and Reality* was the result, begun in 1830 and published the following year. Landon said that "writing poetry is like writing one's native language, and writing prose, writing in a strange tongue."[7] Nevertheless, her novel *Francesca Carrara* (1834) brought praise from the critics and established her as a writer of romantic fiction.

Landon's success also inspired gossip and rumor, fed by her habit of publicly calling male friends such as William Jerdan and the Irish artist David Maclise by their first names and receiving them alone in private. She was said to be romantically involved with William Maginn, a journalist with a jealous wife and four children. Landon lamented, "I have long since discovered that I must be prepared for enmity I have never provoked, and unkindness I have little deserved. God knows that if, when I do go into society, I meet with more homage and attention than most, it is dearly bought. What is my life? One day of drudgery after another; . . . envy, malice, and all uncharitableness, — these are the fruits of a successful literary career for a woman."[8] Feigning indifference, she refused publicly to respond to the accusations. But privately she yearned "for oblivion, and five hundred a year!"[9] In 1834 rumors circulated that Landon, then thirty-two, was engaged to marry John Forster, the twenty-three-year-old editor of the *Daily News* who was to become Dickens's biographer. But the stories that had circulated earlier concerning Maginn revived, and she told Forster, "That I am the object often of malicious misrepresentation, or rather invention, is true; but it is not the public, it is not the general feeling. I can understand that success must bear the penalty of envy, but it is those who know nothing about me, or my habits, who are bitter against me. . . . As regards myself, I have no answer beyond contemptuous silence, an appeal to all who know my past life, and a very bitter sense of innocence and of injury."[10] Yet she broke off the engagement, telling Forster, "I feel that to give up all idea of a near and dear connection, is as much my duty to myself as to you. Why should you be exposed to the annoyance—

7. Ibid., 87.
8. Quoted in Hall, *A Book of Memories,* 266.
9. Blanchard, *Life and Literary Remains,* 1:54.
10. Quoted in ibid., 107–8.

the mortification of having the name of the woman you honour with your regard, coupled with insolent insinuation? — you never would bear it." [11]

In the summer of 1834 Landon visited Paris. When she returned to London, she saw a new painting by Maclise, *Vow of the Peacock* (1835), which inspired her to write a poem on the same topic. Saunders and Otley published *The Vow of the Peacock, and Other Poems* in the autumn of 1835 with an engraving of one of Maclise's three portraits of L.E.L. as the frontispiece. This imperfect likeness was the first published portrait of L.E.L. — the first time her readers had seen her "face." In 1836 Henry Colburn brought out her *Traits and Trials of Early Life,* a collection of prose tales for children; Landon acknowledged that the last story in the book was a thinly veiled description of her own childhood. The following year Colburn published *Ethel Churchill; or, The Two Brides,* a love story, considered by many to be her strongest novel. Meanwhile, Landon continued to publish as prolifically as ever in periodicals and literary annuals. In addition to contributing to the *Literary Gazette,* the *Court Journal,* and the *New Monthly Magazine,* she poetically illustrated *Flowers of Loveliness* for Rudolph Ackermann, the *Book of Beauty* for Charles Heath, and the *Drawing-Room Scrap-Book* for Fisher. Starting in 1836, she contributed annually to Schloss's *Fairy Almanac.*

In October 1836, at the home of an acquaintance in Hampstead, Landon met George Maclean, the governor of Cape Coast, Africa. Even as a child Landon had been interested in Africa, and the two had much to discuss. Rumors circulated about Maclean as well. It was said that he had married a native woman, who lived with him in Cape Coast Castle. Maclean denied that he had ever been married and assured Landon that he had ended his relationship with a native woman. On 7 June 1838, with her brother officiating, the two were married at St. Mary's Church on Bryanstone Square. The event was kept secret at the behest of the bridegroom, who wanted a private wedding. After a few days spent out of town, the couple returned to London, announced their marriage to surprised friends, and then left for Portsmouth to embark on the long sea voyage to Cape Coast, Africa. Landon had agreed to live in Africa for three years, after which time she would be free to return to England if she so wished. On 5 July 1838 she sailed from Portsmouth, planning to continue her literary career from afar.

The voyage took nearly six weeks; oddly, when they landed on 16 August, her arrival was unexpected. She wrote to her brother and to others of how favorably impressed she was with Cape Coast and its castle, surrounded by sea on three sides. Her letters were cheerful and full of hope for the future.

---

11. Ibid., 112.

She reported, "It is like living in the 'Arabian Nights,' looking out upon palm and cocoa-nut trees. . . . If my literary success does but continue, in two or three years I shall have an independence from embarrassment it is long since I have known. It will enable me comfortably to provide for my mother."[12] She said she was happy and well and relieved to find the place better than she had supposed. She was working on a series of descriptive and critical essays on the female characters of Walter Scott; several of these essays had already been printed in the *New Monthly Magazine,* and Heath had agreed to publish a collection of them. But they were never finished.

Only two months after her arrival in Africa, on Monday, 15 October 1838, between 8:00 and 9:00 A.M., a servant discovered Landon collapsed on the floor with an empty bottle of prussic acid in her hand. The efforts of a physician to revive her proved fruitless. A hastily convened coroner's jury ruled that she had died by poison. But the lack of an autopsy and the inadequacy of the inquest caused the verdict to be received with suspicion in England. Had she committed suicide? The tone and content of her letters to family and friends made that seem doubtful. Had she been murdered by the native woman who had borne Maclean's child and had formerly lived in the castle? The coroner's inquest recorded bruises on her cheek and hands. The first announcement in England of L.E.L.'s death appeared in the *Watchman* for 31 December 1838 in a letter from a missionary named Freeman, who insinuated that the jury's verdict was not a conscientious one. The next day this letter was used in the papers to suggest that Landon had been poisoned or had committed suicide. George Maclean maintained that his wife must have accidentally taken an overdose of a medication she used to calm her nerves. His account was met with skepticism, and the English servant who had discovered the poet was later found to be an untrustworthy witness. The puzzle of L.E.L.'s premature death was never solved, adding to the mystique of her posthumous reputation.

MAJOR WORKS: *The Fate of Adelaide, a Swiss Romantic Tale; and Other Poems* (London, 1821); *The Improvisatrice; and Other Poems* (London and Edinburgh, 1824); *The Troubadour; Catalogue of Pictures, and Historical Sketches* (London and Edinburgh, 1825); *The Golden Violet, with its Tales of Romance and Chivalry: and Other Poems* (London, 1827); *The Poetical Works* (London, 1827); *The Venetian Bracelet, The Lost Pleiad, a History of the Lyre, and Other Poems* (London, 1829); *Romance and Reality,* 3 vols. (London, 1831); *The Easter Gift, a Religious Offering* (London, 1832 and 1833); *Fisher's Drawing-Room Scrap-Book,* 8 vols. (London, 1832–39); *Corrine; or, Italy,* by Madame de Staël . . . with metrical versions of the odes by L. E. Landon, trans. Isabel Hill, Standard Novels,

12. Ibid., 166.

no. 24 (London, Edinburgh, Dublin, and Paris, 1833); *Heath's Book of Beauty* (London, 1833); *Francesca Carrara,* 3 vols. (London, 1834); *The Miscellaneous Poetical Works* (London, 1835); *The Vow of the Peacock, and Other Poems* (London, 1835); *Traits and Trials of Early Life* (London, 1836); *A Birthday Tribute [in verse] Addressed to . . . the Princess Alexandrina Victoria, on attaining her Eighteenth Year* (London, [1837]); *Ethel Churchill; or, The Two Brides,* 3 vols. (London, 1837); *Duty and Inclination, a Novel,* 3 vols. (London, 1838); *Flowers of Loveliness. Twelve Groups of Female Figures Emblematic of Flowers: designed by Various Artists, with Poetical Illustrations by LEL* (London, 1838); *The Works of Letitia Elizabeth Landon,* 2 vols. (Philadelphia, 1838); *The Zenana and Minor Poems of L. E. L.; with a Memoir by Emma Roberts* (London, 1839).

TEXTS USED: Texts of "The Oak" and "Home" from *The Improvisatrice; and Other Poems.* Text of "Hannibal's Oath" from *The Troubadour; Catalogue of Pictures, and Historical Sketches.* Texts of "The Altered River" and "Marius at the Ruins of Carthage" from the *Keepsake* for 1829 and 1833, respectively. Text of "Lines of Life" from *The Venetian Bracelet, The Lost Pleiad, a History of the Lyre, and Other Poems.* Texts of "Carrick-a-Rede, Ireland," "Fountain's Abbey," and "The Unknown Grave" from *Fisher's Drawing-Room Scrap-Book* for 1832, 1833, and 1837, respectively.

The Oak

. . . It is the last survivor of a race
Strong in their forest-pride when I was young.
I can remember, when for miles around,
In place of those smooth meadows and corn-fields,
There stood ten thousand tall and stately trees,
Such as had braved the winds of March, the bolt
Sent by the summer lightning, and the snow
Heaping for weeks their boughs. Even in the depth
Of hot July the glades were cool; the grass,
Yellow and parched elsewhere, grew long and fresh,   10
Shading wild strawberries and violets,
Or the lark's nest; and overhead, the dove
Had her lone dwelling, paying for her home
With melancholy songs; and scarce a beech
Was there without a honeysuckle linked
Around, with its red tendrils and pink flowers;
Or girdled by a brier rose, whose buds

Yield fragrant harvest for the honey-bee.
There dwelt the last red deer, those antler'd kings . . .
20   But this is as a dream,—the plough has pass'd
Where the stag bounded, and the day has looked
On the green twilight of the forest-trees.
This oak has no companion! . . .

(1823)

Home

I left my home;—'twas in a little vale,
Sheltered from snow-storms by the stately pines;
A small clear river wandered quietly,
Its smooth waves only cut by the light barks
Of fishers, and but darkened by the shade
The willows flung, when to the southern wind
They threw their long green tresses. On the slope
Were five or six white cottages, whose roofs
Reached not to the laburnum's height, whose boughs
10   Shook over them bright showers of golden bloom.
Sweet silence reigned around:—no other sound
Came on the air, than when the shepherd made
The reed-pipe rudely musical, or notes
From the wild birds, or children in their play
Sending forth shouts or laughter. Strangers came
Rarely or never near the lonely place. . . .
I went into far countries. Years past by,
But still that vale in silent beauty dwelt
Within my memory. Home I came at last.
20   I stood upon a mountain height, and looked
Into the vale below; and smoke arose,
And heavy sounds; and through the thick dim air
Shot blackened turrets, and brick walls, and roofs
Of the red tile. I entered in the streets:

9 laburnum's] A small tree belonging to the family Leguminosae and bearing long pendulous racemes of bright yellow flowers followed by pods of poisonous seeds.

There were ten thousand hurrying to and fro;
And masted vessels stood upon the river,
And barges sullied the once dew-clear stream.
Where were the willows, where the cottages?
I sought my home; I sought and found a city,
Alas! for the green valley!   30

(1824)

Hannibal's Oath*

And the night was dark and calm,
    There was not a breath of air,
The leaves of the grove were still,
    As the presence of death was there;†

Only a moaning sound
    Came from the distant sea;
It was as if, like life,
    It had no tranquillity.

A warrior and a child
    Pass'd through the sacred wood,   10
Which, like a mystery,
    Around the temple stood.

The warrior's brow was worn
    With the weight of casque and plume,
And sun-burnt was his cheek,
    And his eye and brow were gloom.

The child was young and fair,
    But the forehead large and high,
And the dark eyes' flashing light
    Seem'd to feel their destiny.   20

They enter'd in the temple,
    And stood before the shrine,

It stream'd with the victim's blood,
  With incense and with wine.

The ground rock'd beneath their feet,
  The thunder shook the dome,
But the boy stood firm, and swore
  Eternal hate to Rome.

There's a page in history
30   O'er which tears of blood were wept,
And that page is the record
  How that oath of hate was kept.
                                        (1825)

---

*Hannibal (247–c. 183–181 B.C.) was a Carthaginian military leader who fought against the Roman republic. His father, the great Carthaginian general Hamilcar Barca, took him to Spain at an early age and made him swear eternal hostility to Rome. Hannibal became commander in chief of the Carthaginian army at age twenty-six. His greatest military achievement was a surprise attack on the Romans during the Second Punic War, made possible by the ingenious method of having his troops cross the Alps on elephants. In the end he was defeated.

† In the first edition this line ended with the words "were there."

The Altered River

Thou lovely river, thou art now
  As fair as fair can be,
Pale flowers wreathe upon thy brow,
  The rose bends over thee.
Only the morning sun hath leave
  To turn thy waves to light,
Cool shade the willow branches weave
  When noon becomes too bright.
The lilies are the only boats
10   Upon thy diamond plain,

The swan alone in silence floats
    Around thy charm'd domain.
The moss bank's fresh embroiderie,
    With fairie favours starr'd,
Seems made the summer haunt to be
    Of melancholy bard.
Fair as thou art, thou wilt be food
    For many a thought of pain;
For who can gaze upon thy flood,
    Nor wish it to remain   20
The same pure and unsullied thing
    Where heaven's face is as clear
Mirror'd in thy blue wandering
    As heaven's face can be here.
Flowers fling their sweet bonds on thy breast,
    The willows woo thy stay,
In vain,—thy waters may not rest,
    Their course must be away.
In yon wide world, what wilt thou find?
    What all find—toil and care: 30
Your flowers you have left behind
    Far other weight to bear.
The heavy bridge confines your stream,
    Through which the barges toil,
Smoke has shut out the sun's glad beam,
    Thy waves have caught the soil.
On—on—though weariness it be,
    By shoal and barrier cross'd,
Till thou hast reach'd the mighty sea,
    And there art wholly lost.   40
Bend thou, young poet, o'er the stream—
    Such fate will be thine own;
Thy lute's hope is a morning dream,
    And when have dreams not flown?

          (1829)

Lines of Life

Orphan in my first years, I early learnt
To make my heart suffice itself, and seek
Support and sympathy in its own depths.

Well, read my cheek, and watch my eye,—
  Too strictly school'd are they,
One secret of my soul to show,
  One hidden thought betray.

I never knew the time my heart
  Look'd freely from my brow;
It once was check'd by timidness,
  'Tis taught by caution now.

I live among the cold, the false,
  And I must seem like them;
And such I am, for I am false
  As those I most condemn.

I teach my lip its sweetest smile,
  My tongue its softest tone;
I borrow others' likeness, till
  Almost I lose my own.

I pass through flattery's gilded sieve,
  Whatever I would say;
In social life, all, like the blind,
  Must learn to feel their way.

I check my thoughts like curbed steeds
  That struggle with the rein;
I bid my feelings sleep, like wrecks
  In the unfathom'd main.

I hear them speak of love, the deep,
  The true, and mock the name;
Mock at all high and early truth,
  And I too do the same.

I hear them tell some touching tale,
   I swallow down the tear;   30
I hear them name some generous deed,
   And I have learnt to sneer.

I hear the spiritual, the kind,
   The pure, but named in mirth;
Till all of good, ay, even hope,
   Seems exiled from our earth.

And one fear, withering ridicule,
   Is all that I can dread;
A sword hung by a single hair
   For ever o'er the head.   40

We bow to a most servile faith,
   In a most servile fear;
While none among us dares to say
   What none will choose to hear.

And if we dream of loftier thoughts,
   In weakness they are gone;
And indolence and vanity
   Rivet our fetters on.

Surely I was not born for this!
   I feel a loftier mood   50
Of generous impulse, high resolve,
   Steal o'er my solitude!

I gazed upon the thousand stars
   That fill the midnight sky;
And wish, so passionately wish,
   A light like theirs on high.

I have such eagerness of hope
   To benefit my kind;
And feel as if immortal power
   Were given to my mind.   60

I think on that eternal fame,
   The sun of earthly gloom,
Which makes the gloriousness of death,
   The future of the tomb—

That earthly future, the faint sign
   Of a more heavenly one;
—A step, a word, a voice, a look,—
   Alas! my dream is done.

And earth, and earth's debasing stain,
70   Again is on my soul;
And I am but a nameless part
   Of a most worthless whole.

Why write I this? because my heart
   Towards the future springs,
That future where it loves to soar
   On more than eagle wings.

The present, it is but a speck
   In that eternal time,
In which my lost hopes find a home,
80   My spirit knows its clime.

O! not myself,—for what am I?—
   The worthless and the weak,
Whose every thought of self should raise
   A blush to burn my cheek.

But song has touch'd my lips with fire,
   And made my heart a shrine;
For what, although alloy'd, debased,
   Is in itself divine.

I am myself but a vile link
90   Amid life's weary chain;
But I have spoken hallow'd words,
   O do not say in vain!

My first, my last, my only wish,
   Say will my charmed chords
Wake to the morning light of fame,
   And breathe again my words?

Will the young maiden, when her tears
   Alone in moonlight shine—
Tears for the absent and the loved—
   Murmur some song of mine?   100

Will the pale youth by his dim lamp,
   Himself a dying flame,
From many an antique scroll beside,
   Choose that which bears my name?

Let music make less terrible
   The silence of the dead;
I care not, so my spirit last
   Long after life has fled.

                 (1829)

Carrick-a-Rede, Ireland*

He dwelt amid the gloomy rocks,
   A solitary man;
Around his home on every side,
   The deep salt waters ran.
The distant ships sailed far away,
   And o'er the moaning wave
The sea-birds swept, with pale white wings,
   As phantoms haunt the grave:
'Twas dreary on an autumn night,
   To hear the tempest sweep,   10
When gallant ships were perishing
   Alone amid the deep.

He was a stranger to that shore,
  A stranger he remained,
For to his heart, or hearth, or board,
  None ever welcome gained.
Great must have been the misery
  Of guilt upon his mind,
That thus could sever all the ties
20 Between him and his kind.
His step was slow, his words were few,
  His brow was worn and wan;
He dwelt among those gloomy rocks,
  A solitary man.

(1832)

*The romantic anecdote, to which [these] lines have reference, is a true one. A manuscript journal of a Tour through the Western Islands of Scotland, and along the Northern Coast of Ireland, in 1746, contains the following passage:

"Carrick-a-Reid is a great rock, cut off from the shore by a chasm of fearful depth, through which the sea, when vexed by angry winds, boileth with great fury. It is resorted to at this season of the year by fishers, for the taking of salmon, who sling themselves across the perilous gulf by means of a stout rope, or withe, as the name Carrick-a-Reid imports. I was told, that, all through the inclemency of last winter, there dwelled here a solitary stranger, of noble mien, in an unseemly hut, made by his own hands. The people, in speaking of the stranger, called him, from his aspect, "The Man of Sorrow"; and 'tis not unlikely, poor gentleman, he was one of the rebels who fled out of Scotland." In the 2nd volume of "Wakefield's Ireland," a particular account of Carrick-a-Rede, its fishery, and "very extraordinary flying bridge," may be found. *Landon.*

Fountain's Abbey[*]

Never more, when the day is o'er,
Will the lonely vespers sound;
No bells are ringing—no monks are singing,
When the moonlight falls around.

A few pale flowers, which in other hours
May have cheered the dreary mood;
When the votary turned to the world he had spurned,
And repined at the solitude.

Still do they blow 'mid the ruins below,
For fallen are fane and shrine,   10
And the moss has grown o'er the sculptured stone
Of an altar no more divine.

Still on the walls, where the sunshine falls,
The ancient fruit-tree grows;
And o'er tablet and tomb, extends the bloom
Of many a wilding rose.

Fair though they be, yet they seemed to me
To mock the wreck below;
For mighty the tower, where the fragile flower
May now as in triumph blow.   20

Oh, foolish the thought, that my fancy brought;
More true and more wise to say,
That still thus doth spring, some gentle thing,
With its beauty to cheer decay.

(1833)

[*] "Many a garden flower grows wild": amid the ruins of the old monasteries, many a weary hour may their cultivation once have beguiled. At Fountain's Abbey there is still preserved a species of pear peculiar to the place. *Landon.*

Marius at the Ruins of Carthage[*]

He turn'd him from the setting sun,
  Now sinking in the bay:—
He knew that so his course was run,
  But with no coming day;
From gloomy seas and stormy skies
He had no other morn to rise.

He sat, the column at his feet,
  The temple low beside;
A few wild flowers blossom'd sweet
  Above the column's pride;
And many a wave of drifted sand
The arch, the once triumphal, spann'd.

The place of pleasant festival,
  The calm and quiet home,
The senate, with its pillar'd hall,
  The palace with its dome,—
All things in which men boast and trust
Lay prone in the unconscious dust.

Yet this the city which once stood
  A queen beside the sea,
Who said she ruled the ocean flood
  Wherever there might be
Path for bold oar or daring prow:—
Where are her thousand galleys now?

A bird rose up—it was the owl,
  Abroad at close of day;
The wind it brought a sullen howl,
  The wolf is on his way;
The ivy o'er yon turret clings,
And there the wild bee toils and sings.

And yet these once were battlements,
  With watchers proud and bold,

Who slept in war-time under tents
   Of purple and of gold!
This is the city with whose power
Rome battled for earth's sovereign hour!

That hour it now was Rome's, and he
   Who sat desponding there,
Had he not aim'd the soul to be
   Of all that she could dare;   40
The will that led that mighty state,
The greatest, too—where all were great?

An exile and a fugitive,
   The Roman leant alone;
All round him might those lessons give
   The past has ever shown,
With which is all experience fraught,
Still teaching those who are not taught.

He saw and felt wealth, glory, mind
   Are given but for a day;   50
No star but hath in time declined,
   No power but pass'd away!
He witness'd how all things were vain,
And then went forth to war again!

                  (1833)

---

*Gaius Marius (c. 157–86 B.C.) was a Roman general who became a successful politician on the strength of the votes of army veterans. In the year before his death, following an attempt to seize control of the Asian command, Marius was exiled to Africa; he returned the next year, captured Rome, had himself elected consul for the seventh time, and then died.

The Unknown Grave

There is a little lonely grave
   Which no one comes to see,
The foxglove and red orchis wave
   Their welcome to the bee.
There never falls the morning sun,
   It lies beneath the wall,
But there when weary day is done
   The lights of sunset fall,
Flushing the warm and crimson air
As life and hope were present there.

There sleepeth one who left his heart
   Behind him in his song;
Breathing of that diviner part
   Which must to heaven belong.
The language of those spirit chords,
   But to the poet known,
Youth, love, and hope yet use his words,
   They seem to be his own.
And yet he has not left a name,
The poet died without his fame.

How many are the lovely lays
   That haunt our English tongue,
Defrauded of their poet's praise
   Forgotten he who sung.
Tradition only vaguely keeps
   Sweet fancies round his tomb;
Its tears are what the wild flower weeps,
   Its record is that bloom;
Ah, surely nature keeps with her
The memory of her worshipper.

One of her loveliest mysteries
   Such spirit blends at last
With all the fairy fantasies
   Which o'er some scenes are cast.

A softer beauty fills the grove,
  A light is in the grass,
A deeper sense of truth and love
  Comes o'er us as we pass;
While lingers in the heart one line,
The nameless poet hath a shrine.   40
       (1837)

Mary Leadbeater

(1758–1826)

Mary Leadbeater was born in 1758 in the village of Ballitore, County Kildare, Ireland, to Richard Shackleton, a schoolmaster, and his second wife, Elizabeth Carleton. Her parents were Quakers and educated their daughter at home. As a child she wrote poetry, kept a journal, and published some verse anonymously. In 1784 her father took her to London, where she met Edmund Burke (who had been her paternal grandfather's pupil), George Crabbe, and Sir Joshua Reynolds. In 1791 (a year after Joshua Edkins published her work in *A Collection of Poems, Mostly Original, By Several Hands*),[1] she married William Leadbeater, an Irishman of Huguenot descent and a former student of her father's. They remained in Ballitore, where her husband was a landowner and had a small farm and where she ran the local post office. The couple had several children.

Leadbeater's letters show that she was intensely interested in public affairs and social issues such as the abolition of capital punishment, the improvement of living conditions for the poor, and the establishment of savings banks and schools. Her first book, *Extracts and Original Anecdotes for the Improvement of Youth* (1794), published anonymously in Dublin, includes "divine odes" as well as poems on secular subjects and an account of "the people called Quakers." Ballitore was occupied, then sacked, by insurgents in 1798. She and her husband only narrowly escaped death, and for years she had nightmares of massacre. In 1808 she published *Poems,* comprising a collection of sixty-seven poems and a poetic rendition of her husband's prose translation of a fifteenth-century sequel to the *Aeneid*. "The Negro" makes a case against slavery, and other poems concern family, village, friends, and her patron, Edmund Burke, who is the subject of six poems.

In 1811 Leadbeater published *Cottage Dialogues Among the Irish Peasantry,* with an introduction and notes by Maria Edgeworth. Like Edgeworth, she

1. Vol. 2 (Dublin, 1790).

sympathetically portrayed ordinary life among the Irish laboring classes with wit and humor. Edgeworth says in the introduction that the conversations "seem actually to have passed in real life; the thoughts and feelings are natural, the reflections and reasoning such as appear to be suggested by passing circumstances or personal experience." Leadbeater's purpose was didactic, and she urged the poor to practice industry, cleanliness, dutifulness, sobriety, and thrift. The book had gone through four editions by 1813. A sequel directed at the rich, *The Landlord's Friend,* came out in 1813. *Tales for Cottagers* (1814), written with her mother, came out the following year. *Cottage Biography, being a Collection of Lives of the Irish Peasantry* (1822), the last book in the series, traces the lives of real Irish people. In *Memoirs and Letters of Richard and Elizabeth Shackleton* (1822) she edited her parents' letters together with her mother's memoirs. *Biographical Notices of Members of the Society of Friends who were Resident in Ireland* came out in 1823. She died in Ballitore on 27 June 1826 and was interred in the Quaker cemetery.

Annals of Ballitore was published posthumously in 1862 as volume 1 in *The Leadbeater Papers; A Selection from the Mss. and Correspondence of Mary Leadbeater* by Richard Davis Webb, a printer whose purpose was to preserve Irish culture. *Annals* gives an account of life in Ballitore from 1766 to 1823, including a description of the horrors of the rebellion of 1798. The second volume includes Leadbeater's correspondence with Edmund Burke (including letters from him), Melusina Trench, Maria Edgeworth, and George Crabbe.

MAJOR WORKS: *Extracts and Original Anecdotes for the Improvement of Youth* (Dublin, 1794); *Poems . . . to Which is Prefixed her Translation of the Thirteenth Book of the Aeneid; with the Latin Original, Written in the Fifteenth Century, by Maffaeus* (Dublin and London, 1808); *Cottage Dialogues Among the Irish Peasantry* (London, 1811); *The Landlord's Friend* (Dublin, 1813); *Cottage Biography, being a Collection of Lives of the Irish Peasantry* (Dublin, 1822); *Annals of Ballitore,* vol. 1 of *The Leadbeater Papers; A Selection from the Mss. and Correspondence of Mary Leadbeater* (London, 1862).

EDITED WORKS: *Tales for Cottagers,* with Elizabeth Shackleton (Dublin, 1814); *Memoirs and Letters of Richard and Elizabeth Shackleton* (London, 1822).

TEXT USED: Text of "Lines Written in a Bower" from *Poems.*

Lines Written in a Bower

Dear, lovely bow'r, to-morrow morn
    From thee I haste away:
Say, will the sun with smiles adorn
    That melancholy day!

Ah yes! the sun as bright will shine,
    The flow'rs as gaily blow;
Nought but this hapless heart of mine
    Will wear the gloom of wo.

How quickly am I forc'd to haste
    From scenes so fair and new!
Thy charms I just began to taste;
    Sweet Abbeville, adieu.

What though to me more lovely vales
    And sweeter shades are giv'n!—
A pang the parting spirit feels,
    Though leaving earth for Heav'n.

                                    (1808)

Helen Leigh

(fl. 1788, d. before 1795)

What little is known about Helen Leigh comes from the short preface to her *Miscellaneous Poems,* published by subscription in Manchester in 1788. She notes, "Though an Apology is undoubtedly requisite for the Publication of the following Sheets, I must confess that I have, in Reality, no *plausible* one to make, if declaring myself the Wife of a Country Curate, and Mother of seven Children, will not be deemed sufficient." Her husband was George Leigh, curate of Middlewich, Cheshire. The poet must have died before 1795, when her husband remarried.

Her small quarto volume contains within its 101 pages fourteen poems of uncommon variety of style, meter, and genre, including traditional ballads and fables as well as humorous and highly imaginative pieces and a long work on the battle of Agincourt. The poems tackle social issues, often exploring the implications of societal practices. Leigh argues, for example, against dueling and war, highlights the way culture victimizes both illegitimate children and their abandoned mothers, and criticizes the low standards for "female education." The volume had about 750 subscribers, including many members of the clergy but no members of the aristocracy, few people from London, and no well-known writers or notables of any sort.

MAJOR WORK: *Miscellaneous Poems* (Manchester, 1788).

TEXTS USED: All texts from *Miscellaneous Poems.*

The Natural Child*

Let not the title of my verse offend,
   Nor let the Prude contract her rigid brow;
That helpless Innocence demands a friend,
   Virtue herself will cheerfully allow:

And shou'd my pencil prove too weak to paint,
   The ills attendant on the babe ere born;
Whose parents swerv'd from Virtue's mild restraint,
   Forgive th' attempt, nor treat the Muse with scorn.

Yon rural farm, where Mirth was wont to dwell,
10   Of Melancholy, now appears the seat;
Solemn and silent as the hermit's cell—
   Say what, my muse, has caus'd a change so great?

This hapless morn, an Infant first saw light,
   Whose innocence a better fate might claim,
Than to be shunn'd as hateful to the sight,
   And banish'd soon as it receives a name.

No joy attends its entrance into life,
   No smile upon its mother's face appears,
She cannot smile, alas! she is no wife;
20   But vents the sorrows of her heart in tears.

No father flies to clasp it to his breast,
   And bless the pow'r that gave it to his arms;
To see his form, in miniature, express'd,
   Or trace, with ecstacy, its mother's charms.

Unhappy babe! thy father is thy foe!
   Oft shall he wish thee number'd with the dead;
His crime entails on thee a load of woe,
   And sorrow heaps on thy devoted head.

Torn from its mother's breast, by shame or pride,
30.   No matter which—to hireling hands assign'd;

A parent's tenderness, when thus deny'd,
 Can it be thought its nurse is over-kind?

Too many, like this infant may we see,
 Expos'd, abandon'd, helpless and forlorn;
'Till death, misfortune's friend, has set them free,
 From a rude world, which gave them nought but scorn.

Too many mothers—horrid to relate!
 Soon as their infants breathe the vital air,
Deaf to their plaintive cries, their helpless state,
 Led on by shame, and driv'n by despair,   40

Fell murderers become—Here cease, my pen,
 And leave these wretched victims of despair;
But ah! what punishments await the men,
 Who, in such depths of mis'ry, plunge the fair.

          (1788)

---

* *Natural child* was a euphemism for a child born out of wedlock.

The Linnet; a Fable

Young Celia was beauteous, and blithe as the morn,
 On her cheek bloom'd the lilly and rose,
And sweet was her breath as the blossoming thorn,
 When, to hail spring returning it blows.

Her bosom, with love, and with tenderness glow'd,
 But her Linnet was all her delight;
On the sweet little warbler that love she bestow'd,
 And carest him from morning to night.

How oft wou'd she open the door of his cage,
 From which he enraptur'd wou'd fly,   10
And, perch'd on her hand, her attention engage,
 While her lover unheeded stood by!

Yet oft, the ingrate wou'd for Liberty pine,
    As he saw from her window the grove;
And oft wou'd he wish his companions to join,
    Again thro' the woodlands to rove.

Unrestrain'd by his Mistress, one Midsummer morn,
    When Phoebus illumin'd the east,
He flew to some birds, who were perch'd on a thorn,
20   And forsook his wont seat on her breast.

"Ungrateful deserter!" cry'd Celia, "away,
    "And meet the reward of your crime;
"For shou'd you escape the keen sportsman's survey,
    "You'll die of Repentance in time.

"But ah! his departure I ever shall mourn,
    "He was all that was charming and sweet;
"And shou'd the dear fugitive once more return,
    "He shall still greater tenderness meet:

"But vain the suggestion!—for tho' he may fly,
30   "More quick from a gun flies the shot;
"And, so num'rous the engines, prepar'd to destroy,
    "That death is most surely his lot."

Thus, with direful forebodings, was Celia opprest,
    His loss often cost her a tear;
While he, far away from his mistress and rest,
    Silly bird!—found destruction was near.

From a net, which was artfully spread to ensnare,
    He saw a poor bird get away,
And, at some little distance, a kite in the air,
40   Apparently, eager of prey:

In deep consternation, his monstrous beak,
    With wonder a while he survey'd,
Rejoic'd to escape it;—but found his mistake,
    By his former vain notions betray'd.

Said he to himself, in disconsolate strain,
    "How happy, the state I regret!
"Cou'd I my fair mistress's fondness regain—
    "That fondness I ne'er can forget:

"I again shou'd be fed by her delicate hand,
    "As three times I was yesterday,   50
"When she strok'd my smooth feathers—and now here I stand,
    "Neglected—to hunger a prey.

"Ah! Celia, your bosom with kindness replete,
    "Has been cruelly stung by my flight,
"But I'll haste to return, and abjure at your feet
    "My crime, and be blest with your sight."

He spoke—and, like light'ning, flew back to the spot,
    Where his mistress receiv'd him with joy;
He is faithful, she loves him—thus happy his lot,
    He'll never more venture to fly.   60

Like this simple Linnet, how oft may we see,
    The fond youth, and the love-stricken maid,
From their parents embraces imprudently flee,
    By false notions of freedom betray'd!

                        (1788)

The Revenge; from a Fact,
Attested by the Spanish Historians

'Twas night—and darkness all around,
   Her sable curtain spread,
When Claudio sought—and seeking found,
   The mansions of the dead:

For having, in his own defence
   Slain his invet'rate foe,
Ere he cou'd prove his innocence,
   Elsewhere 'twas death to go.

A church's sacred portal gain'd,
   He lean'd against the door—
Surpriz'd!—the door on which he lean'd
   Flew open;—but what more

The wretched wanderer did affright,
   Within the hallow'd dome,
He saw a pale and glimmering light,
   As issuing from a tomb:

Yet still had courage to draw near,
   When, dreadful to behold!
He saw, what chill'd his heart with fear,
   What made his blood run cold—

A beauteous Lady, clad in white,
   With wild and frantic look,
Rose from the grave;—while, at the sight,
   His frame with horror shook:

Who stepping, with a threat'ning tone,
   And with a bloody knife,
To Claudio, almost turn'd to stone,
   Almost bereft of life;

Demanded, what had brought him there,
   At such an hour of night?   30
The tim'rous youth, benumb'd with fear,
   And thinking her a sprite,

The truth, without reserve, confest,
   And why he thither fled—
"Art thou, indeed, so much distrest?"
   The beauteous phantom said.

"'Tis true, thou'rt in my pow'r," she cry'd,
   "But fear no harm from me;
"I am—and own the deed with pride—
   "A murderer like thee.   40

"A Lady of a noble race,
   "By perjur'd man betray'd;
"And doom'd to mis'ry and disgrace,
   "Tho' late a spotless maid.

"The wretch who won my virgin heart,
   "Soon triumph'd o'er my fame;
"Acted the treacherous villain's part,
   "And boasted of my shame.

"I hir'd a ruffian—had him slain—
   "But not with *that* content,   50
"Still greater vengeance to obtain,
   "I to the Sexton went;

"And purchas'd, with a purse of gold,
   "Permission to explore
"His grave;—and *here* that heart behold,
   "The perjur'd villain wore.

"From his vile breast, these hands have torn
   "This heart—Revenge how sweet!"
She said—and with a look of scorn,
   Stamp'd on it with her feet.   60

"Be this," she cry'd, "each traitor's doom
   "Who our weak sex betrays";
Then turn'd—and sought the Convent's gloom,
   To end her wretched days.

                                        (1788)

Isabella Lickbarrow

(fl. 1814–1818)

Robert Southey, William Wordsworth, Thomas De Quincey, Thomas Cookson, and Basil Montague all subscribed to Isabella Lickbarrow's *Poetical Effusions,* published in Kendal, in Westmorland, in 1814. The *Monthly Review* noted, "The introduction to these verses is written with a simplicity and humility which are sufficient to mollify the severest critic; and the compositions, though not brilliant, display much chastened feeling, and a poetical perception of the beauties of nature."[1] Certainly her celebrations of Lake District scenery would have pleased the Wordsworth circle.

Poetical Effusions contains unusual variety for a first book, ranging from the playfully comic to the sublime, from love lyrics to a celebration of dream life. Lickbarrow contemplates the ephemerality of the written word and explores the character and significance of her own poetry. Some poems portray the vulnerability and loneliness of women widowed or alone; some assert the value of single life and its attendant liberty. Often Lickbarrow's protagonists are solitary women facing difficult situations or choices. Works such as "On the Sprint at Garnet Bridge" and "Lines Written on the Banks of the Eden, near Kirkby Stephen" are sensuous and at times erotic.

Information about Lickbarrow's life is scanty. We know that she was self-taught, that she read the poetry of Thomas Chatterton and Elizabeth Smith and the letters of Anne Grant, and that she began writing verse as a child. She and her sisters were orphaned early, and she was much in need of the money the 372 subscribers to her poems provided. She wrote clandestinely, she admits in her preface, "at intervals stolen from repose" after her domestic duties were done. In 1818 she published in Liverpool *A Lament upon the Death of . . . the Princess Charlotte, and Alfred, a Vision,* which appears to have attracted little notice.

1. 76 (February 1815): 211.

MAJOR WORKS: *Poetical Effusions* (Kendal, 1814); *A Lament upon the Death of Her Royal Highness the Princess Charlotte, and Alfred, a Vision* (Liverpool, 1818).

TEXTS USED: All texts from *Poetical Effusions*.

Lines on the Comet

Trav'ller of th' etherial round,
    Hast'ning o'er yon starry plain,
Tell us whither art thou bound,
    What far distant goal to gain?

Say by what resistless force
    Thus thy glowing orb is driven,
Forwards on its rapid course,
    Through the azure fields of heav'n.

What is thy unerring guide,
10   Marking out thy devious way,
Through the trackless ether wide,
    That thou wand'rest not astray?

Borne upon th' elastic air,
    Not the sweeping whirlwind's speed,
Not the lightning's sudden glare,
    The swiftness of thy flight exceed.

Say, (for in thy ceaseless race,
    Ever since the world began,
Thou hast travers'd wilds of space,
20   Far beyond the view of man,)

In what realm, to us unknown,
    Wond'rous trav'ller hast thou been,
Passing many a torrid zone,
    Many a chilling region keen?

Hast thou roll'd thy lucid train
  O'er yon beauteous tract of light,
Yon thickly studded, shining plain,
  With countless constellations bright.

Tell us if thy circuit runs
  Where other planets brighter blaze,   30
Where more powerful burning suns
  Shed around intenser rays.

Hast thou rush'd through dreary realms,
  Lost in dim obscurity,
Where no faint star's glimmering beams
  Tremble o'er the cheerless sky?

Trav'ller, wheresoever bound,
  Or new regions to explore,
Or to trace a former round,
  Trod a thousand years before;   40

Yet awhile within our sphere,
  Beauteous stranger, deign to stay,
Haste not on thy vast career,
  With such rapid speed away.

                              (1814)

---

27 Yon thickly studded, shining plain] The Milky Way. *Lickbarrow.*

On the Fate of Newspapers

What changes time's swift motion brings!
What sad reverse of human things!
What once was valu'd, highly priz'd,
Is in a few short hours despis'd.
I'll but solicit your attention,
While I a single instance mention,
The "*Advertiser,*" you must know,
Fresh from the Mint not long ago,
We welcom'd with abundant pleasure,
10   Impatient for the mighty treasure,
In what an alter'd state forlorn,
'Tis now in scatter'd fragments torn,
Part wrapp'd around the kettle's handle,
Part twisted up to light the candle,
Part given to the devouring fire:
Ah! see line after line expire;
It surely would, beyond a joke,
The patience of a saint provoke,
To think that after all their pains,
20   The rhymes which rack'd the poet's brains,
And all the antiquarian's learning,
Display'd so justly in discerning
The ancient Saxon derivation
Of half the places in the nation,
And the philosopher's vast skill,
In measuring each stupendous hill,
From Sca-fell down to Benson-knot,
And even hills of lesser note;
To think that what such wits have penn'd,
30   Should come to this disgraceful end.

25 philosopher's] During Lickbarrow's time the term *natural philosophy* still covered all that now would be included under the heading "science." This name was first used by Aristotle to describe his Platonic study. Later the term meant the various branches of science, such as logic, physics, botany, animal anatomy, physiology, psychology, and ethics. This usage continued in England when it had become obsolete in other countries.

27 Sca-fell] A mountain in the Lake District, in Cumberland.

27 Benson-knot] A hill in Westmorland, also in the Lake District.

Why 'tis enough to make them vow,
With aspect stern and frowning brow,
They'll such an useless trade resign,
And never write another line.
But stop, good sirs, a nobler fate
May your productions yet await;
A thought just now my head has enter'd,
In which alone my hopes are center'd.
Perhaps, preferr'd the pipe to light,
For some dull heavy witless wight,   40
They'll, with tobacco's fumes, infuse
The inspiration of the muse,
And furnish many an empty brain—
If so, we'll write and sing again.

        (1814)

The Nun's Soliloquy

Yon sun, who runs his annual course
 About earth's varied bound,
While slow revolving seasons roll,
 Their never-ceasing round—

Yon rising sun, whose early beams,
 Returning beauty spreads,
And o'er those lonely convent walls
 A golden lustre sheds—

Adorns a long forsaken world,
 Which I no more must see;   10
Yet that forsaken world contains
 One object dear to me.

The play-mate of my early years,
 Companion of my youth,
In whose mild eye expressive shone
 Intelligence and truth.

Like two fair rose-buds on one stem,
   We grew, nor wish'd to part;
Our hopes, our fears, our joys the same,
20   We only had one heart.

Oh! days of innocent delight!
   Oh! youth so dear to me!
How soon I bade a last adieu
   To social life and thee.

A dying mother claim'd my vow,
   My parting vow I gave,
That here I'd pass my future days,
   And here should be my grave.

But ah! no language can describe
30   The anguish of my heart,
From thee, dear brother of my soul,
   To be compell'd to part.

It griev'd me not to leave a world
   Whose charms were yet unknown—
That world with all its gay delights,
   I lov'd for thee alone.

Nor other joys I wish'd to prove,
   Nor other pleasures know,
Than those thy converse and thy smile,
40   Thy friendship could bestow.

And when my trembling lips pronounc'd
   The irrevocable vow—
That vow which ne'er can be recall'd,
   Which seal'd my doom below.

That from my thoughts, all earthly things
   Henceforth should banish'd be,
I in my bosom's secret shrine
   Reserv'd one thought for thee.

And still in youthful beauty there
   Does thy lov'd image dwell,   50
Its inmate in this lone abode,
   This solitary cell.

Each daily orison enjoin'd,
   Perform'd with duteous care;
Still ere I close my eyes, for thee
   I breathe a secret pray'r.

And sure a love so pure as mine,
   May hope to be forgiv'n,
Should harsh ungenerous mortals blame,
   Sweet pity dwells in heav'n.   60

Perhaps ev'n saints from earth remov'd,
   Some tender thoughts bestow,
And some fond recollections feel,
   Of those they left below.

In that blest world may faithful friends,
   By kindred minds allied,
Meet where no rigid vows forbid,
   No convent walls divide.

                        (1814)

53 orison] Prayer.

On Sleep

Come ye deep shades of night, that from the view
Of an unpitying world the wretched shroud,
That give the harass'd limbs of toil repose,
And bid the way-worn trav'ller turn, and seek
Some place of shelter for his houseless head:
That the tired soldier, from his weary march,
And from the dreadful field of war and death,
A while release; come thou sad mourner night,
I love thy darkness, or the pensive beam
10   The moon's pale lustre sheds upon thy brow.
Now when the clouded light of day presents
Our eyes with nought but scenes of desolation,
I love thee for thy gentle hand-maid Sleep,
Who seals in sweet forgetfulness our eyes,
Transports us from life's sad realities,
To tranquil scenes of happiness and peace.
Such is the mighty necromancer's power
Who o'er Sleep's vast ideal realms presides,
That when from our cold clime is swept away
20   Each summer grace, his pow'rful wand can raise
A lovelier landscape, cloth'd in brighter hues—
Can such magnificence, such charms display,
As waking fancy's boldest thoughts ne'er fram'd—
That pow'rful wand, whose touch can quick erase
The past and present from our memory,
And drive the intruding future from our thoughts;
While visions fair of momentary joy,
Unreal as the seeming silver lake
Which cheats the trav'ller o'er Arabian sands,
30   Seem permanent the portion of our lives.
Oh I have felt such sweet tranquillity,
Such pure sensations of sincere delight,
As if that instant into being wak'd,
With feelings tun'd to joy, and joy alone,
I almost wish'd life could be spent in dreams.
Yet the magician too can be unkind,

Can shut this gay ideal paradise.
Those pleasing regions he displays no more,
But bids around me scenes unlovely rise.

   A dear and honour'd guest would frequent come;   40
And speak in tones so long and well remember'd,
Which once were wont to gladden my young heart,
That days of early pleasure seem'd returned.
In youthful grace, with sweet engaging smile,
Another form belov'd was wont to pay
A short and welcome visit to my dreams;
But comes no more — dear semblance of a friend,
Whom death has hid for ever from my view,
Since I must never more on earth behold
The lov'd original, nor find again   50
Another friend so faithful and so kind,
Come lovely vision to my dreams once more.
Thou bear'st his image, tho' an empty shade,
And thou canst look, and speak, and charm my heart.
                                (1814)

The Widow

How dreary is winter to me,
   Alone all its rigours I bear;
The hand that should shield me lies low;
   I've none in my sorrows to share.

Ye trees that hang over my cot,
   And tremble with each passing breeze,
The sport of the rude whistling winds,
   Which bend your tall heads as they please:

For the ravage of winter you sigh,
   And the loss of your verdure deplore,   10
But your lot's not so wretched as mine,
   My winter will never be o'er.

Thou snowdrop so sickly and sad,
   That droops when the sun is gone down;
Now languid and bending thy head,
   Beneath the pale light of the moon.

Fair flow'ret! too early thy birth,
   Too soon hast thou left thy warm bed,
The hoar-frost will nip thy sweet bud,
20   And soon will thy beauty be fled.

Like thee do I languish and fade,
   But my state is more sad and forlorn;
And ah! hapless me, if I die,
   My loss a sweet infant will mourn.

                                         (1814)

Colin*

Gentle maid, consent to be
A rural bride, and dwell with me,
Where the woodland warblers sing
Songs of love, to hail the spring—
Where sweet wild flowers scent the gale
Round my cottage of the vale.

The jess'mine dark with snowy gems,
Scatter'd o'er its bending stems;
And the woodbine's tendrils twine
10   With the blushing eglantine,
To form a rural bower for thee—
Quit for these thy liberty.

                                         (1814)

   *"Colin" and "Lucy" are a response to the famous ballad "Colin and Lucy," by
Thomas Tickell (1686–1740), the friend of Addison.

Lucy

Shepherd, tho' thy song be sweet,
And thy cottage is complete,
Yet, should I consent to be
A rural bride, and dwell with thee,
Shall good-humour still prevail
In thy cottage of the vale?

Say, shall never frowns or strife
Make me rue a married life?
Wilt thou constant be and kind,
And as now to love inclin'd?   10
Else to me would sweeter be
A single life and liberty.

              (1814)

Lines Written on the Banks of the Eden, near Kirkby Stephen*

From distant moor-land heights descending,
   How swiftly rolls this stream away!
Say, whither, Eden, art thou hasting?
   Stay, impetuous river, stay,

And hear a rural muse address thee,
   Who thy steep woody banks along,
By these rude scenes once more awaken'd,
   Pours again th' unstudied song.

From other plains afar, a wand'rer,
   I thy loud sounding stream have sought,   10
Beside thy darkly rolling waters,
   T' indulge the pensive dreams of thought.

Here, when the full-orb'd moon ascending
   Sheds her radiant light serene,
And round a softer day diffuses
   O'er this wild and rugged scene;

Here would I love unseen to ramble
   Around this rocky lone recess,
Form'd by the windings of the river,
20   A sweet sequester'd wilderness;

Amid the roar of dashing waters,
   That sweep on every side around,
Mingled with the hollow murmurs
   Of the deep current under ground.

Sweet as the voice of sweetest music
   Is the wild torrent's roar to me;
The foam upon its broken surface,
   'Mid pointed crags, I love to see.

But here I may no longer listen
30   This rapid current, nor survey
Its waves down shelving rocks swift tumbling;
   For ev'ning calls my steps away.

Through many a lovely vale meand'ring,
   Of thee shall other poets tell;
I may perhaps no more behold thee,
   Eden, to thy dark stream farewell!

                    (1814)

* Market town situated on the Eden River in Westmorland.

On the Sprint at Garnet Bridge*

Riv'let of the narrow valley,
  Far on ev'ry side resounds
The dashing of thy roaring waters,
  Now confin'd within their bounds.

Here, ev'n now, with strong sensations
  I survey thy rapid flood,
Flowing in foaming waves beneath me,
  Half concealed by the wood.

But when autumn's gather'd tempests
  Burst on those surrounding hills,   10
And the swift descending torrent
  Soon thy rocky channel fills—

When, its narrow bounds disdaining,
  Pent within its banks no more,
Thy stream with sudden fury rushing
  Sweeps its woody margin o'er—

With what mingled joy and terror
  Would I mark thy rapid course,
O'er yon crags in vain opposing,
  Bounding with resistless force.   20

Riv'let of the narrow valley!
  Swiftly rolls thy stream away;
Here though every charm surrounds thee,
  Here, thou must not, canst not stay.

Go, and along yon verdant meadows
  With a gentler current glide;
Then must, sweet stream, thy lucid waters
  Swell a nobler river's pride.

                                    (1814)

28 a nobler river's] The Kent River.

*A river in Westmorland, the Sprint flows through Long Sleddale to the Kent River near Kendal. Garnet Bridge is four miles northwest of Kendal.

The Mountain Flower

If, the rude mountain turf adorning,
   Some lowly flower should chance to rise,
With simple charms to greet the morning;
   Tho' plac'd beneath ungenial skies;

And with no fertile soil to cherish,
   No shade to screen it from the blast;
Expos'd or in the birth to perish,
   Or brave the storm which o'er it past;

Tho' it can never boast the neatness,
10   The varied tints, majestic air,
The rich luxuriance, or the sweetness,
   Which grace the garden's inmates fair:

Oh let the curious florist spare it
   When the lone mountain gem he spies;
Tho' he with those can not compare it,
   Yet it may please some humbler eyes.

Oft have I seen a lovely blossom,
   Rearing its unprotected form
Upon the rugged wild's bleak bosom,
20   Unshelter'd from the piercing storm.

Yet sweetly there it grew and flourish'd,
   In humble charms to deck the waste,
By frequent showers and sunbeams nourish'd;
   And oft I've stay'd my eager haste,

17 lovely blossom] The grass of Parnassus. *Lickbarrow.*

To view the flower so unassuming,
　　So simple, yet so spotless fair,
Which on no higher rank presuming,
　　Blossoms and dies in secret there;

And thought perhaps my artless ditties,
　　Had better like their sister been,　　　　　　　　30
Still all unknown in towns and cities,
　　And had bloom'd and died unseen.
　　　　　　　　(1814)

Lady Hamilton

*According to tradition, the circumstance on which the following Poem is
founded, happened some centuries ago, and Lady Hamilton's apparition
was believed to make its appearance, till part of the building which she
frequented was pulled down and re-built.*

　　Round Sizergh's antique, massy walls,
　　　　Full frequent swept the whistling blast;
　　It sigh'd along the spacious halls,
　　　　And through the tap'stried chambers past.

　　The clock, with solemn-sounding knell,
　　　　Proclaim'd the dreary midnight hour;
　　And loud the deep-ton'd magic bell
　　　　Slow answer'd from the lonely tower.

　　But wherefore, at this silent hour,
　　　　When every eye is clos'd in sleep,　　　　　　　10
　　In yonder lonely desert tower,
　　　　Why tolls the midnight bell so deep?

　　Immur'd within these gloomy walls,
　　　　Here long a gentle lady lay;
　　Far from her dear paternal halls,
　　　　She wept her bloom of life away.

Far from the noble youth she lov'd,
    A youth for matchless constancy,
For worth and valour, long approv'd,
20   For generous deeds and courtesy.

When Albert clasp'd her trembling hand,
    And press'd it to his throbbing heart,
Sighing, that honour's stern command,
    Compell'd such faithful friends to part;

And whisper'd vows of endless truth,
    To soothe the parting sense of pain,
Ah! little thought the gentle youth,
    They never were to meet again.

Hither, allur'd by treach'rous art,
30   Deceiv'd by friendship's specious name,
Hither, with unsuspecting heart,
    In evil hour, fair Marg'ret came.

When first these fatal doors she pass'd,
    On heavy wing the bat flew by;
And hollow moaning rush'd the blast;
    The owlet gave a boding cry.

Then first that sullen peal was rung,
    Loud bursting on the night's dark gloom;
That bell by unseen spirits swung,
40   Foretold fair Hamilton's sad doom.

But guileless, nor suspecting harm,
    These with no terrors struck her mind,
Soon she forgot the slight alarm,
    Which left no lasting fears behind.

A few short days within these walls
    Were heard the festive notes of joy;
Music's sweet strains and sprightly balls
    Conspir'd to please the ear and eye.

Soon those delusive visions past;
    Her few last days of pleasure o'er,   50
(She little dreamt they were her last,)
    Fair Hamilton was seen no more.

But when the chill autumnal breeze
    Swept briskly o'er the curling flood—
Shook the high towering forest trees,
    And of its foliage stript the wood—

O'er all the neighb'ring hamlet round,
    Was heard once more that wizard bell;
And those who heard the dreadful sound,
    Said that it toll'd fair Margaret's knell.   60

E'er since, when o'er this ancient pile
    The deep'ning shades of ev'ning fell,
And lingering day-light's latest smile
    Seem'd loath to bid the world farewell—

Amid the melancholy glooms,
    Her spirit oft was seen to walk,
Through gall'ries long, and spacious rooms,
    And to herself would whisp'ring talk.

In sorrow's sable weeds array'd,
    She mov'd with pensive, solemn grace;   70
Slow was her step, noiseless her tread,
    A sable veil conceal'd her face.

Sometimes she seem'd in thought profound,
    Her head reclining on her arm;
Her eyes still fixt upon the ground,
    As spell-bound by some powerful charm.

When the dim taper's feeble beam
    Around the lone apartment shed,
Of partial light, a sudden gleam—
    Instant the shadowy form was fled.   80

Still as that woful night returns
　　Which seal'd the lovely Margaret's doom;
That bell her cruel exit mourns,
　　In solemn dirges o'er her tomb.

(1814)

Lady Anne Lindsay

(1750–1825)

Lady Anne Lindsay, said to be the child "of a hundred earls," was the author of the single most popular contemporary ballad of the English romantic period, "Auld Robin Gray." Her mother, Anne Dalrymple, was an aristocrat, as was her father, James Lindsay, fifth earl of Balcarras. Born on 8 December 1750, Lady Anne was the eldest of their eleven children. She grew up in Fife, making winter visits to Edinburgh. The extensive family library was hers to use as she liked, and she and her father, who died when she was seventeen, shared a literary camaraderie. Later she remarked that in her youth she would often "scribble away poetically and in prose, till I made myself an artificial happiness, which did very well 'pour passer le temps.'"[1]

Another member of the household was Sophy Johnstone, a relative who came for a visit and stayed thirteen years. She wore men's clothes, walked with a masculine stride, took up blacksmithing, and occasionally swore. She played the fiddle and sang, in a deep voice, a wealth of old Scots ballads, including the ancient air "The Bridegroom Greits When the Sun Gaes Doun." Lady Anne was especially fond of the melody and longed herself to sing it but considered the traditional words too coarse. In early 1772, feeling sad just after her sister Margaret had married and moved to London, Lady Anne composed new words for the old song, trying, as she said, to "give to its plaintive tones some little history of virtuous distress in humble life, such as might suit it."[2] Mischievously she named the lyric after Robin Gray, an old shepherd the children disliked. More than fifty years later, she recounted circumstances of its composition, including the following incident:

1. *Lives of the Lindsays; or a memoir of the houses of Crawford and Balcarres by Lord Lindsay . . . together with personal narratives by his brothers . . . and his sister, Lady Anne Barnard*, 3 vols. (London, 1849), 2:332.

2. Lindsay to Walter Scott, 8 July 1823, quoted in Walter Scott's introduction to *Auld Robin Gray; A Ballad by the Right Honourable Lady Anne Barnard, Born Lady Anne Lindsay of Balcarras*, ed. Walter Scott (Edinburgh, 1825).

I called to my little sister [Elizabeth, twelve or thirteen years Anne's junior, later] Lady Hardwicke, . . . "I have been writing a ballad, my dear; I am oppressing my heroine with many misfortunes. I have already sent her Jamie to sea—and broken her father's arm—and made her mother fall sick—and given her Auld Robin Gray for her lover; but I wish to load her with a fifth sorrow within the four lines, poor thing! Help me to one."—"Steal the cow, sister Anne," said the little Elizabeth. The cow was immediately *lifted* by me, and the song completed. At our fire-side, and amongst our neighbours, "Auld Robin Gray" was always called for. I was pleased in secret with the approbation it met with; but such was *my dread* of being suspected of writing *any thing,* perceiving the shyness it created in those who could write *nothing,* that I carefully kept my own secret.[3]

Evidently Lady Anne kept her secret for other reasons as well. Her narrative about a loveless marriage of convenience too closely paralleled the actual fates of her mother and her sister Margaret, both forced into marriages with substantially older, wealthy men. Her father had been nearly sixty and her mother only twenty-three when they married. The young woman had refused the near-deaf Lord Balcarras, but after he developed a serious fever, made her heir to half his estate, and resolved to die out of "grief and despair," she married him. Then the earl recovered.[4] The life of Lady Anne's sister Margaret was similar in this respect. She fell in love with James Burgess, a man of ambition and intelligence but no fortune, but she was made to give him up, and James left the country. Just before the composition of the ballad, Margaret married Alexander Fordyce of Roehampton, a middle-aged banker, said to be one of the richest in the country.[5] Lady Anne's narrative probably gave voice as well to her anxieties about her own future in a world where women, whether aristocratic or working-class, were still legally treated as property.

"Auld Robin Gray" struck a chord in many people and enjoyed great popularity. Not only was it sung throughout Scotland but it was carried into England by ballad-mongers and strolling players, translated into French, sung by a lunatic in Mary Wollstonecraft's *Maria, or The Wrongs of Woman* and by a milkmaid in Susanna Blamire's "Stoklewath," and printed in every anthology of Scottish verse and song; it even lent its name to the newest fashions, including, one season, the Robin Gray hat. It found its way into print in many versions, with several people, including a clergyman, claiming authorship.

Antiquarians debated whether "Auld Robin Gray" was an ancient ballad

3. Ibid.
4. Madeleine Masson, *Lady Anne Barnard* (London, 1949), 18–19.
5. Ibid., 2.

or of modern origin. Even though they advertised a twenty-guinea reward to anyone who could prove its origin, Lady Anne and Sophy Johnstone remained silent. Eventually the Antiquarian Society dispatched its secretary to visit Lady Anne in an effort to discover the truth. Offended by his "impertinent" questioning, Lady Anne closed the interview with the remark, "The ballad in question has in my opinion met with attentions beyond its deserts. It set off with having a very fine tune put to it by a doctor of music, was sung by youth and beauty for five years and more, had a romance composed from it by a man of eminence, was the subject of a play, of an opera, and of a pantomime, was sung by the united armies in America, acted by Punch, and afterwards danced by dogs in the street—but never more honored than by the present investigation."[6]

Some guessed the poem's origin early on. "Happening to sing it one day at Dalkeith-House, with more feeling perhaps than belonged to a common ballad," Lady Anne recounts, "our friend Lady Frances Scott smiled, and fixing her eyes on me, said, '*You* wrote this song yourself.' The blush that followed confirmed my *guilt*. Perhaps I blushed the more (being then very young) from the recollection of the coarse words from which I borrowed the tune, and was afraid of the raillery which might have taken place if it had been discovered I had ever heard such."[7] The laird of Dalziel also was not deceived. He advised Lady Anne to make the lyrics more authentic. "Instead of singing, 'To make the crown a pound, my Jamie gaed to sea,'" he told her, "say, to make it twenty merks, for a Scottish pund is but twenty pence, and Jamie was na such a gowk as to leave Jenny and gang to sea to lessen his gear. It is that line . . . that tells me that sang was written by some bonnie lassie that didna ken the value of the Scots money quite so well as an auld writer in the town of Edinburgh would have kent it."[8]

Not until half a century after its composition did its author confess the truth to anyone outside her family circle. In the *Pirate* (1821), Walter Scott compares the situation of his character Minna to that of Jennie Gray "the village-heroine in Lady Anne Lindsay's beautiful ballad." He then quotes four lines from an unpublished sequel to the ballad, composed by Lady Anne at her mother's request many years after the original. Curious to know how he could have learned lines she never so much as wrote in manuscript and how he could attribute them to her, Lady Anne wrote to Scott. (His aunt Christy Rutherford, it turned out, was a mutual friend.) Thus began a lively corre-

6. *Lives of the Lindsays,* 2:333. The doctor of music was the Reverend William Leeves, of Wrington, Somerset, who had written a new melody.

7. Lindsay to Walter Scott, 8 July 1823.

8. Ibid.

spondence between the two, resulting in the publication in 1825 of "Auld Robin Gray" with its two inferior sequels and an introduction by Walter Scott in a thin quarto volume for the members of the Bannatyne Club, a society for the preservation of Scottish literature and history. At Scott's request, she also gathered together and prepared for the press a volume entitled *Lays of the Lindsays,* containing more of her poems as well as works by other members of her family. Although she suppressed this book, three copies are known to have survived.[9]

Lady Anne never met Scott, but she did meet and record her conversation with Samuel Johnson when he visited Edinburgh in 1773. She was a friend of David Hume, Henry Mackenzie, William Pitt, Horace Mann, Edmund Burke, Richard Brinsley Sheridan, the prince of Wales, and probably Horace Walpole and Joanna Baillie. For some years she lived in London with her sister Margaret, but in 1793, at the age of forty-three, she married Andrew Barnard, son of the bishop of Limerick. Though not wealthy, he was an accomplished man, somewhat younger than his bride. When he was appointed colonial secretary under Lord MacCartney in 1797, the couple moved to the Cape of Good Hope. There Lady Anne entertained for the unmarried governor and documented her experience in a journal and a sketchbook, both later published. Her husband died in 1807, and Lady Anne lived once again with her sister Margaret in Berkeley Square, London, where their home became a literary salon. It was said that she "could change a disagreeable party into an agreeable one; she could make the dullest speak, the shiest feel happy, and the witty flash fire."[10] When Margaret married a second time in 1812, Lady Anne stayed on alone at Berkeley Square, continuing her father's work by adding her reminiscences to *The Lives of the Lindsays.*

She died in London on 6 May 1825, at the age of seventy-four, remembered most for the lyric she wrote at twenty-one, a work Leigh Hunt called "the most pathetic ballad that ever was written";[11] in 1856 *Blackwood's Edinburgh Magazine* called it "one of those perfect and unimprovable works of genius which . . . the whole world receives into its heart" and noted, "There are lines in Lady Anne's ballad unparalleled, so far as we are aware, in depth of insight and perfect simplicity of expression."[12] William Wordsworth con-

9. See Walter Scott's letter of 3 October [1824] concerning the recall of *Lays of the Lindsays* in *The Letters of Sir Walter Scott,* ed. H. J. C. Grierson, vol. 8 (London, 1935), 386. One copy is now at Abbotsford, Scott's home, and another, imperfect copy is at the National Library of Scotland.

10. Catherine J. Hamilton, *Women Writers: Their Works and Ways,* 1st ser. (London, 1892).

11. Leigh Hunt, "Specimens of British Poetesses," in *Men, Women, and Books: A Selection of Sketches, Essays, and Critical Memoirs from his Uncollected Prose,* new ed. (London, 1891), 284.

12. "Family History," *Blackwood's Edinburgh Magazine* 80 (October 1856): 466.

sidered it one of "the two best Ballads, perhaps of modern times."[13] As late as 1876, in *The Poets and Poetry of Scotland,* James Grant Wilson called it "perhaps the most perfect, tender, and affecting of modern Scottish ballads."[14] William Hazlitt remarked, "The effect of reading this old ballad is as if all our hopes and fears hung upon the last fibre of the heart, and we felt that giving way. What silence, what loneliness, what leisure for grief and despair!"[15] And Walter Scott called it a "real pastoral, which is worth all the dialogues Corydon and Phillis have had together from the days of Theocritus downwards."[16] None of her contemporary commentators, except perhaps Scott, and he only in an oblique way, remarks on the subversive character of a narrative showing how duty and virtue as defined by conventional morality lead to human misery.

MAJOR WORKS: *Lays of the Lindsays; being Poems by the Ladies of the House of Balcarres* (Edinburgh, 1824); *Auld Robin Gray; A Ballad by the Right Honourable Lady Anne Barnard, Born Lady Anne Lindsay of Balcarras,* ed. Walter Scott (Edinburgh, 1825); *Lives of the Lindsays; or, A Memoir of the Houses of Crawford and Balcarres by Lord Lindsay . . . together with Personal Narratives by His Brothers . . . and His Sister, Lady Anne Barnard,* 3 vols. (London, 1849); *South Africa a Century Ago. Letters written from the Cape of Good Hope, 1797–1801,* ed. with a memoir [of Lady Anne Lindsay] and brief notes by W. H. Wilkins (London, 1901); *The Letters of Lady Anne Barnard to Henry Dundas to the Cape and Elsewhere / 1793–1803 Together with her Journal of a Tour into the Interior and Certain Other Letters,* ed. A. M. Lewin Robinson (Cape Town, 1973).

TEXTS USED: Text of "Auld Robin Gray" from *Auld Robin Gray; A Ballad.* Text of "The Highland Storm" from *Lays of the Lindsays,* which also contained the first authorized printed version of "Auld Robin Gray."

13. Letter to Alexander Dyce, 4 December 1833, in *The Letters of William and Dorothy Wordsworth: The Later Years,* ed. Ernest de Selincourt, vol. 2 (Oxford, 1939), 678.

14. *The Poets and Poetry of Scotland; from the earliest to the present time,* 2 vols. (London, 1876), 1, pt. 2: 334.

15. *The Collected Works of William Hazlitt,* eds. A. R. Waller and Arnold Glover, 12 vols. (London, 1902), 5:141.

16. *The Letters of Sir Walter Scott,* ed. H. J. C. Grierson, 13 vols. (London, 1935), 8:37.

Auld Robin Gray

When the sheep are in the fauld, when the cows come hame,
When a' the weary world to quiet rest are gane,
The woes of my heart fa' in showers frae my ee,
Unken'd by my gudeman, who soundly sleeps by me.

Young Jamie loo'd me weel, and sought me for his bride;
But saving ae crown-piece, he'd naething else beside.
To make the crown a pound, my Jamie gaed to sea;
And the crown and the pound, oh! they were baith for me!

Before he had been gane a twelvemonth and a day,
My father brak his arm, our cow was stown away;
My mither she fell sick—my Jamie was at sea—
And Auld Robin Gray, oh! he came a-courting me.

My father cou'dna work—my mother cou'dna spin;
I toil'd day and night, but their bread I cou'dna win;
Auld Rob maintain'd them baith, and, wi' tears in his ee,
Said, "Jenny, oh! for their sakes, will you marry me?"

My heart it said na, and I look'd for Jamie back;
But hard blew the winds, and his ship was a wrack:
His ship it was a wrack! Why didna Jenny dee?
Or, wherefore am I spared to cry out, Woe is me!

My father argued sair—my mother didna speak,
But she look'd in my face till my heart was like to break:
They gied him my hand, but my heart was in the sea;
And so Auld Robin Gray, he was gudeman to me.

I hadna been his wife, a week but only four,
When mournful' as I sat on the stane at my door,

10

20

---

1 fauld] Fold.
4 Unken'd . . . gudeman] Unknown by my husband.
6 ae] One.   23 gied] Gave.
21 sair] Sore.   26 stane] Stone.

I saw my Jamie's ghaist—I cou'dna think it he,
Till he said, "I'm come hame, my love, to marry thee!"

O sair, sair did we greet, and mickle say of a';
Ae kiss we took, nae mair—I bad him gang awa.   30
I wish that I were dead, but I'm no like to dee;
For O, I am but young to cry out, Woe is me!

I gang like a ghaist, and I carena much to spin;
I darena think o' Jamie, for that wad be a sin.
But I will do my best a gude wife aye to be,
For auld Robin Gray, oh! he is sae kind to me.
                              (wr. 1772; pub. 1824)

The Highland Storm*

1

Where, my love, where art thou going?
        Cruven Elin, Evin Oge;
Far's thy home, and late 'tis growing,
        Cruven Elin, Evin Oge.
See the angry sky is scowling,
Hark! the hollow winds are howling,
To their sheds run beast and fowl in,
        Cruven Elin, Evin Oge.

2

Draw not back, my love, I pray thee,
        Cruven Elin, Evin Oge;   10
Do not let the storm dismay thee,
        Cruven Elin, Evin Oge.
Lean on me, I'll keep thee steady;
How it rains! you're wet already,
Creep into my tartan plaidy,
        Cruven Elin, Evin Oge.

29 mickle] Much.

3

Yonder stands a cot forsaken,
    Cruven Elin, Evin Oge;
Let's bide there till morn awaken,
20   Cruven Elin, Evin Oge.
Would you then go there without me?
Oh, my love, how can you doubt me!
Dearest arm! 'tis thrown about me,
    Cruven Elin, Evin Oge.

4

Soft as violets, fresh as roses,
    Cruven Elin, Evin Oge;
Who on Donald's breast reposes,
    Cruven Elin, Evin Oge.
One sweet kiss might I but take it?—
30   No! my love for her is sacred,
Till her daddie honest make it,
    Cruven Elin, Evin Oge.

(1824)

---

* This tune, with words appropriate to it in the Erse language, was sung to me by Sir John M'Pherson, brother to the compiler of the Poems of Ossian. I noted down the tune and its burthen at the time, as he sang it. He promised to translate and versify the words, but died ere he had fulfilled his intentions. I have put a few simple verses to the ditty, and preserve it for the sake of the chieftain, who, had he lived, would have given me the song in *Oscar's own words. Lindsay.*

Janet Little

(1759–1813)

Called "Jennie" by her friends, family, and employers, Janet Little was born in August 1759, the daughter of George Little of Nether Bogside, near Ecclefechan, in Dumfriesshire, Scotland. Her parents were people of modest means, and her formal education was probably minimal. Belying her surname, she grew into an unusually tall, dark-haired woman. One of her contemporaries described her as "no bad representation of some of Sir Walter Scott's gigantic heroines, but without their impudence."[1] She first worked for several years as a servant in the home of a Reverend Johnstone and accompanied his children to Glasgow. Later she became a chambermaid for Frances Anna Wallace Dunlop, the patron of Robert Burns, who took an interest in her and her poetry. Little naturally heard much about Burns in the Dunlop household, admired his work, and was inspired by his example.

After the suicide of the earl of Loudoun in 1786, Little accompanied Dunlop's daughter, Susan Hendrie, to her new home at Loudoun Castle and took charge of the dairy there, earning the nickname "The Scotch Milkmaid." On 12 July 1789, no doubt encouraged by Frances Dunlop, she wrote to Burns:

> You must know, Sir, I am somewhat in love with the Muses, though I cannot boast of any favours they have deigned to confer upon me as yet; my situation in life has been very much against me as to that. . . . As I had the pleasure of perusing your poems, I felt a partiality for the author, which I should not have experienced had you been in a more dignified station. I wrote a few verses of address to you, which I did not then think of ever presenting; but as fortune seems to have favoured me in this, by bringing me into a family by whom you are well known and much esteemed, and where perhaps I may have an opportunity of seeing you, I shall, in hopes of your future friendship, take the liberty to transcribe them.

1. Quoted in [James Paterson], *The Contemporaries of Burns, and the More Recent Poets of Ayrshire, with Selections from their Writings* (Edinburgh and London, 1840), 87–88.

She enclosed a ten-stanza poem in praise of Burns, written partly in Scots dialect, containing the self-deprecating lines,

> Sure Milton's eloquence were faint
> The beauties of your verse to paint:
> My rude unpolish'd strokes but taint
> Their brilliancy;

She closed the letter, "Sir—I hope you will pardon my boldness in this: my hand trembles while I write to you, conscious of my unworthiness of what I would most earnestly solicit, viz. your favour and friendship; yet, hoping you will show yourself possessed of as much generosity and good nature as will prevent your exposing what may justly be found liable to censure in this measure, I shall take the liberty to subscribe myself, Sir, Your most obedient humble servant, Janet Little."[2]

We know that Burns received the letter, for he wrote Frances Dunlop nearly two months later, on 6 September: "I had some time ago an epistle, part poetic, and part prosaic, from your poetess, Mrs. J. L——, a very ingenious but modest composition. I should have written her, as she requested, but for the hurry of this new business. I have heard of her and her compositions in this country; and, I am happy to add, always to the honour of her character. The fact is, I know not well how to write to her: I should sit down to a sheet of paper that I knew not how to stain."[3] Whether Burns ever replied directly to Little is unclear, but later Little made a trip to Dumfriesshire, principally to see Burns at his farm in Ellisland. Little's "On a Visit to Mr. Burns" describes this meeting, which took place shortly after Burns had broken his arm in a fall from a horse:

> With beating breast I view'd the bard;
> All trembling did him greet:
> With sighs bewail'd his fate so hard,
> Whose notes were ever sweet.

In 1792, with Frances Dunlop's help and encouragement, *The Poetical Works of Janet Little, the Scotch Milkmaid,* was published in Ayr by subscription, earning Little about fifty pounds. A 207-page octavo volume dedicated to Flora, Countess of Loudoun, then twelve years old, it contains fifty-four poems and a list of more than six hundred subscribers, including well-respected and influential people from throughout the country. In one poem, "To the Public," Little sets forth her goal:

2. Quoted in ibid., 79–81.
3. *The Letters of Robert Burns,* ed. G. Ross Roy, 2nd ed. (Oxford, 1985), 1:438.

> From the dull confines of a country shade,
> A rustic damsel issues forth her lays;
> There she, in secret, sought the Muse's aid,
> But now, aspiring, hopes to gain the bays.

Around this time Little married a laborer, John Richmond, eighteen years her senior and a widower with five children.

In December 1792, when Burns visited Dunlop House for four days, Frances Dunlop made a point of calling to his attention Little's recently published volume, which contained several poems idolizing him. He was unimpressed. Severely disappointed in his response, Dunlop wrote to him ten weeks later:

> Methinks I hear you ask me with an air that made me feel as I had got a slap in the face, if you must read all the few lines I had pointed out to your notice in poor Jenny's book. How did I upbraid my own conceited folly at that instant that had ever subjected one of mine to so haughty an imperious critic! I never liked so little in my life as at that moment the man whom at all others I delighted to honour. . . . I then felt for Mrs Richmond (Jenny Little), for you, and for myself, and not one of the sensations were such as I would wish to cherish in remembrance.[4]

Of Little's subsequent life, not much is recorded. Her neighbors recalled that she was a fond and attentive stepmother, that she was well liked in the community, belonged to a dissenting church in Galston, and was considered one of its more intelligent and devout members. She was said to have such a good memory that, hearing a sermon read from a prepared text for the second time, several weeks after having first heard it, she could remember the only sentence the speaker omitted. To a query by the Reverend Mr. Schaw of Ayr asking what she thought of a sermon, Little is said to have replied, "I thocht it rather flowery. Ye ken what I mean, Mr. Schaw—a wi' hue mair soun' than sense!" Taken aback by such an astute, plucky assessment by a mere servant woman, Schaw warned on his departure that "*they* would have to beware what kind of sermons they preached, since they had such critics as Janet Little."[5]

Little continued to supervise the dairy at Loudoun Castle even after the departure of Susan Hendrie. In 1807 John Hamilton was appointed factor to the countess of Loudoun, and it was said that Little "became so intimate in the house of that gentleman as to be almost regarded as one of the domes-

---

4. Quoted in Maurice Lindsay, *The Burns Encyclopedia* (New York, 1980), 218.
5. [Paterson], *Contemporaries of Burns*, 88.

tics."[6] One of her last poems was written for Mrs. Hamilton on the birth of her twin sons. Little died in Causey Head at Loudoun Castle on 15 March 1813, after being ill only one day. Her husband survived her by six years. Their remains are marked with a plain stone in the ancestral burying ground of the Loudoun family at Loudoun-Kirk, inscribed with the words: "In memory of John Richmond, who died August 10, 1819, aged 78 years; and Janet Little, his spouse, who died March 15, 1813, aged 54 years." She left behind some poems in manuscript, including "Elegy on T. S.," which contains the lines:

> Can sages say what fascinating charm
>   Binds our attachment to this noxious soil;
> Where poisonous gales are fraught with rude alarm,
>   And disappointment mocks our anxious toil?[7]

MAJOR WORK: *The Poetical Works of Janet Little, the Scotch Milkmaid* (Air, 1792).

TEXTS USED: All texts from *The Poetical Works of Janet Little, the Scotch Milkmaid.*

To the Public

I

From the dull confines of a country shade,
    A rustic damsel issues forth her lays;
There she, in secret, sought the Muse's aid,
    But now, aspiring, hopes to gain the bays.

II

"Vain are her hopes," the snarling critic cries;
    "Rude and imperfect is her rural song."
But she on public candour firm relies,
    And humbly begs they'll pardon what is wrong.

---

6. Ibid.
7. Ibid., 90.
4 bays] The leaves or sprigs of the bay laurel, made into a wreath for a conqueror or poet.

III

And if some lucky thought, while you peruse,
　　Some little beauty strike th' inquiring mind;　　　　　10
In gratitude she'll thank th' indulgent Muse,
　　Nor count her toil, where you can pleasure find.

IV

Upon your voice depends her share of fame,
　　With beating breast her lines abroad are sent:
Of praise she'll no luxuriant portion claim;
　　Give but a little, and she'll rest content.

　　　　　　　　　　　　　　　　　(1792)

Another Epistle to Nell*

　While Phœbus did our summer arbours cheer,
And joys Autumnal crown'd our circling year;
Even then my thoughts to you excursions made,
And ardently the bypast scenes survey'd;
Where oft we met in Eccles' peaceful bow'rs,
While social pleasure mark'd the passing hours.
From these sweet scenes I found myself remov'd,
I fear'd no more remember'd or belov'd.
Forgot by Nell, whose friendship seem'd sincere,
Such cold neglect, who undisturb'd could bear?　　　　10

　Mild Autumn now resigns to rougher skies,
And frightful storms, in wild commotion, rise.
The tempest howls, while dark December reigns,
And scatters desolation o'er the plains.
Just as the sun bursts from the wintry cloud,
Which oft does now his native glory shroud,
Your welcome letter cheers my anxious soul;
For humour, wit, and friendship grace the whole.
Well pleas'd I find you on Parnassus' hill;
The more I read, the more I prize your skill.　　　　　20

The Muses coy, you seem to catch with ease,
And unfatigu'd attain the art to please.

  Go on, dear Nell, the laureate-wreath pursue,
In time perhaps you may receive your due.
We'll beat the bushes for the rustic muse,
Where ev'ry dunce her inspiration sues.
'Mongst the vast crowd, let you and I aspire
To share a little of Apollo's fire.
If Fortune prove, like Cupid, ever blind,
30 We may perhaps some petty favour find;
But if no more we gain by these our lays,
We'll please ourselves with one another's praise.

                                        (1792)

* This poem follows "Epistle to Nell, Wrote from Loudoun Castle" and "Nell's Answer" in *The Poetical Works of Janet Little, the Scotch Milkmaid*.

To My Aunty

My ever dear an' worthy aunty,
Wha n'er o' wit nor lear was vaunty;
Yet often could, like honest grandam,
Unravel dreams; an' whiles, at random,
Did truth in mystic terms declare,
Which made us aft wi' wonder stare.

  Last night, when Morpheus softly hurl'd
His silken sceptre o'er the world,
Some anxious cares within my breast
10 Were silently consign'd to rest;

2 lear] Learning.
2 vaunty] Proud, boastful.
7 Morpheus] According to Greek mythology, one of the sons of Hypnos, or Sleep. He is commonly referred to in literature as the god of sleep and the bringer of dreams.

Yet did in sleep their pow'r retain,
As shews the visions of my brain.

My works I thought appear'd in print,
And were to diff'rent corners sent,
Whare patrons kind, but scant o' skill,
Had sign'd my superscription bill.
Voratious critics by the way,
Like eagles watching for their prey,
Soon caught the verse wi' aspect sour,
An' did ilk feeble thought devour;   20
Nor did its humble, helpless state,
One fraction of their rage abate.

Tom Touchy, one of high pretence
To taste an' learning, wit an' sense,
Was at the board the foremost man,
Its imperfections a' to scan.
Soon as the line he seem'd to doubt,
The meaner critics scratch'd it out;
Still to be nam'd on Touchy's side,
Was baith their int'rest and their pride.   30

Will Hasty, in an unco rage,
Revis'd the volume page by page;
But aft was deem'd a stupid ass,
For cens'ring what alone might pass.

Jack Tim'rous gladly would have spoke,
But quiv'ring lips his sentence broke;
So much he fear'd a brother's scorn,
The whole escap'd his claws untorn.

James Easy calm'd my throbbing heart,
An' whisp'ring told each man apart,   40
That he the volume much esteem'd;
Its little faults he nothing deem'd:

31 unco] Uncouth; also great or remarkable.

An' if his vote they would receive,
It might through countless ages live.

While I poor James's speech admir'd,
Tom Touchy at the sound was fir'd:
And ah! it griev'd me much to find,
He prov'd him senseless, deaf, and blind:
Then quick as thought, ere I could tell him,
50   Ilk critics club was up to fell him;
An' as he, helpless, met the stroke,
I, starting, trembl'd, syne awoke.

Now aunty, see this sad narration,
Which fills my breast wi' fair vexation;
An' if you can some comfort gie me,
Make nae delay, but send it to me:
For I'm commanded by Apollo,
Your sage advice in this to follow.

(1792)

On Reading Lady Mary Montague and Mrs. Rowe's Letters[*]

As Venus by night, so MONTAGUE bright
    Long in the gay circle did shine:
She tun'd well the lyre, mankind did admire;
    They prais'd, and they call'd her divine.

This pride of the times, in far distant climes,
    Stood high in the temple of Fame:
Britannia's shore, then ceas'd to adore,
    A greater the tribute did claim.

To sue for the prize, fam'd ROWE did arise,
10   More bright than Apollo was she:

52 syne] Then.

Superior rays obtain'd now the bays,
    And MONTAGUE bended the knee.

O excellent ROWE, much Britain does owe
    To what you've ingen'ously penn'd:
Of virtue and wit, the model you've hit;
    Who reads must you ever commend.

Would ladies pursue, the paths trod by you,
    And jointly to learning aspire,
The men soon would yield unto them the field,
    And critics in silence admire.   20

(1792)

---

* Lady Mary Wortley Montagu (1689–1762), essayist. She went with her husband to Constantinople, and her *Turkish Letters* (1763) were published posthumously. Elizabeth Rowe (1674–1737) published *Poems on Several Occasions* (1696) but was better known for her epistolary works, such as *Friendship in Death, in Twenty Letters from the Dead to the Living* (1728).

To a Lady Who Sent the Author Some Paper with a Reading of Sillar's Poems *

Dear madam, with joy I read over your letter;
Your kindness still tends to confirm me your debtor;
But can't think of payment, the sum is so large,
Tho' farthings for guineas could buy my discharge.
But, madam, the Muses are fled far away,
They deem it disgrace with a milkmaid to stay.
Let them go if they will, I would scorn to pursue,
And can, without sighing, subscribe an adieu.
Their trifling mock visits, to many so dear,
Is the only disaster on earth I now fear.   10
Sure Sillar much better had banish'd them thence,
Than wrote in despite of good manners and sense:
With two or three more, whose pretensions to fame

Are slight as the bubble that bursts on the stream.
And lest with such dunces as these I be number'd,
The task I will drop, nor with verse be incumber'd;
Tho' pen, ink and paper, are by me in store,
O madam excuse, for I ne'er shall write more.

(1792)

* David Sillar (1760–1830) was a good friend of Robert Burns; his *Poems* (1789) enjoyed little success.

Given to a Lady Who Asked Me
to Write a Poem

In royal Anna's golden days,
Hard was the task to gain the bays:
Hard was it then the hill to climb;
Some broke a neck, some lost a limb.
The vot'ries for poetic fame,
Got aff decrepit, blind, an' lame:
Except that little fellow Pope,
Few ever then got near its top:
An' Homer's crutches he may thank,
10   Or down the brae he'd got a clank.

Swift, Thomson, Addison, an' Young
Made Pindus echo to their tongue,

---

1 In royal Anna's golden days] Anne (1665–1714) was queen of Great Britain from 1702 to 1714.

7–9 Except that little fellow Pope . . . An' Homer's crutches he may thank] Alexander Pope (1688–1744), best known today for his *Rape of the Lock* (1714), suffered when he was twelve a severe illness, probably Pott's disease, that affected his spine; as a result, his health was ruined and his growth stunted.

10 brae] Riverbank.

10 clank] Noise, severe blow.

11 Swift, Thomson, Addison, an' Young] Jonathan Swift (1667–1745), James Thomson (1700–1748), Joseph Addison (1672–1719), Edward Young (1683–1765).

12 Pindus] Probably a reference to Pindar (c. 522–443 B.C.), Greek lyric poet.

In hopes to please a learned age;
But Doctor Johnston, in a rage,
Unto posterity did shew
Their blunders great, their beauties few.
But now he's dead, we weel may ken;
For ilka dunce maun hae a pen,
To write in hamely, uncouth rhymes;
An' yet forsooth they please the times.   20

  A ploughman chiel, Rab Burns his name,
Pretends to write; an' thinks nae shame
To souse his sonnets on the court;
An' what is strange, they praise him for't.
Even folks, wha 're of the highest station,
Ca' him the glory of our nation.

  But what is more surprising still,
A milkmaid must tak up her quill;
An' she will write, shame fa' the rabble!
That think to please wi' ilka bawble.   30
They may thank heav'n, auld Sam's asleep:
For could he ance but get a peep,
He, wi' a vengeance wad them sen'
A' headlong to the dunces' den.

  Yet Burns, I'm tauld, can write wi' ease,
An' a' denominations please;
Can wi' uncommon glee impart
A usefu' lesson to the heart;
Can ilka latent thought expose,
An' Nature trace whare'er she goes: 40
Of politics can talk wi' skill,
Nor dare the critics blame his quill.

14 Doctor Johnston] Samuel Johnson (1709–84).

18 For ilka dunce maun hae a pen] For every dunce must have a pen.

  21 A ploughman chiel, Rab Burns] *Chiel* is Scots for "child," "fellow," or "man." The novelist Henry Mackenzie, writing about the poems of Robert Burns (1759–96) in the *Lounger* (9 December 1786), called him a "heaven-taught ploughman."

  35 Yet Burns, I'm tauld, can write wi' ease] Burns (1759–96) was a prolific writer both in his native Scots and in correct eighteenth-century English.

But then a rustic country quean
To write—was e'er the like o't seen?
A milk maid poem-books to print;
Mair fit she wad her dairy tent;
Or labour at her spinning wheel,
An' do her wark baith swift an' weel.
Frae that she may some profit share,
50 But winna frae her rhyming ware.
Does she, poor silly thing, pretend
The manners of our age to mend?
Mad as we are, we're wise enough
Still to despise sic paultry stuff.

   "May she wha writes, of wit get mair,
An' a' that read an ample share
Of candour ev'ry fault to screen,
That in her dogg'ral scrawls are seen."

   All this and more, a critic said;
60 I heard and slunk behind the shade:
So much I dread their cruel spite,
My hand still trembles when I write.

(1792)

On Seeing Mr. —— Baking Cakes

As Rab, who ever frugal was,
   Some oat-meal cakes was baking,
In came a crazy scribbling lass,
   Which set his heart a-quaking.

"I fear," says he, "she'll verses write,
   An' to her neebors show it:
But troth I need na care a doit,
   Though a' the country knew it.

54 sic] Such.
7 doit] Small Dutch copper coin used in Scotland and considered to be of little value.

My cakes are good, none can object;
   The maids will ca' me thrifty;
To save a sixpence on the peck
   Is just an honest shifty.

They're fair an' thin, an' crump, 'tis true;
   You'll own sae when you see them;
But, what is better than the view,
   Put out your han' an' pree them."

He spoke, an' han'd the cakes about,
   Whilk ev'ry eater prized;
Until the basket was run out,
   They did as he advised.

An' ilka ane that got a share,
   Said that they were fu' dainty;
While Rab cri'd eat, an' dinna spare;
   For I hae cakes in plenty.

And i' the corner stan's a cheese,
   A glass an' bottle by me;
Baith ale and porter, when I please,
   To treat the lasses slily.

Some ca' me wild an' roving youth;
   But sure they are mistaken:
The maid wha gets me, of a truth,
   Her bread will ay be baken.

               (1792)

10

20

30

13 crump] Crisp, brittle.
16 pree] Sample, try out.

The Month's Love

Ye maidens attend to my tale,
   Of love that sly archer take care;
His darts o'er all ranks do prevail,
   The wealthy, the wise, and the fair.

When once his fierce arrow he throws,
   Contentment will bid you adieu;
No potion the doctor bestows,
   Can then be of service to you.

Experience prompts me to tell,
10   I felt his tyrannical sway;
The time I remember too well;
   It was a long month and a day.

The youth, I'll not mention his name,
   Who was the sole cause of my smart,
His deeds were unnotic'd by fame,
   His manners unpolish'd by art.

His person could boast of no charm,
   His words of no conquering power;
Yet his footsteps did give the alarm,
20   Which made my heart beat for an hour.

When absent from him I ador'd,
   One minute as ages did prove;
Though plenty replenish'd my board,
   I fasted and feasted on love.

My couch but augmented my pain;
   No sleep ever closed my eyes;
One glance of my rustic young swain
   Was what I more highly did prize.

None ever bemoan'd my sad case;
30   They laugh'd at the ills I endur'd;

But time did my sorrows efface,
   And spite of the imp I was cur'd.

I saw my lov'd youth in the shade,
   Soft whisp'ring to Susan apart;
Resentment came quick to my aid,
   And I banish'd him quite from my heart.

But be not too forward, ye fair,
   Nor take too much courage from me,
How many have fall'n in the snare
   That got not so easily free?   40

(1792)

Maria Logan

(fl. 1793)

Most of what is known about Maria Logan comes from her *Poems on Several Occasions,* published in 1793 in York with a subscription list that included Anna Letitia Barbauld and her brother, John Aikin, and Henry Mackenzie, the Scottish novelist. The book was successful enough to enjoy a second edition, published in London by Thomas Cadell as well as in York and in Leeds. William Enfield wrote in the *Monthly Review* that Logan's poems "have the intrinsic merit of just and interesting sentiments, pleasing imagery, correct and easy diction and harmonious numbers."[1] The author Capel Lofft also admired her verse.

Poems on Several Occasions opens with the inscription: "To those friends whose tender and unremitted attentions have enlivened seven tedious years of uninterrupted sickness, the following trifles are inscribed by their sincerely grateful and affectionate friend, M. Logan." The poet was probably attended at times by her brother, who trained as a surgeon in London in 1784; she relied on opium to relieve her chronic pain. Her poems often concern themselves with altered states of consciousness and with a yearning for release through death or sleep. One poem ends with the lines:

> While Pain's wan victim sees, with look serene,
> Life's final prospect op'ning to her view;
> And gladly hastens to that promised shore,
> Where sickness, pain, and grief, are known no more.[2]

A 1793 issue of the *European Magazine* included "Sonnet. On Reading 'Poems by Maria Logan,'" which praised her "fortitude unknown to *fictious* woe" and concluded:

> O! may Hygeia, with celestial ray,
> Ere long thy fading stem of life restore;

1. 2 (1793): 214.
2. "On the Spring of a Seventh Year of Uninterrupted Sickness" (1793).

While Friendship shall enraptur'd hail the day
Which gives thee to her joyful arms once more;
And bids thy muse resume her heavenly lyre,
And sweep the sounding strings "with renovated fire." [3]

"To Opium" continued to appear in such periodicals as the *Monthly Magazine* decades after its first publication. [4]

MAJOR WORK: *Poems on Several Occasions* (York, 1793).

TEXTS USED: Texts from *Poems on Several Occasions.*

To Opium

Let others boast the golden spoil,
   Which Indian climes afford;
And still with unavailing toil,
   Increase the shining hoard:—

Still let Golconda's dazzling pride
   On Beauty's forehead glow,
And round the fair, on ev'ry side,
   Sabean odours flow:—

Be mine the balm, whose sov'reign pow'r
   Can still the throb of Pain;   10
The produce of the scentless flow'r,
   That strews Hindostan's plain.*

No gaudy hue its form displays,
   To catch the roving eye;

3. Signed "W.G." and dated "Leeds, May 1793," the poem appears in vol. 23, p. 470.
4. See, e.g., *Monthly Magazine,* 1 June 1816.

5 Golconda's] A ruined city in Hyderabad, India, famous for its fort, its mausoleums of ancient kings, and the diamonds that were cut and polished there.
8 Sabean odours] An ancient people of the pre-Islamic kingdom of Sheba, the Sabeans were merchants of, among other things, spices and perfumes, imported from India.
12 Hindostan's] Land of the Hindus, or northern India.

And Ignorance, with vacant gaze,
    May pass regardless by.

But shall the Muse with cold disdain,
    Its simple charms behold!
Shall she devote the tuneful strain
20   To incense, gems, or gold!

When latent ills the frame pervade,
    And mock the healing art;
Thy friendly balm shall lend its aid,
    And transient ease impart;

Shall charm the restless hour of day,
    And cheer the midnight gloom;
Shall blunt each thorn, which strews the way
    That leads us to the tomb.

And oft, when Reason vainly tries
30   To calm the troubled breast,
Thy pow'r can seal our streaming eyes,
    And bid our sorrows rest.

What tho' this calm must quickly cease,
    And Grief resume its pow'r,
The heart that long has sigh'd for ease,
    Will prize the tranquil hour.

A short oblivion of its care
    Relieves the weary'd mind,
Till suff'ring nature learns to bear
40   The weight by Heav'n assign'd.

Reviv'd by thee, my drooping Muse
    Now pours the grateful strain,
And Fancy's hand sweet flow'rets strews
    Around the bed of Pain.

At her command gay scenes arise
    To charm my raptur'd sight,

While Memory's faithful hand supplies
    Past objects of delight.

Yet Memory's soothing charms were vain,
    Without thy friendly aid;   50
And sportive Fancy's smiling train,
    Would fly Disease's shade —

Did not thy magic pow'r supply,
    A mild, tho' transient ray;
As meteors in a northern sky,
    Shed artificial day.

And shall my humble Muse alone
    Thy peerless worth declare!
A Muse to all the world unknown,
    Whose songs are lost in air.   60

O! may the bard, whose tuneful strain
    Resounds thro' Derwent's vale,
At whose command the hosts of Pain,
    Disease and Sickness, fail —

That sage, to whom the God of Day
    His various gifts imparts,
Whose healing pow'r, whose melting lay,
    United, charm our hearts —

May he devote one tuneful page,
    To thee, neglected Flow'r!   70
Then Fame shall bid each future age,
    Admiring, own thy pow'r! [†]

        (1793)

---

[*] The best Opium is procured from the white poppy of Hindostan. *Logan.*

---

61 the bard] Erasmus Darwin (1731–1802), an English scientist and poet whose *Loves of the Plants* was published in 1789.
  62 Derwent's vale] Vale in the Lake District, near Derwent Water.

† This was written just before the publication of "The Loves of the Plants"; a work which had been long impatiently expected by every one who had been so fortunate as to see any specimen of the Author's poetical abilities. *Logan.*

Verses on Hearing That an Airy and Pleasant Situation,
near a Populous and Commercial Town,
Was Surrounded with New Buildings

There was a time! that time the Muse bewails,
When Sunny-Hill enjoy'd refreshing gales;
When Flora sported in its fragrant bow'rs,
And strew'd with lib'ral hand her sweetest flow'rs!
Now sable vapours, pregnant with disease,
Clog the light pinions of the southern breeze;
Each verdant plant assumes a dusky hue,
And sooty atoms taint the morning dew.
No more the lily rears her spotless head,
10   Health, verdure, beauty, fragrance, all are fled:
Sulphureous clouds deform the rising day,
Nor own the pow'r of Sol's meridian ray;
While sickly damps, from Aire's polluted stream,
Quench the pure radiance of his parting beam.
These are thy triumphs, Commerce!—these thy spoils!
Yet sordid mortals glory in their toils,
Spurn the pure joys which simple Nature yields,
Her breezy hills, dark groves, and verdant fields,
With cold indiff'rence, view her blooming charms,
20   And give youth, ease, and health to thy enfeebling arms.

(1793)

13 Aire's] A river that runs through Leeds.

Christian Milne

(1773–after 1816)

<hr>

According to her own account, Christian Milne was born in Inverness on 15 May 1773. Her mother, Mary Gordon, daughter of a schoolmaster, and her father, Thomas Ross, a cabinetmaker, had at least ten children. She lost her mother at an early age. Her father married shortly thereafter, and the family moved to Auchintoul, Banffshire, where an old woman taught the future poet to read and knit. For one hour a day for six months, at an unspecified period in her childhood, she attended a nearby school, where she wrote and learned arithmetic. She later recalled:

> I delighted so much in writing, that I carried a piece of broken slate always in my pocket, and when I could get out of sight, sat down and wrote upon it, so long, I was afraid to go home. I delighted in copying every thing in the form of verses. . . . My reading and writing was all by stealth, as my step-mother was justly offended with me for neglecting my work. To prevent my scribbling, she would hide my inkstand, behind chests, or where it was least possible for me to think of looking for it. There were a good many books in my father's house: but as I got no time to read, I profited little by them. Those which I liked most, were the Spectator, and Guardian, two old romances, and two or three old plays. There was no poetry in the house, except Allan Ramsay's Gentle Shepherd, and Milton's Paradise Lost. All these I stole out, volume by volume, and fastened them under my frock; and when I was sent on errands, I sat down by the way, and read till I forgot I had to return home; but when I recalled home, and my errand came to mind, I wept bitterly, from fear of the reward due to my thoughtless conduct.[1]

At fourteen Christian was sent to Aberdeen, where she worked as a domestic servant. There, she said, "I had neither books, nor leisure, but I was treated with kindness, and was happy. There I composed many things while I was at work, and wrote them down on the Sunday evenings. After keeping them

<hr>

1. Quoted in Elizabeth Isabella Spence, *Letters from the North Highlands, during the Summer 1816* (London, 1817), 58–59.

for some time, I destroyed them, that it might not be known, that I *fashed* my head with such nonsense."[2]

Christian's father suffered financial disaster at about the same time that his only surviving son drowned at sea on his first voyage as a sailor. Christian, now the only surviving child in her family, accompanied her father, widowed and seriously depressed, on foot all the way from Inverness to Edinburgh. She became seriously ill en route; later she said that this experience "gave my mind that plaintive, dejected cast, which has since been its prominent feature."[3] In Edinburgh she worked as a servant for a lawyer named Steward, and even though her fellow servants ridiculed her, she continued to write poetry. Later she would describe the difficult life of a laboring-class poet:

> But "menial Maid," with no release from Toil,
> And quite estrang'd from Nature's 'witching smile,
> Thro' lanes and dirty streets sent out to roam,
> Or set, like "bottle in the smoke," at home:
> Sure state more adverse to poetic skill
> (With apathy more apt the mind to fill),
> The world knows not. . . .[4]

After her father lost all his money and even his clothes, Christian's wages became their sole support. At nineteen she contracted a serious respiratory illness that prevented her from working for a long while. Once recovered, she set out on her own, returning to Aberdeen to be a house servant; she would never see her father alive again. She worked first for Baillie Cruickshank. Then, when she was twenty-two, she went to work for Professor Jack, the principal of Kings College, Old Aberdeen. Jack and his wife, upon discovering Christian's poetry writing, encouraged her and urged her to preserve what she wrote. Later the poet worked for a widow named Moir.

At twenty-four Christian married Patrick Milne, a journeyman ship carpenter. During their first eight years of marriage they had four children. Even worse than being a servant, she observed, was

> its counterpart,
> That state, more irksome to the feeling heart,
> When *menial maid* becomes a wedded wife,
> Her *term* of slav'ry then the *term* of life![5]

2. Ibid., 60.
3. Preface to Milne, *Simple Poems on Simple Subjects* (Aberdeen, 1805).
4. Ibid.
5. Ibid.

In 1805 a collection of her verse entitled *Simple Poems on Simple Subjects* was published by subscription in Aberdeen, earning her one hundred pounds. She had composed the poems "when I was most busily employed about my washing, baking, or when rocking the cradle with my foot, the inkstand in one hand, the pen in the other, and the paper on my knee, with my children about me. When busy at work, I laid the paper and ink beside me, and wrote the stanza as it came into my mind, and then to my work again."[6] She prefaced the book, which was dedicated to her patron, the duchess of Gordon, with the apology

> Be't known—'mid all who pant for public fame,
> That one more modest ne'er put in a claim
> To be enroll'd an Author, than the mean
> Unletter'd—female bard of Aberdeen!

Apparently the book provoked some public ridicule, for the Aberdeen poet George Smith composed a rejoinder entitled "To the Author of a Pamphlet, entitled 'Remarks on Christian Milne's Poems,'" in which he inquires,

> What mov'd you, sir, in these important days,
> To spend your time in such a needless cause;
> To make a silly woman's wark your sport—
> Was there no better subject? waes me for't.
>
> . . . .
>
> How poorly thus to draw the critic's knife,
> And rip the faults and failings of a wife.
>
> . . . .
>
> Still I'm inclin'd to think her faults are few,[7]

When Elizabeth Spence interviewed her in 1816, Milne had eight children living and had been in poor health for eleven years, bedridden in winter and spring. She was living on the second floor of what Spence termed a "mean house" in the small fishing village of Foot Dee on the river Dee. Milne explained:

> I have suffered many difficulties and much sickness. My husband has been twice taken captive by the Americans, and lost his clothes and wages. But still I have kept my little treasure [profits from her book] untouched. The world may blame me in suffering what I had done to save it, but it was from a good

6. Quoted in Spence, *Letters*, 63.

7. Smith published his poem as one of the "Miscellaneous Pieces" appended to his *Douglas, A Tragedy, in Five Acts by John Home Reduced to Scottish Rhyme, Chiefly in the Broad Buchan Dialect by George Smith* (Aberdeen, 1824), but it had probably seen periodical publication much earlier.

intention; for when I saw so many widows, when I looked around, left by sea-faring men in poverty, I felt, if deprived of my husband, this was intended by a kind Providence to keep me from want, when I should be left a helpless widow with a large family. . . . The half of my husband's wages, which is all I am allowed when he is at sea, proves insufficient for our support, though I teach my girls to read and write myself, but send the boys to proper teachers. When these are paid, there is little left behind to purchase clothes for them, so that I am obliged to descend from Parnassus, and doubling my former diligence, in piecing, darning, and making one thing out of another, that they may be whole and clean.[8]

Her nest egg went into a sixteenth share of a ship built by her husband's employer, a risky investment. Despite the help and encouragement of patrons, she felt embittered by "ridicule and contempt" from her neighbors for what they considered her idle poetic occupation. Evidently, the literary world was equally unappreciative.[9] Milne's later life is undocumented.

MAJOR WORK: *Simple Poems on Simple Subjects* (Aberdeen, 1805).

TEXTS USED: All texts from *Simple Poems on Simple Subjects*.

To a Lady, Who Did Me the Honour to Call at My House

That ne'er-to-be-forgotten day
    You came to see my cottage,
My honest Mate adores you since,
    With fervour next to dotage.

He said, you could have done no more,
    Had I been Pope or Waller;
He walk'd on tiptoe, rais'd his hat,
    And thought he felt much taller:

8. Quoted in Spence, *Letters*, 63–64.
9. See, e.g., the review in *Blackwood's Magazine*, July 1818, 428–29, of Spence, *Letters*, mentioning Milne.

6 Waller] Edmund Waller (1606–87), a precocious poet who wrote "His Majesty's Escape at St Andere" (1625) in heroic couplets—one of the first examples of this form.

Then 'gan to pick the tarry spots,
    That glisten'd on his jacket,   10
And found the tailor much in fault,
    Who did not neater make it.

"But stay," quoth I, "my honest friend,
    "You must not slight your jerkin,
"Tho' you could dress yourself in silk,
    "Tis not so fit to work in!

"And, take my word, I love you more
    "In that blue frock and trouser,
"Than if you wore lac'd hat and cloaths,
    "That won you 'How d'ye do, Sir.'   20

"Ne'er folks like us shew'd foolish pride,
    "But worth and sense despis'd them,
"And justly threw them from the height
    "To which such notice rais'd them."

Now pardon, Ma'am, this silly tale;
    I've often wish'd to drop it;
But when my pen begins to run,
    I try in vain to stop it.

              (1805)

Sent with a Flower Pot, Begging a Slip of Geranium

I've sent my empty pot again,
    To beg another slip;
The last you gave, I'm griev'd to tell,
    December's frost did nip.

I love fair Flora and her train,
    But nurse her children ill;
I tend too little or too much;
    They die from want of skill.

I blush to trouble you again,
10   Who've serv'd me oft before;
But, should this die, I'll break the pot,
    And trouble you no more.

(1805)

On a Lady, Who Spoke with Some Ill-Nature of the Advertisement of My Little Work in the "Aberdeen Journal"

    Says pert Miss Prue,
    There's something new
In Chalmers' weekly papers—
    A Shipwright's Wife,
    In humble life,
Writes *rhyme* by nightly tapers!!

    That folks of taste
    Their time should waste
To read them, makes me wonder!
10   A low-born fool,
    Ne'er bred in school,
What can *she* do but blunder?

    Write rhyme, forsooth!
    Upon my truth
'Twill put it out of fashion;
    She can but paint,
    In colours faint,
Rude Nature's lowest passion.

    A wife so mean
20   Should nurse and clean,
And mend her husband's jacket;
    Not spend her time
    In writing rhyme,
And raising such a racket!

(1805)

To a Gentleman,
Desirous of Seeing My Manuscripts

I'm gratify'd to think that you
   Should wish to see my Songs,
As few would read my Book, who knew
   To whom this Book belongs.

My mean estate, and birth obscure,
   The ignorant will scorn;
Respect, tho' distant, from the good,
   Makes that more lightly borne.

Tho' I could write with Seraph pen—
   Tho' Angels did inspire,   10
None but the candid and humane
   My writings would admire.

The proud wou'd cry, "Such paltry works
   "We will not deign to read;
"The Author's but a Shipwright's Wife,
   "And was a serving Maid."

Inur'd to hardships in my youth,
   If want my age should crown,
I'll never beg the haughty's bread;
   Death's milder than their frown.   20

You'll think but little of my Songs,
   When you have read them o'er;
But say, "They're well enough from her"—
   And I expect no more.

                 (1805)

Song

Tune—"Logan Water"

At eve, when Dee's transparent stream
Flows trembling 'neath the moon's pale beam,
Lone on its banks I sit and mourn,
For him who now will ne'er return!
How blest was I each cheerful morn,
Ere he from me by War was torn!
But now my tears must ever flow
For him who far, far hence lies low!

He grasp'd me to his manly breast—
His love in softest strains exprest,
While down his cheek there stole a tear,
Which spoke his parting pang sincere:
"My love!" said he, "O do not mourn!
"Think on our joys, when I return
"With blooming laurel round my brow!"
But, ah! he far, far hence lies low!

Had we been bound with Hymen's chain,
With freedom then I might complain;
But now the maidens mock my pain,
Who love my dear lamented swain.
Here ev'ry eve I sit alone—
To Dee's soft murmurs tell my moan,
While sighing zephyrs join my woe,
For him who far, far hence lies low!

(1805)

17 Hymen] Ancient Greek god of marriage.

Mary Russell Mitford

(1787–1855)

Best known for her amusing, affectionate, down-to-earth prose sketches of village life, Mary Russell Mitford was also a respected dramatist and poet. Born in Alresford, Hampshire, on 16 December 1787, she was the only child of Mary Russell, a well-read heiress, and George Mitford, a physician with a weakness for gambling and high living.

By the mid 1790s George Mitford had squandered almost all of his wife's inheritance of twenty-eight thousand pounds, and the family was forced to sell furniture and portions of the library to satisfy creditors. But they moved to a grander house in the fashionable resort of Lyme Regis, where the doctor attempted to recover his finances through more gambling. A year later almost all their belongings had to be sold at auction, and they left for dingy apartments in London. On Mary's tenth birthday her father asked her to pick a number for a lottery ticket. Her choice was the twenty-thousand-pound winner. From that day forward Mary would be the chief financial support of her family, which now was able to move to a substantial house in Reading.

Beginning in 1798 Mary attended the same boarding school at 22 Hans Place, London, where Caroline Lamb had once been a pupil and where Letitia Elizabeth Landon later enrolled. There she studied French, English, Italian, Latin, history, geography, dancing, and drawing. Among her teachers was the poet Frances Rowden, who became her mentor and laid the foundation for her love of drama and literature. In 1802 her father purchased an estate near Reading and removed Mary from school. The family lived in town during the four-year renovation of the mansion, which spared no expense. Furnishings included a Gainsborough, a Greuze, and a portrait of Dr. Mitford by John Opie. Meanwhile, Mary continued reading voraciously.

In 1810 she had privately printed a volume titled simply *Poems,* treating politics as well as nature and country life. Reviewers were cordial. But her pleasure was short-lived, for because of her father's extravagant habits creditors were once again closing in. She decided she could earn a livelihood for her family through writing and began working on a long narrative poem about recently revealed incidents on Pitcairn Island after the mutiny on the HMS *Bounty*. Samuel Taylor Coleridge read each canto of *Christina, the Maid of the South Seas* as it was completed and suggested changes. Published by Rivington in 1811, it was popular in America as well as in Britain but did not earn enough to do more than pay immediate financial obligations. In March of that year her father was briefly imprisoned for debt.

Watlington Hill; a Poem (1812) celebrated hunting and country landscape. *Poems on the Female Character,* published by Rivington in 1813 and pirated in America, includes "The Rival Sisters" and the ambitious "Blanche of Castile," read in manuscript by Robert Southey, Thomas Campbell, and Samuel Taylor Coleridge (who encouraged the young author to attempt tragedy). During a stay in London in 1813, Mitford was a guest in the home of James Perry, editor of the *Morning Chronicle,* where she met Thomas Moore and Amelia Opie. In 1818, with family finances still on shaky ground, she began to write prose descriptions of her neighborhood, which appeared in the *Lady's Magazine,* a little-known periodical, beginning in 1819. By March 1820 Dr. Mitford's gambling and extravagant spending had reduced his family to poverty, and they moved a mile away to a labourer's cottage in Three Mile Cross, a village on the turnpike road between Reading and Basingstoke. Mitford was to stay there for thirty years, allowing herself only the luxury of a flower garden.

Meanwhile, Mitford's sketches had become so popular with readers of the *Lady's Magazine* that its circulation had increased eightfold, and the editor begged for more. Since her writing was the only source of income for her family, she was glad to supply them. Her tragedy *Julian,* which had been written with the advice of William Macready and Thomas Talfourd, was performed at Covent Garden on 15 March 1823 with Macready in the title role; it played for eight nights, bringing her two hundred pounds and much acclaim. But the weight of supporting her family was heavy at times. She told Sir William Elford, "I am now chained to a desk, eight, ten, twelve hours a day, at mere drudgery. All my thoughts of writing are for hard money. All my correspondence is on hard business. Oh! pity me, pity me! My very mind is sinking under the fatigue and the anxiety."[1]

In 1824 Mitford collected and polished twenty-four of her *Lady's Magazine* sketches of Berkshire life and published them with George Whittaker under the title *Our Village*. The book took the world by storm, was critically well received, and sold beyond her wildest dreams. Within months Whittaker was

---

1. Letter dated 25 April 1823, quoted in *The Life of Mary Russell Mitford, Told by Herself in Letters to her Friends,* ed. A. G. K. L'Estrange, 2 vols. (New York, 1870), 2:227–28.

asking for a second series, which appeared in 1826; three more volumes, drawing on her experiences at Three Mile Cross, eventually came out at two year intervals. Charles Lamb said that nothing so fresh had appeared for a long time. Harriet Martineau regarded Mitford as the originator of a new style of "graphic description," which Elizabeth Barrett compared to Dutch painting in its detail, light, and humor. H. F. Chorley called Mitford "the Claude of English village life," and Felicia Hemans was cheered by the sketches in sickness.[2]

As Coleridge had predicted, Mitford also excelled at writing tragic drama on historical themes. Her *Foscari* played at Covent Garden for fifteen nights beginning in early November 1826, with Charles Kemble in the leading role. From this production, along with the sale of its copyright, the publication of her *Dramatic Scenes,* and sales to periodicals and annuals she earned more than six hundred pounds for the year. But because of her father's irresponsible spending the family remained poor. And her father was growing personally more difficult. Her success made him jealous of her literary friendships, and he taunted her and treated her friends with contempt. Another tragedy, *Rienzi,* played at Drury Lane to a crowded and rapt house for thirty-four nights in October 1828, earning Mitford four hundred pounds. The printed play sold eight thousand copies and became popular in America. Now her poems and stories began to appear frequently in the literary annuals, including the *Forget-Me-Not, Friendship's Offering,* the *Literary Souvenir,* the *Amulet,* and *Finden's Tableaux* (which she would edit in 1838 and 1839). Her popularity allowed her to command high prices for her work. Whittaker, the publisher of *Our Village,* claimed that Mitford's name "would sell anything." But her father's continuing extravagant spending meant she always felt financially in peril. She told a friend, "I myself hate all my own doings, and consider the being forced to this drudgery as the greatest misery that life can afford. But it is my wretched fate and must be undergone—so long, at least, as my father is spared to me. If I should have the misfortune to lose him, I shall go quietly to the workhouse, and never write another line—a far preferable destiny."[3]

Mitford wrote a scena in English verse, *Mary Queen of Scots,* in 1831 and a blank verse opera libretto, *Sadak and Kalasrade,* which was performed only once at the Lyceum on 20 April 1835 and considered a failure. But her *Charles the First,* produced in July 1834, earned her two hundred pounds. In early 1835 Richard Bentley published in three volumes her novel about the town of Reading, *Belford Regis; or, Sketches of a Country Town.* By this time the first

2. *DNB.*

3. Quoted in W. J. Roberts, *The Life and Friendships of Mary Russell Mitford* (London, 1913), 312.

volume of *Our Village* had gone through fourteen editions. Mary and William Howitt visited that year, and the latter published an appreciative piece in the August *Athenaeum* entitled "A Visit to Our Village." The next year, Mitford dined with William Wordsworth, Robert Browning, and Samuel Rogers and on the same visit to London met Joanna Baillie and Jane Porter. An inveterate letter writer, she carried on a voluminous correspondence with such friends as William Macready, Felicia Hemans, Frances Trollope, Barbara Hofland, Anna Maria Hall, Mary Howitt, Harriet Martineau, Anna Jameson, Benjamin Robert Haydon, Barry Cornwall, Thomas Noon Talfourd, Allan Cunningham, and others. She was such a good conversationalist that some preferred her talk to her books. In 1836 she met Elizabeth Barrett, beginning a long friendship that included the gift to Barrett of her spaniel Flush, later immortalized by Virginia Woolf. Before Barrett showed her *Sonnets to the Portuguese* to Robert Browning, she sent them to Mitford for her criticism and approval.

In 1837 Mitford received a civil list pension of one hundred pounds a year, and in 1842 her eighty-two-year-old father, whom she had nursed through four years of sickness, died. Even though he had squandered during his lifetime about seventy thousand pounds and had never worked for a living, his affectionate daughter always forgave him his faults. Now Mitford was left with a crushing debt of almost a thousand pounds. In 1843, friends, including H. F. Chorley, Thomas Moore, Henry Hart Milman, and others, took up a public subscription that paid the debt and left a small surplus for Mitford. In September 1851 her cottage was no longer habitable, and she moved to Swallowfield, near Reading. *Recollections of a Literary Life* appeared in 1852. A novel, *Atherton, and Other Tales,* published in April 1854, won praise from John Ruskin. In 1854 her plays were published collectively in two volumes with an autobiographical introduction. Mitford died on 10 January 1855 and was buried in the village churchyard. Walter Savage Landor expressed what many felt when he observed in verse that no one could tell "The country's purer charms so well / As Mary Mitford."

MAJOR WORKS: *Poems* (London, 1810); *Christina, the Maid of the South Seas; a Poem* (London, 1811); *Watlington Hill; a Poem* (London, 1812); *Narrative Poems on the Female Character, in the Various Relations of Life* (London, 1813); *Julian, a Tragedy in Five Acts* (London, 1823); *Our Village: Sketches of Rural Character and Scenery,* 5 vols. (London, 1824–32); *Foscari: A Tragedy* (London, 1826); *Dramatic Scenes, Sonnets, and Other Poems* (London, 1827); *Rienzi: A Tragedy, in Five Acts* (London, 1828); *Charles the First, an Historical Tragedy, in Five Acts* (London, 1834); *Belford Regis, or Sketches of a Country Town,* 3 vols. (London, 1835); *Sadak and Kalasrade; or, The Waters of Oblivion. A Romantic Opera in Two Acts* (London, 1835); *Country Stories* (London, 1837); *Inez de Castro: A Tragedy in*

Five Acts (London, 1841); *Recollections of a Literary Life,* 3 vols. (London, 1852); *Atherton, and Other Tales,* 3 vols. (London, 1854); *The Dramatic Works of Mary Russell Mitford,* 2 vols. (London, 1854); *The Life of Mary Russell Mitford, Related in a Selection from her Letters to her Friends,* ed. Rev. A. G. L'Estrange, 3 vols. (London, 1870).

TEXTS USED: Text of "Winter Scenery, January, 1809" from *Poems.* Text of "To Mr. Lucas" from *Friendship's Offering* for 1830.

Winter Scenery, January, 1809

The dark sky lours: a crimson streak
In vain the heavy clouds would break;
The lowing herds desert the plain,
Scatter'd is all the fleecy train;
The feather'd songsters all are gone,
The dear domestic bird alone,
The cheerful robin, seeks his food,
And breaks the death-like solitude:
For, save his notes, no earthly sound
Through the chill air, is heard around;   10

E'en she, whose playful fondness still
Attends my steps on dale or hill,
She, who still wears the victor blue,
Maria of the raven hue!
No longer seeks with frolic glee,
Where'er I roam, to follow me,
But shrinks within her shelter warm,
And hides in straw her graceful form.

Yet lovelier is the magic scene,
Than blooming summer's brightest green: 20
The icicles in crystal row
Suspended from the pent-house low,
O'er the luxuriant ivy fall,
Or glitter on the moss-grown wall;
The level lawn, in dazzling light,

Array'd in pure unsullied white,
Scarce marks, with undulating bend,
With its smooth edge, where waters blend.

Crown'd is each grove with vestal snow.
30   Whilst varied colors gleam below;
The holly's deeply burnish'd green,
With coral berries faintly seen,
The oak's rich leaves of saffron hue,
The tow'ring fir's dark misty blue,
Closer their mingling branches twine,
And through their brilliant burthen shine.

See on the pine the snow arise,
A tap'ring cone, it seeks the skies!
Or wreathes the rugged elm around!
40   Or bends the light broom to the ground!
Or in ethereal lustre gay,
Clothes the pale aspen's flexile spray!

And, still to fancy's eye more dear,
What strange fantastic forms appear!
High arches rise, abrupt and bright,
And gothic fret-work silv'ry light;
There frown dark pillars, slim and tall,
And there the mould'ring turrets fall!
But, emblem true of human joys,
50   Rais'd in an hour, an hour destroys;
Already has the brilliant ray
Melted the fairy scene away;
No fleecy whiteness decks the ground,
No glitt'ring frost work gleams around;
All, all are gone. The swollen flood
Spreads its stain'd waters to the wood;
Each tree, with snowy crest so fair,
That rose with gay fantastic air,
Now waves its dark boughs, rough and bare;
60   And o'er the hills, the groves, the plains,
The daemon Desolation reigns!

                                          (1810)

To Mr. Lucas, Written Whilst Sitting to Him for my Portrait. December 1828*

Oh young and richly gifted! born to claim
No vulgar place amidst the sons of fame;
With shapes of beauty haunting thee like dreams,
And skill to realise Art's loftiest themes;
How wearisome to thee the task must be
To copy these coarse features painfully;
Faded by time and paled by care, to trace
The dim complexion of this homely face;
And lend to a bent brow and anxious eye
Thy patient toil, thine Art's high mastery.   10
Yet by that Art, almost methinks divine,
By touch and colour and the skilful line
Which at a stroke can strengthen and refine,
And mostly by the invisible influence
Of thine own spirit, gleams of thought and sense
Shoot o'er the care-worn forehead, and illume
The heavy eye, and break the leaden gloom:
Even as the sun-beams on the rudest ground
Fling their illusive glories wide around,
And make the dullest scene of nature bright   20
By the reflexion of their own pure light.

(1830)

* Lady Madelina Palmer, patron of John Lucas (1807–74), urged Mitford to pose for the artist and lent her clothes for the occasion. There were at least three sittings in December, and the portrait, which was said to be a strong likeness, was complete by 7 January 1829. Mitford observed, "It was difficult, in painting me, to steer between the Scylla and Charybdis of making me dowdy, like one of my own rustic heroines, or dressed out like a tragedy queen. He has managed the matter with infinite taste, and given to the whole figure the look of a quiet gentlewoman. . . . The face is thoughtful and placid, with the eyes looking away—a peculiarity which, they say, belongs to my expression" (quoted in *The Life of Mary Russell Mitford, Told by Herself in Letters to her Friends,* ed. A. G. K. L'Estrange, 2 vols. [New York, 1870], 2:86). An engraving from the portrait is reproduced opposite p. 290 of W. J. Roberts, *Mary Russell Mitford* (London, 1913). A later portrait of Mitford by Lucas, dated 1852, is owned by the National Portrait Gallery, London.

Elizabeth Moody

(d. 1814)

Elizabeth Moody was born Elizabeth Greenly and married the well-read clergyman Christopher Lake Moody (1753–1815). The couple lived at Turnham Green Terrace, near the home of Ralph Griffiths, editor of the *Monthly Review*. Griffiths published twenty-six of Elizabeth Moody's reviews between 1789 and 1808; she seems to have been the first woman critic to write regularly for that publication. In one early review, she noted, "Of the various species of composition that in course come before us, there are none in which *our* writers of the male sex have less excelled, since the days of Richardson and Fielding, than in the arrangement of a novel. Ladies seem to appropriate to themselves an exclusive privilege in this kind of writing; witness the numerous productions of romantic tales to which female authors have given birth." Anticipating Joanna Baillie's "Introductory Discourse" (1798) and William Wordsworth's preface to the *Lyrical Ballads* (1800), Moody argued that the characters in a novel should be "always natural"; they "should talk, think, and act, as becomes their respective ages, situations, and characters; . . . the language should be easy, correct, and elegant, free from affectation, and unobscured by pedantry."[1]

Moody also published poems in the *General Evening Post* and in the *Gentleman's Magazine*. According to an obituary in the latter, "She took up at an early age a passion for taste in literature, for poetical ingenuity, for wit, and for the charm of style, whether in verse or in prose: . . . Her letters to numerous correspondents had a variety of talent in that branch of written eloquence, which has been seldom equalled in our language by either sex. . . . Whatever she wrote, whether serious or comic, was original, flowing, and beautiful, polished off-hand by taste and good sense."[2] Edward Lovibond (1724–75), of Hampton, Middlesex, mentored her in poetry, and she was the "Miss G——"

1. N.s., 3 (1790): 400.
2. 84 (December 1814): 613. Roger Lonsdale, in *Eighteenth-Century Women Poets,* probably errs in suggesting that this obituary was written by her husband.

to whom Lovibond addressed several poems. Apparently, either Moody or her husband edited Lovibond's posthumous collection *Poems* (1785).[3]

In 1798 Moody published in London, with Cadell and Davies, *Poetic Trifles,* a 186-page volume of fugitive poems previously published anonymously as well as many new works, some on figures as diverse as Samuel Johnson, Joseph Priestley, Robespierre, and John Opie.[4] The *Monthly Magazine* said that many of the poems were "extremely beautiful and delicate," and the *Critical Review* found in the volume "good sense and a lively imagination"; however, both these reviews found fault with her blank verse. The *British Critic* praised the book for "taste and elegance of sentiment," while the *Monthly Visitor* noted, "There is a tenderness in these verses which the reader will feel and admire. They address the heart in a language which cannot fail of being understood." The *New Annual Register* was also approving.[5] Not surprisingly, given her connection, the *Monthly Review* was the most enthusiastic of all, lauding the poet's wit and declaring,

> The polished period in which we live may be justly denominated the Age of ingenious and learned Ladies;—who have excelled so much in the more elegant branches of literature, that we need not to hesitate in concluding that the long agitated dispute between the two sexes is at length determined; and that it is no longer a question,—whether the woman *is* or *is not* inferior to man in natural ability, or less capable of excelling in mental accomplishments.[6]

Moody died on 10 December 1814.

MAJOR WORK: *Poetic Trifles* (London, 1798).

TEXTS USED: All texts from *Poetic Trifles.*

3. See Lonsdale, *Eighteenth-Century Women Poets,* 401.

4. Among the poems originally published anonymously were *The Temptation, Or, Satan in the Country* (1781); "Dr. Johnson's Ghost" (March 1786); and "Anna's Complaint; or, The Miseries of War. Written in the Isle of Thanet, 1794," in George Miller's *War a System of Madness and Irreligion* (1796).

5. *Monthly Magazine,* suppl., 7 (20 July 1799): 537; *Critical Review,* n.s., 25 (1799): 229–30; *British Critic* 14 (July 1799): 72; *Monthly Visitor* 6 (April 1799): 413; *New Annual Register* 19 (1798): 310.

6. 27 (December 1798): 442.

To Dr. Darwin,
On Reading His Loves of the Plants*

No Bard e'er gave his tuneful powers,
Thus to traduce the fame of flowers;
Till Darwin sung his gossip tales,
Of females woo'd by *twenty* males.
Of *Plants* so given to amorous pleasure;
Incontinent beyond all measure.
He sings that in botanic schools,
Husbands† adopt licentious rules;
Plurality of Wives they wed,
And all they like—they take to bed.
That Lovers sigh with *secret* love,
And marriage rites clandestine, prove.
That, fann'd in groves their mutual fire,
They to some Gretna *Green* retire.

Linneus things, no doubt, reveal'd,
Which prudent *Plants* would wish conceal'd;
So free of *families* he spoke,
As must that modest race provoke.
Till he invaded Flora's bowers
None heard of marriage among flowers;
Sexual distinctions were unknown;
Discover'd by the Swede alone.
He blab'd through all the list'ning groves,
The mystick rites of *flow'ry loves.*
He pry'd in every blossom's fold,
And all he saw unseemly—told.
Blab'd tales of many a *feeble* swain;‡
Unmeet to join in Flora's train;
Unless appointed by her care,
Like Turkish guards to watch the fair.
These *vegetable monsters* claim,
Alliance with the Eunuch's name.

10

20

30

15 Linneus] Carolus Linnaeus (1707–78), a Swedish botanist, the first to enunciate the principles for defining genera and species and to adhere to a uniform use of the binomial system for naming plants and animals.

In every herb and tree that grows;
Some frail propensity he shows.

But then in prose Linneus prattles,
And soon forgot is all he tattles.
While memory better pleas'd retains,
The frolicks of poetic brains.

So when the Muse with strains like thine
Enchantment breathes through every line;　　　　　　40
That Reason pausing makes a stand,
Control'd by Fiction's magic hand.
Enamour'd we the verse pursue,
And feel each fair delusion true.

Luxuriant thought thy mind o'ergrows;
Such painting from thy pencil flows;
Warm to my sight the visions rise,
And thy rich fancy mine supplies.
Thy themes rehearsing in my bower;
From those I picture ev'ry flower;　　　　　　50
With thy descriptive forms imprest,
I see them in thy colours drest;
Rememb'ring all thy lays unfold,
The snow-drop⁵ *freezes* me with *cold*.
I hear the *love-sick* violet's sighs,
And see the hare-bell's *azure eyes*.
See *jealous cowslips* hang their heads,
And *virgin lilies*—pine in beds.
The primrose meets my tinctur'd view,
Far paler than before—she grew.　　　　　　60
While Woodbines *wanton* seem to twine,
And reeling shoots the *maud'ling vine*.

If e'er I seek the *Cypress* shade,
Whose branches contemplation aid.
Of learned lore my thoughts possest,
Might dwell on mummies in a chest.

---

62 *maud'ling*] "'Drink deep, sweet youths,' seductive Vitis cries, / The maudlin tear-drop glittering in her eyes." Darwin [3.355–56]. *Moody*.

Unperishable chests 'tis said, ⎫
Where the Egyptian dead were laid, ⎬
Are of the Cypress timber made. ⎭
70   And gates of Rome's fam'd church they say,
Defying mould'ring time's decay;
From Constantine to Pope Eugene,
Eleven hundred years were seen,
In perfect state of sound and good,
Form'd of this Adamantine wood.
Then, DARWIN! were it not for thee,
I sure must venerate this tree.
But as his boughs hang o'er my head, ⎫
I recollect from you I read, ⎬
80   *His wife he exiles from his bed.* ‖ ⎭

    Since thus thy fascinating art,
So takes possession of the heart,
Go bid thy Muse a wreath prepare,
"To bind some charming Chloe's hair."
But tune no more thy Lyre's sweet powers,
To libel harmless trees and flowers.

                                        (1798)

* Erasmus Darwin (1731–1802), an English scientist and poet whose *Loves of the Plants* was published in 1789.
† See classes of Flowers, Polygamy, Clandestine Marriage, &c. *Moody.*
‡ See class — Vegetable Monsters and Eunuchs. *Moody.*

§ How snow-drops cold and blue eye'd hare-bells blend
Their tender tears as o'er the stream they bend
The love-sick violet, and the primrose pale,
Bow their sweet heads and whisper to the gale,
With secret sighs the virgin lily droops,
And jealous cowslips hang their tawny cups.
        Darwin's Loves of the Plants [1.11–16]. *Moody.*

‖ Cupressus dark disdains his dusky bride,
One dome contains them — but two beds divide.
            Darwin [1.9.73–75]. *Moody.*

84 Chloe's] Country maiden in love with Daphnis in the pastoral romance *Daphnis and Chloe*, attributed to the third-century Greek poet Longus.

To Sleep, a Song

A che condizione occhi miei Siete!
Che chiusi il bene, aperti il mal vedete!
—ARIOSTO*

Sleep expand thy downy wing,
Lull my heart's corroding pain;
Soft descend, and with thee bring,
Thy smiling visionary train.

In thy bosom's halcyon calm,
Stormy grief forgets to flow;
Gently drops thy lenient balm,
Sweet as Lethe's draught to woe.

Slumber sooths frail Nature's toils,
Chases Sorrow—chases Care;   10
Conscience of her thorn beguiles,
Smooths the brow of fierce despair.

Joys that waking Sense denies,
Flattering Sleep unfolds to view.
Ah, me! in dreams each barrier flies,
That parts my Soul from *love*—and *you*.
                                   (1798)

* "In what a state are you, my eyes, that when you are closed you see good and
when you are open see evil?" (*Orlando Furioso* 33.62.7–8, from the translation by Allan
Gilbert, 2 vols. [New York, 1954], 2:582).

The Housewife; or, The Muse Learning to Ride the Great Horse Heroic. Addressed to Lysander[*]

O thou that with deciding voice oft sways
The doubtful wand'rings of th' advent'rous Muse!
And oft directs her wav'ring feet, where best
To tread! Whether to climb the steep Parnassian
Mount,—that slippery path where NUMBERS slide
And fall,—or tread with firmer step Prosaic
Ground—Accept this verse! And should the Muse
All insufficient to so new a theme
Fail in her song—If not thy smile, at least
10   Thy patience give! And with unruffled face,
Stern critic furrows banish'd from thy brow,
Attend her flight through regions sacred
To domestic use; where she, guided by truth,
In search of that fair Nymph Economy,
Must now explore.—And quit for these, the more
Inviting paths of fiction—Her once lov'd
Haunts, where she was wont to cull poetic
Sweets, and lure thy fancy to more pleasing dreams.

Now when the Sun in Sagitarius rides,
20   And Morn, her dusky brow in misty vapours
Clad, with ling'ring beams unfolds reluctant
Day.—E'en though the aweful monitor of time
Proclaims the seventh hour; yet sleep his drowzy
Poppies waves o'er all the house, and wraps
The *snoring* Maids in gossip dreams, of *sweet*
Hearts, shows, and *fairs!*—All but the wakeful Housewife!
She late and early plys her busy cares,
And preparation makes for Christmas cheer.

Before the dawn emits one ray of light,
30   Forth from her couch she springs; her pregnant mind
Alert:—for *she* has things of great concern
In view.—Sleep on ye idle fair! ye time

4 Parnassian] Parnassus was the home of Apollo and the poetic Muses.

Destroyers! who live to dress, and flaunt,
And flirt, and waste your silly lives 'mid scenes
Of dissipation!—This useful maid to deeds
Of more importance gives her day, and scorns
The dainty modes of polish'd indolence.

    In garb of russet brown and round-ear'd cap,
With bib and apron of an azure hue,
And bunch of pendent keys that grac'd her side;   40
Which *she* by thrifty rules of Prudence warn'd
Ne'er from her sight would trust, for she was vers'd
In tricks of *vassal-kind,* and knew full well
That those whom we mistaking, *honest* call,
Are oft disloyal to the faith they owe,
And swerve from their allegiance!—tempted
By paltry gain of little price. Thus with
Her economic ensigns deck'd—Say, Muse!
If thou wilt deign to aid so mean a song?
And thou hast not disdain'd to sing, in days   50
Of yore, of Culinary Arts.—Both when
The beauteous Mother of mankind regal'd
Her Angel guest, and from sweet kernels press'd
The dulcet creams—And when the Grecian chiefs
Reserv'd a portion of the victim slain,
And AGAMEMNON help'd to *roast the Beef.*
Say then! Where first the HOUSEWIFE bends her steps!
Whether to that sequester'd Pile, where the cool
Dairy, guarded from Summer's noon-tide beams
Stands in a grove retired? Or to the bright   60
Illumin'd Kitchen? whose chimney issuing
Furious smoke, denotes th' approaching feast,
And fills the passing traveller, I ween,
With many a hungry thought. These, and
Departments many more than these, each in their
Turn, will her attendance claim—for method
And due order rul'd her ways; but pris'ners
Kept for Luxury's repast, require their food
As soon as morning breaks—and haply if not

56 Agamemnon] Legendary leader of the Greeks in the Trojan War.

70 *Fed*—would pine and *die,* which *she,* I trust,
A sore mischance would deem. Her visitation
First to these she pays, and to the Poultry
Court with speed repairs. There, nourish'd by
Violence and cruel art, a group of feather'd
Monsters round her stand, mis-shapen *fowls,*
With *maws protuberant!* There the cram'd Turkey
Groans beneath her care, and loaths the hand that
Ministers to life. *She* calm Spectat'ress
Of the woes she makes, repeats her barb'rous
80 Task; down each reluctant throat the food
She thrusts, then with discerning and unpitying
Eye inspects their bulk,—blows the light feathers
From their snowy breasts—proclaims their fitness
For the circling spit, and signs the warrant
That shall end their pains. The Dairy next demands
Her frugal care. There from the surface of the
Richest milk, the cream she skims; this with due
Labour and unweary'd toil she *churns,* till
To a firm consistence it is wrought, and *bears*
90 The name of *Butter.* Then with some light
Fantastic mould the tiny pats she prints,
And in a china vase, fill'd with clear water
From pellucid spring, her workmanship deposits.

    Now with the nimble step of busy haste
She to the store-room turns her active feet.
To the known manuscripts of ancient fame,
Where from a copious line of eating ancestors
Are cull'd a hoard of choice receipts; and where,
In Grandam spelling of no modern date
100 Recorded stands full many a dainty
Culinary Art, she turns the *time-worn* page
To find that celebrated *Pie,* which from the
Season takes its honour'd name. Then on the board,
With noisy din, the sav'ry meat she chops,
And in some vessel fit, blends th' ingredients.
Spice odoriferous, and luscious plums,
With moist'ning juice of apple, extracted
From the golden rinds of fairest fruit, then

With that potent spirit, sought on Gallia's
Shore, whose power medic'nal from indigestion   110
Guards rebellious food—the dang'rous *mass*
She tempers, and in the patty pans and
Pliant paste, in circling folds envelops.
Cakes too she fashion'd of fantastic forms,
Oblong, round and square; some in the diamond's
Shape compress'd—some in the heart's; some from the
Corriander seed their flavour take—some from
The Plum—*Cakes* of all names! Pound, saffron, lemon,
Orange—And those far fam'd for sweet delicious
Taste, that from the fair SALOPIA take their   120
Name. High above the rest majestic stood,
In size pre-eminent, with sugar'd top,
Graced by a royal Pair, and studded o'er
With choice confection of the Citron's fruit,
That mirth-inspiring *cake* all *children* hail,—
When on Twelfth-tide they meet, with festive glee,
And dance and song, and sportive tricks, to close
The gambols—Time-honour'd gambols! of the Christmas scene.

    What more this busy active dame perform'd,
In the *next Canto* shall the Muse rehearse.   130
The HOUSEWIFE's toils an ample theme supply;
Returning toils that rise with ev'ry Sun.
O days of ALBION! happier far I ween,
When WOMAN's knowledge own'd its boundary *here!*

                            (1798)

* D. 395 B.C. Spartan politician and general during the Peloponnesian War who
played a decisive role in defeating Athens.

120 Salopia] Shropshire.
133 Albion] Celtic name for Great Britain.

Hannah More

(1745–1833)

Hannah More first made a name for herself as an author of poems and plays but ended her long literary career as an influential writer of religious tracts and essays on education and morality. Born on 2 February 1745, she was the fourth of five daughters of Mary Grace and Jacob More, a Gloucestershire schoolmaster. Brought up on stories from the classics, she learned Latin and mathematics from her father and French from an older sister. But her father discontinued her studies when she was ten, fearful of producing an "overeducated" daughter. Around 1757 her eldest sister founded a boarding school in Bristol, and Hannah and her other sisters joined her. Hannah studied Spanish, Italian, and more advanced Latin with the instructors at the school. Her play *The Search after Happiness: A Pastoral Drama,* written when she was sixteen, was published in 1773. For several years Hannah served as an instructor at the school, but she resigned in 1767, when she became engaged to Edward Turner, a wealthy landowner twenty years her senior. But Turner kept putting off the wedding day, and after six years of postponements Hannah broke the engagement. To compensate her, Turner proposed an annuity of two hundred pounds a year, which she rejected; however, her sisters accepted it for her without her knowledge. Shortly thereafter, Hannah refused another offer of marriage. Resolved never to wed, and free from financial worry, she devoted herself to literature.

In 1773 *The Search after Happiness* was successfully produced at Bath. Later that year More went to London, where she became friends with Elizabeth Montagu, Elizabeth Carter, Hester Chapone, and other literary women in the bluestocking circle, as well as with David Garrick, Samuel Johnson, and Sir Joshua Reynolds. In 1776 Thomas Cadell published her ballad "Sir Eldred of the Bower," which probes the moral and psychological implications of love, jealousy, and rage and ends didactically, along with "The Bleeding Rock," an earlier poem. Cadell paid her as much for this volume as he had paid Goldsmith for *The Deserted Village.* Samuel Johnson called More "the most powerful versificatrix" in the English Language.[1] David Garrick became a close friend, and More published the playful *Ode to Dragon, Mr. Garrick's House-Dog, at Hampton* in 1777. Garrick urged her to write for the stage, and the result was the hugely successful *Percy, a Tragedy* (1778), written in blank verse and centering around a virtuous and wronged heroine, Elwina, forced to marry a man she could not love and destroyed by his jealousy. Garrick wrote the prologue and the epilogue, but the emotionally powerful play established More as a writer of some importance. When another drama, *The Fatal Falsehood,* appeared in 1779, Hannah Cowley accused More of having stolen the plot of her tragedy *Albina,* refused by Garrick several years earlier.

With Garrick's death that same year, More withdrew from London society and decided to devote her talents to religion. Though most considered her a Methodist, she was an evangelical who subscribed to the Church of England. Now convinced that the theater was a corrupting influence, she refused to attend a revival of *Percy* in 1784. Although she no longer wrote plays to be performed, in 1782 she produced a volume entitled *Sacred Dramas,* intended for reading. These works dramatize Old Testament stories in blank verse and explore the psychological dimensions of such familiar narratives as David and Goliath, Moses in the bulrushes, and Daniel and Belshazzar. "I rather aspired after moral instruction than the purity of dramatic composition," she wrote in the advertisement. Included in the same volume is "Sensibility, a Poem," extolling sympathetic feeling and the benevolent action that results.

At about this time, More befriended Ann Yearsley, an impoverished poet whose verses she edited and on whose behalf she solicited subscriptions. The relationship would end in misunderstanding, acrimony, and disillusionment on both sides, largely because of More's patronizing behavior toward Yearsley and the latter's offended pride. In 1786 More published two secular poems, both of which dramatize conflicts in her own life. "Florio" features a fashionable young man who vacillates in his choice between two women, one a natural, bright, and affectionate person who represents the values of rural life and the other a worldly woman who symbolizes the city's artificial values. Florio eventually decides in favor of the country and lives happily ever after, just as More would withdraw from London society to a rural cottage near Bristol in 1785. "The Bas Bleu; or, Conversation," dedicated to Elizabeth Vesey, celebrates the members of the bluestocking circle and advocates good conversation by intelligent women as an important moral and social force. Here she juxtaposes aristocratic society's artificiality with the authentic

---

1. James Beattie to Sir William Forbes, 31 July 1784, in Forbes, *An Account of the Life and Writings of James Beattie,* 2nd ed., 3 vols. (Edinburgh, 1807), 2:334.

social interaction of the bluestockings, deeming conversation "That noblest commerce of mankind, / Whose precious merchandise is Mind!"

Accompanied by William Wilberforce, More and her sisters visited the town of Cheddar, where they were shocked by the villagers' poverty, ignorance, and undisciplined behavior. As a result, they established a Sunday school, first in that town and then in many others, that taught laboring-class people to read, to know the Bible, and to follow principles of good conduct. Students were rewarded with gifts of clothing and with festive meals. Although there was much resistance among the moneyed classes to the idea of educating the poor, More managed to win widespread approval and support, largely because she advocated education as a way of instilling values that would support the status quo—piety, frugality, and acceptance by the laboring class of their lower station in life.

Slavery, a Poem (1788), later revised, expanded, and retitled "The Black Slave Trade. A Poem," was written to help Wilberforce with his 1788 opening of the parliamentary campaign against the slave trade. More told her sister, "I grieve I did not set about it sooner; as it must now be done in such a hurry . . . but, good or bad, if it does not come out at the particular moment when the discussion comes on in Parliament, it will not be worth a straw."[2] The poem argues on both an intellectual and an emotional level that the principles of civilized life and the practice of slavery are incompatible. The *Monthly Review* remarked, "The chief excellence of this poem consists in its pathetic appeals to our feelings, in behalf of our sable *fellow-creatures.*"[3] The poem was widely distributed by anti-slavery societies throughout Britain, particularly those organized for women. With her friend Lady Margaret Middleton, More initiated discussions concerning the slave trade at dinner parties attended by prominent politicians in an effort to sway the vote. Together with Lady Middleton, she persuaded the manager of the Drury Lane Theater to put on Thomas Southerne's dramatization of Aphra Behn's *Oroonoko,* with its anti-slavery message, as a way to reach thousands.

In the following years, More produced such didactic prose as *Thoughts on the Importance of the Manners of the Great to General Society* (1788) and *An Estimate of the Religion of the Fashionable World: By One of the Laity* (1791). She published these essays anonymously because, first, she suspected that a woman's ideas on such subjects would not be taken seriously and, second, because she was criticizing the mode of life of many of her friends in London. But the books got

2. Quoted in William Roberts, *Memoirs of the Life and Correspondence of Mrs. Hannah More,* 2 vols. (New York, 1835), I:281.

3. 78 (1788): 246.

a good reception, and she published several more works on educational and moral reform that brought together her conservative goals and progressive ideas. For example, like Mary Wollstonecraft, she advocated a more rigorous and extensive education for women, but, unlike Wollstonecraft, she believed that women should use this education only in traditional roles.

Between 1794 and 1797 More brought out fifty *Cheap Repository Tracts,* pamphlets for a laboring-class audience intended to counteract the influence of French Revolutionary ideas. Couching conservative politics in brief, entertaining stories, these tracts offered a pious alternative to the fiction currently available to the poor in inexpensive chapbooks. The tracts also included moralistic ballads warning against overindulgence in drink, sex, and bad company. Two million copies of More's tracts were published in the first two years; and when More stopped writing them after the danger of Revolutionary politics had passed, others imitated her successful formula for years to come.

More moved to Barley Wood in 1802, and her sisters came to live with her there two years later. In 1808 she published her first and only novel, *Cœlebs in Search of a Wife,* adapting what she considered a degenerate literary form to a worthy moral purpose. The narrative is accompanied by religious instructions telling young people how to live productively and piously and telling their parents how to raise good children. Twelve editions sold out in the first year.

In 1821, after all of her sisters had died, More brought out a children's book summarizing Biblical stories in verse, *Bible Rhymes on the Names of All the Books of the Old and New Testament.* In 1828 she moved to Clifton, where she died of old age on 7 September 1833, having made over thirty thousand pounds from her books. One of the most influential conservative writers of her time, she helped popularize the short story as a literary form, legitimated the novel in the eyes of many religious readers, helped advance the causes of anti-slavery and education for the poor, and argued for women's intellectual abilities. However, she never challenged the prevailing notion that women should remain subservient to men. Even so, Hester Lynch Piozzi called her "the cleverest of all us Female Wits."[4]

MAJOR WORKS: *The Search after Happiness: A Pastoral Drama* (Bristol, 1773); *The Inflexible Captive: A Tragedy* (Bristol, 1774); *Sir Eldred of the Bower, and the Bleeding Rock: Two Legendary Tales* (London, 1776); *Essays on Various Subjects, Principally Designed for Young*

---

4. *Thraliana: The Diary of Mrs. Hester Lynch Thrale (Later Mrs. Piozzi): 1776–1809,* ed. Katharine C. Balderston, 2nd ed., vol. 2 (Oxford, 1951), 699 (entry for 5 December 1787).

Ladies (London, 1777); *Ode to Dragon, Mr. Garrick's House-Dog, at Hampton* (London, 1777); *Percy, a Tragedy* (London, 1778); *The Works of Miss Hannah More in Prose and Verse* (Cork, 1778); *The Fatal Falsehood: A Tragedy* (London, 1779); *Sacred Dramas: Chiefly Intended for Young Persons: the Subjects Taken from the Bible. To Which is Added, Sensibility, a Poem* (London, 1782); *Florio: A Tale, for Fine Gentlemen and Fine Ladies: And, the Bas Bleu; or, Conversation: Two Poems* (London, 1786); *Slavery, a Poem* (London, 1788); *Thoughts on the Importance of the Manners of the Great to General Society* (London, 1788); *An Estimate of the Religion of the Fashionable World: By One of the Laity* (London, 1791); *Cheap Repository Tracts; Entertaining, Moral, and Religious*, 3 vols. (London and Bath, 1798); *Strictures on the Modern System of Female Education: With a View of the Principles and Conduct Prevalent among Women of Rank and Fortune*, 2 vols. (London, 1799); *The Works of Hannah More, Including Several Pieces Never Before Published*, 8 vols. (London, 1801); *Cœlebs in Search of a Wife: Comprehending Observations on Domestic Habits and Manners, Religion and Morals*, 2 vols. (London, 1808); *Practical Piety; or, The Influence of Religion of the Heart on the Conduct of Life* (London, 1811); *Poems* (London, 1816); *The Twelfth of August; or the Feast of Freedom* (London, 1819); *Moral Sketches of Prevailing Opinions and Manners, Foreign and Domestic; with Reflections on Prayer* (London, 1819); *Bible Rhymes on the Names of All the Books of the Old and New Testament: With Allusions to Some of the Principal Incidents and Characters* (London, 1821); *Letters of Hannah More*, ed. R. Brimley Johnson (London, 1925); *The Poetical Works . . . With a Memoir of the Author* (London, 1835).

TEXT USED: Text from *The Works of Hannah More*, vol. 2 (London, 1830).

The Black Slave Trade. A Poem

> —O great design!
> Ye Sons of Mercy! O complete your work;
> Wrench from Oppression's hand the iron rod,
> And bid the cruel feel the pains they give.
> —Thompson's "Liberty" *

If Heaven has into being deign'd to call
Thy light, O LIBERTY! to shine on all;
Bright intellectual Sun! why does thy ray
To earth distribute only partial day?
Since no resisting cause from *spirit* flows
Thy universal presence to oppose;
No obstacles by Nature's hand impress'd,
Thy subtle and ethereal beams arrest;

Not sway'd by *matter* is thy course benign,
Or more direct or more oblique to shine;   10
Nor motion's laws can speed thy active course;
Nor strong repulsion's pow'rs obstruct thy force:
Since there is no convexity in MIND,
Why are thy genial rays to parts confin'd?
While the chill North with thy bright beam is blest,
Why should fell darkness half the South invest?
Was it decreed, fair Freedom! at thy birth,
That thou should'st ne'er irradiate *all* the earth?
While Britain basks in thy full blaze of light,
Why lies sad Afric quench'd in total night?   20
   Thee only, *sober* Goddess! I attest,
In smiles chastis'd, and decent graces dress'd;
To thee alone, pure daughter of the skies,
The hallow'd incense of the Bard should rise:
Not that mad Liberty, in whose wild praise
Too oft he trims his prostituted bays;
Not that unlicens'd monster of the crowd,
Whose roar terrific bursts in peals so loud,
Deaf'ning the ear of Peace; fierce Faction's tool,
Of rash Sedition born, and mad Misrule;   30
Whose stubborn mouth, rejecting Reason's rein,
No strength can govern, and no skill restrain;
Whose magic cries the frantic vulgar draw
To spurn at Order, and to outrage Law;
To tread on grave Authority and Pow'r,
And shake the work of ages in an hour:
Convuls'd her voice, and pestilent her breath,
She raves of mercy, while she deals out death:
Each blast is fate; she darts from either hand
Red conflagration o'er th' astonish'd land;   40
Clamouring for peace, she rends the air with noise,
And, to reform a part, the whole destroys.
Reviles oppression only to oppress,
And, in the act of murder, breathes redress.
Such have we seen on Freedom's genuine coast,
Bellowing for blessings which were never lost.

25 that mad Liberty] Alluding to the riots in London in the year 1800. *More.*

'Tis past, and Reason rules the lucid hour,
And beauteous ORDER reassumes his power:
Lord of the bright ascendant may he reign,
50   Till perfect Peace eternal sway maintain!
          O, plaintive Southerne! whose impassion'd page
Can melt the soul to grief, or rouse to rage;
Now, when congenial themes engage the Muse,
She burns to emulate thy generous views;
Her failing efforts mock her fond desires,
She shares thy feelings, not partakes thy fires.
Strange pow'r of song! the strain that warms the heart
Seems the same inspiration to impart;
Touch'd by th' extrinsic energy alone,
60   We think the flame which melts us is our own;
Deceiv'd, for genius we mistake delight,
Charm'd as we read, we fancy we can write.
          Though not to me, sweet Bard, thy pow'rs belong,
The cause I plead shall sanctify my song.
The Muse awakes no artificial fire,
For Truth rejects what Fancy would inspire:
Here Art would weave her gayest flow'rs in vain,
The bright invention Nature would disdain.
For no fictitious ills these numbers flow,
70   But living anguish, and substantial woe;
No individual griefs my bosom melt,
For millions feel what Oronoko felt:
Fir'd by no single wrongs, the countless host
I mourn, by rapine dragg'd from Afric's coast.
          Perish th' illiberal thought which would debase
The native genius of the sable race!
Perish the proud philosophy, which sought
To rob them of the pow'rs of equal thought!
What! does th' immortal principle within
80   Change with the casual colour of a skin?
Does matter govern spirit? or is MIND
Degraded by the form to which 'tis join'd?
          No: they have heads to think, and hearts to feel,

---

51 Southerne] Author of the Tragedy of Oronoko. *More.* [Thomas Southerne (1660–1746)
based his work (1696) on Aphra Behn's prose narrative *Oroonoko* (1688), about a slave uprising
in Surinam and two Africans who choose death over slavery. *Ed.*]

And souls to act, with firm, though erring zeal;
For they have keen affections, soft desires,
Love strong as death, and active patriot fires:
All the rude energy, the fervid flame
Of high-soul'd passion, and ingenuous shame:
Strong, but luxuriant virtues, boldly shoot
From the wild vigour of a savage root.   90
 Nor weak their sense of honour's proud control,
For pride is virtue in a Pagan soul;
A sense of worth, a conscience of desert,
A high, unbroken haughtiness of heart;
That self-same stuff which erst proud empires sway'd,
Of which the conquerors of the world were made.
Capricious fate of men! that very pride
In Afric scourg'd, in Rome was deified.
 No Muse, O Qua-shi! shall thy deeds relate,
No statue snatch thee from oblivious fate!   100
For thou wast born where never gentle Muse
On Valour's grave the flow'rs of Genius strews;
And thou wast born where no recording page
Plucks the fair deed from Time's devouring rage.
Had Fortune plac'd thee on some happier coast,
Where *polish'd* Pagans souls heroic boast,
To thee, who sought'st a voluntary grave,
Th' uninjur'd honours of thy name to save,
Whose generous arm thy barbarous Master spar'd,
Altars had smok'd, and temples had been rear'd.   110
 Whene'er to Afric's shores I turn my eyes,
Horrors of deepest, deadliest guilt arise;

99 Qua-shi] It is a point of honour among Negroes of a high spirit to die rather than to suffer their glossy skin to bear the mark of the whip. Qua-shi had somehow offended his master,
a young planter, with whom he had been bred up in the endearing intimacy of a play-fellow.
His services had been faithful; his attachment affectionate. The master resolved to punish him,
and pursued him for that purpose. In trying to escape, Qua-shi stumbled and fell; the master
fell upon him: they wrestled long with doubtful victory; at length Qua-shi got uppermost,
and, being firmly seated on his master's breast, he secured his legs with one hand, and with
the other drew a sharp knife: then said, "Master, I have been bred up with you from a child;
I have loved you as myself; in return, you have condemned me to a punishment of which I
must ever have borne the marks—thus only I can avoid them;" so saying, he drew the knife
with all his strength across his own throat, and fell down dead, without a groan, on his master's
body. [James] Ramsay's *Essay on the Treatment [and Conversion] of African Slaves [in the British Sugar
Colonies* (1784)]. *More.*

I see, by more than Fancy's mirror shown,
The burning village, and the blazing town:
See the dire victim torn from social life,
See the scar'd infant, hear the shrieking wife!
She, wretch forlorn! is dragg'd by hostile hands,
To distant tyrants sold, in distant lands:
Transmitted miseries, and successive chains,
120   The sole sad heritage her child obtains.
E'en this last wretched boon their foes deny,
To weep together, or together die.
By felon hands, by one relentless stroke,
See the fond vital links of Nature broke!
The fibres twisting round a parent's heart,
Torn from their grasp, and bleeding as they part.
    Hold, murderers! hold! nor aggravate distress;
Respect the passions you yourselves possess:
Ev'n you, of ruffian heart, and ruthless hand,
130   Love your own offspring, love your native land;
Ev'n you, with fond impatient feelings burn,
Though free as air, though certain of return.
Then, if to you, who voluntary roam,
So dear the memory of your distant home,
O think how absence the lov'd scene endears
To him, whose food is groans, whose drink is tears;
Think on the wretch whose aggravated pains
To exile misery adds, to misery chains.
If warm *your* heart, to British feelings true,
140   As dear his land to him as yours to you;
And Liberty, in you a hallow'd flame,
Burns, unextinguish'd, in his breast the same.
Then leave him holy Freedom's cheering smile,
The heav'n-taught fondness for the parent soil;
Revere affections mingled with our frame,
In every nature, every clime the same;
In all, these feelings equal sway maintain;
In all, the love of HOME and FREEDOM reign:
And Tempe's vale, and parch'd Angola's sand,

---

149 Tempe's vale] Valley in Greece between the Olympus and Ossa Mountains; laurel from
Tempe was used for the first temple of Apollo at Delphi.

One equal fondness of their sons command.   150
Th' unconquer'd Savage laughs at pain and toil,
Basking in Freedom's beams which gild his native soil.
  Does thirst of empire, does desire of fame,
(For these are specious crimes,) our rage inflame?
No: sordid lust of gold their fate controls,
The basest appetite of basest souls;
Gold, better gain'd by what their ripening sky,
Their fertile fields, their arts, and mines supply.
  What wrongs, what injuries does Oppression plead,
To smooth the crime and sanctify the deed?   160
What strange offence, what aggravated sin?
They stand convicted—of a darker skin!
Barbarians, hold! th' opprobrious commerce spare,
Respect His sacred image which they bear.
Though dark and savage, ignorant and blind,
They claim the common privilege of *kind;*
Let Malice strip them of each other plea,
They still are men, and men should still be free.
Insulted Reason loathes th' inverted trade—
Loathes, as she views the human purchase made;   170
The outrag'd Goddess, with abhorrent eyes,
Sees MAN the traffic, SOULS the merchandize!
Man, whom fair Commerce taught with judging eye,
And liberal hand, to barter or to buy,
Indignant Nature blushes to behold,
Degraded Man himself, truck'd, barter'd, sold;
Of ev'ry native privilege bereft,
Yet curs'd with ev'ry wounded feeling left.
Hard lot! each brutal suff'ring to sustain,
Yet keep the sense acute of human pain.   180
Plead not, in reason's palpable abuse,
Their sense of feeling callous and obtuse:
From heads to hearts lies Nature's plain appeal,
Though few can reason, all mankind can feel.
Though wit may boast a livelier dread of shame,

---

158 their arts] Besides many valuable productions of the soil, cloths and carpets of exquisite manufacture are brought from the coast of Guinea. *More.*

182 Their sense of feeling] Nothing is more frequent than this cruel and stupid argument, that they do not *feel* the miseries inflicted on them as Europeans would do. *More.*

A loftier sense of wrong refinement claim;
Though polish'd manners may fresh wants invent,
And nice distinctions nicer souls torment;
Though these on finer spirits heavier fall,
190   Yet natural evils are the same to all.
Though wounds there are which reason's force may heal,
There needs no logic sure to make us feel.
The nerve, howe'er untutor'd, can sustain
A sharp, unutterable sense of pain;
As exquisitely fashion'd in a slave,
As where unequal fate a sceptre gave.
Sense is as keen where Gambia's waters glide,
As where proud Tiber rolls his classic tide.
Though verse or rhetoric point the feeling line,
200   They do not whet sensation, but define.
Did ever wretch less feel the galling chain,
When Zeno prov'd there was no ill in pain?
In vain the sage to smooth its horror tries;
Spartans and Helots see with different eyes;
Their miseries philosophic quirks deride,
Slaves groan in pangs disown'd by Stoic pride.

When the fierce Sun darts vertical his beams,
And thirst and hunger mix their wild extremes;
When the sharp iron wounds his inmost soul,
210   And his strain'd eyes in burning anguish roll;
Will the parch'd Negro own, ere he expire,
No pain in hunger, and no heat in fire?

For him, when agony his frame destroys,
What hope of present fame or future joys?
For *that* have Heroes shorten'd Nature's date;
For *this* have Martyrs gladly met their fate;
But him, forlorn, no Hero's pride sustains,
No Martyr's blissful visions soothe his pains;
Sullen, he mingles with his kindred dust,
220   For he has learn'd to dread the Christian's trust;
To him what mercy can that GOD display,

202 Zeno] C. 340–c. 265 B.C. Greek philosopher; founder of the Stoic school of thought.
    209 When the sharp iron] This is not said figuratively. The writer of these lines has seen a
complete set of chains, fitted to every separate limb of these unhappy, innocent, men; together
with instruments for wrenching open the jaws, contrived with such ingenious cruelty as would
gratify the tender mercies of an inquisitor. *More.*

Whose servants murder, and whose sons betray?
Savage! thy venial error I deplore,
They are *not* Christians who invest thy shore.
  O thou sad spirit, whose preposterous yoke
The great deliverer Death, at length, has broke!
Releas'd from misery, and escap'd from care,
Go, meet that mercy man denied thee here.
In thy dark home, sure refuge of th' oppress'd,
The wicked vex not, and the weary rest.   230
And, if some notions, vague and undefin'd,
Of future terrors have assail'd thy mind;
If such thy masters have presum'd to teach,
As terrors only they are prone to preach;
(For should they paint eternal Mercy's reign,
Where were th' oppressor's rod, the captive's chain?)
If, then, thy troubled soul has learn'd to dread
The dark unknown thy trembling footsteps tread;
On HIM, who made thee what thou art, depend;
HE, who withholds the means, accepts the end.   240
Thy mental night thy Saviour will not blame,
He died for those who never heard his name.
Not *thine* the reckoning dire of LIGHT abus'd,
KNOWLEDGE disgrac'd, and LIBERTY misus'd;
On *thee* no awful judge incens'd shall sit
For parts perverted, and dishonour'd wit.
Where ignorance will be found the safest plea,
How many learn'd and wise shall envy *thee!*
  And thou, WHITE SAVAGE! whether lust of gold
Or lust of conquest rule thee uncontroll'd!   250
Hero, or robber!—by whatever name
Thou plead thy impious claim to wealth or fame;
Whether inferior mischief be thy boast,
A tyrant trader rifling *Congo's* coast:
Or bolder carnage track thy crimson way,
Kings dispossess'd, and provinces thy prey;
Whether thou pant to tame earth's distant bound;
All Cortez murder'd, all Columbus found;
O'er plunder'd realms to reign, detested Lord,

258 Cortez murder'd] Hernando Cortez (1485–1547), Spanish explorer whose invasion,
conquest, and enslavement of Mexicans involved enormous slaughter.

260 Make millions wretched, and thyself abhorr'd:—
     Whether Cartouche in forests break the law,
     Or bolder Caesar keep the world in awe;
     In Reason's eye, in Wisdom's fair account,
     Your sum of glory boasts a like amount:
     The means may differ, but the end's the same;
     Conquest is pillage with a nobler name.
     Who makes the sum of human blessings less,
     Or sinks the stock of general happiness,
     Though erring fame may grace, though false renown
270 His life may blazon or his memory crown,
     Yet the last audit shall reverse the cause,
     And God shall vindicate his broken laws.

         Had those advent'rous spirits who explore
     Through ocean's trackless wastes, the far-sought shore;
     Whether of wealth insatiate, or of pow'r,
     Conquerors who waste, or ruffians who devour;
     Had these possess'd, O Cook! thy gentle mind,
     Thy love of arts, thy love of human kind;
     Had these pursued thy mild and liberal plan,
280 Discoverers had not been a curse to man.
     Then, bless'd Philanthropy! thy social hands
     Had link'd dissever'd worlds in brothers' bands;
     Careless, if colour, or if clime divide;
     Then, lov'd and loving, man had liv'd, and died.
     Then with pernicious skill we had not known
     To bring their vices back and leave our own.

         The purest wreaths which hang on glory's shrine,
     For empires founded, peaceful Penn! are thine;
     No blood-stain'd laurels crown'd thy virtuous toil,
290 No slaughter'd natives drench'd thy fair-earn'd soil.
         Still thy meek spirit in thy flock survives,

---

261 Cartouche] Louis Dominque Cartouche (1693–1721), a notorious French criminal whose career began with a theft when he was eleven, after which he hid in a wood. Eventually something of a popular hero, he was captured and executed on the wheel in 1721.

277 Cook] James Cook (1728–79) English explorer of Canada, South America, Australia, New Zealand, Hawaii, the west coast of North America, and the Antarctic. Anna Seward wrote an *Elegy on Captain Cook* (1780).

288 Penn] William Penn (1644–1718), founder of the colony of Pennsylvania.

291 thy flock] The Quakers have emancipated all their slaves throughout America. *More.*

Consistent still, *their* doctrines rule their lives;
Thy followers only have effac'd the shame
Inscrib'd by SLAVERY on the Christian name.
   Shall Britain, where the soul of Freedom reigns,
Forge chains for others she herself disdains?
Forbid it, Heaven! O let the nations know
The liberty she tastes she will bestow;
Not to herself the glorious gift confin'd,
She spreads the blessing wide as human kind;   300
And scorning narrow views of time and place,
Bids all be free in earth's extended space.
   What page of human annals can record
A deed so bright as human rights restor'd?
O may that god-like deed, that shining page
Redeem OUR fame, and consecrate OUR age,
And let this glory mark our favour'd shore,
To curb FALSE FREEDOM and the TRUE restore!
   And see the cherub MERCY from above,
Descending softly, quits the sphere of love!   310
On Britain's Isle she sheds her heavenly dew,
And breathes her spirit o'er th' enlighten'd few;
From soul to soul the generous influence steals,
Till every breast the soft contagion feels.
She speeds, exulting, to the burning shore,
With the best message Angel ever bore;
Hark! 'tis the note which spoke a Saviour's birth,
Glory to God on high, and peace on Earth!
She vindicates the Pow'r in Heaven ador'd,
She stills the clank of chains, and sheathes the sword;   320
She cheers the mourner, and with soothing hands
From bursting hearts unbinds th' Oppressor's bands;
Restores the lustre of the Christian name,
And clears the foulest blot that dimm'd its fame.
   As the mild Spirit hovers o'er the coast,
A fresher hue the wither'd landscapes boast;
Her healing smiles the ruin'd scenes repair,
And blasted Nature wears a joyous air;
While she proclaims through all their spicy groves,
"Henceforth your fruits, your labours, and your loves,   330
"All that your Sires possess'd, or you have sown,

"Sacred from plunder—all is now YOUR OWN."
    And now, her high commission from above,
Stamp'd with the holy characters of love,
The meek-ey'd spirit waving in her hand,
Breathes manumission o'er the rescu'd land:
She tears the banner stain'd with blood and tears,
And, LIBERTY! thy shining standard rears!
As the bright ensign's glory she displays,
340   See pale OPPRESSION faints beneath the blaze!
The giant dies! no more his frown appals,
The chain, untouch'd, drops off, the fetter falls.
Astonish'd echo tells the vocal shore,
Oppression's fall'n, and Slavery is no more!
The dusky myriads crowd the sultry plain,
And hail that MERCY long invok'd in vain.
Victorious pow'r! she bursts their two-fold bands,
And FAITH and FREEDOM spring from Britain's hands.
    And THOU! great source of Nature and of Grace,
350   Who of one blood didst form the human race,
Look down in mercy in thy chosen time,
With equal eye on Afric's suff'ring clime:
Disperse her shades of intellectual night,
Repeat thy high behest—LET THERE BE LIGHT!
Bring each benighted soul, great GOD, to Thee,
And with thy wide Salvation make them free!
                                            (1788)

* By James Thomson (1700–1748), best known for *The Seasons.*

Countess of Morley

(1781–1857)

Records show that the countess of Morley was born Frances Talbot in 1781 and that she was the only daughter of Thomas Talbot of Norfolk, but nothing else about her childhood has come to light. On 22 August 1809 she became the second wife of John Parker, baron of Morley, who had divorced his first wife the preceding year. In 1815 he was made Viscount Boringdon and earl of Morley. Their son, Edmund, was born on 10 June 1810, and upon his father's death in 1840 he inherited his title. The couple apparently also had a daughter. During the 1830s the family lived in London at Kent-house, in South Place, Knightsbridge, and had a country home, Boringdon-house, in Saltram, Devonshire.[1]

An obituary in the *Gentleman's Magazine* describes the countess of Morley as "a woman of strong mind and considerable literary and artistic abilities."[2] A notice in the *Athenaeum* observes that she showed "a sufficiency of grace and talent to have given their writer a fair place among authoresses had she taken time and pains to try for it. As it was, she stood first among the first of talkers," well known for her "readiness in repartee — her vivacity and good nature in raillery — her power of keeping up the ball, however strong and lively might be the other playmate, will not be forgotten by any one enumerating the Thrales, the Corks, the Berrys, the Fanshawes, who have enlived London society during the past half-century."[3]

The countess's literary works include *Dacre*, a silver-fork novel published in three volumes by Longmans in 1834.[4] The title page lists her merely as the editor, but such a subterfuge was common in this period, and the book

---

1. George Boyle, ed., *Boyle's Fashionable Court and Country Guide, and Town Visiting Directory* (London, January 1835, January 1839).

2. 204 (January 1858): 117.

3. December 1857, 1553.

4. The copy of *Dacre* in the Humanities Research Center at the University of Texas was owned by Maria Theresa Lister, who lived at the same address in Knightsbridge.

was widely known to have been her work. The *Quarterly Review* remarked that the manners of the time could not have been "any more vividly or more faithfully portrayed" than they were in this book and that it displayed not only "a thoughtful insight into the feelings and ways of mankind" but also a "faultlessness in point of taste, and an ease and lightness of style."[5] The *Edinburgh Review* noted,

> a remarkable degree of truth and keeping, both in the incidents, the characters, and sentiments; that nothing is distorted or overdrawn; that the plot, without being too intricate or complex, is well constructed, and the interest well sustained to the last; that all the hopes, fears, and anxieties of love, are depicted with the skill and tenderness which only a woman's hand could impart to the picture; that the occasional sketches of natural scenery which are introduced, are graphic and picturesque; that the style is clear, unaffected, and terse.[6]

Other novels include *A Man without a Name* (1852), *Nina* (c. 1850), and possibly *The Divorced* and *Family Records*. She is also said to have written proverbs and comedies. Sarah J. Hale observes that the countess's novels "attained considerable popularity both in England and America."[7] She had privately printed, interleaved with illustrations, two verse pamphlets, *The Nose, a Poem, in Six Stanzas . . . Dedicated to All Unmarried Ladies Who May Profit by the Example, and Take Warning from the Fate of Dorothy Spriggins* (1831) and *The Flying Burgermaster. A Legend of the Black Forest* (1832), and she was probably the author of another, *Some Account of Lord Boringdon's Accident* ([1818]). Walter Sneyd's *Portraits of the Spruggins Family* (1829) contains her lithographs.

The countess of Morley died at Saltram on 6 December 1857 at the age of seventy-six and was interred in the family vault at the church of Plympton St. Mary. She is said to have left a large collection of paintings. The following two poems appeared in the *Keepsake*.

MAJOR WORKS: *The Nose, a Poem, in Six Stanzas . . . Dedicated to All Unmarried Ladies Who May Profit by the Example, and Take Warning from the Fate of Dorothy Spriggins* ([London], 1831); *The Flying Burgermaster. A Legend of the Black Forest* ([London], 1832); *Dacre; a Novel* 3 vols. (London, 1834); *A Man without a Name: a Tale*, 2 vols. (London, 1852); *Nina, a Tale* ([London?], c. 1850).

Uncertain attributions include *Some Account of Lord Boringdon's Accident, on 21st July, 1817, and its Consequences* (n.p., [1818]); *The Divorced, A Novel* ([London?], n.d.); and *Family Records* ([London?], n.d.).

5. 52 (November 1834): 488–95.
6. 59 (July 1834): 475–76.
7. Sarah J. Hale, *Woman's Record; or, Sketches of all Distinguished Women, from the Creation to A.D. 1868. Arranged in Four Eras. With Selections from Authoresses of Each Era.* 3rd ed., rev. (New York, 1870), 848.

TEXTS USED: Text of "A Party of Pleasure up the River Tamer" from the *Keepsake* for 1832; text of "Epilogue" from the *Keepsake* for 1834.

A Party of Pleasure up the River Tamer

> —Proudly riding on the azure realm,
> In gallant trim the gilded vessel goes—
> Youth at the prow, and Pleasure at the helm—
> Regardless of the sweeping whirlwind's sway,
> That waits in grim repose his evening's prey.
> —Gray*

The clock strikes nine—nor has the sun,
Since from the east his course begun,
    Deign'd once to show his face;
Low on the hills the mist descends,
A certain sign which rain portends
    Ere he has run his race.

Fie, Phoebus, fie! on such a day,
Thus spiteful, to withhold thy ray
    Seems at the best suspicious;
But if that frown betrays intent   10
In thee t'oppose the government,
    'Tis surely most flagitious.

That thou, the sky's great potentate,
Shouldst scowl on ministers of state,
    Appears such strange behavior!
One would have thought the brightest beam
That from thy summer's smile could gleam
    Had shone to show them favour.

That morning many a lovely eye,
Bright as thyself, beheld the sky   20
    With doubt and trepidation;

7 Phoebus] Apollo, Greek god of music and prophecy.
14 ministers of state] A Secretary of State was one of the party. *Frederic Mansel Reynolds.*

And many a gay and gallant spark
Contemplated the horizon dark
    With undisguised vexation.

But souls like ours, of courage high,
Will triumph, though prosperity
    Seems threat'ning to desert us.
Let black'ning clouds the skies deform,
Dauntless, we brave the gathering storm,
30   "*In arduis viget virtus.*"

See then the gallant bark unmoor'd:
Graceful the ladies step on board;
    (What lovely themes for sonnets!)
Those airy forms and beaming faces
Have quite the ton of Nymphs and Graces
    Disguised in cloaks and bonnets.

Proud Egypt's queen might boast of old
Her royal galley deck'd with gold—
    We venture not to blame her,
40   Though we suspect her far-famed crew
Had dowdies been, compared to you,
    Ye ladies of the Tamer.

Flow on, fair stream! thy rapid tide
Swiftly the painted bark will guide
    Along thy sinuous way,
To where high banks of tufted wood,
And tow'ring crags o'ershade the flood
    From the broad glare of day.

That day, alas! such shade was vain,
50   As umbrellas from the rain
    Was all the shelter needed;
For still the pelting torrent pours,
And Tamer's wild and woody shores
    Were pass'd in fogs unheeded.

---

30 *In arduis viget virtus*] "Virtue flourishes in adversities."

Council was held, and all agreed
'Twould show more spirit to proceed
    Till we had reach'd Pentilly,
Than dastardly to turn the boat;
As going back, when once afloat,
    Would seem so very silly.   60

Ply then your oars, ye gallant crew!
For see, — Pentilly full in view,
    Rising from yon dark wood,
Majestic from the mountain's brow,
Frowns on her battlements below,
    Reflected in the flood.

Steer for yon little shelter'd glade,
Where underneath the mountain's shade
    That lonely cottage stands;
Some light repast of milk and fruits,   70
Such as that lowly dwelling suits,
    Our famish'd state demands.

But, lo! beneath the humble shed,
Surprised we find a banquet spread
    Of dainties quite patrician:
The *Baron* there of beef the prime,
And stately *Sir* Loin tower'd sublime, —
    But where was the magician?

No magic power was here exerted,
Or nature from her course diverted: 80
    A tourist from the east
Had saunter'd out to take an airing,
Just whilst his servants were preparing
    For *him* this tempting feast.

Fain would I here a fact conceal
Which truth compels me to reveal,
    To this conclusion leading: —
That e'en amidst the most polite
There's no controlling appetite —
    Hunger devours good breeding.   90

Dishes so savoury and alluring
Increased our hunger past enduring,
    Till, to refrain unable,
We all at once, like hungry hawks,
Pounced on the meal of Mr. Fawkes,
    And quickly clear'd the table.

Scarce had we finish'd, when on high
The sun in cloudless majesty
    Shone forth on saint and sinner:
It really seem'd as if, in spite,
He only shone to bring to light
    That dark and guilty dinner.

And conscience-stricken off we flew,
To gain the boat ere yet in view
    The injured Fawkes appear'd;
And quickly as the dashing oars
Bore us from those unhallow'd shores,
    Straight for Cotele we steer'd.

The clouds in airy tumult fly,
And opening show a dappled sky —
    (An omen inauspicious);
And that bright sun-beam on the flood,
Which gilds the water, rocks, and wood,
    Is treacherous — not propitious.

Onward we go — the rapid tide
Lashes the vessel's painted side,
    And bubbles round the keel;
Whilst lovelier still the landscape grows,
Through which the mazy river flows,
    Which leads us to Cotele.

We land — and up the steep we climb,
To gain that ancient pile, where time
    Vainly asserts his rights;
We view those gloomy-vaulted halls,
The winding stairs, the tapestried walls,
    Fit haunt for ghosts and sprites.

In such a scene, 'tis not surprising
Our thoughts should turn to moralizing
    On fleeting earthly pleasure—
On human vanity and pride;   130
Though for such thoughts the ebbing tide
    Left us but little leisure.

As on our voyage homeward bent,
Some ominous presentiment
    Seem'd to oppress the party;
Flatter and flatter grew the jest,
Fainter the laugh, and lost the zest
    For punning and ecarté.

The hollow wind, midst rushes sighing,
Brushing the wave, the sea-mew flying—   140
    All shook our resolution;
For, thinking on that stolen repast,
We fear'd, whilst listening to the blast,
    The hour of retribution.

More loud and dread the storm approaches,
And gloomy twilight fast encroaches
    On the fair light of day;
Anxious we spread the fluttering sail,
But court in vain the changeful gale
    To speed us on our way.   150

That fatal dinner ill-digested,
With direful qualms the fair molested,
    Who, pale, despairing, lost,
Stretch'd on the deck await their doom,
Like roses, in their op'ning bloom,
    Nipt by untimely frost.

Awful to hear the wild wind raging,
And with the waves' dread warfare waging,
    As darker grows the night;
The blackening clouds in torrents pouring—   160

138 ecarté] Card game for two persons played with thirty-two cards.

When, lo! to cheer a scene so lowering,
    Behold a distant light.

The ladies from their lowly beds
Like drooping lilies raised their heads
    To hail that beam of hope;
So, when he first emits his ray,
Turns fondly to the lord of day
    His cherish'd Heliotrope.

That scene so dismal, dark, and dreary—
Ourselves so frighten'd, wet, and weary,
    Seems now a troubled dream;
Hope smiles where lately frown'd despair,
And joy assumes the place of fear,
    All by that magic gleam.

And nearer as the beacon blazes
Eager the weary seaman gazes,
    And briskly plies his oar;
Whilst we, despising dangers past,
Scorning the billows and the blast,
    Triumphant reach the shore.

But who shall paint the joyous faces,
The greetings, chidings, smiles, embraces,
    Which our return awaited!
The eager looks, the exclamations
Of anxious friends and dear relations
    At all we then narrated.—

MORAL

Learn hence, ye fair, on pleasure bent,
When guilt allures, that punishment
    Treads closely on his heel:
Not all that tempts the greedy eyes

---

168 His cherish'd Heliotrope] The flowers of the heliotrope turn to follow the sun.

Or hungry stomach 's lawful prize—
'Tis better starve than steal.

(1832)

---

* Quoted imprecisely from Thomas Gray, *The Bard, a Pindaric Ode* (1757) 2.2.72–76.

Epilogue*

And must I then—the fatal knot once tied—
Become the meek, submissive, pattern bride?
Forego the short-lived triumph of my sex,
Renounce the glorious privilege to vex—
To tease the teaser—to befool the wise,
And o'er the future tyrant—tyrannize?
Why—for the brief dominion of an hour
Should fate accord us weapons of such power?
Eyes darting fire—legions of conquering graces—
Squadrons of charms:—look, heroes, in our faces   10
And own yourselves the humblest of our slaves.
You smile assent—but you're such treacherous knaves,
There's something in your very smiles would say,
"We have our safety in the word—*obey*";
But if you hold us by this legal tether,
And fancy love and law can go together,
We may contrive such galling chains to loose,
And when you least expect it—slip the noose.
(Aside.) A friendly hint, dear ladies, in your ear,
Which, if you'll follow (husbands must not hear),   20
You still may rule them with despotic sway:
Always—in trifles—let them have their way.
On soups and *entrées*—bow to their opinion;
O'er dogs and horses—grant them full dominion;
Protest you think their arguments so clever
On game and corn-laws—you're convinced for ever.
Give them in politics no molestation,
But whilst you rule them—let them rule the nation.

Your tyrant thus deceived becomes your tool,
30   Still, though you rule him, never show you rule:
Rivals in love they naturally hate—
Rivals in power they cannot tolerate.
Who calls to order? How am I transgressing?
The ladies only, sir, I was addressing.
I see you tremble lest I go too far,
Encouraging revolt and civil war—
The fearful fruits of our emancipation—
Allow me then a word in explanation.
I dread, like you, reforms and revolutions,
40   'Tis to support established institutions,
As ancient as the siege of Troy, I speak—
The great Atrides was a Jerry Sneak.
Nay, I could cite, but that I dread to bore ye,
Examples without end from ancient story,
Occurrences as old as the creation,
Proving the rule of *man*—the innovation.
(Aside.) (But am I wise and prudent—on reflection—
Suing for public favour and protection,
One half my audience thus by taunts provoking.)
50   Believe me, gentlemen, I am only joking.
You know too well—howe'er we scorn and flout you,
We had all rather die than live without you.
Your praise we covet—your applause we prize,
E'en "as the light that visits these bright eyes."
Nay, *I*—with all my airs of domination
Claim at your hands one clap of approbation.
Be generous then, exceed the boon I ask,
And if you deem we well have done our task,
Let cheers and bravos echo from the walls,
60   To crown our triumph as the curtain falls.

(1834)

---

* This Epilogue is supposed to be spoken by a Coquette, who marries at the termination of a comedy, of which she is the heroine. *Frederic Mansel Reynolds.*

42 The great Atrides was a Jerry Sneak] Agamemnon, who, upon his return from Troy, was murdered by his wife's lover, Aegisthus, while his wife, Clytemnestra, killed his war prize, Cassandra. A "Jerry Sneak" is a henpecked husband.

Carolina, Baroness Nairne

(1766–1845)

Carolina, Baroness Nairne, was born in the Scottish Highlands, in Gask, Perthshire, on 16 August 1766, the third of six children. Her father was Laurence Oliphant, laird of Gask, and her mother was his first cousin, Margaret Robertson, eldest daughter of Duncan Robertson of Strowan, chief of the Clan Donnochy. Both were ardent Jacobites; they christened their daughter after Prince Charles Stuart and regaled her with stories of the Rebellions of 1715, in which her grandfather had taken part; both father and grandfather were veterans of the Rebellion of 1745. Her mother died when Carolina was eight.

Carolina's governess found that she learned well the practice of "ye needle, principles of religion, and loyalty, a good carriage, and talking tolerable good English."[1] Carolina was fond of dancing, painting, singing, and playing the harpsichord; she became known as "the Flower of Strathearn." Through visits to the poor at Gask she became familiar with the manners, customs of rural life, and speech patterns of the common people. She was among the first to recognize Burns's genius, and in 1786 she persuaded her brother Laurence to subscribe to his poems.

Early on, Carolina began rewriting the earthy words to traditional Scottish national songs with a view toward making them suitable for the drawing room. In 1792, when her father died, she was called upon to preside over her brother Laurence's house. At his accession to the estates, he entertained the Gask tenantry by singing Carolina's new version of the old Scottish song "The Ploughman"; though the author remained anonymous, the song was an immediate hit. "The Land o' the Leal," one of her most popular songs, dates from the time of her brother Charles's death in Paris in 1797 and the death a year later of the infant daughter of her best friend, Mary Ann Erskine Colquhoun, to whom she sent the song in a letter of condolence. To this early

---

1. Sarah Tytler and J. C. Watson, 2 vols., *The Songstresses of Scotland* (London, 1871), 2:115.

period before her marriage belong such comic songs as "John Tod" and "The Laird o' Cockpen" as well as many of her ardent Jacobite songs.

Captain William Murray Nairne, a landless Irishman nine years her senior and a second cousin, was a frequent visitor at Gask. In the spring of 1806 he was promoted to major and became assistant inspector-general of barracks in Scotland; this was the career advancement the couple had been long awaiting in order to marry. The bride was forty-one and the groom fifty when they took their vows on 2 June 1806 at the family home in Gask. Her uncle bought them a villa at Wester Duddingston, not far from Edinburgh, which they named Carolina Cottage. There Carolina gave birth to her only child, William Murray, in 1808. Carolina and her husband were also given the use of a house in town and later received a grant of royal apartments in Holyrood Palace. Even so, she did not participate in the lettered society of Edinburgh. She met Walter Scott infrequently, but no close friendship developed between them even though they came to be related by marriage. She appears not to have known Joanna Baillie, Anne Grant of Laggan, or Elizabeth Hamilton, who were all living nearby. Sir John Watson painted the famous portrait of the poet with her son sometime around 1817.

In 1821 Robert Purdie, a music publisher, decided to bring out a collection of national airs edited by R. A. Smith, with the lyrics sanitized for polite company. Under the assumed name of "Mrs. Bogan, of Bogan," Carolina Nairne joined with a group of women committed to "purifying" the national minstrelsy. Her contributions to the early parts of the *Scottish Minstrel* are signed "B.B." After a while, fearful of detection, she stopped signing her contributions; they appear in the later volumes as the work of "S.M." (for Scottish Minstrel) or of "unknown" authorship. She jealously guarded the secret of her authorship, even going so far as to alter her handwriting and to don a disguise to meet the publisher Robert Purdie. "I cannot help," she observed, "in some degree undervaluing beforehand what is said to be a feminine production."[2] To one of her few confidantes she confessed, "I have not even told Nairne lest he blab."[3] In the preface to the sixth and last volume, published in 1824, the editors remark that they "would have felt happy in being permitted to enumerate the many original and beautiful verses that adorn their pages, for which they are indebted to the author of the much-admired song, 'The Land of the Leal,' but they fear to wound a delicacy which shrinks from all

2. Ibid., 136.

3. [Margaret Stewart Simpson], *The Scottish Songstress: Caroline Baroness Naire* (Edinburgh, 1894), 6.

observation." Despite heated controversies in the newspapers concerning the identity of "B.B." and entreaties as late as the 1840s, Carolina Nairne refused to acknowledge that she had composed these works.

In return for surrendering their claim to their apartments in Holyrood Palace for King George IV's visit to Edinburgh in 1822, the authorities granted the Nairnes a lifetime annuity of three hundred pounds. The story may be apocryphal, but tradition has it that Lady Nairne's song "The At-tainted Scottish Nobles" was sung to the king during his visit and motivated him to seek the restoration of the Nairne title. In any case, in 1824 Major Nairne's peerage was restored, whereupon Carolina became known as Baron-ess Nairne. She devoted herself to educating her son until he was fifteen. On 9 July 1830 Lord Nairne died; Lady Nairne spent six months with relatives at Clifton, near Bristol, before moving her household to Ireland—to Kings-town, near Dublin, for a short time and then to Enniskerry, county Wicklow. She spent the summer of 1834 in Edinburgh and elsewhere in Scotland but left with her son in the autumn of 1834 for a tour of the Continent, visiting France, Italy, Switzerland, Germany, and Belgium. Her son fell victim to the influenza epidemic in the spring of 1837 and died early that December in Brussels, leaving the poet inconsolable.

Eventually she was persuaded to resume her Continental tour with her sister and niece; she did not return to Scotland until April 1842, when she went to live in Gask with her nephew, James Blair Oliphant, and his new wife. At the age of seventy-six she wrote "Would you be Young Again? So Would Not I." She died at Gask on 26 October 1845 at the age of seventy-nine, having guarded her literary anonymity to the grave. As a result, her songs were frequently attributed to Burns, Hogg, Ferrier, or Tannahill.[4]

Only a few family members and close friends knew of her authorship dur-ing her lifetime. But before she died she agreed to allow her songs to be collected and published in book form, on the condition that her name not be revealed, and she supplied some of her previously unpublished compositions. Shortly after her death, while the volume was still in press, her surviving sister gave permission for Lady Nairne's name to be published with her work; some of it had been written more than half a century earlier. The book was entitled *Lays from Strathearn, by Carolina, Baroness Nairne. Arranged with symphonies and accompaniments for the pianoforte, by Finlay Dun* and contained seventy of her songs. Later editions added others. T. L. Kingston Oliphant wrote a life of the poet, which was published in 1869 as *Life and Songs of the Baroness Nairne,*

4. Rev. George Henderson, *Lady Nairne and Her Songs,* enl. ed. (Paisley, [1905]), 9.

edited by Charles Rogers. Thomas Wilson Bayne, in his entry on Lady Nairne in the *Dictionary of National Biography,* maintains that

> her admirable command of lowland Scotch enabled her to write for the Scottish people, and her ease of generalisation gave breadth of significance to special themes. In her "Land o' the Leal," "Laird o' Cockpen," and "Caller Herrin," she is hardly, if at all, second to Burns himself. . . . Lady Nairne ranks with Hogg in her Jacobite songs, but in several she stands first and alone. Nothing in the language surpasses the exuberant buoyancy of her "Charlie is my darling," the swift triumphant movement of "The Hundred Pipers," and the wail of forlorn desolation in "Will ye no' come back again?" Excellent in structure, these songs are enriched by strong conviction and natural feeling. The same holds true of all Lady Nairne's domestic verses and occasional pieces.

While her Scottish evokes the flavor of working-class speech, it cannot help but betray the language patterns of a more privileged class that habitually spoke and wrote English. Nevertheless, some of Lady Nairne's songs continue to this day to be among the most popular in English, and Scots schoolchildren still enjoy her enduringly humorous satire of the pompous, self-important laird of Cockpen.

MAJOR WORK: *Lays from Strathearn, by Carolina, Baroness Nairne. Arranged with symphonies and accompaniments for the pianoforte, by Finlay Dun* (London, [1846]).

TEXTS USED: All texts from *The Modern Scottish Minstrel; or, The Songs of Scotland of the Past Half Century,* ed. Charles Rogers, vol. 1 (Edinburgh, 1855).

The Laird o' Cockpen*

Tune: "When she came ben, she bobbit."†

The Laird o' Cockpen he's proud and he's great,
His mind is ta'en up with the things o' the state;
He wanted a wife his braw house to keep,
But favour wi' wooin' was fashious to seek.

Down by the dyke-side a lady did dwell,
At his table-head he thought she'd look well;
M'Clish's ae daughter o' Claverse-ha' Lee,
A penniless lass wi' a lang pedigree.

His wig was weel pouther'd, and as gude as new;
His waistcoat was white, his coat it was blue;   10
He put on a ring, a sword, and cock'd hat,
And wha' could refuse the Laird wi' a' that?

He took the gray mare, and rade cannily—
And rapp'd at the yett o' Claverse-ha' Lee;
"Gae tell Mistress Jean to come speedily ben,
She's wanted to speak to the Laird o' Cockpen."

Mistress Jean was makin' the elder-flower wine,
"And what brings the Laird at sic a like time?"
She put aff her apron, and on her silk gown,
Her mutch wi' red ribbons, and gaed awa' down.   20

1 Laird] Lord, landed property owner, or chief.
3 braw] Fine.
4 fashious] Troublesome.
7 M'Clish's] Perhaps a whimsical reference to the "parish minister at Gask, who, in 1746, refused to pray for the family, and rode to Perth to bring on them the vengeance of the Duke of Cumberland. . . . She must often have heard her father deprecate the conduct of the heartless ecclesiastic" (Rogers, *Life and Songs,* 284).
7 ae] One.
13 cannily] Gently.
14 yett] Gate.
15 ben] Into the room.
18 sic] Such.
20 mutch] Headdress, cap.

And when she cam' ben, he bowed fu' low,
And what was his errand he soon let her know;
Amazed was the Laird when the lady said "Na";
And wi' a laigh curtsie she turned awa'.

Dumbfounder'd he was, nae sigh did he gie;
He mounted his mare—he rade cannily;
And aften he thought, as he gaed through the glen,
She's daft to refuse the Laird o' Cockpen.‡

(c. 1822)

* An older version of this song, entitled "Cockpen," belonged to the reign of
Charles II. For the earlier version of the song, see Cromek's *Select Songs of Scotland*
(1810) and Herd's *Scottish Songs* (1776); for a discussion of the possible identity of the
Laird of Cockpen, see Henderson, *Lady Nairne and Her Songs,* 55–56, 57n.

† When she came into the parlor, she curtsied.

‡ Susan Ferrier, the Scottish novelist, was rumored to have written the following
two stanzas, sometimes appended to "The Laird o' Cockpen," though she probably
was not the author (see Henderson, *Lady Nairne and Her Songs,* 55):

And now that the Laird his exit had made,
Mistress Jean she reflected on what she had said;
"Oh! for ane I'll get better, it's waur I'll get ten,
I was daft to refuse the Laird o' Cockpen."

Next time that the Laird and the Lady were seen,
They were gaun arm-in-arm to the kirk on the green;
Now she sits in the ha' like a weel-tappit° hen,   well laying (plump)
But as yet there's nae chickens appear'd at Cockpen.

24 laigh] Low.
25 gie] Give.

Caller Herrin'[*]

Wha'll buy caller herrin'?
They're bonnie fish and halesome farin';
Wha'll buy caller herrin',
New drawn frae the Forth?

When ye were sleepin' on your pillows,
Dream'd ye ought o' our puir fellows,
Darkling as they faced the billows,
A' to fill the woven willows.

   Buy my caller herrin',
   New drawn frae the Forth.   10

Wha'll buy my caller herrin'?
They're no brought here without brave daring;
Buy my caller herrin',
Haul'd thro' wind and rain.

   Wha'll buy caller herrin'? &c

Wha'll buy my caller herrin'?
Oh, ye may ca' them vulgar farin'!
Wives and mithers, maist despairin',
Ca' them lives o' men.

   Wha'll buy caller herrin'? &c   20

When the creel o' herrin' passes,
Ladies, clad in silks and laces,
Gather in their braw pelisses,
Cast their heads, and screw their faces.

   Wha'll buy caller herrin'? &c

1 caller] Fresh.
2 halesome] Healthful, wholesome.
4 the Forth] River in Scotland.

21 creel] Fish basket.
23 braw pelisses] Beautiful furs.

Caller herrin's no got lightlie;
Ye can trip the spring fu' tightlie;
Spite o' tauntin', flauntin', flingin',
Gow has set you a' a-singin'.

30   Wha'll buy caller herrin'? &c

Neebour wives, now tent my tellin',
When the bonny fish ye're sellin',
At ae word be in yer dealin'—
Truth will stand when a' thing's failin'.

Wha'll buy caller herrin'?
They're bonnie fish and halesome farin';
Wha'll buy caller herrin',
New drawn frae the Forth?

(c. 1822)

* Written to benefit Nathaniel Gow, musical composer and son of the violinist and composer Neil Gow, and dedicated to the duchess of Athole. The tune represents the chime of the bells of the Tron Kirk at Edinburgh. Both Philip Knapton and Charles Czerny arranged it for the pianoforte, and John Wilson's vocal renditions were well known (Rogers, *Life and Songs,* 282–83; idem, *Modern Scottish Minstrel,* 195).

29 Gow] Nathaniel Gow (1766–1831), Scots composer.
31 tent] Heed.
33 ae] One.

The Lass o' Gowrie*

Air—"Loch Erroch Side"

'Twas on a summer's afternoon,
A wee afore the sun gaed down,
A lassie, wi' a braw new gown,
    Cam' ower the hills to Gowrie.
The rose-bud, wash'd in summer's shower,
Bloom'd fresh within the sunny bower;
But Kitty was the fairest flower
    That e'er was seen in Gowrie.

To see her cousin she cam' there,
An', oh, the scene was passing fair!   10
For what in Scotland can compare
    Wi' the Carse o' Gowrie?
The sun was setting on the Tay,
The blue hills melting into gray;
The mavis' and the blackbird's lay
    Were sweetly heard in Gowrie.

Oh, lang the lassie I had woo'd!
An' truth and constancy had vow'd,
But cam' nae speed wi' her I lo'ed,
    Until she saw fair Gowrie.   20
I pointed to my faither's ha',
Yon bonnie bield ayont the shaw,
Sae loun' that there nae blast could blaw;
    Wad she no bide in Gowrie?

Her faither was baith glad and wae;
Her mither she wad naething say;

3 braw] Fine.
12 Carse] A stretch of flat fertile land near a river.
15 mavis'] Thrush.
22 bield ayont the shaw] Shelter beyond the birchen wood.
23 Sae loun'] So warm.
25 wae] Sorrowful.

The bairnies thocht they wad get play
　　If Kitty gaed to Gowrie.
　　She whiles did smile, she whiles did greet,
30　　The blush and tear were on her cheek;
　　She naething said, an' hung her head;
　　　But now she's Leddy Gowrie.
　　　　　　　　　(c. 1822)

*At least three other versions of this song exist—one published in 1797 by William Reid, of Glasgow, entitled "Kate o' Gowrie"; another by Dr. Thomas Lyle, who revised a work ascribed to Col. James Ramsay, of Stirling Castle; and a third by an unknown author, whose first two stanzas are almost identical to those of Lady Nairne.

John Tod *

He's a terrible man, John Tod, John Tod,
　　He's a terrible man, John Tod;
　　　He scolds in the house,
　　　He scolds at the door,
He scolds on the vera hie road, John Tod,
　　He scolds on the vera hie road.

The weans a' fear John Tod, John Tod,
　　The weans a' fear John Tod;
　　　When he's passing by,
10　　　The mithers will cry,—
Here's an ill wean, John Tod, John Tod,
　　Here's an ill wean, John Tod.

The callants a' fear John Tod, John Tod,
　　The callants a' fear John Tod;
　　　If they steal but a neep,

27 bairnies] Children.　　　　　　13 callants] Boys.
7 weans] Wee anes, or children.　　15 neep] Turnip.

The callant he'll whip,
And it's unco weel done o' John Tod, John Tod,
  It's unco weel done o' John Tod.

An' saw ye nae wee John Tod, John Tod?
  Oh, saw ye nae wee John Tod?   20
    His bannet was blue,
    His shoon maistly new,
An' weel does he keep the kirk road, John Tod,
  Oh, weel does he keep the kirk road.

How is he fendin', John Tod, John Tod?
  How is he wendin', John Tod?
    He's scourin' the land,
    Wi' his rung in his hand,
An' the French wadna frighten John Tod, John Tod,
  An' the French wadna frighten John Tod.   30

Ye're sun-brunt and batter'd, John Tod, John Tod
  Ye're tautit and tatter'd, John Tod;
    Wi' your auld strippit coul,
    Ye look maist like a fule,
But there's nouse i' the lining, John Tod, John Tod,
  But there's nouse i' the lining, John Tod.

He's weel respeckit, John Tod, John Tod,
  He's weel respeckit, John Tod;
    He's a terrible man,
    But we'd a' gae wrang   40
If e'er he sud leave us, John Tod, John Tod,
  If e'er he sud leave us, John Tod.

                (c. 1822)

17 unco] Uncommonly.
23 kirk] Church.
28 rung] Heavy staff, cudgel.

32 tautit] Rough, shaggy.
33 strippit coul] Striped nightcap.
35 nouse] Good sense.

* The protagonist of this song is said to be the Reverend John Tod, pastor of Ladykirk, Berwickshire. He married a daughter of Sir Patrick Home's, and their grandson
inherited the estate of Wedderburn. Lady Nairne was a friend of the Wedderburn
family, among whom stories of the great worth but uncouth manners of the minister of Ladykirk had been passed down (Rogers, *Life and Songs,* 295; Henderson, *Lady
Nairne and Her Songs,* 59).

The Land o' the Leal*

I'm wearin' awa', John,
Like snaw wreaths in thaw, John;
I'm wearin awa'
    To the land o' the leal.
There's nae sorrow there, John;
There's neither cauld nor care, John;
The day's aye fair
    I' the land o' the leal.

Our bonnie bairn's there, John;
10   She was baith gude and fair, John;
And, oh! we grudged her sair
    To the land o' the leal.
But sorrow's sel' wears past, John,
And joy's a-comin' fast, John—
The joy that's aye to last
    In the land o' the leal.

Sae dear's that joy was bought, John,
Sae free the battle fought, John,
That sinfu' man e'er brought
20   To the land o' the leal.
Oh, dry your glist'ning e'e, John!
My saul langs to be free, John;

4 leal] Land of the true-hearted or home of the faithful, i.e., heaven.
9 bairn's] Child.
11 sair] Sorely.

And angels beckon me
    To the land o' the leal.

Oh, haud ye leal and true, John!
Your day it's wearin' thro', John;
And I'll welcome you
    To the land o' the leal.
Now, fare ye weel, my ain John,
This warld's cares are vain, John;   30
We'll meet, and we'll be fain,
    In the land o' the leal.
    (wr. c. 1798; pub. c. 1822)

---

*The tune is said to date from the reign of James IV. The verse beginning "Sae dear's that joy was bought, John" (line 17) appears to have been composed some years after the other stanzas and reflects the poet's later religious convictions. In old age Lady Nairne said of this poem, "I wrote it merely because I liked the air so much, and I put these words to it, never fearing questions as to the authorship. However, a lady would know and took it down, and I had not Sir Walter's art of denying. I was present when it was asserted that Burns composed it on his death-bed, and that he had it *Jean* instead of 'John'; but the parties could not decide why it never appeared in his works, as his last song should have done. I never answered." During a visit to Edinburgh in 1834, she was entertained by a young lady who remarked before singing the song, "I am very fond of this air, and I am sure you will like it." Lady Nairne remained silent. The song was translated into Greek verse by the Reverend J. Riddell, fellow of Balliol College, Oxford (Rogers, *Life and Songs,* 35, 41, 48, 279–82).

25 haud] Hold.
31 fain] Joyful.

Caroline Norton

(1808–1877)

Caroline Elizabeth Sarah Sheridan Norton, one of seven children of Thomas and Caroline Henrietta Callander Sheridan, from the beginning seemed destined for fame. Richard Brinsley Sheridan was her paternal grandfather; her paternal grandmother was the soprano Elizabeth Linley; and her mother was the author of *Aims and Ends, Carwell,* and other novels well known in their time. Today she is best known as a political reformer who played a pivotal role in influencing the passage through Parliament of the Infants' Custody Bill (1839) and the Marriage and Divorce Act of 1857. But Norton was known in her own time not only as the author of important political pamphlets but as a poet, a fiction writer, an essayist, an editor, and a fashionable celebrity at the center of a major political scandal.

Caroline Norton was born in London on 22 March 1808, a year before her family lost its fortune in the Drury Lane Theatre fire. When she was only five, she and several of her siblings were sent to Scotland to live with her mother's family. Her parents went to live at the Cape of Good Hope for the health of her father, who was seriously ill, and so that he could assume the position of colonial secretary. When he died in 1817, her mother's fiction writing became the family's major source of income. Even so, Norton grew up in privileged surroundings, for the duke of York gave her mother apartments in Hampton Court Palace, and the family eventually moved to Great George Street, Westminster, for part of the year. She was sent for a short time to school at Wonersh, Surrey, and she published a *jeu d'esprit* entitled *The Dandies' Rout,* illustrated with her own drawings, at age thirteen. When she was introduced to London society in 1826, Thomas Moore was among her admirers, singling her out as "the handsomest of any."[1] He appreciated her Irish wit as much as her beauty and in 1831 dedicated to her his poem "Summer Fete."

---

1. See his diary entry for 31 May 1826 in *The Journals of Thomas Moore,* ed. Wilfred S. Dowden, 5 vols. (Newark, N.J., 1983), 3:943.

There was as much tragedy in Norton's life, however, as glitter. It began in the summer of 1827, when, at age nineteen, yielding to family pressure and the reality that she had no dowry, she married George Chapple Norton, a barrister M.P. for Guildford and the younger son of the first Lord Grantley. She regretted the marriage almost immediately. He was moody, violent, selfish, coarse, and childish, once setting fire to her writing materials to "discipline" her even though the family was supported mainly by her literary earnings. The realities of her public and private lives could not have been more different. To the world she was "the ornament of brilliant society."[2] Edward Bulwer Lytton, Samuel Rogers, Edward John Trelawny, Isaac Disraeli, Mary Shelley, and Lord Melbourne all attended Norton's salon at her home in Storey's Gate. The actress and author Frances Kemble described Norton at this period as a woman with "a deep, sweet, contralto voice" and

> an un-English character of beauty, her rather large and heavy head and features recalling the grandest Grecian and Italian models, to the latter of whom her rich coloring and blue-black braids of hair gave her an additional resemblance. . . . [She] was extremely epigrammatic in her talk, and comically dramatic in her manner of narrating things. I do not know whether she had any theatrical talent, though she sang pathetic and humorous songs admirably, and I remember shaking in my shoes when, soon after I came out, she told me she envied me, and would give anything to try the stage herself. I thought, as I looked at her wonderful, beautiful face, "Oh, if you should, what would become of me!"[3]

Mary Shelley told Trelawny, "I do not wonder at your not being able to deny yourself the pleasure of Mrs. Norton's society—I never saw a woman I thought so fascinating—Had I been a man I should certainly have fallen in love with her."[4] Privately, though, Norton was the victim of continuing mental and physical abuse from her husband.

Writing became Norton's refuge, and the world increasingly saw her as a major player on the literary stage. She had published anonymously in 1829 *The Sorrows of Rosalie. A Tale. With Other Poems,* praised by James Hogg;[5] according to Norton, "The first expenses of my son's life were defrayed from that first creation of my brain."[6] In 1830 she acknowledged on the title page her authorship of *The Undying One,* a poem based on the legend of the Wan-

2. *Fraser's Magazine* 3 (March 1831): 222.

3. See Kemble's *Records of a Girlhood* (New York, 1879), 174–75.

4. Letter dated 12 October 1835, in *The Letters of Mary Wollstonecraft Shelley,* ed. Betty T. Bennett, 3 vols. (Baltimore, 1980–88), 2:256.

5. In the *Noctes Ambrosianae* in *Blackwood's Edinburgh Magazine* 48 (April 1830), reprinted in 5 vols. (New York, 1863), 3:458.

6. *DNB.*

dering Jew and condemning corporeal punishment of children, the harsh educational system, and inhumane prison conditions. *Fraser's,* the *Edinburgh Review,* and the *New Monthly Magazine* all praised it.[7] In May of the following year, Covent Garden produced her play *The Gypsy Father.* In the early thirties she earned as much as fourteen hundred pounds a year publishing poems and prose works in the annuals, editing gift books such as the *English Annual* (1834–35), and editing *La Belle Assemblée; or, Bell's Court and Fashionable Magazine* (1832–37).

In June 1836 Norton's private misery was broadcast to the world in the most public way imaginable: George Norton filed a ten-thousand-pound lawsuit against the prime minister, Lord Melbourne, for allegedly committing adultery with his wife. He had originally encouraged his wife's friendship with Melbourne, then home secretary, who had helped him land a judgeship paying one thousand pounds a year in the Lambeth division of the Metropolitan Police courts. The jury threw the case out, never even asking the accused to testify. Many considered the suit a Tory ploy to unseat the prime minister, but it was the scandal of the year, and Caroline Norton paid the usual price of women caught in such a web — excoriating journalistic attacks on her character, including fabricated stories of adventures not only with Lord Melbourne but with other men as well. Worse than the assault on her reputation was the separation from her three sons — Fletcher, born in 1829, Thomas Brinsley, born in 1831, and William, born in 1833. George Norton, from whom she was never to be divorced, refused her all access to them. She discovered that she had no legal redress under English law. Even the most vicious and unprincipled husband had indisputable custody of minor children; moreover, George Norton, not she, owned the copyrights to her books and was entitled to keep her literary earnings as well as all her personal possessions, including her jewelry, clothing, books, and letters.

Outraged that her husband could legally keep her from seeing her children, Caroline Norton decided to change the law, tirelessly lobbying politically powerful friends, writing and circulating pamphlets such as *Observations on the Natural Claim of the Mother to the Custody of her Infant Children* (1837) and *A Plain Letter to the Lord Chancellor on the Infant Custody Bill* (1839). She wrote directly to the lord chancellor, to the queen, to every peer, to every member of Parliament, and to the *Times.* Thomas Noon Talfourd introduced in Parliament the Infant Custody Bill, and after a long and stormy debate it passed in 1839, granting women the right to apply to the courts for custody of their children. Eventually, after six years and the death of her youngest son, Nor-

7. *Fraser's Magazine* 3 (March 1831): 222; *Edinburgh Review* 53 (June 1831): 361–69; *New Monthly Magazine* 31 (January 1831): 180–83.

ton was able to be with the two remaining children for part of the year. Educated by her own suffering, Norton continued to publish more pamphlets, poems, and books of fiction to awaken the social consciousness of her readers. Her long poems, *A Voice from the Factories* (1836) and *The Child of the Islands* (1845), condemn child labor and argue for better living and working conditions for the poor. Her imaginative writing continued to earn respect. Henry Nelson Coleridge, in the *Quarterly Review,* called her the "Byron of our modern poetesses" and praised her sonnets as "worthy to be laid up in cedar with the best in our language."[8] Richard Hengist Horne thought her the equal of Elizabeth Barrett.[9] Many of her songs, some of which she set to music, enjoyed popularity, especially "I Do Not Love Thee;"[10] several of her poems, including "The Arab's Farewell to His Horse" and "Bingen on the Rhine," were standard anthology pieces well into the twentieth century.

In 1851 Norton's husband, having heard that her mother had left her a small legacy, terminated her allowance. In the ensuing dispute he learned that she had received a legacy from Lord Melbourne in 1848. Once more, this time in the pages of the *Times,* he accused her of adultery. Discovering that she had no legal right to her legacies, she determined once again to challenge the system. Her moving pleas for women's rights in pamphlets such as *English Laws for Women in the Nineteenth Century* (1854) and *A Letter to the Queen on Lord Chancellor Cranworth's Marriage and Divorce Bill* (1855) played a crucial role in the passage by Parliament of the Marriage and Divorce Act

---

8. "Modern English Poetesses," *Quarterly Review* 66 (September 1840): 376, 381. Later in the century, D. M. Moir would refine this judgment by saying that "in her tenderer moods she pitches on a key somewhat between Goldsmith and Rogers—with here the sunset glow of the first, and there the twilight softness of the latter: in her more passionate ones we have a reflex of Byron; but it is a reflex of the pathos, without the misanthropy of that great poet" (*Sketches of the Poetical Literature of the Past Half Century* [Edinburgh, 1851], 275).

9. Horne wrote, "The imagination of Mrs. Norton is chiefly occupied with domestic feelings and images, and breathes melodious plaints or indignations over the desecrations of her sex's loveliness; that of Miss Barrett often wanders amidst the supernatural darkness of Calvary sometimes with anguish and tears of blood, sometimes like one who echoes the songs of triumphal choirs. Both possess not only great mental energies, but that description of strength which springs from a fine nature, and manifests itself in productions which evidently originated in genuine impulses of feeling. The subjects they both choose appear spontaneous, and not resulting from study or imitation, though cast into careful moulds of art. The one records and laments the actual; the other creates and exults in the ideal. Both are excellent artists; the one in dealing with subjects of domestic interest; the other in designs from sacred subjects, poems of religious tendency, or of the supernatural world. Mrs. Norton is beautifully clear and intelligible in her narrative and course of thought and feeling; Miss Barrett has great inventiveness, but not an equal power in construction. The one is all womanhood; the other all wings" (*A New Spirit of the Age* [London, 1907], 338–43).

10. For a list of fifty-five of her songs see Jane Gray Perkins, *The Life of the Honourable Mrs. Norton* (New York, 1909), 300–301.

of 1857, allowing a woman to be treated as a legal entity distinct from her husband, with the right to own property, enter into contracts, sue, bequeath and inherit in her own right, and protect her earnings from the demands of her husband. An English divorce would now be more accessible, no longer requiring an act of Parliament. Although she did not consider herself a feminist, Caroline Norton probably accomplished more for women's legal rights in England than any other woman of her time. When Daniel Maclise painted a fresco in the House of Lords, he used Caroline Norton as the model for his depiction of Justice.

Like her poems, her four novels and many short stories reflect the realities of her own life, centering on loss and on love turned painful or tragic. Her women struggle to achieve their own identity in a patriarchal culture and are often betrayed or abandoned. But there are some notable exceptions. "The Lost Election," for example, is a witty and amusing political satire. Sometimes, as in her novel *Lost and Saved,* a rebellious "ruined" heroine goes on to live happily ever after, defying conventional wisdom. In the novel *Old Sir Douglas* Norton achieves literary revenge on her husband, portraying him as the selfish and brutish Kenneth Ross. Her last major poem was *The Lady of La Garaye,* published in 1861.

Norton's personal journey was not entirely bleak, though her own story has a plot worthy of fiction. (George Meredith, who admired Norton as a writer, used what was purported to be an incident in her life as an inspiration for *Diana of the Crossways* [1885]; Dickens is said to have based "Bardell vs. Pickwick" on the 1836 trial that made Norton the subject of controversy; and Tennyson is said to have used Norton as the prototype for his Princess Ida in *The Princess* [1847].) In 1870 Norton had the pleasure of seeing Parliament pass the Married Women's Property Act. In February 1875 George Norton died, and on 1 March 1877 Caroline Norton, aged sixty-nine, married her intimate friend of nearly thirty years, the Scottish historian Sir William Stirling-Maxwell. She died fourteen weeks later, on 15 June 1877.

MAJOR WORKS: *The Sorrows of Rosalie. A Tale. With Other Poems* (London, 1829); *The Undying One, and Other Poems* (London, 1830); *The Coquette, and Other Tales and Sketches, in Prose and Verse,* 2 vols. (London, 1835); *The Wife, and Woman's Reward,* 3 vols. (London, 1835); *A Voice from the Factories. In Serious Verse* (London, 1836); *Observations on the Natural Claim of the Mother to the Custody of her Infant Children* (London, 1837); *The Separation of Mother and Child by the Law of "Custody of Infants," Considered* (London, 1838); *A Plain Letter to the Lord Chancellor on the Infant Custody Bill* (London, 1839); *The Dream, and Other Poems* (London, 1840); *The Child of the Islands. A Poem* (London, 1845); *Stuart of Dunleath. A Story of Modern Times,* 3 vols. (London, 1847); *Tales and Sketches, in Prose and Verse* (London, 1850); *English Laws for Women in the Nineteenth*

Century (London, 1854); *A Letter to the Queen on Lord Chancellor Cranworth's Marriage and Divorce Bill* (London, 1855); *The Lady of La Garaye* (Cambridge, 1861); *Lost and Saved*, 3 vols. (London, 1863); *Old Sir Douglas*, 3 vols. (London, 1867).

EDITED WORKS: *Fisher's Drawing-Room Scrap-Book* (1846–49); *English Annual* (1834–35); *La Belle Assemblée; or, Bell's Court and Fashionable Magazine* (1832–37); *Keepsake* (1836).

TEXTS USED: Text of "I Do Not Love Thee" from *The Sorrows of Rosalie*. Texts of "The Faithless Knight," "We Have Been Friends Together," and "The Arab's Farewell to His Horse" from *The Undying One*, 2nd ed.

I Do Not Love Thee

I do not love thee!—no! I do not love thee!
And yet when thou art absent I am sad;
   And envy even the bright blue sky above thee,
Whose quiet stars may see thee and be glad.

I do not love thee!—yet, I know not why,
Whate'er thou dost seems still well done, to me—
   And often in my solitude I sigh—
That those I *do* love are not more like thee!

I do not love thee!—yet, when thou art gone
I hate the sound (though those who speak be dear)   10
   Which breaks the lingering echo of the tone
Thy voice of music leaves upon my ear.

I do not love thee!—yet thy speaking eyes,
With their deep, bright, and most expressive blue—
   Between me and the midnight heaven arise,
Oftener than any eyes I ever knew.

I *know* I do not love thee!—yet, alas!
Others will scarcely trust my candid heart;
   And oft I catch them smiling as they pass,
Because they see me gazing where thou art.   20

             (1829)

The Faithless Knight

The lady she sate in her bower alone,
And she gaz'd from the lattice window high,
Where a white steed's hoofs were ringing on,
With a beating heart, and a smother'd sigh.
Why doth she gaze thro' the sunset rays—
Why doth she watch that white steed's track—
While a quivering smile on her red lip plays?
'Tis her own dear knight—will he not look back?

The steed flew fast—and the rider past—
Nor paus'd he to gaze at the lady's bower;
The smile from her lip is gone at last—
There are tears on her cheek—like the dew on a flower!
And "plague on these foolish tears," she said,
"Which have dimm'd the view of my young love's track;
For oh! I am sure, while I bent my head,
It was then—it was *then* that my knight look'd back."

On flew that steed with an arrow's speed;
He is gone—and the green boughs wave between:
And she sighs, as the sweet breeze sighs through a reed,
As she watches the spot where he last has been.
Oh! many a sun shall rise and set,
And many an hour may she watch in vain,
And many a tear shall that soft cheek wet,
Ere that steed and its rider return again!

(1830)

We Have Been Friends Together

We have been friends together,
In sunshine and in shade;
Since first beneath the chesnut trees
In infancy we played.
But coldness dwells within thy heart,
A cloud is on thy brow;
We have been friends together—
Shall a light word part us now?

We have been gay together;
We have laughed at little jests;   10
For the fount of hope was gushing
Warm and joyous in our breasts.
But laughter now hath fled thy lip,
And sullen glooms thy brow;
We have been gay together—
Shall a light word part us now?

We have been sad together,
We have wept with bitter tears,
O'er the grass-grown graves, where slumbered
The hopes of early years.   20
The voices which are silent there
Would bid thee clear thy brow;
We have been *sad* together—
Oh! what shall part us now?

(1830)

The Arab's Farewell to His Horse

My beautiful! my beautiful! that standest meekly by
With thy proudly arched and glossy neck, and dark and fiery
　　eye;
Fret not to roam the desert now, with all thy winged
　　speed—
I may not mount on thee again—thou'rt sold, my Arab
　　steed!
Fret not with that impatient hoof—snuff not the breezy
　　wind—
The further that thou fliest now, so far am I behind;
The stranger hath thy bridle rein—thy master hath *his*
　　gold—
Fleet-limbed and beautiful! farewell!—thou'rt sold, my
　　steed—thou'rt sold!

Farewell! those free untired limbs, full many a mile must
　　roam,
To reach the chill and wintry sky, which clouds the stranger's
　　home;
Some other hand, less fond, must now thy corn and bed
　　prepare;
The silky mane I braided once, must be another's care!
The morning sun shall dawn again, but never more with
　　thee
Shall I gallop through the desert paths, where we were wont
　　to be:
Evening shall darken on the earth; and o'er the sandy plain
Some other steed, with slower step, shall bear me home
　　again.

Yes, thou must go! the wild free breeze, the brilliant sun and
　　sky,
Thy master's home—from all of these, my exiled one must
　　fly.
Thy proud dark eye will grow less proud, thy step become
　　less fleet,

And vainly shalt thou arch thy neck, thy master's hand to
    meet.   20
Only in sleep shall I behold that dark eye, glancing bright —
Only in sleep shall hear again that step so firm and light:
And when I raise my dreaming arm to check or cheer thy
    speed,
Then must I starting wake, to feel — thou'rt *sold,* my Arab
    steed!

Ah! rudely then, unseen by me, some cruel hand may chide,
Till foam-wreaths lie, like crested waves, along thy panting
    side:
And the rich blood, that is in thee swells, in thy indignant
    pain,
Till careless eyes, which rest on thee, may count each started
    vein.
Will they ill-use thee? If I thought — but no, it cannot be —
Thou art so swift, yet easy curbed; so gentle, yet so free.   30
And yet, if haply when thou'rt gone, my lonely heart should
    yearn —
Can the hand which casts thee from it now, command thee
    to return?

Return! — alas! my Arab steed! what shall thy master do,
When thou who wert his all of joy, hast vanished from his
    view?
When the dim distance cheats mine eye, and through the
    gath'ring tears
Thy bright form, for a moment, like the false mirâge appears.
Slow and unmounted will I roam, with weary foot alone,
Where with fleet step, and joyous bound, thou oft hast
    bourne me on;
And, sitting down by that green well, I'll pause and sadly
    think,
"It was *here* he bowed his glossy neck, when last I saw him
    drink!"   40

"When last I saw thee drink! — away! the fevered dream is
    o'er —

I could not live a day, and *know,* that we should meet no
  more!
They tempted me, my beautiful! for hunger's power is
  strong—
They tempted me, my beautiful! but I have loved too long.
Who said that I had given thee up? Who said that thou wert
  sold?
'Tis false—'tis false, my Arab steed! I fling them back their
  gold!
Thus, *thus,* I leap upon thy back, and scour the distant plains;
Away! who overtakes us now, shall claim *thee* for his pains!

                                                          (1830)

Henrietta O'Neill

(1758–1793)

Close friend and patron of both Charlotte Smith and Sarah Siddons, Henrietta O'Neill was the only daughter of Susanna Hoare and Charles Boyle, Viscount Dungarvan. In October 1777 she married the wealthy politician John O'Neill, nationalist representative to the Irish Parliament, of Shane's Castle, county Antrim. An actress, in 1780 she set up a private theater in her home, launched with her own prologue and epilogue.

O'Neill is the author of an epilogue to *Cymbeline* (in which she and Lord Edward Fitzgerald performed), published in *The Private Theatre of Kilkenny* (1825). At Charlotte Smith's request she composed "Ode to the Poppy," which Smith published in her novel *Desmond* (1792) and reprinted along with O'Neill's "Verses Written . . . on Seeing Her Two Sons at Play" in the second volume of *Elegiac Sonnets, and Other Poems* (1797).[1] In November 1793 the *Anthologia Hibernica* reprinted "Ode to the Poppy," having referred to it the previous month as "perhaps the most beautiful lyric production of the age."[2] It enjoyed considerable popularity and appears in many periodicals of the time.

When only eighteen, O'Neill befriended the struggling young actress Sarah Siddons, whom she discovered playing in Otway's *Venice Preserved* in Cheltenham. She encouraged her not only by praising her talent but also by giving her expensive clothes, supervising her wardrobe, and even sewing some of her costumes herself. Through her stepfather, Lord Bruce, she was responsible for bringing Siddons to Garrick's attention, thus launching Siddons's distinguished acting career. The two women were lifelong friends;

1. The sons were Charles-Henry-St. John, born on 22 January 1779, and John-Bruce-Richard, born on 30 December 1780.
2. The quotation appeared in vol. 2, p. 320. The poem was reprinted in vol. 2, pp. 384–85. The November issue also included "Verses on the Death of the Right Hon. Mrs. O'Neil," by Thomas Dermody.

in her account of a 1784 visit Siddons provides a description of O'Neill's home in Ireland, Shane's Castle, on the Antrim shore of Lough Neagh:

> Here were assembled all the talent and rank and beauty of Ireland. . . . It is scarce possible to conceive the splendour of this almost Royal Establishment, except by recollecting the circumstances of an Arabian Nights entertainment. . . . The table was servd with a profusion and elegance to which I have never known anything comparable. The side-boards [were] decorated with adequate magnificence, at which appeared several immense silver Flagons containing Claret. A fine band of musicians played during the whole of the repast. They were stationed in the Corridor which led from the dining room into a fine Conservatory, where we pluckd our desert from numerous trees of the most exquisite fruits, and where the waves of a superb Lake washd its feet while its cool delicious murmers were accompanyd with strains of celestial harmony from the Corridor.[3]

O'Neill traveled several times to Portugal for her health and died at the Caldas de Rainha, near Lisbon, on 3 September 1793; she was buried in the English Cemetery there, near the grave of Henry Fielding. Charlotte Smith said that losing her friend, whom she called "Harriet," was "a deprivation which has rendered *my* life a living death." In the second volume of her *Elegiac Sonnets,* Smith published a poem entitled "Verses, on the Death of the Same Lady, Written in September, 1794." There she observes,

> Wit, that no sufferings could impair,
> Was thine, and thine those mental powers
> Of force to chase the fiends that tear
> From Fancy's hands her budding flowers.[4]

Sarah Siddons told Annabella Milbanke, the future Lady Byron, that "Ode to the Poppy" was written

> by the friend of my early youth, who found me in obscurity, and who, gifted herself with extraordinary Talents, cherishd and encouraged them in others, with a generous warmth of feeling, peculiar to her own aimiable mind and exalted understanding. She finishd that Lovely Poem in her Sick bed, while I sat by her anxiously watching every turn and change, of that countenance whose radient intelligence the united attacks of Sickness, pain, and Sorrow,

3. Sarah Kemble Siddons, *The Reminiscences of Sarah Kemble Siddons, 1778–1785,* ed. William Van Lennep (Cambridge, 1942), 27–28.

4. The lady in the title was clearly O'Neill, for it followed a poem titled "Verses Written by the Same Lady on Seeing Her Two Sons at Play," which followed "Ode to the Poppy. Written by a Deceased Friend." Smith also published "Sonnet . . . Sent to the Honorable Mrs. O'Neill, with Painted Flowers" in later editions of *Elegiac Sonnets.*

could not diminish; in compliance with her desire I corrected some little mistakes, occasiond by the uneasy position in which she was obligd to write it: . . . If it is not arrogant to say so, She lovd me while She had life and while I live, her memory will be most dear and sacred to me. I cannot define the feeling that took possession of my mind, upon seeing the beginning of that Ode copied by your hand [in a letter to Siddons], or the comparison it led me to make between you. She was wonderfully endowd with mental power, She was young, and lovely, and belovd; here thank God the comparison ends! for She was unhappy. May God preserve you my sweet young friend from the errors and misfortunes of an exalted but misguided imagination!!![5]

Although few of O'Neill's poems survive, the British Library owns two in manuscript: "Ambrosia Breathes in Every Sigh" and "To a Lady Who Requested the Description of a Gentleman," beginning "Sweet Ann revoke thy vain request."[6] Leigh Hunt mentions her in "Specimens of British Poetesses," snidely suggesting that she and Charlotte Smith were both opium addicts.[7] Her husband, made a baron shortly after her death and a viscount three years later, died fighting against insurgents in the Irish Rebellion of 1798.

TEXT USED: "Ode to the Poppy" from Charlotte Smith's novel *Desmond* (London, 1792).

5. Quoted in Malcolm Elwin, *Lord Byron's Wife* (New York, 1963), 80–81.
6. The latter is a copy made after the poet's death, shelfmark BL 37934, f. 92.
7. In Hunt's *Men, Women, and Books: A Selection of Sketches, Essays, and Critical Memoirs from his Uncollected Prose Writings* (London, 1847).

Ode to the Poppy

Not for the promise of the labor'd field,
Not for the good the yellow harvests yield,
    I bend at Ceres' shrine;
  For dull, to humid eyes appear,
  The golden glories of the year;
Alas!—a melancholy worship's mine!

I hail the Goddess for her scarlet flower!
    Thou brilliant weed,
    That dost so far exceed,
10   The richest gifts gay Flora can bestow;
Heedless I pass'd thee, in life's morning hour,
    (Thou comforter of woe,)
'Till sorrow taught me to confess thy power.

    In early days, when Fancy cheats,
     A various wreath I wove;
    Of laughing springs luxuriant sweets,
     To deck ungrateful love:
    The rose, or thorn, my numbers crown'd,
    As Venus smil'd, or Venus frown'd;
20   But Love, and Joy, and all their train, are flown;
    E'en languid Hope no more is mine,
    And I will sing of thee alone;
Unless, perchance, the attributes of grief,
    The cypress bud, and willow leaf,
Their pale, funereal foliage, blend with thine.

    Hail, lovely blossom!—thou can'st ease,
    The wretched victims of disease;
Can'st close those weary eyes, in gentle sleep,
    Which never open but to weep;
30   For, oh! thy potent charm,
    Can agonizing pain disarm;

---

3 Ceres'] Ceres was the Roman goddess of corn or of the earth and its fertility; known as
Demeter in Greek mythology, she was widely worshipped as an earth-mother figure.

Expel imperious memory from her seat,
And bid the throbbing heart forget to beat.

Soul-soothing plant!—that can such blessings give,
   By thee the mourner bears to live!
    By thee the hopeless die!
   Oh! ever "friendly to despair,"
   Might sorrow's palid votary dare,
Without a crime, that remedy implore,
Which bids the spirit from its bondage fly,   40
I'd court thy palliative aid no more;
   No more I'd sue, that thou shouldst spread,
   Thy spell around my aching head,
   But would conjure thee to impart,
   Thy balsam for a broken heart;
   And by thy soft Lethean power,
    (Inestimable flower)
Burst these terrestrial bonds, and other regions try.

(1792)

46 Lethean power] In classical mythology, the Lethe was a river in the underworld. Drinking its waters brought forgetfulness.

Amelia Opie
(1769–1853)

Amelia Opie, the only child of Amelia Briggs and her physician husband James Alderson, was born on 12 November 1769 in Norwich, where she was to grow up and spend almost all her long life. Her mother, an invalid, taught her courage and sympathy. When the child recoiled from a skeleton, she encouraged her to hold it in her lap and to play with it. When the skin color of a black footman frightened her, her mother recounted "the sad tale of negro wrongs and negro slavery" and had the child make friends with the man.[1] Amelia's fear of two mentally ill women was met by the insistence that she shake hands with one and give money to the other. She not only conquered her fears but came to be fascinated by those living on the margins of society; eventually they would inhabit her writings. Her father, who treated four hundred patients a week, many of them poor, also taught her compassion.

Opie had no formal education, but she was trained in dancing, drawing, and music. Her singing was said to be unusually appealing and distinctive. She also learned French, a language in which she would eventually become fluent. The writings of William Hayley and Madame de Genlis were among the favorites of Opie and her mother, who frequently read together.

Opie's childhood ended abruptly with her mother's death on 31 December 1784. Although Opie was only fifteen, she stepped into her mother's shoes, managing her father's household, entertaining, and accompanying her father to the theater and to the weekly balls and cotillions of Norwich. Her powerful devotion to her father became the overriding force in her life. Mrs. Taylor, wife of John Taylor, the Norwich yarnmaker, and a highly intelligent older woman, became her mentor and adviser. Through her father and the Taylors she met the literary circle of Norwich, then a provincial center of culture. When she sent her poems to John Aikin for his opinion and recommenda-

---

1. Margaret Eliot Macgregor, *Amelia Alderson Opie: Worldling and Friend*, Smith College Studies in Modern Languages 14, no. 1–2 (Northhampton, Mass., 1933), 4.

tions, he told his sister, Anna Letitia Barbauld, " 'The Virgin's First Love' is indeed a very pretty idea, and in some parts beautifully worked up; but I want a *finished piece* from this clever lass." [2] Opie eventually published this poem, along with some others, in the *Cabinet*, signing her contributions "N." [3] Three plays also are among Opie's early experiments in writing. *Adelaide*, a verse tragedy set in Paris, was produced in 1791 in the private Norwich theater of Anne Plumptre and her sister Annabella but was never printed. Opie's first book-length publication was an anonymous novel, *The Dangers of Coquetry*, brought out in two volumes by W. Lane (1790). Even though Prince Hoare considered dramatizing it, it attracted almost no attention. The *Critical Review* noted, "The moral to be drawn from this work is so good, that we are blind to the dulness, the insipidity, and improbability of the narrative." [4]

It was Opie's habit to visit the assizes in Norwich, for she relished the drama of a courtroom. In 1794 in London she attended the treason trials of Thomas Hardy, John Horne Tooke, and John Thelwall, partly because she shared her father's ardent republicanism and partly because he had said that if the prisoners were convicted, he would emigrate to America. It was rumored that Opie walked up to Tooke after his acquittal and kissed him, but she denied it. She spent so much time in London with Elizabeth Inchbald, Thomas Holcroft, and William Godwin that rumors circulated of a ménage à quatre. Opie recorded that according to Elizabeth Inchbald, "the report of the world is, that Mr. Holcroft is in love with her, *she* with Mr. Godwin, Mr. Godwin with *me*, and I am in love with Mr. Holcroft!" [5] It may have been that both Godwin and Holcroft were in love with Opie, though the suggestion that Godwin proposed marriage is almost certainly incorrect. [6] Holcroft apparently did, but with no success. Opie appears to have had a long and discreet affair with an older married man, possibly the J. Boddington of Southgate whose home she visited frequently during the 1790s. [7] During her London visits she also spent time with Sarah Siddons, Anna Letitia Barbauld, and, in 1796, Mary Wollstonecraft, who became a close friend.

2. Mary E. Martin, *Memoirs of Seventy Years* (London and New York, 1883), 73–74.

3. See Macgregor, *Amelia Alderson Opie*, 12, for a catalog of fifteen Opie poems published in the *Cabinet*. Macgregor includes an inventory of other periodical publications on 132–33.

4. 70 (1790): 339.

5. Cecilia Lucy Brightwell, *Memorials of the Life of Amelia Opie, Selected and Arranged from her Letters, Diaries, and Other Manuscripts* (Norwich, 1854).

6. See William St. Clair, *The Godwins and the Shelleys* (Baltimore, 1989), 164; and Todd, *Dictionary*.

7. See Donald J. Reiman, introduction to Opie's *Elegy to the Memory of the Late Duke of Bedford Written on the Evening of His Interment*, ed. Reiman (New York, 1978), vi; and Julia Kavanagh, *English Women of Letters: Biographical Sketches*, 2 vols. (London, 1863), 2:245–46.

In 1797 Amelia met John Opie, an acclaimed painter and a self-educated man, son of a Cornish carpenter. James Northcote once said of John Opie, "While other artists painted to live, Opie lived to paint."[8] They married on 8 May 1798 and went to live at 8 Berners Street, London. Even though he made the impressive sum of nearly one thousand pounds a year, the couple continued to live nearly as frugally as he had before his marriage. With his encouragement (motivated in part by his desire to reconcile her to a less active social life), she set about attempting to earn a reputation as an author. "Knowing at the time of our marriage that my most favourite amusement was writing, he did not check my ambition to become an author," she said; "on the contrary he encouraged it, and our only quarrel was not that I wrote too much, but that I did not write more and better."[9]

In 1801 Opie published with Davis, Wilks, and Taylor *The Father and Daughter, a Tale in Prose,* accompanied by some poems, including "The Maid of Corinth." Unlike her first book, this one, dedicated to her father, bore her name on the title page and was a huge success. Walter Scott said it made him weep, and the novel was widely acclaimed for its pathos. It had gone through ten editions by 1844, was translated into French and Portuguese, and was the basis for one of the most popular Italian operas of the time, Paer's *Agnese,* and for a five-act comedy entitled *Smiles and Tears* by Frances Kemble's mother, Maria Theresa deCamp Kemble. Opie's hero, Agnes, runs off and is seduced and then abandoned; she returns home to find her father literally gone mad as a result of her actions. For the powerful emotional landscape of the novel, Opie clearly drew on her own worst fears and anxieties, separated as she was, for the first time in her life, from her own father.

The following year, she brought out *Elegy to the Memory of the Late Duke of Bedford; Written on the Evening of his Interment,* published by Longmans. Donald J. Reiman has called it "her masterpiece—a moving poem of great structural and symbolic sophistication."[10] Another volume, simply titled *Poems,* was published in 1802 by Taylor and Wilks. Despite reservations, in the first issue of the *Edinburgh Review* Dr. Thomas Brown lauded the "uncommon elegance" of "the tender song of sentiment and pathos."[11] According to the *Critical Review,* Opie was in the same league as Charlotte Smith, Anna Seward, and Anna Letitia Barbauld.[12] Sir James Mackintosh, writing from India, said of "Go, Youth Beloved," one of the lyrics in the volume, "Tell the fair Opie

---

8. John Jope Rogers, *Opie and His Works* (Truro, 1878), 34.

9. Brightwell, *Memorials,* 70.

10. See Reiman, introduction, xv.

11. 1 (October 1802): 114.

12. 36 (1802): 413–18.

that if she would address such pretty verses to me . . . I think she might bring me back from Bombay." Several years later, at the Royal Institution, Sydney Smith, in one of his lectures on moral philosophy, applauded the same lyric for illustrating "the true language of nature and of feeling."[13] "Go, Youth Beloved" continued to be a favorite anthology piece throughout the next century. Opie was now a literary celebrity in London. Henry Crabb Robinson records that "titled folk, and learned folk, and rich folk" noticed and courted her, and her drawing room was filled with "poets, painters, players, playwriters, members of parliament, titled men and women, beauties, and fine ladies."[14]

In August 1802, during the Peace of Amiens, when France was once again open to British travelers, the Opies visited Paris with Anne Plumptre and others to see the effects of the revolution and to examine the art newly deposited at the Louvre. There Opie spent time with Benjamin West, Charles James Fox, General Kosciusko, and Helen Maria Williams. In 1804 Opie published her most ambitious novel, *Adeline Mowbray; or, The Mother and Daughter.* Although it is not strictly biographical, the main characters are based loosely on Mary Wollstonecraft and William Godwin, and the plot concerns Adeline's attempt to live according to Godwin's early idealistic views. Harriet Westbrook gave a copy to Percy Bysshe Shelley in her successful effort to convince him to marry her. The book ostensibly shows the error of cohabitation without marriage, but some contemporary commentators noticed that Adeline was happiest when she and Glenmurray were unmarried lovers. When she obeys his dying wish and marries, her life becomes a nightmare. The reviewer for the *Critical Review* observed, "What we have to object to are the fascinating colours thrown over the erroneous virtues of Adeline and Glenmurray, 'making . . . vice, more dangerous by giving it an air of respectability.' "[15] Mackintosh said that "it may as well be taken to be a satire on our prejudices in favour of marriage as on the paradoxes of sophists against it."[16] The *Monthly Review* praised the book's design and execution, and the *Edinburgh Review* called the second volume "perhaps the most pathetic and most natural in its pathos of any fictitious narrative in the language."[17] In the spring of 1805 Opie brought out a volume called *Simple Tales.* The *Edinburgh*

13. Quoted in Brightwell, *Memorials,* 87; and Sydney Smith, *Elementary Sketches on Moral Philosophy,* 2nd ed. (London, 1850), 156, respectively.

14. Macgregor, *Amelia Alderson Opie,* 36.

15. 3rd ser., 4 (1805): 219–21.

16. Robert James Mackintosh, ed., *Memoirs of the Life of the Right Honourable Sir James Mackintosh,* 2 vols. (London, 1835), 1:255.

17. *Edinburgh Review* 8 (1806): 465; *Monthly Review* 51 (1806): 320–21.

Review noticed similarities to *Adeline Mowbray,* observing "the same truth and delicacy of sentiment; the same graceful simplicity in the dialogue . . . and the same happy art of presenting ordinary feelings and occurrences in a manner that irresistibly commands our sympathy and affection. Mrs. Opie has no great share of invention, either in incident or in character. We often see through the whole story from its first opening; and few of her personages can be said to be original, or even uncommon. . . . however . . . they are strictly true to general nature, and are rarely exhibited, except in interesting situations."[18] The *Critical Review* called the tales tedious and insipid and suggested that Opie had either written the *Edinburgh Review* article herself or had had a friend do it.[19]

Meanwhile, as Amelia Opie's writing career was reaching its pinnacle, so was her husband's. Their mutually supportive relationship had a great deal to do with the success of each. Friends told John Opie that his "representation of female beauty" had improved considerably thanks to Amelia's influence; he painted at least ten portraits of his wife. When John Opie was elected professor of painting at the Royal Academy, he agreed to deliver lectures on his art. From September to February he painted feverishly during the day and wrote at night, delivering several well-received lectures from mid-February to early March. He fell ill a few days after the last one and died on 9 April 1807. John Opie was buried in St. Paul's Cathedral; his funeral was a public pageant.

Amelia Opie sold the house in Berners Street, auctioned off many of her husband's paintings, and returned to a quiet life in Norwich near her father. John Opie had left her completely independent, with an estate worth ten thousand pounds. In 1808 she published *The Warrior's Return, and Other Poems,* which was praised by the *Gentleman's Magazine* for "originality and polished meter, animated by the genuine fire of the Poet," and panned by the *Universal Magazine* as "the refuse of her writing desk."[20] Meanwhile, she was composing a memoir of her husband to accompany her edition of his lectures, published in 1809. The critics were harsh. William Hazlitt said "that nobody but Mrs. Opie" would have thought to publish the lectures, and Mary Russell Mitford said of the memoir, "Dead angels are common enough."[21] In 1812 she published *Temper,* which most reviewers agreed was not as successful as

18. *Edinburgh Review* 8 (1806): 465–71.

19. 3rd ser., 8 (1806): 443–46.

20. *Gentleman's Magazine* 78 (July 1808): 612; *Universal Magazine,* n.s., 9 (April 1808): 306.

21. Hazlitt is quoted in Macgregor, *Amelia Alderson Opie,* 50; Mitford in A. G. K. L'Estrange, *The Life of Mary Russell Mitford,* 2 vols. (New York, 1870), 1:81.

Opie's earlier fiction. Her next effort, *Tales of Real Life* (1813), written for young readers, was more highly regarded.

In 1813 Opie met Germaine de Staël in London and became engaged to Lord Herbert Stuart, second son of John, fourth earl of Bute; however, she broke the engagement. During her yearly London visits she met Byron, Keats, Wordsworth, Scott, Southey, Caroline Lamb, Hannah More, Charles Lamb, and others. At home in Norwich, she spent eight to ten hours a day writing. Her didactic tale *Valentine's Eve* (1816) was not well received. Joseph John Gurney objected that it alluded to "adultery, seduction . . . a house of ill fame, things not to be named, especially by a woman," and that she was "making the minds of young women *impure.*"[22] In 1818 she published *New Tales,* translated into French the same year. One of the tales, "The Ruffian Boy," was dramatized and produced by Edward Fitzball, first in Norwich and later in London, at the Surrey Theatre and later at Drury Lane.[23] In 1820 Opie brought out *Tales of the Heart.* The increasingly didactic nature of her fiction owes much to her developing relationship with Joseph Gurney, a humorless Quaker leader nineteen years her junior, who worked to convert Opie to his faith and with whom she seems to have had a serious romance. In the end, though, she urged him to marry someone else.

When James Alderson fell ill in December 1820, Opie devoted all of her time to caring for him. Her isolation and loneliness, the prospect of losing her father, and the pressure of the Gurney family led her to more serious religious questioning. She published several fictional works anonymously during this period— *The Only Child* (1821), *Much to Blame* (1824), and possibly *Self-Delusion; or, Adelaide D'Hauteroche* (1823).[24] *Madeline* (1822), an epistolary love story, was published under her own name. This vacillation about acknowledging her fiction reflects her ambivalence during this period about embracing the tenets of the Society of Friends. Another novel, *The Painter and his Wife,* though advertised by the publisher, was never finished, for Opie abandoned it, as she had abandoned her family's Unitarianism, when she decided in 1824 to join the Society of Friends, whose meetings she had been attending for

22. Macgregor, *Amelia Alderson Opie,* 65.

23. The play was renamed *Gerald Durald, the Bandit of Bohemia* for the Drury Lane production of 8 September 1821 (ibid., 68–69).

24. Opie acknowledged *The Only Child* to be hers in an unpublished letter dated 21 June 1839 to Sir John Gurney, in the possession of the editor. Peter Garside has suggested in a letter to me, I believe accurately, that the unnamed anonymous novel that Opie acknowledges as hers and describes in this letter is *Much to Blame* (1824). *Self-Delusion* is attributed to Opie in a review of the book in the *Ladies' Monthly Museum* 18 (1823): 220–22, 284.

a decade. Her father died on 20 October 1825, only a few months after the Quakers accepted her into membership.

To assuage her grief Opie turned to the devotional poetry of Felicia Hemans and Anna Letitia Barbauld and set about doing good works such as visiting the poor, the sick, the imprisoned, the homeless, and the mentally ill. After her conversion her literary popularity waned. *Illustrations of Lying, in All its Branches* (1825) and *Detraction Displayed* (1828), both published by Longmans, were highly didactic and not generally well received, although the former was widely reprinted in America. Catharine Maria Sedgwick noted that the "elaborate simplicity and the fashionable little train to her pretty satin gown indicated how much easier it is to adopt a theory than to change one's habits."[25] But Opie's conversion was genuine. She now wrote to educate youngsters about the injustices of slavery and brought out *The Negro Boy's Tale, a Poem, Addressed to Children* (1824) and *The Black Man's Lament; or, How to Make Sugar* (1826), both published by Harvey and Darton. When Opie returned to Paris in June 1829, the first time in a quarter-century, she got to know her childhood hero, the marquis de Lafayette. On a trip the next year, she met James Fenimore Cooper and Madame de Genlis. In 1832 she sold her home and for the following decade traveled extensively, to Cornwall, John Opie's home, as well as to Scotland, Belgium, Switzerland, France, and Germany. In 1834 she brought out *Lays for the Dead,* poems in memory of lost friends and relatives; the *Monthly Review* said that little could be said in its favor but that some of the pieces were "very sweet and tender."[26] In 1840 Opie attended the antislavery convention; she appears in Benjamin Robert Haydon's painting of the delegates, now in the National Portrait Gallery, London. In May 1851 she attended the Great Exhibition in London, where she saw Mary Berry, also in a wheelchair. She was seventy-nine years old, but she had not lost her sense of fun and jokingly challenged Berry to a chair race.

After a trip to Cromer in September 1852, Opie became ill and never left her house again. She died on 2 December 1853. For nearly a week afterwards her body lay in state in her drawing room surrounded by portraits of Lafayette, Sarah Siddons, Germaine de Staël, James Fenimore Cooper, and others she had known and admired. She was buried in the Friends' cemetery in Norwich, in the same grave as her father.

MAJOR WORKS: *The Dangers of Coquetry, A Novel,* 2 vols. (London, 1790); *The Father and Daughter, a Tale in Prose: With an Epistle from the Maid of Corinth to her Lover; and*

25. *DNB.*
26. N.s., 2 (1834): 538.

Other Poetical Pieces (London, 1801); *Elegy to the Memory of the Late Duke of Bedford; Written on the Evening of his Interment* (London, 1802); *Poems* (London, 1802); *Adeline Mowbray; or, the Mother and Daughter, A Tale,* 3 vols. (London, 1804); *Simple Tales,* 4 vols. (London, 1806); *The Warrior's Return, and Other Poems* (London, 1808); *Temper; or, Domestic Scenes, a Tale,* 3 vols. (London, 1812); *Tales of Real Life,* 3 vols. (London, 1813); *Valentine's Eve,* 3 vols. (London, 1816); *New Tales,* 4 vols. (London, 1818); *Tales of the Heart,* 4 vols. (London, 1820); *The Only Child; or, Portia Bellenden. A Tale* (London, 1821); *Madeline, a Tale,* 2 vols. (London, 1822); possibly *Self-Delusion; or, Adelaide D'Hauteroche: A Tale,* 2 vols. (London, 1823); *Much to Blame, A Tale,* 3 vols. (London, 1824); *The Negro Boy's Tale, a Poem, Addressed to Children* (London, 1824); *Illustrations of Lying, in All its Branches,* 2 vols. (London, 1825); *Tales of the Pemberton Family; for the Use of Children* (London, 1825); *The Black Man's Lament; or, How to Make Sugar* (London, 1826); *Detraction Displayed* (London, 1828); *Happy Faces; or, Benevolence and Selfishness, and The Revenge* (London, [1830?]); *Lays for the Dead* (London, 1834); *Lines to the Memory of John Cubitt, Rector of Overstrand* (Norwich, [1842]).

TEXTS USED: Texts of "Ode: Written on the Opening of the Last Campaign" and "Allen Brooke, of Windermere" from the *Cabinet* 1 (1795): 309–10 and 2 (1795): 317–18, respectively, signed "N." Texts of "Stanzas Written under Aeolus's Harp," "Song (I know you false)," "Song (Go, youth beloved)," and "The Despairing Wanderer" from the 2nd ed. of *Poems* (London, 1803). Text of "An Evening Walk at Cromer, 1791" from *The Annual Anthology,* 2 vols. (Bristol, 1799–1800), 2:131–33.

Ode: Written on the Opening of the Last Campaign[*]

> Spring! thy impatient bloom restrain,
> Nor wake so soon thy genial pow'r,
> For, deeds of death must hail thy reign,
> And clouds of fate around thee low'r.
> Alas! not all thy store of charms
> For patriot hearts can comfort find,
> Or lull to peace the dread alarms
> Which rack the friends of human kind.
> In vain thy balmy breath to me
> Scents with its sweets the ev'ning gale;   10
> In vain the violet's charms I see,
> Or fondly mark thy primrose pale.
> To me thy softest zephyrs breathe,

Of sorrow's soul-distracting tone,
To me thy most attractive wreath
Seems ting'd with human blood alone.
Arrest thy steps, thou source of love,
Thou genial friend of joy and life!
Let not thy smile propitious prove
20   To works of carnage, scenes of strife.
Bid Winter all his frowns recall,
And back his icy footsteps trace;
Again the soil in frost enthrall,
And check the War-fiend's murd'rous chace.
Ah, fruitless pray'r! thy hand divine
MUST on the teeming season lead,
And (contrast dire!) at War's red shrine
Must bid unnumber'd victims bleed.
But not in vain—if on this hour
30   The fate of Freedom shall depend—
If o'er this earth th' Eternal Pow'r
The scale of Justice now extend.
For then, O Spring, thy sun shall see
The patriot flame triumphant shine;
GALLIA shall bid the world be free,
And WAR his blood-stain'd throne resign!

(1795)

---

* Opie published this poem anonymously in the *Cabinet,* 3 vols. (Norwich, 1795), 1:309–10, signing herself "N."

Stanzas Written under Aeolus's Harp[*]

Come, ye whose hearts the tyrant sorrows wound;
Come, ye whose breasts the tyrant passions tear,
And seek this harp, ... in whose still-varying sound
Each woe its own appropriate plaint may hear.

Solemn and slow yon murmuring cadence rolls,
Till on the attentive ear it dies away, ...
To your fond griefs responsive, ye, whose souls
O'er loved lost friends regret's sad tribute pay.

But hark! in regular progression move
Yon silver sounds, and mingle as they fall;   10
Do they not wake thy trembling nerves, O Love,
And into warmer life thy feelings call?

Again it speaks; . . . . but, shrill and swift, the tones
In wild disorder strike upon the ear:
Pale Phrensy listens, ... kindred wildness owns,
And starts appalled the well known sounds to hear:

Lo! e'en the gay, the giddy and the vain
In deep delight these vocal wires attend, ...
Silent and breathless watch the varying strain,
And pleased the vacant toils of mirth suspend.   20

So, when the lute on Memnon's statue hung
At day's first rising strains melodious poured
Untouched by mortal hands, the gathering throng
In silent wonder listened and adored.

But the wild cadence of these trembling strings
The enchantress Fancy with most rapture hears;

21 So, when the lute on Memnon's statue hung] A colossal statue of the Egyptian king
Amenophis near Thebes was looked upon by the Greeks as a statue of Memnon, the son of Eos,
who in the *Odyssey* and Hesiod slew Antilochus, the son of Nestor, at Troy. Made of black stone,
the statue depicts a sitting figure, its feet close together and its hands leaning on its seat. When
the rays of the sun hit the statue, it produced a sound resembling that of a breaking chord.

At the sweet sound to grasp her wand she springs,
And lo! her band of airy shapes appears!

She, rapt enthusiast, thinks the melting strains
30   A choir of angels breathe, in bright array
Bearing on radiant clouds to yon blue plains
A soul just parted from its silent clay.

And oft at eve her wild creative eye
Sees to the gale their silken pinions stream,
While in the quivering trees soft zephyrs sigh,
And through the leaves disclose the moon's pale beam.

O breathing instrument! be ever near
While to the pensive muse my vows I pay;
Thy softest call the inmost soul can hear,
40   Thy faintest breath can Fancy's pinions play.

And when art's laboured strains my feelings tire,
To seek thy simple music shall be mine;
I'll strive to win its graces to my lyre,
And make my plaintive lays enchant like thine.

                                    (1795)

---

*In the mythological history of Greece, Aeolus ruled over the winds. This poem was first published in the *Cabinet*, 3:128–30, as "To Eolus's Harp." Opie revised it for *Poems* (1802). The text printed here is from the second edition (1803); among her alterations were the deletion of the original first eight lines and a major reworking of the concluding four lines. The 1795 version opened with the lines

> Sure, 'tis a voice divine that wakes yon strings,
> And calls the power of music from her cell,

and it concluded with the lines

> Then oft from busy crowds, o'erjoy'd, I'll steal
>   To where my hand has rais'd thy tuneful shrine;
> There, from thy varying tones I'll learn to feel,
>   And, sweet inspirer, own no aid but THINE.

Allen Brooke, of Windermere*

Say, have you in the valley seen
A gentle youth of pensive mien?
And have you mark'd his pallid cheek,
That does his secret sorrow speak?
Perhaps you'd wish his name to hear—
'Tis Allen Brooke, of Windermere.

But, ah! the *cause* that prompts his sigh,
That dims with tears his sparkling eye;
That bids his youthful cheek turn pale,
And *sorrow's* hue o'er *health's* prevail;   10
That cause from *me* you must not hear—
Ask Allen Brooke, of Windermere.

Yet *needless* were his *words* to prove
This sorrow springs from hopeless love;
Go to the youth—of *Jessy* speak,
Then mark the *crimson* on his cheek;
That blush will make the secret clear
Of Allen Brooke, of Windermere.

And, oh! believe his Jessy's breast
Is still with *answ'ring* cares oppress'd;   20
But know, a father's stern command
Withholds from him my willing hand:
All but a *father's frown* I'd bear
For Allen Brooke, of Windermere.

Then, gentle stranger, seek the youth,
And tell him of his Jessy's truth;
Say that you saw my alter'd cheek,
My faithful bosom's anguish speak;
Say that till death, I'll hold most dear
My Allen Brooke, of Windermere.   30

(1795)

---

* In *Poems* (1802), Opie includes the note, "The burthen and the two first lines of this ballad were taken from a song written some years ago by Mr. G. S. Carey."

An Evening Walk at Cromer, 1795

Hail scene sublime! along the Eastern hills
Night draws her veil, and lo! the circling lamp
That guides the vessel thro' the ambush'd rocks,
Hangs in bright contrast on her dusky brow,
And smiles away its gloom. — See from the West,
A branching stream of silver radiance flows
On Ocean's bosom, till it emulates
The trembling lustre of the milky way;
While the dark cliffs projecting o'er the waves,
10   And frowning, (Fancy whispers) envious seem
Of the soft light they share not. In the South,
The star of evening sheds her pallid rays;
While from the humble cottages that skirt
Yon hill's uneven side, lights *redly* shine
Contrasting Art with Nature, and fill up
The chain of objects that leads captive sight,
And to the shrine of meditation draws
The wanderer's soul. — But hark! the awaken'd Owl
Majestic, slow, on sounding wing sails by,
20   And, rous'd to active life, enjoys the hour
That gives his winking eyelids leave to rest,
While his bright eye, dim in day's dazzling light
Now into distance shoots its beams, and guides
The unwieldy spoiler to his creeping prey,
Which having seiz'd, again on murmuring wing
He cleaves the tranquil air, and to his nest
Proudly bears home the feast, he toil'd to gain;
Then from the bosom of some thick-wove tree
Breathes in dull note his votive strain to Night,
30   Friend of his daring, season of his joy.

Here could I stay, now list'ning, gazing now,
Till all that crowded, busy, life can give
Sunk from my view, lost in the splendid vast
Of Nature's pure magnificence, that still
Will shine and charm for ages. FASHION's hand

---

2 circling lamp] The light in Cromer light-house revolves. *Opie.*

Which, in the world's gay scenes omnipotent,
Makes, and destroys, and the same object bids
Delight one moment, and disgust the next,
Here can no influence boast; but here true TASTE
To FASHION rarely known, enamour'd roves   40
And rapt, becomes DEVOTION, while the tear
Steals the flush'd cheek adown, as on the rose
Glitters the dew-drop. Hail again, bright scene!
On the moist gale of Eve shall I breathe forth
The song of praise to thee, responsive still
To Ocean's solemn roar? or shall I stand
In SACRED SILENCE bound, Devotion's friend,
And list'ning, let my eager ear drink in
The distant, mingling sounds that Fancy loves,
'Till every thought's thanksgiving, and the lips   50
Can only murmur praise? And lo! my lips
In utterance fail, and SILENCE I am thine.

                                            (1800)

Song

I know you false, I know you vain,
Yet still I cannot break my chain:
Though with those lips so sweetly smiling,
Those eyes so bright and so beguiling,
On every youth by turns you smile,
And every youth by turns beguile,
Yet still enchant and still deceive me,
Do all things, fatal fair, ... but leave me.

Still let me in those speaking eyes
Trace all your feelings as they rise;   10
Still from those lips in crimson swelling,
Which seem of soft delights the dwelling,
Catch tones of sweetness, which the soul
In fetters ever new control;
Nor let my starts of passion grieve thee, ...
Though death to stay, 't were death to leave thee.

                                            (1802)

Song

Go, youth beloved, in distant glades,
New friends, new hopes, new joys to find!
Yet sometimes deign, midst fairer maids,
To think on her thou leav'st behind.
Thy love, thy fate, dear youth, to share
Must never be my happy lot;
But thou mayst grant this humble prayer,
Forget me not, forget me not!

Yet, should the thought of my distress
10   Too painful to thy feelings be,
Heed not the wish I now express,
Nor ever deign to think on me:
But, oh! if grief thy steps attend,
If want, if sickness be thy lot,
And thou require a soothing friend,
Forget me not! forget me not!

                   (1802)

The Despairing Wanderer

Oh! 't is an hour to misery dear!
No noise but dashing waves I hear,
Save hollow blasts that rush around,
For Midnight reigns with horrors crowned.

Lo! clouds in swarthy grandeur sweep
Portentous o'er the troubled deep:
O'er the tall rocks' majestic heads,
See, billowy vapour slowly spreads:

And lo! fantastic shapes seem near,
10   The rocks with added height appear,
And from the mist, to seek the tide,

Gigantic figures darkly glide;
While, with quick step and hurried mien,
The timid fly the fearful scene.
Again loud blasts I shuddering hear,
Which to my mournful soul appear
To toll some shipwrecked sailor's knell!
Of fear, of grief, of death, they tell.
Perhaps they bade yon foaming tide
Unheard-of misery scatter wide.   20
Hail! dread idea, fancy-taught, ...
To me with gloomy pleasure fraught!
I should rejoice the world to see
Distrest, distracted, lost, like me.

Oh! why is phrensy called a curse?
I deem the sense of misery worse:
Come, Madness, come! though pale with fear
Be joy's flusht cheek when thou art near,
On thee I eager glances bend;
Despair, O Madness, calls thee friend!   30
Come, with thy visions cheer my gloom, ...
Spread o'er my cheek thy feverish bloom,
To my weak form thy strength impart,
From my sunk eye thy lightnings dart!
O come, and on the troubled air
Throw rudely my disordered hair;
Arm me with thy supporting pride,
Let me all ills, all fears deride!
O bid me roam in tattered vest,
Bare to the wintry wind my breast,   40
Horrors with dauntless eye behold,
And stalk in fancied greatness bold!
Let me, from yonder frowning rock,
With thy shrill scream the billows mock;
With fearless step ascend the steep
That totters o'er the encroaching deep;
And while the swelling main along
Blue lightning's awful splendours throng, ...
And while within each warring wave
Unnumbered victims find a grave,   50

And thunders rend the ear of Night,
Which happy wanderers' souls affright, ...
Let ME the mountain torrent quaff,
And midst the war of nature . . . laugh!

(1802)

Isabel Pagan

(c. 1741–1821)

Born in the parish of New Cumnock, Ayrshire, Scotland, around 1741, Isabel (or "Tibbie") Pagan was an alehouse keeper who had been abandoned by her well-connected family in early life and began earning her own living at the age of fourteen. She had almost no formal education; as she put it, "My learning it can soon be told, / Ten weeks when I was seven years old." An old religious woman taught her to read from the Bible, and young Tibbie subsequently devoted all the time she could spare to reading. Vivacious, with an excellent singing voice, Pagan suffered from infancy from a physical disability that impaired her walking. She had a child by a man named Campbell, who deserted her on the eve of their marriage. For most of her life she lived near Muirkirk, Scotland, first in a cottage on the property of Muirsmill, then for more than thirty years in what had once been a warehouse for a tar works on the banks of Garpal Water within short walking distance of the village, given to her rent free by Admiral Keith Steward.

A spirited woman who lived alone, Pagan was unapologetically promiscuous, habitually drunk, and irreverent toward religion, though, unlike many believers, she could recite much of the Bible by heart. She entertained her alehouse guests with improvised dramatic monologues and amusing songs, some old but many her own compositions. According to James Paterson's 1840 account,

> Night after night the vaulted roof of [Pagan's] humble dwelling rung with the voice of licentious mirth, and the revelries of bacchanalian worshippers, among whom she was the administering priestess. Famed for her sarcastic wit, as well as for her vocal powers, her cottage may be truly said to have been the favorite *howff* of all the drunken wags and "drouthy neebors" in the district. She had no license for the retail of spirits, but usually kept a bottle for the supply of her customers; and by this means she contrived to eke out a subsistence which must otherwise have been sustained from charity.[1]

1. [James Paterson], *The Contemporaries of Burns, and the More Recent Poets of Ayrshire, with Selections from their Writings* (Edinburgh, 1840), 116.

Pagan's alehouse was especially crowded and noisy in August, when aristocrats came to the Muirkirk moors for grouse shooting. According to Paterson, "Many of the sportsmen not only frequented her cottage, but occasionally sent for her to Muirkirk, where, in return for her songs, her wit, and wicked sarcasm, she was of course well plied with liquor and rewarded with money. From such visits it was no uncommon thing for Isobel to return to her lonely habitation at midnight, or beyond it, deeply intoxicated, and by a path not the most easy of access." When a local minister hazarded a visit to the "wicket Tibbie Pagan," he noticed that "she had her Bible at her elbow. She told us of a satire that had been written on her, which stated that she was a strumpet when only twelve years of age, and that she would go to hell. 'Oh!' quo Tibbie, 'was not that great nonsense?' She sang a song to us, which she had composed by way of retaliation."[2]

Clergy themselves did not escape Pagan's penchant for critique. One Sabbath she passed a minister preaching in the open air and overheard him earnestly trying to clear up "some knotty 'point o' faith.'" Leaning upon her crutch and "casting a sarcastic look" at him, she "exclaimed in a truly satiric tone — 'Ye're *borin'* awa' I see!'"[3] Although her behavior violated community norms, few were willing to risk offending her; those who did were made the object of her ridicule. For example, of a farmer who spoke harshly of her she sang:

> Mr ———— in the Kyle,
>   Ca'd me a common ____;
> But if he had not tried himsel',
> He wadna been sae sure![4]

In 1803, in her early sixties, Pagan published in Glasgow *A Collection of Songs and Poems on Several Occasions,* printed by Niven, Napier, and Khull of Trongate, containing forty-six favorite songs in her repertoire, such as James Boswell's "The Laird o' Glenlee," and many original works. Unable to write herself, she dictated the volume to her amanuensis, said to be William Gemmell, a tailor. Printed on extremely thin paper and containing only seventy-six pages in all, the volume was just the right size to fit in a hunter's pocket. There are love songs, both tender and passionate, but other songs are teasing, sometimes bawdy, filled with "in" jokes and the ambiance and good humor of a rural Scottish alehouse; often she makes herself the butt of her sarcasm or humor. In "A Hunting Song" she mentions regulars by name, describing

2. Ibid., 116–17.
3. Ibid., 121.
4. Quoted in ibid., 122.

their exploits comically though never disrespectfully. But her themes also deal with the problems of a person living on society's margin—the high cost of milk, the difficulty of selling inferior herring, merchants who cheat working-class customers. Some poems, such as "Muirkirk Light Weights," speak out against injustice. "The Spinning Wheel" condemns British governmental policy. Some are filled with gleeful jibes at conventional morality. Others, such as "A New Song on the Times," are devoted entirely to praise of her patrons, suggesting the delicate balancing act between insubordination and subordination that marks her work. (One of her patrons appears to have treated her to a long trip outside of Scotland.)

Although she apologizes repeatedly for her lack of education, she seems quite aware of the literary tradition of Burns and Ramsay, which legitimizes her own poetic voice. Some of her lyrics would have been considered obscene by the standards of the middle-class drawing room. For example, in the song "The Duke of Gordon's Fencibles" she writes:

> There's one call'd F——r I have seen,
> A verse from me he may expect,
> One night at Cumnock fell late,
> A lass convoy'd me near Affleck.
>
> And F——r she did take with her,
> To crack to her as she gaed hame,
> And as his kilt was short before,
> Think ye he wad na _____ her wame.

Paterson claimed that in both subject matter and language many of her best and wittiest sayings were too coarse for him to reprint; her amanuensis is said to have sanitized many of her lyrics for publication.

Not included in her book are the well-known song attributed to her called "The Crook and Plaid" and her most famous song, "Ca' the Ewes to the Knowes."[5] (Usually omitted in nineteenth-century sources because of its "indelicacy" is the fourth stanza of the latter.) Robert Burns "discovered" the song, according to his account, in 1787, when he heard it sung by the Reverend John Clunie. He had it transcribed, added a final stanza, "mended" others, and eventually had the poem published in volume 3 of James Johnson's *The Scots Musical Museum* (1790), acknowledging Pagan's authorship only in later editions. "This beautiful song," he said, "is in the true old Scotch taste, yet I do not know that either air or words were in print before. It has a border sound."[6] For George Thomson's *Select Collection of Original Scottish Airs* (1793–

5. For a discussion of the attribution, see ibid., 114.
6. Robert Burns, *The Works of Robert Burns,* ed. John Wilson, 2 vols. (Glasgow, 1852), 32.

99) Burns substantially altered the poem once again, much to its detriment. His second attempt at revision retains only the first stanza of the original, followed by twenty new lines, beginning "Hark the mavis' evening sang" and closing with the original first stanza repeated.[7] By 1845 Pagan's book had become so rare that Alex Whitelaw, doing research for a volume on Scottish song, was unable to locate a copy or even to confirm its contents.[8] However, he recorded that the tune for "Ca' the Ewes to the Knowes" was still familiar and that the song was still being sung.

Despite what many considered a dissolute existence, Pagan lived to be eighty years old, dying on 3 November 1821. Because she was such a well-known eccentric, her funeral was an event of considerable local interest, and people from all walks of life paid their respects. "Ca' the Ewes to the Knowes" is widely taught to Scottish schoolchildren to this day.

MAJOR WORK: *A Collection of Songs and Poems on Several Occasions* (Glasgow, 1803).

TEXTS USED: Text of "Ca' the Ewes to the Knowes" from James Johnson, *The Scots Musical Museum,* 6 vols. (Edinburgh, 1787–1803), 3:273. Text of "The Crook and Plaid" from *The Contemporaries of Burns, and the More Recent Poets of Ayrshire, with Selections from their Writings,* by [James Paterson] (Edinburgh, 1840), 119–20. All other poems from Pagan's *Collection of Songs and Poems on Several Occasions.*

7. See Burns to George Thomson, September 1794, in which he includes this revision, in ibid.

8. Writing in 1840, Paterson said that he had an incomplete copy and that he doubted that another could be found anywhere; however, the British Library now owns a complete copy.

Ca' the Ewes to the Knowes

Ca' the ewes to the knowes,
Ca' them whare the heather grows,
Ca' them whare the burnie rowes,
  My bonnie dearie.

As I gaed down the water-side,
There I met my shepherd-lad,
He row'd me sweetly in his plaid,
  An he ca'd me his dearie.
    Chos. Ca' the ewes &c.

Will ye gang down the water-side   10
And see the waves sae sweetly glide
Beneath the hazels spreading wide,
  The moon it shines fu' clearly.
    Chos. Ca' the ewes &c.

I was bred up at nae sic school,
My shepherd-lad, to play the fool,
And a' the day to sit in dool,
  And nae body to see me.
    Chos. Ca' the ewes &c.

Ye sall get gowns and ribbons meet,   20
Cauf-leather shoon upon your feet,
And in my arms ye'se lie and sleep,
  And ye sall be my dearie.
    Chos. Ca' the ewes &c.

If ye'll but stand to what ye've said,
I'se gang wi' you, my shepherd-lad,

1 Knowes] Knolls.
3 whare the burnie rowes] Where the stream rolls.
7 row'd me . . . in his plaid] Wrapped me . . . in his tartan (a euphemism for sexual intimacy).
15 nae sic school] No such school.
17 dool] Sadness.

And ye may rowe me in your plaid,
And I sall be your dearie.
Chos. Ca' the ewes &c.*
(wr. c. 1787; pub. 1790)

* When he published the poem in the *Scots Musical Museum* (1790), Robert Burns
added to the ending the following stanza, considerably altering the meaning of
the whole.

While waters wimple° to the sea;	meander, ripple
While day blinks° in the lift° sae hie;	shines heaven
Till clay-cauld death sall blin'° my e'e,	close
Ye sall be my dearie.	

The Crook and Plaid

Ilk lassie has a laddie she lo'es aboon the rest,
Ilk lassie has a laddie, if she like to confess't,
That is dear unto her bosom whatever be his trade;
But my lover's aye the laddie that wears the crook and plaid.

Ilk morn he climbs the mountains, his fleecy flocks to view,
And hears the lav'rocks chanting, new sprung frae 'mang the dew;
His bonnie wee bit doggie, sae frolicsome and glad,
Rins aye before the laddie that wears the crook and plaid.

And when that he is wearied, and lies upon the grass,
10   What if that in his plaidie he hide a bonnie lass?—
Nae doubt there's a preference due to every trade,
But commen' me to the laddie that wears the crook and plaid.

And when in summer weather he is upon the hill,
He reads in books of history that learns him meikle skill;

1 Ilk lassie] Each girl.
6 lav'rocks] Larks.
14 meikle] Much.

There's nae sic joyous leisure to be had at ony trade,
Save that the laddie follows that wears the crook and plaid.

What though in storms o' winter part o' his flock should die,
My laddie is aye cheerie, and why should not I?
The prospect o' the summer can weel mak' us glad;
Contented is the laddie that wears the crook and plaid.   20

King David was a shepherd while in the prime o' youth,
And following the flocks he ponder'd upon truth;
And when he came to be a king, and left his former trade,
'Twas an honour to the laddie that wears the crook and plaid.

(wr. c. 1787; pub. 1790)

Account of the Author's Lifetime

I was born near four miles from Nith-head,
Where fourteen years I got my bread;
My learning it can soon be told,
Ten weeks when I was seven years old
With a good old religious wife,
Who liv'd a quiet and sober life;
Indeed she took of me more pains
Than some does now of forty bairns.
With my attention, and her skill,
I read the Bible no that ill;   10
And when I grew a wee thought mair,
I read when I had time to spare.
But a' the whole tract of my time,
I found myself inclin'd to rhyme;
When I see merry company,
I sing a song with mirth and glee,

15 sic] Such.

21 King David was a shepherd] The Biblical king of the Hebrew people; as a child he was in charge of his father's sheep and displayed his courage by killing both a lion and a bear that attacked the flock.

8 bairns] Children.

And sometimes I the whisky pree,
But 'deed its best to let it be.
A' my faults I will not tell,
20   I scarcely ken them a' mysel;
I've come thro' various scenes of life,
Yet never was a married wife.

(1803)

A New Love Song, with the Answer

I have travell'd the country both early and late,
My travels were many, my sorrows were great,
I courted a fair maid who did me disdain,
She aften deny'd me, but I'll try her again.

I own that her parents they were very rich,
As I am not their equal it troubles me much,
But will you leave father and mother also,
And thro' the wise world with your darling love go.

O Johnny, dear, Johnny, love, that will not do,
10   For to leave my parents, love, and go with you,
To leave my relations to mourn for my sake,
And thro' the wide world to follow a rake.

Some says I am rakish, some says I am wild,
Some says the fair damsels I often beguile,
For that is a falsehood, and that I will prove,
I'm guilty of nothing, but innocent love.

I'm sorry, I'm sorry, my fortune's so bad,
That I have been slighted by any false maid,
'Tis false information that I may think on,
20   It makes me lament, love, for what I have done.

17 pree] Try, sample.
20 ken] Know.

My love she is proper, though not very tall,
Her decent behavior it far exceeds all,
She has my heart bound, that it cannot get free,
She has too many sweethearts for to marry me.

Farewell to this country, I bid it adieu,
Wherever I go, love, I will think on you,
For sleeping, or waking, you're still in my mind,
To sail to America is my whole design.

(1803)

The Answer

My Johnny is left me and gone to the sea,
I mourn for the absence of his company,
My parents was rich, and they did him despise,
And they advised me to do so likewise.

Alas! he has gone the wide world to range,
And were he but here now, my mind would soon change,
For sleeping and waking, I'm never at rest,
To think on my Johnny my mind's sore oppress'd.

My love he is handsome in every degree,
Good natur'd and sober was his company,   10
He is voic'd like a blackbird, and eyed like a dove,
He is every way handsome the man that I love.

And dearly I lov'd him, as I lov'd my life,
Although 'tis decreed that I am not his wife,
Yet he has my heart in his bosom secure,
We are all born to troubles, I must that endure.

(1803)

On Burns and Ramsay

Now Burns and Ramsay both are dead,
Although I cannot them succeed;
Yet here I'll try my natural skill,
And hope you will not take it ill.

You know their learning was not sma',
And mine is next to nane at a';
Theirs must be brighter far than mine,
Because I'm much on the decline.

I hope the public will excuse
10   What I have done here by the Muse;
As diff'rent men are of diff'rent minds,
My meter is of diff'rent kinds.

                    (1803)

1 Burns and Ramsay] Allan Ramsay (1686–1758) was a Scots poet who helped revive vernacular Scots poetry with publications such as *The Tea-Table Miscellany* (1724–
37), a collection of surviving traditional songs and ballads, and *The Ever Green* (1724),
containing work by the great poets of late medieval Scotland. Robert Burns (1759–
96), author of *Poems, Chiefly in the Scottish Dialect* (1786), was lionized by Edinburgh's
literary and aristocratic society as a peasant poet, though he was well educated. He
developed a passion for collecting old Scots songs for *The Scots Musical Museum* and
contributed some original compositions as well. He was much influenced by Ramsay
and could write with ease both in correct eighteenth-century English and in his
native Scots.

A Letter

Sir, be pleas'd these lines to read,
    Pray take it not amiss,
And, if you please, I wish to know
    How Captain L_____n is.

For he was cheerfu' on the moors,
    With music in his heart,
And with his money I am sure,
    Was never swear to part.

I thank you for your bottle, Sir,
    But woes my heart its dry,   10
'Tis in your power to fill't again,
    The next time you come by.

It is my lot to live my lane,
    And sometimes I think lang,
Sometimes I do amuse myself
    With making of a song.

Were I in power to publish them,
    To be sung when I'm dead,
And while I am upon the stage,
    Might help to merit bread.   20

Let this be shown to Lady Kirk,
    That noble hearted chiel,
God bless him and his family,
    I thank him for his meal.

Sir, by misfortune of a dog,
    Old chucky lost her life,
Disturbed Robin's family,
    Especially his wife.

13 my lane] Alone; without a mate.

'Deed I'm afraid she'll break her heart,
30   Sir, I maun let you ken,
For aye when I see her she cries,
       Alas! the old muir-hen.

(1803)

The Spinning Wheel

When I sit at my spinning wheel,
    And think on every station,
I think I'm happiest myself,
    At my small occupation.
No court, nor freet, nor dark debate,
    Can e'er attend my dwelling,
While I make cloth of diff'rent sorts,
    Which is an honest calling.

Indeed ye know the nights are lang,
10   And sometimes I do weary,
But, as they'll shortly turn again,
    I hope I'll grow more cheery.
I'll sing a song with noble glee,
    And tune that I think canty,
But I sing best, it is no jest,
    When the tobacco's plenty.

I live content, I pay no rent,
    In my quiet habitation,
For B——e he did order it,
20   Which shews his great discretion.
To favor one so low as me,
    While I was no relation;
But now he's dead, and in the clay,
    I hope he's won the blessing.

30 maun let you ken] Must let you know.
5 freet] Fret; vexation.
14 canty] Cheerful, lively, neat and small.

M'A—m brave, agrees to this
   Kind, honest disposition,
He's charitable, just and true,
   Not like most men of fashion.
I have no reason here to fret,
   That I was never married,   30
Since I a free possession get,
   Of freedom I'm not wearied.

For when around me I do look,
   And see the merchants dealing,
For they do triple profit take
   For every thing they're selling;
For honesty is grown so weak,
   It is so old a fashion,
'Tis not regarded in our day,
   'Tis scarce throughout the nation.   40

Kind Providence sent a good crop
   For to support our nation,
But Satan's crew sent it abroad,
   Which is a sad vexation,
That e'er such blackguard vagabonds
   Should have a habitation
Below our British government,
   That takes this occupation.
                 (1803)

A Love Letter

If you desir'd my bosom friend,
    Now if you can think it so,
Pray yield all pleasures to my mind,
    And make much happiness to flow.

Sure its decreed by the pow'rs above,
    As I'm now oblig'd to think,
We'll lay aside all flattering words,
    And close in love's embraces link.

What though envy and lying tongues,
10   'Gainst you their utmost forces bend,
And some makes money all their hope,
    While love, you know's, a lasting friend.

When absent from your company,
    'Tis great uneasiness to me,
But hope again makes love remain,
    I'm still rejoicing thee to see.

At night when I go to my rest,
    Thinking to get some sweet repose,
Your image still is with me there,
20   Sweeter far than any rose.

But yet far short of the sweet joys,
    That love's embraces now have press'd,
In thy soft arms to be enclos'd,
    And there in silence sleep to rest.

I will guard thee round about,
    Myself, I'm sure, shall be the door,
And if thy heart chance to steal out,
    I vow I'll never love thee more.

Though father fret, and mother scold,
30   Although that all my friends should frown,

All that I have thou art sure of,
   And well may think it all thine own.

I have not time to make more rhyme,
   So well's my judgment could express,
But I am thine, and heart and mind,
   Sincerely hope the Lord will bless.

If you'll be true as I'm to you,
   So shall you find me evermore,
I add no more, but so I rest,
   Sincere your true love and your dear.   40
               (1803)

Muirkirk Light Weights

In Muirkirk there lives a taylor,
He scrimpit weight for greed of filler;
He scrimpit weight, he counts not fair,
Till he's made three hundred pounds and mair.

The year the sugar has come down,
Three pounds give less nor half-a-crown,
And a' the dealers round about
Came to the taylor in great doubt,
Whether to hang themselves or no.
Some said they would, and some said no;   10
Some said, I think we will set a day,
We'll fast and sigh, and read and pray,
Perhaps the gods will please that well,
If we turn to them frae the de'il.

The taylor said, with heart right fair,
I fear for me God will not care,
For I within my coat do wear

2 scrimpit] Shaved.

Ten thousand curses every year.
There's something I'll confess and tell,
Beside me I do keep a mell,
And now and then my weights do hit,
And whiles break aff a gay wee bit.

The oldest dealer he did say,
What will be said at the last day?

The taylor said, ne'er mind the last,
If we can but make money fast;
There will be large allowance gaun
For every dealer in the land.

Then every one thought to themsell
'Tis good for us to keep a mell,
So they struck a' their weights right fair,
Some broke off less, and some broke mair.
This practice did so long prevail,
Till poor workmen were like to fail.

Some told the Dean of Guild of Ayr
That Muirkirk weights they were not fair;
To try the same was his intent,
The standard to Muirkirk he sent.

The day was short, the road was wet,
For depute, he employ'd C——t,
Who thought it was his only chance
To seize the merchants all at once,
And bring them all unto one place,
And do them justice to their face.

O man, it was a pleasant sight,
The works of darkness brought to light.
How bravely I their names could tell,
Who had been busy with the mell;

20 mell] hammer.

But this at present, I will spare,
And hope they will do so nae mair. 50

Thanks to the gentlemen and judges that were there,
I'm sure they acted honourably, no person they did spare;
Long may they live, and happy be, and aye to good inclin'd,
And aye when 'tis convenient, their standard they should mind.

(1803)

Ann Radcliffe

(1764–1823)

Ann Radcliffe is best known today as the founder of an exceedingly in-fluential and popular school of gothic fiction whose villains prefigured the Byronic hero and whose success inspired many imitations and parodies, the best known among them Jane Austen's *Northanger Abbey.* During the 1790s Radcliffe was the best-selling of all British novelists—read and translated more than any other. When she died, the *Edinburgh Magazine and Literary Miscellany* observed, "Mrs Radcliffe has long borne undisputed, an almost solitary sway over the regions of romance."[1] Walter Scott said, "Mrs Radcliffe has a title to be considered as the first poetess of romantic fiction."[2]

But Radcliffe's personal history is as obscure as her fame was wide. The *Edinburgh Review* noted that "the fair authoress kept herself almost as much incognito as the Author of *Waverley;* nothing was known of her but her name on the title page. She never appeared in public, nor mingled in private society, but kept herself apart, like the sweet bird that sings its solitary notes."[3] This may have been a slight exaggeration, but many years after Radcliffe's death, when Christina Rossetti attempted a biography of her predecessor, whom she admired, she was forced to give up the project for lack of information about her reclusive subject.

To this day, because of Radcliffe's self-imposed seclusion only basic infor-mation is available about her life. She was born in London on 9 July 1764, the only daughter of Ann Oates and William Ward, a businessman. A frequent visitor was her uncle, Thomas Bentley, a widely traveled, liberal, highly cul-tured man and partner of Josiah Wedgwood. He introduced Ann to Elizabeth Montagu and Hester Lynch Piozzi. Ann was living at Bath during the time when Sophia and Harriet Lee were running their school, but whether she attended is unclear. Judging from the epigraphs and allusions in her work, she

1. 18 (1826): 703.
2. Quoted in Robert Miles, *Ann Radcliffe: The Great Enchantress* (Manchester, 1995), 7.
3. 76 (May 1823): 360n.

read all of the standard eighteenth-century poets and was steeped in Shakespeare. She seems to have held conservative views on politics and religion
but opposed the slave trade. In 1787 at Bath she married William Radcliffe,
an Oxford graduate and law student. Soon afterward the couple moved to
London, where William became owner and editor of the *English Chronicle*.
During the evenings, editorial work frequently demanded William's time,
leaving Ann on her own. He had admired the prose sketches of scenery she
had been in the habit of composing and encouraged her to spend her solitary
time writing.

Within two years of her marriage, which seems to have been a happy one,
she produced *The Castles of Athlin and Dunbayne* (1789), a melodramatic tale
with a medieval setting. *A Sicilian Romance* followed in 1790. Both novels
were published anonymously, and both were given a lukewarm critical reception. *The Romance of the Forest: Interspersed with Some Pieces of Poetry* (1791)
represented an artistic advance over the earlier works, and the reviews were
more positive. By 1795 it had gone through four editions, had been translated into Italian and French, and had been adapted for the stage by John
Boaden (*Fountainville Forest*, 1794). It was in an advertisement for the second
edition of *The Romance of the Forest* that Radcliffe's name was first linked to
her fiction. *The Mysteries of Udolpho, A Romance; Interspersed with Some Pieces
of Poetry*, for which Cadell paid her five hundred pounds, took the world by
storm, becoming a sensation not only in Britain but on the Continent as
well. Radcliffe was now established as a major novelist.

Radcliffe's work owes much not only to Renaissance romance but to the
early novels of Charlotte Smith. Both authors write about virtuous women
of sensibility who are isolated within and threatened by a cold, aristocratic
patriarchy, whose dangers they meet with quiet courage. Radcliffe also drew
on Clara Reeve's *Old English Baron* (1777), Horace Walpole's *Castle of Otranto*
(1765), and Sophia Lee's *Recess* (1783–85), but although she used many standard conventions, such as secret passageways, gloomy castles, and claustro-
phobic spaces, Radcliffe's gothicism was distinctively her own. She was one of
the most skillful practitioners of the art of suspense, interweaving complex
plots and often keeping readers hanging for hundreds of pages. For depictions
of a consciousness subjected to terror her writing is unsurpassed. Her heroines are passionate about music and picturesque landscapes but also studious,
proper, and sensitive. Her fiction explores the realm of female fantasy, and the
psyches of her heroines, sometimes pushed to the extremes of human emotion, are drawn with psychological sophistication. Her villains are brooding,
dark, authoritarian male characters who imprison the heroines and threaten
sexual violation. There is always a loyal servant, and the antics of laboring-

class characters often provide comic relief to the suspense. Radcliffe's clever, self-reliant, and gutsy heroines emerge triumphant from their travails, physically unscathed, and reunited with their true loves. Apparently supernatural events inspire terror but are eventually rationally explained. However, her ghosts are generally more convincing than her explanations. Tension between the allure of imagination and feeling and the need for rational control infuses her plots. Thus, her heroines are women of sensibility who are also tough-minded and resolute. Several of her heroines write poetry, which is inserted in the narrative and operates both to delay the action (thereby increasing suspense) and to examine the act and context of women's poetic composition.

During the summer of 1794 Radcliffe and her husband journeyed down the Rhine to the Swiss border, where they were turned back for bureaucratic reasons. Thus, Radcliffe never set foot in Switzerland or Italy and never got to see for herself the landscapes that are the settings for much of her fiction; she knew them only from pictures and travel literature. She and William returned to England and contented themselves with a tour of the Lake District. Ann Radcliffe published her impressions in *A Journey Made in the Summer of 1794, Through Holland and the Western Frontier of Germany, With a Return Down the Rhine: To Which Are Added Observations During a Tour to the Lakes of Lancashire, Westmoreland, and Cumberland* (1795).

Samuel Taylor Coleridge remarked, "In reviewing the *Mysteries of Udolpho,* we hazarded an opinion, that, if a better production could appear, it must come only from the pen of Mrs. Radcliffe."[4] Radcliffe received the enormous sum of eight hundred pounds for her next novel, *The Italian, or the Confessional of the Black Penitents. A Romance* (1797). John Boaden wrote a dramatic adaptation entitled the *Italian Monk,* which was produced on 15 August 1797 at the Haymarket Theatre in London. Despite such critical, popular, and economic success, at the age of only thirty-three Radcliffe stopped publishing, though she would live another two and a half decades. Many rumours circulated about why Radcliffe abandoned her writing career at the height of her fame. Some reported her to be disgusted by her imitators or appalled by her own celebrity. Others alleged that an overexuberant and morbid imagination had caused her death or led to madness. She was said to be in Derbyshire, confined in Haddon Hall. Radcliffe felt it indecorous to explain her silence or reply to rumors of her mental or physical demise. In truth, she had inherited money when her father died that left her financially independent, with no further incentive to put her name before the public.

After Radcliffe died of an asthma attack on 7 February 1823, the *New*

4. *Critical Review,* n.s., 23 (June 1798): 166–69.

Monthly Magazine claimed that she had died "under a gradual decay of her mental and bodily powers."[5] Although Radcliffe stopped publishing, she continued to write for pleasure in the last quarter-century of her life; her last novel, *Gaston de Blondeville,* was composed in 1802. It is the only one of her novels in which the supernatural is not rationally explained away in the end. Her husband published it, along with a memoir and other of her works, in *Gaston de Blondeville, or the Court of Henry III Keeping Festival in Ardenne, a Romance. St. Alban's Abbey, a Metrical Tale with Some Poetical Pieces* (1826).

Although the poetic nature of Radcliffe's verbal landscapes is acknowledged in critical commentary, that she was a poet seems all but forgotten in our time. But Walter Scott pointed to *A Sicilian Romance* (1790) as the first example in modern English of the poetic novel.[6] And Radcliffe herself considered poetry such an essential part of her fiction that the titles of her two most important novels make specific reference to the poems within them— *The Romance of the Forest: Interspersed with Some Pieces of Poetry* (1791) and *The Mysteries of Udolpho, A Romance; Interspersed with Some Pieces of Poetry* (1794). Moreover, the volume containing *Gaston de Blondeville* includes a lengthy metrical tale along with other poetic pieces.

Leigh Hunt said of Radcliffe that "in her verses she is a tinselled nymph in a pantomime, calling up commonplaces with a wand";[7] in fact, her poetry was astonishingly innovative in its experimentation with freer form and language. Poetry plays an essential function in the novels, setting mood, illuminating the interior landscape of characters, and describing the conditions for imaginative production, among other things. But the poems are not merely an extension of her fictional voice. They can and did function independently of the novels. A collected edition of her poetry appeared in 1815 and was of enough interest to be reissued in 1834, 1845, and 1852, though apparently Radcliffe herself never chose to publish her poems separately. (The only book of her verse published during her lifetime was pirated, the poems having been extracted from the novels by an unknown compiler).

MAJOR WORKS: *The Castles of Athlin and Dunbayne. A Highland Story* (London, 1789); *A Sicilian Romance,* 2 vols. ([London, 1790]); *The Romance of the Forest: Interspersed with Some Pieces of Poetry,* 3 vols. (London, 1791); *The Mysteries of Udolpho, A Romance; Interspersed with Some Pieces of Poetry,* 4 vols. (London, 1794); *A Journey Made in the Summer of 1794, through Holland and the Western Frontier of Germany, with a Return Down the*

5. 9 (May 1823): 232.

6. *DNB;* strictly speaking, Scott was incorrect.

7. Leigh Hunt, *Men, Women, and Books: A Selection of Sketches, Essays, and Critical Memoirs from his Uncollected Prose,* new ed. (London, 1891), 278.

Rhine, to which are added Observations during a tour to the Lakes of Lancashire, Westmoreland, and Cumberland (London, 1795); The Italian, or the Confessional of the Black Penitents. A Romance, 3 vols. (London, 1797); The Poems of Mrs. A. Radcliffe (London, 1815); The Posthumous Works of Ann Radcliffe, 4 vols. (London, 1833); The Poetical Works of Ann Radcliffe, 2 vols. (London, 1834); Gaston de Blondeville, or the Court of Henry III. Keeping Festival in Ardenne, A Romance. St. Alban's Abbey, a Metrical Tale; with Some Poetical Pieces . . . To Which is Prefixed a Memoir of the Author, with Extracts from her Journals, 4 vols. (London, 1826).

TEXTS USED: Texts of "To the Nightingale," "Song of a Spirit," and "Sunset" from *The Romance of the Forest*. Texts of "The First Hour of Morning," "Sonnet (Now the bat circles on the breeze of eve)," "To Melancholy," "The Sea-Nymph," "Rondeau," and "Storied Sonnet" from *The Mysteries of Udolpho, A Romance*. "Shakspeare's Cliff," "To the River Dove," "The Sea-Mew," "On a First View of the Group Called the Seven Mountains," and "A Second View of the Seven Mountains" were composed around 1800 but first published in *Gaston de Blondeville*, from which these texts are taken.

To the Nightingale

Child of the melancholy song!
O yet that tender strain prolong!

Her lengthen'd shade, when Ev'ning flings,
   From mountain-cliffs and forest's green,
And sailing slow on silent wings
   Along the glimm'ring West is seen;
I love o'er pathless hills to stray,
   Or trace the winding vale remote,
And pause, sweet Bird! to hear thy lay
   While moon-beams on the thin clouds float,
Till o'er the mountain's dewy head
Pale Midnight steals to wake the dead.

Far through the Heav'ns' ætherial blue,
   Wafted on Spring's light airs you come,
With blooms, and flow'rs, and genial dew,
   From climes where Summer joys to roam,
   O! welcome to your long-lost home!

10

"Child of the melancholy song!"
   Who lov'st the lonely woodland-glade
To mourn, unseen, the boughs among,
   When Twilight spreads her pensive shade,
Again thy dulcet voice I hail!   20
      O! pour again the liquid note
That dies upon the ev'ning gale!
   For Fancy loves the kindred tone;
   Her griefs the plaintive accents own.
    She loves to hear thy music float
At solemn Midnight's stillest hour,
   And think on friends for ever lost,
   On joys by disappointment crost,
And weep anew Love's charmful pow'r!

Then Memory wakes the magic smile,   30
   Th' impassion'd voice, the melting eye,
That won't the trusting heart beguile,
   And *wakes again* the hopeless sigh!
Her skill the glowing tints revive
   Of scenes that Time had bade decay;
She bids the soften'd Passions live—
   The Passions urge again their sway.
Yet o'er the long-regretted scene
   Thy song the grace of sorrow throws;
A melancholy charm serene,
   More rare than all that mirth bestows.
Then hail, sweet Bird! and hail thy pensive tear!
To Taste, to Fancy, and to Virtue, dear!

                    (1791)

Song of a Spirit

In the sightless air I dwell,
    On the sloping sun-beams play;
Delve the cavern's inmost cell,
    Where never yet did day-light stray:

Dive beneath the green sea waves,
    And gambol in briny deeps;
Skim ev'ry shore that Neptune laves,
    From Lapland's plains to India's steeps.

Oft I mount with rapid force
10   Above the wide earth's shadowy zone;
Follow the day-star's flaming course
    Through realms of space to thought unknown:

And listen oft celestial sounds
    That swell the air unheard of men,
As I watch my nightly rounds
    O'er woody steep, and silent glen.

Under the shade of waving trees,
    On the green bank of fountain clear,
At pensive eve I sit at ease,
20   While dying music murmurs near.

And oft, on point of airy clift,
    That hangs upon the western main,
I watch the gay tints passing swift,
    And twilight veil the liquid plain.

Then, when the breeze has sunk away,
    And ocean scarce is heard to lave,
For me the sea-nymphs softly play
    Their dulcet shells beneath the wave.

Their dulcet shells! I hear them now,
30   Slow swells the strain upon mine ear;

Now faintly falls—now warbles low,
   Till rapture melts into a tear.

The ray that silvers o'er the dew,
   And trembles through the leafy shade,
And tints the scene with softer hue,
   Calls me to rove the lonely glade;

Or hie me to some ruin'd tower,
   Faintly shewn by moon-light gleam,
Where the lone wanderer owns my power
   In shadows dire that substance seem;   40

In thrilling sounds that murmur woe,
   And pausing silence make more dread;
In music breathing from below
   Sad solemn strains, that wake the dead.

Unseen I move—unknown am fear'd!
   Fancy's wildest dreams I weave;
And oft by bards my voice is heard
   To die along the gales of eve.

                (1791)

Sunset

Soft o'er the mountain's purple brow
   Meek Twilight draws her shadows gray;
From tufted woods, and vallies low,
   Light's magic colours steal away.
Yet still, amid the spreading gloom,
   Resplendent glow the western waves
   That roll o'er Neptune's coral caves,
A zone of light on Ev'ning's dome.
   On this lone summit let me rest,
And view the forms to Fancy dear,   10
   Till on the Ocean's darken'd breast

The stars of Ev'ning tremble clear;
Or the moon's pale orb appear,
   Throwing her line of radiance wide,
   Far o'er the lightly-curling tide,
   That seems the yellow sands to chide.
No sounds o'er silence now prevail,
   Save of the dying wave below,
Or sailor's song borne on the gale,
20   Or oar at distance striking slow.
So sweet! so tranquil! may my ev'ning ray
Set to this world—and rise in future day!

(1791)

The First Hour of Morning

How sweet to wind the forest's tangled shade,
   When early twilight, from the eastern bound,
Dawns on the sleeping landscape in the glade,
   And fades as morning spreads her blush around!

When ev'ry infant flower, that wept in night,
   Lifts its chill head soft glowing with a tear,
Expands its tender blossom to the light,
   And gives its incense to the genial air.

How fresh the breeze that wafts the rich perfume,
10   And swells the melody of waking birds;
The hum of bees, beneath the verdant gloom,
   And woodman's song, and low of distant herds!

Then, doubtful gleams the mountain's hoary head,
   Seen through the parting foliage from afar;
And, farther still, the ocean's misty bed,
   With flitting sails, that partial sun-beams share.

But, vain the sylvan shade—the breath of May,
   The voice of music floating on the gale,

And forms, that beam through morning's dewy veil,
  If health no longer bid the heart be gay!   20
O balmy hour! 'tis thine her wealth to give,
Here spread her blush, and bid the parent live!

                         (1794)

Sonnet

Now the bat circles on the breeze of eve,
That creeps, in shudd'ring fits, along the wave,
And trembles 'mid the woods, and through the cave
Whose lonely sighs the wanderer deceive;
For oft, when melancholy charms his mind,
He thinks the Spirit of the rock he hears,
Nor listens, but with sweetly-thrilling fears,
To the low, mystic murmurs of the wind!
Now the bat circles, and the twilight dew
Falls silent round, and, o'er the mountain-cliff,   10
The gleaming wave and far-discover'd skiff,
Spreads the gray veil of soft, harmonious hue.
So falls o'er Grief the dew of pity's tear
Dimming her lonely visions of despair.

                         (1794)

To Melancholy

    Spirit of love and sorrow—hail!
    Thy solemn voice from far I hear,
    Mingling with evening's dying gale;
    Hail, with this sadly-pleasing tear!

    O! at this still, this lonely hour,
    Thine own sweet hour of closing day,
    Awake thy lute, whose charmful pow'r
    Shall call up Fancy to obey:

To paint the wild romantic dream,
10   That meets the poet's musing eye,
As, on the bank of shadowy stream,
He breathes to her the fervid sigh.

O lonely spirit! let thy song
Lead me through all thy sacred haunt;
The minster's moon-light aisles along,
Where spectres raise the midnight chaunt.

I hear their dirges faintly swell!
Then, sink at once in silence drear,
While, from the pillar'd cloister's cell,
20   Dimly their gliding forms appear!

Lead where the pine-woods wave on high,
Whose pathless sod is darkly seen,
As the cold moon, with trembling eye,
Darts her long beams the leaves between.

Lead to the mountain's dusky head,
Where, far below, in shade profound,
Wide forests, plains, and hamlets spread,
And sad the chimes of vesper sound.

Or guide me, where the dashing oar
30   Just breaks the stillness of the vale,
As slow it tracks the winding shore,
To meet the ocean's distant sail:

To pebbly banks, that Neptune laves,
With measur'd surges, loud and deep,
Where the dark cliff bends o'er the waves,
And wild the winds of Autumn sweep.

There pause at midnight's spectred hour,
And list the long-resounding gale;
And catch the fleeting moon-light's pow'r,
40   O'er foaming seas and distant sail.

(1794)

The Sea-Nymph

Down, down a thousand fathom deep,
Among the sounding seas I go;
Play round the foot of ev'ry steep
Whose cliffs above the ocean grow.

There, within their secret caves,
I hear the mighty rivers roar;
And guide their streams through Neptune's waves
To bless the green earth's inmost shore:

And bid the freshen'd waters glide,
For fern-crown'd nymphs of lake, or brook,   10
Through winding woods and pastures wide,
And many a wild, romantic nook.

For this the nymphs, at fall of eve,
Oft dance upon the flow'ry banks,
And sing my name, and garlands weave
To bear beneath the wave their thanks.

In coral bow'rs I love to lie,
And hear the surges roll above,
And through the waters view on high
The proud ships sail, and gay clouds move.   20

And oft at midnight's stillest hour,
When summer seas the vessel lave,
I love to prove my charmful pow'r
While floating on the moon-light wave.

And when deep sleep the crew has bound,
And the sad lover musing leans
O'er the ship's side, I breathe around
Such strains as speak no mortal means!

O'er the dim waves his searching eye
Sees but the vessel's lengthen'd shade;   30

Above—the moon and azure sky;
Entranc'd he hears, and half afraid!

Sometimes, a single note I swell,
That, softly sweet, at distance dies;
Then wake the magic of my shell,
And choral voices round me rise!

The trembling youth, charm'd by my strain,
Calls up the crew, who, silent, bend
O'er the high deck, but list in vain;
40   My song is hush'd, my wonders end!

Within the mountain's woody bay,
Where the tall bark at anchor rides,
At twilight hour, with tritons gay,
I dance upon the lapsing tides:

And with my sister-nymphs I sport,
Till the broad sun looks o'er the floods;
Then, swift we seek our crystal court,
Deep in the wave, 'mid Neptune's woods.

In cool arcades and glassy halls
50   We pass the sultry hours of noon,
Beyond wherever sun-beam falls,
Weaving sea-flowers in gay festoon.

The while we chant our ditties sweet
To some soft shell that warbles near;
Join'd by the murmuring currents, fleet,
That glide along our halls so clear.

There, the pale pearl and sapphire blue,
And ruby red, and em'rald green,
Dart from the domes a changing hue,
60   And sparry columns deck the scene.

When the dark storm scowls o'er the deep,
And long, long peals of thunder sound,

On some high cliff my watch I keep
O'er all the restless seas around:

Till on the ridgy wave afar
Comes the lone vessel, labouring slow,
Spreading the white foam in the air,
With sail and top-mast bending low.

Then, plunge I 'mid the ocean's roar,
My way by quiv'ring lightnings shewn,   70
To guide the bark to peaceful shore,
And hush the sailor's fearful groan.

And if too late I reach its side
To save it from the 'whelming surge,
I call my dolphins o'er the tide,
To bear the crew where isles emerge.

Their mournful spirits soon I cheer,
While round the desert coast I go,
With warbled songs they faintly hear,
Oft as the stormy gust sinks low.   80

My music leads to lofty groves,
That wild upon the sea-bank wave;
Where sweet fruits bloom, and fresh spring roves,
And closing boughs the tempest brave.

Then, from the air spirits obey
My potent voice they love so well,
And, on the clouds, paint visions gay,
While strains more sweet at distance swell.

And thus the lonely hours I cheat,
Soothing the ship-wreck'd sailor's heart,   90
Till from the waves the storms retreat,
And o'er the east the day-beams dart.

Neptune for this oft binds me fast
To rocks below, with coral chain,

Till all the tempest's over-past,
And drowning seamen cry in vain.

Whoe'er ye are that love my lay,
Come, when red sun-set tints the wave,
To the still sands, where fairies play;
There, in cool seas, I love to lave.

(1794)

100 (left margin, line 100)

Rondeau[*]

Soft as yon silver ray, that sleeps
Upon the ocean's trembling tide;
Soft as the air, that lightly sweeps
Yon sail, that swells in stately pride:

Soft as the surge's stealing note,
That dies along the distant shores,
Or warbled strain, that sinks remote—
So soft the sigh my bosom pours!

True as the wave to Cynthia's ray,
True as the vessel to the breeze,
True as the soul to music's sway,
Or music to Venetian seas:

Soft as yon silver beams, that sleep
Upon the ocean's trembling breast;
So soft, so true, fond Love shall weep,
So soft, so true, with *thee* shall rest.

(1794)

10 (left margin, line 10)

9 Cynthia's] A name for the moon personified as a goddess.

*A rondeau is a French verse form having only two rhymes throughout, with the opening words used twice as a refrain. Radcliffe takes some liberties with the form here, which, strictly speaking, consists of only thirteen lines.

Storied Sonnet

The weary traveller, who, all night long,
Has climb'd among the Alps' tremendous steeps,
Skirting the pathless precipice, where throng
Wild forms of danger; as he onward creeps
If, chance, his anxious eye at distance sees
The mountain-shepherd's solitary home,
Peeping from forth the moon–illumin'd trees,
What sudden transports to his bosom come!
But, if between some hideous chasm yawn,
Where the cleft pine a doubtful bridge displays,   10
In dreadful silence, on the brink, forlorn
He stands, and views in the faint rays
Far, far below, the torrent's rising surge,
And listens to the wild impetuous roar;
Still eyes the depth, still shudders on the verge,
Fears to return, nor dares to venture o'er.
Desperate, at length the tottering plank he tries,
His weak steps slide, he shrieks, he sinks—he dies!

(1794)

Shakspeare's Cliff

Here, all along the high sea-cliff,
   Oh, how sweet it is to go!
When Summer lures the light-winged skiff
   Over the calm expanse below,—

And tints, with shades of sleepy blue,
   Misty ocean's curving shores;
And with a bright and gleaming hue,
   Dover's high embattled towers.

How sweet to watch the blue haze steal
10   Over the whiteness of yon sail;
O'er yon fair cliffs, and now conceal
   Boulogne's walls and turrets pale!

Oh! go not near that dizzy brink,
   Where the mossed hawthorn hangs its root,
To look how low the sharp crags sink,
   Before the tide they overshoot.

Nor listen for their hollow sound—
   Thou canst not hear the surges mourn,
Nor see how high the billows bound
20   Among the caves their rage has worn.

Yet, yet forbear! thou canst not spring,
   Like fay, from off this summit high,
And perch upon the out-stretched wing
   Of the sea-mew passing by,

And safely with her skirt the clouds;
   Or, sweeping downward to the tide,
Frolic amid the seaman's shrouds,
   Or on a bounding billow ride.

Ah! no; all this I cannot do;
    Yet I will dare the mountain's height,   30
Seas and shores and skies to view,
    And cease but with the dim day-light.

For fearful-sweet it is to stand
    On some tall point 'tween earth and heaven,
And view, far round, the two worlds blend,
    And the vast deep by wild winds riven.

And fearful-sweet it is to peep
    Upon the yellow strands below,
When on their oars the fishers sleep,
    And calmer seas their limits know.   40

And bending o'er this jutting ridge,
    To look adown the steep rock's sides,
From crag to crag, from ledge to ledge,
    Down which the samphire-gatherer glides.

Perhaps the blue-bell nods its head,
    Or poppy trembles o'er the brink,
Or there the wild-briar roses shed
    Their tender leaves of fading pink.

Oh fearful-sweet it is, through air
    To watch their scattered leaves descend,   50
Or mark some pensile sea-weed dare
    Over the perilous top to bend,

And, joyous in its liberty,
    Wave all its playful tresses wide,
Mocking the death, that waits for me,
    If I but step one foot aside.

44 samphire-gatherer] Samphire, or *Crithmum maritimum,* is an aromatic plant with fleshy leaves (used in pickling) that grows on rocks by the sea. The name could also refer to other maritime plants, such as glasswort.
    51 pensile] Pendulous, hanging down.

Yet I can hear the solemn surge
   Sounding long murmurs on the coast;
And the hoarse waves each other urge,
60   And voices mingling now, then lost.

The children of the cliffs I hear,
   Free as the waves, as daring too;
They climb the rocky ledges there,
   To pluck sea-flowers of humble hue.

Their calling voices seem to chime;
   Their choral laughs rise far beneath;
While, who the dizziest point can climb,
   Throws gaily down the gathered wreath.

I see their little upward hands,
70   Outspread to catch the falling flowers,
While, watching these, the little bands
   Sing welcomes to the painted showers.

And others scramble up the rocks,
   To share the pride of him, who, throned
On jutting crag, at danger mocks,
   King of the cliffs and regions round.

Clinging with hands and feet and knee,
   How few that envied height attain!
Not half-way up those urchins, see,
80   Yet ply their perilous toil in vain.

Fearless their hero sports in air,
   A rival almost of the crows,
And weaves fresh-gathered blossoms there,
   To bind upon his victor-brows.

The broad sea-myrtle glossy bright,
   Mixed with the poppy's scarlet bell,
And wall-flowers, dipt in golden light,
   Twine in his sea-cliff coronal.

The breeze has stolen his pageant-crown;
  He leans to mark how low it falls; 90
Oh, bend not thou! lest, headlong down,
  Thou paint'st with death these fair sea-walls!

Now, o'er the sky's concave I glance,
  Now o'er the azure deep below,
Now on the long-drawn shores of France,
  And now on England's coast I go,

To where old Beachy's beaked head,
  High peering in the utmost West,
Bids the observant seaman dread,
  Lest he approach his guarded rest. 100

What fairy hand hangs loose that sail
  In graceful fold of sunny light?
Beneath what tiny figures move,
  Traced darkly on the wave's blue light?

It is the patient fisher's sloop,
  Watching upon the azure calm;
They are his wet sea-boys, that stoop,
  And haul the net with bending arm.

But on this southern coast is seen,
  From Purbeck hills to Dover piers, 110
No foam-tipt wave so clearly green,
  No rock so dark as Hastings rears.

How grand is that indented bay,
  That sweeps to Romney's sea-beat wall,
Whose marshes slowly stretch away,
  And slope into some green hill small.

Now North and East I bend my sight
  To where the flats of Flanders spread;
And now where Calais cliffs are bright,
  Made brighter by the sunset red. 120

Shows not this towering point so high
    To him, who in mid-channel sails;
For the slant light from western sky
    Ne'er on its awful front prevails.

But mark! on *this* cliff Shakspeare stood,
    And waved around him Prosper's wand,
When straight from forth the mighty flood
    The Tempest "rose, at his command!"
              (wr. bef. 1823; pub. 1826)

To the River Dove

Oh! stream beloved by those,
    With Fancy who repose,
And court her dreams 'mid scenes sublimely wild,
    Lulled by the summer-breeze,
    Among the drowsy trees
Of thy high steeps, and by thy murmurs mild,

    My lonely footsteps guide,
    Where thy blue waters glide,
Fringed with the Alpine shrub and willow light;
    'Mid rocks and mountains rude,
    Here hung with shaggy wood,
And there upreared in points of frantic height.

    Beneath their awful gloom,
    Oh! blue-eyed Nymph, resume
The mystic spell, that wakes the poet's soul!
    While all thy caves around
    In lonely murmur sound,
And feeble thunders o'er these summits roll.

    O shift the wizard scene
    To banks of pastoral green

10

20

19 wizard] Enchanted.

When mellow sun-set lights up all thy vales;
   And shows each turf-born flower,
   That, sparkling from the shower,
Its recent fragrance on the air exhales.

   When Evening's distant hues
   Their silent grace diffuse
In sleepy azure o'er the mountain's head;
   Or dawn in purple faint,
   As nearer cliffs they paint,
Then lead me 'mid thy slopes and woodland shade.   30

   Nor would I wander far,
   When Twilight lends her star,
And o'er thy scenes her doubtful shades repose;
   Nor when the Moon's first light
   Steals on each bowery height,
Like the winged music o'er the folded rose.

   Then, on thy winding shore,
   The fays and elves, once more,
Trip in gay ringlets to the reed's light note;
   Some launch the acorn's *ring,*   40
   Their sail—Papilio's wing,
Thus shipped, in chace of moon-beams, gay they float.

   But, at the midnight hour,
   I woo thy thrilling power,
While silent moves the glow-worm's light along,
   And o'er the dim hill-tops
   The gloomy red moon drops,
And in the grave of darkness leaves thee long.

   Even then thy waves I hear,
   And own a nameless fear,   50
As, 'mid the stillness, the night winds do swell,
   Or (faint from distance) hark
   To the lone watch-dog's bark!
Answering a melancholy far sheep bell.

41 Papilio's wing] The butterfly's wing.

O! Nymph fain would I trace
    Thy sweet awakening grace,
When summer dawn first breaks upon thy stream;
    And see thee braid thy hair;
    And keep thee ever there,
60 Like thought recovered from an antique dream!
                    (wr. bef. 1823; pub. 1826)

The Sea-Mew

Forth from her cliffs sublime the sea-mew goes
To meet the storm, rejoicing! To the woods
She gives herself; and, borne above the peaks
Of highest head-lands, wheels among the clouds,
And hears Death's voice in thunder roll around,
While the waves far below, driven on the shore,
Foaming with pride and rage, make hollow moan.
Now, tossed along the gale from cloud to cloud,
She turns her silver wings touched by the beam,
10 That through a night of vapours darts its long,
Level line; and, vanishing 'mid the gloom,
Enters the secret region of the storm;
But soon again appearing, forth she moves
Out from the mount'nous shapes of other clouds,
And, sweeping down them, hastens to new joys.
It was the wailing of the deep she heard!
No fears repel her: when the tumult swells,
Ev'n as the spirit-stirring trumpet glads
The neighing war-horse, is the sound to her.
20 O'er the waves hovering, while they lash the rocks,
And lift, as though to reach her, their chafed tops,
Dashing the salt foam o'er her downy wings,
Higher she mounts, and from her feathers shakes
The shower, triumphant. As they sink, she sinks,
And with her long plumes sweeps them in their fall,
As if in mockery; then, as they retreat,
She dances o'er them, and with her shrill note
Dares them, as in scorn.

It is not thus she meets their summer smiles;
Then, skimming low along the level tide,   30
She dips the last point of her crescent wings,
At measured intervals, with playful grace,
And rises, as retreating to her home.
High on yon 'pending rock, but poised awhile
In air, as though enamoured of the scene,
She drops, at once, and settles on the sea.
On the green waves, transparent then she rides,
And breathes their freshness, trims her plumage white,
And, listening to the murmur of the surge,
Doth let them bear her wheresoe'er they will.   40

Oh! bird beloved of him, who, absent long
From his dear native land, espies thee ere
The mountain tops o'er the far waters rise,
And hails thee as the harbinger of home!
Thou bear'st to him a welcome on thy wings.
His white sail o'er th' horizon thou hast seen
And hailed it, with thy oft-repeated cry,
Announcing England. "England is near!" he cries,
And every seaman's heart an echo beats,
And "England—England!" sounds along the deck,   50
Mounts to the shrouds, and finds an answering voice,
Ev'n at the top-mast head, where, posted long,
The "look out" sailor clings, and with keen eye,
By long experience finely judging made,
Reads the dim characters of air-veiled shores.
O happy bird! whom Nature's changing scenes
Can ever please; who mount'st upon the wind
Of Winter and amid the grandeur soar'st
Of tempests, or sinkest to the peaceful deep,
And float'st with sunshine on the summer calm!   60
O happy bird! lend me thy pinions now.
Thy joys are mine, and I, like thee, would skim
Along the pleasant curve of the salt bays,
Where the blue seas do now serenely sleep;
Or, when they waken to the Evening breeze,
And every crisping wave reflects her tints
Of rose and amber,—like thee, too, would I
Over the mouths of the sea-rivers float,

70
Or watch, majestic, on the tranquil tide,
The proud ships follow one another down,
And spread themselves upon the mighty main,
Freighted for shores that shall not dawn on sight,
Till a new sky uplift its burning arch,
And half the globe be traversed. Then to him,
The home-bound seaman, should my joyous flight
Once more the rounding river point,—to him
Who comes, perchance, from coasts of darkness, where
Grim Ruin, from his throne of hideous rocks,
O'ercanopied with pine, or giant larch,

80
Scowls on the mariner, and Terror wild
Looks through the parting gloom with ghastly eye,
Listens to woods, that groan beneath the storm,
And starts to see the river-cedar fall.

How sweet to him, who from such strands returns,
How sweet to glide along his homeward stream
By well-known meads and woods and village cots,
That lie in peace around the ivied spire
And ancient parsonage, where the small, fresh stream
Gives a safe haven to the humbler barks

90
At anchor, just as last he viewed the scene.
And soft as then upon the surface lies
The sunshine, and as sweet the landscape
Smiles, as on that day he sadly bade farewell
To those he loved. Just so it smiles, and yet
How many other days and months have fled,
What shores remote his steps have wandered o'er,
What scenes of various life unfolded strange,
Since that dim yesterday! The present scene
Unchanged, though fresh, appears the only truth,

100
And all the interval a dream! May those
He loves still live, as lives the landscape now;
And may to-morrow's sun light the thin clouds
Of doubt with rainbow-hues of hope and joy!

Bird! I would hover with thee o'er the deck,
Till a new tide with thronging ships should tremble;
Then, frightened at their strife, with thee I'd fly

To the free waters and the boundless skies,
And drink the light of heaven and living airs;
Then with thee haunt the seas and sounding shores,
And dwell upon the mountain's beaked top,   110
Where nought should come but thou and the wild winds.
There would I listen, sheltered in our cell,
The tempest's voice, while midnight wraps the world.
But, if a moon-beam pierced the clouds, and shed
Its sudden gleam upon the foaming waves,
Touching with pale light each sharp line of cliff,
Whose head towered darkly, which no eye could trace,—
Then downward I would wheel amid the storm,
And watch, with untired gaze, the embattled surges
Pouring in deep array, line after line,   120
And hear their measured war-note sound along
The groaning coast, whereat the winds above
Answer the summons, and each secret cave,
Untrod by footsteps, and each precipice,
That oft had on the unconscious fisher frowned,
And every hollow bay and utmost cape
Sighs forth a fear for the poor mariner.
He, meanwhile, hears the sound o'er waters wide;
Lashed to the mast, he hears, and thinks of home.

O bird! lend me thy wings,   130
That swifter than the blast I may out-fly
Danger, and from yon port the life-boat call.
And see! e'en now the guardian bark rides o'er
The mountain-billows, and descends through chasms
Where lurks Destruction eager for his prey,
With eyes of flashing fire and foamy jaws.
He, by strange storm-lights shown, uplifts his head,
And, from the summit of each rising wave,
Darts a grim glance upon the daring crew,
And sinks the way their little boat must go!   140
But she, with blessings armed, best shield! as if
Immortal, surmounts the abyss, and rides
The watery ridge upon her pliant oars,
Which conquer the wild, raging element
And that dark demon, with angelic power.

Wave after wave, he sullenly retreats,
With oft repeated menace, and beholds
The poor fisherman, with all his fellows,
Borne from his grasp in triumph to the shore—
150   There Hope stands watchful, and her call is heard
Wafted on wishes of the crowd. Hark! hark!
Is that her voice rejoicing? 'Tis her song
Swells high upon the gale, and 'tis her smile,
That gladdens the thick darkness. THEY ARE SAVED.

Bird of the winds and waves and lonely shores,
Of loftiest promontories—and clouds,
And tempests—Bird of the sun-beam, that seeks
Thee through the storm, and glitters on thy wings!
Bird of the sun-beam and the azure calm,
160   Of the green cliff, hung with gay summer plants,
Who lov'st to sit in stillness on the bough,
That leans far o'er the sea, and hearest there
The chasing surges and the hushing sounds,
That float around thee, when tall shadows tremble,
And the rock-weeds stream lightly on the breeze.
O bird of joy! what wanderer of air
Can vie with thee in grandeur of delights,
Whose home is on the precipice, whose sport
Is on the waves? O happy, happy bird!
170   Lend me thy wings, and let thy joys be mine!
                              (wr. bef. 1823; pub. 1826)

On a First View of the Group
Called the Seven Mountains;
in the Approach to Cologne from Xanten

When first I saw ye, Mountains, the broad sun
In cloudy grandeur sunk, and showed, far off,
A solemn vision of imperfect shapes
Crowding the southward sky and stalking on
And pointing us "the way that we should go."
Dark thunder-mists dwelt on ye; and your forms,
Obscurely towering, stood before the eye,
Like some strange thing portentous and unknown.
I watched the coming storm. The sulphurous gloom
Clung sullenly round me, and a dull tinge   10
Began to redden through these mournful shades.
A low imperfect murmur o'er ye rolled.
Doubtful, I listened. On the breathless calm
Again I heard it—then, ye Mountains vast,
Amid the tenfold darkness ye withdrew,
And vanished quite, save that your high tops smoked,
And from your clouds the arrowy lightnings burst,
While peals resistless shook the trembling world!—
                         (wr. bef. 1823; pub. 1826)

A Second View of the Seven Mountains

Mountains! when next I saw ye it was Noon,
     And Summer o'er your distant steeps had flung
     Her veil of misty light: your rock-woods hung
Just green and budding, though in pride of June,

And pale your many-spiring tops appeared,
     While, here and there, soft tints of silver grey
     Marked where some jutting cliff received the ray;
Or long-lived precipice its brow upreared.

Beyond your tapering pinnacles, a show
10   Of other giant-forms more dimly frowned,
       Hinting the wonders of that unknown ground,
And of deep wizard-vales, unseen below.

Thus, o'er the long and level plains ye rose
       Abrupt and awful, when my raptured eye
       Beheld ye. Mute I gazed! 'Twas then a sigh
Alone could speak the soul's most full repose;

For of a grander world ye seemed the dawn,
       Rising beyond where Time's tired wing can go,
As, bending o'er the green Rhine's liquid lawn,
20   Ye watched the ages of the world below.
                                   (wr. bef. 1823; pub. 1826)

12 wizard-vales] Enchanted valleys.

Emma Roberts

(1794?–1840)

Born after the death of her father, Captain William Roberts, to a mother with strong literary interests, Emma Roberts grew up in Bath with an older sister. She met Letitia Elizabeth Landon while studying at the British Museum, and the two became good friends, eventually sharing a house in Hans Place with other literary women for a year, a year that Roberts later termed "one of the happiest of my life."[1]

The *Monthly Review* called Roberts's first book, *Memoirs of the Rival Houses of York and Lancaster, or the White and Red Roses* (1827), "the most full and lively picture which we possess of the state of English society during the fourteenth and fifteenth centuries."[2] The *New Monthly Magazine* observed, "The glow of romance is shed over, but never allowed to diminish, the sober truth of history; and the judgment of the writer is everywhere evinced by her just discrimination between the conflicting authorities."[3] The *London Literary Gazette* also reviewed the book favorably.[4]

In February 1828, her mother having died, Roberts went to India with her sister and brother-in-law, Captain Robert Adair McNaghten of the Sixty-first Bengal Infantry, spending the next two years in Agra, Cawnpore, and Etawah. Beginning in December 1832 she described these places in articles for the *Asiatic Journal,* a periodical to which she contributed until the end of her life. She later published a selection of these articles as *Scenes and Characteristics of Hindostan, with Sketches of Anglo-Indian Society* (1835).[5] The *London Quarterly*

---

1. See her introduction to Letitia Elizabeth Landon, *The Zenana and Minor Poems of L.E.L.: with a Memoir by Emma Roberts* (London, 1839).

2. September 1827, 37–47.

3. 21 (1 August 1827): 328.

4. 2 June 1827, 337–39.

5. This edition was published in three volumes by Allen & Company, London. It was reprinted in Philadelphia in 1836.

Review described the book as "animated and interesting."[6] According to a notice in the *Calcutta Literary Gazette,*

> She had a peculiar readiness in receiving, and a singular power of retaining, first impressions of the most minute and evanescent nature. She walked through a street or a bazaar, and everything that passed over the mirror of her mind left a clear and lasting trace. She was thus enabled, even years after a visit to a place of interest, to describe everything with the same freshness and fidelity as if she had taken notes upon the spot. They who have gone over the same ground are delighted to find . . . their own vague and half-faded impressions revived and defined by her magic glass; while the novelty and vividness of her foreign pictures make her home readers feel that they are nearly as much entitled to be called travellers as the fair authoress herself.[7]

Roberts also described in painful detail the isolation and unhappiness of many young women who, thinking to escape the privations of a limited income in England for a luxurious exotic life in the east, followed a family member to a faraway, tropical post. On arriving, she found that three was a crowd, that it was too hot to garden or do needlework, that the warm air had destroyed her guitar and piano, that insects devoured her music books, and that drawing supplies were scarce. Moreover, "her brother and sister are domestic, and do not sympathise in her *ennui;* they either see little company, or invite guests merely with a view to be quit of an incumbrance. . . . Few young women who have accompanied their married sisters to India possess the means of returning home; however strong their dislike may be to the country, their lot is cast in it, and they must remain in a state of miserable dependence, with the danger of being left unprovided for before them, until they shall be rescued . . . by an offer of marriage."[8]

Roberts was happier and more productive at Cawnpore than in the remote jungle post of Etawah; she sent to press *Oriental Scenes, Dramatic Sketches and Tales, with Other Poems* (1830), dedicated to Letitia Landon (L.E.L.) and republished in London in 1832. Its most memorable poem, "The Rajah's Obsequies," condemns suttee. After her sister died in 1831, Roberts moved to Calcutta, where she devoted herself to literature and journalism and edited a newspaper, the *Oriental Observer.*

The next year, for health reasons she returned to London, where she continued writing for the *Asiatic Journal;* she also edited for John Murray the

6. Quoted in Allibone, *Critical Dictionary.*

7. Quoted in Mrs. Anne Katherine Elwood's *Memoirs of Literary Ladies of England, from the Commencement of the Last Century,* 2 vols. (London, 1843), 2:335.

8. Quoted in ibid., 338–39.

sixty-fourth edition of Mrs. Rundell's *A New System of Domestic Cookery, Founded on Principles of Economy, and Adapted to the Use of Private Families* (1840), including nearly one thousand new recipes. Also during this period she contributed almost three dozen poems, tales, and dramatic sketches to literary annuals, including the *Forget-Me-Not, Friendship's Offering,* the *Literary Souvenir,* the *Amulet,* and the *Pledge of Friendship,* among others. She published a travel-advice book, *The East India Voyages,* in 1839. *Fisher's Drawing-Room Scrap-Book* for 1840 included her biographical sketch of Landon, later reprinted with *The Zenana and Minor Poems of L.E.L.* A book of drawings by Robert Elliot entitled *Views in India, China, and on the Shores of the Red Sea* (1835) used her descriptions.

On 1 September 1839 Roberts and a female companion set out unaccompanied on an arduous overland journey to India through Egypt. She had previously arranged to send back to the *Asiatic Journal* a series of articles describing their travels. They crossed the desert on donkeys, and by 29 October they had reached Bombay, settling in Parell. While there, Roberts edited a new weekly paper, *The Bombay United Service Gazette,* and worked on a book about the presidency and a plan to provide employment for Indian women. She became ill in April 1840 and died at Poona on 16 September 1840. The last travel article in her series for the *Asiatic Journal* appeared in the issue announcing her death. Later the series was reprinted in London as *Notes of an Overland Journey Through France and Egypt to Bombay* (1841). Roberts was buried in India near the grave of another literary Englishwoman, Dorothy Wordsworth's friend Maria Jane Jewsbury.

MAJOR WORKS: *Almegro, a Poem, in Five Cantos* (London, 1819); *Memoirs of the Rival Houses of York and Lancaster, or the White and Red Roses,* 2 vols. (London, 1827); *Oriental Scenes, Dramatic Sketches and Tales, with Other Poems* (Calcutta, 1830); *Scenes and Characteristics of Hindostan, with Sketches of Anglo-Indian Society,* 3 vols. (London, 1835); *The East India Voyager, or Ten Minutes' Advice to the Outward Bound* (London, 1839); *Notes of an Overland Journey Through France and Egypt to Bombay* (London, 1841); *Hindostan: its Landscapes, Palaces, Temples, Tombs; the Shores of the Red Sea; and the . . . Scenery of the Himalaya Mountains, Illustrated in a Series of Views,* 2 vols. (London, [1850]).

TEXT USED: Text from the *Forget-Me-Not* for 1830.

Song

Upon the Ganges' regal stream,
    The sun's bright splendours rest;
And gorgeously the noon-tide beam
    Reposes on its breast:
But in a small secluded nook,
    Beyond the western sea,
There rippling glides a narrow brook,
    That's dearer far to me.

The lory perches on my hand,
    Caressing to be fed,
And spreads its plumes at my command,
    And stoops its purple head;
But where the robin, humble guest,
    Comes flying from the tree,
Which bears its unpretending nest,
    Alas! I'd rather be.

The fire-fly flashes through the sky,
    A meteor swift and bright;
And the wide space around, on high,
    Gleams with its emerald light;
Though glory tracks that shooting star,
    And bright its splendours shine,
The glow-worm's lamp is dearer far
    To this sad heart of mine.

Throughout the summer year, the flowers
    In all the flush of bloom,
Clustering around the forest bowers,
    Exhale their rich perfume.
The daisy, and the primrose pale,
    Though scentless they may be,

10

20

30

---

1 Ganges'] River in India.
  9 lory] Parrotlike bird of the family Loriinae with brilliant plumage, from Southeast Asia and Australia.

That gem a far, far distant vale,
    Are much more prized by me.

The lotus opes its chalices,
    Upon the tank's broad lake,
Where India's stately palaces
    Their ample mirrors make:
But reckless of each tower and dome,
    The splendid and the grand,
I languish for a cottage home,
    Within my native land.   40
                    Benares, 1828
                     (1830)

34 tank's] Indian term for a reservoir for irrigation and drinking water.

Mary Robinson

(1758–1800)

Mary Robinson's prolific literary career spanned a quarter-century, from her first book in 1775 to her last collection, *Lyrical Tales,* published shortly before her death in 1800. She was not only a poet but also a novelist, actress, playwright, translator, noted beauty, and, for a time, paramour of the Prince of Wales, the future King George IV. Robinson was born in Bristol on 27 November 1758 to Mary Seys and John Darby, a prosperous American sea captain, who left his family to pursue commercial schemes in Lapland and America when Robinson was not quite seven. He returned to England, though not to his family, three years later, his fortune lost. Robinson had been a pupil in the school run by Hannah More's sisters but now was sent to Chelsea to become the student of Meribah Lorrington, a learned woman and an alcoholic, who was to profoundly influence her student. When Robinson's mother then established her own small school in Little Chelsea, Robinson taught English. After only eight months, though, Robinson's father forbade his wife to work and closed the school.

As a child Robinson read the poems of Anna Letitia Barbauld "with rapture; I thought them the most beautiful Poems I had ever seen, and considered the woman who could invent such poetry, as the most to be envied of human creatures."[1] At fifteen Robinson attracted the attention of David Garrick, the manager of the Drury Lane Theatre, who wanted her to play Cordelia opposite his Lear. Instead, her mother pressured her into marrying Thomas Robinson on 12 April 1774 at St. Martin's in the Fields. Thomas Robinson was an articled clerk at Lincoln's Inn and a gambler who borrowed heavily. They lived a fashionable life for a short time, until 1775, when he was sentenced to debtor's prison; Robinson and her infant daughter, Maria, stayed with him there for fifteen months. During this period she wrote a long poem, aptly

---

1. Mary Robinson, *Perdita: The Memoirs of Mary Robinson,* ed. M. J. Levy (London, 1994), 54–55.

titled *Captivity.* Georgiana, wife of the fifth Duke of Devonshire, became her patron, introducing her to Charles James Fox and Richard Brinsley Sheridan.

Shortly after his release from prison, Thomas Robinson agreed to allow Mary to pursue the stage career she had earlier forgone. Sheridan encouraged her, and Garrick, now retired from the stage, became her tutor. She debuted as Juliet on 10 December 1776. The next day the *Morning Post* noted that "her person is genteel, her voice harmonious and admitting of various modulations;—and her features, when properly animated, are striking and expressive.—At present she discovers a theatrical genius in the rough; which, however, in elocution as well as action, seems to require considerable polishing." The second time she played the part, she was paid the handsome sum of twenty pounds.[2] Robinson was to play three dozen parts during four seasons on the stage. In the summer of 1778 the birth of her second daughter, Sophia, who died at six weeks, prevented her from playing in the premiere of *A School for Scandal.* But she was back on stage by November, and on 30 April 1778 she played Lady Macbeth in a performance for her benefit, the evening concluding with her own composition, *The Lucky Escape,* a musical farce; only the songs appear to have survived. During the 1779–80 season she was on stage for fifty-five nights.

Robinson's performance of 3 December 1779 was the turning point of her life. She played Perdita in Garrick's alteration of *The Winter's Tale* at a command performance for the royal family. The Prince of Wales, then only seventeen, found her captivating, and in the spring of 1780 she became his lover; their much publicized affair made her the object of both scandal and satire, earning her the sobriquet "Perdita." By December the prince had lost interest, and she was seven thousand pounds in debt. But she continued to live the fashionable life, and it was during this period that Romney, Gainsborough, and Reynolds all painted her portrait. From October to December 1781 she was in Paris, feted as "la belle Anglaise"; there she met the queen, Marie Antoinette. Although her daughter claims that Robinson never returned to the stage, in fact she did for most of the 1782–83 season, playing Rosamond in *Henry the Second* at Covent Garden on 31 December 1782 and Alicia in Nicholas Rowe's *Jane Shore* on 27 January 1783. The *Morning Herald* for 29 March 1783 praises her Victoria in Hannah Cowley's comedy *A Bold Stroke for a Husband;* she also added to her repertoire Oriana in *The Knight of Malta* and Alinda in *The Pilgrim.* The king granted her five thousand pounds in cash (reputedly in return for the prince's love letters) and eventually a life-time annuity of five hundred pounds a year in lieu of a bond the prince had signed promising her twenty thousand pounds when he came of age.

Robinson settled at Windsor with Col. Banastre Tarleton (1754–1833), a well-known British officer who had fought in the American War of Independence but also an inveterate gambler.[3] By 1783 her five-hundred-pound "lifetime annuity" had ceased, and in June Tarleton retired from the army on half-pay, his gambling debts still mounting.[4] Robinson fell seriously ill, either from rheumatic fever (as her daughter insists) or from a miscarriage (as others suggest). Whatever the case, she was bedridden for six months, with both legs paralyzed. She and Tarleton eventually went to France, and her belongings were sold at auction on 7 January 1785.[5] From February to May 1787 she played several roles in Edinburgh, including Lady Macbeth, Alicia in *Jane Shore,* and the title role in *The Irish Widow.*

Robinson's literary career began in earnest in 1788. Like Lord Byron, she was a notorious personality, her life and works inextricably linked in the public consciousness, each contributing to the interest and success of the other. She is said to have composed extemporaneously "Lines to Him Who Will Understand Them" for Richard Burke, son of Edmund Burke, who published the poem in the *Annual Register.* During the winter of 1790 Robinson carried on a poetical correspondence with Robert Merry, the Della Cruscan. In reply to his "Laurel of Liberty," she composed, reputedly in only twelve hours, her *Ainsi va le Monde.* Her *Poems* (1791) had nearly six hundred subscribers, headed by the Prince of Wales. The *Analytical Review* wrote, "If a great variety of refined sentiments, sometimes of the tender but more commonly of the plaintive kind, adorned with rich and beautiful imagery, and expressed in sweetly harmonious verse, can entitle the Poetical Productions of a Female Pen to public praise, Mrs. Robinson's Poems will obtain no inconsiderable share of applause."[6]

Eventually Robinson became known as the "English Sappho." Her poetic works, comprising more than a dozen volumes, portray vividly what she was to term in her memoirs "this world of duplicity and sorrow." Works such as "The Lascar" and "The Negro Girl" champion the plight of the disenfranchised while chronicling the moral bankruptcy surrounding and victimizing them. She explores the irrational—the realm of madness and dreams—in poems such as "The Maniac" and "The Lady of the Black Tower." Here, as in

---

3. He became the Whig M.P. for Liverpool in 1790 and was made a baronet in 1815.

4. Highfill, Burnim, and Langhans, *Biographical Dictionary,* 13:36.

5. Whitley Papers, British Library; Robert D. Bass, *The Green Dragoon: The Lives of Banastre Tarleton and Mary Robinson* (New York, 1957), 238.

6. 10 (1791): 279.

Keats, the line between the waking world and the dream world blurs, leaving the nature of reality itself in question. Her settings are often gothic, peopled by those such as the Alien Boy—the isolated, the abandoned, the confined, the despairing—tormented people who long for oblivion. Robinson's universe is littered with shipwrecks, drownings, stabbings, and murderers lying in wait. Injustice prevails, merit goes unrecognized and unrewarded, and love fails to triumph. Nature offers no consolation to human woes, and psychic pain seems strangely pointless. God is nowhere in evidence, and religious institutions only offer another form of tyranny. Her best poems, such as "London's Summer Morning," heap image upon image with striking energy, concreteness, and immediacy to make a cacophony of human experience. Her poems are often not without humor, as she pokes holes in the facade of conventional life, exposing its hypocrisy and emptiness. Many of her poems first appeared in periodicals under pseudonyms.[7] In 1799 she became poetry editor of the *Morning Post,* where she published a series of satirical odes.

Robinson was the friend of William Godwin, Mary Wollstonecraft, John Wolcot (Peter Pindar), and Samuel Taylor Coleridge, who called her "A woman of undoubted genius" and observed, "I never knew a human being with so *full* a mind—bad, good, & indifferent, I grant you, but full, & overflowing."[8] We know that in 1799 Coleridge showed her an early draft, now lost, of "Kubla Khan," for she quotes parts of it in her poetic tribute, "To The Poet Coleridge."[9] After her *Lyrical Tales* appeared in 1800, Wordsworth seriously considered changing the title of the second edition of his *Lyrical Ballads.* The first of at least eight novels, *Vancenza; or, The Dangers of Credulity* (1792), sold out in one day, and five more editions quickly followed. *The False Friend, a Domestic Story* (1799) includes an unflattering portrait of Tarleton, who had left her in 1798 to marry well.

Not every work met with acclaim. *Nobody,* her farce about fashionable life, was condemned on 29 November 1794 at Drury Lane by an audience composed mostly of those she satirized. The prompter noted that "the dissatisfaction to the Piece being so great [Mrs Jordan] was so much agitated as to be unable to repeat above one half of the Epilogue, which, from the Opposition of Hisses and Applauses, not scarcely three lines of that could be distinctly heard."[10] *The Sicilian Lover,* a five-act tragedy in verse, was never performed, though it was published in 1796.

---

7. These included Laura, Laura Maria, Julia, Perdita, Tabitha Bramble, Anne Frances Randall, Oberon, and Horace Juvenal.

8. Coleridge to Robert Southey, quoted in the introduction to Robinson, *Perdita,* vii.

9. According to Jack Stillinger, no known draft of "Kubla Khan" conforms to Robinson's quotations (private conversation with author, December 1991).

10. Highfill, Burnim, and Langhans, *Biographical Dictionary,* 13:37.

By the spring of 1800 Robinson's health had deteriorated seriously, and she gave up her London life and moved to a cottage near Windsor to be with her daughter. Here, on 17 July 1800, she witnessed the military spectacle she would describe in her poetic tour de force, "The Camp," published two weeks after the event under the pseudonym Oberon in the *Morning Post* and later retitled "Winkfield Plain; or, A Description of a Camp in the Year 1800" for its posthumous reprinting in *The Wild Wreath*. During the final year of her life Robinson wrote many of her best poems, including "The Haunted Beach" and "The Poet's Garret." On 18 December, her last poem, "All Alone," appeared in the *Morning Post*. She died on 26 December 1800 of pulmonary edema and was buried in the churchyard of Old Windsor. Engraved on her tomb is one of her own poems, concluding with the lines

No wealth had she, no power to sway;
Yet rich in worth, and learning's store:
She *wept her summer hours away,*
She heard the wintry storm no more.

Yet o'er this low and silent spot,
Full many a bud of Spring shall wave,
While she, by all, save ONE, forgot,
SHALL SNATCH A WREATH BEYOND THE GRAVE!

The only literary friends at her small funeral were William Godwin and John Wolcot. Her daughter, Maria Elizabeth, a novelist, completed Robinson's memoirs and in 1801 published them in four volumes along with several other works. Maria Elizabeth's 1804 volume, *The Wild Wreath*, lists her mother as a major "contributor." And in 1806 Robinson's *Poetical Works* appeared in three volumes, including many of her previously uncollected or unpublished poems (but, interestingly, not the provocative "The Camp" ["Winkfield Plain"]), as well as poems by others written in tribute to Robinson, including "A Stranger Minstrel" by Samuel Taylor Coleridge.

MAJOR WORKS: *Poems* (London, 1775); *Captivity, a Poem. And Celadon and Lydia, a Tale* (London, [1777]); *Ainsi va le monde, a Poem,* 2nd ed. (London, 1790); *Impartial Reflections on the Present Situation of the Queen of France; by a Friend to Humanity* (London, 1791); *Poems,* 2 vols. (London, 1791–93); *Monody to the Memory of Sir Joshua Reynolds* (London, 1792); *Vancenza; or, The Dangers of Credulity* (London, 1792); *Modern Manners, a Poem. In Two Cantos* (London, 1793); *Monody to the Memory of the Late Queen of France* (London, 1793); *An Ode to the Harp of the Late Accomplished and Amiable Louisa Hanway* (London, 1793); *Sight, the Cavern of Woe, and Solitude. Poems* (London, 1793); *The Widow, or A Picture of Modern Times. A Novel, in a Series of Letters,* 2 vols. (London, 1794); *Angelina; a Novel,* 3 vols. (London, 1796); *Hubert de Sevrac; a Romance of the Eighteenth Century,* 3 vols. (London, 1796); *Sappho and Phaon. In a Series of Legitimate Sonnets, with Thoughts on Poetical Subjects, and Anecdotes of the Grecian Poetess* (London, 1796); *The Sicilian Lover. A Tragedy. In Five Acts* (London, 1796); *Walsingham; or, The Pupil of Nature. A Domestic Story* (London, 1797); *The False Friend: a Domestic Story,* 4 vols. (London, 1799); *The Natural Daughter. With Portraits of the Leadenhead Family. A Novel,* 2 vols. (London, 1799); *Thoughts on the Condition of Women, and on the Injustice of Mental Subordination* (London, 1799); *Lyrical Tales* (London and Bristol, 1800); *Memoirs of the Late Mrs. Robinson, Written by Herself. With Some Posthumous Pieces,* ed. Maria Elizabeth Robinson, 4 vols. (London, 1801); *The Wild Wreath,* ed. M.[aria] E.[lizabeth] Robinson (London, 1804); *The Poetical Works of the Late Mrs. Mary Robinson, including many Pieces Never Before Published,* ed. Maria Elizabeth Robinson, 3 vols. (London, 1806).

TEXTS USED: Text of "The Linnet's Petition" from *Poems* (1775). Text of "Second Ode to the Nightingale" from *Poems,* vol. 1 (1791). Texts of "The Maniac," "Stanzas Written after Successive Nights of Melancholy Dreams," "London's Summer Morning," "January 1795," "Marie Antoinette's Lamentation," "The Lascar," "The Negro Girl," "The Alien Boy," "The Haunted Beach," "To the Poet Coleridge," "The Poet's Garret," and "The Lady of the Black Tower" from *The Poetical Works of the Late Mary Robinson* (1806). Text of "The Camp" from *Morning Post,* 1 August 1800. Judith Pascoe and Martin Levy helped with the dating of Robinson's poems.

The Linnet's Petition

I

As Stella sat the other day,
　　Beneath a myrtle shade,
A tender bird in plaintive notes,
　　Address'd the pensive maid.

II

Upon a bough in gaudy cage,
　　The feather'd warbler hung,
And in melodious accents thus,
　　His fond petition sung.

III

"Ah! pity my unhappy fate,
　　"And set a captive free,　　　　　　　　10
"So may you never feel the loss,
　　"Of peace, or liberty."

IV

"With ardent pray'r and humble voice,
    "Your mercy now I crave,
"Your kind compassion and regard,
    "My tender life to save."

V

"Ah! wherefore am I here confin'd,
    "Ah! why does fate ordain,
"A life so innocent as mine,
20   "Should end in grief and pain."

VI

"I envy every little bird,
    "That warbles gay and free,
"The meanest of the feather'd race,
    "Is happier far than me."

VII

"Sweet liberty by heaven sent,
    "From me, alas! is torn,
"And here without a cause confin'd,
    "A captive doom'd I mourn."

VIII

"When bright Aurora's silver rays,
30   "Proclaim the rising morn,
"And glitt'ring dew drops shine around,
    "Or gild the flow'ring thorn."

IX

"When every bird except myself,
    "Went forth his mate to see,
"I always tun'd my downy throat,
    "To please, and gladden thee."

X

"Beneath thy window each new day,
    "And in the myrtle bow'r,
"I strove to charm thy list'ning ear,
40   "With all my little pow'r."

XI

"Ah! what avails this gaudy cage,
  "Or what is life to me,
"If thus confin'd, if thus distress'd,
  "And robb'd of liberty."

XII

"I who the greatest fav'rite was
  "Of all the feather'd race,
"Think, Stella think, the pain I feel,
  "And pity my sad case."

XIII

"While here condemn'd to sure despair,
  "What comfort have I left,   50
"Or how can I this fate survive,
  "Of every joy bereft."

XIV

"My harmless life was ever free,
  "From mischief and from ill,
"My only wish on earth to prove,
  "Obedient, to your will."

XV

"Then pity my unhappy fate,
  "And set a captive free,
"So may you never feel the loss,
  "Of peace, or liberty."   60

XVI

On Stella's breast compassion soon,
  Each tender feeling wrought,
Resolv'd to give him back with speed,
  That freedom which he sought.

XVII

With friendly hand she ope'd the cage,
  By kindred pity mov'd,
And sympathetic joys divine,
  Her gentle bosom prov'd.

XVIII

When first she caught the flutt'ring thing,
  She felt strange extasy,
70
But never knew so great a bliss,
  As when she set him free.

        (1775)

Second Ode to the Nightingale

Blest be thy song, sweet NIGHTINGALE,
Lorn minstrel of the lonely vale!
Where oft I've heard thy dulcet strain
In mournful melody complain;
When in the POPLAR's trembling shade,
At Evening's purple hour I've stray'd,
While many a silken folded flow'r
Wept on its couch of Gossamer,
And many a time in pensive mood
Upon the upland mead I've stood,
To mark grey twilight's shadows glide
Along the green hill's velvet side;
To watch the perfum'd hand of morn
Hang pearls upon the silver thorn,
Till rosy day with lustrous eye
In saffron mantle deck'd the sky,
And bound the mountain's brow with fire,
And ting'd with gold the village spire:
While o'er the frosted vale below
The amber tints began to glow:
And oft I seek the daisied plain
To greet the rustic nymph and swain,
When cowslips gay their bells unfold,
And flaunt their leaves of glitt'ring gold,
While from the blushes of the rose
A tide of musky essence flows,
And o'er the odour-breathing flow'rs
The woodlands shed their diamond show'rs,

When from the scented hawthorn bud
The BLACKBIRD sips the lucid flood,   30
While oft the twitt'ring THRUSH essays
To emulate the LINNET's lays;
While the poiz'd LARK her carol sings
And BUTTERFLIES expand their wings,
And BEES begin their sultry toils
And load their limbs with luscious spoils,
I stroll along the pathless vale,
And smile, and bless thy soothing tale.

    But ah! when hoary winter chills
The plumy race—and wraps the hills   40
In snowy vest, I tell my pains
Beside the brook in icy chains
Bound its weedy banks between,
While sad I watch night's pensive queen,
Just emblem of MY weary woes:
For ah! where'er the virgin goes,
Each flow'ret greets her with a tear
To sympathetic sorrow dear;
And when in black obtrusive clouds
The chilly MOON her pale cheek shrouds,   50
I mark the twinkling starry train
Exulting glitter in her wane,
And proudly gleam their borrow'd light
To gem the sombre dome of night.
Then o'er the meadows cold and bleak,
The glow-worm's glimm'ring lamp I seek,
Or climb the craggy cliff to gaze
On some bright planet's azure blaze,
And o'er the dizzy height inclin'd
I listen to the passing wind,   60
That loves my mournful song to seize,
And bears it to the mountain breeze.
Or where the sparry caves among
Dull ECHO sits with aëry tongue,
Or gliding on the ZEPHYR's wings

63 sparry caves] *Spar* is a general term for a number of lustrous crystalline minerals.

From hill to hill her cadence flings,
O, then my melancholy tale
Dies on the bosom of the gale,
While awful stillness reigning round
70   Blanches my cheek with chilling fear;
Till from the bushy dell profound,
    The woodman's song salutes mine ear.

    When dark NOVEMBER's boist'rous breath
Sweeps the blue hill and desart heath,
When naked trees their white tops wave
O'er many a famish'd REDBREAST's grave,
When many a clay-built cot lays low
Beneath the growing hills of snow,
Soon as the SHEPHERD's silv'ry head
80 Peeps from his tottering straw-roof'd shed,
To hail the glimm'ring glimpse of day,
    With feeble steps he ventures forth
    Chill'd by the bleak breath of the North,
And to the forest bends his way,
To gather from the frozen ground
Each branch the night-blast scatter'd round.—
If in some bush o'erspread with snow
He hears thy moaning wail of woe,
A flush of warmth his cheek o'erspreads,
90 With anxious timid care he treads,
And when his cautious hands infold
Thy little breast benumb'd with cold,
"Come, plaintive fugitive," he cries,
While PITY dims his aged eyes,
"Come to my glowing heart, and share
"My narrow cell, my humble fare,
"Tune thy sweet carol—plume thy wing,
"And quaff with me the limpid spring,
"And peck the crumbs my meals supply,
100 "And round my rushy pillow fly."

    O, MINSTREL SWEET, whose jocund lay
Can make e'en POVERTY look gay,
Who can the poorest swain inspire

And while he fans his scanty fire,
When o'er the plain rough Winter pours
Nocturnal blasts, and whelming show'rs,
Canst thro' his little mansion fling
The rap'trous melodies of spring.
To THEE with eager gaze I turn,
   Blest solace of the aching breast;   110
Each gaudy, glitt'ring scene I spurn,
   And sigh for solitude and rest,
For art thou not, blest warbler, say,
   My mind's best balm, my bosom's friend?
Didst thou not trill thy softest lay,
   And with thy woes my sorrows blend?
Yes, darling Songstress! when of late
   I sought thy leafy-fringed bow'r,
The victim of relentless fate,
   Fading in life's dark ling'ring hour,   120
Thou heard'st my plaint, and pour'd thy strain
   Thro' the sad mansion of my breast,
   And softly, sweetly lull'd to rest
The throbbing anguish of my brain.

   AH! while I tread this vale of woe,
Still may thy downy measures flow,
To wing my solitary hours
With kind, obliterating pow'rs;
And tho' my pensive, patient heart
No wild, extatic bliss shall prove,   130
Tho' life no raptures shall impart,
No boundless joy, or, madd'ning love,
Sweet NIGHTINGALE, thy lenient strain
Shall mock Despair, AND BLUNT THE SHAFT OF PAIN.

          (1791)

The Maniac

Ah! what art thou, whose eye-balls roll
Like Heralds of the wand'ring soul,
While down thy cheek the scalding torrents flow?
    Why does that agonizing shriek
    Thy mind's unpitied anguish speak?
O tell me, thing forlorn! And let me share thy woe.

Why dost thou rend thy matted hair,
And beat thy burning bosom bare?
Why is thy lip so parch'd, thy groan so deep?
10   Why dost thou fly from cheerful light,
    And seek in caverns mid-day night,
And cherish thoughts untold, and banish gentle sleep?

Why dost thou from thy scanty bed
Tear the rude straw to crown thy head,
And nod with ghastly smile, and wildly sing?
    While down thy pale distorted face
    Thy crystal drops each other chase,
As though thy brain were drown'd in one eternal spring?

Why dost thou climb yon craggy steep,
20   That frowns upon the clam'rous deep,
And howl, responsive to the waves below?
    Or on the margin of the rock
    Thy Sov'reign Orb exulting mock,
And waste the freezing night in pacing to and fro?

Why dost thou strip the fairest bow'rs,
To dress thy scowling brow with flow'rs,
And fling thy tatter'd garment to the wind?
    Why madly dart from cave to cave,
    Now laugh and sing, then weep and rave,
30   And round thy naked limbs fantastic fragments bind?

23 Thy Sov'reign Orb] The moon.

Why dost thou drink the midnight dew,
 Slow trickling from the baneful yew,
Stretch'd on a pallet of sepulchral stone;
  While, in her solitary tow'r,
  The Minstrel of the witching hour
Sits half congeal'd with fear, to hear thy dismal moan?

 Thy form upon the cold earth cast,
 Now grown familiar with the blast,
Defies the biting frost and scorching sun:
  All Seasons are alike to thee;   40
  Thy sense, unchain'd by Destiny,
Resists, with dauntless pride, all miseries but one!

 Fix not thy steadfast gaze on me,
 Shrunk atom of mortality!
Nor freeze my blood with thy distracted groan;
  Ah! quickly turn those eyes away,
  They fill my soul with dire dismay,
For dead and dark they seem, and almost chill'd to stone!

 Yet, if thy scatter'd senses stray
 Where Reason scorns to lend a ray,   50
Or if Despair supreme usurps her throne,
  Oh! let me all thy sorrows know;
  With thine my mingling tear shall flow,
And I will share thy pangs, and make thy griefs my own.

 Hath Love unlock'd thy feeling breast,
 And stol'n from thence the balm of rest?
Then far away on purple pinions borne,
  Left only keen regret behind,
  To tear with poison'd fangs thy mind,
While barb'rous Mem'ry lives, and bids thee hopeless mourn? 60

 Does Fancy to thy straining arms
 Give thee false Nymph in all her charms,
And with her airy voice beguile thee so,
  That Sorrow seems to pass away,

Till the blithe harbinger of day
Awakes thee from thy dream, and yields thee back to woe?

Say, have the bonds of Friendship fail'd,
Or jealous pangs thy mind assail'd;
While black Ingratitude, with ranc'rous tooth,
70   Pierc'd the fine fibres of thy heart,
And fest'ring every sensate part,
Dim'd with contagious breath the crimson glow of youth?

Or has stern Fate, with ruthless hand,
Dash'd on some wild untrodden strand
Thy little bark, with all thy fortunes fraught;
While thou didst watch the stormy night
Upon some bleak rock's fearful height,
Till thy hot brain consum'd with desolating thought?

Ah! wretch forlorn, perchance thy breast,
80   By the cold fangs of Avarice press'd,
Grew hard and torpid by her touch profane;
Till Famine pinch'd thee to the bone,
And mental torture made thee own
That thing the most accurs'd, who drags her endless chain!

Or say, does flush'd Ambition's wing
Around thy fev'rish temples fling
Dire incense, smoking from th' ensanguin'd plain,
That, drain'd from bleeding warriors' hearts,
Swift to thy shatter'd sense imparts
90   The victor's savage joy, that thrills through ev'ry vein?

Does not the murky gloom of night
Give to thy view some murd'rous sprite,
Whose poniard gleams along thy cell forlorn;
And when the Sun expands his ray,
Dost thou not shun the jocund day,
And mutter curses deep, and hate the ruddy Morn?

93 poniard] Dagger.

And yet the Morn on rosy wing
  Could once to thee its raptures bring,
And Mirth's enliv'ning song delight thine ear;
    While Hope thine eye-lids could unclose   100
    From the sweet slumbers of repose,
To tell thee Love's gay throng of tender joys were near!

  Or hast thou stung with poignant smart
  The orphan's and the widow's heart,
And plung'd them in cold Poverty's abyss;
    While Conscience, like a vulture, stole
    To feed upon thy tortur'd soul,
And tear each barb'rous sense from transitory bliss?

  Or hast thou seen some gentle maid,
  By thy deluding voice betray'd,   110
Fade like a flow'r, slow with'ring with remorse?
    And didst thou then refuse to save
    Thy victim from an early grave,
Till at thy feet she lay a pale and ghastly corse?

  Oh! tell me, tell me all thy pain;
  Pour to mine ear thy frenzied strain,
And I will share thy pangs, and soothe thy woes!
    Poor MANIAC! I will dry thy tears,
    And bathe thy wounds, and calm thy fears,
And with soft Pity's balm enchant thee to repose.   120

(1793)

Stanzas Written after Successive Nights
of Melancholy Dreams

Ye airy Phantoms, by whose pow'r
  Night's curtains spread a deeper shade;
Who, prowling in the murky hour,
  The weary sense with spells invade;
Why round the fibres of my brain
  Such desolating miseries fling,
And with new scenes of mental pain
Chase from my languid eye sleep's balm-dispensing wing?

Ah! why, when o'er the darken'd globe
10   All Nature's children sink to rest—
Why, wrapp'd in Horror's ghastly robe,
  With shad'wy hand assail my breast?
Why conjure up a tribe forlorn,
  To menace, where I bend my way?
Why round my pillow plant the thorn,
Or fix the Demons dire in terrible array?

Why, when the busy day is o'er—
  A day, perhaps of *tender thought*—
Why bid my eager gaze explore
20   New prospects, with new anguish fraught?
Why bid my madd'ning sense descry
  The Form in silence I adore?
His magic smile, his murd'rous eye!
Then bid me wake to prove the fond illusion o'er!

When, fev'rish with the throbs of pain,
  And bath'd with many a trickling tear,
I close my cheated eyes again,
  Despair's wild bands are hov'ring near:
Now borne upon the yelling blast,
30   O'er craggy Peaks I bend my flight;
Now on the yawning Ocean cast,
I plunge unfathom'd depths, amid the shades of night!

Or, borne upon the billows' Ire,
　　O'er the vast waste of waters drear,
Where shipwreck'd Mariners expire,
　　No friend their dying plaints to hear,
I view far off the craggy cliff,
　　Whose white top mingles with the skies;
While at its base the shatter'd Skiff,
Wash'd by the foaming wave, in many a fragment lies.　　　40

Oft, when the Morning's gaudy beams
　　My lattice gild with sparkling light,
O'erwhelm'd with agonizing dreams,
　　And bound in spells of fancied Night,
I start, convulsive, wild, distraught!
　　By some pale Murd'rer's poniard press'd,
Or by the grinning Phantom caught,
Wake from the madd'ning grasp with horror-freezing breast!

Then down my cold and pallid cheek
　　The mingling tears of joy and grief　　　50
The soul's tumultuous feeling speak,
　　And yield the struggling heart relief;
I smile to know the danger past,
　　But soon the radiant moment flies—
Soon is the transient Day o'ercast,
And hope steals trembling from my languid eyes!

If thus, for moments of repose,
　　Whole hours of mis'ry I must know;
If, when each sunny day shall close,
　　I must each gleam of peace forego!　　　60
If for one little morn of mirth,
　　This breast must feel long nights of pain,
Oh! Life, thy joys are nothing worth!
Then let me sink to rest—AND NEVER WAKE AGAIN!

(1793)

46 poniard] Dagger.

Marie Antoinette's Lamentation,
in Her Prison of the Temple*

When on my bosom Evening's ruby light
   Thro' my thrice-grated window warmly glows,
Why does the cheerful ray offend my sight,
   And with its lustre mock my weary woes?
Alas! because on my sad breast appears
A dreadful record—written with my tears!

When awful Midnight, with her ebon wand,
   Charms Nature's poorest meanest child to peace,
Why cannot I one little hour command,
10   When gentle sleep may bid my anguish cease?
Alas! because, where'er I lay my head,
A dreary couch I find, with many a thorn o'erspread.

When the sun, rising in the eastern skies,
   Awakes the feather'd race to songs divine,
Why does remembrance picture to these eyes
   The jocund morn of life, that once was mine?
Alas! because, in sorrow doom'd to mourn,
I ne'er shall see that blissful morn return!

When I behold my darling infants sleep,
20   Fair spotless blossoms, deck'd in op'ning charms,
Why do I start aghast, and wildly weep,
   And madly snatch them to my eager arms?
Ah me! because my sense, o'erwhelm'd with dread,
Views the sweet cherubs on their funeral bed!

Why, when they ope their eyes to gaze on me,
   And fondly press me in their dear embrace,
Hang on my neck, or clasp my trembling knee,
   Why do maternal sorrows drench my face?
Alas! because inhuman hands unite
30 To tear from my fond soul its last delight!

Oh, fell Barbarity! yet spare a while
    The sacred treasures of my throbbing breast;
Oh, spare their infant hearts, untouch'd by guile,
    And let a widow'd mother's darlings rest!
Though you have struck your faulchions at the root,
Oh, give the tender branches time to shoot!

The lightning, by the angry tempest cast,
    Strikes at the lofty pine, and lays it low;
While the small flow'ret 'scapes the deadly blast,
    A while its od'rous breath around to throw!   40
Then let distracted GALLIA's lilies bloom,
Tho' but to deck with sweets a dungeon's gloom!

O my poor innocents! all bath'd in tears,
    Like with'ring flow'rets wash'd with chilling dew,
Sleep on, nor heed a frantic mother's fears:
    The savage tigers will not injure you!
Your harmless bosoms not a crime can know,
Scarce born to greatness—ere consign'd to woe!

When left forlorn, dejected, and alone,
    Imperfect sounds my pensive soul annoy;   50
I hear in every distant mingling tone
    The merry bells—the boist'rous songs of joy!
Ah! then I contemplate my loathsome cell,
Where meagre grief and scowling horror dwell!

The rabble's din, the tocsin's fateful sound,
    The cannon thund'ring thro' the vaulted sky,
The curling smoke, in columns rising round,
    Which from my iron lattice I descry,
Rouse my lethargic mind! I shriek in vain,
My tyrant jailor only mocks my pain!   60

35 faulchions] Swords.
41 GALLIA's lilies] France's fleur de lys.
55 tocsin's] Signal or alarm, especially the ringing of a bell.

Yet bear thy woes, my soul, with proud disdain,
   Meet the keen lance of Death with stedfast eye;
Think on the glorious tide that fills each vein,
   And throbbing bids me tremble not, to die!
Yet, shall I from my friendless children part?
Oh, all the mother rushes to my heart!

Where'er I turn, a thousand ills appear,
   Arm'd at all points, in terrible array:
Pale hood-wink'd murder ever lurking near,
70   And coward cruelty that shuns the day!
See, see, they pierce, with many a recreant sword,
The mangled bosom of my bleeding Lord!

Oh, dreadful thought! Oh, agony supreme!
   When will the sanguinary scene be o'er?
When will my soul, in sweet Oblivion's dream,
   Fade from this orb to some more peaceful shore?
When will the cherub Pity break the snare,
And snatch one victim from the last despair?

(1793)

* Marie Antoinette (1755–93), whom Robinson met in 1781, was the Austrian queen consort of Louis XVI of France. In 1792, following the French Revolution, the queen, along with the rest of the royal family, was kept a prisoner in the Temple; and after 1 August 1793 she was placed in solitary confinement in the Conciergerie. Even after the execution of the king she showed courage. She was guillotined in Paris in the Place de la Revolution on 16 October 1793.

London's Summer Morning

Who has not wak'd to list the busy sounds
Of summer's morning, in the sultry smoke
Of noisy London? On the pavement hot
The sooty chimney-boy, with dingy face
And tatter'd covering, shrilly bawls his trade,
Rousing the sleepy housemaid. At the door
The milk-pail rattles, and the tinkling bell
Proclaims the dustman's office; while the street
Is lost in clouds impervious. Now begins
The din of hackney-coaches, waggons, carts;   10
While tinmen's shops, and noisy trunk-makers,
Knife-grinders, coopers, squeaking cork-cutters,
Fruit-barrows, and the hunger-giving cries
Of vegetable venders, fill the air.
Now ev'ry shop displays its varied trade,
And the fresh-sprinkled pavement cools the feet
Of early walkers. At the private door
The ruddy housemaid twirls the busy mop,
Annoying the smart 'prentice, or neat girl,
Tripping with band-box lightly. Now the sun   20
Darts burning splendour on the glitt'ring pane,
Save where the canvas awning throws a shade
On the gay merchandize. Now, spruce and trim,
In shops (where beauty smiles with industry),
Sits the smart damsel; while the passenger
Peeps thro' the window, watching ev'ry charm.
Now pastry dainties catch the eye minute
Of humming insects, while the limy snare
Waits to enthral them. Now the lamp-lighter
Mounts the tall ladder, nimbly vent'rous,   30
To trim the half-fill'd lamp; while at his feet
The pot-boy yells discordant! All along
The sultry pavement, the old-clothes-man cries
In tone monotonous, and side-long views
The area for his traffic: now the bag

20 band-box] Cardboard box made to hold hats, caps, collars, or millinery.

Is slily open'd, and the half-worn suit
(Sometimes the pilfer'd treasure of the base
Domestic spoiler), for one half its worth,
Sinks in the green abyss. The porter now
40   Bears his huge load along the burning way;
And the poor poet wakes from busy dreams,
To paint the summer morning.

                                          (1795)

January, 1795

Pavement slipp'ry, people sneezing,
Lords in ermine, beggars freezing;
Titled gluttons dainties carving,
Genius in a garret starving.

Lofty mansions, warm and spacious;
Courtiers cringing and voracious;
Misers scarce the wretched heeding;
Gallant soldiers fighting, bleeding.

Wives who laugh at passive spouses;
10   Theatres, and meeting-houses;
Balls, where simp'ring misses languish;
Hospitals, and groans of anguish.

Arts and sciences bewailing;
Commerce drooping, credit failing;
Placemen mocking subjects loyal;
Separations, weddings royal.

Authors who can't earn a dinner;
Many a subtle rogue a winner;
Fugitives for shelter seeking;
20   Misers hoarding, tradesmen breaking.

15 Placemen] Political appointees who have sought the position from self-interest rather
than because of fitness for the job.

Taste and talents quite deserted;
All the laws of truth perverted;
Arrogance o'er merit soaring;
Merit silently deploring.

Ladies gambling night and morning;
Fools the works of genius scorning;
Ancient dames for girls mistaken,
Youthful damsels quite forsaken.

Some in luxury delighting;
More in talking than in fighting;   30
Lovers old, and beaux decrepid;
Lordlings empty and insipid.

Poets, painters, and musicians;
Lawyers, doctors, politicians:
Pamphlets, newspapers, and odes,
Seeking fame by diff'rent roads.

Gallant souls with empty purses,
Gen'rals only fit for nurses;
School-boys, smit with martial spirit,
Taking place of vet'ran merit.   40

Honest men who can't get places,
Knaves who shew unblushing faces;
Ruin hasten'd, peace retarded;
Candour spurn'd, and art rewarded.

(1795)

The Lascar*

In two parts.

"Another day, Ah! me, a day
   Of dreary Sorrow is begun!
And still I loath the temper'd ray,
   And still I hate the sickly Sun!
Far from my native Indian shore,
I hear our wretched race deplore;
I mark the smile of taunting Scorn,
And curse the hour when I was born!
I weep, but no one gently tries
To stop my tear, or check my sighs;
For while my heart beats mournfully,
Dear Indian home, I sigh for Thee!

"Since, gaudy Sun! I see no more
   Thy hottest glory gild the day;
Since, sever'd from my burning shore,
   I waste the vapid hours away;
O! darkness come! come deepest gloom!
Shroud the young Summer's op'ning bloom!
Burn, temper'd Orb, with fiercer beams
This northern world! and drink the streams
That thro' the fertile vallies glide
To bathe the feasted Fiends of Pride!
Or hence, broad Sun! extinguish'd be!
For endless night encircles Me!

"What is to me the City gay?
   And what the board profusely spread?
I have no home, no rich array,
   No spicy feast, no downy bed!
I with the dogs am doom'd to eat,
To perish in the peopl'd street,
To drink the tear of deep despair,
The scoff and scorn of fools to bear!
I sleep upon the pavement stone,

10

20

30

Or pace the meadows, wild—alone!
And if I curse my fate severe
Some Christian Savage mocks my tear!

"Shut out the Sun, O! pitying Night!
   Make the wide world my silent tomb!
O'ershade this northern, sickly light,
   And shroud me in eternal gloom!   40
My Indian plains now smiling glow,
There stands my Parent's hovel low,
And there the tow'ring aloes rise,
And fling their perfumes to the skies!
There the broad palm trees covert lend,
There Sun and Shade delicious blend;
But here, amid the blunted ray,
Cold shadows hourly cross my way.

"Was it for this, that on the main
   I met the tempest fierce and strong,   50
And steering o'er the liquid plain,
   Still onward, press'd the waves among?
Was it for this the LASCAR brave
Toil'd like a wretched Indian Slave;
Preserv'd your treasures by his toil,
And sigh'd to greet this fertile soil?
Was it for this, to beg, to die!
Where plenty smiles, and where the sky
Sheds cooling airs; while fev'rish pain
Maddens the famish'd LASCAR's brain?   60

"Oft I the stately Camel led,
   And sung the short-hour'd night away;
And oft, upon the top-mast's head,
   Hail'd the red Eye of coming day.
The Tanyan's back my mother bore;
And oft the wavy Ganges roar
Lull'd her to rest, as on she past,
'Mid the hot sands and burning blast!

65 Tanyan's] A variation of *tanghan* or *tangun,* a strong, sure-footed pony native to Tibet and Bhutan.

And oft beneath the Banyan tree
70   She sate and fondly nourish'd me;
And while the noontide hour past slow
I felt her breast with kindness glow.

"Where'er I turn my sleepless eyes
    No cheek so dark as mine I see;
For Europe's Suns with softer dyes
    Mark Europe's favour'd progeny!
Low is my stature, black my hair,
The emblem of my Soul's despair!
My voice no dulcet cadence flings,
80   To touch soft pity's throbbing strings;
Then wherefore, cruel Briton, say,
Compel my aching heart to stay?
To-morrow's Sun may rise to see
The famish'd LASCAR blest as thee!"

The morn had scarcely shed its rays,
    When from the City's din he ran;
For he had fasted four long days,
    And faint his Pilgrimage began!
The LASCAR now, without a friend,
90   Up the steep hill did slow ascend;
Now o'er the flow'ry meadows stole,
While pain and hunger pinch'd his soul;
And now his fev'rish lip was dried,
And burning tears his thirst supply'd,
And ere he saw the Ev'ning close,
Far off, the City dimly rose.

Again the Summer Sun flam'd high,
    The plains were golden far and wide;
And fervid was the cloudless sky,
100   And slow the breezes seem'd to glide:
The gossamer, on briar and spray,
Shone silv'ry in the solar ray;
And sparkling dew-drops, falling round,
Spangled the hot and thirsty ground;
The insect myriads humm'd their tune

To greet the coming hour of noon,
While the poor LASCAR Boy, in haste,
Flew, frantic, o'er the sultry waste.

And whither could the wand'rer go?
    Who would receive a stranger poor?   110
Who, when the blasts of night should blow,
    Would ope to him the friendly door?
Alone, amid the race of man,
The sad, the fearful alien ran!
None would an Indian wand'rer bless;
None greet him with the fond caress;
None feed him, though with hunger keen
He at the lordly gate were seen
Prostrate, and humbly forc'd to crave
A shelter for an Indian Slave.   120

The noon-tide Sun, now flaming wide,
    No cloud its fierce beam shadow'd o'er,
But what could worse to him betide
    Than begging at the proud man's door?
For clos'd and lofty was the gate,
And there, in all the pride of state,
A surly Porter turn'd the key,
A man of sullen soul was he —
His brow was fair; but in his eye
Sat pamper'd scorn, and tyranny;   130
And near him a fierce Mastiff stood,
Eager to bathe his fangs in blood.

The weary LASCAR turn'd away,
    For trembling fear his heart subdued,
And down his cheek the tear would stray,
    Though burning anguish drank his blood!
The angry Mastiff snarl'd as he
Turn'd from the house of luxury;
The sultry hour was long, and high
The broad-sun flam'd athwart the sky —   140
But still a throbbing hope possess'd
The Indian wand'rer's fev'rish breast,

When from the distant dell a sound
Of swelling music echo'd round.

It was the church-bell's merry peal;
   And now a pleasant house he view'd:
And now his heart began to feel
   As though it were not quite subdu'd!
No lofty dome shew'd loftier state,

150   No pamper'd Porter watch'd the gate,
No Mastiff like a tyrant stood,
Eager to scatter human blood;
Yet the poor Indian wand'rer found,
E'en where Religion smil'd around,
That tears had little pow'r to speak
When trembling on a *sable cheek!*

With keen reproach, and menace rude,
   The LASCAR Boy away was sent;
And now again he seem'd subdu'd,

160   And his soul sicken'd as he went.
Now on the river's bank he stood;
Now drank the cool refreshing flood;
Again his fainting heart beat high;
Again he rais'd his languid eye;
Then from the upland's sultry side
Look'd back, forgave the wretch, and sigh'd!
While the proud pastor bent his way
To preach of CHARITY—and PRAY!

Part Second

The LASCAR Boy still journey'd on,

170   For the hot Sun HE well could bear,
And now the burning hour was gone,
   And Evening came, with softer air.
The breezes kiss'd his sable breast,
While his scorch'd feet the cold dew prest;
The waving flow'rs soft tears display'd,
And songs of rapture fill'd the glade;
The South-wind quiver'd, o'er the stream

Reflecting back the rosy beam;
While as the purpling twilight clos'd,
On a turf bed—the boy repos'd.   180

And now, in fancy's airy dream,
    The LASCAR Boy his Mother spied;
And from her breast a crimson stream
    Slow trickled down her beating side:
And now he heard her wild, complain,
As loud she shriek'd—but shriek'd in vain!
And now she sunk upon the ground,
The red stream trickling from her wound;
And near her feet a murd'rer stood,
His glitt'ring poniard tipp'd with blood!   190
And now, "farewell, my son!" she cried,
Then clos'd her fainting eyes—and died!

The Indian Wand'rer, waking, gaz'd,
    With grief, and pain, and horror, wild;
And tho' his fev'rish brain was craz'd,
    He rais'd his eyes to Heav'n, and smil'd:
And now the stars were twinkling clear,
And the blind Bat was whirling near,
And the lone Owlet shriek'd, while he
Still sate beneath a shelt'ring tree;   200
And now the fierce-ton'd midnight blast
Across the wide heath howling past,
When a long cavalcade he spied
By torch-light near the river's side.

He rose, and hast'ning swiftly on,
    Call'd loudly to the sumptuous train,
But soon the cavalcade was gone,
    And darkness wrapp'd the scene again.
He follow'd still the distant sound;
He saw the lightning flashing round;   210
He heard the crashing thunder roar;
He felt the whelming torrents pour;
And now, beneath a shelt'ring wood,
He listen'd to the tumbling flood—

And now, with falt'ring, feeble breath,
The famish'd LASCAR pray'd for Death.

And now the flood began to rise,
　　And foaming rush'd along the vale;
The LASCAR watch'd, with stedfast eyes,
220　　　The flash descending quick and pale;
And now again the cavalcade
Pass'd slowly near the upland glade;
But HE was dark, and dark the scene,
The torches long extinct had been;
He call'd, but in the stormy hour
His feeble voice had lost its pow'r,
Till, near a tree, beside the flood,
A night-bewilder'd Trav'ller stood.

The LASCAR now with transport ran,
230　　　"Stop! stop!" he cried, with accents bold;
The Trav'ller was a fearful man,
　　And next his life he priz'd his gold.
He heard the wand'rer madly cry;
He heard his footsteps following nigh;
He nothing saw, while onward prest,
Black as the sky, the Indian's breast
Till his firm grasp he felt; while cold
Down his pale cheek the big drop roll'd;
Then, struggling to be free, he gave
240　A deep wound to the LASCAR Slave.

And now he groan'd, by pain opprest,
　　And now crept onward, sad and slow:
And while he held his bleeding breast
　　He feebly pour'd the plaint of woe:
"What have I done!" the LASCAR cried
"That Heaven to me the pow'r denied
To touch the soul of man, and share
A brother's love, a brother's care?
Why is this dingy form decreed
250　To bear oppression's scourge and bleed?

Is there a GOD in yon dark Heav'n,
And shall such monsters be forgiv'n?

"Here, in this smiling land we find
    Neglect and mis'ry sting our race;
And still, whate'er the LASCAR's mind,
    The stamp of sorrow marks his face!"
He ceas'd to speak; while from his side
Fast roll'd life's sweetly-ebbing tide,
And now, though sick and faint was he,
He slowly climb'd a tall elm tree,   260
To watch if near his lonely way
Some friendly Cottage lent a ray,
A little ray of cheerful light,
To gild the LASCAR's long, long night!

And now he hears a distant bell,
    His heart is almost rent with joy!
And who but such a wretch can tell
    The transports of the Indian boy?
And higher now he climbs the tree,
And hopes some shelt'ring Cot to see;   270
Again he listens, while the peal
Seems up the woodland vale to steal;
The twinkling stars begin to fade,
And dawnlight purples o'er the glade;
And while the sev'ring vapours flee
The LASCAR Boy looks chearfully.

And now the Sun begins to rise
    Above the Eastern summit blue;
And o'er the plain the day-breeze flies,
    And sweetly bloom the fields of dew.   280
The wand'ring wretch was chill'd, for he
Sate shivering in the tall elm tree;
And he was faint, and sick, and dry,
And blood-shot was his fev'rish eye;
And livid was his lip, while he
Sate silent in the tall elm tree,

And parch'd his tongue, and quick his breath,
And his dark cheek was cold as Death!

And now a Cottage low he sees,
290   The chimney smoke, ascending grey,
Floats lightly on the morning breeze
       And o'er the mountain glides away.
And now the Lark, on flutt'ring wings,
Its early song, delighted, sings;
And now, across the upland mead,
The Swains their flocks to shelter lead;
The shelt'ring woods wave to and fro;
The yellow plains far distant glow;
And all things wake to life and joy,
300   All! but the famish'd Indian Boy!

And now the village throngs are seen,
       Each lane is peopled, and the glen
From ev'ry op'ning path-way green
       Sends forth the busy hum of men.
They cross the meads, still, all alone,
They hear the wounded Lascar groan!
Far off they mark the wretch, as he
Falls, senseless, from the tall elm tree!
Swiftly they cross the river wide,
310   And soon they reach the elm tree's side;
But ere the sufferer they behold,
His wither'd Heart is DEAD — *and* COLD!

                                   (1800)

*A lascar was an East Indian sailor.

The Negro Girl

Dark was the dawn, and o'er the deep
   The boist'rous whirlwinds blew;
The Sea-bird wheel'd its circling sweep,
   And all was drear to view—
When on the beach that binds the western shore
The love-lorn ZELMA stood, list'ning the tempest's roar.

Her eager Eyes beheld the main,
   While on Her DRACO dear
She madly call'd, but call'd in vain,
   No sound could DRACO hear,   10
Save the shrill yelling of the fateful blast,
While ev'ry Seaman's heart quick shudder'd as it past.

White were the billows, wide display'd
   The clouds were black and low;
The Bittern shriek'd, a gliding shade
   Seem'd o'er the waves to go!
The livid flash illum'd the clam'rous main,
While ZELMA pour'd, unmark'd her melancholy strain.

"Be still!" she cries, "loud tempest cease!
   O! spare the gallant souls!"   20
The thunder rolls—the winds increase—
   The Sea like mountains rolls.
While from the deck the storm-worn victims leap,
And o'er their struggling limbs the furious billows sweep.

"O! barb'rous Pow'r! relentless Fate!
   Does Heaven's high will decree
That some should sleep on beds of state—
   Some in the roaring Sea?
Some nurs'd in splendour deal Oppression's blow,
While worth and DRACO pine—in Slavery and woe!   30

15 Bittern] Long-legged, wading bird of the order *Grallatores,* related to the heron but smaller, with a distinctive, booming mating call.

"Yon vessel oft has plough'd the main
   With human traffic fraught;
Its cargo—our dark Sons of pain—
   For worldly treasure bought!
What had they done? O Nature tell me why
Is taunting scorn the lot of thy dark progeny?

"Thou gav'st, in thy caprice, the Soul
   Peculiarly enshrin'd;
Nor from the ebon Casket stole
40   The Jewel of the mind!
Then wherefore let the suff'ring Negro's breast
Bow to his fellow MAN, in brighter colours drest.

"Is it the dim and glossy hue
   That marks him for despair?
While men with blood their hands embrue,
   And mock the wretch's pray'r,
Shall guiltless Slaves the scourge of tyrants feel,
And, e'en before their GOD! unheard, unpitied kneel.

"Could the proud rulers of the land
50   Our Sable race behold;
Some bow'd by Torture's giant hand,
   And others basely sold!
Then would they pity Slaves, and cry, with shame,
What'er their TINTS may be, their SOULS are still the same!

"Why seek to mock the Ethiop's face?
   Why goad our hapless kind?
Can features alienate the race—
   Is there no kindred mind?
Does not the cheek which vaunts the roseate hue
60   Oft blush for crimes that Ethiops never knew?

"Behold! the angry waves conspire
   To check the barb'rous toil!
While wounded Nature's vengeful ire
   Roars round this trembling Isle!
And hark! her voice re-echoes in the wind—
Man was not form'd by Heav'n to trample on his kind!

"Torn from my mother's aching breast,
   My Tyrant sought my love—
But in the grave shall ZELMA rest,
   Ere she will faithless prove;   70
No, DRACO!—Thy companion I will be
To that celestial realm where Negros shall be free!

"The Tyrant WHITE MAN taught my mind
   The letter'd page to trace;
He taught me in the Soul to find
   No tint, as in the face:
He bade my reason blossom like the tree—
But fond affection gave the ripen'd fruits to thee.

"With jealous rage he mark'd my love;
   He sent thee far away;   80
And prison'd in the plantain grove
   Poor ZELMA pass'd the day;
But ere the moon rose high above the main
ZELMA and Love contriv'd to break the Tyrant's chain.

"Swift, o'er the plain of burning Sand
   My course I bent to thee;
And soon I reach'd the billowy strand
   Which bounds the stormy Sea.
DRACO! my Love! Oh yet thy ZELMA's soul
Springs ardently to thee, impatient of controul.   90

"Again the lightning flashes white
   The rattling cords among!
Now, by the transient vivid light,
   I mark the frantic throng!
Now up the tatter'd shrouds my DRACO flies,
While o'er the plunging prow the curling billows rise.

"The topmast falls—three shackled slaves
   Cling to the Vessel's side!
Now lost amid the madd'ning waves—
   Now on the mast they ride—   100
See! on the forecastle my DRACO stands,
And now he waves his chain, now clasps his bleeding hands.

"Why, cruel WHITE-MAN! when away
   My sable Love was torn,
Why did you let poor ZELMA stay,
   On Afric's sands to mourn?
No! ZELMA is not left, for she will prove
In the deep troubled main her fond—her faithful Love."

The lab'ring Ship was now a wreck,
110   The shrouds were flutt'ring wide;
The rudder gone, the lofty deck
   Was rock'd from side to side—
Poor ZELMA's eyes now dropp'd their last big tear,
While from her tawny cheek the blood recoil'd with fear.

Now frantic, on the sands she roam'd,
   Now shrieking stopp'd to view
Where high the liquid mountains foam'd
   Around the exhausted crew—
'Till, from the deck, her DRACO's well-known form
120   Sprung 'mid the yawning waves, and buffetted the storm.

Long, on the swelling surge sustain'd,
   Brave DRACO sought the shore,
Watch'd the dark Maid, but ne'er complain'd,
   Then sunk, to gaze no more!
Poor ZELMA saw him buried by the wave,
And, with her heart's true Love, plung'd in a wat'ry grave.

                         (1800)

The Haunted Beach

Upon a lonely desart Beach,
   Where the white foam was scatter'd,
A little shed uprear'd its head,
   Though lofty barks were shatter'd.
The sea-weeds gath'ring near the door,
   A sombre path display'd;
And, all around, the deaf'ning roar
Re-echo'd on the chalky shore,
   By the green billows made.

Above a jutting cliff was seen   10
   Where Sea Birds hover'd, craving;
And all around the craggs were bound
   With weeds—for ever waving.
And here and there, a cavern wide
   Its shad'wy jaws display'd;
And near the sands, at ebb of tide,
A shiver'd mast was seen to ride
   Where the green billows stray'd.

And often, while the moaning wind
   Stole o'er the Summer Ocean;   20
The moonlight scene was all serene,
   The waters scarce in motion;
Then, while the smoothly slanting sand
   The tall cliff wrapp'd in shade,
The Fisherman beheld a band
Of Spectres gliding hand in hand—
   Where the green billows play'd.

And pale their faces were as snow,
   And sullenly they wander'd;
And to the skies with hollow eyes   30
   They look'd as though they ponder'd.
And sometimes, from their hammock shroud,
   They dismal howlings made,
And while the blast blew strong and loud

The clear moon mark'd the ghastly croud,
    Where the green billows play'd!

And then above the haunted hut
    The Curlews screaming hover'd;
And the low door, with furious roar,
    The frothy breakers cover'd.
For in the Fisherman's lone shed
    A MURDER'D MAN was laid,
With ten wide gashes in his head,
And deep was made his sandy bed
    Where the green billows play'd.

A shipwreck'd Mariner was he,
    Doom'd from his home to sever
Who swore to be thro' wind and sea
    Firm and undaunted ever!
And when the wave resistless roll'd,
    About his arm he made
A packet rich of Spanish gold,
And, like a British sailor bold,
    Plung'd where the billows play'd!

The Spectre band, his messmates brave,
    Sunk in the yawning ocean,
While to the mast he lash'd him fast,
    And brav'd the storm's commotion.
The winter moon upon the sand
    A silv'ry carpet made,
And mark'd the Sailor reach the land,
And mark'd his murd'rer wash his hand
    Where the green billows play'd.

And since that hour the Fisherman
    Has toil'd and toil'd in vain;
For all the night the moony light
    Gleams on the specter'd main!
And when the skies are veil'd in gloom,
    The Murd'rer's liquid way
Bounds o'er the deeply yawning tomb,

And flashing fires the sands illume,
  Where the green billows play!

Full thirty years his task has been,
  Day after day more weary;
For Heav'n design'd his guilty mind
  Should dwell on prospects dreary.
Bound by a strong and mystic chain,
  He has not pow'r to stray;
But destin'd mis'ry to sustain,
He wastes, in Solitude and Pain,   80
  A loathsome life away.

                                    (1800)

The Alien Boy

'Twas on a mountain, near the western main,
An ALIEN dwelt. A solitary hut
Built on a jutting crag, o'erhung with weeds,
Mark'd the poor exile's home. Full ten long years
The melancholy wretch had liv'd unseen
By all, save HENRY, a lov'd little son,
The partner of his sorrows. On the day
When persecution, in the sainted guise
Of liberty, spread wide its venom'd pow'r,
The brave saint HUBERT fled his lordly home,   10
And, with his baby son, the mountain sought.
Resolv'd to cherish in his bleeding breast
The secret of his birth—Ah! birth too high
For his now humbled state!—from infancy
He taught him labour's task: he bade him cheer
The dreary day of cold adversity
By patience and by toil. The summer morn
Shone on the pillow of his rushy bed;
The noontide sultry hour he fearless past
On the shagg'd eminence; while the young kid   20
Skipp'd to the cadence of his minstrelsey.

At night young HENRY trimm'd the faggot fire,
While oft Saint HUBERT wove the ample net
To snare the finny victim. Oft they sang
And talk'd, while sullenly the waves would sound,
Dashing the sandy shore. Saint HUBERT's eyes
Would swim in tears of fondness, mix'd with joy,
When he observ'd the op'ning harvest rich
Of promis'd intellect, which HENRY's soul,
30   Whate'er the subject of their talk, display'd.

Oft the bold youth, in question intricate,
Would seek to know the story of his birth;
Oft ask, who bore him: and with curious skill
Enquire, why he, and only one beside,
Peopled the desert mountain? Still his sire
Was slow of answer, and, in words obscure,
Varied the conversation. Still the mind
Of HENRY ponder'd; for, in their lone hut,
A daily journal would Saint HUBERT make
40   Of his long banishment: and sometimes speak
Of friends forsaken, kindred massacred;
Proud mansions, rich domains, and joyous scenes
For ever faded,—lost!
                              One winter time,
'Twas on the eve of Christmas, the shrill blast
Swept o'er the stormy main; the boiling foam
Rose to an altitude so fierce and strong,
That their low hovel totter'd. Oft they stole
To the rock's margin, and with fearful eyes
50   Mark'd the vex'd deep, as the slow rising moon
Gleam'd on the world of waters. 'Twas a scene
Would make a stoic shudder! For, amid
The wavy mountains, they beheld, *alone,*
A LITTLE BOAT, now scarcely visible;
And now not seen at all; or, like a buoy,
Bounding, and buffeting, to reach the shore!

Now the full moon, in crimson lustre shone
Upon the outstretch'd ocean. The black clouds
Flew swiftly on, the wild blast following,
60   And, as they flew, dimming the angry main

With shadows horrible! Still the small boat
Struggled amid the waves, a sombre speck
Upon the wide domain of howling death!
Saint HUBERT sigh'd! while HENRY's speaking eye
Alternately the stormy scene survey'd,
And his low hovel's safety. So past on
The hour of midnight,—and, since first they knew
The solitary scene, no midnight hour
E'er seem'd so long and weary.
     While they stood,   70
Their hands fast link'd together, and their eyes
Fix'd on the troublous ocean, suddenly
The breakers, bounding on the rocky shore,
Left the small wreck; and crawling on the side
Of the rude crag,—a HUMAN FORM was seen!
And now he climb'd the foam-wash'd precipice,
And now the slipp'ry weeds gave way, while he
Descended to the sands. The moon rose high—
The wild blast paus'd, and the poor shipwreck'd man
Look'd round aghast, when on the frowning steep 80
He mark'd the lonely exiles. Now he call'd;
But he was feeble, and his voice was lost
Amid the din of mingling sounds that rose
From the wild scene of clamour.
     Down the steep
Saint HUBERT hurried, boldly venturous,
Catching the slimy weeds from point to point,
And unappall'd by peril. At the foot
Of the rude rock, the fainting mariner
Seiz'd on his outstretch'd arm, impatient, wild 90
With transport exquisite! But ere they heard
The blest exchange of sounds articulate,
A furious billow, rolling on the steep,
Engulph'd them in oblivion!
     On the rock
Young HENRY stood, with palpitating heart,
And fear-struck, e'en to madness! Now he call'd,
Louder and louder, as the shrill blast blew;
But, 'mid the elemental strife of sounds,
No human voice gave answer! The clear moon 100
No longer quiver'd on the curling main,

But, mist-encircled, shed a blunted light,
Enough to shew all things that mov'd around,
Dreadful, but indistinctly! The black weeds
Wav'd, as the night-blast swept them; and along
The rocky shore, the breakers sounding low,
Seem'd like the whisp'ring of a million souls
Beneath the green-deep mourning.
                              Four long hours
110   The lorn boy listen'd! four long tedious hours
Pass'd wearily away, when, in the east,
The grey beam coldly glimmer'd. All alone
Young HENRY stood aghast, his eye wide fix'd;
While his dark locks, uplifted by the storm,
Uncover'd, met its fury. On his cheek
Despair sate terrible! for, 'mid the woes
Of poverty and toil, he had not known,
Till then, the horror-giving cheerless hour
Of TOTAL SOLITUDE!
120   He spoke—he groan'd,
But no responsive voice, no kindred tone,
Broke the dread pause: for now the storm had ceas'd,
And the bright sun-beams glitter'd on the breast
Of the green placid ocean. To his hut
The lorn boy hasten'd; there the rushy couch,
The pillow still indented, met his gaze,
And fix'd his eye in madness.—From that hour
A maniac wild the alien boy has been;
His garb with sea-weeds fring'd, and his wan cheek,
130   The tablet of his mind, disorder'd, chang'd,
Fading, and worn with care. And if, by chance,
A sea-beat wand'rer from the outstretch'd main
Views the lone exile, and with gen'rous zeal
Hastes to the sandy beach, he suddenly
Darts 'mid the cavern'd cliffs, and leaves pursuit
To track him, where no footsteps but his own
Have e'er been known to venture! YET HE LIVES
A melancholy proof, that man may bear
All the rude storms of fate, and still suspire
140   By the wide world forgotten!
                                        (1800)

To the Poet Coleridge

Rapt in the visionary theme!
   SPIRIT DIVINE! with THEE I'll wander,
Where the blue, wavy, lucid stream,
   'Mid forest glooms, shall slow meander!
With THEE I'll trace the circling bounds
   Of thy NEW PARADISE extended;
And listen to the varying sounds
   Of winds, and foamy torrents blended.

Now by the source which lab'ring heaves
   The mystic fountain, bubbling, panting,   10
While Gossamer its net-work weaves,
   Adown the blue lawn slanting!
I'll mark thy *sunny dome,* and view
Thy *Caves of Ice,* thy fields of dew!
Thy ever-blooming mead, whose flow'r
Waves to the cold breath of the moonlight hour!
Or when the day-star, peering bright
On the grey wing of parting night;
While more than vegetating pow'r
Throbs grateful to the burning hour,   20
As summer's whisper'd sighs unfold
Her million, million buds of gold;
Then will I climb the breezy bounds,
   Of thy NEW PARADISE extended,
And listen to the distant sounds
   Of winds, and foamy torrents blended!

SPIRIT DIVINE! with THEE I'll trace
Imagination's boundless space!
With thee, beneath thy *sunny dome,*
   I'll listen to the minstrel's lay,   30
   Hymning the gradual close of day;
In *Caves of Ice* enchanted roam,
Where on the glitt'ring entrance plays
The moon's-beam with its silv'ry rays;
   Or, when glassy stream,
      That thro' the deep dell flows,

Flashes the noon's hot beam;
    The noon's hot beam, that midway shows
Thy flaming Temple, studded o'er
With all PERUVIA's lustrous store!
There will I trace the circling bounds
    Of thy NEW PARADISE extended!
And listen to the awful sounds,
    Of winds, and foamy torrents blended!

And now I'll pause to catch the moan
    Of distant breezes, cavern-pent;
Now, ere the twilight tints are flown,
Purpling the landscape, far and wide,
On the dark promontory's side
    I'll gather wild flow'rs, dew besprent,
And weave a crown for THEE,
GENIUS OF HEAV'N-TAUGHT POESY!
While, op'ning to my wond'ring eyes,
Thou bidst a new creation rise,
I'll raptur'd trace the circling bounds
    Of thy RICH PARADISE extended,
And listen to the varying sounds
    Of winds, and foaming torrents blended.

And now, with lofty tones inviting,
Thy NYMPH, her dulcimer swift smiting,
Shall wake me in ecstatic measures!
Far, far remov'd from mortal pleasures!
    In cadence rich, in cadence strong,
Proving the wondrous witcheries of song!
      I hear her voice! thy *sunny dome,*
    Thy *caves of ice,* loud repeat,
    Vibrations, madd'ning sweet,
      Calling the visionary wand'rer home.
She sings of THEE, O favour'd child
Of *Minstrelsy,* SUBLIMELY WILD!
Of thee, whose soul can feel the tone
Which gives to airy dreams *a magic* ALL THY OWN!

                        (1800)

The Camp

Tents, *marquees,* and baggage waggons;
Suttling houses, beer in flaggons;
Drums and trumpets, singing, firing;
Girls seducing, *beaux* admiring;
Country lasses gay and smiling,
City lads their hearts beguiling;
Dusty roads, and horses frisky;
Many an *Eton boy* in whisky;
Tax'd carts full of farmers' daughters;*
Brutes condemn'd, and man—who slaughters!   10
Public-houses, booths, and castles;
Belles of fashion, serving vassals;
Lordly Gen'rals fiercely staring,
Weary soldiers, sighing, swearing!
Petit maitres always dressing—
In the glass themselves caressing;
Perfum'd, painted, patch'd and blooming
Ladies—manly airs assuming!
Dowagers of fifty, simp'ring
Misses, for a lover whimp'ring—   20
Husbands drill'd to household tameness;
Dames heart sick of wedded sameness.
Princes setting girls a-madding—
Wives for ever fond of gadding—
Princesses with lovely faces,
Beauteous children of the Graces!
Britain's pride and Virtue's treasure,
Fair and gracious, beyond measure!
Aid de Camps, and youthful pages—
Prudes, and vestals of all ages!—   30
Old coquets, and matrons surly,
Sounds of distant *hurly burly!*
Mingled voices uncouth singing;
Carts, full laden, forage bringing;
Sociables, and horses weary;

---

2 Suttling houses] Establishments serving food and drink to soldiers.

Houses warm, and dresses airy;
Loads of fatten'd poultry; pleasure
Serv'd (TO NOBLES) without measure.
Doxies, who the waggons follow;
40   Beer, for thirsty hinds to swallow;
Washerwomen, fruit-girls cheerful,
ANTIENT LADIES—*chaste* and *fearful!*
Tradesmen, leaving shops, and seeming
More of *war* than profit dreaming;
Martial sounds, and braying asses;
Noise, that ev'ry noise surpasses!
All confusion, din, and riot—
NOTHING CLEAN—and NOTHING QUIET.

                                        (1800)

* In the original this read "farmer's daughters."

The Poet's Garret

Come, sportive fancy! come with me, and trace
The poet's attic home! the lofty seat
Of the heav'n-tutor'd nine! the airy throne
Of bold imagination, rapture fraught
Above the herds of mortals. All around
A solemn stillness seems to guard the scene,
Nursing the brood of thought—a thriving brood
In the rich mazes of the cultur'd brain.
Upon thy altar, an old worm-eat board,
10   The pannel of a broken door, or lid
Of a strong coffer, plac'd on three-legg'd stool,
Stand quires of paper, white and beautiful!
Paper, by destiny ordain'd to be
Scrawl'd o'er and blotted; dash'd, and scratch'd, and torn;

39 Doxies] Prostitutes, paramours.
3 the heav'n-tutor'd nine!] The muses.

Or mark'd with lines severe, or scatter'd wide
In rage impetuous! Sonnet, song, and ode,
Satire, and epigram, and smart charade;
Neat paragraph, or legendary tale,
Of short and simple metre, each by turns
Will there delight the reader.　　　　　　　　　　20
　　　　　　　　　On the bed
Lies an old rusty suit of "solemn black," —
Brush'd thread-bare, and, with brown, unglossy hue,
Grown somewhat ancient. On the floor is seen
A pair of silken hose, whose footing bad
Shews they are trav'llers, but who still bear
Marks somewhat *holy*. At the scanty fire
A chop turns round, by packthread strongly held;
And on the blacken'd bar a vessel shines
Of batter'd pewter, just half fill'd, and warm,　　30
With Whitbread's bev'rage pure. The kitten purs,
Anticipating dinner; while the wind
Whistles thro' broken panes, and drifted snow
Carpets the parapet with spotless garb,
Of vestal coldness. Now the sullen hour
(The fifth hour after noon) with dusky hand
Closes the lids of day. The farthing light
Gleams thro' the cobwebb'd chamber, and the bard
Concludes his pen's hard labour. Now he eats
With appetite voracious! nothing sad　　　　　　40
That he with costly plate, and napkins fine,
Nor china rich, nor fork of silver, greets
His eye or palate. On his lyric board
A sheet of paper serves for table-cloth;
An heap of salt is serv'd, — oh! heav'nly treat!
On ode Pindaric! while his tuneful puss
Scratches his slipper for her fragment sweet,
And sings her love-song soft, yet mournfully.
Mocking the pillar Doric, or the roof

31 Whitbread's bev'rage] Beer.
　37 farthing] A quarter of a penny; figuratively, a very little, a bit.
　46 ode Pindaric] Pindar (c. 518–c. 438 B.C.) was a Greek choral lyricist who composed,
among other things, epinician odes, with three-part stanzas containing a characteristic strophe,
antistrophe, and epode, imitated by Congreve, Jonson, and Gray.

50   Of architecture Gothic, all around
The well-known ballads flit, of Grub-street fame!
The casement, broke, gives breath celestial
To the long dying-speech; or gently fans
The love-inflaming sonnet. All around
Small scraps of paper lie, torn vestiges
Of an unquiet fancy. Here a page
Of flights poetic—there a dedication—
A list of dramatis personæ, bold,
Of heroes yet unborn, and lofty dames
60   Of perishable compound, light as fair,
But sentenc'd to oblivion!
                      On a shelf,
(Yclept a mantle-piece) a phial stands,
Half fill'd with potent spirits!—spirits strong,
Which sometimes haunt the poet's restless brain,
And fill his mind with fancies whimsical.
Poor poet! happy art thou, thus remov'd
From pride and folly! for in thy domain
Thou can'st command thy subjects; fill thy lines;
70   Wield th' all-conqu'ring weapon heav'n bestows
On the grey goose's wing! which, tow'ring high,
Bears thy sick fancy to immortal fame!
                    (wr. 1800; pub. 1801)

51 Grub-street fame] According to Samuel Johnson, Grub Street was "originally the name of a street near Moorfields in London, much inhabited by writers of small histories, dictionaries, and temporary poems, whence any mean production is called *grubstreet*." The term came to mean literary hackwork.

63 Yclept] Called.

70–71 th' all-conqu'ring weapon . . . On the grey goose's wing] A goose-quill pen.

The Lady of the Black Tower

"Watch no more the twinkling stars;
   Watch no more the chalky bourne;
Lady! from the Holy wars
    Never will thy Love return!
      Cease to watch, and cease to mourn,
      Thy Lover never will return!

"Watch no more the yellow moon,
   Peering o'er the mountain's head;
Rosy day, returning soon,
    Will see thy Lover, pale and dead!   10
      Cease to weep, and cease to mourn,
      Thy Lover will no more return!

"Lady, in the Holy wars,
   Fighting for the Cross, he died;
Low he lies, and many scars
    Mark his cold and mangled side;
      In his winding-sheet he lies,
      Lady! check those rending sighs.

"Hark! the hollow sounding gale
   Seems to sweep in murmurs by,   20
Sinking slowly down the vale;
    Wherefore, gentle Lady, sigh?
      Wherefore moan, and wherefore sigh?
      Lady! all that live must die.

"Now the stars are fading fast:
   Swift their brilliant course are run;
Soon shall dreary night be past:
    Soon shall rise the cheering sun!
      The sun will rise to gladden thee:
      Lady, Lady, cheerful be."   30

17 winding-sheet] Burial shroud.

So spake a voice! While sad and lone,
    Upon a lofty tower, reclin'd,
A Lady sat: the pale moon shone,
    And sweetly blew the summer wind;
        Yet still, disconsolate in mind,
        The lovely Lady sat reclin'd.

The lofty tow'r was ivy clad;
    And round a dreary forest rose;
The midnight bell was tolling sad—
40   'Twas tolling for a soul's repose!
        The Lady heard the gates unclose,
        And from her seat in terror rose.

The summer moon shone bright and clear;
    She saw the castle gates unclose;
And now she saw four monks appear,
    Loud chanting for a soul's repose.
        Forbear, oh, Lady! look no more—
        They pass'd—a livid corpse they bore.

They pass'd, and all was silent now;
50   The breeze upon the forest slept;
The moon stole o'er the mountain's brow;
    Again the Lady sigh'd, and wept:
        She watch'd the holy fathers go
        Along the forest path below.

And now the dawn was bright, the dew
    Upon the yellow heath was seen;
The clouds were of a rosy hue,
    The sunny lustre shone between:
        The Lady to the chapel ran,
60   While the slow matin prayer began.

And then, once more, the fathers grey
    She mark'd, employ'd in holy prayer:
Her heart was full, she cou'd not pray,
    For love and fear were masters there.
        Ah, Lady! thou wilt pray ere long
        To sleep those lonely aisles among!

And now the matin prayers were o'er;
  The barefoot monks, of order grey,
Were thronging to the chapel door,
    When there the Lady stopp'd the way: 70
      "Tell me," she cried, "whose corpse so pale,
      Last night ye bore along the vale?"

"Oh, Lady! question us no more:
  No corpse did we bear down the dale!"
The Lady sunk upon the floor,
    Her quivering lip was deathly pale.
      The barefoot monks now whisper'd, sad,
      "God grant our Lady be not mad."

The monks departing, one by one,
  The chapel gates in silence close;   80
When from the alter steps, of stone,
    The trembling Lady feebly goes:
      While the morning sheds a ruby light,
      The painted windows glowing bright.

And now she heard a hollow sound;
  It seem'd to come from graves below;
And now again she look'd around,
    A voice came murm'ring sad and slow;
      And now she heard it feebly cry,
      "Lady! all that live must die!"   90

"Watch no more from yonder tow'r,
  Watch no more the star of day!
Watch no more the dawning hour,
    That chases sullen night away!
      Cease to watch, and cease to mourn,
      Thy Lover will no more return!"

She look'd around, and now she view'd,
  Clad in a doublet gold and green,
A youthful knight: he frowning stood
    And noble was his mournful mien;   100
      And now he said, with heaving sigh,
      "Lady, all that live must die!"

She rose to quit the altar's stone,
　She cast a look to heaven and sigh'd,
When lo! the youthful knight was gone;
　And, scowling by the Lady's side,
　　With sightless skull and bony hand,
　　She saw a giant spectre stand!

His flowing robe was long and clear,
110　His ribs were white as drifted snow:
The Lady's heart was chill'd with fear;
　She rose, but scarce had power to go:
　　The spectre grinn'd a dreadful smile,
　　And walk'd beside her down the aisle.

And now he wav'd his rattling hand;
　And now they reach'd the chapel door,
And there the spectre took his stand;
　While, rising from the marble floor,
　　A hollow voice was heard to cry,
120　"Lady, all that live must die!"

"Watch no more the evening star!
　Watch no more the glimpse of morn!
Never from the Holy War,
　Lady, will thy Love return!
　　See this bloody cross; and see
　　His bloody scarf he sends to thee!"

And now again the youthful knight
　Stood smiling by the Lady's side;
His helmet shone with crimson light,
130　His sword with drops of blood was dy'd:
　　And now a soft and mournful song
　　Stole the chapel aisles among.

Now from the spectre's paley cheek
　The flesh began to waste away;
The vaulted doors were heard to creek,
　And dark became the Summer day!
　　The spectre's eyes were sunk, but he
　　Seem'd with their sockets still to see!

The second bell is heard to ring:
    Four barefoot monks, of orders grey, 140
Again their holy service sing;
    And round the chapel altar pray:
        The Lady counted o'er and o'er,
        And shudder'd while she counted—*four!*

"Oh! Fathers, who was he, so gay,
    That stood beside the chapel door?
Oh! tell me fathers, tell me pray."
    The monks replied, "We fathers four,
        Lady *no other* have we seen,
        Since in this holy place we've been!" 150

Part Second

Now the merry bugle horn
    Thro' the forest sounded far;
When on the lofty tow'r, forlorn,
    The Lady watch'd the evening star;
        The evening star that seem'd to be
        Rising from the dark'ned sea!

The Summer sea was dark and still,
    The sky was streak'd with lines of gold,
The mist rose grey above the hill,
    And low the clouds of amber roll'd: 160
        The Lady on the lofty tow'r
        Watch'd the calm and silent hour.

And, while she watch'd, she saw advance
    A ship, with painted streamers gay:
She saw it on the green wave dance,
    And plunge amid the silver spray;
        While from the forest's haunts, forlorn,
        Again she heard the bugle horn.

The sails were full; the breezes rose;
    The billows curl'd along the shore; 170
And now the day began to close;—
    The bugle horn was heard no more,

But, rising from the wat'ry way,
　　An airy voice was heard to say:

"Watch no more the evening star;
　　Watch no more the billowy sea;
Lady, from the Holy War
　　Thy lover hastes to comfort thee:
　　　　Lady, Lady, cease to mourn;
180　　　　Soon thy lover will return."

Now she hastens to the bay;
　　Now the rising storm she hears;
Now the sailors smiling say,
　　"Lady, Lady, check your fears:
　　　　Trust us, Lady; we will be
　　　　Your pilots o'er the stormy sea."

Now the little bark she view'd,
　　Moor'd beside the flinty steep;
And now, upon the foamy flood,
190　　The tranquil breezes seem'd to sleep.
　　　　The moon arose; her silver ray
　　　　Seem'd on the silent deep to play.

Now music stole across the main:
　　It was a sweet but mournful tone;
It came a slow and dulcet strain;
　　It came from where the pale moon shone:
　　　　And, while it pass'd across the sea,
　　　　More soft, and soft, it seem'd to be.

Now on the deck the Lady stands;
200　　The vessel steers across the main;
It steers towards the Holy Land,
　　Never to return again:
　　　　Still the sailors cry, "We'll be
　　　　Your pilots o'er the stormy sea."

Now she hears a low voice say,
　　"Deeper, deeper, deeper still;

Hark! the black'ning billows play;
   Hark! the waves the vessel fill:
     Lower, lower, down we go;
     All is dark and still below." *   210

Now a flash of vivid light
   On the rolling deep was seen!
And now the Lady saw the Knight,
   With doublet rich of gold and green:
     From the sockets of his eyes,
     A pale and streaming light she spies!

And now his form transparent stood,
   Smiling with a ghastly mien;—
And now the calm and boundless flood
   Was, like the emerald, bright and green;   220
     And now 'twas of a troubled hue,
     While, "Deeper, deeper," sang the crew.

Slow advanced the morning-light,
   Slow they plough'd the wavy tide;
When, on a cliff of dreadful height,
   A castle's lofty tow'rs they spied:
     The Lady heard the sailor-band
     Cry, "Lady, this is Holy Land."

"Watch no more the glitt'ring spray;
   Watch no more the weedy sand;   230
Watch no more the star of day;
   Lady, this is Holy Land:
     This castle's lord shall welcome thee;
     Then Lady, Lady, cheerful be!"

Now the castle-gates they pass;
   Now across the spacious square,
Cover'd high with dewy grass,
   Trembling steals the Lady fair:
     And now *the castle's lord* was seen,
     Clad in a doublet gold and green.   240

He led her thro' the gothic hall,
  With bones and skulls encircled round;
"Oh, let not this thy soul appal!"
  He cried, "for this is Holy Ground."
    He led her thro' the chambers lone,
    'Mid many a shriek and many a groan.

Now to the banquet-room they came:
  Around a table of black stone
She mark'd a faint and vapoury flame;
250   Upon the horrid feast it shone—
    And there, to close the madd'ning sight,
    Unnumber'd spectres met the light.

Their teeth were like the brilliant, bright;
  Their eyes were blue as sapphire clear;
Their bones were of a polish'd white;
  Gigantic did their ribs appear!—
    And now the Knight the Lady led,
    And plac'd her at the table's head!—

Just now the Lady WOKE:—for she
260   Had slept upon the lofty tow'r,
And dreams of dreadful phantasie
  Had fill'd the lonely moon-light hour:
    Her pillow was the turret-stone,
    And on her breast the pale moon shone.

But now a *real* voice she hears:
  It was her lover's voice;—for he,
To calm her bosom's rending fears,
  That night had cross'd the stormy sea:
    "I come," said he, "from Palestine,
270   To prove myself, *sweet Lady,* THINE."

                                    (1804)

*The closing quotation marks in lines 210 and 228 were absent in the original poem.

Anna Seward

(1742–1809)

George Washington once dispatched a special envoy to dissuade Anna Seward from her published opinion of him. Friend of Helen Maria Williams, Erasmus Darwin, William Hayley, Walter Scott, and a host of other writers, Seward, known as the "Swan of Lichfield," was a widely respected poet and woman of letters who helped to revive the sonnet in English.

Anna Seward was born in Eyam, Derbyshire, near Sheffield, on 12 December 1742 to Elizabeth Hunter and the Reverend Thomas Seward.[1] Called Nancy by her family and close friends, she had been introduced by the age of three to the works of Shakespeare, Milton, and other English writers. When she was nine, she could recite from memory, with an inflection that showed understanding, the first three books of *Paradise Lost*. She was seven when her father became canon of the cathedral at Lichfield, a major provincial cultural center. The Reverend Seward was a man of learning and taste, popular in literary circles; he contributed an essay entitled "The Female Right to Literature" to Dodsley's *Collection* (1748) and edited the works of Beaumont and Fletcher in ten volumes (1750). The Sewards entertained widely.

The family moved in 1754 to the bishop's palace, in the cathedral close, where Anna was to live for more than half a century, until the end of her life. Several siblings died in infancy, but she shared her childhood with her sister Sarah, two years younger, and, after she was thirteen, with her foster sister, Honora Sneyd, eight years younger. Erasmus Darwin, the prominent physician, naturalist, and poet, who lived nearby, encouraged her in her writing once she had convinced him that the verses she showed him were hers rather than her father's. But when Darwin tactlessly told her father that he thought Anna's poetry better than Dr. Seward's own, the latter forbade her

---

1. *The Dictionary of National Biography* and other reference books are incorrect in giving her date of birth as 1747. For a full discussion of the evidence, see Margaret Ashmun, *The Singing Swan: An Account of Anna Seward and Her Acquaintance with Dr. Johnson, Boswell and Others of Their Time* (New Haven, 1931), 5.

to compose verse any more. Anna's sister Sarah, pressured into becoming engaged to a man she did not love, a relative of Samuel Johnson's, died before the marriage could take place. This event, which occurred when Anna was twenty-two, was the first serious bereavement of her life. After it, her attachment to Honora Sneyd became especially intense.

At about this time Anna began taking harpsichord lessons from John Saville, and later in the year she went to London for a month. There she accidentally renewed her friendship with a young soldier of modest means; the two soon fell in love, but her father considered the match unsuitable and had her break the engagement. Later, Anna fell in love with Cornet Richard Vyse, who courted her for three months and then grew cool. After this rejection, she turned down further offers of marriage to pursue the life of the mind. She was widely read in literature, politics, and religion. And her warm personal charm, considerable conversational skills, and talent for dramatic recitation made her popular both as a guest and a hostess.

Richard Lovell Edgeworth wooed and won Honora Sneyd in 1773. Anna Seward fought the marriage as hard as she could, as a result of which she and Sneyd became forever estranged. Seward never fully recovered from this profound loss and bitterly blamed Edgeworth.

In 1777 Erasmus Darwin planted an elaborate garden with botanical specimens and invited Seward to visit. Moved by the scene, she celebrated it in a poem. Darwin suggested that it be published and even expanded into a longer, visionary work propounding the Linnaean system. When Seward refused the assignment, Darwin set to work on his own. The *Gentleman's Magazine* published Seward's poem in 1783 after Darwin had "fixed" it by adding eight lines at the end. Later Darwin published the larger project as *The Botanic Garden,* a work that would bring him wide fame. Seward's lines appear in this work without acknowledgment.

In 1778 Seward met Lady Anna Miller, who encouraged her to write more poetry, published some of it in her *Batheaston Miscellany,* and urged her to send more to the London journals. Seward's *Elegy on Captain Cook,* published in 1780 by J. Dodsley, won the grudging approval of Samuel Johnson. The reviewer for the *Critical Review* noted, "There is a pathetic tenderness in this Elegy, joined to a persuasive harmony of numbers."[2] Just as Seward was beginning to garner the respect of the larger literary world, however, death entered her life powerfully. Honora Sneyd, Maria Edgeworth's first stepmother, died in May 1780. Seward's mother died in July, and the following autumn a friend, Major John André, was hanged in America as a traitor for

2. 50 (1780): 69.

conspiring with Benedict Arnold. Seward's accumulated pain and rage found expression in her *Monody on the Death of Major Andrè,* a long elegy, published the following year. She invented the poetic form that she called "monody," which Darwin termed "epic elegy." The poem paints André as the victim of treachery and strongly reproaches George Washington for his part in condemning him to death. The poem was in tune with wartime public feeling and won Seward instant fame. Once peace was made with England, Washington sent an officer to tell Seward that "no circumstance of his life had been so mortifying as to be censured in the Monody on André, as the pitiless author of his ignominious fate."[3] The emissary produced documents showing that Washington had tried to save André. The papers restored Seward's former admiration for Washington, and filled her "with contrition" for the "rash injustice of her censure."[4]

Seward was a prolific contributor to literary periodicals, especially the *Gentleman's Magazine,* and just as prolific a letter writer. One of her correspondents was William Hayley, best known in the twentieth century as patron to William Blake but regarded in his lifetime as a poet. In the summer of 1782 Seward spent six weeks visiting Hayley; while she was there she met George Romney, who painted her portrait and presented it to his host. Romney also painted a full-length portrait of her and gave it to Seward's father in 1788. In April 1782 the *European Magazine* acknowledged Seward's celebrity by featuring a biographical article on her.

In 1784 Seward published *Louisa, a Poetical Novel, in Four Epistles,* begun when she was nineteen and laid aside at her father's command until years later. In her introduction Seward says she wished "to unite the impassioned fondness of Pope's Eloisa" with the "tenderness of Prior's Emma; avoiding the voluptuousness of the first, and the too conceding softness of the second."[5] About one woman who wrongs another, a tale of forgiveness with a happy ending, the book was an important experiment at a time when the role of poetry in fictional narrative was still being determined. Had Seward's concept of a fictional narrative in verse caught on, the history of the novel might have been quite different. James Boswell reviewed it favorably, but the *European Magazine* savaged it;[6] in general, though, it was well received and went through five editions, but no one imitated the form, and it became a dead end in the history of the novel. In March 1790 Seward's father died.

3. Ashmun, *The Singing Swan,* 85.
4. Ibid., 86.
5. *The Poetical Works of Anna Seward; with Extracts from her Literary Correspondence,* ed. Walter Scott, 3 vols. (Edinburgh and London, 1810), 2:219.
6. 1 August 1784, 106.

She had cared for him assiduously throughout his last decade. "He seems," she wrote, "at once my parent and my child."[7] He left her a comfortable income of four hundred pounds a year, and with it the freedom to come and go as she chose. Jane West described Seward as living "in an elegant hospitable way."[8]

The love of Seward's life was John Saville, vicar choral of Lichfield Cathedral, an enthusiastic botanist and gardener who had lived almost next-door to her from the time she was twelve and he was twenty. Seward called him Giovanni and said of him, "Mr. Saville's songs are always exquisite. Of all our public singers, while many are masterly, many elegant, many astonishing, *he* only is sublime!"[9] Her devotion to him over the course of many years was complete even though he had a wife and two daughters and despite the gossip of neighbors.

Llangollen Vale, published in 1796 with several other poems and six sonnets, commemorates her friendship with Lady Eleanor Butler and Sarah Ponsonby. The reviewer for the *Gentleman's Magazine* for May 1796 said that "there are few to whom the lovers of poetry owe greater obligations than to Miss Seward"; the *British Critic,* however, was scornful.[10] Her Miltonic *Original Sonnets on Various Subjects; and Odes Paraphrased from Horace* appeared in 1799. Seward demonstrated her technical prowess by reverting to the strict rules of sonnet form; at the same time she took liberties with Horace, for, being an essentially self-taught woman, she knew neither Greek nor Latin. Capel Lofft praised the sonnets warmly in the *Critical Review,* and the *Gentleman's Magazine* was equally laudatory. Even Leigh Hunt liked her "December Morning, 1782."[11]

While Seward became the center of the intellectual and literary circle in Lichfield, not everyone was enamoured. Her uneasy literary association with Samuel Johnson and James Boswell is her most famous and problematic relationship. She knew Johnson for much of her life. Her maternal grandfather had taught him at Lichfield school, and Johnson had once been her mother's unsuccessful suitor. Johnson had even less patience for Seward than for other literary women. Seward knew Johnson at his worst and did not fear to document it. For the 27 December 1784 *General Evening Post* she wrote an unsigned "character" of Johnson, pointing out his shortcomings and arguing that he did not merit others' admiration. In 1786 she replied in *Urban's Maga-*

7. Ashmun, *The Singing Swan,* 188.

8. Margaret Ashmun, *The Singing Swan: An Account of Anna Seward and Her Acquaintance with Dr. Johnson, Boswell and Others of Their Time* (1931; reprint, New York, 1968), 177.

9. Ibid., 181.

10. *Gentleman's Magazine* 66 (1796): 413–14; *British Critic* 7 (1796): 404–7.

11. See *Critical Review,* n.s., 26 (May 1799): 33–38.

zine to a review of Boswell's *Tour of the Hebrides,* offering a corrective to the lavish praise of Johnson and pointing to Johnson's bigotry and his injustices to others. "Dr. Johnson's own veracity was too often the victim of his malevolent passions," she argued, and she signed the letter "Benvolio."[12] Three months later, using the same signature in the *Gentleman's Magazine,* she attempted to discredit Hester Lynch Piozzi's contention that Johnson was charitable and honest by citing instances of his ingratitude, sarcasm, ill temper, and delight in wounding the feelings of others.[13] Boswell did not reply. Six years later Seward published a full-page letter in the *Gentleman's Magazine* defending her position and once more complaining about Boswell's rudeness.[14] This time Boswell was not silent. His two-page satiric reply in the November issue included the aspersion that Johnson despised her. In December she replied, elaborating upon her judgment of Johnson's character defects and decrying Boswell's hypocrisy. He retaliated in January, accusing her of envy and malice, alluding to her ignorance of foreign languages, particularly the classical, describing her as a minor versifier, referring to her overfamiliarly as "Nancy Seward," and using derisively the adulatory term "Swan of Lichfield." In what was probably a veiled reference to her liaison with Saville, he remarked that "poetesses . . . have too often been not of the most exemplary lives."[15] She could not risk a reply.

In 1799 Walter Scott, then relatively unknown, wrote to Seward, and the two began corresponding. Scott thought so highly of her "Ballad in the Ancient Scotch Dialect, Auld Willie's Farewell," an imitation of the poetry in his *Minstrelsy of the Scottish Border,* that he published it in the third volume. After Erasmus Darwin died, Seward set down her recollections in a series of anecdotes. Joseph Johnson brought out her *Memoirs of the Life of Dr. Darwin* in 1804, describing not only her old friend but much about the intellectual life of Lichfield. The *Edinburgh Review* for April 1804 savaged the book. Seward wrote Walter Scott, "Ignorance and envy are the only possible parents of such criticisms as disgrace the publication which assumes the name of your city. In putting them forth, their author is baser than a thief, since to blight the early sale of an eminent work by unjust criticism is to rob the bard of his remuneration, while the arrested progress of his fame must inflict severer mortification."[16]

12. 10 January 1786.

13. 61 (April 1786): 302. She acknowledged authorship of the Benvolio letter in the *Gentleman's Magazine* for December 1793 and for October 1794.

14. 63, pt. 2 (October 1793): 875.

15. Quoted in Ashmun, *The Singing Swan,* 206.

16. Seward to Scott, 20 June 1806, quoted in ibid., 237.

In December 1801 John Saville suffered a paralytic seizure. Seward took him into her house for more than a month, despite gossip. On 2 August 1803 he died suddenly. Seward never fully recovered from her bereavement. When she first heard of Saville's death, she had in her hand a letter to Scott. As he later told Joanna Baillie, "The crossest thing I ever did in my life was to poor dear Miss Seward; she wrote me in an evil hour (I had never seen her, mark that!) a long and most passionate epistle upon the death of a dear friend, whom I had never seen, neither, concluding with a charge not to attempt answering the said letter, for she was dead to the world, etc., etc., etc. Never were commands more literally obeyed. I remained as silent as the grave, till the lady made so many inquiries after me, that I was afraid of my death being prematurely announced by a sonnet or an elegy. When I did see her, however, she interested me very much."[17] Scott visited Seward in May of 1807, intending only to spend a few hours; but he was so taken with her that he stayed for two nights. "Such visits," said Seward "are the most high-prized honours which my writings have procured for me."[18]

Seward died on 25 March 1809, at the age of sixty-six, and was buried in the cathedral at Lichfield. The *Gentleman's Magazine* called her "the justly celebrated Miss Seward" and marked her passing with a "Biographical Sketch of the Late Miss Seward."[19] As he had promised her, Walter Scott edited Seward's *Poetical Works* with extracts from her literary correspondence and penned a biographical preface, published in 1810 by John Ballantyne in Edinburgh and Longmans in London. The *Letters of Anna Seward, Written between the Years 1784 and 1807* were edited and published in a six-volume set by Archibald Constable in 1811. Seward had revised them extensively for publication, and Walter Scott had made many deletions. Robert Southey thought the silent emendations misrepresented Seward and was indignant that Constable had violated the conditions of her bequest by publishing the letters so soon.[20] Seward's letters caused much talk. Lady Charlotte Bury's judgment is typical, "I think them very entertaining, though the style is too labored and affected. . . . She is a clever woman, and they contain much reflection and criticism; there is more in them than the generality of published letters, but not one atom of simplicity or nature."[21] Bishop Percy of Dromore, Ireland,

17. Quoted in ibid., 252–53.
18. Quoted in ibid., 255.
19. 79 (April 1809): 378.
20. Southey's letter to Walter Savage Landor, summarized and partly quoted in Ashmun, *The Singing Swan*, is dated Keswick, 5 June 1811. The 1762 portrait of Seward by Kettle, reproduced as a frontispiece for the first volume of her letters, is now in the National Portrait Gallery in London.
21. Lady Charlotte Campbell Bury, *The Diary of a Lady in Waiting* (London, 1908), 125.

saw in them "vanity, egotism, and . . . malignity," evidenced in "her abuse of Mr. Pitt," "her illiberal treatment of Dr. Johnson," "her improper attachment to Saville," her "disrespect for parsons and the hierarchy," and "her cruel censure" of works she disliked.[22] Jane West called her "the British Sappho," defended "the sweetness and sublimity of the most part of her poetry; her wit and taste, not always pure indeed, but always original and ingenious; the ardour with which she supports the cause of genius; her perfect freedom from envy . . . her acute sensibility, and elegant manners," and argued that these "entitle her I think to as high a place as the Ninon de l'Enclos, or Madame Deffand, of France."[23]

MAJOR WORKS: *Elegy on Captain Cook. To Which is Added, an Ode to the Sun* (London, 1780); *Monody on Major Andrè. To Which are Added Letters Addressed to Her by Major Andrè, in the Year 1769* (Lichfield, 1781); *Poem to the Memory of Lady Miller* (London, 1782); *Louisa, a Poetical Novel, in Four Epistles* (Lichfield, 1784); *Ode on General Eliott's Return from Gibraltar* (London, 1787); *Llangollen Vale, with Other Poems* (London, 1796); *Original Sonnets on Various Subjects; and Odes Paraphrased from Horace* (London, 1799); *Memoirs of the Life of Dr. Darwin, Chiefly during his Residence in Lichfield, with Anecdotes of his Friends and Criticisms on his Writings* (London, 1804); *Blindness, a Poem . . . Written at the Request of an Artist, Who Lost his Sight by the Gutta Serena, in his Twenty-eighth Year, and Who was Therefore Obliged to Change his Profession for That of Music* (Sheffield, 1806); *The Poetical Works of Anna Seward; with Extracts from her Literary Correspondence,* ed. Walter Scott, 3 vols. (Edinburgh, 1810); *Letters of Anna Seward, Written between the Years 1784 and 1807,* ed. A. Constable, 6 vols. (Edinburgh, 1811).

TEXTS USED: Texts of "Sonnet IV. To Honora Sneyd, Whose Health Was Always Best in Winter," "Sonnet VII ('By Derwent's rapid stream as oft I stray'd')," "Sonnet X. To Honora Sneyd," "Sonnet XV. Written on Rising Ground near Lichfield," "Sonnet XIX. To ———," "Sonnet LXVII. On Doctor Johnson's Unjust Criticisms in His Lives of the Poets," "Sonnet LXVIII. On the Posthumous Fame of Doctor Johnson," "Sonnet LXXI. To the Poppy," "Sonnet LXXXI. On a Lock of Miss Sarah Seward's Hair Who Died in Her Twentieth Year," and "Sonnet XCV ('On the damp margin of the sea-beat shore')" from *Original Sonnets on Various Subjects; and Odes Paraphrased from Horace,* 2nd ed. (London: G. Sael, 1799). Text of "Sonnet XVIII. An Evening in November, Which Had Been Stormy, Gradually Clearing Up, in a Mountainous Country" from *The Poetical Works of Anna Seward; with Extracts from her Literary Correspondence.*

22. Quoted in Ashmun, *The Singing Swan,* 274.
23. West to Bishop Percy, 22 August 1811, quoted in Ashmun, *The Singing Swan.*

Sonnet IV
To Honora Sneyd,*
Whose Health Was Always Best in Winter

And now the youthful, gay, capricious Spring,
   Piercing her showery clouds with crystal light,
   And with their hues reflected streaking bright
   Her radiant bow, bids all her Warblers sing;
The Lark, shrill caroling on soaring wing;
   The lonely Thrush, in brake, with blossoms white,
   That tunes his pipe so loud; while, from the sight
   Coy bending their dropt heads, young Cowslips fling
Rich perfume o'er the fields. — It is the prime
10   Of Hours that Beauty robes: — yet all they gild,
   Cheer, and delight in this their fragrant time,
For thy dear sake, to me less pleasure yield
   Than, veil'd in sleet, and rain, and hoary rime,
   Dim Winter's naked hedge and plashy field.
                          (wr. May 1770; pub. 1799)

*Afterwards Mrs. Edgeworth. *Seward.* [Honora Sneyd became Maria Edgeworth's stepmother. *Ed.*]

14 plashy] Marshy, swampy, boggy.

Sonnet VII

By Derwent's rapid stream as oft I stray'd,
  With Infancy's light step and glances wild,
  And saw vast rocks, on steepy mountains pil'd,
  Frown o'er th'umbrageous glen; or pleas'd survey'd
The cloudy moonshine in the shadowy glade,
  Romantic Nature to th'enthusiast Child
  Grew dearer far than when serene she smil'd,
  In uncontrasted loveliness array'd.
But O! in every Scene, with sacred sway,
  Her graces fire me; from the bloom that spreads   10
  Resplendent in the lucid morn of May,
To the green light the little Glow-worm sheds
  On mossy banks, when midnight glooms prevail,
  And softest Silence broods o'er all the dale.
                        (wr. 1771–72; pub. 1799)

Sonnet X
To Honora Sneyd

Honora, should that cruel time arrive
  When 'gainst my truth thou should'st my errors poize,
  Scorning remembrance of our vanish'd joys;
  When for the love-warm looks, in which I live,
But cold respect must greet me, that shall give
  No tender glance, no kind regretful sighs;
  When thou shalt pass me with averted eyes,
  Feigning thou see'st me not, to sting, and grieve,
And sicken my sad heart, I could not bear
  Such dire eclipse of thy soul-cheering rays;   10
  I could not learn my struggling heart to tear
From thy loved form, that thro' my memory strays;
  Nor in the pale horizon of Despair
  Endure the wintry and the darken'd days.
                        (wr. April 1773; pub. 1799)

4 umbrageous] Shady.

Sonnet xv
Written on Rising Ground near Lichfield

The evening shines in May's luxuriant pride,
    And all the sunny hills at distance glow,
    And all the brooks, that thro' the valley flow,
    Seem liquid gold. — O! had my fate denied
Leisure, and power to taste the sweets that glide
    Thro' waken'd minds, as the soft seasons go
    On their still varying progress, for the woe
    My heart has felt, what balm had been supplied?
But where great NATURE smiles, as *here* she smiles,
10   'Mid verdant vales, and gently swelling hills,
    And glassy lakes, and mazy, murmuring rills,
And narrow wood-wild lanes, her spell beguiles
    Th'impatient sighs of Grief, and reconciles
    Poetic Minds to Life, with all her ills.
                      (wr. May 1774; pub. 1796)

Sonnet xviii
An Evening in November, Which Had Been Stormy, Gradually Clearing Up, in a Mountainous Country

Ceas'd is the rain; but heavy drops yet fall
    From the drench'd roof; — yet murmurs the sunk wind
    Round the dim hills; can yet a passage find
    Whistling thro' yon cleft rock, and ruin'd wall.
Loud roar the angry torrents, and appal
    Tho' distant. — A few stars, emerging kind,
    With green rays tremble thro' their misty shrouds;
    And the moon gleams between the sailing clouds
On half the darken'd hill. — Now blasts remove
10   The shadowing clouds, and on the mountain's brow,
    Full-orb'd she shines. Half sunk within its cove
Heaves the lone boat, with gulphing sound: — and lo!

Bright rolls the settling lake, and brimming rove
The vale's blue rills, and glitter as they flow!

(1799)

Sonnet XIX
To ————

Farewell, false Friend!—our scenes of kindness close!
   To cordial looks, to sunny smiles farewell!
   To sweet consolings, that can grief expel,
   And every joy soft sympathy bestows!
For alter'd looks, where truth no longer glows,
   Thou hast prepar'd my heart;—and it was well
   To bid thy pen th' unlook'd for story tell,
   Falsehood avow'd, that shame, nor sorrow knows—
O! when we meet,—(to meet we're destin'd, try
   To avoid it as thou may'st) on either brow,   10
   Nor in the stealing consciousness of eye,
Be seen the slightest trace of what, or how
   We once were to each other;—nor one sigh
   Flatter with weak regret a broken vow!

(1799)

Sonnet LXVII
On Doctor Johnson's Unjust Criticisms
in His Lives of the Poets*

Could aweful JOHNSON want poetic ear,
    Fancy, or judgment?—no! his splendid strain,
    In prose, or rhyme, confutes that plea.—The pain
    Which writh'd o'er GARRICK's fortunes, shows us clear
Whence all his spleen to Genius.—Ill to bear
    A Friend's renown, that to his *own* must reign,
    Compar'd, a Meteor's evanescent train,
    To Jupiter's fix'd orb, proves that each sneer,
Subtle and fatal to poetic Sense,
10   Did from insidious Envy meanly flow,
    Illumed with dazzling hues of eloquence,
And Sophist-Wit, that labour to o'er-throw
    Th' awards of Ages, and new laws dispense
    That lift the *mean,* and lay the Mighty low.

                                 (1799)

* When Johnson's idolaters are hard pressed concerning his injustice in those *fallacious* though *able* pages;—when they are reminded that he there tells us the perusal of Milton's Paradise Lost is a *task,* and never a *pleasure;*—reminded also of his avowed contempt of that exquisite Poem, the Lycidas;—of his declaration that Dryden's absurd Ode on the death of Mrs. Anne Killegrew, written in Cowley's *worst* manner, is the *noblest* Ode in this Language;—of his disdain of Gray as a *lyric* Poet; of the superior respect he pays to *Yalden, Blackmore,* and *Pomfret;*—When these things are urged, his Adorers seek to acquit him of *wilful* misrepresentation by alleging that he wanted ear for lyric numbers, and taste for the *higher* graces of Poetry:—but it is impossible to believe, when we recollect that even his *prose* abounds with poetic efflorescence, metaphoric conception, and harmonious cadence, which in the highest degree adorn it, without diminishing its strength. We must look for the source of his injustice in

4 o'er Garrick's fortunes] David Garrick (1717–79) was Samuel Johnson's pupil at Edial and accompanied him when he moved from Lichfield to London. He became a well-respected actor, versatile in playing both comic and tragic parts. In 1747 he joined the management of the Drury Lane Theatre, where he produced many Shakespearean dramas. He wrote farces and was a member of Johnson's Literary Club. He lies buried in Westminster Abbey.
14 That lift the *mean,* and lay the Mighty low] See Virgil, *Aeneid* 6.853.

the envy of his temper. When Garrick was named a candidate for admission into the Literary Club, Dr. Johnson told Mr. Thrale he would black-ball him. "*Who,* Sir? Mr. Garrick! Companion of your Youth! your acknowledged Friend!"—"Why, Sir, I love my little David better than any, or all of his Flatterers love him; but surely we ought to sit in a society like ours, unelbow'd by a Gamester, Pimp, or Player." See Supplement to Dr Johnson's Letters, published by Mrs Piozzi. The blended hypocrisy and malice of this sally show the man. Johnson knew, at times, how to coax without sincerity as well as to abuse without justice. His seeming fondness for Mrs. C—— of Lichfield, on his visits to that City, and the contempt with which he spoke of her to her townspeople, was another instance of the same nature. *Seward.* [Samuel Johnson published his *Lives of the Poets* from 1779 to 1781. *Ed.*]

Sonnet LXVIII
On the Posthumous Fame of Doctor Johnson

Well it becomes thee, Britain, to avow
   JOHNSON's high claims!—yet boasting that his fires
   Were of *unclouded* lustre, Truth retires
   Blushing, and Justice knits her solemn brow;
The eyes of Gratitude withdraw the glow
   His moral strain inspired.—Their zeal requires
   That thou should'st better guard the sacred Lyres,
   Sources of thy bright fame, than to bestow
Perfection's wreath on him, whose ruthless hand,
   Goaded by jealous rage, the laurels tore,   10
   That Justice, Truth, and Gratitude demand
Should deck those Lyres till Time shall be no more.—
   A radiant course did JOHNSON's Glory run,
   But large the spots that darken'd on its Sun.

(1799)

Sonnet LXXI
To the Poppy

While Summer Roses all their glory yield
   To crown the Votary of Love and Joy,
   Misfortune's Victim hails, with many a sigh,
   Thee, scarlet Poppy of the pathless field,
Gaudy, yet wild and lone; no leaf to shield
   Thy flaccid vest, that, as the gale blows high,
   Flaps, and alternate folds around thy head. —
   So stands in the long grass a love-craz'd Maid,
Smiling aghast; while stream to every wind
   Her garish ribbons, smear'd with dust and rain;
   But brain-sick visions cheat her tortured mind,
And bring false peace. Thus, lulling grief and pain,
   Kind dreams oblivious from thy juice proceed,
   Thou flimsy, shewy, melancholy weed.

(1799)

Sonnet LXXXI
On a Lock of Miss Sarah Seward's Hair
Who Died in Her Twentieth Year

My Angel Sister, tho' thy lovely form
   Perish'd in Youth's gay morning, yet is mine
   This precious Ringlet! — still the soft hairs shine,
   Still glow the nut-brown tints, all bright and warm
With sunny gleam! — Alas! each kindred charm
   Vanish'd long since; deep in the silent shrine
   Wither'd to shapeless Dust! — and of their grace
   Memory alone retains the faithful trace. —
Dear Lock, had thy sweet Owner liv'd, ere now
   Time on her brow had faded thee! — My care
   Screen'd from the sun and dew thy golden glow;
And thus her early beauty dost thou wear,

Thou *all* of that fair Frame my love could save
From the resistless ravage of the Grave!
(1799)

Sonnet xcv

On the damp margin of the sea-beat shore
   Lonely at eve to wander;—or reclin'd
   Beneath a rock, what time the rising wind
   Mourns o'er the waters, and, with solemn roar,
Vast billows into caverns surging pour,
   And back recede alternate; while combin'd
   Loud shriek the sea-fowls, harbingers assign'd,
   Clamorous and fearful, of the stormy hour;
To listen with deep thought those awful sounds;
   Gaze on the boiling, the tumultuous waste,   10
   Or promontory rude, or craggy mounds
Staying the furious main, delight has cast
   O'er my rapt spirit, and my thrilling heart,
   Dear as the softer joys green vales impart.
(wr. 1790; pub. 1799)

Mary Wollstonecraft Shelley

(1797–1851)

Author of *Frankenstein,* Mary Wollstonecraft Godwin Shelley seemed destined from birth for distinction in the world of letters. Her mother was Mary Wollstonecraft, pioneering feminist author of *The Vindication of the Rights of Woman* (1792), and her father was William Godwin, whose treatise *An Enquiry concerning Political Justice* (1793) made him the leading British philosopher of his time. Both wrote novels and were part of a circle of radical London intellectuals who espoused egalitarian principles inspired by the American and French revolutions. Although both Wollstonecraft and Godwin were opposed to the institution of marriage, for the sake of their unborn child they wed five months before her birth in London on 30 August 1797. Wollstonecraft died from complications of childbirth, and Mary spent her earliest years in the care of relatives and friends.

When Mary was four Godwin married Mary Jane Clairmont; finally Mary had a stable home, if not an altogether happy one. She and her stepmother never got along, and her father, whom she adored, was a remote parent. Mary could often be found sitting in nearby St. Pancras churchyard by the grave of her mother, whom she idolized but had never known, reading and rereading Wollstonecraft's and Godwin's works. Mary had no formal schooling, but being part of the Godwin household was an excellent education in itself. Her father knew all of the leading writers and intellectuals, and Mary grew up surrounded by books and enlightened discussion. One night she heard Samuel Taylor Coleridge recite "The Rime of the Ancient Mariner."

In 1812 Percy Bysshe Shelley, an aristocratic disciple of both Wollstonecraft and Godwin, came to Skinner Street to sit at the feet of the author of *Political Justice.* At the time he took little notice of fourteen-year-old Mary, who shortly thereafter went for the sake of her health to Scotland. However, in the spring of 1814, when Mary next encountered the twenty-one-year-old Shelley, she had blossomed into an engaging and attractive young woman of sixteen. Before long, over Mary Wollstonecraft's grave, they declared their love for one another. Ignoring the conventions of the world and her father's wishes, on 28 July 1814 Mary eloped with Shelley, beginning the nomadic existence she would know for the whole of her life with him. Mary's stepsister, Claire Clairmont, joined them. The threesome traveled across France, among the first English tourists to witness firsthand the devastation and human misery left by the ravages of the Napoleonic Wars, and Switzerland. They returned to London in mid-September to suffer the severe social consequences of their action.

William Godwin refused to see Mary or to communicate with her in any way. Former friends, scandalized by her behavior, would have nothing to do with her. Harriet Shelley, Percy Bysshe Shelley's wife, hired a lawyer. For a time Shelley was in danger of being imprisoned for debt. In February 1815 Mary gave birth to a premature infant, whom the doctor said could not live. But Mary read Germaine de Staël's *Corinne* and nursed the baby. Two weeks later she found the infant dead. Soon afterwards she recorded in her journal, "Dream that my little baby came to life again—that it had only been cold & that we rubbed it by the fire & it lived—."[1] That August, a year after their first elopement, with financial matters settled for the time being, the lovers set up their first household in Bishopsgate, near Windsor. There Mary gave birth to their son William in January 1816. Thomas Love Peacock was a frequent visitor, but Mary Godwin's family still refused to see her. Nevertheless, William Godwin demanded that Shelley continue to provide him with financial support.

The couple left for Switzerland in May 1816. From the beginning their life together had included a rigorous program of reading, both to each other and alone, in poetry, fiction, drama, history, travel writing, biography, philosophy, and classical literature, which they pursued during an unusually cold and rainy summer near Lake Geneva. They met Lord Byron at Secheron at the end of May and soon saw him almost daily at his Villa Diodati; Mary, Shelley, and Byron himself were all to be deeply affected, both from a personal and a literary standpoint, by the close relationship that developed between them.

In June Byron proposed a contest for writing the best ghost story, and the next day he and Shelley each began one. Eighteen-year-old Mary, feeling the pressure of her distinguished literary parentage and intimidated by the fame of Byron and the literary talent of her partner, could not think of a story for a week. However, a discussion of the possibility of reanimating corpses through galvanism, along with Mary Godwin's own sublimated longing for

---

1. Entry for 19 March 1815, *The Journals of Mary Shelley,* ed. Paula R. Feldman and Dina Scott-Kilvert, 2 vols. (Oxford, 1987), 1:70.

her dead mother and infant as well as anxiety about her literary abilities, came together to inspire a horrific "waking dream." She later recalled, "I saw the pale student of unhallowed arts kneeling beside the thing he had put together. I saw the hideous phantasm of a man stretched out, and then, on the working of some powerful engine, show signs of life, and stir with an uneasy, half-vital motion. . . . His success would terrify the artist."[2] Mary Shelley knew she had found the germ of her story, and after Byron and Shelley set off for a trip around Lake Geneva she sat down and began, "It was on a dreary night of November, that I beheld the accomplishment of my toils." When Shelley returned, Mary showed him her short prose tale, and he urged her to expand it.

The mythic novel she crafted over the next nine months, *Frankenstein; or, The Modern Prometheus,* expresses in the veiled and transmuted manner of a nightmarish dream its author's own fears, anxieties, and emotional response to her excommunication from her family. It is the story of failed parenthood, artistic inadequacy, and knowledge misused, which produce a creature shunned by humanity, an outcast longing for love and acceptance but experiencing only the cruelest rejection. The book implicitly calls attention to the shortcomings of Godwin's philosophy. The psychological landscape of the novel was also shaped by traumatic events that took place during its composition, the suicides of her half-sister, Fanny Imlay, and Harriet Shelley. Victor Frankenstein, the "creator," the solitary artist, and the creature's double, neglects his family as he pursues his Promethean ambition and is responsible for the deaths of those close to him, inspiring the guilt and despair Mary Shelley herself knew all too well. Though some commentators have tried to argue that the success of the novel owes much to Percy Bysshe Shelley's editorial suggestions, in fact his contribution was no greater than that of many editors, and Mary Shelley did not always adopt his suggestions.[3] Despite its awkwardnesses, the power of *Frankenstein* owes much to its having fulfilled its author's wish to "speak to the mysterious fears of our nature."[4] The publishing firms of John Murray and Charles Ollier rejected the novel, but Lackington published it in 1818. Although some denounced it for impiety, Walter Scott gave it high praise in *Blackwood's Edinburgh Review,* unaware, like others, that the anonymous novel had been authored by a young woman. When Mary Shelley revealed her authorship to Scott, the news enhanced the

2. From Mary Shelley's introduction to *Frankenstein,* Standard Novels (London, 1831), x.

3. For a discussion of this issue, see Emily Sunstein, *Mary Shelley: Romance and Reality* (Boston, 1989), 127, 430–31.

4. Introduction to *Frankenstein,* ix.

book's sensation. The first science-fiction novel, it was a popular success from the beginning.

In August 1816 the couple returned to England and settled in Bath. They married on 30 December 1816. In March the Shelleys moved to Marlow, and in September Mary gave birth to a daughter, Clara Everina. At the end of the year Mary published anonymously with Thomas Hookham a travel book, *History of a Six Weeks' Tour,* drawn from the journal the couple had kept during their elopement, with extracts from the letters written on their journey. Shortly thereafter the family moved to London, but by mid-March they were off to Italy. They migrated from Milan to Pisa to Leghorn to Bagni di Lucca.

In September 1818 one-year-old Clara Everina died from dysentery. Mary, grief-stricken, remained depressed and withdrawn for months. All her maternal affections were now focused on three-year-old William. The family traveled to Rome, then to Venice, then back to Rome again. In early June 1819 William contracted a serious fever and died on 7 June. Having lost her two children within a year, Mary, who was pregnant, sank into a severe, suicidal depression and withdrew from all those around her, including her husband. He wrote:

> My dearest Mary, wherefore hast thou gone,
> And left me in this dreary world alone?
> Thy form is here indeed—a lovely one—
> But thou art fled, gone down the dreary road,
> That leads to Sorrow's most obscure abode;
> Thou sittest on the hearth of pale despair, where
> For thine own sake I cannot follow thee.[5]

It was in this context that in August 1819 Mary Shelley began drafting "The Fields of Fancy," later retitled *Matilda,* a tragic tale of incestuous love between a father and his daughter. In November she gave birth to a son, Percy Florence, but her depression did not lift until the end of the following summer. Nursing her child, she revised her novella, hoping to raise funds through its sale to relieve her father's financial difficulties. In the spring of 1820 she sent the manuscript to Godwin. Aghast, he would not submit it to a publisher, and he refused to return the manuscript; as a result, *Matilda* was not published until 1959.[6]

In early 1820, soon after Mary moved with her family to Pisa, she began composing a historical novel based upon the life of the fourteenth-century

5. "To Mary Shelley."
6. *Mathilda,* ed. Elizabeth Nitchie (Chapel Hill, 1959).

Castruccio Castracani, duke of Lucca. One of the fictional heroines is the republican countess of Valperga, after whom Mary entitled the novel. The Shelleys moved to Leghorn in June 1820 and during the next year migrated back and forth from Bagni San Giuliano to Pisa. By the end of July 1821 Mary had finished a draft of *Valperga,* and six months later she sent a corrected copy to England.

At the end of April 1822 the Shelleys moved to a place just outside Lerici, where Mary suffered a near-fatal miscarriage in mid-June. On 8 July Shelley, who could not swim, sailed from Leghorn harbor with two others into an approaching storm. It was ten agonizing days before his body was found washed up on shore at Viareggio, where he was cremated. Mary, now twenty-four years old, found herself widowed with no financial resources. Shelley's family, blaming her for their son's alienation from his first wife, refused her any support.

During a prolonged period of severe, suicidal depression Mary began her next diary notebook with the lines, "The Journal of Sorrow—Begun 1822 / But for my Child it could not / End too soon."[7] In July 1823 in Genoa, where she had moved in mid-September to live with Leigh Hunt and his family, she composed a long poem addressed to her late husband entitled "The Choice," expressing not only her grief but her guilt and remorse at having become emotionally withdrawn from him during their last years together. She acknowledged

> . . . cold neglect, averted eyes
> That blindly crushed thy heart's fond sacrifice:—
> My heart was all thine own—but yet a shell
> Closed in its core, which seemed impenetrable,
> Till sharp:toothed Misery tore the husk in twain
> Which gaping lies nor may unite again—
> Forgive me! let thy love descend in dew
> Of soft repentance and regret most true;—[8]

Her goal became to make the world aware of Shelley's literary worth by editing and publishing his works. In the process, she collected and preserved holograph copies of his poems and, with the peculiar skill of one intimately familiar with his habits of composition and accustomed to reading his difficult handwriting, she sometimes painstakingly reconstructed drafts of poems where no fair copy existed. Often the work was emotionally trying, for Shelley had written not only about his pain at finding Mary remote and un-

---

7. *Journals of Mary Shelley,* 2:428.
8. "The Choice," lines 33–40, ibid., 491.

responsive but also about his love for other women. *Posthumous Poems of Percy Bysshe Shelley* appeared in mid-June 1824 and included sixty-five works never before published. It was an important step in the process of inspiring public respect for a man condemned during his lifetime as an immoral author of obscure works.

Valperga, sold to Whittaker for four hundred pounds, had been published in February 1823. Despite some positive critical response, it enjoyed only a modest sale. Mary returned to London in late August 1823 to discover that *Frankenstein* had made her famous. A dramatic adaptation was enjoying success at the English Opera House, and within four days of her arrival she attended a performance. Her most serious concern, however, and her reason for returning to England, was financial: how to provide for herself and her son. She reapplied for support to Sir Timothy Shelley, her late husband's father, and was told she could expect one hundred pounds a year for Percy Florence but nothing for herself. Still, this was enough to relieve her immediate needs and to provide a foundation to be supplemented by literary earnings. She began writing professionally in earnest, contributing fiction to the *London Magazine.* Soon she began publishing stories and then poems in such well-paying literary annuals as the *Forget-Me-Not,* the *Keepsake,* and *Heath's Book of Beauty.* Flora Tristan, the French feminist, described Mary Shelley's verse as "pleins de melodie et de sentiment," but most of it is fairly undistinguished compared with her fiction.[9] In the 1830s Mary would also write biographical sketches for Dionysius Lardner's Cabinet Cyclopedia.

Mary's *roman à clef, The Last Man,* imaginatively projects the psychic landscape of her personal past into a futuristic, twenty-first-century science-fiction plot. The story is narrated by Lionel Verney, the last man alive after a plague has decimated the human race, and features a hot-air balloon trip across the Atlantic Ocean as well as idealized portraits of Percy Bysshe Shelley (Adrian) and Lord Byron (Lord Raymond), whose recent death in Greece had shaken Mary and reinforced her conviction that she, like Lionel Verney, was the last survivor of a race. In January 1826 Henry Colburn published *The Last Man,* for which Mary earned three hundred pounds, less than *Valperga* had brought. Despite initial demand and some positive reviews, most critics and readers panned the novel for the grimness of its subject. Demoralized, Mary Shelley wrote articles for the *Westminster Review* and the *London Magazine.*

Mary's next novel, *The Fortunes of Perkin Warbeck,* published in May 1830, was a historical romance set in medieval times about a pretender to the English throne and his wife, Katherine Gordon. Criticized by reviewers for

9. Quoted in Sunstein, *Mary Shelley,* 340.

its pessimism, the book was a commercial failure. The *Athenaeum* named Mary Shelley the most distinguished living British woman author, but such praise did not pay the bills. Richard Bentley published her substantially revised text of *Frankenstein* in his Standard Novels series in November 1831, for which Mary wrote an introduction recalling the circumstances of the novel's composition.

Lodore, published by Bentley in April 1835, contains three heroines, including Fanny Derham, an intellectual who fights for the oppressed using the power of language but who lacks the financial resources to be independent. Critics praised the novel for its originality, style, and energy and liked it better than anything she had written since *Frankenstein.* Mary Shelley's last novel, *Falkner,* published by Saunders and Otley in February 1837, features the heroine Elizabeth Raby, adopted daughter of Falkner, a man haunted by a secret crime. Raby defies conventional notions of female conduct and, unlike Mary Shelley's other heroines, finds happiness in the end in a loving family circle that includes both husband and father. Some criticized the book for defending criminal behavior or for moralizing, but most reviewers liked it.

Now that conditions were right, she turned to the difficult task of editing *The Poetical Works of Percy Bysshe Shelley* in four volumes with biographical and critical notes on the poems, seeing as her goal "to lay the first stone of a monument due to Shelley's genius, his sufferings, and his virtues."[10] Edward Moxon paid her five hundred pounds for the copyright. After the first volume appeared in January 1839, she was criticized for omissions she believed Shelley himself would have wanted and for others demanded by the publisher. Moreover, writing the notes unearthed painful memories, as did love poems such as *Epipsychidion,* inspired by other women, and she suffered another severe and extended period of depression. Still, she completed all four volumes of *The Poetical Works* as well as two volumes of Shelley's prose, *Essays, Letters from Abroad, Translations and Fragments,* for publication in 1839. These editions played a crucial role in establishing Percy Bysshe Shelley as a major English poet.

Mary Shelley's last book, *Rambles in Germany and Italy, in 1840, 1842, and 1843* (1844), dedicated to Samuel Rogers, describes two tours of the Continent she made with her son and others. The critics were favorable, and though he disliked it, Robert Browning sent a copy to Elizabeth Barrett. Richard Hengist Horne devoted an appreciative chapter to Mary Shelley in *The New Spirit of the Age,* and Balzac in *La Muse du Département* (1843) pointed to her and to

---

10. Mary Shelley, preface to *The Poetical Works of Percy Bysshe Shelley,* 4 vols. (London, 1839), 1:xvi.

Ann Radcliffe as proof that women surpass men in the realm of imaginative creation.

In April 1844 Sir Timothy Shelley died, and Percy Florence inherited the title and estate. However, Mary Shelley's years of financial security were brief. She died of a brain tumor on 1 February 1851, at the age of fifty-three, and was buried in Bournemouth in a common grave with William Godwin and Mary Wollstonecraft.

MAJOR WORKS: *Frankenstein: or, The Modern Prometheus,* 3 vols. (London, 1818); *Valperga: Or, the Life and Adventures of Castruccio, Prince of Lucca,* 3 vols. (London, 1823); *The Last Man,* 3 vols. (London, 1826); *The Fortunes of Perkin Warbeck, A Romance,* 3 vols. (London, 1830); *Lodore,* 3 vols. (London, 1835); *Falkner. A Novel,* 3 vols. (London, 1837); *Rambles in Germany and Italy, in 1840, 1842, and 1843,* 2 vols. (London, 1844).

WITH PERCY BYSSHE SHELLEY: *History of a Six Weeks' Tour through a Part of France, Switzerland, Germany, and Holland: with Letters Descriptive of a Sail round the Lake of Geneva, and of the Glaciers of Chamouni* (London, 1817).

EDITED WORKS: Percy Bysshe Shelley, *The Poetical Works of Percy Bysshe Shelley,* 4 vols. (London, 1839) and *Essays, Letters from Abroad, Translations and Fragments,* 2 vols. (London, 1840).

TEXT USED: "Stanzas" from the *Keepsake* for 1839.

Stanzas

O, come to me in dreams, my love!
   I will not ask a dearer bliss;
Come with the starry beams, my love,
   And press mine eyelids with thy kiss.

'Twas thus, as ancient fables tell,
   Love visited a Grecian maid,
Till she disturbed the sacred spell,
   And woke to find her hopes betrayed.

But gentle sleep shall veil my sight,
   And Psyche's lamp shall darkling be,   10

When, in the visions of the night,
   Thou dost renew thy vows to me.

Then come to me in dreams, my love,
   I will not ask a dearer bliss;
Come with the starry beams, my love,
   And press mine eyelids with thy kiss.

(1839)

Charlotte Smith

(1749–1806)

Recognized as one of the foremost poets and novelists of her time, Charlotte Smith grew up with every advantage of wealth and social position. The eldest child of Nicholas Turner and his first wife, Anna Towers, she was born on 4 May 1749 in London and spent her infancy at Stoke. Her father, a member of the landed gentry with holdings in Surrey and Sussex, was also a poet; a man of wit and fashion, he was cultured and intellectual and had a love of nature and poetry, which he passed on to his daughter. When Charlotte was three, her mother died from complications during childbirth; not long afterwards, her unmarried maternal aunt, Lucy Towers, became her foster mother and directed her education. Charlotte first went to school in Chichester and then attended a school in Kensington, London.

When Charlotte was ten the family moved to Bignor Park in Sussex, near the river Arun and the South Downs. The landscape captivated her imagination, and she later recreated it in her sonnets (see especially sonnet v, "To the South Downs") and in "Beachy Head"; she came to associate the happiness and freedom of childhood with this countryside. Charlotte left school at the age of twelve, but she had tutors in music, drawing, dancing, and French and read fiction and poetry voraciously. When the family was in London, she began to attend the theater and the opera with her father, who encouraged her poetry writing and, when she was fourteen, urged her to send some of her verses to the editor of the *Lady's Magazine*.

The poet's happy childhood ended abruptly, however, when she was fifteen. Contemplating his own remarriage, on 23 February 1765 her father hastily married Charlotte off to Benjamin Smith, second son of Richard Smith, a West Indian merchant and a director of the East India Company. The marriage, in which there was no fondness on either side, was a disaster, and the cause of almost all her future misery. Forced to leave her beloved South Downs for one of the filthiest streets in London, she was now surrounded by people who did not share her interests. Their living quarters, over her father-in-law's business, were large and well furnished but sunless. There in 1766 she gave birth to a son, who died one year later, at just about the time when a second son was born. Charlotte was only seventeen. Unable to love her husband, she had loved her child inordinately, and her intense grief at the baby's death endangered her health. Her father-in-law, Richard Smith, who had grown particularly fond of her, granted her request to leave London. She moved with her family to Southgate, where her health improved. Charlotte indulged her love of reading and gave birth to two more sons at Southgate; eventually the family moved to Tottenham, within five miles of London where three more children were born. At the age of twenty-five, Charlotte Smith had been unhappily married for nine years and had six children living, the oldest only seven years old. The care of so many little children, which often included her husband's orphaned nieces and nephews, might have seemed burdensome to some, but children were the only joy in Charlotte Smith's marriage.

When the family had grown to ten children the Smiths moved to Lys Farm in Hampshire, near Sussex. There they lived for nine years, and there, away from his father's supervision, Benjamin Smith spent large sums on building projects and experimental farming. His wife had no power to stop his inevitable plunge into financial ruin as he squandered the large fortune she had brought into the marriage. Her father-in-law, who had become a close friend and protector, died in October 1776. The intricacies of his will and the machinations of lawyers prevented her children from coming into their inheritance for many years and thrust Charlotte Smith, named as a joint executor, into a distressing quagmire of legal dissension. In 1777 her eldest son, ten-year-old Benjamin Berney, an intelligent but sickly child upon whom Smith doted, died. Another blow came in December 1783, when Benjamin Smith's irresponsible spending caught up with him; without his father to bail him out, he was thrown into King's Bench prison for debt. Friends and relatives deserted Charlotte Smith in the face of this humiliation, but her brother, Nicholas Turner, took over the care of her children at Bignor Park when she accompanied her husband to prison.

From this time forward Smith supported her husband and family of nine children through authorship. After several rejections of her first book, she sought out William Hayley, whom she had never met but who lived within seven miles of Bignor Park. He encouraged her and gave her advice; she, in turn, dedicated the book to him. To a friend's suggestion that the public might prefer poems of a lively cast, she replied, " 'Are grapes gathered from

thorns, or figs from thistles?' Or can the *effect* cease, while the *cause* remains?"[1]
Dodsley, in Pall Mall, the most fashionable publisher in London, printed at
Smith's own expense *Elegiac Sonnets, and Other Essays.* The thin, quarto volume came out on 10 May 1784, and its profits temporarily relieved Smith
and her family; a second edition was called for within the year.

The book sold well and enjoyed critical success. Smith sparked a controversy by stretching the sonnet form beyond its traditional confines, including many irregular as well as Shakespearean sonnets in her collection.
This experimental work profoundly influenced the history and development
of the sonnet in English.[2] The *Gentleman's Magazine* observed, "A very trifling compliment is paid Mrs. Smith, when it is observed how much her
Sonnets exceed those of *Shakespeare* and *Milton.* She has undoubtedly con-
ferred honour on a species of poetry which most of her predecessors in this
country have disgraced."[3] Anna Seward was less impressed. She wrote to a
friend shortly after reading this review, "Such praise may vie, as an offering at the shrine of dulness. . . . You say Mrs. Smith's sonnets are pretty:—
so say I; *pretty* is the proper word; pretty tuneful cantos from our various
poets, without anything original. All the lines that are not the lines of others
are weak and unimpressive; and these hedge-flowers to be preferred, by a
critical dictator, to the roses and amaranths of the first poets the world has
produced!!!—It makes me sick."[4] But many believed, as did the reviewer for
the *Critical Review,* that Smith had shown "that a species of poetry, the most
artificial, might be rendered natural and pleasing in our language, by taste
and judgment."[5] And in his "Essay on the English Sonnet" published in the
Universal Magazine, "J.T." defends Smith against the criticism of the Reverend
Henry White, a cousin of Anna Seward's, by observing that Smith's sonnets
"display a more touching melancholy, a more poetical simplicity, nay I will
venture to say, a greater vigour and correctness of genius, than any other
English poems I have ever seen, under the same denomination: and I certainly do not mean to except the sonnets of Milton."[6] For the third edition

1. From Smith's preface to the sixth edition of *Elegiac Sonnets* (London, 1792), quoted
in Florence May Anna Hilbish, *Charlotte Smith, Poet and Novelist (1794-1806)* (Philadelphia,
1941), 106.

2. See Hilbish, *Charlotte Smith,* 246–49; and Daniel Robinson, "Reviving the Sonnet: Women
Romantic Poets and the Sonnet Claim," *European Romantic Review* 6 (summer 1995): 98–123.

3. 56 (April 1786): 334. See also *Monthly Review* 71 (November 1784): 368.

4. *Letters of Anna Seward,* 6 vols. (London, 1811), 1:162–63.

5. 65 (appendix, January–June 1788): 531.

6. 91 (December 1792), 412–13; Hilbish, *Charlotte Smith,* 241. Other enthusiastic reviews appeared in the *European Magazine* (1789) and in Nathan Drakes's *Literary Hours or Sketches Critical*

Smith shortened the original title to reflect her having included only sonnets and added twenty more. In response to the charge of plagiarism made by Seward and others, she also annotated the sonnets, explicitly acknowledging lines and ideas taken from elsewhere.[7] Although Smith remained sensitive to the charge of plagiarism for the rest of her career (see, for example, the extensive notes to *Beachy Head*), the controversy helped to bring her work to public attention. The fifth edition (1787) included more sonnets and some additional poems as well as five engraved plates. Among the 817 subscribers were Horace Walpole, Henrietta O'Neil, William Hayley, William Cowper, the archbishop of Canterbury, and William Pitt. In 1795, a seventh edition, with more sonnets and other poems, appeared in London. Stothard reissued the fifth edition in 1797 (by subscription for a guinea) along with plates and a new second volume. The ninth edition (1800) includes ninety-two sonnets and twenty-seven additional poems and was the last that Smith personally superintended. But the enduring popularity of *Elegiac Sonnets* is attested to by its posthumous republication in a tenth edition in 1811 and an eleventh edition in 1851. Still, in 1784, the initial profits from Smith's book were not sufficient to protect Smith's husband from creditors.

Benjamin Smith left prison on 2 July 1784. Within three months he faced the unhappy choice between further imprisonment and flight. He left for Upper Normandy, renting a dilapidated château nine miles from the nearest town. There, lacking access to fuel to warm the comfortless house, the Smiths suffered during the winter of 1785, and there Charlotte gave birth to another son. She also translated Prevost's *Manon L'Escaut* from the French. In the spring of 1785, when her youngest child was barely two months old, she returned to England, pacified her husband's creditors, and settled in Sussex. After Cadell published *Manon L'Escaut,* critic George Stevens attacked Smith for translating an "immoral" work, and she was forced to withdraw the book. In the spring of 1786 her eldest son, William Towers, then seventeen or eighteen, received an appointment in Bengal; bitter and depressed, Smith grieved that she might never see him again. Soon after William's departure her second son, Braithwaite, died of a fever, having been ill for only thirty-six hours.

In 1787, after twenty-three years of unhappy marriage, Smith obtained an "amicable separation" from her husband. This move subjected her to severe criticism, but her sister, Catherine Ann Dorset, said that those who knew the

---

and Narrative (Sudbury, 1798) and David Rivers's *Literary Memoirs of Living Authors of Great Britain* (London, 1798).

　　7. For a discussion of the nature of Smith's borrowings, see Hilbish, *Charlotte Smith,* 242–46.

true causes "could only regret that the measure had not been adopted years before."[8] Smith continued to give her husband money, and their relationship remained amicable. Having become involved in fresh troubles, Benjamin Smith tried to persuade the poet to return to him, but when she refused, he left for the Continent. Elizabeth Carter reported that Charlotte Smith "has been obliged to purchase her freedom from a vile husband, by giving up part of the little fortune she had left; so that she has at present little more than a hundred a year to support herself and six or seven children."[9] Still, despite the hardship, Smith could now freely pursue her writing. She translated from the French *Les causes célèbres,* by Francois Gayot de Pitaval, in 1787 and published these stories under the title *The Romance of Real Life.* The book was popular with reviewers and the public alike. She began work on a novel, *Emmeline, the Orphan of the Castle,* in the summer of 1787 and published it eight months later, in the spring of 1788. She had interwoven her own poems into the narrative, and reviewers were enthusiastic. The fifteen hundred copies of the first edition sold so rapidly that the book immediately went into a second edition, and a third edition followed the next year. Walter Scott called it "happily conceived, and told in a most interesting manner. It contained a happy mixture of humour, and of bitter satire mingled with pathos, while the characters, both of sentiment and of manners, were sketched with a firmness of pencil, and liveliness of colouring, which belong to the highest branch of fictitious narrative."[10] Sir Samuel Egerton Brydges recalled, "It displayed such a simple energy of language, such an accurate and lively delineation of character, such a purity of sentiment, and such exquisite scenery of a picturesque and rich, yet most unaffected imagination, as gave it a hold upon all readers of true taste, of a new and most captivating kind."[11] Within a year Smith had written and published her five-volume second novel, *Ethelinde, the Recluse of the Lake* (1789). A second edition followed the same year, and in 1805 Montagne published a French translation. The critic for the *Analytical Review* noted, "The same quick sensibility which enabled [Smith] to produce such apt similes in her sonnets, led her to catch all those alluring charms of nature, which form such enchanting backgrounds to the historical part of the pictures she displays in these volumes and gives them sentiment and interest."[12] In the next two years Smith produced another novel, *Celestina* (1791),

8. From Dorset's biographical contribution to "Charlotte Smith," in Walter Scott's *Lives of the Novelists* (reprint; London, n.d.), 321.

9. Carter to Elizabeth Montague, 30 June 1788, quoted in Hilbish, *Charlotte Smith,* 128.

10. From Scott's commentary in "Charlotte Smith," 328.

11. Quoted in Hilbish, *Charlotte Smith,* 131.

12. 5 (December 1789): 484.

close in style to its predecessors and similarly highly praised. The critic for the *Critical Review,* confessing that he wept over the novel, remarked, "In the modern school of novel-writers, Mrs. Smith holds a very distinguished rank; and, if not the first, she is so near as scarcely to be styled an inferior. Perhaps, with Miss Burney she may be allowed to hold 'a divided sway': and, though on some occasions below her sister-queen, yet, from the greater number of her works, she seems to possess a more luxuriant imagination, and a more fertile invention."[13] Smith's next novel, *Desmond,* supported the French revolution, though by 1792, when it was published, feeling against the French was running high. Her aristocratic friends were offended, and the controversial subject matter inspired more negative reviews than had any of Smith's other works of fiction. Even so, a second London edition, along with a Dublin edition, was called for that same year, with a French edition following.

Smith spent part of August and September 1792 at William Hayley's home at Eartham as part of a group that included the artist George Romney and the poet William Cowper. She would compose part of the text of *The Old Manor House* in the mornings and read it to the group in the evenings. Hayley observed, "It was delightful to hear her read what she had just written; for she read as she wrote, with simplicity and grace."[14] Cowper inspired Smith's long poem *The Emigrants,* published in two books in the summer of 1793. The *Monthly Review* observed, "The style of the poem is seldom highly poetical, and sometimes is even nearly prosaic; yet the general effect is truly pleasing; and there are passages which do credit to the elegant pen that wrote the justly admired Elegiac Sonnets."[15] When *The Old Manor House* came out that same year, she won back many of the friends she had alienated with *Desmond.* But the reviewers were not as forgiving and found little to praise. Walter Scott, however, considered this novel her *chef-d'oeuvre* and especially admired the character of Mrs. Rayland, whom he thought "without a rival."[16] Anna Letitia Barbauld selected it for her British Novelists series.

In September 1793 Smith's favorite daughter, Anna Augusta, married the chevalier de Faville, a French officer to whom the hero of Smith's next novel, *The Banished Man,* published in August 1794, bears a striking resemblance. Critics considered *The Banished Man* inferior to her previous fiction. Despite worsening arthritis in her hands, she persisted in what was becoming the physically difficult task of writing, publishing *Montalbert* in July 1795, only eleven months after she had concluded *The Banished Man.* Within this short

13. 3 (November 1791): 318–23.
14. As cited in the *American Whig Review* 9 (June 1849): 628.
15. N.s., 12 (1793): 375–76.
16. Scott, *Lives of the Novelists,* 330.

period she also published two other works, the seventh edition of *Elegiac Sonnets,* with additional sonnets and other poems, as well as the first of her books for children, *Rural Walks: in Dialogues. Intended for the Use of Young Persons,* written for her thirteen-year-old daughter, Harriet. *Montalbert* contains the fewest personal allusions of all her novels, largely because Smith was in great emotional pain. Though grieving for her son Charles Dyer, who had lost a leg in the siege of Dunkirk, and for her favorite daughter, Anna Augusta, who had died shortly after giving birth, she could not afford the luxury of slowing the pace of her publication. In 1796 she brought out another children's book, *Rambles Farther: A Continuation of Rural Walks: in Dialogues. Intended for the Use of Young Persons,* and a novel, *Marchmont.*

In the previous eight years Smith had produced thirty-two volumes of novels, four volumes of prose for children, and a two-volume poem, as well as additional poems for various editions of *Elegiac Sonnets.* In 1798 her last novel, *The Young Philosopher,* appeared. The reviews were more positive than they had been for a long time, but her highly critical portrayal of lawyers was not popular with the reading public. Ironically, this was the same year that Smith and her children first began to collect some of the settlement from Richard Smith's estate. But this legal matter, which harassed her for the last thirty years of her life and deprived her children of the support due them, was not entirely concluded until six months after Charlotte Smith's own death, long after most of her children had reached adulthood. In 1801 she was still forced to write for subsistence. Two volumes of *The Letters of a Solitary Wanderer* came out in 1799, and three more followed in the next several years. Though tired and ill, Smith remained feisty. In response to the writer for the *Critical Review* of May 1801, she replied in her 1802 preface to this novel, "It is observed . . . that 'Mrs. Smith is too fond of representing the distress of *middle-aged ladies;* and has given the same character, under different names, in almost all her novels.' I never imagined, till I read this judicious criticism, that no interest could be excited but by love stories that relate to girls of fifteen." In 1801 her widowed daughter and three children came to live with her, and her son Charles Dyer died in Barbados.

Her health failing, Smith moved to Surrey so that she could be buried with her mother and father's family in the parish church at Stoke. There, in great physical pain, she wrote *Conversations Introducing Poetry: Chiefly on Subjects of Natural History. For the Use of Children and Young Persons,* her most enduring children's book. Her estranged husband, Benjamin Smith, died on 22 February 1806, allowing Smith for the first time to have possession of her own earnings and inheritance. But she died not long afterwards, on 28 October 1806, at Tilford House at the age of fifty-seven, having single-handedly for nearly two decades supported ten children and later three grandchildren. Six of her twelve children survived her. Obituaries appeared in the leading periodicals, including the *Annual Register*, the *Gentleman's Magazine*, the *European Magazine*, the *Monthly Magazine*, and the *Universal Magazine*. Her sister, Catherine Dorset, claimed that "the sweepings of her closet were, without exception, committed to the flames."[17] But two works, *The Natural History of Birds, Intended Chiefly for Young Persons* (1807) and Smith's tour de force, *Beachy Head: With Other Poems* (1807), were published posthumously. According to the publisher's advertisement, Smith had delivered the manuscript of the latter book the previous May, but her illness had slowed publication. The *Annual Review* observed,

> It is with a kind of melancholy pleasure that we prepare to pay a tribute of posthumous applause to the elegant genius of Mrs. Charlotte Smith. On the 28th of October last, the world was deprived of this delightful poet and interesting woman; long a sufferer from pain, sickness, and misfortune. As a descriptive writer, either in verse or prose, she was surpassed by few. Gifted in no ordinary degree, with taste, with fancy, and with feeling she well knew how to select the most striking features from the face of nature; to add the accompaniment and to lay on the tints best suited to the cast of sentiment in which it soothed her to indulge, and to extract from the whole food for a most delicious melancholy.[18]

MAJOR WORKS: *Elegiac Sonnets, and Other Essays* (London, 1784); *Emmeline, the Orphan of the Castle*, 4 vols. (London, 1788); *Ethelinde, the Recluse of the Lake*, 5 vols. (London, 1789); *Celestina, a Novel*, 4 vols. (London, 1791); *Desmond, a Novel*, 3 vols. (London, 1792); *The Emigrants, a Poem, in Two Books* (London, 1793); *The Old Manor House: A novel*, 4 vols. (London, 1793); *The Banished Man. A Novel*, 4 vols. (London, 1794); *The Wanderings of Warwick* (London, 1794); *Montalbert. A Novel*, 3 vols. (London, 1795); *Rural Walks: in Dialogues. Intended for the Use of Young Persons*, 2 vols. (London, 1795); *Marchmont, a Novel*, 4 vols. (London, 1796); *A Narrative of the Loss of the Catharine, Venus, and Piedmont Transports, and the Thomas, Golden Grove, and Aeolus Merchant Ships, near Weymouth, on Wednesday the 18th of November Last* (London, 1796); *Rambles Farther: A Continuation of Rural Walks: in Dialogues. Intended for the Use of Young Persons*, 2 vols. (London, 1796); *Minor Morals, Interspersed with Sketches of Natural History, Historical Anecdotes, and Original Stories*, 2 vols. (London, 1798); *The Young Philosopher: a Novel*, 4 vols. (London, 1798); *The Letters of a Solitary Wanderer: Containing Narratives of Various Description*, 5 vols. (London, 1800–1802); *Conversations Introducing Poetry: Chiefly on Subjects of Natural History. For the Use of Children and Young Persons*, 2 vols. (London, 1804); *The History of England, from the Earliest Records to the Peace of Amiens. In a Series of Letters to a Young Lady at School*, 3 vols. (London, 1806); *Beachy Head: With Other Poems*

17. From Dorset's biographical contribution to "Charlotte Smith," in ibid., 326.
18. 6 (1807): 536–38.

(London, 1807); *The Natural History of Birds, Intended Chiefly for Young Persons,* 2 vols. (London, 1807); *The Poems of Charlotte Smith,* ed. Stuart Curran (New York, 1993).

TEXTS USED: Sonnets I and V first appeared in the *European Magazine* for 1782. The first edition of Charlotte Smith's *Elegiac Sonnets, and Other Essays* was published in 1784; the texts of all the sonnets printed below are from the fifth edition (1789) with the exception of sonnets LXVII and LXX, from the first edition of volume 2 (1797). Texts of "The Swallow" and "Beachy Head" from *Beachy Head: With Other Poems.*

Sonnet I
The Partial Muse

The partial Muse, has from my earliest hours
 Smil'd on the rugged path I'm doom'd to tread,
And still with sportive hand has snatch'd wild flowers,
 To weave fantastic garlands for my head:
But far, far happier is the lot of those
 Who never learn'd her dear delusive art;
Which, while it decks the head with many a rose,
 Reserves the thorn, to fester in the heart.
For still she bids soft Pity's melting eye
 Stream o'er the ills she knows not to remove,   10
Points every pang, and deepens every sigh
 Of mourning friendship, or unhappy love.
Ah! then, how dear the Muse's favors cost,
 If those paint sorrow best—who feel it most!

             (1782)

---

14 *If those paint sorrow best—who feel it most!*] The well sung woes shall soothe my pensive ghost; He best can paint them, who shall feel them most. *Pope's Eloisa to Abelard, 366th line. Smith.*

Sonnet II
Written at the Close of Spring

The garlands* fade that Spring so lately wove,
 Each simple flower, which she had nurs'd in dew,
Anemonies, that spangled every grove,
 The primrose wan, and hare-bell, mildly blue.
No more shall violets linger in the dell,
 Or purple orchis variegate the plain,
Till Spring again shall call forth every bell,
 And dress with humid hands her wreaths again.—
Ah! poor humanity! so frail, so fair,
10 Are the fond visions of thy early day,
Till tyrant passion, and corrosive care,
 Bid all thy fairy colours fade away!
Another May new buds and flowers shall bring;
Ah! why has happiness——no second Spring?
          (1784)

*Originally this read "garland's," which was clearly an error; it was corrected in later editions.

Sonnet III
To a Nightingale

Poor melancholy bird——that all night long
 Tell'st to the Moon thy tale of tender woe;
  From what sad cause can such sweet sorrow flow,
And whence this mournful melody of song?

3 Anemonies] Anemony Nemeroso. The wood Anemony. *Smith.*

1 Poor melancholy bird——that all night long] The idea from the 43rd sonnet of Petrarch. Secondo parte. Quel rosigniuol, che si soave piagne. *Smith.* [Petrarch's sonnet begins, "That nightingale who so tenderly weeps" (Petrarch, *Sonnets and Songs,* trans. Anna Maria Armi [New York, 1946], 433). *Ed.*]

Thy poet's musing fancy would translate
    What mean the sounds that swell thy little breast,
    When still at dewy eve thou leav'st thy nest,
Thus to the listening night to sing thy fate?

Pale Sorrow's victims wert thou once among,
    Tho' now releas'd in woodlands wild to rove?   10
    Say—hast thou felt from friends some cruel wrong,
Or died'st thou——martyr of disastrous love?
Ah! songstress sad! that such my lot might be,
To sigh and sing at liberty——like thee!

                  (1784)

Sonnet IV
To the Moon

Queen of the silver bow!—by thy pale beam,
    Alone and pensive, I delight to stray,
And watch thy shadow trembling in the stream,
    Or mark the floating clouds that cross thy way.
And while I gaze, thy mild and placid light
    Sheds a soft calm upon my troubled breast;
And oft I think,——fair planet of the night,
    That in thy orb, the wretched may have rest:
The sufferers of the earth perhaps may go,
    Releas'd by death——to thy benignant sphere,   10
And the sad children of despair and woe
    Forget in thee, their cup of sorrow here.
Oh! that I soon may reach thy world serene,
Poor wearied pilgrim——in this toiling scene!
                  (1784)

Sonnet v
To the South Downs

Ah! hills belov'd!——where once, an happy child,
    Your beechen shades, "your turf, your flowers among,"
I wove your blue-bells into garlands wild,
    And woke your echoes with my artless song.
Ah! hills belov'd!——your turf, your flow'rs remain;
    But can they peace to this sad breast restore,
For one poor moment soothe the sense of pain,
    And teach a breaking heart to throb no more?
And you, Aruna!——in the vale below,
10   As to the sea your limpid waves you bear,
Can you one kind Lethean cup bestow,
    To drink a long oblivion to my care?
Ah! no!——when all, e'en Hope's last ray is gone,
There's no oblivion——but in death alone!

                      (1782)

2 "your turf, your flowers among"] Whose turf, whose shades, whose flowers among.—
Gray. *Smith.* [See Thomas Gray's "Ode on a Distant Prospect of Eton College," line 8. *Ed.*]
   9 Aruna] The river Arun. *Smith.*
  11 Lethean cup] Cup of the waters of forgetfulness. In classical mythology, the waters of the
river Lethe brought forgetfulness of previous life for souls returning to earth to be reborn.

Sonnet VII
On the Departure of the Nightingale

Sweet poet of the woods——a long adieu!
　Farewel, soft minstrel of the early year!
Ah! 'twill be long ere thou shalt sing anew,
　And pour thy music on the "night's dull ear."
Whether on Spring thy wandering flights await,
　Or whether silent in our groves you dwell,
The pensive muse shall own thee for her mate,
　And still protect the song, she loves so well.
With cautious step, the love-lorn youth shall glide
　Thro' the lone brake that shades thy mossy nest;　　10
And shepherd girls, from eyes profane shall hide
　The gentle bird, who sings of pity best:
For still thy voice shall soft affections move,
And still be dear to sorrow, and to love!

(1784)

---

4 on the "night's dull ear"] *Shakespeare. Smith.* [See Shakespeare, *King Henry V,* act 4, line 11. *Ed.*]

5 Spring] Alludes to the supposed migration of the Nightingale. *Smith.*

7 The pensive muse shall own thee for a mate] Whether the Muse or Love call thee his mate, / Both them I serve, and of their train am I.—Milton's *First Sonnet. Smith.* [Smith quotes the final two lines of John Milton's sonnet "O Nightingale!" *Ed.*]

Sonnet VIII
To Spring

Again the wood, and long withdrawing vale,
   In many a tint of tender green are drest,
Where the young leaves unfolding, scarce conceal
   Beneath their early shade, the half-form'd nest
Of finch or wood-lark; and the primrose pale,
   And lavish cowslip, wildly scatter'd round,
Give their sweet spirits to the sighing gale.
    Ah! season of delight!——could aught be found
     To soothe awhile the tortur'd bosom's pain,
10   Of Sorrow's rankling shaft to cure the wound,
      And bring life's first delusions once again,
'Twere surely met in thee!——thy prospect fair,
Thy sounds of harmony, thy balmy air,
Have power to cure all sadness——but despair.

                  (1784)

---

14 Have power to cure all sadness——but despair] To the heart inspires / Vernal delight
and joy, able to drive / All sadness but despair. — *Paradise Lost, Fourth Book* [lines 155–56]. *Smith.*

Sonnet XXI
Supposed to Be Written by Werter*

Go! cruel tyrant of the human breast!
    To other hearts, thy burning arrows bear;
Go, where fond hope, and fair illusion rest!
    Ah! why should love inhabit with despair!
Like the poor maniac I linger here,
    Still haunt the scene, where all my treasure lies;
Still seek for flowers, where only thorns appear,
    "And drink delicious poison from her eyes!"
Towards the deep gulph that opens on my sight
    I hurry forward, passion's helpless slave!   10
And scorning reason's mild and sober light,
    Pursue the path that leads me to the grave!
So round the flame the giddy insect flies,
And courts the fatal fire, by which it dies!

(1784)

* Werter is the sensitive, melancholy artist protagonist in Wolfgang von Goethe's extremely popular novel *The Sorrows of Young Werter* (1774); Werter eventually commits suicide over his hopeless love for Charlotte, a woman betrothed and then married to someone else.

5 Like the poor maniac] See the Story of the Lunatic. "Is this the destiny of man? Is he only happy before he possesses his reason, or after he has lost it?—Full of hope you go to gather flowers in Winter, and are grieved not to find any—and do not know why they cannot be found." *Sorrows of Werter. Volume Second. Smith.*

8 "And drink delicious poison from her eyes!"] "And drink delicious poison from thine eye." *Pope. Smith.* [Alexander Pope's "Eloisa to Abelard" reads, "Still drink delicious poison from thy eye" (line 22). *Ed.*]

Sonnet XXXIX
To Night

I love thee, mournful sober-suited night,
  When the faint moon, yet lingering in her wane,
And veil'd in clouds, with pale uncertain light
  Hangs o'er the waters of the restless main.
In deep depression sunk, the enfeebled mind
  Will to the deaf, cold elements complain,
  And tell the embosom'd grief, however vain,
To sullen surges and the viewless wind.
Tho' no repose on thy dark breast I find,
  I still enjoy thee—cheerless as thou art;
  For in thy quiet gloom, the exhausted heart
Is calm, tho' wretched; hopeless, yet resign'd.
While, to the winds and waves its sorrows given,
May reach—tho' lost on earth—the ear of Heaven!

                 (1784)

10

Sonnet XLIV
Written in the Church-Yard at Middleton in Sussex

Press'd by the Moon, mute arbitress of tides,
  While the loud equinox its power combines,
  The sea no more its swelling surge confines,
But o'er the shrinking land sublimely rides.
The wild blast, rising from the Western cave,
  Drives the huge billows from their heaving bed;
  Tears from their grassy tombs the village dead,
And breaks the silent sabbath of the grave!
With shells and sea-weed mingled, on the shore

7 Tears from their grassy tombs the village dead] Middleton is a village on the margin of the sea in Sussex, containing only two or three houses. There were formerly several acres of ground between its small church and the sea; which now, by its continual encroachments, approaches within a few feet of this half ruined and humble edifice. The wall, which once surrounded the church yard, is entirely swept away, many of the graves broken up, and the remains of bodies interred washed into the sea: whence human bones are found among the sand and shingles on the shore. *Smith.*

Lo! their bones whiten in the frequent wave;   10
But vain to them the winds and waters rave;
They hear the warring elements no more:
While I am doom'd—by life's long storm opprest,
To gaze with envy, on their gloomy rest.

(1784)

Sonnet LXVII
On Passing over a Dreary Tract of Country, and near the Ruins of a Deserted Chapel, during a Tempest[*]

Swift fleet the billowy clouds along the sky,
  Earth seems to shudder at the storm aghast;
While only beings as forlorn as I,
  Court the chill horrors of the howling blast.
Even round yon crumbling walls, in search of food,
  The ravenous Owl foregoes his evening flight,
And in his cave, within the deepest wood,
  The Fox eludes the tempest of the night.
But to *my* heart congenial is the gloom
  Which hides me from a World I wish to shun;   10
That scene where Ruin saps the mouldering tomb,
  Suits with the sadness of a wretch undone.
Nor is the deepest shade, the keenest air,
Black as my fate, or cold as my despair.

(1797)

[*]Printed in [Montalbert]. *Smith.*

Sonnet LXX
On Being Cautioned against Walking
on an Headland Overlooking the Sea,
Because It Was Frequented by a Lunatic

Is there a solitary wretch who hies
 To the tall cliff, with starting pace or slow,
And, measuring, views with wild and hollow eyes
 Its distance from the waves that chide below;
Who, as the sea-born gale with frequent sighs
 Chills his cold bed upon the mountain turf,
With hoarse, half-utter'd lamentation, lies
 Murmuring responses to the dashing surf?
In moody sadness, on the giddy brink,
 I see him more with envy than with fear;
He has no *nice felicities* that shrink
 From giant horrors; wildly wandering here,
He seems (uncursed with reason) not to know
The depth or the duration of his woe.

(1797)

10

---

11 *He* has no *nice felicities* that shrink] " 'Tis delicate felicity that shrinks / When rocking winds are loud."—Walpole. *Smith.* [The lines are from Horace Walpole's *The Mysterious Mother, a Tragedy,* 2.3.5–6. *Ed.*]

The Swallow

The gorse is yellow on the heath,
    The banks with speedwell flowers are gay,
The oaks are budding; and beneath,
The hawthorn soon will bear the wreath,
    The silver wreath of May.

The welcome guest of settled Spring,
    The Swallow too is come at last;
Just at sun-set, when thrushes sing,
I saw her dash with rapid wing,
    And hail'd her as she pass'd.   10

Come, summer visitant, attach
    To my reed roof your nest of clay,
And let my ear your music catch
Low twittering underneath the thatch
    At the gray dawn of day.

As fables tell, an Indian Sage,
    The Hindostani woods among,
Could in his desert hermitage,
As if 'twere mark'd in written page,
    Translate the wild bird's song.   20

I wish I did his power possess,
    That I might learn, fleet bird, from thee,
What our vain systems only guess,
And know from what wide wilderness
    You came across the sea.

---

1 gorse] The Gorse-Furze. — Ulex Europæus. Called so in many counties of England. *Smith.*
2 speedwell flowers] Veronica chamœdrys. — This elegant flower, though not celebrated like the Primrose, Cowslip, and Daisy, is in all its varieties one of the most beautiful of our indigenous plants. *Smith.*
16 As fables tell, an Indian Sage] There are two or three fables that relate the knowledge acquired by some Indian recluse, of the language of birds. *Smith.*

I would a little while restrain
    Your rapid wing, that I might hear
Whether on clouds that bring the rain,
You sail'd above the western main,
30   The wind your charioteer.

In Afric, does the sultry gale
    Thro' spicy bower, and palmy grove,
Bear the repeated Cuckoo's tale?
Dwells *there* a time, the wandering Rail
    Or the itinerant Dove?

Were you in Asia? O relate,
    If there your fabled sister's woes
She seem'd in sorrow to narrate;
Or sings she but to celebrate
40   Her nuptials with the rose?

I would enquire how journeying long,
    The vast and pathless ocean o'er,
You ply again those pinions strong,
And come to build anew among
    The scenes you left before;

But if, as colder breezes blow,
    Prophetic of the waning year,
You hide, tho' none know when or how,
In the cliff's excavated brow,
50   And linger torpid here;

    33–35 Cuckoo's tale . . . the itinerant Dove] The Cuckoo, the Rail, and many species of Doves, are all emigrants. *Smith.*

    37–40 fabled sister's woes . . . nuptials with the rose?] Alluding to the Ovidian fable of the Metamorphosis of Procne and Philomela into the Swallow and the Nightingale; and to the oriental story of the Loves of the Nightingale and the Rose; which is told with such elegant extravagance in the Botanic Garden. *Smith.* [For the story of Procne and Philomela, see Ovid's *Metamorphoses* 6.428–674; on the loves of the nightingale and the rose, see Erasmus Darwin's *Botanic Garden,* pt. 2 ("The Loves of the Plants"), canto 4, lines 305–20. *Ed.*]

    44 And come to build anew] Accurate observers have remarked, that an equal number of these birds return every year to build in the places they frequented before; and that each pair set immediately about repairing a particular nest. *Smith.*

    49 In the cliff's excavated brow] Many persons have supported the idea, that the Hirundines linger concealed among rocks and hollows in a torpid state, and that all do not emigrate. *Smith.*

Thus lost to life, what favouring dream
  Bids you to happier hours awake;
And tells, that dancing in the beam,
The light gnat hovers o'er the stream,
  The May-fly on the lake?

Or if, by instinct taught to know
  Approaching dearth of insect food;
To isles and willowy aits you go,
And crouding on the pliant bough,
  Sink in the dimpling flood: 60

How learn ye, while the cold waves boom
  Your deep and ouzy couch above,
The time when flowers of promise bloom,
And call you from your transient tomb,
  To light, and life, and love?

Alas! how little can be known,
  Her sacred veil where Nature draws;
Let baffled Science humbly own,
Her mysteries understood alone,
  By *Him* who gives her laws.   70
             (1807)

58 To isles and willowy aits you go] Another opinion is, that the Swallows, at the time they disappear, assemble about rivers and ponds, and a number of them settling on the pliant boughs of willow and osier, sink by their weight into the water; at the bottom of which they remain torpid till the ensuing spring. For the foundation of these various theories, see "White's History of Selbourne." *Smith.* [An ait is an islet or small island, especially in a river. Smith refers here to English naturalist Gilbert White's *Natural History and Antiquities of Selbourne* (1789). White (1720–93) was known especially for his knowledge of birds. *Ed.*]

Beachy Head*

On thy stupendous summit, rock sublime!
That o'er the channel rear'd, half way at sea
The mariner at early morning hails,
I would recline; while Fancy should go forth,
And represent the strange and awful hour
Of vast concussion; when the Omnipotent
Stretch'd forth his arm, and rent the solid hills,
Bidding the impetuous main flood rush between
The rifted shores, and from the continent
Eternally divided this green isle.
Imperial lord of the high southern coast!
From thy projecting head-land I would mark
Far in the east the shades of night disperse,
Melting and thinned, as from the dark blue wave
Emerging, brilliant rays of arrowy light
Dart from the horizon; when the glorious sun
Just lifts above it his resplendent orb.
Advances now, with feathery silver touched,
The rippling tide of flood; glisten the sands,
While, inmates of the chalky clefts that scar
Thy sides precipitous, with shrill harsh cry,
Their white wings glancing in the level beam,
The terns, and gulls, and tarrocks, seek their food,
And thy rough hollows echo to the voice
Of the gray choughs, and ever restless daws,
With clamour, not unlike the chiding hounds,

    1–3 stupendous summit . . . The mariner at early morning hails] In crossing the Channel
from the coast of France, Beachy-Head is the first land made. *Smith*.
    5–6 the strange and awful hour / Of vast concussion] Alluding to an idea that this Island was
once joined to the continent of Europe, and torn from it by some convulsion of Nature. I confess I never could trace the resemblance between the two countries. Yet the cliffs about Dieppe,
resemble the chalk cliffs on the Southern coast. But Normandy has no likeness whatever to the
part of England opposite to it. *Smith*.
    23 The terns, and gulls, and tarrocks] Terns.—Sterna hirundo, or Sea Swallow. Gulls.—
Larus canus. Tarrocks.—Larus tridactylus. *Smith*.
    25 gray choughs] Gray Choughs.—Corvus Graculus, Cornish Choughs, or, as these birds are
called by the Sussex people, Saddle-backed Crows, build in great numbers on this coast. *Smith*.

While the lone shepherd, and his baying dog,
Drive to thy turfy crest his bleating flock.

The high meridian of the day is past,
And Ocean now, reflecting the calm Heaven,   30
Is of cerulean hue; and murmurs low
The tide of ebb, upon the level sands.
The sloop, her angular canvas shifting still,
Catches the light and variable airs
That but a little crisp the summer sea,
Dimpling its tranquil surface.

                   Afar off,
And just emerging from the arch immense
Where seem to part the elements, a fleet
Of fishing vessels stretch their lesser sails;   40
While more remote, and like a dubious spot
Just hanging in the horizon, laden deep,
The ship of commerce richly freighted, makes
Her slower progress, on her distant voyage,
Bound to the orient climates, where the sun
Matures the spice within its odorous shell,
And, rivalling the gray worm's filmy toil,
Bursts from its pod the vegetable down;
Which in long turban'd wreaths, from torrid heat
Defends the brows of Asia's countless casts.   50
There the Earth hides within her glowing breast
The beamy adamant, and the round pearl
Enchased in rugged covering; which the slave,
With perilous and breathless toil, tears off
From the rough sea-rock, deep beneath the waves.
These are the toys of Nature; and her sport
Of little estimate in Reason's eye:

---

48 the vegetable down] Cotton. (Gossypium herbaceum.) *Smith.*

52 The beamy adamant] Diamonds, the hardest and most valuable of precious stones. For the extraordinary exertions of the Indians in diving for the pearl oysters, see the account of the Pearl Fisheries in Percival's View of Ceylon. *Smith.* [Robert Percival (1765–1826) published *An Account of Ceylon, with the Journal of an Embassy to the Court of Candy* (1803). *Beamy* means emitting beams of light; radiant. *Ed.*]

And they who reason, with abhorrence see
Man, for such gaudes and baubles, violate
60   The sacred freedom of his fellow man—
Erroneous estimate! As Heaven's pure air,
Fresh as it blows on this aërial height,
Or sound of seas upon the stony strand,
Or inland, the gay harmony of birds,
And winds that wander in the leafy woods;
Are to the unadulterate taste more worth
Than the elaborate harmony, brought out
From fretted stop, or modulated airs
Of vocal science.—So the brightest gems,
70   Glancing resplendent on the regal crown,
Or trembling in the high born beauty's ear,
Are poor and paltry, to the lovely light
Of the fair star, that as the day declines,
Attendant on her queen, the crescent moon,
Bathes her bright tresses in the eastern wave.
For now the sun is verging to the sea,
And as he westward sinks, the floating clouds
Suspended, move upon the evening gale,
And gathering round his orb, as if to shade
80   The insufferable brightness, they resign
Their gauzy whiteness; and more warm'd, assume
All hues of purple. There, transparent gold
Mingles with ruby tints, and sapphire gleams,
And colours, such as Nature through her works
Shews only in the ethereal canopy.
Thither aspiring Fancy fondly soars,
Wandering sublime thro' visionary vales,
Where bright pavilions rise, and trophies, fann'd
By airs celestial; and adorn'd with wreaths
90   Of flowers that bloom amid elysian bowers.
Now bright, and brighter still the colours glow,
Till half the lustrous orb within the flood
Seems to retire: the flood reflecting still
Its splendor, and in mimic glory drest;
Till the last ray shot upward, fires the clouds

59 gaudes] Playthings; something gaudy; finery.

With blazing crimson; then in paler light,
Long lines of tenderer radiance, lingering yield
To partial darkness; and on the opposing side
The early moon distinctly rising, throws
Her pearly brilliance on the trembling tide.   100

The fishermen, who at set seasons pass
Many a league off at sea their toiling night,
Now hail their comrades, from their daily task
Returning; and make ready for their own,
With the night tide commencing:—The night tide
Bears a dark vessel on, whose hull and sails
Mark her a coaster from the north. Her keel
Now ploughs the sand; and sidelong now she leans,
While with loud clamours her athletic crew
Unload her; and resounds the busy hum   110
Along the wave-worn rocks. Yet more remote,
Where the rough cliff hangs beetling o'er its base,
All breathes repose; the water's rippling sound
Scarce heard; but now and then the sea-snipe's cry
Just tells that something living is abroad;
And sometimes crossing on the moonbright line,
Glimmers the skiff, faintly discern'd awhile,
Then lost in shadow.

              Contemplation here,
High on her throne of rock, aloof may sit,   120
And bid recording Memory unfold
Her scroll voluminous—bid her retrace
The period, when from Neustria's hostile shore
The Norman launch'd his galleys, and the bay
O'er which that mass of ruin frowns even now

112 Where the rough cliff hangs beetling o'er its base] *Beetling* refers to lowered, scowling eyebrows. It can also mean the prominent brow of a mountain; thus, Smith personifies the cliff while naming it.

114 the sea-snipe's cry] In crossing the channel this bird is heard at night, uttering a short cry, and flitting along near the surface of the waves. The sailors call it the Sea Snipe; but I can find no species of sea bird of which this is the vulgar name. A bird so called inhabits the Lake of Geneva. *Smith.*

123 Neustria's hostile shore] Normandy.

125 that mass of ruin] Pevensey Castle. *Smith.*

> In vain and sullen menace, then received
> The new invaders; a proud martial race,
> Of Scandinavia the undaunted sons,

128 Scandinavia] The Scandinavians [Scandinavia.—Modern Norway, Sweden, Denmark, Lapland, &c.], and other inhabitants of the north, began towards the end of the 8th century, to leave their inhospitable climate in search of the produce of more fortunate countries.

The North-men made inroads on the coasts of France; and carrying back immense booty, excited their compatriots to engage in the same piratical voyages: and they were afterwards joined by numbers of necessitous and daring adventurers from the coasts of Provence and Sicily.

In 844, these wandering innovators had a great number of vessels at sea; and again visiting the coasts of France, Spain, and England, the following year they penetrated even to Paris: and the unfortunate Charles the Bald, king of France, purchased at a high price, the retreat of the banditti he had no other means of repelling.

These successful expeditions continued for some time; till Rollo, otherwise Raoul, assembled a number of followers, and after a descent on England, crossed the channel, and made himself master of Rouen, which he fortified. Charles the Simple, unable to contend with Rollo, offered to resign to him some of the northern provinces, and to give him his daughter in marriage. Neustria, since called Normandy, was granted to him, and afterwards Brittany. He added the more solid virtues of the legislator to the fierce valour of the conqueror—converted to Christianity, he established justice, and repressed the excesses of his Danish subjects, till then accustomed to live only by plunder. His name became the signal for pursuing those who violated the laws; as well as the cry of Haro, still so usual in Normandy. The Danes and Francs produced a race of men celebrated for their valour; and it was a small party of these that in 983, having been on a pilgrimage to Jerusalem, arrived on their return at Salerno, and found the town surrounded by Mahometans, whom the Salernians were bribing to leave their coast. The Normans represented to them the baseness and cowardice of such submission; and notwithstanding the inequality of their numbers, they boldly attacked the Saracen camp, and drove the infidels to their ships. The prince of Salerno, astonished at their successful audacity, would have loaded them with the marks of his gratitude; but refusing every reward, they returned to their own country, from whence, however, other bodies of Normans passed into Sicily [anciently called Trinacria.]; and many of them entered into the service of the emperor of the East, others of the Pope, and the duke of Naples was happy to engage a small party of them in defence of his newly founded dutchy. Soon afterwards three brothers of Coutance, the sons of Tancred de Hauteville, Guillaume Fier-a-bras, Drogon, and Humfroi, joining the Normans established at Aversa, became masters of the fertile island of Sicily; and Robert Guiscard joining them, the Normans became sovereigns both of Sicily and Naples [Parthenope]. How William, the natural son of Robert, duke of Normandy, possessed himself of England, is too well known to be repeated here. William sailing from St. Valori, landed in the bay of Pevensey; and at the place now called Battle, met the English forces under Harold: an esquire (ecuyer) called Taillefer, mounted on an armed horse, led on the Normans, singing in a thundering tone the war song of Rollo. He threw himself among the English, and was killed on the first onset. In a marsh not far from Hastings, the skeletons of an armed man and horse were found a few years since, which are believed to have belonged to the Normans, as a party of their horse, deceived in the nature of the ground, perished in the morass. *Smith*. [Charles I (823–77), king of France from 843 to 877, was called Charles II as Western (Holy Roman) Emperor from 875 to 877. Rollo, also known as Rudolph, duke of Burgundy, was king of France from 923 to 936. His reign was little more than an unending series of battles. Charles III (879–929) was the only surviving grandson

Whom Dogon, Fier-a-bras, and Humfroi led
To conquest: while Trinacria to their power   130
Yielded her wheaten garland; and when thou,
Parthenope! within thy fertile bay
Receiv'd the victors —

                 In the mailed ranks
Of Normans landing on the British coast
Rode Taillefer; and with astounding voice
Thunder'd the war song daring Roland sang
First in the fierce contention: vainly brave,
One not inglorious struggle England made —
But failing, saw the Saxon heptarchy   140
Finish for ever.——Then the holy pile,
Yet seen upon the field of conquest, rose,
Where to appease heaven's wrath for so much blood,
The conqueror bade unceasing prayers ascend,
And requiems for the slayers and the slain.
But let not modern Gallia form from hence
Presumptuous hopes, that ever thou again,
Queen of the isles! shalt crouch to foreign arms.
The enervate sons of Italy may yield;
And the Iberian, all his trophies torn   150
And wrapp'd in Superstition's monkish weed,
May shelter his abasement, and put on
Degrading fetters. Never, never thou!

---

of Charles the Bald, so he had a claim to the French throne. He was crowned king of France in 893. Tancred (d. 1194) was king of Sicily from 1190. As a natural son of King Roger II's son Roger, duke of Apulia, he was of the Norman dynasty of Hauteville. He was a petty Norman noble who held a fief of ten men-at-arms at Hauteville-la-Guicharde, near Coutances. Robert Guiscard (d. 1085), a son of Tancred, was duke of Apulia from 1059. In southern Italy Guiscard led the life of a robber chief and was known for his violence. William I the Conquerer (c. 1028–87) was duke of Normandy and king of England. He was also referred to as "the Bastard," since he was the illegitimate son of Duke Robert I of Normandy. *Ed.*]

   129 Dogon] Probably Drogo, the second son of Tancred by his first wife, Murialla. In 1048 he was recognized as leader of the Apulian Normans.

   129 Humfroi] Probably Humphrey, another son of Tancred and Murialla.

   137 daring Roland] Roland was the most famous of the "Paladins of Charlemagne."

   141 Then the holy pile] Battle Abbey was raised by the Conqueror, and endowed with an ample revenue, that masses might be said night and day for the souls of those who perished in battle. *Smith.*

Imperial mistress of the obedient sea;
But thou, in thy integrity secure,
Shalt now undaunted meet a world in arms.

England! 'twas where this promontory rears
Its rugged brow above the channel wave,
Parting the hostile nations, that thy fame,
160   Thy naval fame was tarnish'd, at what time
Thou, leagued with the Batavian, gavest to France
One day of triumph—triumph the more loud,
Because even then so rare. Oh! well redeem'd,
Since, by a series of illustrious men,
Such as no other country ever rear'd,
To vindicate her cause. It is a list
Which, as Fame echoes it, blanches the cheek
Of bold Ambition; while the despot feels
The extorted sceptre tremble in his grasp.

170   From even the proudest roll by glory fill'd,
How gladly the reflecting mind returns
To simple scenes of peace and industry,

161–62 gavest to France / One day of triumph] In 1690, King William being then in Ireland, Tourville, the French admiral, arrived on the coast of England. His fleet consisted of seventy-eight large ships, and twenty-two fire-ships. Lord Torrington, the English admiral, lay at St. Helens, with only forty English and a few Dutch ships; and conscious of the disadvantage under which he should give battle, he ran up between the enemy's fleet and the coast, to protect it. The queen's council, dictated to by Russel, persuaded her to order Torrington to venture a battle. The orders Torrington appears to have obeyed reluctantly: his fleet now consisted of twenty-two Dutch and thirty-four English ships. Evertson, the Dutch admiral, was eager to obtain glory; Torrington, more cautious, reflected on the importance of the stake. The consequence was, that the Dutch rashly sailing on were surrounded, and Torrington, solicitous to recover this false step, placed himself with difficulty between the Dutch and French;—but three Dutch ships were burnt, two of their admirals killed, and almost all their ships disabled. The English and Dutch declining a second engagement, retired towards the mouth of the Thames. The French, from ignorance of the coast, and misunderstanding among each other, failed to take all the advantage they might have done of this victory. *Smith.* [Anne Hilarion de Cotentin, Tourville (1642–1701), was the French admiral who commanded the French fleet of more than seventy ships in the battle of Beachy Head in 1690. Arthur Herbert Torrington (1647–1716) was the English admiral who commanded the Anglo-Dutch fleet. During the battle, Torrington retreated into the Thames, for which he was tried by court martial. He was acquitted on the defense that he had maintained his "fleet in being," so that no invasion could be attempted while it remained intact. Edward Russell (1653–1727) was admiral of the British fleet. C. Evertzen commanded the Dutch fleet. *Ed.*]

Where, bosom'd in some valley of the hills
Stands the lone farm; its gate with tawny ricks
Surrounded, and with granaries and sheds,
Roof'd with green mosses, and by elms and ash
Partially shaded; and not far remov'd
The hut of sea-flints built; the humble home
Of one, who sometimes watches on the heights,
When hid in the cold mist of passing clouds,   180
The flock, with dripping fleeces, are dispers'd
O'er the wide down; then from some ridged point
That overlooks the sea, his eager eye
Watches the bark that for his signal waits
To land its merchandize:—Quitting for this
Clandestine traffic his more honest toil,
The crook abandoning, he braves himself
The heaviest snow-storm of December's night,
When with conflicting winds the ocean raves,
And on the tossing boat, unfearing mounts   190
To meet the partners of the perilous trade,
And share their hazard. Well it were for him,
If no such commerce of destruction known,
He were content with what the earth affords
To human labour; even where she seems
Reluctant most. More happy is the hind,
Who, with his own hands rears on some black moor,
Or turbary, his independent hut
Cover'd with heather, whence the slow white smoke
Of smouldering peat arises——A few sheep,   200
His best possession, with his children share
The rugged shed when wintry tempests blow;
But, when with Spring's return the green blades rise

179 one, who sometimes watches on the heights] The shepherds and labourers of this tract
of country, a hardy and athletic race of men, are almost universally engaged in the contraband
trade, carried on for the coarsest and most destructive spirits, with the opposite coast. When
no other vessel will venture to sea, these men hazard their lives to elude the watchfulness of
the Revenue officers, and to secure their cargoes. *Smith.*
  186 Clandestine traffic] Smuggling in England during the eighteenth century threatened
the very structure of finance and government. From the coast of Sussex gangs left for London
to sell contraband more frequently and more regularly than the stagecoaches.
  196 hind] Farm servant, for whom a cottage is provided; rustic.
  198 turbary] Peat bog.

Amid the russet heath, the household live
Joint tenants of the waste throughout the day,
And often, from her nest, among the swamps,
Where the gemm'd sun-dew grows, or fring'd buck-bean,
They scare the plover, that with plaintive cries
Flutters, as sorely wounded, down the wind.
210   Rude, and but just remov'd from savage life
Is the rough dweller among scenes like these,
(Scenes all unlike the poet's fabling dreams
Describing Arcady)—But he is free;
The dread that follows on illegal acts
He never feels; and his industrious mate
Shares in his labour. Where the brook is traced
By crouding osiers, and the black coot hides
Among the plashy reeds, her diving brood,
The matron wades; gathering the long green rush
220   That well prepar'd hereafter lends its light
To her poor cottage, dark and cheerless else
Thro' the drear hours of Winter. Otherwhile
She leads her infant group where charlock grows
"Unprofitably gay," or to the fields,
Where congregate the linnet and the finch,
That on the thistles, so profusely spread,
Feast in the desert; the poor family
Early resort, extirpating with care
These, and the gaudier mischief of the ground;
230   Then flames the high rais'd heap; seen afar off
Like hostile war-fires flashing to the sky.
Another task is theirs: On fields that shew
As angry Heaven had rain'd sterility,
Stony and cold, and hostile to the plough,

207–8 the gemm'd sun-dew . . . the plover] Sun-dew.—Drosera rotundifolia. Buck-bean.—
Menyanthes trifoliatum. Plover.—Tringa vanellus. *Smith.*

217 osiers] A species of willow.

217 coot] Coot.—Fulica aterrima. *Smith.*

224 "Unprofitably gay"] "With blossom'd furze, unprofitably gay." *Goldsmith. Smith.* [Oliver
Goldsmith, *The Deserted Village,* line 194. *Ed.*]

231 Like hostile war-fires] The Beacons formerly lighted up on the hills to give notice of
the approach of an enemy. These signals would still be used in case of alarm, if the Telegraph
now substituted could not be distinguished on account of fog or darkness. *Smith.*

Where clamouring loud, the evening curlew runs
And drops her spotted eggs among the flints;
The mother and the children pile the stones
In rugged pyramids;—and all this toil
They patiently encounter; well content
On their flock bed to slumber undisturb'd   240
Beneath the smoky roof they call their own.
Oh! little knows the sturdy hind, who stands
Gazing, with looks where envy and contempt
Are often strangely mingled, on the car
Where prosperous Fortune sits; what secret care
Or sick satiety is often hid,
Beneath the splendid outside: *He* knows not
How frequently the child of Luxury
Enjoying nothing, flies from place to place
In chase of pleasure that eludes his grasp;   250
And that content is e'en less found by him,
Than by the labourer, whose pick-axe smooths
The road before his chariot; and who doffs
What *was* an hat; and as the train pass on,
Thinks how one day's expenditure, like this,
Would cheer him for long months, when to his toil
The frozen earth closes her marble breast.

Ah! who *is* happy? Happiness! a word
That like false fire, from marsh effluvia born,
Misleads the wanderer, destin'd to contend   260
In the world's wilderness, with want or woe—
Yet *they* are happy, who have never ask'd
What good or evil means. The boy
That on the river's margin gaily plays,
Has heard that Death is there—He knows not Death,
And therefore fears it not; and venturing in
He gains a bullrush, or a minnow—then,
At certain peril, for a worthless prize,
A crow's, or raven's nest, he climbs the boll
Of some tall pine; and of his prowess proud,   270

235 curlew] Curlew.—Charadrius oedicnemus. *Smith.*
269 boll] Trunk.

Is for a moment happy. Are *your* cares,
Ye who despise him, never worse applied?
The village girl is happy, who sets forth
To distant fair, gay in her Sunday suit,
With cherry colour'd knots, and flourish'd shawl,
And bonnet newly purchas'd. So is he
Her little brother, who his mimic drum
Beats, till he drowns her rural lovers' oaths
Of constant faith, and still increasing love;
280   Ah! yet a while, and half those oaths believ'd,
Her happiness is vanish'd; and the boy
While yet a stripling, finds the sound he lov'd
Has led him on, till he has given up
His freedom, and his happiness together.
I once was happy, when while yet a child,
I learn'd to love these upland solitudes,
And, when elastic as the mountain air,
To my light spirit, care was yet unknown
And evil unforeseen:—Early it came,
290   And childhood scarcely passed, I was condemned,
A guiltless exile, silently to sigh,
While Memory, with faithful pencil, drew
The contrast; and regretting, I compar'd
With the polluted smoky atmosphere
And dark and stifling streets, the southern hills
That to the setting Sun, their graceful heads
Rearing, o'erlook the frith, where Vecta breaks
With her white rocks, the strong impetuous tide,
When western winds the vast Atlantic urge
300   To thunder on the coast—Haunts of my youth!
Scenes of fond day dreams, I behold ye yet!
Where 'twas so pleasant by thy northern slopes
To climb the winding sheep-path, aided oft
By scatter'd thorns: whose spiny branches bore
Small woolly tufts, spoils of the vagrant lamb
There seeking shelter from the noon-day sun;

---

297 Vecta] The Isle of Wight, which breaks the force of the waves when they are driven
by south-west winds against this long and open coast. It is somewhere described as "Vecta
shouldering the Western Waves." *Smith.*

And pleasant, seated on the short soft turf,
To look beneath upon the hollow way
While heavily upward mov'd the labouring wain,
And stalking slowly by, the sturdy hind   310
To ease his panting team, stopp'd with a stone
The grating wheel.

          Advancing higher still
The prospect widens, and the village church
But little, o'er the lowly roofs around
Rears its gray belfry, and its simple vane;
Those lowly roofs of thatch are half conceal'd
By the rude arms of trees, lovely in spring,
When on each bough, the rosy-tinctur'd bloom
Sits thick, and promises autumnal plenty.   320
For even those orchards round the Norman farms,
Which, as their owners mark the promis'd fruit,
Console them for the vineyards of the south,
Surpass not these.

          Where woods of ash, and beech,
And partial copses, fringe the green hill foot,
The upland shepherd rears his modest home,
There wanders by, a little nameless stream
That from the hill wells forth, bright now and clear,
Or after rain with chalky mixture gray,   330
But still refreshing in its shallow course,
The cottage garden; most for use design'd,
Yet not of beauty destitute. The vine
Mantles the little casement; yet the briar
Drops fragrant dew among the July flowers;
And pansies rayed, and freak'd and mottled pinks
Grow among balm, and rosemary and rue:
There honeysuckles flaunt, and roses blow
Almost uncultured: Some with dark green leaves

318 By the rude arms of trees, lovely in spring] Every cottage in this country has its orchard; and I imagine that not even those of Herefordshire, or Worcestershire, exhibit a more beautiful prospect, when the trees are in bloom, and the "Primavera candida e vermiglia," is every where so enchanting. *Smith.* ["Primavera candida e vermiglia," or "Pure and rosy spring," is from Petrarch, sonnet 310, line 4. *Ed.*]

340   Contrast their flowers of pure unsullied white;
             Others, like velvet robes of regal state
             Of richest crimson, while in thorny moss
             Enshrined and cradled, the most lovely, wear
             The hues of youthful beauty's glowing cheek.—
             With fond regret I recollect e'en now
             In Spring and Summer, what delight I felt
             Among these cottage gardens, and how much
             Such artless nosegays, knotted with a rush
             By village housewife or her ruddy maid,
350   Were welcome to me; soon and simply pleas'd.

             An early worshipper at Nature's shrine,
             I loved her rudest scenes—warrens, and heaths,
             And yellow commons, and birch-shaded hollows,
             And hedge rows, bordering unfrequented lanes
             Bowered with wild roses, and the clasping woodbine
             Where purple tassels of the tangling vetch
             With bittersweet, and bryony inweave,
             And the dew fills the silver bindweed's cups—
             I loved to trace the brooks whose humid banks
360   Nourish the harebell, and the freckled pagil;
             And stroll among o'ershadowing woods of beech,
             Lending in Summer, from the heats of noon
             A whispering shade; while haply there reclines
             Some pensive lover of uncultur'd flowers,
             Who, from the tumps with bright green mosses clad,
             Plucks the wood sorrel, with its light thin leaves,
             Heart-shaped, and triply folded; and its root
             Creeping like beaded coral; or who there
             Gathers, the copse's pride, anémones,

356 vetch] Vetch.—Vicia sylvatica. *Smith.*

357 bittersweet, and bryony] Bittersweet.—Solanum dulcamara. Bryony.—Bryonia alba.
Smith.

358 bindweed's cups] Bindweed.—Convolvulus sepium. *Smith.*

360 the harebell, and the freckled pagil] Harebell.—Hyacinthus non scriptus. Pagil.—
Primula veris. *Smith.*

365 tumps] Hill or mound; sometimes a clump of trees, shrubs, or grass.

366 wood sorrel] Oxalis acetosella. *Smith.*

369 anémones] Anemóne nemorosa.—It appears to be settled on late and excellent authorities, that this word should not be accented on the second syllable, but on the penultima. I have

With rays like golden studs on ivory laid   370
Most delicate: but touch'd with purple clouds,
Fit crown for April's fair but changeful brow.

Ah! hills so early loved! in fancy still
I breathe your pure keen air; and still behold
Those widely spreading views, mocking alike
The Poet and the Painter's utmost art.
And still, observing objects more minute,
Wondering remark the strange and foreign forms
Of sea-shells; with the pale calcareous soil
Mingled, and seeming of resembling substance.   380
Tho' surely the blue Ocean (from the heights
Where the downs westward trend, but dimly seen)
Here never roll'd its surge. Does Nature then
Mimic, in wanton mood, fantastic shapes
Of bivalves, and inwreathed volutes, that cling
To the dark sea-rock of the wat'ry world?
Or did this range of chalky mountains, once
Form a vast bason, where the Ocean waves
Swell'd fathomless? What time these fossil shells,
Buoy'd on their native element, were thrown   390
Among the imbedding calx: when the huge hill
Its giant bulk heaved, and in strange ferment
Grew up a guardian barrier, 'twixt the sea
And the green level of the sylvan weald.

---

however ventured the more known accentuation, as more generally used, and suiting better the nature of my verse. *Smith.*

379 calcareous] Chalky.

379–80 Of sea-shells; . . . seeming of resembling substance] Among the crumbling chalk I have often found shells, some quite in a fossil state and hardly distinguishable from chalk. Others appeared more recent; cockles, muscles, and periwinkles, I well remember, were among the number; and some whose names I do not know. A great number were like those of small land snails. It is now many years since I made these observations. The appearance of sea-shells so far from the sea excited my surprise, though I then knew nothing of natural history. I have never read any of the late theories of the earth, nor was I ever satisfied with the attempts to explain many of the phenomena which call forth conjecture in those books I happened to have had access to on this subject. *Smith.*

387 Or did this range of chalky mountains] The theory here slightly hinted at, is taken from an idea started by Mr. White. *Smith.* [Gilbert White, the English naturalist. *Ed.*]

388 bason] Variation of *basin.*

391 calx] Chalk, limestone.

Ah! very vain is Science' proudest boast,
And but a little light its flame yet lends
To its most ardent votaries; since from whence
These fossil forms are seen, is but conjecture,
Food for vague theories, or vain dispute,
400   While to his daily task the peasant goes,
Unheeding such inquiry; with no care
But that the kindly change of sun and shower,
Fit for his toil the earth he cultivates.
As little recks the herdsman of the hill,
Who on some turfy knoll, idly reclined,
Watches his wether flock; that deep beneath
Rest the remains of men, of whom is left
No traces in the records of mankind,
Save what these half obliterated mounds
410   And half fill'd trenches doubtfully impart
To some lone antiquary; who on times remote,
Since which two thousand years have roll'd away,
Loves to contemplate. He perhaps may trace,
Or fancy he can trace, the oblong square
Where the mail'd legions, under Claudius, rear'd
The rampire, or excavated fossé delved;
What time the huge unwieldy Elephant

406 wether] Male sheep, ram; especially a castrated ram.

407 remains of men] These Downs are not only marked with traces of encampments, which from their forms are called Roman or Danish; but there are numerous tumuli [sepulchral mounds] among them. Some of which having been opened a few years ago, were supposed by a learned antiquary to contain the remains of the original natives of the country. *Smith.*

415 the mail'd legions, under Claudius] That the legions of Claudius [10 B.C.–A.D. 54] were in this part of Britain appears certain. Since this emperor received the submission of Cantii, Atrebates, Irenobates, and Regni, in which latter denomination were included the people of Sussex. *Smith.*

416 rampire] Rampart, barrier.

416 fossé] Trench, ditch.

417 What time the huge unwieldy Elephant] In the year 1740, some workmen digging in the park at Burton in Sussex, discovered, nine feet below the surface, the teeth and bones of an elephant; two of the former were seven feet eight inches in length. There were besides these, tusks, one of which broke in removing it, a grinder not at all decayed, and a part of the jaw-bone, with bones of the knee and thigh, and several others. Some of them remained very lately at Burton House, the seat of John Biddulph, Esq. Others were in possession of the Rev. Dr. Langrish, minister of Petworth at that period, who was present when some of these bones were taken up, and gave it as his opinion, that they had remained there since the universal deluge. The Romans under the Emperor Claudius probably brought elephants into Britain. Milton,

Auxiliary reluctant, hither led,
From Afric's forest glooms and tawny sands,
First felt the Northern blast, and his vast frame   420
Sunk useless; whence in after ages found,
The wondering hinds, on those enormous bones
Gaz'd; and in giants dwelling on the hills
Believed and marvell'd—

                Hither, Ambition, come!
Come and behold the nothingness of all
For which you carry thro' the oppressed Earth,
War, and its train of horrors—see where tread
The innumerous hoofs of flocks above the works
By which the warrior sought to register   430
His glory, and immortalize his name—
The pirate Dane, who from his circular camp
Bore in destructive robbery, fire and sword
Down thro' the vale, sleeps unremember'd here;
And here, beneath the green sward, rests alike
The savage native, who his acorn meal
Shar'd with the herds, that ranged the pathless woods;

---

in the Second Book of his History, in speaking of the expedition, says that "He like a great eastern king, with armed elephants, marched through Gallia." This is given on the authority of Dion Cassius, in his Life of the Emperor Claudius. It has therefore been conjectured, that the bones found at Burton might have been those of one of these elephants, who perished there soon after its landing; or dying on the high downs, one of which, called Duncton Hill, rises immediately above Burton Park, the bones might have been washed down by the torrents of rain, and buried deep in the soil. They were not found together, but scattered at some distance from each other. The two tusks were twenty feet apart. I had often heard of the elephant's bones at Burton, but never saw them; and I have no books to refer to. I think I saw, in what is now called the National Museum at Paris, the very large bones of an elephant, which were found in North America: though it is certain that this enormous animal is never seen in its natural state, but in the countries under the torrid zone of the old world. I have, since making this note, been told that the bones of the rhinoceros and hippopotamus have been found in America. *Smith.* [Claudius I invaded Britain in A.D. 43. *Ed.*]

423 in giants] The peasants believe that the large bones sometimes found belonged to giants, who formerly lived on the hills. The devil also has a great deal to do with the remarkable forms of hill and vale: the Devil's Punch Bowl, the Devil's Leaps, and the Devil's Dyke, are names given to deep hollows, or high and abrupt ridges, in this and the neighbouring county. *Smith.*

432 The pirate Dane] The incursions of the Danes were for many ages the scourge of this island. *Smith.*

436 The savage native] The Aborigines of this country lived in woods, unsheltered but by trees and caves; and were probably as truly savage as any of those who are now termed so. *Smith.*

And the centurion, who on these wide hills
Encamping, planted the Imperial Eagle.
440   All, with the lapse of Time, have passed away,
Even as the clouds, with dark and dragon shapes,
Or like vast promontories crown'd with towers,
Cast their broad shadows on the downs: then sail
Far to the northward, and their transient gloom
Is soon forgotten.

                                    But from thoughts like these,
By human crimes suggested, let us turn
To where a more attractive study courts
The wanderer of the hills; while shepherd girls
450   Will from among the fescue bring him flowers,
Of wonderous mockery; some resembling bees
In velvet vest, intent on their sweet toil,
While others mimic flies, that lightly sport
In the green shade, or float along the pool,
But here seem perch'd upon the slender stalk,
And gathering honey dew. While in the breeze
That wafts the thistle's plumed seed along,
Blue bells wave tremulous. The mountain thyme
Purples the hassock of the heaving mole,
460   And the short turf is gay with tormentil,

450 fescue] The grass called Sheep's Fescue, (Festuca ovina,) clothes these Downs with the softest turf. *Smith.*

451 some resembling bees] Ophrys apifera, Bee Ophrys, or Orchis found plentifully on the hills, as well as the next. *Smith.*

453 While others mimic flies] Ophrys muscifera. — Fly Orchis. Linnæus, misled by the variations to which some of this tribe are really subject, has perhaps too rashly esteemed all those which resemble insects, as forming only one species, which he terms Ophrys insectifera. See English Botany. *Smith.*

458 Blue bells] (Campanula rotundifolia.) The mountain thyme] Thymus serpyllum. "It is a common notion, that the flesh of sheep which feed upon aromatic plants, particularly wild thyme, is superior in flavour to other mutton. The truth is, that sheep do not crop these aromatic plants, unless now and then by accident, or when they are first turned on hungry to downs, heaths, or commons; but the soil and situations favourable to aromatic plants, produce a short sweet pasturage, best adapted to feeding sheep, whom nature designed for mountains, and not for turnip grounds and rich meadows. The attachment of bees to this, and other aromatic plants, is well known." Martyn's Miller. *Smith.* [Quotation from Thomas Martyn, *The Gardener's and Botanist's Dictionary . . . by the late Philip Miller . . . To Which Are Now Added a Complete Enumeration and Description of All Plants* (1797–1807). *Ed.*]

460 tormentil] Tormentilla reptans. *Smith.*

And bird's foot trefoil, and the lesser tribes
Of hawkweed; spangling it with fringed stars. —
Near where a richer tract of cultur'd land
Slopes to the south; and burnished by the sun,
Bend in the gale of August, floods of corn;
The guardian of the flock, with watchful care,
Repels by voice and dog the encroaching sheep—
While his boy visits every wired trap
That scars the turf; and from the pit-falls takes
The timid migrants, who from distant wilds,   470
Warrens, and stone quarries, are destined thus
To lose their short existence. But unsought
By Luxury yet, the Shepherd still protects
The social bird, who from his native haunts
Of willowy current, or the rushy pool,
Follows the fleecy croud, and flirts and skims,
In fellowship among them.

           Where the knoll
More elevated takes the changeful winds,
The windmill rears its vanes; and thitherward   480
With his white load, the master travelling,
Scares the rooks rising slow on whispering wings,
While o'er his head, before the summer sun
Lights up the blue expanse, heard more than seen,
The lark sings matins; and above the clouds
Floating, embathes his spotted breast in dew.

461–62 And bird's foot trefoil, and the lesser tribes of hawkweed] Bird's foot trefoil.—
Trifolium ornithopoides. Hawkweed.—Hieracium, many sorts. *Smith.*

466 The guardian of the flock, with watchful care] The downs, especially to the south,
where they are less abrupt, are in many places under the plough; and the attention of the
shepherds is there particularly required to keep the flocks from trespassing. *Smith.*

468 every wired trap] Square holes cut in the turf, into which a wire noose is fixed, to catch
Wheatears. Mr. White says, that these birds (Motacilla oenanthe) are never taken beyond the
river Adur, and Beding Hill; but this is certainly a mistake. *Smith.*

470 The timid migrants] These birds are extremely fearful, and on the slightest appearance
of a cloud, run for shelter to the first rut, or heap of stones, that they see. *Smith.*

474 The social bird] The Yellow Wagtail.—Motacilla flava. It frequents the banks of rivulets
in winter, making its nest in meadows and corn-fields. But after the breeding season is over, it
haunts downs and sheepwalks, and is seen constantly among the flocks, probably for the sake
of the insects it picks up. In France the shepherds call it *La Bergeronette,* and say it often gives
them, by its cry, notice of approaching danger. *Smith.*

Beneath the shadow of a gnarled thorn,
Bent by the sea blast, from a seat of turf
With fairy nosegays strewn, how wide the view!
490 Till in the distant north it melts away,
And mingles indiscriminate with clouds:
But if the eye could reach so far, the mart
Of England's capital, its domes and spires
Might be perceived—Yet hence the distant range
Of Kentish hills, appear in purple haze;
And nearer, undulate the wooded heights,
And airy summits, that above the mole
Rise in green beauty; and the beacon'd ridge
Of Black-down shagg'd with heath, and swelling rude
500 Like a dark island from the vale; its brow
Catching the last rays of the evening sun
That gleam between the nearer park's old oaks,
Then lighten up the river, and make prominent
The portal, and the ruin'd battlements
Of that dismantled fortress; rais'd what time
The Conqueror's successors fiercely fought,
Tearing with civil feuds the desolate land.

488 Bent by the sea blast] The strong winds from the south-west occasion almost all the trees, which on these hills are exposed to it, to grow the other way. *Smith.*

489 how wide the view!] So extensive are some of the views from these hills, that only the want of power in the human eye to travel so far, prevents London itself being discerned. Description falls so infinitely short of the reality, that only here and there, distinct features can be given. *Smith.*

494–95 the distant range / Of Kentish hills] A scar of chalk in a hill beyond Sevenoaks in Kent, is very distinctly seen of a clear day. *Smith.*

497 And airy summits] The hills about Dorking in Surry; over almost the whole extent of which county the prospect extends. *Smith.*

498–99 and the beacon'd ridge . . . shagg'd with heath] This is an high ridge, extending between Sussex and Surry. It is covered with heath, and has almost always a dark appearance. On it is a telegraph. *Smith.*

504 and the ruin'd battlements] In this country there are several of the fortresses or castles built by Stephen of Blois, in his contention for the kingdom, with the daughter of Henry the First, the empress Matilda. Some of these are now converted into farm houses. *Smith.* [Stephen, king of England from 1135 to 1154, was the third son of Stephen, count of Blois and Chartres. In 1127 and again in 1133 Stephen and other English magnates were persuaded or forced by Henry I to take oaths of fealty to his daughter, the empress Matilda, as heir to the throne and to recognize the hereditary right of her son Henry of Anjou, the future Henry II. These oaths were later forsaken, which led to a civil war in 1139 over the crown between Matilda and her half-brother Robert of Gloucester, on the one hand, and Stephen. *Ed.*]

But now a tiller of the soil dwells there,
And of the turret's loop'd and rafter'd halls
Has made an humbler homestead—Where he sees,   510
Instead of armed foemen, herds that graze
Along his yellow meadows; or his flocks
At evening from the upland driv'n to fold—

In such a castellated mansion once
A stranger chose his home; and where hard by
In rude disorder fallen, and hid with brushwood
Lay fragments gray of towers and buttresses,
Among the ruins, often he would muse—
His rustic meal soon ended, he was wont
To wander forth, listening the evening sounds   520
Of rushing milldam, or the distant team,
Or night-jar, chasing fern-flies: the tir'd hind
Pass'd him at nightfall, wondering he should sit
On the hill top so late: they from the coast
Who sought bye paths with their clandestine load,
Saw with suspicious doubt, the lonely man
Cross on their way: but village maidens thought
His senses injur'd; and with pity say
That he, poor youth! must have been cross'd in love—
For often, stretch'd upon the mountain turf   530

522 chasing fern-flies] Dr. Aikin remarks, I believe, in his essay "On the Application of Natural History to the Purposes of Poetry," how many of our best poets have noticed the same circumstance, the hum of the Dor Beetle (Scaraboeus stercorarius,) among the sounds heard by the evening wanderer. I remember only one instance in which the more remarkable, though by no means uncommon noise, of the Fern Owl, or Goatsucker, is mentioned. It is called the Night Hawk, the Jar Bird, the Churn Owl, and the Fern Owl, from its feeding on the Scaraboeus solstitialis, or Fern Chafer, which it catches while on the wing with its claws, the middle toe of which is long and curiously serrated, on purpose to hold them. It was this bird that was intended to be described in the Forty-second Sonnet (Smith's Sonnets). I was mistaken in supposing it as visible in November; it is a migrant, and leaves this country in August. I had often seen and heard it, but I did not then know its name or history. It is called Goatsucker (Caprimulgus), from a strange prejudice taken against it by the Italians, who assert that it sucks their goats; and the peasants of England still believe that a disease in the backs of their cattle, occasioned by a fly, which deposits its egg under the skin, and raises a boil, sometimes fatal to calves, is the work of this bird, which they call a Puckeridge. Nothing can convince them that their beasts are not injured by this bird, which they therefore hold in abhorrence. *Smith.* [John Aikin (1747–1822), father of Lucy Aikin and brother of Anna Letitia Barbauld, wrote *An Essay on the Application of Natural History to Poetry* (1777). *Ed.*]

With folded arms, and eyes intently fix'd
Where ancient elms and firs obscured a grange,
Some little space within the vale below,
They heard him, as complaining of his fate,
And to the murmuring wind, of cold neglect
And baffled hope he told. — The peasant girls
These plaintive sounds remember, and even now
Among them may be heard the stranger's songs.

    Were I a Shepherd on the hill
540   And ever as the mists withdrew
    Could see the willows of the rill
    Shading the footway to the mill
      Where once I walk'd with you —

    And as away Night's shadows sail,
      And sounds of birds and brooks arise,
    Believe, that from the woody vale
    I hear your voice upon the gale
      In soothing melodies;

    And viewing from the Alpine height,
550   The prospect dress'd in hues of air,
    Could say, while transient colours bright
    Touch'd the fair scene with dewy light,
      'Tis, that *her* eyes are there!

    I think, I could endure my lot
      And linger on a few short years,
    And then, by all but you forgot,
    Sleep, where the turf that clothes the spot
      May claim some pitying tears.

    For 'tis not easy to forget
560   One, who thro' life has lov'd you still,
    And you, however late, might yet
    With sighs to Memory giv'n, regret
      The Shepherd of the Hill.

Yet otherwhile it seem'd as if young Hope
Her flattering pencil gave to Fancy's hand,
And in his wanderings, rear'd to sooth his soul
Ideal bowers of pleasure—Then, of Solitude
And of his hermit life, still more enamour'd,
His home was in the forest; and wild fruits
And bread sustain'd him. There in early spring   570
The Barkmen found him, e'er the sun arose;
There at their daily toil, the Wedgecutters
Beheld him thro' the distant thicket move.
The shaggy dog following the truffle hunter,
Bark'd at the loiterer; and perchance at night
Belated villagers from fair or wake,
While the fresh night-wind let the moonbeams in
Between the swaying boughs, just saw him pass,
And then in silence, gliding like a ghost
He vanish'd! Lost among the deepening gloom.—   580
But near one ancient tree, whose wreathed roots
Form'd a rude couch, love-songs and scatter'd rhymes,
Unfinish'd sentences, or half erased,
And rhapsodies like this, were sometimes found—

    Let us to woodland wilds repair
       While yet the glittering night-dews seem
    To wait the freshly-breathing air,
       Precursive of the morning beam,
    That rising with advancing day,
    Scatters the silver drops away.   590

    An elm, uprooted by the storm,
       The trunk with mosses gray and green,
    Shall make for us a rustic form,
       Where lighter grows the forest scene;

571 The Barkmen] As soon as the sap begins to rise, the trees intended for felling are cut and barked. At which time the men who are employed in that business pass whole days in the woods. *Smith.*

572 the Wedgecutters] The wedges used in ship-building are made of beech wood, and great numbers are cut every year in the woods near the Downs. *Smith.*

574 the truffle hunter] Truffles are found under the beech woods, by means of small dogs trained to hunt them by the scent. *Smith.*

And far among the bowery shades,
Are ferny lawns and grassy glades.

Retiring May to lovely June
   Her latest garland now resigns;
The banks with cuckoo-flowers are strewn,
600   The woodwalks blue with columbines,
And with its reeds, the wandering stream
Reflects the flag-flower's golden gleam.

There, feathering down the turf to meet,
   Their shadowy arms the beeches spread,
While high above our sylvan seat,
   Lifts the light ash its airy head;
And later leaved, the oaks between
Extend their boughs of vernal green.

The slender birch its paper rind
610   Seems offering to divided love,
And shuddering even without a wind
   Aspins, their paler foliage move,
As if some spirit of the air
Breath'd a low sigh in passing there.

The Squirrel in his frolic mood,
   Will fearless bound among the boughs;
Yaffils laugh loudly thro' the wood,
   And murmuring ring-doves tell their vows;
While we, as sweetest woodscents rise,
620   Listen to woodland melodies.

And I'll contrive a sylvan room
   Against the time of summer heat,

---

599 cuckoo-flowers] Lychnis dioica. *Smith.*

600 columbines] Aquilegia vulgaris. Shakespeare describes the Cuckoo buds as being yellow. He probably meant the numerous Ranunculi, or March marigolds (Caltha palustris,) which so gild the meadows in Spring; but poets have never been botanists. The Cuckoo flower is the Lychnis floscuculi. *Smith.* [See *Love's Labour's Lost* 5.2.894. *Ed.*]

602 flag-flower's] Flag-flower. — Iris pseudacorus. *Smith.*

617 Yaffils] Yaffils. — Woodpeckers (Picus): three or four species in Britain. *Smith.*

Where leaves, inwoven in Nature's loom,
    Shall canopy our green retreat;
And gales that "close the eye of day"
Shall linger, e'er they die away.

And when a sear and sallow hue
    From early frost the bower receives,
I'll dress the sand rock cave for you,
    And strew the floor with heath and leaves,   630
That you, against the autumnal air
May find securer shelter there.

The Nightingale will then have ceas'd
    To sing her moonlight serenade;
But the gay bird with blushing breast,
    And Woodlarks still will haunt the shade,
And by the borders of the spring
Reed-wrens will yet be carolling.

The forest hermit's lonely cave
    None but such soothing sounds shall reach,   640
Or hardly heard, the distant wave
    Slow breaking on the stony beach;
Or winds, that now sigh soft and low,
Now make wild music as they blow.

And then, before the chilling North
    The tawny foliage falling light,
Seems, as it flits along the earth,
    The footfall of the busy Sprite,
Who wrapt in pale autumnal gloom,
Calls up the mist-born Mushroom.   650

624 And gales that "close the eye of day"] "And [Thy] liquid notes that close the eye of day."
Milton. The idea here meant to be conveyed is of the evening wind, so welcome after a hot day
of Summer, and which appears to sooth and lull all nature into tranquillity. *Smith.* [Milton's
sonnet I, "O Nightingale," line 5. *Ed.*]

635 the gay bird with blushing breast] The Robin, (Motacilla rubecula,) which is always
heard after other songsters have ceased to sing. *Smith.*

636 Woodlarks] The Woodlark, (Alauda nemorosa,) sings very late. *Smith.*

638 Reed-wrens] Reed-wrens, (Motacilla arundinacea,) sing all the summer and autumn,
and are often heard during the night. *Smith.*

Oh! could I hear your soft voice there,
    And see you in the forest green
All beauteous as you are, more fair
    You'ld look, amid the sylvan scene,
And in a wood-girl's simple guise,
Be still more lovely in mine eyes.

Ye phantoms of unreal delight,
    Visions of fond delirium born!
Rise not on my deluded sight,
660   Then leave me drooping and forlorn
To know, such bliss can never be,
Unless Amanda loved like me.

The visionary, nursing dreams like these,
Is not indeed unhappy. Summer woods
Wave over him, and whisper as they wave,
Some future blessings he may yet enjoy.
And as above him sail the silver clouds,
He follows them in thought to distant climes,
Where, far from the cold policy of this,
670   Dividing him from her he fondly loves,
He, in some island of the southern sea,
May haply build his cane-constructed bower
Beneath the bread-fruit, or aspiring palm,
With long green foliage rippling in the gale.
Oh! let him cherish his ideal bliss—
For what is life, when Hope has ceas'd to strew
Her fragile flowers along its thorny way?
And sad and gloomy are his days, who lives
Of Hope abandon'd!

---

671 in some island of the southern sea] An allusion to the visionary delights of the new[ly]
discovered islands, where it was at first believed men lived in a state of simplicity and happiness;
but where, as later enquiries have ascertained, that exemption from toil, which the fertility
of their country gives them, produces the grossest vices; and a degree of corruption that late
navigators think will end in the extirpation of the whole people in a few years. *Smith.* [Dur-
ing the eighteenth century British explorers competed with the French to chart the islands
of Polynesia. In 1767 the British captain Samuel Wallis discovered the island now known as
Tahiti. *Ed.*]

Just beneath the rock 680
Where Beachy overpeers the channel wave,
Within a cavern mined by wintry tides
Dwelt one, who long disgusted with the world
And all its ways, appear'd to suffer life
Rather than live; the soul-reviving gale,
Fanning the bean-field, or the thymy heath,
Had not for many summers breathed on him;
And nothing mark'd to him the season's change,
Save that more gently rose the placid sea,
And that the birds which winter on the coast 690
Gave place to other migrants; save that the fog,
Hovering no more above the beetling cliffs
Betray'd not then the little careless sheep
On the brink grazing, while their headlong fall
Near the lone Hermit's flint-surrounded home,
Claim'd unavailing pity; for his heart
Was feelingly alive to all that breath'd;
And outraged as he was, in sanguine youth,
By human crimes, he still acutely felt
For human misery. 700

Wandering on the beach,
He learn'd to augur from the clouds of heaven,
And from the changing colours of the sea,
And sullen murmurs of the hollow cliffs,
Or the dark porpoises, that near the shore
Gambol'd and sported on the level brine
When tempests were approaching: then at night
He listen'd to the wind; and as it drove

682–83 Within a cavern . . . / Dwelt one] In a cavern almost immediately under the cliff called Beachy Head, there lived, as the people of the country believed, a man of the name of Darby, who for many years had no other abode than this cave, and subsisted almost entirely on shell-fish. He had often administered assistance to ship-wrecked mariners; but venturing into the sea on this charitable mission during a violent equinoctial storm, he himself perished. As it is above thirty years since I heard this tradition of Parson Darby (for so I think he was called): it may now perhaps be forgotten. *Smith.*

691–93 the fog . . . betray'd not then the little careless sheep] Sometimes in thick weather the sheep feeding on the summit of the cliff, miss their footing, and are killed by the fall. *Smith.*

705 Or the dark porpoises] Delphinus phocœna. *Smith.*

The billows with o'erwhelming vehemence
710 He, starting from his rugged couch, went forth
And hazarding a life, too valueless,
He waded thro' the waves, with plank or pole
Towards where the mariner in conflict dread
Was buffeting for life the roaring surge;
And now just seen, now lost in foaming gulphs,
The dismal gleaming of the clouded moon
Shew'd the dire peril. Often he had snatch'd
From the wild billows, some unhappy man
Who liv'd to bless the hermit of the rocks.
720 But if his generous cares were all in vain,
And with slow swell the tide of morning bore
Some blue swol'n cor'se to land; the pale recluse
Dug in the chalk a sepulchre—above
Where the dank sea-wrack mark'd the utmost tide,
And with his prayers perform'd the obsequies
For the poor helpless stranger.

     One dark night
The equinoctial wind blew south by west,
Fierce on the shore;—the bellowing cliffs were shook
730 Even to their stony base, and fragments fell
Flashing and thundering on the angry flood.
At day-break, anxious for the lonely man,
His cave the mountain shepherds visited,
Tho' sand and banks of weeds had choak'd their way—
He was not in it; but his drowned cor'se
By the waves wafted, near his former home
Receiv'd the rites of burial. Those who read
Chisel'd within the rock, these mournful lines,
Memorials of his sufferings, did not grieve,
740 That dying in the cause of charity
His spirit, from its earthly bondage freed,
Had to some better region fled for ever.

          (1807)

---

*Beachy Head is a promontory on the southern coast of Sussex, three miles
southwest of Eastbourne.

Agnes Strickland

(1796–1874)

She earned her fame as a biographer, but Agnes Strickland's literary career began with poetry and children's stories, and these, like all else in her life, were steeped in her love of history. Born in London on 19 August 1796, she was the daughter of Thomas Strickland, a dock manager, and his second wife, Elizabeth Homer; the couple had nine children, six of whom became writers.[1] Agnes and Elizabeth (1794–1875), the eldest girls, were educated by their father, who taught them Greek, Latin, mathematics, and a passionate Stuart partisanship. The children read Plutarch's *Lives,* Rapin's *History of England,* Clarendon's *History of the Rebellion,* Pope's translation of Homer's *Iliad,* and, on the sly, Shakespeare's plays. Agnes's nickname was "the dictionary." She wrote her first poem at age nine, persevering despite her father's disapproval of "juvenile versifying." In 1808 the family moved from Norwich to Reydon Hall, an Elizabethan mansion near Southwold in Suffolk; however, Thomas Strickland's work soon took the family back to Norwich for part of each year.

Agnes Strickland's first published poem, "Monody upon the Death of the Princess Charlotte of Wales," appeared anonymously in 1817 in the *Norwich Mercury.* When Thomas Strickland died in 1818, having only recently lost most of his money, Agnes and Elizabeth decided to write children's stories to support themselves. Agnes's historical fiction for young people included *True Stories from Ancient History* (1819), *Guthred: The Widow's Slave. The Druid's Retreat* (1821), *The Tell-Tale* (1823), *Prejudice Reproved* (1826), *The Rival Crusoes; or, The Shipwreck* (1826), *Tales of the Schoolroom* ([1835?]), *The Pilgrims of Walsingham* (1835), *Tales and Stories from History* (1836), and others—some no doubt still unidentified, for much was published anonymously.

Agnes began to visit London in 1827, sometimes staying with a bachelor cousin in Newman Street who taught her Italian and with whom she read Dante, Ariosto, Tasso, and Petrarch, sometimes staying with another cousin,

---

1. Agnes, Elizabeth, Jane Margaret, Samuel, Susanna, and Catherine.

Mrs. Leverton in Bloomsbury, who introduced her to other writers. Soon her circle of friends included Letitia Elizabeth Landon, Lady Morgan, Sir Walter Scott, Mary Howitt, William Jerdan (editor of *The Literary Gazette*), John Mitford (editor of *The Gentleman's Magazine,* to which she sometimes contributed), Anna Jameson, Barbara Hofland, Jane Porter, Alaric A. Watts, and Thomas Pringle. Thomas Campbell, editor of the *New Monthly Magazine,* published some of her translations of Petrarch's sonnets. Her metrical romance in four cantos, *Worcester Field; or, The Cavalier,* was published by subscription in 1826, though it had been completed by 1818. In 1827 she brought out *The Seven Ages of Woman, and Other Poems,* dedicated to Mrs. Leverton.

In the late 1820s and early 1830s Agnes contributed prolifically to the literary annuals, especially to the *Keepsake,* the *Forget-Me-Not,* and *Friendship's Offering.* When she stayed in Bloomsbury, she would go daily to the British Museum Library to read history, and there she and Elizabeth learned paleography. Her prose romance *The Pilgrims of Walsingham* was well reviewed and went into a second edition in America but was not a financial success. She and Bernard Barton edited *Fisher's Juvenile Scrapbook* from 1837 to 1839, and she contributed several articles to Charles Dickens's *Pic-Nic Papers* (1841).

Meanwhile, Elizabeth had become editor of the *Court Journal,* for which she wrote biographical sketches of several queens. When Agnes suggested that they write a book together containing similar biographies of the English queens, Elizabeth agreed, but because she disliked publicity, she asked Agnes to handle all of the correspondence and to claim sole authorship.[2] Their motto was, "Facts not Opinions," but their strong Stuart partisanship nevertheless shows through. *Lives of the Queens of England from the Norman Conquest, with Anecdotes of their Courts, now First Published from Official Records and other Authentic Documents, Private as Well as Public* appeared in two volumes in 1840. The *Times* said *Lives of the Queens* was "written by a lady of considerable learning, indefatigable industry, and careful judgment. . . . it will be a matter of surprise to most readers how large a mass of information, in many respects entirely novel, has been collected. . . . The volumes have the fascination of romance united to the integrity of history. The reader is instructed and pleased at the same time, and when it is considered that this charm is produced by the judicious arrangement and application of materials from which preceding writers have extracted little beyond the dull sobriety of chronological narrative, the merit of the lady who has made so judicious a use of

---

2. For a breakdown of who wrote which biographies in this and future volumes, see Una Pope-Hennessy's *Agnes Strickland: Biographer of the Queens of England, 1796–1874* (London, 1940), 319.

her talent and learning will be the more enhanced, and her claim to praise proportionably the greater."[3]

Thomas Macaulay, who preferred to think of history as the military maneuvers of kings, not the domestic lives of queens, attacked the Stuart volumes in a twenty-six-page article in the *Edinburgh Review,* making such observations as that "she excuses the coarse absurdities of James I and exhausts her benevolent interest to credit James II with a sincere wish for religious toleration."[4] But biographer Antonia Fraser credits Agnes Strickland with founding "a whole new school of vivid utterly readable history, aimed to capture the general reader who felt himself inadequately served in the 1840s either by the pedantic scholar or the over-imaginative historical novelist."[5] The authors reaped little reward from the immense popularity of the work because of the poor financial arrangement with Henry Colburn, the publisher. Finally, after Agnes insisted on renegotiating terms, Colburn agreed to pay £150 for each future volume. By the time *Lives of the Queens* was completed in 1848, it comprised twelve volumes. Agnes was presented at court in 1840, a measure of the sisters' literary success, but shortly thereafter she earned the queen's disfavor because of factual errors in her subsequent two-volume *Queen Victoria from her Birth to her Bridal.*[6] Still, she enjoyed her new-found celebrity, while the retiring Elizabeth jealously guarded her obscurity. Although they acknowledged joint authorship in the preface to the revised edition of *Lives of the Queens,* the title pages still listed Agnes only; despite their distinctive writing styles, the public never seemed to realize that the author "Agnes Strickland" was more than one person.

Gaining access to research materials was often fraught with difficulty. The Stricklands liked to work as much as possible from primary, often unpublished, materials, but many documents rested in private hands, making travel to historic homes all over England necessary. Governmental records posed significant problems as well. For example, while writing biographies of Henry VIII's consorts, they asked to see state papers, but the Home Secretary, Lord John Russell, denied permission. After Lord Normanby intervened, the Stricklands were permitted access to the documents. In 1844 François Guizot had to arrange for Agnes to use French archives in Paris.

Meanwhile, Agnes had been editing the *Letters of Mary, Queen of Scots,* in three volumes (1842–43), the third volume of which she dedicated to Jane

3. *Times* (London), 5 September 1840, 3.

4. *Edinburgh Review,* July 1847.

5. Introduction to Agnes Strickland, *Lives of the Queens of England,* 8 vols., facs. ed. (Bath, 1972), 1:v.

6. The queen's copy, with her penciled corrections, is in the Royal Library, Windsor Castle.

Porter. She spent the decade of the 1850s working with Elizabeth on the lucrative *Lives of the Queens of Scotland and English Princesses Connected with the Regal Succession of Great Britain,* in 8 vols. (1850–59), published by William Blackwood, followed in 1861 by *Lives of the Bachelor Kings of England.* When Henry Colburn died in 1856, Longmans bought the copyright to *Lives of the Queens* for what was then the enormous sum of £6,900. In 1865 Bentley paid Agnes £250 for the three-volume novel *Althea Woodville; or, How Will it End?* She and Elizabeth together wrote *Lives of the Seven Bishops* (1866) and *Lives of the Tudor Princesses* (1868), but Agnes was the sole author of *Lives of the Last Four Princesses of the Royal House of Stuart* (1872), for which she traveled to Holland in 1869 to do research. She was granted a civil list pension of £100 per year in 1870. On 13 July 1874 Agnes died from a stroke; she was buried in the Southwold churchyard. Her writing career had spanned more than half a century. Proudly emblazoned on her tomb are the words "Agnes Strickland, Historian of the Queens of England."

MAJOR WORKS: *Monody on the Death of the Princess Charlotte of Wales* (London, 1817); *True Stories from Ancient History . . . From the Creation of the World to the Death of Charlemagne* (London, 1819); *The Moss-House: in which Many of the Works of Nature are Rendered a Source of Amusement to Children* (London, 1822); *The Tell-Tale: An Original Collection of Moral and Amusing Stories* (London, 1823); *The Rival Crusoes; or, the Shipwreck. Also, A Voyage to Norway; and The Fisherman's Cottage, etc.* (London, 1826); *Worcester Field; or, The Cavalier. A Poem in Four Cantos, with Historical Notes* (London, [1826]); *The Juvenile Forget-Me-Not* (London, 1827); *The Seven Ages of Woman, and Other Poems* (London, 1827); *Sketches from Nature; or Hints to Juvenile Naturalists* (London, 1830); *Demetrius: a Tale of Modern Greece: In Three Cantos. With Other Poems* (London, 1833); *The Broken Heart; and The Bridal* (London, [1835?]); *The Pilgrims of Walsingham, or Tales of the Middle Ages; An Historical Romance,* 2 vols. (London, 1835); *Tales of the Schoolroom* (London, [1835?]); *Floral Sketches, Fables, and Other Poems* (London, [1836]); *Tales and Stories from History,* 2 vols. (London, 1836); *Queen Victoria from her Birth to her Bridal,* 2 vols. (London, 1840); *Alda, The British Captive* (London, 1841); *Historic Scenes and Poetic Fancies* (London, 1850); *The Sea Side Offering* (Edinburgh, 1856); *How Will it End?* 3 vols. (London, 1865); *Lives of the Last Four Princesses of the Royal House of Stuart* (London, 1872).

WITH ELIZABETH STRICKLAND: *Historical Tales of Illustrious British Children* (London, 1833); *Lives of the Queens of England, from the Norman Conquest,* 12 vols. (London, 1840–48); *Lives of the Queens of Scotland and English Princesses Connected with the Regal Succession of Great Britain,* 8 vols. (Edinburgh, 1850–59); *Lives of the Bachelor Kings of England* (London, 1861); *Lives of the Seven Bishops Committed to the Tower in 1688* (London, 1866); *Lives of the Tudor Princesses, including Lady Jane Gray and her Sisters* (London, 1868).

EDITED WORKS: [with Bernard Barton], *Fisher's Juvenile Scrapbook* (London, 1837–39); *Letters of Mary, Queen of Scots*, 2 vols. (London, 1842).

TEXTS USED: Texts of "The Earthquake of Callao," "To the Spirit of Dreams," and "The Enfranchised; or, The Butterfly's First Flight" from *The Seven Ages of Woman, and Other Poems.* Text of "The Self-Devoted" from the *Keepsake* for 1832.

The Earthquake of Callao*

Along the vast Pacific day's last smile
Reflected many a bay and verdant isle,
And spicy grove that from its rocky steep
Stretched its luxuriant branches o'er the deep,
And softly shadowed in the waters blue,
In mirror'd landscapes met the downward view;
The billows, sleeping on the ocean's breast,
Forgot to murmur in their placid rest;
The languid breeze was lulled on vale and hill,
And every leaf lay motionless and still;　　　　10
The flowers, from blossomed boughs to lowly beds,
Had closed their bells and hung their beauteous heads;
And Nature, plunged in lethargy profound,
Seemed as when in primeval slumbers bound,
Ere o'er her silent bosom void and vast
The quickening spirit of creation past.
The lonely watcher on the flagstaff's height
With musing eye surveyed the lovely sight,
When the departing sun shed glory down
On tranquil ocean, convent, tower, and town;　　　　20
And then his task resuming, half unfurl'd
Spain's haughty standard to the watery world;
But ere the dull and languid air could raise
One drooping fold, his desultory gaze
Returns where, in the splendour of Peru,
A moment back the town had met his view,
With domes, and palaces, and walls of might,
Reposing in a flood of rosy light.

But like the fading of a meteor's beam,
30   Or the delusive pageant of a dream,
'Tis gone! and ere mute Wonder can demand
The how? or when? or Reason understand
The awful change—the reeling mountains swim
Before his dizzy sight, confused and dim;
Dense clouds obscure the sunset—and that sound
Which bursts from the cavernous depths profound
Of earth's rent bosom, with terrific roar,
Tells the appalling tale from shore to shore.
Mixed with the sullen echoes of the bells,
40   Tolling from crashing towers their own deep knells;
And, oh! in that last dismal clangour rings
The fearful dirge-note of all living things.
Within that fated town, united there
In one dread gulph of ruin and despair,
The grave hath oped its jaws, and young and old,
And high and low, in its insatiate fold
Are mingling crushed.—The hopes and cares of life,
Its busy projects and its restless strife,
And all its social joys, with them are o'er,
50   And they have left no mourner to deplore
Their general doom, save that unhappy one
Who, of its breathing thousands, was alone
Spectator of that town's sad overthrow;
The only victim conscious of his woe,
Preserved by cruel miracle of Fate,
To see his native land made desolate,
And all he ever loved, on that dread day,
Pass like a drama's shifting scene away,
And his whole race in one tremendous doom
60   Involved, and hurried living to the tomb.

Heartstruck, he drops from his relaxing hands
The useless ensign—and bewildered stands,
With glazing eyeballs and with stiffened neck,
A living statue gazing on the wreck
Of all his joys—nor now discerns the spot
Where once arose in peace his humble cot,
Endeared by every tender spell that lies
In home's sweet bound, and love's delightful ties;

But wife and children, happiness and home,
For him exist no longer—he must roam   70
Through the wide world in utter loneliness,
Without one friend to sooth, one hope to bless.
All, all are strangers now—there is no face
To him familiar of the human race;
Nor aught remains to charm, to cheer, or throw
A ray of interest on his path of woe.

   Yet months shall pass, and spring restore again
The flowers and blighted verdure of the plain;
Another town in time's due course shall rise,
And prouder structures greet the morning skies;   80
Long silent echoes shall again rejoice
To hear gay childhood's shout and silvery voice;
The smiling bridegroom and the flower-crowned bride
Shall tread new streets adorned in nuptial pride;
Arts bloom afresh, and commerce bring once more
The flush of wealth and plenty to the shore;
And busy population, far and wide
Extend an eager and increasing tide.
But *he,* lone relic of a vanished race,
Shall flee like troubled spirit from the place,   90
To pore in cureless anguish on the flood
That flows where once the town in splendour stood,
And rolls its sullen, melancholy waves
O'er his last home, and his loved kindred's graves.

                             (1827)

*At the destruction of Callao, in 1747, no more than one of the inhabitants escaped; and he, by a providence the most extraordinary. This man was on the fort that overlooked the harbour, going to strike the flag, when he perceived the sea to retire to a considerable distance; and then, swelling mountain high, it returned with great violence. The people ran from their houses in terror and confusion: he heard a cry of *Miserere* rise from all parts of the city; and immediately all was silent—the sea had entirely overwhelmed it, and buried it for ever in its bosom. But the same wave that destroyed it, drove a little boat by the place where he stood, into which he threw himself and was saved. *Strickland.* [Callao is a port city on the Pacific coast of Peru, about eight miles west of Lima. In 1746 it was destroyed by an earthquake and tidal waves. *Ed.*]

To the Spirit of Dreams

Spirit! who to shrouded eyes
Bringest such wild fantasies
As no waking glances yet,
In this work-day world, have met;
Thou, who o'er the mind and brain,
With thy bright ideal train,
Wrapt in slumber's mantle stealest,
And such wond'rous power revealest,
That Earth's proudest children still
10   Are the puppets of thy will,
In the moment when each sense
Bows to thine omnipotence.

In thy mystic dramas we
Must perforce the actors be,
And submit to every change,
Be it ne'er so wild and strange.
Taking at thy will the shape
Of owlet, kitten, bat, or ape.
Mightiest monarchs, in the hour
20   Of thy *more* despotic power,
Lay aside their regal state
For a wandering beggar's fate;
Whilst the landless wight in thee
Grasps imperial dignity.
Through the fen, the flood, the fire,
We must go at thy desire,
Over desert, rock, and mountain,
Treach'rous sands and frozen fountain,
Deep in gloomy caves of ocean,
30   Where the waves with restless motion
Howl above with ceaseless roar,
From bleak Norway's stormy shore;
For we passively obey
Thy unknown mysterious sway.

23 wight] Creature; being.

Oft thou dost to lovers bring
All the trembling hopes that spring
In the bosom's sealed recess,
Nurst in tearful tenderness;
Which they, waking, dare not own,
And confess to thee alone.   40
Thou, to eyes that weep in vain,
Bring'st the loved and lost again,
In angelic looks revealing
All the warmth of earthly feeling,
Lingering in the radiant breast
Of the purified and blest;
But thou dost with visions drear
Shake the murderer's couch with fear;
Who indeed could aptest tell
All the terrors of thy spell,   50
Which doth far too dreadful seem
For thy coinage, Airy dream!

Spirit, who, in gay confusion,
Through the regions of illusion
Lead'st in brilliant flights the mind,
By dull Reason unconfined;
Who, poor, grave, reflective elf,
Loves not sparklers like thyself,
But presumes not e'er to throw
Chills on thy poetic flow;   60
For the scene which thou dost grace,
Is for her no time or place.
When through fairy land thou rangest,
And as wind unfettered changest,
With the flash of Fancy's wing,
To some wild fantastic thing
Yet unthought-of, but all-glowing
With magic lights of thine own throwing,
Which in hues divine and bright,
After thou hast ta'en thy flight,   70
Long and lovely leave behind
Shades of glory on the mind.

(1827)

The Enfranchised; or,
The Butterfly's First Flight

Thou hast burst from thy prison,
    Bright child of the air,
Like a spirit just risen
    From its mansion of care.

Thou art joyously winging
    Thy first ardent flight,
Where the gay lark is singing
    Her notes of delight.

Where the sunbeams are throwing
10   Their glories on thine,
Till thy colours are glowing
    With tints more divine.

Then tasting new pleasure
    In Summer's green bowers,
Reposing at leisure
    On fresh opened flowers;

Or delighted to hover
    Around them, to see
Whose charms, airy rover!
20   Bloom sweetest for thee;

And fondly exhaling
    Their fragrance, till day
From thy bright eye is failing
    And fading away.

Then seeking some blossom
    Which looks to the west,
Thou dost find in its bosom
    Sweet shelter and rest,

And there dost betake thee
   Till darkness is o'er,   30
And the sunbeams awake thee
   To pleasure once more.
              (1827)

The Self-Devoted

She hath forsaken courtly halls and bowers
   For his dear sake:—ay, cheerfully resign'd
   Country and friends for him, and hath entwined
Her fate with his in dark and stormy hours,
As the fond ivy clings to ruin'd towers
   With generous love; and never hath inclined
   Round gilded domes and palaces to wind,
Or flung her wintry wreath midst summer flowers.
Her cheek is pale—it hath grown pale for him;
   Her all of earthly joy, her heaven below—   10
   He fades before her—fades in want and wo;
She sees his lamp of life wax faint and dim,
   Essays to act the Roman matron's part,
   And veils with patient smiles a breaking heart.
              (1832)

Ann Taylor

(1782–1866)

and

Jane Taylor

(1783–1824)

Ann Taylor and her younger sister Jane belonged to the literary family known as the Taylors of Ongar, whose members produced or made substantial contributions to almost a hundred books, many of them for children. The Taylor sisters were educated at home in astronomy, anatomy, geography, geometry, mechanics, and general history. To save money, in 1786 the family moved from London, where the girls had been born, to Lavenham, in Suffolk; they stayed there until 1796, when they moved to Colchester, where their father was to be the minister of a nonconformist congregation. Beginning in 1797 the sisters worked with their parents and later with their younger siblings at the family business—engraving book illustrations on copper plates, an occupation Jane, at least, did not relish. Always precocious, Jane once presented her parents with a petition for a garden in five well-crafted stanzas. She later recalled, "I know I have sometimes lived so much in a *castle,* as almost to forget that I lived in a *house.*"[1]

In 1798 Ann bought a copy of the *Minor's Pocket Book,* jotted down solutions to the enigma, charade, and other puzzles, and, using the pseudonym "Juvenilia," sent them to the Quaker publisher, William Darton. In each of the following years, Ann, Jane, and their brother Isaac sent solutions in verse, and Darton published several of Ann's compositions. In 1803 Darton accepted Jane's poem "The Beggar Boy" for publication in the 1804 issue and wrote

1. Letter of 24 September 1806, quoted in Isaac Taylor, *Memoirs and Poetical Remains of the Late Jane Taylor,* 2 vols. (London, 1825), 1:6–7, also 2:152.

to their father asking for more "specimens of easy Poetry for young children. . . . What would be most likely to please little minds must be well known to every one of those who have written such pieces as we have already seen from thy family." He offered to pay in cash or books. The Taylors sent enough poems to fill a volume, which was published early in 1804 as *Original Poems, for Infant Minds,* by "Several Young Persons." Darton paid ten pounds for the poems. When the book appeared, the Taylors were displeased to find that Darton had included seventeen poems by Adelaide O'Keeffe (1776–1855) and one by Barnard Barton (1784–1849) in addition to the twenty poems by Ann, twenty by Jane, and three by their brother, Isaac Jr., who also engraved the volume's frontispiece. But the book was an immense success. It "awoke the nurseries of England, and those in charge of them,"[2] earning enthusiastic praise from Walter Scott, Robert Southey, and Maria Edgeworth. These were among the first original poems in English written specifically for the enjoyment of children rather than primarily for educational or didactic purposes.

Original Poems, for Infant Minds went through eighteen English editions in the first fourteen years; by 1865 there had been eighty English and American editions, as well as Dutch, French, German, and Russian translations. The poems' influence was enormous. Generations of children, including many future authors, grew up reading, reciting, and singing them. Kate Greenaway illustrated them in 1883; and in 1925 Edith Sitwell introduced a selection. Their success inspired a slew of imitations, including ones by Sara Coleridge and by Charles and Mary Lamb. In November 1804 Darton solicited a second volume of *Original Poems* from the Taylors, for which they received £15. This volume contained sixteen poems by Adelaide O'Keeffe as well as twenty-nine by Ann, twenty-two by Jane, and three by Isaac. The Taylors appear to have earned £440 for their contributions to the various editions of *Original Poems* by 1844.[3]

When their next volume was in preparation, Jane acquired her own room in the attic. Her brother Isaac later recalled that the window "commanded a view of the country, and a 'tract of sky' as a field for that nightly soaring of the fancy of which she was so fond."[4] *Rhymes for the Nursery,* published in 1806,

---

2. F. J. Harvey Darton, *Children's Books in England: Five Centuries of Social Life* (Cambridge, 1932), 187.

3. The authors of each of the poems in these and other Taylor volumes are identified by Christina Duff Stewart in *The Taylors of Ongar: An Analytical Bio-Bibliography,* 2 vols. (New York, 1975). Stewart also describes the revisions that took place from one edition to another and the sums received.

4. Isaac Taylor, *Memoirs and Poetical Remains of the Late Jane Taylor,* 1:86.

included Jane's poem "The Star," still a staple in our present-day repertoire of poetry for children. Known now by its first line, "Twinkle, twinkle, little star," its opening stanza persists as if it were folklore, the name of its creator now almost entirely forgotten. The first publication of this book brought the Taylors forty pounds; by 1881 it had gone through forty-one editions.

In 1807, on a visit to London, the young sisters stopped at Newington to meet the elderly Anna Letitia Barbauld and her brother, John Aikin. The sisters' *Hymns for Infant Minds,* for which Ann engraved the frontispiece, appeared in 1810. The hymns almost immediately made their way into Sunday school anthologies, often without acknowledgment. *Hymns* had gone through more than fifty editions in England by the 1880s and nearly fifty in America by the 1860s. In the first year, the authors earned £150. In 1811 the family moved to Ongar, in Essex, and in 1812 Ann and Jane published *Original Hymns for Sunday Schools* with Josiah Conder. Though the language of these hymns is highly simplified, they were not easy to write. Isaac Jr. remarked that "if one might judge by the appearance of the manuscript copy of these hymns—its intricate interlineations, and multiplied revisions, it would seem that, many of them cost the author more labour than any other of her writings."[5]

In December 1813 Ann married the Reverend Joseph Henry Gilbert (1779–1852), the liberal Congregationalist pastor of the Nether Chapel in Sheffield. She suspended her writing career in the early years of her marriage in order to devote herself to her family, which eventually came to include eight children. Separated now from her older sister, Jane turned to writing a work of fiction. Isaac Jr. later recalled, "It was her custom, in a solitary ramble among the rocks, for half an hour after breakfast, to seek that pitch of excitement without which she never took up the pen:—this fever of thought was usually exhausted in two or three hours of writing."[6] In August 1815 *Display. A Tale for Young People* appeared. This was the first work Jane had authored alone and also the first work bearing her name on the title page. Her mother could no longer object to her daughter being known publicly as an author, as she had herself the previous year made her own debut in the world of letters, publishing now having displaced engraving as the more lucrative family business. Although modern readers find *Display* overly didactic, it was popular enough in its own time to go through three editions in the first six months. Soon after its publication, Jane began working on a book of poems for an adult audience. Isaac noted that she hesitated to express her opinions on serious

5. Ibid., 116.
6. Ibid., 137.

subjects in prose, but "in verse, she felt as if sheltered. She therefore determined to write what she thought and felt, with less reserve than hitherto; but under the cover of poetry."[7] The result was *Essays in Rhyme, on Morals and Manners,* published by Taylor and Hessey and Josiah Conder in 1816. John Keats wrote to his fourteen-year-old sister, Fanny, "How do you like Miss Taylor's essays in Rhyme—I just look'd into the Book and it appeared to me suitable to you—especially since I remember your liking for those pleasant little things the Original Poems."[8] The next year Jane collaborated with her mother to pen the daughter's part of *Correspondence Between a Mother and Her Daughter at School* (1817). This was Jane's last book. Around the time of its publication she discovered the breast cancer that would eventually claim her life. Her physician forbade all writing for fear that excitement would weaken her. Nevertheless, for the next five years, under the signature "Q.Q.," she continued to contribute poems, essays, and stories to the *Youth's Magazine.* These pieces, including her famous story "How It Strikes a Stranger," about a visit by a man from another planet, were collected and published shortly after her death on 13 April 1824.[9] *The Contributions of Q.Q. to a Periodical Work: with Some Pieces Not Before Published* had gone through thirteen British editions by 1866. In 1825 Isaac Jr. published a biography of his sister and edited more works in the two-volume *Memoirs and Poetical Remains of the Late Jane Taylor: with Extracts from her Correspondence,* drawing the silhouette of Jane for the frontispiece to volume 1.

Though principally occupied with her family, Ann published in 1827 *Original Anniversary Hymns* and in 1839 *The Convalescent; Twelve Letters on Recovery from Sickness,* occasioned by the serious illness of her daughter and several others. Isaac Jr. wrote congratulating his sister on the book's publication, expressing his "particular pleasure in finding that you have at length returned to your vocation, and left . . . the mending of stockings to hands that cannot so well handle a pen."[10] Ann contributed more than one hundred hymns to Leifchild's *Original Hymns* (1842). In 1843 her youngest son nearly died; she wrote *Seven Blessings for Little Children* during his illness and recuperation. Family duties and problems and the poor health of her husband kept Ann too busy to publish much for the next decade. Her husband died on 12 December

7. Ibid., 147.

8. John Keats, *The Letters of John Keats: 1814–1821,* ed. Hyder Edward Rollins, vol. 1 (Cambridge, Mass., 1958), 155.

9. Robert Browning borrowed the title for his poem "How It Strikes a Contemporary," used the substance of the story for his poem "Rephan," and modeled Lazarus in "An Epistle" on Taylor's main character (Stewart, 2:713).

10. Quoted in Stewart, *The Taylors of Ongar,* 1:540.

1852, and in 1853, at the age of seventy-one, she was forced to give up her house. But as workmen were dismantling her household, she wrote a memoir of her husband, published as *A Biographical Sketch of the Rev. Joseph Gilbert.* Ann enjoyed travel and made the journey to Scotland and Devon at the age of eighty-two. She also wrote the preface for her daughter Caroline's book *A Child's Walk Through the Year,* published in 1858. Ann died in 1866 at the age of eighty-five; her son Josiah Gilbert edited and completed the autobiography she had written for her family and published it in 1874 under the title *Autobiography and Other Memorials of Mrs. Gilbert (Formerly Ann Taylor).*

Although Ann Taylor's "My Mother" became one of the best-known, most frequently imitated and parodied poems of the nineteenth century, Jane is generally considered to be the more significant poet. Her dissenting vision was both democratic and inclusive; those with physical and mental disabilities, ordinary women, the poor, all inhabit her work. She wrote about and for real, not mythologized or sentimentalized, children, who speak the language of the common child and, like real children, are capable of thoughtlessness, even cruelty. She was a poet unabashedly of and for the British middle class; but just as she was a dissenter in religion, a Congregationalist, so she dissented from some of the most pervasive bourgeois values of her time, despising materialism and its social trappings, along with pretension of any sort. The rising middle class, she believed, was so enmeshed in a self-indulgent quest for more and ever more things that it was in danger of forgetting the moral soil in which it had germinated and of losing its humanity. She would be its social conscience, its minister. Through imaginative sympathy she sought to sensitize readers to the everyday life of the disenfranchised. Her contributions to *Original Poems* include titles such as "Crazy Robert" and "Poverty," and *Rhymes for the Nursery* contains "The Old Beggar Man," "The Little Beggar Girl," and "Poor Children." Companion poems such as "One Little Boy" and "Another Little Boy" not only show the dignity and worth of the common laborer's contribution to society while exposing the spiritual sterility of aristocratic values but also dramatize the mutual contempt of these classes for one another, a theme she revisits for adult readers in "A Pair."

Taylor was well aware how women's intellectual and artistic potential frequently drowned in the menial demands of everyday life and how through subtle coercion women come to embrace the constraints on their lives. Two years after she published "The Cow and the Ass," a poem that explores this issue, she wrote to a friend: "I do believe the reason why so few men, even among the intelligent, wish to encourage the mental cultivation of women, is their excessive love of the *good things* of this life: they tremble for their dear stomachs, concluding that a woman who could taste the pleasures of poetry or sentiment, would never descend to pay due attention to those exquisite flavors in pudding or pie, that are so gratifying to their philosophic palates; and yet . . . it is a thousand pities they should be so mistaken."[11]

MAJOR WORKS:

Ann Taylor: *The Wedding Among the Flowers* (London, 1808); *Original Anniversary Hymns, Adapted to the Public Services of Sunday Schools and Sunday School Unions* (London, 1827); *The Convalescent; Twelve Letters on Recovery from Sickness* (London, 1839); *Seven Blessings for Little Children* (London, 1844); *A Biographical Sketch of the Rev. Joseph Gilbert. By his Widow. With Recollections of The Discourses of his closing Years, from Notes at the Time, by One of His Sons* (London, 1853); *Autobiography and Other Memorials of Mrs. Gilbert (formerly Ann Taylor),* ed. Josiah Gilbert (London, 1874).

Jane Taylor: *Display. A Tale for Young People* (London, 1815); *Essays in Rhyme, on Morals and Manners* (London, 1816); *The Contributions of Q.Q. to a Periodical Work: with some Pieces not before Published,* 2 vols. (London, 1824); *Memoirs and Poetical Remains of the Late Jane Taylor: with Extracts from her Correspondence,* ed. Isaac Taylor, 2 vols. (London, 1825).

COLLABORATIVE WORKS: *Original Poems, for Infant Minds* [Jane Taylor, Ann Taylor, Isaac Taylor Jr., Bernard Barton, and Adelaide O'Keeffe], 2 vols. (London, 1804–5); *Rural Scenes: or, A Peep into the Country, for Good Children* [Jane Taylor, Ann Taylor, and Isaac Taylor Jr.] (London, 1805); *City Scenes: or, A Peep into London, for Good Children* [Jane Taylor, Ann Taylor, and Isaac Taylor Jr.] (London, 1806); *Rhymes for the Nursery* [Jane and Ann Taylor] (London, 1806); *Limed Twigs, to Catch Young Birds* [Jane and Ann Taylor, illustrations by Isaac Taylor Jr.] (London, 1808); *The New Cries of London* [Jane Taylor, Ann Taylor, and Isaac Taylor Jr.] (London, 1808); *Hymns for Infant Minds* [Jane Taylor, Ann Taylor, and Isaac Taylor Jr.] (Bucklersbury, 1810); *Signor Topsy-Turvy's Wonderful Magic Lantern; or, The World Turned Upside Down* [Jane Taylor, Ann Taylor, and Rev. Isaac Taylor] (London, 1810); *The Mother's Fables, In Verse. Designed, Through the Medium of Amusement, to Correct some of the Faults and Follies of Children* [Jane Taylor, Ann Taylor, and possibly Isaac Taylor Jr. or Jefferys Taylor] (London, 1812); *Original Hymns for Sunday Schools* [Jane Taylor and Ann Taylor] (London, 1812); *Correspondence between a Mother and her Daughter at School* [Jane Taylor and her mother, Mrs. Ann Taylor] (London, 1817); *The Linnet's Life. Twelve Poems with a Copper Plate Engraving to Each* [Jane Taylor, Ann Taylor, Rev. Isaac Taylor, and possibly Isaac Taylor Jr.] (London, 1822); *The Family Pen. Memorials, Biographical and Literary, of the Taylor Family, of Ongar,* ed. Rev. Isaac Taylor [with selections from the works of Isaac Taylor Sr., Jane Taylor, Jefferys Taylor, and Ann Taylor], 2 vols. (London, 1867); *Meddlesome Matty and Other Poems for Infant Minds,* [Jane and Ann Taylor, with an introduction by Edith Sitwell] (London, 1925).

11. Letter of 2 June 1808, quoted in Isaac Taylor, *Memoirs and Poetical Remains of the Late Jane Taylor,* 2:178.

TEXTS USED: Texts of "The Little Bird's Complaint to His Mistress" and "The Mistress's Reply to Her Little Bird," both by Ann Taylor, and "The Cow and the Ass," by Jane Taylor, from *The "Original Poems" and Others,* ed. E. V. Lucas (London, 1903). Text of "The Star," by Jane Taylor, from *Rhymes for the Nursery,* 10th ed. (1818). Texts of "Recreation," "The Squire's Pew," and "A Pair," by Jane Taylor, from *Essays in Rhyme, on Morals and Manners.* Text from "Philip: A Fragment," by Jane Taylor, from *Memoirs and Poetical Remains of the Late Jane Taylor: with Extracts from her Correspondence.*

The Little Bird's Complaint to His Mistress

Here in this wiry prison where I sing,
    And think of sweet green woods, and long to fly,
Unable once to try my useless wing,
    Or wave my feathers in the clear blue sky,

Day after day the selfsame things I see,
    The cold white ceiling, and this dreary house;
Ah! how unlike my healthy native tree,
    Rocked by the winds that whistled through the boughs.

Mild spring returning strews the ground with flowers,
10   And hangs sweet May-buds on the hedges gay,
That no kind sunshine cheers my gloomy hours,
    Nor kind companion twitters in the spray!

Oh! how I long to stretch my listless wings,
    And fly away as far as eye can see!
And from the topmost bough, where Robin sings,
    Pour my wild songs, and be as blithe as he.

Why was I taken from the waving nest,
    From flowery fields, wide woods, and hedges green;
Torn from my tender mother's downy breast,
20   In this sad prison-house to die unseen?

Why must I hear, in summer evenings fine,
    A thousand happier birds in merry choirs?
And I, poor lonely I, in grief repine,
    Caged by these wooden walls and golden wires!

Say not, the tuneful notes I daily pour
    Are songs of pleasure, from a heart at ease;—
They are but wailings at my prison door,
    Incessant cries, to taste the open breeze!

Kind mistress, come, with gentle, pitying hand,
    Unbar that curious grate, and set me free;   30
Then on the whitethorn bush I'll take my stand,
    And sing sweet songs to freedom and to thee.
                  (1805)

The Mistress's Reply to Her Little Bird

Dear little bird, don't make this piteous cry,
    My heart will break to hear thee thus complain;
Gladly, dear little bird, I'd let thee fly,
    If that were likely to relieve thy pain.

Base was the boy who climbed the tree so high,
    And took thee, bare and shivering, from thy nest;
But no, dear little bird, it was not I,
    There's more of soft compassion in my breast.

But when I saw thee gasping wide for breath,
    Without one feather on thy callow skin,   10
I begged the cruel boy to spare thy death,
    Paid for thy little life, and took thee in.

Fondly I fed thee, with the tenderest care,
    And filled thy gaping beak with nicest food,
Gave thee new bread and butter from my share,
    And then with chickweed green thy dwelling strewed.

Soon downy feathers dressed thy naked wing,
    Smoothed by thy little beak with beauish care;
And many a summer's evening wouldst thou sing,
    And hop from perch to perch with merry air.   20

But if I now should loose thy prison door,
    And let thee out into the world so wide,
Unused to such a wondrous place before,
    Thou'dst want some friendly shelter where to hide.

Thy brother birds would peck thy little eyes,
    And fright the stranger from their woods away;
Fierce hawks would chase thee trembling through the skies,
    Or crouching pussy mark thee for her prey.

Sad, on the lonely blackthorn wouldst thou sit,
30   Thy mournful song unpitied and unheard;
And when the wintry wind and driving sleet
    Came sweeping o'er, they'd kill my pretty bird.

Then do not pine, my favourite, to be free,
    Plume up thy wings, and clear that sullen eye;
I would not take thee from thy native tree,
    But now 'twould kill thee soon, to let thee fly.

                                (1805)

The Cow and the Ass

Beside a green meadow a stream used to flow,
So clear, one might see the white pebbles below;
To this cooling brook the warm cattle would stray,
To stand in the shade on a hot summer's day.

A cow, quite oppressed by the heat of the sun,
Came here to refresh, as she often had done,
And standing quite still, stooping over the stream,
Was musing perhaps; or perhaps she might dream.

But soon a brown ass, of respectable look,
10   Came trotting up also, to taste of the brook,
And to nibble a few of the daisies and grass:
"How d'ye do?" said the cow; "How d'ye do?" said the ass.

"Take a seat," said the cow, gently waiving her hand;
"By no means, dear madam," said he, "while you stand."
Then stooping to drink, with a complaisant bow,
"Ma'am, your health," said the ass:—"Thank you, sir," said the cow.

When a few of these compliments more had been passed,
They laid themselves down on the herbage at last;
And waiting politely (as gentlemen must),
The ass held his tongue, that the cow might speak first.   20

Then, with a deep sigh, she directly began,
"Don't you think, Mr. Ass, we are injured by man?
'Tis a subject which lies with a weight on my mind:
We really are greatly oppressed by mankind.

"Pray what is the reason (I see none at all)
That I always must go when Jane chooses to call?
Whatever I'm doing ('tis certainly hard)
I'm forced to leave off, to be milked in the yard.

"I've no will of my own, but must do as they please,
And give them my milk to make butter and cheese;   30
Sometimes I endeavour to kick down the pail,
Or give her a box on the ear with my tail."

"But, Ma'am," said the ass, "not presuming to teach—
Oh dear, I beg pardon—pray finish your speech;
Excuse my mistake," said the complaisant swain,
"Go on, and I'll not interrupt you again."

"Why, sir, I was just then about to observe,
Those hard-hearted tyrants no longer I'll serve;
But leave them for ever to do as they please,
And look somewhere else for their butter and cheese."   40

Ass waited a moment, his answer to scan,
And then, "Not presuming to teach," he began,
"Permit me to say, since my thoughts you invite,
I always saw things in a different light.

"That you afford man an important supply,
No ass in his senses would ever deny:
But then, in return, 'tis but fair to allow,
They are of *some* service to you, Mistress Cow.

50   " 'Tis their pleasant meadow in which you repose,
And they find you a shelter from wintery snows.
For comforts like these, we're indebted to man;
And for him, in return, should do all that we can."

The cow, upon this, cast her eyes on the grass,
Not pleased to be schooled in this way by an ass:
"Yet," said she to herself, "though he's not very bright,
I really believe that the fellow is right." *

                                        (1805)

---

* In later editions of *Original Poems for Infant Minds,* the volume in which "The Cow and the Ass" first appeared, the poem's last two lines were revised to read, " 'Yet,' thought she, 'I'm determin'd I'll benefit by 't, / For I really believe that the fellow is right.' " Ann Taylor may well have been responsible for this revision.

The Star

Twinkle, twinkle, little star,
How I wonder what you are!
Up above the world so high,
Like a diamond in the sky.

When the blazing sun is gone,
When he nothing shines upon,
Then you show your little light,
Twinkle, twinkle, all the night.

10   Then the trav'ller in the dark,
Thanks you for your tiny spark:
He could not see which way to go,
If you did not twinkle so.

In the dark blue sky you keep,
And often through my curtains peep,
For you never shut your eye,
'Till the sun is in the sky.

As your bright and tiny spark,
Lights the trav'ller in the dark,—
Though I know not what you are,
Twinkle, twinkle, little star.   20

(1806)

Recreation

"—We took our work, and went, you see,
To take an early cup of tea.
We did so now and then, to pay
The friendly debt, and so did they.
Not that our friendship burnt so bright
That all the world could see the light;
'Twas of the ordinary *genus,*
And little love was lost between us:
We lov'd, I think, about as true,
As such near neighbours mostly do.   10

At first, we all were somewhat dry;—
Mamma felt cold, and so did I:
Indeed, that room, sit where you will,
Has draught enough to turn a mill.
"I hope you're warm," says Mrs. G.
"O, quite so," says mamma, *says she;*
"I'll take my shawl off by and by."—
"This room is always warm," *says I.*

At last the tea came up, and so,
With that, our tongues began to go.   20
Now, in that house you're sure of knowing
The smallest scrap of news that's going;

We find it *there* the wisest way,
To take some care of what we say.

 —Says she, "there's dreadful doings still
In that affair about the *will;*
For now the folks in Brewer's Street,
Don't speak to *James's,* when they meet.
Poor Mrs. *Sam* sits all alone,
30 And frets herself to skin and bone.
For months she manag'd, she declares,
All the old gentleman's affairs;
And always let him have his way,
And never left him night nor day;
Waited and watch'd his every look,
And gave him every drop he took.
Dear Mrs. *Sam,* it was too bad!
He might have left her all he had."

 "Pray ma'am," says I, "has poor Miss A.
40 Been left as *handsome* as they say?"
"My dear," says she, "'tis no such thing,
She'd nothing but a mourning ring.
But is it not *uncommon* mean,
To wear that rusty bombazeen!"
"She had," says I, "the very same,
Three years ago, for—what's his name?"—
"The Duke of *Brunswick,*—very true,
And has not bought a thread of new,
I'm positive," said Mrs. G.—
50 So then we laugh'd, and drank our tea.

 "So," says mamma, "I find it's true
What Captain P. intends to do;
To hire that house, or else to buy—"
"Close to the tan-yard, ma'am," says I;
"Upon my word it's very strange,
I wish they mayn't repent the change!"

 44 bombazeen] A twilled dress material composed of silk and worsted, cotton and worsted, or worsted alone. Black bombazeen was frequently worn for mourning.

"My dear," says she, " 'tis very well
You know, if *they* can bear the smell."

    "Miss F." says I, "is said to be
A sweet young woman, Mrs. G."   60
"O, excellent! I hear," she cried;
"O, truly so!" mamma replied.
"How old should you suppose her, pray?
She's older than she looks, they say."
"Really," says I, "she seems to me
Not more than twenty-two or three."
"O, then you're wrong," says Mrs. G.
"Their upper servant told our *Jane,*
She'll not see twenty-nine again."
"Indeed, so old! I wonder why   70
She does not marry, then," says I;
"So many thousands to bestow,
And such a beauty, too, you know."
"A beauty! O, my dear Miss B.
You must be joking, now," says she;
"Her *figure's* rather pretty," —— "Ah!
That's what *I* say," replied mamma.

    "Miss F." says I, "I've understood,
Spends all her time in doing good:
The people say her coming down   80
Is quite a blessing to the town."
At that our hostess fetch'd a sigh,
And shook her head; and so, says I,
"It's very kind of her, I'm sure,
To be so generous to the poor."
"No doubt," says she, " 'tis very true;
Perhaps there may be *reasons* too: —
You know some people like to pass
For *patrons* with the lower class."

    And here I break my story's thread,   90
Just to remark, that what she said,
Although I took the other part,
Went like a cordial to my heart.

Some inuendos more had pass'd,
Till out the scandal came at last.
"Come then, I'll tell you something more,"
Says she,—"Eliza, shut the door.—
I would not trust a creature here,
For all the world, but you, my dear.
100 Perhaps it's false—I wish it may,
—But let it go no further, pray!"
"O," says mamma, "You need not fear,
We never mention what we hear."
"Indeed we shall not, Mrs. G."
Says I, again, impatiently:
And so, we drew our chairs the nearer,
And whispering, lest the child should hear her,
She told a tale, at least too *long*,
To be repeated in a song;
110 We, panting every breath between,
With curiosity and spleen.
And how we did enjoy the sport!
And echo every faint report,
And answer every candid doubt,
And turn her motives inside out,
And holes in all her virtues pick,
Till we were sated, almost sick.

—Thus having brought it to a close,
In great good humour, we arose.
120 Indeed, 'twas more than time to go,
Our boy had been an hour below.
So, warmly pressing Mrs. G.
To fix a day to come to tea,
We muffled up in cloke and plaid,
And trotted home behind the lad."

(1816)

The Squire's Pew

A slanting ray of evening light
   Shoots through the yellow pane;
It makes the faded crimson bright,
   And gilds the fringe again:
The window's gothic frame-work falls
In oblique shadow on the walls.

And since those trappings first were new,
   How many a cloudless day,
To rob the velvet of its hue,
   Has come and pass'd away!   10
How many a setting sun hath made
That curious lattice-work of shade!

Crumbled beneath the hillock green,
   The cunning hand must be,
That carv'd this fretted door, I ween,
   Acorn, and *fleur-de-lis;*
And now the worm hath done her part,
In mimicking the chisel's art.

—In days of yore (as now we call)
   When the first *James* was king;   20
The courtly knight from yonder hall,
   Hither his train did bring;
All seated round in order due,
With broider'd suit and buckled shoe.

On damask cushions, set in fringe,
   All reverently they knelt:
Prayer-books, with brazen hasp and hinge,
   In ancient English spelt,
Each holding in a lily hand,
Responsive at the priest's command.   30

20 When the first *James* was king] James I (1566–1625) was the first Stuart king of England, succeeding Queen Elizabeth in 1603.

—Now, streaming down the vaulted aisle,
　The sunbeam, long and lone,
Illumes the characters awhile
　Of their inscription stone;
And there, in marble hard and cold,
The knight and all his train behold.

Outstretch'd together, are express'd
　He and my lady fair;
With hands uplifted on the breast,
40　　In attitude of prayer;
Long visag'd, clad in armor, he,
With ruffled arm and bodice, she.

Set forth, in order as they died,
　The numerous offspring bend;
Devoutly kneeling side by side,
　As though they did intend
For past omissions to atone,
By saying endless prayers in stone.

Those mellow days are past and dim,
50　　But generations new,
In regular descent from him,
　Have fill'd the stately pew;
And in the same succession go,
To occupy the vault below.

And now, the polish'd, modern squire,
　And his gay train appear;
Who duly to the hall retire,
　A season, every year;
And fill the seats with belle and beau,
60　As 'twas so many years ago.

Perchance, all thoughtless as they tread
　The hollow sounding floor,
Of that dark house of kindred dead,
　Which shall, as heretofore,
In turn, receive, to silent rest,
Another, and another guest.

The feather'd hearse and sable train,
   In all its wonted state,
Shall wind along the village lane,
   And stand before the gate;   70
—Brought many a distant county thro',
To join the final rendezvous.

And when the race is swept away,
   All to their dusty beds;
Still shall the mellow evening ray
   Shine gaily o'er their heads:
While other faces, fresh and new,
Shall occupy the squire's pew.

               (1816)

A Pair

   There was a youth—but woe is me!
I quite forget his name, and he
Without some label round his neck,
Is like one pea among a peck.
Go search the country up and down,
Port, city, village, parish, town,
And, saving just the face and name,
You shall behold the very same,
Wherever pleasure's train resorts,
From the Land's-End to *Johnny Groats';*   10
And thousands such have swell'd the herd,
From *William,* down to *George* the Third.

   To life he started—thanks to fate,
In contact with a good estate:
Provided thus, and quite at ease,
He takes for granted all he sees;
Ne'er sends a thought, nor lifts an eye,

12 From *William,* down to *George* the Third] From William the Conqueror (c. 1027–87) to George III (1738–1820), i.e., from the earliest English king to the most recent.

To ask what am I? where? and why?—
All that is no affair of his,
Somehow he came—and there he is!
Without such prosing, stupid stuff,
Alive and well, and that's enough.

    Thoughts! why, if all that crawl like trains
Of caterpillars through his brains,
With every syllable let fall,
Bon mot, and compliment, and all,
Were melted down in furnace fire,
I doubt if shred of golden wire,
To make, amongst it all would linger,
A ring for *Tom Thumb's* little finger.
Yet, think not that he comes below
The modern, average ratio—
The current coin of fashion's mint—
The common, ball-room-going stint.
Of trifling cost his stock in trade is,
Whose business is to please the ladies;
Or who to honours may aspire,
Of a town beau or country squire.
The cant of fashion and of vice
To learn, slight effort will suffice;
And he was furnish'd with that knowledge,
Even *before* he went to college.
And thus, without the toil of thought,
Favour and flattery may be bought.
No need to win the laurel, now,
For lady's smile or vassal's bow;
To lie exposed in patriot camp,
Or study by the midnight lamp.

    Nature and art might vainly strive
To keep his intellect alive.
—'Twould not have forc'd an exclamation,
Worthy a note of admiration,
If he had been on Gibeon's hill,

53 Gibeon's hill] The hill overlooking the town of Gibeon, not far from Jerusalem, is mentioned in 2 Samuel 2:13 for having a famous spring on its southeast side.

20

30

40

50

And seen the sun and moon stand still.
What prodigy was ever known,
To raise the pitch of fashion's tone!
Or make it yield, by any chance,
That studied air of *nonchalance,*
Which after all, however grac'd,
Is apathy, and want of taste.   60

   The *vulgar* every station fill,
St. Giles' or *James's*—which you will;
Spruce drapers in their masters'* shops,
Rank with right honorable fops;
No real distinction marks the kinds—
The *raw material* of their minds.
But *mind* claims rank that cannot yield
To blazon'd arms and crested shield:
Above the need and reach it stands,
Of diamond stars from royal hands;   70
Nor waits the nod of courtly state,
To bid it be, or not be great.
The regions where it wings its way,
Are set with brighter stars than they:
With calm contempt it thence looks down
On fortune's favour or its frown;
Looks down on those, who vainly try,
By strange inversion of the eye,
From that poor mole-hill where they sit,
To cast a downward look on it: 80
As robin, from his pear-tree height,
Looks *down* upon the eagle's flight.

   Before our youth had learnt his letters,
They taught him to despise his betters;
And if *some* things have been forgot,
That lesson certainly has not.
The haunts his genius chiefly graces,
Are tables, stables, taverns, races;—
The things of which he most afraid is,
Are tradesmen's bills, and learned ladies: 90
He deems the first a grievous bore,
But loathes the latter even more

Than solitude or rainy weather,
Unless they happen both together.

Soft his existence rolls away,
To-morrow plenteous as today:
He lives, enjoys, and lives anew,—
And when he dies,—what shall we do!

K.K.

Down a close street, whose darksome shops display,
100   Old clothes and iron on both sides the way;
Loathsome and wretched, whence the eye in pain,
Averted turns, nor seeks to view again;
Where lowest dregs of human nature dwell,
More loathsome than the rags and rust they sell;—
A pale mechanic rents an attic floor;
By many a shatter'd stair you gain the door:
'Tis one poor room, whose blacken'd walls are hung
With dust that settled there when he was young.
The rusty grate two massy bricks displays,
110   To fill the sides and make a frugal blaze.
The door unhing'd, the window patch'd and broke;
The panes obscur'd by half a century's smoke:
There stands the bench at which his life is spent;
Worn, groov'd, and bor'd, and worm-devour'd, and bent:
Where daily, undisturb'd by foes or friends,
In one unvaried attitude he bends.
His tools, long practis'd, seem to understand
Scarce less their functions, than his own right hand.
With these he drives his craft with patient skill;
120   Year after year would find him at it still:
The noisy world around is changing all,
War follows peace, and kingdoms rise and fall;
France rages now, and Spain, and now the Turk;
Now victory sounds;—but there he sits at work!
A man might see him so, then bid adieu,—
Make a long voyage to China or Peru;
There traffic, settle, build; at length might come,
Alter'd, and old, and weather-beaten home,
And find him on the same square foot of floor,
130   On which he left him twenty years before.

—The self same bench, and attitude, and stool,
The same quick movement of his cunning tool;
The very distance 'twixt his knees and chin,
As though he had but stepp'd just out and in.

　Such is his fate—and yet you might descry
A latent spark of meaning in his eye.
—That crowded shelf beside his bench, contains
One old, worn, volume that employs his brains:
With algebraic lore its page is spread,
Where *a* and *b* contend with *x* and *z*:—　　　　140
Sold by some *student* from an Oxford hall,
—Bought by the pound upon a broker's stall.
On this it is his sole delight to pore,
Early and late, when working time is o'er:
But oft he stops, bewilder'd and perplex'd,
At some hard problem in the learned text;
Pressing his hand upon his puzzled brain,
At what the dullest school-boy could explain.

　From needful sleep the precious hour he saves,
To give his thirsty mind the stream it craves:　　　　150
There, with his slender rush beside him plac'd,
He drinks the knowledge in with greedy haste.
At early morning, when the frosty air
Brightens Orion and the northern Bear,
His distant window mid the dusky row,
Shews a dim light to passenger below.
—A light more dim is flashing on his mind,
That shows its darkness, and its views confin'd.
Had science shone around his early days,
How had his soul expanded in the blaze!　　　　160
But penury bound him, and his mind in vain
Struggles and writhes beneath her iron chain.

　—At length the taper fades, and distant cry
Of early sweep bespeaks the morning nigh;
Slowly it breaks,—and that rejoicing ray,
That wakes the healthful country into day,
Tips the green hills, slants o'er the level plain,

Reddens the pool, and stream, and cottage pane,
And field, and garden, park, and stately hall,—
170   Now darts obliquely on his wretched wall.
He knows the wonted signal; shuts his book,
Slowly consigns it to its dusty nook;
Looks out awhile, with fixt and absent stare,
On crowded roofs, seen through the foggy air;
—Stirs up the embers, takes his sickly draught,
Sighs at his fortunes, and resumes his craft.

(1816)

* In the original this read "masters."

from "Philip—A Fragment"

Peggy, his sole domestic, slowly grew
To be, in fact, his sole companion too.
When first she came she never thought—nor he—
With her odd master she could make so free:—
She was not pert:—he wished not to confer
With any living—doubtless, not with her.
But man is social, e'en against his will;
And woman kind, whatever rank she fill.
Her master came a lonely stranger here;
10   Feeble, dejected, friendless—'twould appear.
She pitied;—woman does; nor pitied less,
For knowing not the cause of his distress.
She was not young; and had her troubles known;
So that she felt his sorrows with her own;
And soon resolved to labour, all she could,
To cheer his spirits, and to do him good.

Though few and mean the attainments she could boast,
Peggy had passed her life upon the coast;
And she could thoughts and sentiments disclose,

Such as the inland peasant rarely knows.   20
On squally nights, or when it blew a gale,
Long she would stand, recounting tale on tale,
Of wreck or danger, or of rescue bold,
That she had witnessed, or her kindred told;
Bringing each long-lost circumstance to mind:
And genuine feeling taught her where to find
Terms more expressive, though of vulgar use,
Than hours of patient study will produce.
Her native eloquence would place in view
The very scene, and all its terrors too.   30
Meantime, to excuse her stay, she used to stand,
The tidy hearth still trimming—brush in hand:
Till he, with kind, though not familiar air,
Would interrupt with—"Peggy, take a chair."
A chair she took;—less easy when she had;
But soon resumed her tale, and both were glad.
Thus she became, at length, a parlour guest;
And he was happier, though 'twas ne'er confessed:
Rocks, sea, and hills, were here his friends by choice;
—But there is music in the human voice.   40

  So passed their evenings oft; but now and then,
As the mood seized him, he would take a pen;
Wherewith, though slowly, into form was cast
A brief unfinished record of the past.
Whene'er for this her master gave the word,
His faithful Peggy neither spoke nor stirred:
She took her knitting—chose a distant seat,
And there she sat so still, and looked so neat,
'Twas quite a picture;—there was e'en a grace
In the trim border round her placid face.   50

  When Philip wrote he never seemed so well,
—Was startled even if a cinder fell,
And quickly worried;—Peggy saw it all,
And felt the shock herself, if one did fall.
Of knowledge, she had little in her head;
But a nice feeling often serves instead;
And she had more than many better bred.

But now he felt, like men of greater note,
The harmless wish of reading what he wrote:—
60   Not to the world;—no, that he could not bear;
But here sat candid Peggy, in her chair:
And so it was, that he, whose inward woe
Was much too sacred for mankind to know,
He—so refined, mysterious, and so proud,
To a poor servant read his life aloud.
How weak is man, amused with things like these!
Or else, how vain are writers! which you please.

All Peggy heard she deemed exceeding good;
But chiefly praised the parts she understood.
70   At these, by turns, she used to smile or sigh;
And, with full credit, pass the other by:
While he, like men and wits of modern days,
Felt inly flattered by her humble praise.
Yet vigour failed to accomplish the design;
And 'twas but seldom he would add a line:
But when he died—some years ago at Lea,
Old Peggy sent the manuscript to me.

(1825)

Mary Tighe

(1772–1810)

Born in Dublin on 9 October 1772, Mary Tighe was the daughter of Theodosia Tighe Blachford, an aristocrat active in the Irish Methodist movement, who gave her a progressive and unusually good education in Italian, French, and literary classics as well as training in music and drawing. She was never to know her father, the Reverend William Blachford, a wealthy Anglican clergyman and librarian of Marsh's Library and St. Patrick's Library in Dublin, who died only half a year after her birth. Her great uncle was Edward Tighe, whom Lady Morgan called "the finest dramatic critic of the day, from whose judgment there was no appeal." [1]

Mary Tighe became romantically involved with her handsome and highly educated first cousin, Henry Tighe of Woodstock, County Wicklow, a member of the Irish Parliament, representing Inistioge from 1790 to 1801. In her diary for 4 October 1793, just before her marriage to Henry Tighe, she wrote, "My soul draws back in terror and awe at the idea of the event which is to take place to-morrow." [2] For the first eight years of their marriage the couple lived mostly in London, pursuing an intensely social and, later, literary life. Mary Tighe was not happy, however. Her mother described Henry Tighe as a man who "sought only for amusement for himself and his wife at water-drinking places, in England during some Summers and in Dublin during several Winters. . . . I often thought him much to be pitied as he saw that his wife did not love him though he loved her. She always spent her mornings in study and it was from her hours of study with him that she acquired her knowledge of Latin." [3] Mary Tighe faulted herself for finding it "impossible to resist the temptations of being admired and showing the world that I am

1. Sydney, Lady Morgan, *Lady Morgan's Memoirs: Autobiography, Diaries and Correspondence,* 2nd ed., rev., 2 vols. (London, 1863), 1:12–13.

2. Quoted in Patrick Henchy, *The Works of Mary Tighe, Published and Unpublished,* Bibliographical Society of Ireland Publications 6, no. 6 (Dublin, 1957), 6.

3. From Theodosia Tighe's diary, quoted in ibid.

so,"[4] but she eventually forsook the ballroom and the theater for literary pursuits. Between 1801 and 1803, during visits to Rosanna, County Wicklow, Mary Tighe composed *Psyche; or, The Legend of Love,* a dreamlike allegory of Love and the Soul, based on the story of Cupid and Psyche as related in Apuleius's *Golden Ass.* Fifty copies were privately printed in 1805 for friends and family and circulated widely.[5] A six-canto allegory in Spenserian stanzas, *Psyche* avoids archaic diction; its language is rich, and its descriptions are elegant and highly polished. Her good friend Thomas Moore appreciatively wrote "To Mrs. Henry Tighe on Reading her 'Psyche,'" beginning "Tell me the witching tale again."

By 1804 Tighe began showing symptoms of tuberculosis; Moore wrote to his mother on 6 February 1805, "Poor Mrs. Tighe has had a most dreadful attack of fever, and a very serious struggle for life: her surmounting it gives me great hopes that she has got stamina enough for recovery." But in August Moore wrote, "Poor Mrs. T is ordered to the Madeiras, which makes me despair of her, for she *will not* go, and another *winter* will inevitably be her death."[6] Though she would fight tuberculosis for the next five years, she would never again be well.

She did eventually leave London permanently, not for the Madeiras, but for a house on Dominick Street in her native Dublin, where she was visited by Sydney Owenson (later Lady Morgan), Thomas Moore, and many other members of Dublin society. In 1808 she moved to Rosanna, and the following summer she went to Woodstock, County Kilkenny. The last poem she wrote was "On Receiving a Branch of Mezereon, which Flowered at Woodstock. December 1809." As the poem predicts, she never would see May again, for she died on 24 March 1810, at the age of thirty-seven, at Woodstock, in the home of William Tighe, her brother-in-law. According to William Tighe,

> For many days before her death she frequently uttered this mournful lamentation, *Thy rebukes have broken my heart,* and thirty-six hours before her departure, in the presence of her husband, her mother, her brother, and her affectionate attendant, she cheered their desponding souls, by assuring them, with a most animated countenance, that her terrors of death were entirely removed, and that she felt *God was the strength of her heart, and would be her portion for ever, and*

4. From Mary Tighe's unpublished journal, quoted in ibid., 5.

5. Apuleius's story (*Metamorphoses* 4.28–6.24) is itself taken from Hellenic and folk tale sources. The British Library has what appears to be Mary Tighe's own copy of the 1805 first edition of *Psyche,* and the National Library of Ireland has a copy inscribed by Tighe to a friend.

6. *The Letters of Thomas Moore,* ed. Wilfred S. Dowden, 2 vols. (Oxford, 1964), 1:84, 86, 87, 90.

ever, and ever. After this she spoke but little, but all was peace and kindness, patience, and a cheerful desire to depart, observing that death was but one dark speck in our existence; though before this period she always expressed her wish to continue in a state of the extremest suffering, rather than to be released by death.—She evidently retained the perfect use of her faculties to the very last breath, which was without a struggle, or a pang, so as to appear only as if she had fainted.[7]

Mary Tighe was buried in the churchyard of Inistioge, where a monument sometimes attributed to John Flaxman marks her grave.[8]

Tighe left a large part of her literary production unpublished. Her long novel about fashionable life, "Selena," written at about the same time as *Psyche,* is a story of love, intrigue, and vengeance. A villainous father treats his beautiful and gifted but inexperienced young daughter, Selena, as a pawn in a game to torment his brother, an old enemy. Lord Dallamore, one of the main characters, is a precursor to the Byronic hero, a man of habitual indolence: "Left to himself and devoted to pleasure, with every blessing of fortune except the art of enjoyment he became a prey to ennui, a jest to the fools he called his friends while he shared with them his fortune, and yawned through his tedious existence." In the end, Selena finds love, and the story ends with her wedding. The epigraphs are an index to Tighe's wide reading in classical as well as seventeenth- and eighteenth-century literature; they include quotations from Charlotte Smith, Mary Wortley Montagu, Jane Porter, Anna Seward, Joanna Baillie, and Hannah More, as well as Shakespeare, Milton, Dryden, Petrarch, Beaumont, and Fletcher. The work has many gothic elements as well as much melodrama, and it contains some interesting poems by Tighe, but it is not a successful work of fiction. Still unpublished, the 2,451-page manuscript, in five volumes, is now in the National Library of Ireland.[9]

In 1811 William Tighe privately published *Mary, a Series of Reflections During Twenty Years,* containing eighteen poems by Mary Tighe, carefully selected to show religious devotion, along with a first-person narrative of a childhood dream of the Last Judgment, and a brief biographical commentary. William Tighe's holograph note in the copy at Harvard University's Houghton Library remarks that the editor had only "a very few copies of this selection printed

7. Quoted in Mary Tighe, *Mary, A Series of Reflections During Twenty Years* ([Rosanna?], 1811), 29.

8. Henry Fothergill Chorley, *Memorials of Mrs. Hemans, with Illustrations of her Literary Character from her Private Correspondence,* 2 vols. (London, 1836), 2:174.

9. Shelfmark MS 4742–6. Quoted courtesy of the National Library of Ireland.

privately by a friend to be given only to her most partial & serious friends." [10] Mary Tighe's diary was destroyed, but a cousin, Caroline Tighe Hamilton, copied out extracts in her journal. [11]

Thomas Moore commemorated Mary Tighe's death in the lines included in the fourth number of *Irish Melodies,* beginning "I saw thy form in youthful prime." A year after her death, her brother-in-law, William Tighe, edited and published with Longman's her *Psyche, with Other Poems.* The frontispiece to the 1811 edition is an engraving by Caroline Watson from a miniature after a portrait of Tighe by Romney, showing Tighe's hair long and unrestrained. The book was so popular that it went into a third edition that same year, with a fourth edition the following year and a fifth in 1816. It was reprinted in Philadelphia and in Edinburgh in 1812. [12] The *Annual Register,* surveying all the best poetry published in 1811, chose to reprint some stanzas from *Psyche* along with Tighe's shorter lyric, "The Lily." [13]

Psyche, with Other Poems was widely reviewed and highly praised by all the most important periodicals. According to the *British Critic,* "The elegant poem of Psyche was so long circulated in one or two private editions, that to descant upon it as a new performance would be to repeat only what the majority of our readers already know; and to accumulate superfluous praise, where abundance has already been bestowed." Undeterred, the *Quarterly Review,* which later would savage Keats's *Endymion,* said *Psyche* had "few rivals in delicacy of sentiment, style, or versification" and was reminiscent of Ariosto and compared favorably with Spenser's *Fairie Queene* and James Thompson's *Castle of Indolence.* The *Gentleman's Magazine* took strong issue with Tighe's claim in the preface to "deficiency of genius," saying that not only was this untrue but the work displayed "a fancy seldom excelled. . . . the memory of this regretted lady will long be celebrated by the admirers of genuine poetry"; *Psyche,* it said, rendered "as near as possible what Spenser would have written had he lived at present." The *Eclectic Review* preferred Tighe to La Fontaine and Apuleius and believed her poetry "scarcely inferior" to the "pre-eminently distinguished" poets Ariosto, Tasso, and Spenser. The *Critical Review* lamented Tighe's allegorical form but lauded her "delicate, simple and unaffected" style, adding that "she seldom thrills, surprises, or deeply engages her reader, but often casts him into a voluptuous and soothing trance," and that some of her description rivaled "the beautiful vignettes of Ovid in

10. Shelfmark *EC8 .T4484 .811m. Quoted by permission of the Houghton Library, Harvard University.

11. *Anecdotes of our Family Written for my Children,* National Library of Ireland, MS 4810.

12. It was also republished in 1843, 1844, 1853, 1876, and 1889.

13. Pp. 601–4.

his Metamorphoses." The *British Review* devoted twenty-one pages to *Psyche,* finding its spell "potent and its fascination irresistible," its poetry "not only elevated and refined, but pure and correct; chastened by good sense, and directed by a constant reference to the realities of life." Commending its "many passages of exquisite feeling" and its "genuine pathos," it observed that *Psyche* had more "the easy, equable, and majestic flow of one of our southern rivers, than the bold, broken, and vehement stream of a northern torrent; and consequently its effect is rather gradual than instantaneous, it does not command, but wins our admiration. . . . It has a natural elegance, a sustained dignity, and occasionally an uncommon degree of richness."[14] Sir James Mackintosh called the last three cantos exquisitely beautiful and "beyond all doubt the most faultless series of verses ever produced by a woman."[15] Even Leigh Hunt gave the poem grudging praise.

John Keats must have been sixteen when he first encountered Tighe's luxuriously sensuous poetry. "To Some Ladies," a poem in his 1817 volume, mentions Tighe by name; though he disavowed her in a famous letter (31 December 1818), her influence, both in conception and style, even on his most mature poetry, has been well documented.[16] As would be the case with Keats, Tighe's protracted and premature death from a wasting disease contributed to her popular appeal.

Felicia Hemans was one of Tighe's most ardent admirers. In 1828 Hemans published "The Grave of a Poetess," a poem about Tighe included in *Records of Woman: with other Poems,* in which she said of Tighe:

> Thou hast left sorrow in thy song,
> 　A voice not loud, but deep!
> The glorious bowers of earth among,
> 　How often didst thou weep!
>
> Where couldst thou fix, on mortal ground
> 　Thy tender thoughts and high? —
> Now peace the woman's heart hath found,
> 　And joy the poet's eye.

14. *British Critic* 38 (December 1811): 631–32; *Quarterly Review* 5 (May 1811): 471–85; *Gentleman's Magazine* 82 (November 1812): 464–67; *Eclectic Review,* 9 (March 1813): 217–29; *Critical Review,* 4th ser., 1 (June 1812): 606–9; *British Review* 1 (June 1811): 277–98. The book also received favorable notices in the *New Annual Register* 32 (1811): 364 and the *Poetical Register* 8 (1811): 604.

15. Quoted in *DNB.*

16. See esp. Earle Vonard Weller, *Keats and Mary Tighe: The Poems of Mary Tighe with Parallel Passages from the Work of John Keats* (New York, 1928); and Claude Lee Finney, *The Evolution of Keats's Poetry,* 2 vols. (Cambridge, Mass., 1936).

In 1831 Hemans went to Woodstock to see her brother and made a pilgrimage to the grave she had only imagined three years earlier. This experience inspired two more poems: "I Stood Where the Life of Song Lay Low" (published among her *National Lyrics*) and "Written after Visiting a Tomb near Woodstock, in the County of Kilkenny." She also saw the house in which Tighe died, accompanied by Tighe's widower and other members of the family. Having read with great interest a collection of Mary Tighe's early poems in manuscript, Hemans was inspired to write her sonnet "On Records of Immature Genius," published in her *Poetical Remains*.[17] "Lines for the Album at Rosanna," beginning "Where a sweet spirit once in beauty moved," was also inspired by this visit. Hemans once said of Tighe, "Her poetry has always touched me greatly, from a similarity which I imagine I discover between her destiny and my own."[18]

MAJOR WORKS: *Pysche; or, The Legend of Love* (London, 1805); *Psyche, with Other Poems*, ed. William Tighe (London, 1811); *Mary, a Series of Reflections during Twenty Years*, ed. William Tighe ([Rosanna?], 1811); "Selena," 5 vols., MS 4742–6, National Library of Ireland, Dublin.

TEXTS USED: Texts of *Psyche*, canto 2, "On Receiving a Branch of Mezereon Which Flowered at Woodstock," "Written at Scarborough. August, 1799," "Sonnet" ("As one who late hath lost a friend adored") and "Address to My Harp" from *Psyche, with Other Poems* (1811). Text of "Sonnet, March 1791" from *Mary, A Series of Reflections During Twenty Years*. Text of "Sonnet" (" 'Tis past the cruel anguish of suspence") from "Selena."

17. Chorley, *Memorials of Mrs. Hemans*, 2:173–82.
18. Ibid., 176.

Psyche, canto 2

Argument

Introduction—Dangers of the World—Psyche conveyed by Zephyrs awakes once more in the paternal mansion—Envy of her Sisters—They plot her ruin—Inspire her with suspicion and terror—Psyche's return to the Palace of Love—Her disobedience—Love asleep—Psyche's amazement—The flight of Love—Sudden banishment of Psyche from the island of Pleasure—Her lamentations—Comforted by Love—Temple of Venus—Task imposed on Psyche conditional to her reconciliation with Venus—Psyche soothed and attended by Innocence—Psyche wandering as described in the opening of the first Canto.

Oh happy you! who blest with present bliss
See not with fatal prescience future tears,
Nor the dear moment of enjoyment miss
Through gloomy discontent, or sullen fears
Foreboding many a storm for coming years;
Change is the lot of all. Ourselves with scorn
Perhaps shall view what now so fair appears;
And wonder whence the fancied charm was born
Which now with vain despair from our fond grasp is torn!

Vain schemer, think not to prolong thy joy!   10
But cherish while it lasts the heavenly boon;
Expand thy sails! thy little bark shall fly
With the full tide of pleasure! though it soon
May feel the influence of the changeful moon,
It yet is thine! then let not doubts obscure
With cloudy vapours veil thy brilliant noon,
Nor let suspicion's tainted breath impure
Poison the favouring gale which speeds thy course secure!

Oh, Psyche, happy in thine ignorance!
Couldst thou but shun this heart tormenting bane;   20
Be but content, nor daringly advance
To meet the bitter hour of threatened pain;

Pure spotless dove! seek thy safe nest again;
Let true affection shun the public eye,
And quit the busy circle of the vain,
For there the treacherous snares concealed lie;
Oh timely warned escape! to safe retirement fly!

Bright shone the morn! and now its golden ray
Dispelled the slumbers from her radiant eyes,
30   Yet still in dreams her fancy seems to play,
For lo! she sees with rapture and surprise
Full in her view the well-known mansion rise,
And each loved scene of first endearment hails;
The air that first received her infant sighs
With wondring ecstasy she now inhales,
While every trembling nerve soft tenderness assails.

See from the dear pavilion, where she lay,
Breathless she flies with scarce assured feet,
Swift through the garden wings her eager way,
40   Her mourning parents ravished eyes to greet
With loveliest apparition strange and sweet:
Their days of anguish all o'erpaid they deem
By one blest hour of ecstasy so great:
Yet doubtingly they gaze, and anxious seem
To ask their raptured souls, "Oh, is this all a dream?"

The wondrous tale attentively they hear,
Repeated oft in broken words of joy,
She in their arms embraced, while every ear
Hangs on their Psyche's lips, and earnestly
50   On her is fixed each wonder speaking eye;
Till the sad hour arrives which bids them part,
And twilight darkens o'er the ruddy sky;
Divinely urged they let their child depart,
Pressed with a fond embrace to each adoring heart.

Trusting that wedded to a spouse divine
Secure is now their daughter's happiness,
They half contentedly their child resign,
Check the complaint, the rising sigh suppress,

And wipe the silent drops of bitterness.
Nor must she her departure more delay,   60
But bids them now their weeping Psyche bless;
Then back to the pavilion bends her way
Ere in the fading west quite sinks expiring day.

But, while her parents listen with delight,
Her sisters hearts the Furies agitate:
They look with envy on a lot so bright,
And all the honours of her splendid fate,
Scorning the meanness of their humbler state;
And how they best her ruin may devise
With hidden rancour much they meditate,   70
Yet still they bear themselves in artful guise,
While 'mid the feigned caress, concealed the venom lies.

By malice urged, by ruthless envy stung,
With secret haste to seize their prey they flew,
Around her neck as in despair they clung;
Her soft complying nature well they knew,
And trusted by delaying to undo;
But when they found her resolute to go,
Their well laid stratagem they then pursue,
And, while they bid their treacherous sorrows flow,   80
Thus fright her simple heart with images of woe.

"Oh, hapless Psyche! thoughtless of thy doom!
"Yet hear thy sisters who have wept for thee,
"Since first a victim to thy living tomb,
"Obedient to the oracle's decree,
"Constrained we left thee to thy destiny.
"Since then no comfort could our woes abate;
"While thou wert lulled in false security
"We learned the secret horrors of thy fate,
"And heard prophetic lips thy future ills relate.   90

"Yet fearing never to behold thee more,
"Our filial care would fain the truth conceal;
"But from the sages cell this ring we bore,
"With power each latent magic to reveal:

"Some hope from hence our anxious bosoms feel
"That we from ruin may our Psyche save,
"Since Heaven propitious to our pious zeal,
"Thee to our frequent prayers in pity gave,
"That warned thou yet mayest shun thy sad untimely grave.

100   "Oh! how shall we declare the fatal truth?
"How wound thy tender bosom with alarms?
"Tell how the graces of thy blooming youth,
"Thy more than mortal, all-adored charms
"Have lain enamoured in a sorcerer's arms?
"Oh, Psyche! seize on this decisive hour,
"Escape the mischief of impending harms!
"Return no more to that enchanted bower,
"Fly the magician's arts, and dread his cruel power.

"If, yet reluctant to forego thy love,
110   "Thy furtive joys and solitary state,
"Our fond officious care thy doubts reprove,
"At least let some precaution guard thy fate,
"Nor may our warning love be prized too late;
"This night thyself thou mayst convince thine eyes,
"Hide but a lamp, and cautiously await
"Till in deep slumber thy magician lies,
"This ring shall then disclose his foul deformities.

"That monster by the oracle foretold,
"Whose cursed spells both gods and men must fear,
120   "In his own image thou shalt then behold,
"And shuddering hate what now is prized so dear;
"Yet fly not then, though loathsome he appear,
"But let this dagger to his breast strike deep;
"Thy coward terrors then thou must not hear,
"For if with life he rouses from that sleep
"Nought then for thee remains, and we must hopeless weep."

Oh! have you seen, when in the northern sky
The transient flame of lambent lightning plays,
In quick succession lucid streamers fly,
130   Now flashing roseate, and now milky rays,

While struck with awe the astonished rustics gaze?
Thus o'er her cheek the fleeting signals move,
Now pale with fear, now glowing with the blaze
Of much indignant, still confiding love,
Now horror's lurid hue with shame's deep blushes strove.

On her cold, passive hand the ring they place,
And hide the dagger in her folding vest;
Pleased the effects of their dire arts to trace
In the mute agony that swells her breast,
Already in her future ruin blest: 140
Conscious that now their poor deluded prey
Should never taste again delight or rest,
But sickening in suspicion's gloom decay,
Or urged by terrors rash their treacherous will obey.

While yet irresolute with sad surprise,
Mid doubt and love she stands in strange suspense,
Lo! gliding from her sisters wondering eyes
Returning Zephyrs gently bear her thence;
Lost all her hopes, her joys, her confidence,
Back to the earth her mournful eyes she threw,   150
As if imploring pity and defence;
While bathed in tears her golden tresses flew,
As in the breeze dispersed they caught the precious dew.

Illumined bright now shines the splendid dome,
Melodious accents her arrival hail:
But not the torches' blaze can chase the gloom,
And all the soothing powers of music fail;
Trembling she seeks her couch with horror pale,
But first a lamp conceals in secret shade,
While unknown terrors all her soul assail.   160
Thus half their treacherous counsel is obeyed,
For still her gentle soul abhors the murderous blade.

And now, with softest whispers of delight,
Love welcomes Psyche still more fondly dear;
Not unobserved, though hid in deepest night,
The silent anguish of her secret fear.

He thinks that tenderness excites the tear
By the late image of her parents' grief,
And half offended seeks in vain to cheer,
170   Yet, while he speaks, her sorrows feel relief,
Too soon more keen to sting from this suspension brief!

Allowed to settle on celestial eyes
Soft Sleep exulting now exerts his sway,
From Psyche's anxious pillow gladly flies
To veil those orbs, whose pure and lambent ray
The powers of heaven submissively obey.
Trembling and breathless then she softly rose
And seized the lamp, where it obscurely lay,
With hand too rashly daring to disclose
180   The sacred veil which hung mysterious o'er her woes.

Twice, as with agitated step she went,
The lamp expiring shone with doubtful gleam,
As though it warned her from her rash intent:
And twice she paused, and on its trembling beam
Gazed with suspended breath, while voices seem
With murmuring sound along the roof to sigh;
As one just waking from a troublous dream,
With palpitating heart and straining eye,
Still fixed with fear remains, still thinks the danger nigh.

190   Oh, daring Muse! wilt thou indeed essay
To paint the wonders which that lamp could shew?
And canst thou hope in living words to say
The dazzling glories of that heavenly view?
Ah! well I ween, that if with pencil true
That splendid vision could be well exprest,
The fearful awe imprudent Psyche knew
Would seize with rapture every wondering breast,
When Love's all potent charms divinely stood confest.

All imperceptible to human touch,
200   His wings display celestial essence light,
The clear effulgence of the blaze is such,
The brilliant plumage shines so heavenly bright

That mortal eyes turn dazzled from the sight;
A youth he seems in manhood's freshest years;
Round his fair neck, as clinging with delight,
Each golden curl resplendently appears,
Or shades his darker brow, which grace majestic wears.

Or o'er his guileless front the ringlets bright
Their rays of sunny lustre seem to throw,
That front than polished ivory more white!   210
His blooming cheeks with deeper blushes glow
Than roses scattered o'er a bed of snow:
While on his lips, distilled in balmy dews,
(Those lips divine that even in silence know
The heart to touch) persuasion to infuse
Still hangs a rosy charm that never vainly sues.

The friendly curtain of indulgent sleep
Disclosed not yet his eyes' resistless sway,
But from their silky veil there seemed to peep
Some brilliant glances with a softened ray,   220
Which o'er his features exquisitely play,
And all his polished limbs suffuse with light.
Thus through some narrow space the azure day
Sudden its cheerful rays diffusing bright,
Wide darts its lucid beams, to gild the brow of night.

His fatal arrows and celestial bow
Beside the couch were negligently thrown,
Nor needs the god his dazzling arms, to show
His glorious birth, such beauty round him shone
As sure could spring from Beauty's self alone;   230
The gloom which glowed o'er all of soft desire,
Could well proclaim him Beauty's cherished son;
And Beauty's self will oft these charms admire,
And steal his witching smile, his glance's living fire.

Speechless with awe, in transport strangely lost
Long Psyche stood with fixed adoring eye;
Her limbs immoveable, her senses tost
Between amazement, fear, and ecstasy,

She hangs enamoured o'er the Deity.
240   Till from her trembling hand extinguished falls
The fatal lamp—He starts—and suddenly
Tremendous thunders echo through the halls,
While ruin's hideous crash bursts o'er the affrighted walls.

Dread horror seizes on her sinking heart,
A mortal chillness shudders at her breast,
Her soul shrinks fainting from death's icy dart,
The groan scarce uttered dies but half exprest,
And down she sinks in deadly swoon opprest:
But when at length, awaking from her trance,
250   The terrors of her fate stand all confest,
In vain she casts around her timid glance,
The rudely frowning scenes her former joys enhance.

No traces of those joys, alas, remain!
A desert solitude alone appears.
No verdant shade relieves the sandy plain,
The wide spread waste no gentle fountain cheers,
One barren face the dreary prospect wears;
Nought through the vast horizon meets her eye
To calm the dismal tumult of her fears,
260   No trace of human habitation nigh,
A sandy wild beneath, above a threatening sky.

The mists of morn yet chill the gloomy air,
And heavily obscure the clouded skies;
In the mute anguish of a fixed despair
Still on the ground immoveable she lies;
At length, with lifted hands and streaming eyes,
Her mournful prayers invoke offended Love,
"Oh, let me hear thy voice once more," she cries,
"In death at least thy pity let me move,
270   "And death, if but forgiven, a kind relief will prove.

"For what can life to thy lost Psyche give,
"What can it offer but a gloomy void?
"Why thus abandoned should I wish to live?
"To mourn the pleasure which I once enjoyed,

"The bliss my own rash folly hath destroyed;
"Of all my soul most prized, or held most dear,
"Nought but the sad remembrance doth abide,
"And late repentance of my impious fear;
"Remorse and vain regret what living soul can bear!

"Oh, art thou then indeed for ever gone!   280
"And art thou heedless of thy Psyche's woe!
"From these fond arms for ever art thou flown,
"And unregarded must my sorrows flow!
"Ah! why too happy did I ever know
"The rapturous charms thy tenderness inspires?
"Ah! why did thy affections stoop so low?
"Why kindle in a mortal breast such fires,
"Or with celestial love inflame such rash desires?

"Abandoned thus for ever by thy love,
"No greater punishment I now can bear,   290
"From fate no farther malice can I prove;
"Not all the horrors of this desert drear,
"Nor death itself can now excite a fear;
"The peopled earth a solitude as vast
"To this despairing heart would now appear;
"Here then, my transient joys for ever past,
"Let thine expiring bride thy pardon gain at last!"

Now prostrate on the bare unfriendly ground,
She waits her doom in silent agony;
When lo! the well known soft celestial sound   300
She hears once more with breathless ecstasy,
"Oh! yet too dearly loved! Lost Psyche! Why
"With cruel fate wouldst thou unite thy power,
"And force me thus thine arms adored to fly?
"Yet cheer thy drooping soul, some happier hour
"Thy banished steps may lead back to thy lover's bower.

"Though angry Venus we no more can shun,
"Appease that anger and I yet am thine!
"Lo! where her temple glitters to the sun;
"With humble penitence approach her shrine,   310

"Perhaps to pity she may yet incline;
"But should her cruel wrath these hopes deceive,
"And thou, alas! must never more be mine,
"Yet shall thy lover ne'er his Psyche leave,
"But, if the fates allow, unseen thy woes relieve.

"Stronger than I, they now forbid my stay;
"Psyche beloved, adieu!" Scarce can she hear
The last faint words, which gently melt away;
And now more faint the dying sounds appear,
320   Borne to a distance from her longing ear;
Yet still attentively she stands unmoved,
To catch those accents which her soul could cheer,
That soothing voice which had so sweetly proved
That still his tender heart offending Psyche loved!

And now the joyous sun had cleared the sky,
The mist dispelled revealed the splendid fane;
A palmy grove majestically high
Screens the fair building from the desert plain;
Of alabaster white and free from stain
330   Mid the tall trees the tapering columns rose;
Thither, with fainting steps, and weary pain,
Obedient to the voice at length she goes,
And at the threshold seeks protection and repose.

Round the soft scene immortal roses bloom,
While lucid myrtles in the breezes play;
No savage beast did ever yet presume
With foot impure within the grove to stray,
And far from hence flies every bird of prey;
Thus, mid the sandy Garamantian wild,
340   When Macedonia's lord pursued his way,
The sacred temple of great Ammon smiled,
And green encircling shades the long fatigue beguiled:

326 fane] Temple.

339 Garamantian wild] Garamantes were the southernmost people known to the ancients
in North Africa (modern Libya). Their capital city was Garamia. Herodotus mentions them in
The Histories as a reclusive, pacifist people (4.183).

341 The sacred temple of great Ammon smiled] Ammon was a god of ancient Egypt some-

With awe that fearfully her doom awaits
Still at the portal Psyche timid lies,
When lo! advancing from the hallowed gates
Trembling she views with reverential eyes
An aged priest. A myrtle bough supplies
A wand, and roses bind his snowy brows:
"Bear hence thy feet profane (he sternly cries)
"Thy longer stay the goddess disallows,   350
"Fly, nor her fiercer wrath too daringly arouse!"

His pure white robe imploringly she held,
And, bathed in tears, embraced his sacred knees;
Her mournful charms relenting he beheld,
And melting pity in his eye she sees;
"Hope not (he cries) the goddess to appease,
"Retire at awful distance from her shrine,
"But seek the refuge of those sheltering trees,
"And now thy soul with humble awe incline
"To hear her sacred will, and mark the words divine."   360

"Presumptuous Psyche! whose aspiring soul
"The God of Love has dared to arrogate;
"Rival of Venus! whose supreme control
"Is now asserted by all ruling fate,
"No suppliant tears her vengeance shall abate
"Till thou hast raised an altar to her power,
"Where perfect happiness, in lonely state,
"Has fixed her temple in secluded bower,
"By foot impure of man untrodden to this hour!

"And on the altar must thou place an urn   370
"Filled from immortal Beauty's sacred spring,
"Which foul deformity to grace can turn,
"And back to fond affection's eyes can bring
"The charms which fleeting fled on transient wing;
"Snatched from the rugged steep where first they rise,

---

times represented as a ram with large curving horns and sometimes as a ram-headed man. His
chief temple, with a famous oracle, stood in an oasis in the Libyan desert, a twelve-day journey
from Memphis. The Greeks identified Ammon with Zeus.

"Dark rocks their crystal source o'ershadowing,
"Let their clear water sparkle to the skies
"Where cloudless lustre beams which happiness supplies!

"To Venus thus for ever reconciled,
380   "(This one atonement all her wrath disarms,)
"From thy loved Cupid then no more exiled
"There shalt thou, free from sorrow and alarms,
"Enjoy for ever his celestial charms.
"But never shalt thou taste a pure repose,
"Nor ever meet thy lover's circling arms,
"Till, all subdued that shall thy steps oppose,
"Thy perils there shall end, escaped from all thy foes."

With meek submissive woe she heard her doom,
Nor to the holy minister replied;
390   But in the myrtle grove's mysterious gloom
She silently retired her grief to hide.
Hopeless to tread the waste without a guide,
All unrefreshed and faint from toil she lies:
When lo! her present wants are all supplied,
Sent by the hand of Love a turtle flies,
And sets delicious food before her wondering eyes.

Cheered by the favouring omen, softer tears
Relieve her bosom from its cruel weight:
She blames the sad despondence of her fears,
400   When still protected by a power so great,
His tenderness her toils will mitigate.
Then with renewed strength at length she goes,
Hoping to find some skilled in secret fate,
Some learned sage who haply might disclose
Where lay that blissful bower the end of all her woes.

And as she went, behold, with hovering flight
The dove preceded still her doubtful way;
Its spotless plumage of the purest white,
Which shone resplendent in the blaze of day,
410   Could even in darkest gloom a light display;
Of heavenly birth, when first to mortals given

Named Innocence. But ah! too short its stay;
By ravenous birds it fearfully was driven
Back to reside with Love, a denizen of heaven.

Now through the trackless wild, o'er many a mile
The messenger of Cupid led the fair,
And cheered with hope her solitary toil,
Till now a brighter face the prospects wear,
Past are the sandy wastes and deserts bare,
And many a verdant hill, and grassy dale,   420
And trace, that mortal culture might declare,
And many a wild wood dark, and joyous vale
Appeared her soul to sooth, could soothing scenes avail.

But other fears her timid soul distress,
Mid strangers unprotected and alone,
The desert wilderness alarmed her less
Than cities, thus unfriended and unknown;
But where the path was all by moss o'ergrown,
There still she chose her solitary way,
Where'er her faithful Dove before had flown   430
Fearful of nought she might securely stray,
For still his care supplied the wants of every day.

And still she entered every sacred grove
And homage paid to each divinity,
But chief the altar of almighty Love
Weeping embraced with fond imploring eye;
To every oracle her hopes apply,
Instructions for her dangerous path to gain:
Exclaiming oft, with a desponding sigh,
"Ah! how through all such dangers, toil and pain,   440
"Shall Psyche's helpless steps their object e'er attain!"

And now remote from every peopled town
One sultry day a cooling bower she found:
There, as I whilom sung, she laid her down,
Where rich profusion of gay flowers around

444 whilom] At times.

Had decked with artless shew the sloping ground;
There the wild rose and modest violet grow,
There all thy charms, Narcissus! still abound:
There wrapt in verdure fragrant lilies blow,
450   Lilies that love the vale, and hide their bells of snow.

Thy flowers, Adonis! bright vermilion shew;
Still for his love the yellow Crocus pines;
There, while indignant blushes seem to glow,
Beloved by Phœbus his Acanthus shines;
Reseda still her drooping head reclines
With faithful homage to his golden rays,
And, though mid clouds their lustre he resigns,
An image of the constant heart displays,
While silent still she turns her fond pursuing gaze.

460   And every sweet that Spring with fairy hands
Scatters in thy green path, enchanting May!
And every flowering shrub there clustering stands
As though they wooed her to a short delay,
Yielding a charm to sooth her weary way;
Soft was the tufted moss, and sweet the breeze,
With lulling sound the murmuring waters play,
With lulling sound from all the rustling trees
The fragrant gale invites to cool refreshing ease.

---

448 Narcissus] Handsome son of the river god Cephissus. Nemesis punished him for rejecting the love of Echo by inspiring him with a love for his own reflection (see Ovid's *Metamorphoses* 3.341–510). Narcissus pined away and was turned into a flower of the same name, a symbol of death and fragility.

451 Adonis] Son of Cinyras by his daughter Smyrna, Adonis was a handsome young man beloved by Aphrodite. He died of a wound inflicted by a boar during a chase. The flower anemone sprang from his blood.

452 Crocus] A youth who pined away because he was unable to obtain the object of his affections, the nymph Smilax. He was changed into the crocus flower, or saffron. Smilax was herself metamorphosed into a flower, the smilax, or bindweed (Ovid, *Metamorphoses,* 4.283).

454 Phœbus] Apollo, god of poetry and music.

454 Acanthus] Genus of about twenty species of plants having leaves with sharp points, celebrated by the ancient Greeks, who carved representations of the leaves on the capitals of Corinthian columns.

455 Reseda] Extensive genus of some five dozen plants native to Europe and the Mediterranean.

There as she sought repose, her sorrowing heart
Recalled her absent love with bitter sighs;   470
Regret had deeply fixed the poisoned dart,
Which ever rankling in her bosom lies;
In vain she seeks to close her weary eyes,
Those eyes still swim incessantly in tears,
Hope in her cheerless bosom fading dies,
Distracted by a thousand cruel fears,
While banished from his love for ever she appears.

Oh! thou best comforter of that sad heart
Whom fortune's spite assails; come, gentle Sleep,
The weary mourner sooth! for well the art   480
Thou knowest in soft forgetfulness to steep
The eyes which sorrow taught to watch and weep;
Let blissful visions now her spirits cheer,
Or lull her cares to peace in slumbers deep,
Till from fatigue refreshed and anxious fear
Hope like the morning star once more shall re-appear.

(1805)

On Receiving a Branch of Mezereon Which Flowered at Woodstock. December, 1809

Odours of Spring, my sense ye charm
   With fragrance premature;
And, mid these days of dark alarm,
   Almost to hope allure.
Methinks with purpose soft ye come
   To tell of brighter hours,
Of May's blue skies, abundant bloom,
   Her sunny gales and showers.

Alas! for me shall May in vain
   The powers of life restore;   10
These eyes that weep and watch in pain
   Shall see her charms no more.

No, no, this anguish cannot last!
   Beloved friends, adieu!
The bitterness of death were past,
   Could I resign but you.

But oh! in every mortal pang
   That rends my soul from life,
That soul, which seems on you to hang
20   Through each convulsive strife,
Even now, with agonizing grasp
   Of terror and regret,
To all in life its love would clasp
   Clings close and closer yet.

Yet why, immortal, vital spark!
   Thus mortally opprest?
Look up, my soul, through prospects dark,
   And bid thy terrors rest;
Forget, forego thy earthly part,
30   Thine heavenly being trust:—
Ah, vain attempt! my coward heart
   Still shuddering clings to dust.

Oh ye! who sooth the pangs of death
   With love's own patient care,
Still, still retain this fleeting breath,
   Still pour the fervent prayer:—
And ye, whose smile must greet my eye
   No more, nor voice my ear,
Who breathe for me the tender sigh,
40   And shed the pitying tear,

Whose kindness (though far far removed)
   My grateful thoughts perceive,
Pride of my life, esteemed, beloved,
   My last sad claim receive!
Oh! do not quite your friend forget,
   Forget alone her faults;
And speak of her with fond regret
   Who asks your lingering thoughts.
                (1811)

Written at Scarborough. August, 1799

As musing pensive in my silent home
  I hear far off the sullen ocean's roar,
  Where the rude wave just sweeps the level shore,
Or bursts upon the rocks with whitening foam,
I think upon the scenes my life has known;
  On days of sorrow, and some hours of joy;
  Both which alike time could so soon destroy!
And now they seem a busy dream alone;
While on the earth exists no single trace
  Of all that shook my agitated soul,   10
  As on the beach new waves for ever roll
And fill their past forgotten brother's place:
  But I, like the worn sand, exposed remain
  To each new storm which frets the angry main.

                       (1811)

Sonnet

As one who late hath lost a friend adored,
  Clings with sick pleasure to the faintest trace
  Resemblance offers in another's face,
Or sadly gazing on that form deplored,
Would clasp the silent canvas to his breast:
  So muse I on the good I have enjoyed,
  The wretched victim of my hopes destroyed;
On images of peace I fondly rest,
Or in the page, where weeping fancy mourns,
  I love to dwell upon each tender line,   10
  And think the bliss once tasted still is mine;
While cheated memory to the past returns,
  And, from the present leads my shivering heart
  Back to those scenes from which it wept to part.

                       (1811)

Address to My Harp

Oh, my loved Harp! companion dear!
   Sweet soother of my secret grief,
No more thy sounds my soul must cheer,
   No more afford a soft relief.

When anxious cares my heart oppressed,
   When doubts distracting tore my soul,
The pains which heaved my swelling breast
   Thy gentle sway could oft control.

Each well remembered, practised strain,
10   The cheerful dance, the tender song,
Recalled with pensive, pleasing pain
   Some image loved and cherished long.

Where joy sat smiling o'er my fate,
   And marked each bright and happy day,
When partial friends around me sat,
   And taught my lips the simple lay;

And when by disappointment grieved
   I saw some darling hope o'erthrown,
Thou hast my secret pain relieved;
20   O'er thee I wept, unseen, alone.

Oh! must I leave thee, must we part,
   Dear partner of my happiest days?
I may forget thy much-loved art,
   Unused thy melody to raise,

But ne'er can memory cease to love
   Those scenes where I thy charms have felt,
Though I no more thy power may prove,
   Which taught my softened heart to melt.

Forced to forego with thee this spot,
30   Endeared by many a tender tie,

When rosy pleasure blessed my lot,
 And sparkled in my cheated eye.

Yet still thy strings, in Fancy's ear,
 With soothing melody shall play;
Thy silver sounds I oft shall hear,
 To pensive gloom a silent prey.
       (1811)

Sonnet, March 1791

As the frail bark, long tossed by stormy winds,
Wearied and scattered a calm haven finds,
So from a heavy load of cares set free,
At length, O Lord! my soul returns to thee!
Oh sun of light illume my doubtful way,
And let me from thy paths no longer stray,
Now hearken kindly to my mournful cries,
From the dark world now turn to thee mine eyes:
Oh food of sweetness that can never cloy,
Banish my sorrows with thine holy joy!   10
Thou gentle stream of soft consoling peace
O'erflow this heart, and all my tears shall cease,
Cleanse my repenting soul at mercy's shrine,
And then, adorn her with thy grace divine.
       (1811)

Sonnet

'Tis past the cruel anguish of suspence
Shall vex my soul no more—I know him lost
For ever lost to me—and all that most
On earth I valued, bought with dear expense
Of peaceful nights, and days of innocence
Lies withered in my grasp—Oh idle cost
Of squandered hours! oh vows of anguish tost
To the wild winds, that mocked the eloquence
Of grief indignant, yet constrained to speak!
Now all is past, the desolating storm
No longer may the bowers of bliss deform
Its furious malice has no more to seek
Each high aspiring hope lies all laid low
Sweep on ye powerless winds, o'er your fall'n trophies blow!—

(wr. c. 1805)

Charlotte Elizabeth Tonna

(1790–1846)

Influential social critic, evangelical writer, editor, social-realist novelist, poet, and author of children's stories, Charlotte Elizabeth Tonna described the squalor of urban slums, the exploitation of child laborers, and the dehumanization of the factories; her work anticipates Dickens and contributed to Parliament's passage of the 1844 Factory Bill. Harriet Beecher Stowe said of Tonna's *Personal Recollections* (1841), "We know of no piece of autobiography in the English language which can compare with this in richness of feeling and description, and power of exciting interest."[1]

Born in Norwich on 1 October 1790, the only daughter of the Reverend Michael Browne, minor canon of the cathedral and rector of St. Giles, Tonna suffered several months of temporary but total blindness before she was six. Her home remained, however, a stimulating environment. "My father," she recalled,

> delighted in the society of literary men: and he was himself of a turn so argumentative, so overflowing with rich conversation, so decided in his political views, so alive to passing events, so devotedly and so proudly the Englishman, that with such associates as he gathered about him at his own fireside, I don't see how the little blind girl, whose face was ever turned up towards the unseen speaker, and whose mind opened to every passing remark, could avoid becoming a thinker, a reasoner, a tory and a patriot.[2]

Once her sight returned, her lively imagination fed itself on fairy tales, Shakespeare, the Bible, and martyrs' stories. Her health was seriously impaired, however, by the mercury used to treat her blindness, and at age ten she lost her hearing completely and permanently. Now unable to engage in conversation or to hear the music she loved, she voraciously read British

---

1. H. B. Stowe, introduction to *The Works of Charlotte Elizabeth*, 3 vols. (New York, 1844–45), 1:v.

2. *Personal Recollections* (New York, 1843), 18.

poetry. For the sake of Charlotte Elizabeth's health, the family moved to the country outside Norwich, where she lived an active and unusually free out-door life. She and her father shared a love for politics and literature, and she came to look principally to him for companionship. Thus, his death from a stroke was a severe blow.[3] Although the family had a small annuity, it was not enough, and Charlotte Elizabeth decided to be the provider by writing fiction. She later observed, "I should probably have succeeded very well, but it pleased God to save me from this snare."[4]

Saved perhaps from one snare, she fell into another. On a visit to London she met Captain George Phelan, and within six months they were married. She followed him and his regiment to Nova Scotia in the summer of 1816, en-raptured on the voyage over by what she termed "the terrific grandeur" of the sea.[5] Tonna spent two years in Nova Scotia, delighted by the wilderness and befriending the indigenous people. Her neighbors in Annapolis Royal saw Captain Phelan not only translating the Sunday sermon into sign language for his wife but also on occasion beating her.

The couple left Nova Scotia on 9 July 1818. By early 1819 Tonna had fol-lowed her husband to his native Ireland, where she fell in love with the Irish people and conceived her lifelong hatred for the Roman Catholic Church. She spent most of her five years in Ireland in what she was to call "perfect seclusion, and uninterrupted solitude," neglected by her husband, who was usually off in Dublin, and by her neighbors.[6] It was here that she experi-enced a religious conversion and also began her literary career by writing a tract for the Dublin Tract Society. She chose not to follow her husband, who was sent abroad, and instead settled in Kilkenny with her mother. There she began earning a living for them both by writing penny and two-penny tracts and tales for children. She produced many didactic children's books as well as a long poem, *Osric: A Missionary Tale* ([1825?]). She adopted one of the four deaf children she taught, John, or "Jack," Britt, who lived with her until his death in 1831, and whose story she tells in *The Happy Mute: or, The Dumb Child's Appeal* (bef. 1833). After more than five years in Ireland, Tonna returned to England, settling with Jack near Bristol and enduring what she termed the "incipient derangement" of her husband.[7] There she met Hannah More, who encouraged her in her instruction of the deaf and to whom she dedicated *Osric*.

3. Ibid., 77.
4. Ibid., 78.
5. *Personal Recollections* (London, 1841), 82.
6. *Personal Recollections* (1843), 113.
7. *Personal Recollections* (1841), 208.

In 1826 Tonna went to live with her brother John and his family in Sand-hurst, where she was happy and productive, turning out several dozen small books, tracts, and articles in the course of only a few years. To shield her earnings from her husband's claims, she published under the pen name Char-lotte Elizabeth. In 1828 her brother drowned, and she adopted his two sons, the eldest only five years old. She became a public figure in 1831, when she founded the Irish Episcopal Church in the London slum of St. Giles and launched there a "campaign against starvation and popery."[8] In 1836 she be-came the sole editor of the *Christian Lady's Magazine,* in whose pages she graphically described the squalor and filth of St. Giles. Her magazine clothed instruction in popular entertainment and, for the next ten years, took up in editorials some of the most pressing political issues of the day—the treat-ment of factory workers, the degradation of prostitutes, the indifference of both the church and the rich toward the poor. She advocated the official recognition of the Irish language (enlisting Robert Southey in her cause) and the repatriation of Jews to Israel, in 1844 even presenting an appeal to Em-peror Nicholas on behalf of his Jewish subjects. Her anti-Catholic bigotry was inspired by terrorist activities she witnessed in Ireland during the Roman Catholic agitations, when Protestants were threatened with death unless they converted. She wrote two of the best-known songs for the Orange cause, "The Maiden City" and "No Surrender." By the early 1840s Tonna's books were appearing in New York in the same year that they were published in London. Still editing the *Christian Lady's Magazine,* she took up the editor-ship of the *Protestant Magazine,* the official organ of the Protestant Association from July 1841 to December 1844.

George Phelan died in Dublin in 1837. In 1840 Tonna wrote a spiritual autobiography, *Personal Recollections,* published the following year, filled with humor, candor, and riveting description and considered by many to be her finest work. *Helen Fleetwood,* a novel about children in the cotton mills, had been earlier serialized but came out in book form in 1841. *Judah's Lion* (1843), a religious novel, was Tonna's most popular book; it was translated into French, Dutch, and Swedish and reprinted many times on both sides of the Atlantic through the turn of the century. *The Wrongs of Woman* (1843–44) is hardly a feminist work, but it does portray the exploitation of women and children in manufacturing and even depicts a lacemaker giving her new-born infant opiates so that she can work undisturbed. Tonna published her most influential work anonymously. *The Perils of the Nation. An Appeal to the Legislature, the Clergy, and the Higher and Middle Classes* (1843) takes issue with

8. Ibid., 336.

Harriet Martineau and Malthus and looks at working conditions in manufacturing, mining, and agriculture, advocating national education, covered
sewers, clean water, and paved streets; it smoothed the way in Parliament for
the Ten Hour Bill and the Health of Towns Bill.

In 1841, when Tonna was in her early fifties, she married fellow millenarian
Lewis Hippolytus Joseph Tonna, twenty-two years her junior, secretary to
the United Service Institution. M. W. Dodd published *The Works of Charlotte
Elizabeth* in New York in 1844 and 1845, with an appreciative introduction by
Harriet Beecher Stowe. Tonna died of cancer in Ramsgate on 13 July 1846.
She had raised three children, provided for her aged mother, and authored
altogether some 130 titles.

MAJOR WORKS: *The Shepherd Boy, and the Deluge* (London, 1823); *Osric: A Missionary Tale; with the Garden, and Other Poems* (Dublin, [1825?]); *Izram, a Mexican Tale;
and Other Poems* (London, 1826); *The Happy Mute: or, The Dumb Child's Appeal* (bef.
1833; 2nd ed., rev., London, 1833); *Helen Fleetwood* (London, 1841); *Personal Recollections*
(London, 1841); *Judah's Lion* (London, 1843); *The Wrongs of Woman,* 4 pts. (London,
1843); *The Perils of the Nation; an Appeal to the Legislature, the Clergy and the Higher and
Middle Classes* (London, 1843); *Works of Charlotte Elizabeth,* with an introduction by
H. B. Stowe, 3 vols. (New York, 1844–45).

TEXTS USED: The first twenty-six lines from *Osric, A Missionary Tale* from *The Works
of Charlotte Elizabeth.*

from *Osric, A Missionary Tale,* canto 1

'Tis eve:—ascending high, the ocean storm
Spreads in dark volumes his portentous form;
His hollow breezes, bursting from the clouds,
Distend the sail, and whistle through the shrouds.
Roused by the note of elemental strife,
The swelling waters tremble into life;
Lo! through the tumult of the dashing spray,
The storm beat vessel labours on her way.
With bending mast, rent sail, and straining sides,
High on the foaming precipice she rides,
Then reeling onward with descending prow,

10

In giddy sweep, glides to the gulf below:
Her fragile form conflicting billows rock,
Her timbers echo to the frequent shock,
While bursting o'er the deck, each roaring wave
Bears some new victim to a hideous grave.
The voice of thunder rides upon the blast,
And the blue death-fire plays around the mast:
Beneath the pennon of a riven sail,
That vessel drives, abandoned to the gale.   20
Above, more darkly frowns the brow of night,
Beneath, the waters glow more fiercely bright:
Ploughing a track of mingled foam and fire,
Fast flies the ship before the tempest's ire,
While reeling to and fro the hapless crew
Gaze on the wild abyss, and shudder at the view.

(1825 or 1826)

19 pennon] Long, narrow flag or streamer.

Elizabeth Trefusis

(1763–1808)

Elizabeth Trefusis was the daughter of Anne St. John and Robert Cotton Trefusis of Trefusis, Cornwall; her brother was Robert George William, seventeenth baron Clinton (1791). Trefusis lost her mother before 1778, when her father remarried. Known as Ella, she grew up in privileged surroundings, and while still young she wrote two novels, "Claribell" and "Eudora," and a pastoral romance, "The Cousins." Little is known about her childhood. In adulthood her literary friends included Anna Seward, Hester Lynch Piozzi, and Helen Maria Williams. Trefusis fell in love with Major Barry, son of the Irish Shakespearean actor, but her family forbade the match. She lived for a time at Bletsoe, Bedfordshire, and later in James Street, Westminster. Like Percy Bysshe Shelley, she annoyed family and friends by her tendency to give away whatever she had to those in need; she was partial to struggling poets. Her close friend the writer and editor William Gifford encouraged her to publish her verse, and in 1808, when she brought out her two-volume *Poems and Tales,* she dedicated the book to him.

In part because of Gifford's championing but also probably because of the provocative subject matter (many of her poems sympathetically portray women injured by cold-hearted men), the book was widely reviewed. The *Critical Review,* dissenting from the book's generally favorable reception, recommended "to this fair lady the making of pastry, in preference to the making of poetry." And the *Eclectic Review* recognized that she possessed "powers of fancy, an elegant taste in expression, and a facility of versification" but deplored her "wretched waste of mental resources," complaining, "Miss Trefusis has only aspired to flutter in idle compliments, and sigh in amatory canzonets."[1]

But the *British Critic* extolled the "refined taste, extraordinary sensibility, and superior elegance" of her work and observed that some of the best pas-

---

1. *Critical Review,* 3rd ser., 14 (August 1808): 443; *Eclectic Review* 4 (September 1808): 846.

786

sages "may, in tenderness and delicacy, vie with the very best things of the kind in our language. Many of the songs also are exquisitely delicate and truly poetical." It promised that those "who love genuine poetry, produced by the most unsophisticated sensibility, where every line speaks feeling, truth, and nature, will have a delicious feast." The critic for the *Antijacobin Review* found "no gaudy colouring, nothing exaggerated, nothing but what is perfectly correct and natural" and speculated that the poet herself, displaying "genius and . . . talent undefiled by meretricious ornaments, and undeformed by affection," must be a "pure, unsophisticated child of Nature, who *feels* what she writes, and expresses herself with that simple eloquence of the heart which appeals most forcibly to the understanding, as well as to the feelings." Although it maintained that Trefusis "appears to have had but a small compass of thought, little fertility of invention, and probably no great variety of knowledge," so that "she often sinks into monotony, and not unfrequently deviates into affection," the *Annual Review* acknowledged that "her style is correct, her verse melodious; her ideas are sometimes beautiful; and she speaks of love in a manner which irresistibly persuades us that she must have deeply felt his power." The *Poetical Register* said that her poems "possess great feeling, simplicity, and elegance. Miss Trefusis was a woman of taste, and of a polished mind. Her compositions will cause her name to be remembered with honour."[2]

She survived the publication of her poems by only a few months, succumbing, according to her obituary in the *Gentleman's Magazine,* after "a long and severe illness."[3] William Gifford was her executor. It was said that at her death she left in manuscript novels, pastoral romances, and dramas, but they were never published. A copy of her book in the British Library contains five handwritten, unpublished poems. William Beloe devotes three chapters of his 1817 memoir *The Sexagenarian* to an account of Trefusis, but it is highly colored and unreliable.[4]

MAJOR WORKS: *Poems and Tales,* 2 vols. (London, 1808).

TEXTS USED: Texts from *Poems and Tales.*

---

2. *British Critic* 32 (August 1808): 126, 128–29; *Antijacobin Review* 30 (July 1808): 256, 258; *Annual Review* 7 (1808): 524; *Poetical Register* 7 (1808): 557.

3. *Gentleman's Magazine* 78, pt. 2 (September 1808): 859.

4. William Beloe, *The Sexagenarian; or, The Recollections of a Literary Life,* 2 vols. (London, 1817), 368–84.

Aurora, or the Mad Tale Madly Told

'Tis night. And this the fearful hour
  When yawning graves resign their dead;
Oblivion's god asserts his pow'r,
  And slowly rising from his bed,
O'er all extends a magic hand,
And gently waves his leaden wand;
All nature owns the powerful sway,
Man, beast, and bird, the god obey.
The streams scarce murmur as they flow,
10   The bellowing winds forget to blow,
The light waves gently kiss the shore,
And noise and tumult wake no more.

      No sound is heard,
    Save when the melancholy bird
Flaps her dull wing, and wheels her heavy flight
Through the dark regions of the shadowy night. —
    But who is she, with looks so wild,
      Whose white robes catch the moon's pale beam?
    Sure she is sorrow's favourite child!
20   Of peace bereft, of hope beguil'd,
      Her dim eyes faintly gleam!
Yet ever and anon they pour forth sorrow's stream.
      Poor girl! thine are no common woes!
      See how to heaven her arms she throws,
      Now to the church-yard bends her way,
And crowns her frantic head with flowers;
Then, on her taper fingers counts the long-resounding hours!
    Aurora.
    "Full thirteen moons are gone and past,
30   "And this the place, and this the day
      "Of happiness, too great to last!
    " 'Twas here Alindor, perjured youth,
    "To young Aurora pledged his truth;
    "Yet, ere the ceremony ends,
"Truth and Alindor seem no longer friends!
    "O my poor brain's on fire! —

"Yes, yes, I laugh'd to see
   "This triumph of duplicity!
"Saw you yon mincing dame in proud attire?
    "The bold one claim'd his vows!   40
"Woman, avaunt! thou never wert his spouse.
  "But wherefore wax his cheeks so pale?
   "Why close those eyes of heavenly blue?
  "My life! my love! I scorn the tale;
   "Aurora still believes thee true!
"She loves thee, dearest! loving thee—confides:
"Who shall dare say Alindor has two brides?
    "Or who shall say that candid smile
     "Was but the spurious babe of art?
    "Sure heavenly natures know no guile;   50
     "Thine was no false, no canker'd heart.
"O thou art pure, as are the blest above,
"And I were much to blame to doubt thy love!
    "But wherefore wax his cheeks so pale?
     "Why close those eyes of heavenly blue?
    "Conviction hangs upon the tale!
     "O all ye gods! yes, yes—'tis true!
   "And see, he bends, he sinks to earth!
    "Lovely in death!—
   "When parching Eurus, with destructive breath,   60
    "Gives the mad whirlwind birth,
  "And wide around her leafy honours throws,
 "So bends, in beautiful decay, the withering rose!
   "Come, let me warm thee with a burning sigh!
    " 'Tis for Aurora, not for thee to die!
   "For what is she?—a poor deserted maid!
   "To love, to grief, to infamy betray'd!
    "Unclose those eyes! I can forgive—
    "But must not, dare not live!
    "Stranger, sit thee down awhile,   70
 "I have a tale to tell shall make thee smile.
"Close in the king-cup hides the generous bee,
  "The honey sips, but never harms the flow'r:
"While here, the type of murderous man we see!

60 Eurus] The southeast wind.

"Here the fell spider wantons in his pow'r,
"Forgets the kindly shelter he receives,
"And poisons the poor plant, whose breast that shelter gives!
"My tale is told, my task is done,
"My life is spent, my hour-glass run!
80   "Behold, on yon swift-sailing cloud
"He rides! triumphant o'er the grave!
"He beckons me, he calls aloud;
"Light on the gale his amber ringlets wave,
"The sweets of paradise perfume his breath!
"See how these two new meteors grace the skies!
"Astrologers suspect not they're his eyes!
"Poor knaves! but little knowing, much they'll own!
"This science was reserved for love alone!
"Love penetrates the caves of death!
90   "Old Neptune's secret haunts explores,
"Rides on a billow to his distant shores,
"Mounts to the stars, inspects the moon;
"And if the cold, but fickle fair,
"Detains some wandering lover there,
"Love claims him soon!
"Yet still night's queen her influence maintains,
"And though she yields his heart, she gambols in his brains.
"My tale is told, my task is done,
"My life is spent, my hour-glass run.
100   "Stranger, adieu! I must away,
"My loved Alindor blames Aurora's stay."

Light as the thistle-down she flew
To Neptune's pebbly shore;
The stranger rush'd to save
The lovely maniac from a wat'ry grave;
Round her fair form his sheltering arms he threw.
Horror of horrors! she was seen no more!
He but embraced—a shroud!—
Wild peals of laughter, long and loud,
110   Convulsed the air!—and church-yard records say
This maniac had been dead a year, a month, and day!

(1808)

The Quarrel

I

What have I done? in what have I offended?
  That thus with alter'd looks, and cold regards,
My doom is fixt, ere yet my trial's ended,
  And scorn the truest tenderness rewards!
I ask not for thy love, or would obtain thee;
  Honour forbids that blessing should be mine:
Yet I so dote, that I would die to gain thee,
  Were we both free, and poverty was thine!

II

If it be sin in secret to adore thee,
  Hide latent passion under friendship's guise;   10
If it be sin thus humbly to implore thee,
  And read love's volume in those speaking eyes;
If it be sin these agonies to prove,
  T'exhale my very being in a sigh;
If it be sin to love—as angels love!
  Gods! gods! how great a criminal am I!

(1808)

Jane West

(1758–1852)

Jane West, the only child of Jane and John Iliffe, was born in London on 30 April 1758 in a building that later in the century became St. Paul's Coffee House. When she was eleven the family moved to Desborough in Northamptonshire, the region where she was to spend the rest of her long life. Self-taught, she told her friend Bishop Percy, "I berhymed the seven first chapters of the Acts at 13; I read Martin's Philosophy soon after, and composed an astronomic poem. Pope's Homer inspired me with the epic strain at 16; and I sung (or rather howled) the glories of Caractacus. The catalogue of my compositions previous to my attaining 20 would be formidable. Thousands of lines flowed in very easy measure; I scorned correction, and never blotted."[1]

In the late 1770s or very early 1780s Jane married Thomas West, a yeoman farmer from Little Bowden, and bore three sons.[2] Even when her children were small she published books of verse, including *Miscellaneous Poetry Written at an Early Period in Life* (1786), *The Humours of Brighthelmstone* (1788), *Miscellaneous Poems, and a Tragedy* (1791), *An Elegy on the Death of the Right Honourable Edmund Burke* (1797), *Poems and Plays* (1799–1805), and *The Mother: A Poem, in Five Books* (1809), as well as plays and novels. She published her early novels under the pseudonym Prudentia Homespun, a name earlier used by the Irish poet Charlotte McCarthy. She also wrote conduct books and essays and became a regular contributor to the *Gentleman's Magazine*. Anna Seward admired West's poetry but was critical of her drama *Edmund*. West's anonymously published novel *A Gossip's Story* was the main source for Jane Austen's *Sense and Sensibility;* Mary Wollstonecraft admired the way it showed "the small causes which destroy matrimonial felicity and peace"[3] and asked

---

1. Jane West to Dr. Percy, bishop of Dromore, 1800, quoted in the obituary notice for West in *Gentleman's Magazine* 38 (July 1852): 99.

2. Thomas, born 21 September 1783, John, born 15 January 1787, and Edward, born 24 March 1794.

3. Quoted in Gina Luria, introduction to West's *Letters to a Young Lady in Which the Duties and Character of Women are Considered* (1806; reprint, New York, 1974), 6.

Mary Hays to review it for the *Analytical Review.* West described her verse as "inelegant and crude / Confus'd in sense, in diction rude,"[4] but Bishop Percy told her, "Your 'Odes on Poetry' are of the first-rate excellence; nor could I read them without emotions which I have seldom experienced. They are sublime, animated, rich in imagery, and, what I could scarce have expected from a lady's pen, learned."[5]

But West always protested that domestic duties took precedence over literary occupation. She told Percy, "My season for study and composition . . . is winter. I am engaged in the duties of active life, and to those duties my pleasures ever have been subservient. You noticed my pile of stockings; they were not affectedly introduced. My needle always claims the pre-eminence of my pen. I hate the name of 'rhyming slattern.'"[6] Even so, her pen was a productive one. Percy sent West's poems to Dr. Anderson, editor of the British Poets, in Edinburgh, who told him, "They do credit to the genius, taste, piety, and benevolence of the amiable and elegant writer. They do not, in general, possess the spirit and elevation of the higher poetry; but they abound in tender, interesting, and moral sentiments, elegantly expressed in easy numbers, and adorned with pleasing imagery. In some instances, as in the Ode to Poetry, she soars far above mediocrity, and approaches to sublimity."[7]

West's anti-Jacobinism became explicit in her second novel, *A Tale of the Times* (1799), whose villain is a supporter of the French Revolution. In 1800 she asked Percy to review her conduct book *Letters Addressed to a Young Man.* She had written in the preface that her "secluded life afforded her few opportunities of profiting by literary conversation, or the collision of minds actuated by a similar taste, and engaged in congenial pursuits." It was, however, at about this time that she began corresponding with Sarah Trimmer. Percy wrote a long and enthusiastic piece for the November 1801 issue of the *British Critic,* in which he reported that a gentleman who had accidentally called upon West the previous year had found her not "absorbed in books, and surrounded with papers, with all the paraphernalia of a professed *authoress.*" Instead she was "looking over the linen of her large family, and regulating its economy, in one of the neatest mansions he ever entered; she herself being a perfect pattern of neatness in her person and dress, and of unaffected simplicity in her manners and character."[8]

There was some dispute, however, among West's reading public regarding her station in life. She described herself as "a charmer / Self-taught, and

---

4. "To the Hon. Mrs. C-E.," in West, *Miscellaneous Poems, and a Tragedy* (York, 1791).
5. Quoted in obituary for West, *Gentleman's Magazine* 38 (July 1852): 100.
6. West to Percy, 1800 (see n. 1).
7. Ibid., 101.
8. *British Critic* 18 (November 1801): 528.

married to a farmer; / Who wrote all kind of verse with ease, / Made pies and puddings, frocks and cheese, / Her situation, tho' obscure, / Was not contemptible or poor. / Her conversation spoke a mind / Studious to please, but unrefin'd."[9] In January 1802 the *Gentleman's Magazine* published a letter claiming that West "pays the greatest care and attention to her farm, manages her dairy, and even carries her butter to market."[10] The following month, another reader wrote to object that West was too much of a gentlewoman to be personally engaged in trade, insisting that she *supervised* the sending of cheese to market "while knitting stockings for her husband and sons."[11] The latter correspondent is far likelier to have been correct. In 1805 West inherited land from her father that she did not bother to sell until 1812, at which time she realized at least three thousand pounds, a sum that would have supported a gentlewoman comfortably for a decade. Her fiction sold well. Bishop Percy reported to her in 1800 that at Brighton her novels had "the entire possession of this first of watering-places. Here are three circulating libraries, and the demand for your novels is very great in them all. In the shop where I have been waiting for my turn in your 'Tale of the Times,' I was told there were three sets; nor was it till last night that I could procure the first volume of one of them, although the season is scarce here begun."[12]

West's last novel, *Ringrove: or, Old Fashioned Notions,* was published by Longmans in 1827. In 1833 she brought out a volume of *Sacred Poems* but was already thinking of herself as "an old Q in a corner whom the rest of the world has forgotten."[13] She outlived her husband, who died on 23 January 1823, and all three sons. On 25 March 1852, at the age of ninety-three, she died at Little Bowden, near Market Harborough, and was buried next to her parents in the West family plot at St. Nicholas Church. In a will dated 1846 she left all her letters, unpublished works, and manuscripts to her executor and grandson, the Reverend Edward West, but the whereabouts of these manuscripts are now unknown.

MAJOR WORKS: *Miscellaneous Poetry . . . Written at an Early Period of Life* (London, 1786); *The Humours of Brighthelmstone* (London, 1788); *Miscellaneous Poems, and a Tragedy* (York, 1791); *The Advantages of Education; or, the History of Maria Williams, a Tale for*

9. "To the Hon. Mrs. C-E."

10. Quoted in Pamela Lloyd, "Some New Information on Jane West," *N&Q,* n.s., 31 (December 1984): 469.

11. Ibid.

12. Quoted in *Gentleman's Magazine* 38 (July 1852): 100.

13. Jane West to Miss H., 11 July 1834, *Miscellaneous Fragments, Letters and Papers,* British Museum Manuscript Room, Additional MSS 41567, f. 63, quoted in Lloyd, "Some New Information on Jane West," 470.

Misses and Their Mammas (London, 1793); *A Gossip's Story, and a Legendary Tale* (London, 1796); *An Elegy on the Death of the Right Honourable Edmund Burke* (London, 1797); *A Tale of the Times*, 2 vols. (London, 1799); *Poems and Plays*, 4 vols. (London, 1799–1805); *Letters Addressed to a Young Man, on his First Entrance into Life, and Adapted to the Peculiar Circumstances of the Present Times*, 3 vols. (London, 1801); *The Infidel Father*, 3 vols. (London, 1802); *The Sorrows of Selfishness; or, The History of Miss Richmore* (London, 1802); *Letters to a Young Lady, in which the Duties and Character of Women are Considered, Chiefly with a Reference to Prevailing Opinions*, 3 vols. (London, 1806); *The Mother: A Poem, in Five Books* (London, 1809); *The Refusal*, 3 vols. (London, 1810); *The Loyalists: An Historical Novel* (London, 1812); *Alicia de Lacy; an Historical Romance*, 4 vols. (London, 1814); *Scriptural Essays, Adapted to the Holydays of the Church of England* (London, 1816); *Ringrove; or, Old Fashioned Notions*, 2 vols. (London, 1827).

TEXTS USED: Text of "On the Sonnets of Mrs. Charlotte Smith" from *Miscellaneous Poems, and a Tragedy*. Text of "Sonnet to May" from *A Tale of the Times*.

On the Sonnets of Mrs. Charlotte Smith

The widow'd turtle, mourning for her love,
    Breathes the soft plaintive melody of woe:
And streams, that gently steal along the grove,
    In murmurs dear to melancholy flow.

Yet to thy strains, sweet nymph of Arun's vale,
    Harsh is the turtle's note, and harsh the stream,
Ev'n when their echos die upon the gale,
    Or catch attention by the lunar beam.

Thy strains soul-harrowing melting pity hears,
    Yet fears to break thy privacy of pain,   10
She blots thy page with sympathetic tears,
    And while she mourns thy wrongs enjoys thy strain.

Hast thou indeed no solace? does the earth
    Afford no balm thy anguish to relieve?

1 turtle] Turtle-dove, noted for its affection toward its mate.
5 Arun's] River in southeastern England.

Still must thou feel the pang of suff'ring worth,
   Taught by refinement but to charm and grieve.

Oh! if despair directs thy pensive eyes
   To where death terminates terrestrial woes,
May faith from thence exalt them to the skies,
20   Where glory's palm for suffering virtue grows.

There may thy lyre, whose sweetly magic pow'rs
   From pain'd attention forc'd applauding tears,
With hallelujahs fill the eternal bowers,
   The theme prolonging through eternal years.

                         (1791)

Sonnet to May

Come May, the empire of the earth assume,
   Be crown'd with flowers as universal queen;
   Take from fresh budded groves their tender green,
Bespangled with Pomona's richest bloom,
And form thy vesture. Let the sun illume
   The dew-drops glittering in the blue serene,
   And let them hang, like orient pearls, between
Thy locks besprent with Flora's best perfume.
Attend your sovereign's steps, ye balmy gales!
10   O'er her ambrosial floods of fragrance pour;
Let livelier verdure animate the vales,
   And brighter hues embellish every flower;
And hark, the concert of the woodland hails,
   All gracious May! thy presence, and thy power.

                         (1799)

---

4 Pomona] Roman goddess of fruits and fruit trees.
8 besprent] Besprinkled; strewn with.
8 Flora] Roman goddess of spring and flowers.

Helen Maria Williams

(1761?–1827)

Helen Maria Williams, best known for her eyewitness chronicles of the French Revolution and her influential salon in Paris, was also a poet who could not resist weaving verse into her novels and even into her translation of another author's work. She received her education from her Scots mother, Helen Hay. Her father, Charles Williams, a Welsh army officer, died when she was still a child, and her mother took her and her younger sister, Cecilia, to live in Berwick-upon-Tweed, on the border with Scotland. In 1781 Helen went to London. Andrew Kippis, a leading dissenting minister and family friend, became her mentor and introduced her to Elizabeth Montagu, Frances Burney, Anna Seward, Benjamin Franklin, George Romney, William Hayley, and other writers and intellectuals. Just as important, he edited and helped her publish her first book, *Edwin and Eltruda,* in 1782. A long antiwar poem, it recounts the tale of a woman who loses her lover and her father to a pointless war. The poem's success enabled Williams's mother and sister to join her in London. Eventually Williams's London circle came to include William Godwin, Hester Lynch Piozzi, Samuel Johnson, Sarah Siddons, and Edmund Burke.

An Ode on the Peace (1783) welcomes the end of the American Revolution and foresees a time when Britain will achieve similar democratic and economic prosperity, fostering a new age for the arts. It was published by subscription and was well received. *Peru: a Poem. In Six Cantos* (1784) is an epyllion about the conquered indigenous peoples of South America, examining the impact of war on domestic life and on the sensibilities of its victims. Anna Seward admired it enough to publish "Sonnet To Miss Williams, on her Epic Poem Peru," beginning "Poetic sister, who with daring hand . . . Hast seiz'd the Epic lyre — with art divine."[1] Williams included all of her previously published poetry along with some new pieces in a two-volume collection

---

1. First published in *European Magazine* 6 (1784): 236–37.

simply entitled *Poems* (1786), dedicated to the Queen. The nearly fifteen hundred subscribers, whose names fill seventy-six pages, include Joanna Baillie, the duchess of Devonshire, David Hume, Hannah More, Sir Joshua Reynolds, George Romney, Anna Seward, Sarah Siddons, Horace Walpole, and Thomas Wharton. Among the poems are "An Epistle to Dr. Moore," who had treated her during a serious illness, an elegy, hymns, scriptural paraphrases, and songs, as well as the "Sonnet to Twilight," which William Wordsworth admired and later anthologized. Wordsworth's earliest published poem, in fact, was entitled "Sonnet, on Seeing Miss Helen Maria Williams Weep at a Tale of Distress" (1787).[2]

In 1788 Williams published *A Poem on the Bill Lately Passed for Regulating the Slave Trade,* which, in the stylized manner of much antislavery literature, portrays the domestic realm victimized by commerce and war. That same year Williams visited her sister, Cecilia, who had married a Protestant minister, Athanase Coquerel, and gone to live in France. Williams arrived just before the Festival of the Federation. "The impressions of this unforgetable day," she wrote, "determined my political opinions forever."[3] Her novel, *Julia,* rewrites Rousseau's *Julie; ou, la nouvelle Héloïse* and contains "The Bastille," a poem espousing the ideals of the French Revolution. Her heroine is a cultivated woman of sensibility who struggles against an illicit love. The narrative is interwoven with poems expressing libertarian ideals, the joys of nature, and the pleasure of philanthropic acts. Mary Wollstonecraft was delighted with the novel, and reviewers praised it.

Letters Written in France in the Summer of 1790, to a Friend in England (1790) describes revolutionary events with enthusiasm and highlights the love story of Williams's friends Monique Coquerel and her husband, Augustin du Fossé. She wrote, "I am glad you think that a friend's having been persecuted, imprisoned, maimed, and almost murdered under the antient government of France, is a good excuse for loving the revolution. What, indeed, but friendship, could have led my attention from the annals of imagination to the records of politics; from the poetry to the prose of human life?"[4] The epistolary form of the work gives a sense of spontaneity and immediacy to her argument that the English have misunderstood the Revolution and that they can learn from it. The book made a splash among a British reading public eager for firsthand news of France.

Before revisiting Paris, Williams published *A Farewell, for Two Years, to*

2. Published under the pseudonym "Axiologus" in ibid., 7:202.

3. "Les impressions de cette journée memorable ont fixé pour toujours mes opinions politiques", translated by Gary Kelly in *Women, Writing, and Revolution, 1790–1827* (Oxford, 1993), 35.

4. Quoted in ibid., 35–36.

England (1791), a poem answering recent criticism of the French Revolution. She traveled back and forth across the channel several times before returning to Paris in the summer of 1792, in time to witness the monarchy's overthrow. There her romantic involvement with John Hurford Stone, a married man who had subscribed to her *Poems* (1786), caused talk back home. But in the spirit of revolutionary times, Williams rejected the values of bourgeois respectability.

She knew most of the Jacobin and Girondist leaders, including especially Marie Roland, the most politically powerful woman in Paris, as well as Thomas Paine and Mary Wollstonecraft, who attended her salons. Wollstonecraft told her sister, Everina, "Miss Williams has behaved very civilly to me and I shall visit her frequently, because I *rather* like her, and I meet french company at her house. Her manners are affected, yet the *simple* goodness of her hearts [*sic*] continually breaks through the varnish, so that one would be more inclined, at least I should, to love than admire her. — Authorship is a heavy weight for female shoulders especially in the sunshine of prosperity." [5] After 1792 Williams lived abroad permanently, never to return to England. For the next quarter-century she recorded her impressions of all the major political events in France for British readers and not only became a major conduit of information but also had significant influence on public opinion.

Williams's association with the Girondists colored her accounts. "To Dr. Moore" was written for her friend Dr. John Moore, a well-known British social critic. The poem argues that even though they are far apart geographically, she in France and he in England, they are bonded by their sympathy for the Revolution, undaunted by British criticism of political events. *Letters from France: Containing Many New Anecdotes Relative to the French Revolution, and the Present State of French Manners* (1792) implicitly replies to Edmund Burke's *Reflections on the Revolution in France*. Williams argues that France has learned the lesson of freedom from Britain but will soon surpass its mentor. Laetitia Matilda Hawkins published a book-length attack on Williams and the Revolution in her *Letters on the Female Mind, Its Powers and Pursuits; Addressed to Miss H. M. Williams, with Particular Reference to her Letters from France* (1793).

In 1793 the Girondists were defeated, and Marie Roland and others close to Williams were executed. Williams herself was arrested in October, as were other British citizens. She was incarcerated in the Luxembourg prison along with her mother and sister, but after the intervention of friends, she was sent to an English convent, and in November she was placed under house arrest.

---

5. Letter of 24 December 1792, in *Collected Letters of Mary Wollstonecraft*, ed. Ralph M. Wardle (Ithaca, 1979), 226.

During her imprisonment Williams translated her friend Bernardin de Saint-Pierre's novel *Paul et Virginie* (1788). In *Paul and Virginia* (1795) she excised some of Saint-Pierre's prose and interjected some of her own original sonnets. *Paul and Virginia* became Williams's most frequently reprinted work, popular throughout the nineteenth century. The reviews were generally positive. The *Critical Review* found Williams qualified "not only to transfuse every beauty of the original, but to embellish it with new and peculiar graces."[6] In Williams's next collection of letters she described her experiences in prison, along with those of other prisoners. Many who had known her in England, including Anna Seward and Hester Lynch Piozzi, found disturbing Williams's *Letters Containing a Sketch of the Politics of France from the Thirty-first of May 1793 till the Twenty-eighth of July 1794,* for she continued to support the Revolution despite her revulsion at its violence. "Liberty," declared Williams, "is innocent of the outrages committed under its borrowed sanction."[7] Her reputation suffered as her work and character were savaged by the *Gentleman's Magazine* and the *Anti-Jacobin Review.* Horace Walpole called her a "scribbling trollop."[8]

After her release from custody, strangers were barred from Paris, and Williams moved to Versailles. Then, fearing persecution, she and Stone fled to Switzerland. It may have been simply her anti-Jacobinism that made her vulnerable, but there is some indication that she or Stone may have been involved in spying. She documented the six months she spent in Switzerland in *A Tour of Switzerland* (1798), a book as much about politics as about travel. After the fall of Robespierre in the summer of 1794 Williams and Stone returned to Paris. In 1798 her sister died, and Williams adopted her two young nephews. Initially impressed by Napoleon, Williams later abhorred him. Her "Ode on the Peace of Amiens" (1801) offended the emperor, and as a result she and her family were briefly detained. The British government intercepted letters sent by Williams and Stone to Joseph Priestley and, in an effort to further discredit its critics, published them as *Copies of Original Letters Recently Written by Persons in Paris to Dr. Priestley in America, Taken on Board of a Neutral Vessel* (1798). That same year Richard Polwhele, in *The Unsex'd Females,* called Williams "an intemperate advocate for Gallic licentiousness."[9] Hester Lynch Piozzi referred to her as "a wicked little Democrate."[10] But her press was not all bad. The *Critical Review* for January 1796 observed of her *Letters* that if they

---

6. N.s., 18 (October 1796): 183.
7. Quoted in Todd, *Dictionary.*
8. Ibid.
9. *The Unsex'd Females: A Poem* (London, 1798), 19n.
10. Quoted in Kelly, *Women, Writing, and Revolution,* 77.

want the profound investigation of the statesman or legislator,—if they are destitute of those political discussions, in which historians of the higher order are fond of indulging,—they will be found to contain what is more valuable,—a picture of the times. What they lose in stateliness they gain in interest; if they plunge not deeply into the intrigues of cabinets or the views of politicians, they delineate correctly the fluctuations of popular sentiment; and if they enter but little on the disgusting and generally tiresome details of senatorial debates or military exploits, they paint the manners, and, by a variety of engaging anecdotes, expose the human heart.[11]

Sketches of the State of Manners and Opinions in the French Republic, Towards the Close of the Eighteenth Century in a Series of Letters (1801) picks up the narrative where *A Tour in Switzerland* left off. It includes "The History of Perourou; or, The Bellows-Mender, Written by Himself," a comic tale about the breakdown of class barriers in which a laboring-class man is transformed into a gentleman and achieves domestic happiness in a bourgeois world. One of Williams's most popular stories, it was pirated in chapbooks in London, Dublin, and Edinburgh, and in 1838 Edward Bulwer Lytton used it as the basis for his popular stage play, *The Lady of Lyons*. The *New Annual Register* for 1801 reprinted "On the State of Women in the French Republic," a feminist treatise published within *Sketches* that calls for expanded rights for women and highlights their heroism in the Revolution and their intellectual abilities. *Sketches* provoked a strong but mixed response. The *Critical Review* acknowledged that Williams's "admirers are not confined to this island, nor indeed to this quarter of the globe," but the *Monthly Review* faulted her for "too strong and too poetical colouring," wrong information, borrowing from the work of others, and "an affectation of sentiment and sensibility." The *British Critic* classed her among the "wretches," the "abandoned shameless women," from throughout Europe who were promoting "the views of France against their respective countries" in a revolutionary effort "subversive of the manners and morals of their native country."[12] In 1802 Valentine Browne Lawless described Williams's salon, for many years an important institution in Parisian culture, as "chiefly composed of liberal republicans and anti-Bonapartists."[13]

In 1803, mistakenly thinking the politically motivated forgeries of Louis XVI's letters were authentic, Williams edited them as *The Political and Confidential Correspondence of Lewis the Sixteenth,* adding her own republican

11. N.s., 16 (January 1796): 1.

12. *Critical Review,* n.s., 31 (February 1801): 183–84; *Monthly Review,* n.s., 35 (May 1801): 82–83; *British Critic* 17 (June 1801): 582–83.

13. Quoted in Kelly, *Women, Writing, and Revolution,* 200.

commentary on each letter. British periodicals reviled her for this effort. A. F. Bertrand de Moleville published a book-length attack, translated into English by R. C. Dallas as *A Refutation of the Libel on the Memory of the Late King of France, Published by Helen Maria Williams* (1804). Williams and Stone toured Normandy in 1810, and she was saddened by the death of her mother two years later. The prosperous life the couple had been living came to a halt when Stone lost his money in a business speculation. Williams then became the family's main financial support. With the fall of Napoleon, British travelers flocked to Paris, and Williams's salon was one of the places where they gathered. Freed by the changed political landscape to resume her role as the foremost British commentator on French politics, in 1815 she published *Narrative of Events Which have Taken place in France from the Landing of Napoleon Bonaparte.* Reaction in Britain was mixed. The *Quarterly Review* evaluated a selection of books about Napoleon's "hundred days" and preferred Williams's to the rest, declaring that it was "written with accuracy, with a free and, we had almost said, an impartial spirit." But the *Monthly Review* saw the book as impious, sentimental, and not real history and charged Williams with lax personal morals.[14] In order to raise money, Williams also translated works by her friends Friedrich H. A. von Humboldt and Aimé Bonpland. She published a pamphlet, *On the Late Persecution of the Protestants in the South of France* (1816), to help avert calls for military intervention by Britain.

In 1817 Williams and Stone were struggling financially, and Henry Crabb Robinson asked the editor of the *Times* to give her work.[15] Stone died in May 1818, and Williams was cheated out of what remained of their joint assets. A few years later Crabb Robinson remarked that she looked unhappy and ill. He helped her place her next book, *Letters on the Events which have Passed in France, Since the Restoration in 1815* (1819). The *Monthly Review* found the book insightful, wished it were longer, and declared Williams "an original writer" who should not have to stoop to translating the work of others. The *British Critic,* however, said of her style, "She obviously can hardly write without the tears streaming down her cheeks; notes of admiration conclude every sentence; Oh!'s and Ah!'s choke her utterance before she can begin them." It called her an "ex-jacobin" and said the book was full of nonsense and cant, derivative, and in "extremely bad taste."[16]

14. *Quarterly Review* 14 (October 1815): 69; *Monthly Review,* n.s., 78 (November 1815): 300–309.

15. Henry Crabb Robinson, *Henry Crabb Robinson on Books and Their Writers,* ed. Edith J. Morley, 3 vols. (London, 1938), 1:176, 182.

16. *Monthly Review,* n.s., 90 (September 1819): 32–36; *British Critic,* n.s., 12 (October 1819): 392–99.

The Charter, composed for her nephew, Athanase Laurent Charles Co-querel, on his wedding day, calls for egalitarian marriage. Williams went to live with the young couple in Amsterdam, where her nephew served as minister to a congregation of French Protestants. Williams's *Poems on Various Subjects* (1823), a collected and revised edition of her verse, received little notice. The *Monthly Review* thought her more recent poems inferior to earlier ones, admired the "force and elegance" of the book's introduction, but thought her verse generally inferior to her prose.[17] Still, two of her devotional poems found their way into church hymn books—one beginning "My God! all nature owns thy sway, / Thou giv'st the night, and thou the day," and another beginning

> Whilst thee I see, protecting Power!
> Be my vain wishes stilled;
> And may this consecrated hour
> With better hopes be filled.

William Wordsworth could recite from memory her sonnet "To Hope."[18]

Williams's last work, another collection of political letters, *Souvenirs de la révolution française* (1827), was never published in English; it appeared only in Paris in her nephew's French translation. Williams died in Paris on 15 December 1827 and, as she had wished, was buried beside Stone in Père Lachaise cemetery. Looking back on her long career in 1823, Williams observed in the introduction to *Poems on Various Subjects:* "I have long renounced any attempts in verse, confining my pen almost entirely to sketches of the events of the Revolution. I have seen what I relate, and therefore I have written with confidence; I have there been treading on the territory of History, and a trace of my footsteps will perhaps be left. My narratives make a part of that marvellous story which the eighteenth century has to record to future times, and the testimony of a witness will be heard."[19]

MAJOR WORKS: *Edwin and Eltruda: A Legendary Tale,* [ed. Andrew Kippis] (London, 1782); *An Ode on the Peace* (London, 1783); *Peru: a Poem. In Six Cantos* (London, 1784); *Poems,* 2 vols. (London, 1786); *A Poem on the Bill Lately Passed for Regulating the Slave Trade* (London, 1788); *Julia; a Novel. Interspersed with Some Poetical Pieces,* 2 vols. (London, 1790); *Letters Written in France in the Summer of 1790, to a Friend in England; Containing Various Anecdotes Relative to the French Revolution; and Memoirs of Mons. and Madame du F——* (London, 1790); *A Farewell, for Two Years, to England. A Poem* (Lon-

17. N.s., 102 (September 1823): 20–23.
18. Helen Maria Williams, *Poems on Various Subjects* (London, 1823), 203n.
19. Ibid., ix–x.

don, 1791); *Letters Containing a Sketch of the Politics of France from the Thirty-first of May 1793 till the Twenty-eighth of July 1794,* 2 vols. (London, 1795); *A Tour in Switzerland; or, a View of the Present State of the Governments and Manners of those Cantons: with Comparative Sketches of the Present State of Paris,* 2 vols. (London, 1798); *Sketches of the State of Manners and Opinions in the French Republic Towards the Close of the Eighteenth Century. In a Series of Letters,* 2 vols. (London, 1801); *Verses Addressed by H. M. W. to her Two Nephews, on Saint Helen's Day* (Paris, 1809); *A Narrative of the Events which have Taken Place in France, from the Landing of Napoleon Bonaparte, on the 1st of March 1815, till the Restoration of Louis XVIII. With an Account of the Present State of Society and Public Opinion* (London, 1815); *On the Late Persecution of the Protestants in the South of France* (London, 1816); *The Charter: Lines Addressed by H. M. W. to her Nephew, Athanase C. L. Coquerel, on his Wedding Day* (Paris, 1819); *Letters on the Events which have Passed in France, Since the Restoration in 1815* (London, 1819); *Poems on Various Subjects, with Introductory Remarks on the Present State of Science and Literature in France* (London, 1823); *Souvenirs de la révolution française,* trans. Charles Coquerel (Paris, 1827).

TRANSLATIONS: J. H. B. de Saint-Pierre, *Paul and Virginia* (London, 1795); Friedrich H. A. von Humboldt, *Researches, Concerning the Institutions and Monuments of the Ancient Inhabitants of America, with Descriptions and Views of Some of the Most Striking Scenes in the Cordilleras,* 2 vols. (London, 1814); Friedrich H. A. von Humboldt and Aimé Bonpland, *Personal Narrative of Travels to the Equinoctial Regions of the New Continent during the Years 1799–1804,* 5 vols. (London, 1814–21); Francois Xavier de Maistre, *The Leper of the City of Aoste* (London, 1817).

TEXTS USED: Text from *Peru: a Poem,* from the concluding lines of canto 5, lines 1119–34. Texts of "Sonnet to Twilight," "Elegy on a Young Thrush," "Sonnet to the Moon," "To Dr. Moore, in Answer to a Poetical Epistle Written to Me by Him in Wales," "Hymn, Written among the Alps," "To James Forbes," and "To A Friend" from *Poems on Various Subjects.* Text from "An Epistle to Dr. Moore," lines 93–112, and text of "A Song" ("No riches from his scanty store") from *Poems.* Text from *A Farewell, for Two Years, To England. A Poem* from lines 29–124. "Sonnet to the Curlew," "Sonnet to the White-Bird of the Tropic," and "Sonnet, To the Torrid Zone" from the second edition of Williams's translation of Bernardin Saint-Pierre's *Paul and Virginia* (1796).

from *Peru,* canto 5

Did e'er the human bosom throb with pain
Th' enchanting Muse has sought to sooth in vain?
She, who can still with Harmony its sighs,
And wake the sound at which Affliction dies!
Can bid the stormy Passions backward roll,
And o'er their low-hung Tempests lift the soul;
With magic touch paint Nature's various Scene,
Dark on the Mountain, in the Vale serene;
Can tinge the breathing Rose with brighter bloom,
Or hang the sombrous Rock in deeper gloom;   10
Explore the Gem whose pure, reflected ray
Throws o'er the central Cave a paler Day;
Or soaring view the Comet's fiery frame
Rush o'er the sky, and fold the sphere in flame;
While the charm'd Spirit, as her accents move,
Is wrapt in Wonder, or dissolv'd in Love.

(1784)

Sonnet to Twilight

Meek Twilight! soften the declining day,
    And bring the hour my pensive spirit loves;
When o'er the mountain slow descends the ray
    That gives to silence and to night the groves.
Ah, let the happy court the morning still,
    When, in her blooming loveliness array'd,
She bids fresh beauty light the vale or hill,
    And rapture warble in the vocal shade.
Sweet is the odour of the morning's flower,
    And rich in melody her accents rise;   10
Yet dearer to my soul the shadowy hour
    At which her blossoms close, her music dies:
For then, while languid Nature droops her head,
She wakes the tear 'tis luxury to shed.

(1784)

from "An Epistle to Dr. Moore"*

There, dress'd in each sublimer grace
Geneva's happy scene I trace;
Her lake, from whose broad bosom thrown
Rushes the loud impetuous Rhone,
And bears his waves with mazy sweep
In rapid torrents to the deep—
Oh for a Muse less weak of wing,
High on yon Alpine steeps to spring,
And tell in verse what they disclose
As well as you have told in prose;
How wrapt in snows and icy showers,
Eternal winter, horrid lowers
Upon the mountain's awful brow,
While purple summer blooms below;
How icy structures rear their forms
Pale products of ten thousand storms;
Where the full sun-beam powerless falls
On crystal arches, columns, walls,
Yet paints the proud fantastic height
With all the various hues of light.
Why is no poet call'd to birth
In such a favour'd spot of earth?
How high his vent'rous Muse might rise,
And proudly scorn to ask supplies
From the Parnassian hill, the fire
Of verse, *Mont Blanc* might well inspire.
O SWITZERLAND! how oft these eyes
Desire to view thy mountains rise;
How fancy loves thy steeps to climb,
So wild, so solemn, so sublime;
And o'er thy happy vales to roam,
Where freedom rears her humble home.

(1786)

---

*John Moore (1729–1802), physician and author of *A View of Society and Manners
in France, Switzerland, and Germany* (1779) and *A View of Society and Manners in Italy*

(1781), relating in a series of letters his travels on the Continent with Douglas, the duke of Hamilton, from 1772 to 1777. Like Williams, he was later to write about his observations of France after the Revolution.

A Song

I

No riches from his scanty store
  My lover could impart;
He gave a boon I valued more——
  He gave me all his heart!

II

His soul sincere, his gen'rous worth,
  Might well this bosom move;
And when I ask'd for bliss on earth,
  I only meant his love.

III

But now for me, in search of gain
  From shore to shore he flies: 10
Why wander riches to obtain,
  When love is all I prize?

IV

The frugal meal, the lowly cot
  If blest my love with thee!
That simple fare, that humble lot,
  Were more than wealth to me.

V

While he the dang'rous ocean braves,
  My tears but vainly flow:
Is pity in the faithless waves
  To which I pour my woe?   20

VI

The night is dark, the waters deep,
    Yet soft the billows roll;
Alas! at every breeze I weep——
    The storm is in my soul.

(1786)

Elegy on a Young Thrush, Which Escaped from the Writer's Hand, and Falling Down the Area of a House,* Could Not Be Found

Mistaken Bird, ah whither hast thou stray'd?
    My friendly grasp why eager to elude?
This hand was on thy pinion lightly laid,
    And fear'd to hurt thee by a touch too rude.

Is there no foresight in a Thrush's breast,
    That thou down yonder gulph from me wouldst go?
That gloomy area lurking cats infest,
    And there the dog may rove, alike thy foe.

I would with lavish crumbs my bird have fed,
10   And brought a crystal cup to wet thy bill;
I would have made of down and moss thy bed,
    Soft, though not fashion'd with a Thrush's skill.

Soon as thy strengthen'd wing could mount the sky,
    My willing hand had set my captive free;
Ah, not for her who loves the Muse, to buy
    A selfish pleasure, bought with pain to thee!

The vital air, and liberty, and light
    Had all been thine; and love, and rapt'rous song,
And sweet parental joys, in rapid flight,
20   Had led the circle of thy life along.

Securely to my window hadst thou flown,
    And ever thy accustom'd morsel found;
Nor should thy trusting breast the wants have known
    Which other Thrushes knew when winter frown'd.

Fram'd with the wisdom nature lent to thee,
    Thy house of straw had brav'd the tempest's rage,
And thou through many a Spring hadst liv'd to see
    The utmost limit of a Thrush's age.

Ill-fated bird!—and does the Thrush's race,
    Like Man's, mistake the path that leads to bliss?   30
Or, when his eye that tranquil path can trace,
    The good he well discerns through folly miss?

                        (1790)

* Sunken court that gives access to the basement of a house, shut off from the street by a railing and reached by steps from the pavement.

Sonnet to the Moon

The glitt'ring colours of the day are fled;
Come, melancholy orb! that dwell'st with night,
    Come! and o'er earth thy wand'ring lustre shed,
Thy deepest shadow, and thy softest light;
    To me congenial is the gloomy grove,
When with faint light the sloping uplands shine;
    That gloom, those pensive rays alike I love,
Whose sadness seems in sympathy with mine!
    But most for this, pale orb! thy beams are dear,
For this, benignant orb! I hail thee most: 10
    That while I pour the unavailing tear,
And mourn that hope to me in youth is lost,
    Thy light can visionary thoughts impart,
    And lead the Muse to soothe a suff'ring heart.

                        (1790)

from *A Farewell, for Two Years, to England.*
A Poem

My native scenes! can aught in time, or space,
From this fond heart your lov'd remembrance chase?
Link'd to that heart by ties for ever dear,
By Joy's light smile, and Sorrow's tender tear;
By all that ere my anxious hopes employ'd,
By all my soul has suffer'd, or enjoy'd!
Still blended with those well-known scenes, arise
The varying images the past supplies;
The childish sports that fond attention drew,
10　　And charm'd my vacant heart when life was new;
The harmless mirth, the sadness robb'd of power
To cast its shade beyond the present hour—
And that dear hope which sooth'd my youthful breast,
And show'd the op'ning world in beauty drest;
That hope which seem'd with bright unfolding rays
(Ah, vainly seem'd!) to gild my future days;
That hope which, early wrapp'd in lasting gloom,
Sunk in the cold inexorable tomb!—
And Friendship, ever powerful to controul
20　　The keen emotions of the wounded soul,
To lift the suff'ring spirit from despair,
And bid it feel that life deserves a care.
Still each impression that my heart retains
Is link'd, dear Land! to thee by lasting chains.

She too, sweet soother of my lonely hours!
Who gilds my thorny path with fancy's flowers,
The Muse, who early taught my willing heart
To feel with transport her prevailing art;
Who deign'd before my infant eyes to spread
30　　Those dazzling visions she alone can shed;
She, who will still be found where'er I stray,
The lov'd companion of my distant way;
'Midst foreign sounds, her voice, that charms my ear,
Breath'd in my native tongue, I still shall hear;

'Midst foreign sounds, endear'd will flow the song
Whose tones, my ALBION, will to thee belong!

And when with wonder thrill'd, with mind elate,
I mark the change sublime in GALLIA's state!
Where new-born Freedom treads the banks of Seine,
Hope in her eye, and Virtue in her train!   40
Pours day upon the dungeon's central gloom,
And leads the captive from his living tomb;
Tears the sharp iron from his loaded breast,
And bids the renovated land be blest—
My thoughts shall fondly turn to that lov'd Isle,
Where Freedom long has shed her genial smile.
Less safe in other lands the triple wall,
And massy portal, of the Gothic hall,
Than in that favour'd Isle the straw-built thatch,
Where Freedom sits, and guards the simple latch.   50

Yet, ALBION! while my heart to thee shall spring,
To thee its first, its best affections bring;
Yet, when I hear exulting millions pour
The shout of triumph on the GALLIC shore;
Not without sympathy my pensive mind
The bounds of human bliss enlarg'd, shall find;
Not without sympathy my glowing breast
Shall hear, on any shore, of millions blest!
Scorning those narrow souls, whate'er their clime,
Who meanly think that sympathy a crime;   60
Who, if one wish for human good expand
Beyond the limits of their native land,
And from the worst of ills would others free,
Deem that warm wish, my Country! guilt to thee.
Ah! why those blessings to one spot confine,
Which, when diffus'd, will not the less be thine?
Ah! why repine if far those blessings spread
For which so oft thy gen'rous sons have bled?
Shall ALBION mark with scorn the lofty thought,
The love of Liberty, herself has taught?   70
Shall *her* brave sons, in this enlighten'd age,

Assume the bigot-frown of papal rage,
Nor tolerate the vow to Freedom paid,
If diff'ring from the ritual *they* have made?
Freedom! who oft on ALBION's fost'ring breast
Has found *her* friends in stars and ermine drest,
Allows that some among her chosen race
Should there the claim to partial honours trace,
And in the long-reflected lustre shine
80   That beams thro' Ancestry's ennobled line;
While she, with guardian wing, can well secure
From each proud wrong the undistinguish'd poor.
On GALLIA's coast, where oft the robe of state
Was trail'd by those whom Freedom's soul must hate;
Where, like a comet, rank appear'd to glow
With dangerous blaze, that threaten'd all below;
There Freedom now, with gladden'd eye, beholds
The simple vest that flows in equal folds.

And tho' on Seine's fair banks a transient storm
90   Flung o'er the darken'd wave its angry form;
That purifying tempest now has past,
No more the trembling waters feel the blast;
The bord'ring images, confus'dly trac'd
Along the ruffled stream, to order haste;
The vernal day-spring bursts the partial gloom,
And all the landscape glows with fresher bloom.

(1791)

To Dr. Moore, in Answer to a Poetical Epistle Written to Me by Him in Wales, September 1791

While in long exile far from you I roam,
To soothe my heart with images of home,
For me, my friend, with rich poetic grace
The landscapes of my native Isle you trace;
Her cultur'd meadows, and her lavish shades,
The rivers winding through her lovely glades;
Far as where, frowning on the flood below,
The rough Welsh mountain lifts its craggy brow.*
Meanwhile my steps have stray'd where Autumn yields
A purple harvest on the sunny fields;   10
Where, bending with their luscious weight, recline
The loaded branches of the clust'ring vine;
There, on the Loire's sweet banks, a joyful band
Cull'd the rich produce of the fruitful land;
The youthful peasant, and the village maid,
And age and childhood lent their feeble aid.
The labours of the morning done, they haste
Where in the field is spread the light repast;†
The vintage-baskets serve, revers'd, for chairs,
And the gay meal is crown'd with tuneless airs.‡   20

Delightful land! ah, now with gen'ral voice,
Thy village sons and daughters may rejoice;
Thy happy peasant, now no more a slave,
Forbad to taste one good that nature gave,
No longer views with unavailing pain
The lavish harvest, ripe for him in vain.
Oppression's cruel hand shall dare no more
To seize its tribute from his scanty store;
And from his famish'd infants wring the spoils,
Too hard-earn'd produce of his useful toils;   30
For now on Gallia's plain the peasant knows
Those equal rights impartial heav'n bestows;
He now, by freedom's ray illumin'd, taught
Some self-respect, some energy of thought,

Discerns the blessings that to all belong,
And lives to guard his humble shed from wrong.

    Auspicious Liberty! in vain thy foes
Deride thy ardour, and thy force oppose;
In vain refuse to mark thy spreading light,
40   While, like the mole, they hide their heads in night,
Or hope their eloquence with taper-ray
Can dim the blaze of philosophic day;
Those reas'ners, who pretend that each abuse,
Sanction'd by precedent, has some blest use!
Does then a chemic power to time belong,
Extracting by some process right from wrong?
Must feudal governments for ever last,
Those Gothic piles, the work of ages past?
Nor may obtrusive reason dare to scan,
50   Far less reform, the rude, misshapen plan?
The winding labyrinths, the hostile towers,
Whence danger threatens, and where horror lowers;
The jealous drawbridge, and the mote profound,
The lonely dungeon in the cavern'd ground;
The sullen dome above those central caves,
Where liv'd one despot and a host of slaves?—
Ah, Freedom, on this renovated shore
That fabric frights the moral world no more!
Shook to its basis by thy powerful spell,
60   Its triple walls in massy fragments fell;
While, rising from the hideous wreck, appears
The temple thy firm arm sublimely rears;
Of fair proportions, and of simple grace,
A mansion worthy of the human race.
For me, the witness of those scenes, whose birth
Forms a new era in the storied earth;
Oft, while with glowing breast those scenes I view,
They lead, ah friend belov'd, my thoughts to you!
Still every fine emotion they impart
70   With your idea mingles in my heart;[§]
You, whom I oft have heard, with gen'rous zeal,
With all that truth can urge, or pity feel,
Refute the pompous argument, that tried

The common cause of millions to deride;
With reason's force the plausive sophist hit,
Or dart on folly the bright flash of wit;[∥]
And warmly share, with philosophic mind,
The great, the glorious triumph of mankind.

(1792)

[*] In 1792 the following lines appeared after line 8: "Where nature throws aside her softer charms, / And with sublimer views the bosom warms."

[†] In 1792 the following lines followed line 18 and preceded the present lines 19 and 20: "Around the soup of herbs a circle make, / And all from one vast dish at once partake:"

[‡] In 1792 the present lines 19 and 20 were followed by the following lines: "For each in turn must sing with all his might; / And some their carols pour in nature's spite."

[§] In 1792 the following lines followed line 70: "You, whose warm bosom, whose expanded mind, / Have shar'd this glorious triumph of mankind;"

[∥] In 1792 the following lines followed line 76:

Too swift, my friend, the moments wing'd their flight,
That gave at once instruction and delight;
That ever from your ample stores of thought
To my small stock some new accession brought.
How oft remembrance, while this bosom bleeds,
My pensive fancy to your dwelling leads;
Where, round your cheerful hearth, I weeping trace
The social circle, and my vacant place!—
When to that dwelling friendship's tie endears,
When shall I hasten with the "joy of tears"?
That joy whose keen sensation swells to pain,
And strives to utter what it feels, in vain.

Sonnet to the Curlew

Sooth'd by the murmurs on the sea-beat shore,
His dun-grey plumage floating to the gale,
The Curlew blends his melancholy wail,
With those hoarse sounds the rushing waters pour—
Like thee, congenial bird! my steps explore
The bleak lone sea-beach, or the rocky dale,
And shun the orange bower, the myrtle vale,
Whose gay luxuriance suits my soul no more.
I love the ocean's broad expanse, when drest
10   In limpid clearness, or when tempests blow;
When the smooth currents on its placid breast
Flow calm as my past moments used to flow;
Or, when its troubled waves refuse to rest,
And seem the symbol of my present woe.

(1795)

Sonnet to the White-Bird of the Tropic

Bird of the Tropic! thou, who lov'st to stray,
Where thy long pinions sweep the sultry line,
Or mark'st the bounds which torrid beams confine
By thy averted course, that shuns the ray
Oblique, enamour'd of sublimer day—
Oft on yon cliff thy folded plumes recline,
And drop those snowy feathers Indians twine
To crown the warrior's brow with honours gay—
O'er trackless oceans what impels thy wing?
10   Does no soft instinct in thy soul prevail?
No sweet affection to thy bosom cling,
And bid thee oft thy absent nest bewail?—
Yet thou again to that dear spot canst spring—
But I my long-lost home no more shall hail!

(1795)

Sonnet to the Torrid Zone[*]

Pathway of light! o'er thy empurpled zone,
With lavish charms perennial summer strays;
Soft 'midst thy spicy groves the zephyr plays,
While far around the rich perfumes are thrown;
The amadavid-bird for thee alone,
Spreads his gay plumes that catch thy vivid rays;
For thee the gems with liquid lustre blaze,
And nature's various wealth is all thy own.
But, ah! not thine is twilight's doubtful gloom,
Those mild gradations, mingling day with night;   10
Here, instant darkness shrouds thy genial bloom,
Nor leaves my pensive soul that ling'ring light,
When musing mem'ry would each trace resume
Of fading pleasures in successive flight.

(1795)

* The region of the earth between the tropic of Cancer and the tropic of Capricorn.

Hymn, Written among the Alps

Creation's God! with thought elate,
    Thy hand divine I see
Impressed on scenes, where all is great,
    Where all is full of thee!

Where stern the Alpine mountains raise
    Their heads of massive snow;
When on the rolling storm I gaze,
    That hangs—how far below!

5 amadavid-bird] The amadavat *(Estrilda amandava)*, an Indian songbird, brown with white spots.

Where on some bold, stupendous height,
    The Eagle sits alone;
Or soaring wings his sullen flight
    To haunts yet more his own:

Where the sharp rock the Chamois treads,
    Or slippery summit scales;
Or where the whitening Snow-bird spreads
    Her plumes to icy gales:

Where the rude cliff's steep column glows
    With morning's tint of blue;
Or evening on the glacier throws
    The rose's blushing hue:

Or where by twilight's softer light,
    The mountain's shadow bends;
And sudden casts a partial night,
    As black its form descends:

Where the full ray of noon alone
    Down the deep valley falls:
Or where the sunbeam never shone
    Between its rifted walls:

Where cloudless regions calm the soul,
    Bid mortal cares be still,
Can passion's wayward wish controul,
    And rectify the will:

Where midst some vast expanse the mind,
    Which swelling virtue fires,
Forgets that earth it leaves behind,
    And to its* heaven aspires:

Where far along the desart air
    Is heard no creature's call:
And undisturbing mortal ear
    The avalanches fall:

13 Chamois] Type of antelope inhabiting the highest parts of the Alps; known for its agility.

Where rushing from their snowy source,
　　The daring torrents urge
Their loud-toned waters headlong course,
　　And lift their feathered surge:

Where swift the lines of light and shade
　　Flit o'er the lucid lake:
Or the shrill winds its breast invade,
　　And its green billows wake:

Where on the slope, with speckled dye
　　The pigmy herds I scan;　　　　　　　　　　　50
Or soothed, the scattered *Chalets* spy,
　　The last abode of man:

Or where the flocks refuse to pass,
　　And the lone peasant mows,
Fixed on his knees, the pendent grass,
　　Which down the steep he throws:

Where high the dangerous pathway leads
　　Above the gulph profound,
From whence the shrinking eye recedes,
　　Nor finds repose around:　　　　　　　　　　60

Where red the mountain-ash reclines
　　Along the clifted rock;
Where firm the dark unbending pines
　　The howling tempests mock:

Where, level with the ice-ribb'd bound
　　The yellow harvests glow;
Or vales with purple vines are crown'd
　　Beneath impending snow:

Where the rich min'rals catch the ray,
　　With varying lustre bright,　　　　　　　　　70
And glittering fragments strew the way
　　With sparks of liquid light:

Or where the moss forbears to creep
Where loftier summits rear
Their untrod snow, and frozen sleep
Locks all the uncolour'd year:

In every scene, where every hour
Sheds some terrific grace,
In Nature's vast o'erwhelming power,
80   THEE, THEE, my GOD, I trace!
(1798)

* The original text of the poem reads "And to *it's* heaven aspires:" which is
clearly wrong.

To James Forbes, Esq. on His Bringing Me Flowers
from Vaucluse, and Which He Had Preserved by Means
of an Ingenious Process in Their Original Beauty*

Sweet spoils of consecrated bowers,
How dear to me these chosen flowers!
I love the simplest bud that blows,
I love the meanest weed that grows:
Symbols of nature—every form
That speaks of her this heart can warm;
But ye, delicious flowers, assume
In fancy's eye a brighter bloom;
A dearer pleasure ye diffuse,
10   Cull'd by the fountain of Vaucluse!
For ye were nurtur'd on the sod
Where PETRARCH mourn'd, and LAURA trod;
Ye grew on that inspiring ground
Where love has shed enchantment round;

12 Where PETRARCH mourn'd, and LAURA trod] Petrarch (1304–74) was one of the most
popular Italian poets of the Renaissance. In Avignon in 1327 he met the woman he calls Laura,
who inspired his love poetry. Her true identity is unknown.

Where still the tear of passion flows,
Fond tribute to a poet's woes!
Yet, cherish'd flowers, with love and fame
This wreath entwines a milder name;
Friendship, who better knows than they
The spells that smooth our length'ning way,— 20
Friendship the blooming off'ring brought;
When FORBES the classic fountain sought,
For me he cull'd the fresh-blown flowers,
And fix'd their hues with potent powers;
Their pliant forms with skilful care
He seized, and stamp'd duration there;
His gift shall ever glad the eye,—
Nor, like my verse is born to die.

(1823)

*James Forbes (1749–1819) went to India in 1775 as private secretary to Colonel Keating and returned to England in 1784 with fifty-two thousand pages of sketches and notes on the plants and animals, religion, archeology, and customs of India. He published his *Oriental Memoirs* in four quarto volumes in 1813–15. After being detained in France for almost a year during the Napoleonic Wars, he returned to England in 1804 and published his *Letters from France* in 1806.

To a Friend, Who Sent Me Flowers, When Confined by Illness

While sickness still my step detains
From scenes where vernal pleasure reigns,
Where Spring has bath'd with dewy tear
The blossoms of the op'ning year;
To soothe confinement's languid hours,
You send a lavish gift of flowers,
Midst whose soft odours mem'ry roves
O'er all the images she loves.
Not long their sweetness shall prevail,
Their rosy tints shall soon be pale, 10

Yet fancy in their fading hues
No emblem of our friendship views;
Its firm fidelity shall last,
When all the flowers of spring are past;
And when life's summer shall be o'er,
That summer which returns no more,
Still friendship, with perennial bloom,
Shall soften half the winter's gloom!

(1823)

Dorothy Wordsworth

(1771–1855)

Only in the twentieth century has the literary production of Dorothy Words-worth become widely known. During her lifetime, readership of her journals and poems was, with few exceptions, confined to those within her intimate circle of family and friends. Only five of her poems were published during her lifetime, all anonymously in collections by her brother, William; never-theless, she was from the beginning an important literary influence: aspects of her style and many of her ideas and images, both from written work and conversation, found their way into the writings of William Wordsworth and Samuel Taylor Coleridge.

Born on Christmas Day, 1771, Dorothy was the third child and only daugh-ter of Ann Cookson and John Wordsworth, attorney to Sir James Lowther, Cockermouth. After her mother died in 1778, six-year-old Dorothy was separated from her siblings and sent to live in Halifax, Yorkshire, with her mother's cousin Elizabeth Threlkeld. "Aunt Threlkeld," as Dorothy called her, gave the little girl a loving home in a household of six children, the others from ten to seventeen years old. As the youngest, Dorothy was the favorite. The Halifax Old Subscription Library was housed for some years in Elizabeth Threlkeld's haberdashery shop, and Threlkeld, whom Dorothy came to idol-ize, taught her an early love of reading as well as skill in cooking, sewing, accounting, and general household management. Dorothy briefly attended a boarding school two miles from town in 1781, when she was nine, but then became a day student in Halifax. She attended the Unitarian chapel regularly with Threlkeld.

On 30 December 1783 Dorothy's father died. She had not seen him in the years since her mother's death, but his death was to change her life pro-foundly. John Wordsworth had died without a will and with a major sum owed to him by Sir James Lowther, who refused to make good on his debt. The executors were forced to sue, but in the meantime far less money was made available for Dorothy's support than had been forthcoming in the past.

As an economy, in May of 1787 she was sent to live for a brief but unhappy period with her mother's parents in Penrith over their draper's shop. Her grandmother found her "intractible and wild." Afterward Dorothy went to live for six years in Norfolk to help care for the growing family of her aunt Dorothy Cowper and her uncle William Cookson.

Dorothy and her brother William, who was twenty months her senior, had long dreamed of setting up a household together, and in 1795 they were able to do this at Racedown Lodge, Dorset, near the Devon border. As Thomas DeQuincey later observed, the mission Dorothy saw for herself was "to wait upon him [William] as the tenderest and most faithful of domestics; to love him as a sister; to sympathize with him as a confidante; to counsel him as one gifted with a power of judging that stretched as far as his own for producing; to cheer him and sustain him by the natural expression of her feelings — so quick, so ardent, so unaffected — upon the probable effect of whatever thoughts, plans, images he might conceive."[1] At Racedown Dorothy also cared for the toddler Basil Montagu, and in 1797 she and her brother met and established a close friendship and eventually an intellectual and literary collaboration with Samuel Taylor Coleridge. The Wordsworths were so taken with Coleridge that they moved to Alfoxden House in Somerset to be near him in Nether Stowey; Dorothy kept a journal now referred to as the Alfoxden Journal, from 20 January to 22 May 1798, a period of great poetic creativity in the household. DeQuincey describes her at this time as "too ardent and fiery a creature to maintain the reserve essential to dignity; and dignity was the last thing one thought of in the presence of one so artless, so fervent in her feelings, and so embarrassed in their utterance — "; he also recalls her "originality and native freshness of intellect, which settled with so bewitching an effect upon some of her writings, and upon many a sudden remark or ejaculation, extorted by something or other that struck her eye, in the clouds, or in colouring, or in accidents of light and shade, of form, or combination of form."[2] Coleridge referred to her as Wordsworth's "exquisite Sister" and described "her eye watchful in minutest observation of nature — and her taste a perfect electrometer — it bends, protrudes, and draws in at subtlest beauties and most recondite faults."[3] William said of Dorothy:

> She, in the midst of all, preserv'd me still
> A Poet, made me seek beneath that name
> My office upon earth, and no where else.[4]

1. *Tait's Edinburgh Magazine* 6 (1839): 252.
2. Ibid., 251, 253.
3. Robert Gittings and Jo Manton, *Dorothy Wordsworth* (Oxford, 1985), 65.
4. *The Prelude* (London, 1850), bk. 11, lines 346–48.

After a dispiriting winter in Germany, Dorothy and William returned to the Lake District, to Dove Cottage, Grasmere, in 1799. There on 14 May 1800 Dorothy began another journal "because I shall give William pleasure by it."[5] In later years she explained her own apparent lack of poetic ambition:

> —I *reverenced* the Poet's skill,
> And *might have* nursed a mounting Will
> To imitate the tender Lays
> Of them who sang in Nature's praise;
> But bashfulness, a struggling shame
> A fear that elder heads might blame
> —Or something worse—a lurking pride
> Whispering my playmates would deride
> Stifled ambition, checked the aim
> If e'er by chance "The numbers came"[6]

Even so, many modern readers have been struck by the poetic nature of Dorothy Wordsworth's prose in her Grasmere and Alfoxden Journals. Indeed, in her later journals she experiments by arranging passages in verse form. But as Susan Levin points out, Dorothy would not have thought of these passages as poems. And William's patronizing attitude toward women poets also played a part in her decision to turn her own talents largely to prose. Just as William criticized Felicia Hemans for being "totally ignorant of house-wifery," Dorothy shows her own anxiety about female authorship when, for example, she lauds Joanna Baillie for being not simply a "literary Lady" but a person devoted to her home.[7] But in 1940 Hyman Eigerman published short passages from Dorothy Wordsworth's journals arranged in verse form to show that in such a format they resembled imagist poems. Read in this way, Dorothy Wordsworth seems to anticipate by many years the work of Wallace Stevens, Baudelaire, and Ezra Pound.

Writing was not only an essential part of Dorothy Wordsworth's everyday life; it was crucial to her self-definition. Clearly, from the start she envisioned that her own literary production would contribute to the household she and William planned to set up, for her Aunt Rawson remarked disapprovingly, "Dorothy and Wm. have now a scheme of living together in London, and maintaining themselves by their literary talents, writing and translating. . . . We think it a very bad wild scheme."[8] William Wordsworth's own poetry

5. *Journals of Dorothy Wordsworth,* ed. E. de Selincourt, 2 vols. (London, 1952), 1:37.
6. "Irregular Verses," lines 60–69; the entire poem appears in Susan Levin, *Dorothy Wordsworth and Romanticism* (New Brunswick, N.J., 1987), 202–3.
7. Levin, *Dorothy Wordsworth,* 155–56.
8. Ibid., 58.

became simpler, more concrete, less traditional, and less ornate after he began living with his sister. That is to say, his style came more to resemble her own. Although Dorothy's work remained, for the most part, unpublished during her lifetime, she was an active participant in the collaboration that led to the publication in 1798 of the *Lyrical Ballads,* by William Wordsworth and Samuel Taylor Coleridge. Both for this project and on other occasions, the two male poets mined her journal for poetic images and ideas and liberally borrowed from her verbal observations of the natural world. For both men, she was a sounding board, a critic, an amanuensis, and a significant literary influence.

In August 1802 the Wordsworths visited France, and in Paris Dorothy met William's French daughter, Caroline, now nine years old, and her mother, Annette Vallon, from whom William had been separated by political events. Dorothy kept her journal during the trip, but as part of the conspiracy of silence William imposed on this chapter of his life, she omitted the month in Paris. The Grasmere Journal ends on 16 January 1803, not long after William's marriage on 4 October 1802 to Dorothy's friend Mary Hutchinson, an event of such import in her life that Dorothy was unable to bring herself to attend. But Dorothy remained in the household, continuing to play a crucial part in William's life. Eventually she was to become a second mother to William and Mary's five children.

Was William and Dorothy's relationship an incestuous one? Certainly some of their neighbors thought so, and many modern commentators have voiced similar suspicions. Clearly their relationship was closer and emotionally more intense than is usual between sister and brother. But whether that bond was physically consummated is something we may never know for certain. It is, however, unlikely to have been. And perhaps Coleridge was responding to such rumors when he said of Dorothy,

> In every motion her most innocent soul
> Outbeams so brightly, that who saw would say,
> Guilt was a thing impossible to her— [9]

In 1803 Dorothy made a tour of Scotland with her brother and Samuel Taylor Coleridge, meeting Walter Scott along the way. After the fact, to share the experience with friends, Dorothy wrote *Recollections of a Tour Made in Scotland;* by May 1805 she had produced a complete draft, which she revised and added to in early 1806. Thomas DeQuincey maintained that this book was "in very deed a monument to her power of catching and expressing all the hidden beauties of natural scenery with a felicity of diction, a truth, and strength,

9. See Gittings and Manton, *Dorothy Wordsworth,* 65. For a discussion of local rumors of incest between Dorothy and William, see ibid., 105.

that far transcend Gilpin, or professional writers on those subjects. . . . This book . . . is absolutely unique in its class."[10] On 5 February 1805 Dorothy's younger brother John, captain of an East India ship, drowned in Weymouth Bay. To lift her despondency she began riding a pony, and in November she took a week's riding excursion with William in the countryside around Ullswater. William mined the short journal she kept and later used some of her prose passages in his *Guide to the Lakes* (1822). In March 1808, when her neighbors George and Sarah Green perished in a snowstorm, Dorothy wrote a narrative account of their deaths and the courage of their children to help raise money for their relief. Although it circulated in manuscript at the time, it was not published until 1936.

Dorothy Wordsworth wrote some of what she considered verse—short rhymed, metrical pieces—for the children in her household, for female friends, in letters, and in literary albums and commonplace books. "An Address to a Child in a High Wind" and "To My Niece Dorothy, a Sleepless Baby," were probably composed between 1805 and 1807; they were published anonymously, along with Dorothy's "The Mother's Return," with William's poems of 1815. William took the liberty of altering the original names and titles to distance the world of Dorothy's poems from his own world. For example, in "An Address to a Child in a High Wind" he changed Dorothy's "Johnny," a reference to his own son, John Wordsworth, to "Edward"; and "To My Niece Dorothy" became in his hands the more generalized "A Cottager to Her Infant." Moreover, in his published version of the latter poem William added two stanzas that interject into the poem the issue of social class. Tellingly, in the Rydal notebook Dorothy vigorously crossed out these additional stanzas.[11] After the volume appeared, Charles Lamb wrote William, "We were glad to see the poems by a female friend. The one of the wind is masterly, but not new to us. Being only three [poems], perhaps you might have clapt a *D.* at the corner and let it have past as a print[e]rs mark to the uninitiated, as a delightful hint to the better-instructed."[12]

In 1810 William Wordsworth and Samuel Taylor Coleridge had a serious falling out. As a result, Dorothy did not see her close friend Coleridge for the next decade. She converted to orthodox Christianity in 1811, a faith sorely tested when two of the Wordsworths' children died the following year. The household moved to Rydal Mount in May 1813, where Dorothy, William, and Mary would spend the remainder of their lives. Dorothy climbed Scafell

10. *Tait's Edinburgh Magazine* 6 (1839): 253.

11. Levin, *Dorothy Wordsworth*, 115.

12. *The Letters of Charles and Mary Anne Lamb,* ed. Edwin W. Marrs Jr., 3 vols. (Ithaca, 1975–78), 3:141.

Pike with a friend and guide in 1818 and wrote an account of her experience. William revised the piece and published it in his *Guide to the Lakes* (1822) as an "extract from a letter to a Friend."

From July to November 1820 Dorothy traveled with William and Mary and another couple through France, Belgium, Germany, Switzerland, and Italy, taking in the Alps; from April to August 1821 Dorothy wrote a journal of the tour, which she recopied in October. In the fall of 1822 she took a seven-week trip to Scotland with Joanna Hutchinson, and in hopes of making money for a future journey, she revised her *Recollections* of her first Scottish trip after Samuel Rogers suggested publication. This work was not published until 1874, when the 1806 version, not the revised version, was published. Her journal entries from 1824 to 1833 were sparse. In 1828 she traveled to the Isle of Man with Joanna Hutchinson and her brother Henry. In April of that year, while keeping house for a nephew in Leicestershire, she was overcome by a severe gallstone attack from which she never fully recovered. She was seriously ill again in December 1831, and around this time she began taking laudenum regularly for pain. She had another relapse in 1833. In 1832 Dorothy composed "Loving and Liking. Irregular Verses Addressed to a Child," published by William in his *Poems* (1836). Another of her poems, "The Floating Island at Hawkshead," appeared in William's 1842 collection, the author now identified as "D.W."

In 1835 Dorothy began to show signs of the presenile dementia from which she would suffer for the two decades preceding her death on 25 January 1855. During this twenty-year period she was lovingly cared for by William and Mary. Lucid at intervals, she was sometimes able to write short letters. She also accurately recited long passages of verse and obsessively made copies of her own poetry.

MAJOR WORKS: *Recollections of a Tour Made in Scotland A.D. 1803*, ed. J. C. Sharp (Edinburgh, 1874); *George and Sarah Green. A Narrative*, ed. Ernest de Selincourt (Oxford, 1936); *Journals of Dorothy Wordsworth. The Alfoxden Journal, 1798. The Grasmere Journals, 1800–1803*, ed. Mary Moorman (London, 1971); *The Letters of William and Dorothy Wordsworth*, ed. Ernest de Selincourt, rev. Alan G. Hill, 8 vols. (Oxford, 1978–93).

TEXTS USED: Texts of "An Address to a Child in a High Wind" and "To My Niece Dorothy" from Susan Levin, *Dorothy Wordsworth and Romanticism* (New Brunswick, N.J., 1987), 179–80.

An Address to a Child in a High Wind

What way does the wind come? what way does he go?
He rides over the water and over the snow,
Through the valley, and over the hill
And roars as loud as a thundering Mill.
He tosses about in every bare tree,
As, if you look up you plainly may see
But how he will come, and whither he goes
There's never a Scholar in England knows.

He will suddenly stop in a cunning nook
And rings a sharp larum:—but if you should look   10
There's nothing to see but a cushion of snow,
Round as a pillow and whiter than milk
And softer than if it were cover'd with silk.

Sometimes he'll hide in the cave of a rock;
Then whistle as shrill as a buzzard cock;
—But seek him and what shall you find in his place
Nothing but silence and empty space
Save in a corner a heap of dry leaves
That he's left for a bed for beggars or thieves.

As soon as 'tis daylight tomorrow with me   20
You shall go to the orchard & there you will see
That he has been there, & made a great rout,
And cracked the branches, & strew'd them about:
Heaven grant that he spare but that one upright twig
That look'd up at the sky so proud & so big
All last summer, as well you know
Studded with apples, a beautiful shew!

Hark! over the roof he makes a pause
And growls as if he would fix his claws
Right in the slates, and with a great rattle   30
Drive them down like men in a battle.
—But let him range round; he does us no harm

10 larum] Tumultuous noise.

We build up the fire; we're snug and warm,
Old Madam has brought us plenty of coals
And the Glazier has closed up all the holes
In every window that Johnny broke
And the walls are tighter than Molly's new cloak.

Come, now we'll to bed, and when we are there
He may work his own will, & what shall we care.
40   He may knock at the door—we'll not let him in
May drive at the windows—we'll laugh at his din
Let him seek his own home wherever it be
Here's a canny warm house for Johnny and me.
                              (wr. 1806; pub. 1815)

To My Niece Dorothy,[*] a Sleepless Baby

The days are cold; the nights are long
The north wind sings a doleful song
Then hush again upon my breast;
All *merry* things are now at rest
    Save thee my pretty love!

The kitten sleeps upon the hearth;
The crickets long have ceased their mirth
There's nothing stirring in the house
Save one wee hungry nibbling mouse
10   Then why so busy thou?

Nay, start not at that sparkling light
'Tis but the moon that shines so bright
On the window-pane bedropp'd with rain
Then, little Darling, sleep again
    And wake when it is Day.
                              (wr. c. 1805 to 1807; pub. 1815)

---

[*] Mary and William Wordsworth's daughter Dorothy (1804–47), later known as
Dora to avoid confusion with her aunt.

43 canny] Snug.

Ann Yearsley

(1752–1806)

Ann Yearsley, poet, novelist, and playwright, was born in 1752 at Clifton, near Bristol, to John and Ann Cromartie. She never attended school but read tombstones and later the Bible, Milton, Thomson, and Pope, along with whatever other books her mother could borrow from employers. With the help of her brother, she learned to write and began to pen verses. In 1774 she married John Yearsley, and the couple eventually had six children; her husband appears not to have prospered as a laborer and does not figure prominently in her works or in her own accounts of her life. By 1783 the family was impoverished. Ann Yearsley sold milk, garden produce, and livestock, gleaning fields for extra food and gathering firewood where she could, but her efforts proved insufficient. The brutal winter of 1783–84 found the family without adequate heat or food, with no furniture, work, or income, possibly homeless. Family and friends had long admired her verse; now this talent became Yearsley's only economic resource, and she carefully managed to bring her poetry to the attention of Bristol's literary elite.

In February 1784 Richard Vaughn of Bristol heard some of Yearsley's poems read aloud at a friend's house and admired them as "far above the level of a person in the situation of a milk-woman." After dining, he went to visit the poet. Finding her with her children and mother in desperate circumstances in a rude hut, he sent a horse loaded with provisions. According to one account, "The gratitude which Mr. V.'s benevolence excited was expressed in language which astonished every one to whom Mrs. Yearsley's letters were shewn."[1] Hannah More recalled that "a copy of verses was shewn me, said to be written by a poor illiterate woman in this neighbourhood, who sells milk from door to door. The story did not engage my faith, but the verses excited my attention; for, though incorrect, they breathed the genuine spirit of Poetry, and were rendered still more interesting, by a certain natural

---

1. The *Weekly Entertainer* of Sherborne published an account under the title "Anecdotes of Mrs. Yearsley" in its 14 February 1785 issue.

and strong expression of misery, which seemed to fill the heart and mind of the Author."[2] Elizabeth Montagu also was taken with Yearsley's poetry, exclaiming, "Indeed, she is one of nature's miracles. What force of imagination! what harmony of numbers!"[3]

Convinced that she had discovered a natural genius, whom she dubbed "the Milkwoman of Clifton near Bristol," More decided to help Yearsley. During the fall of 1784 and into the early months of 1785 More wrote influential friends asking them to subscribe to a volume of poems, often sending transcriptions of Yearsley's verse. Horace Walpole warned that Yearsley "must remember that she is a Lactilla, not a Pastora, and is to tend real cows, not Arcadian sheep";[4] it is clear that, although they hoped to aid Yearsley, More and her circle of friends had no intention of encouraging a life of letters for the milkwoman or of accepting her as an equal. Yearsley's poetry appeared in many periodicals during this time, including the *Scots Magazine* and *London Magazine.* According to Chauncey Brewster Tinker, "All social London and half literary London put its name on the list of subscribers," which numbered almost a thousand.[5] *Poems, on Several Occasions,* containing sixteen poems, half of which, obsequious and full of hyperbole, express gratitude to subscribers, was published in June 1785. Addressed largely to aristocratic and upper-middle-class readers, Yearsley's poetic voice both echoes the established values of her audience and subtly critiques the conditions of her relationship with them, a pattern that would persist throughout her career. Having actually labored in the fields, Yearsley had a view of rural life that did not match the pastoral ideal; "Clifton Hill," for example, vividly describes the hardships of agricultural labor.

The reviews were enthusiastic, though most, such as the review in the *Gentleman's Magazine,* mixed their praise with condescension. In the *Monthly Review,* Andrew Badcock wrote, "On the whole these Poems present us with a very striking picture of a vigorous and aspiring genius, struggling with its own feelings. We see an ardent mind exerting itself to throw off every incumbrance that oppresses it, and to burst from the cloud that obscures its lustre." The reviewer for the *Critical Review* was also encouraging: "Stephen [Duck] was merely a rhymer: the protection he obtained proceeded from the

2. From "A Prefatory Letter to Mrs. Montagu," by Hannah More, 20 October 1784, published in Yearsley's first book, *Poems, on Several Occasions,* iv, and reprinted in *Poems on Various Subjects* (1787), viii.

3. William Roberts, *Memoirs of the Life and Correspondence of Mrs. Hannah More,* 2 vols. (New York, 1835), 1:204.

4. *Horace Walpole's Correspondence,* ed. W. S. Lewis, 48 vols. (New Haven, 1971), 31:221.

5. *Nature's Simple Plan: A Phase of Radical Thought in the Mid-Eighteenth Century* (1922; reprint, New York, 1964), 100–101.

peculiarity of a thresher's writing verse, not on account of the verses themselves. . . . The poems before us are entitled to a superior degree of praise;
there are evident traces to be found in them of a strong and fervid imagination." The *European Magazine* reprinted "Clifton Hill" and More's "Prefatory
Letter" in their entirety. The *London Chronicle* filled its front page and most of
its second with a review, devoting more space to Yearsley than to Cowper's
The Task the following month.[6] This first edition made £350.[7]

Just as the second edition was being prepared, a dispute over financial
control of the profits caused a breach with More and put an end to the generosity of Yearsley's first set of subscribers. Naively and in haste, on 10 June
1785 Yearsley and her husband had signed the deed of trust More presented to
them. Having anticipated financial independence, the poet now found that
she would receive an annual allowance of only eighteen pounds (interest on
the principal), so that instead of being able to read and improve her poetry,
she would be forced back into manual labor. When Yearsley approached More
with a proposal to modify the deed to allow her to serve as joint trustee with
More and Elizabeth Montagu, More was insulted to find her judgment and
good intentions questioned by a social "inferior." Yearsley felt that she was
being denied the fruits of her labor and the means to improve the lives of
her children. Both women lost their temper.

During the summer and fall of 1785 More engaged in a letter-writing campaign against Yearsley, portraying her as intemperate, ungrateful, and likely
to squander her earnings. Even so, she resigned the trust in December, and the
money came under Yearsley's control. The fourth edition of *Poems, on Several
Occasions* (1786) contained an indignant prefatory narrative replying point by
point to More's version of the dispute, countering what Yearsley saw as slander, misrepresentation, and injustice. Casting More as insensitive, arrogant,
and a bit dishonest, she promised to show with her performance in *Poems
on Various Subjects* that the quality of her poetry owed virtually nothing to
More's corrections and instruction. She reprinted this narrative, along with
a copy of the deed of trust and the prefatory letter from More to Montagu,
in her next collection. The twentieth-century critic Mary Waldron explains
the dispute by suggesting that in order to attract subscribers to her book,
Yearsley had been willing to groom herself into the milkwoman phenome-
non More announced; in actuality she was a member of the lower middle

6. *Gentleman's Magazine* 55 (1785): 812–13; *Monthly Review* 73 (1785): 221; *Critical Review* 60
(1785): 148.

7. The profits from all four editions would total more than six hundred pounds (see Eliza
Dawson Fletcher, *Autobiography of Mrs. Fletcher with Letters and Other Family Memorials*, edited by
the Survivor of her Family, 3rd ed. [Edinburgh, 1876], 29; and Roberts, *Memoirs of Mrs. Hannah
More*, 1:206).

class, only somewhat recently reduced in circumstances. Thus, her defiance can be explained as resentment against a middle-class woman she considered more her equal than her superior.[8]

Early in 1786 Yearsley established a relationship with the bookseller George Robinson, whose sponsorship helped her achieve independence from a restrictive patronage system and who published most of the poet's subsequent books. That summer, Eliza Dawson (later Fletcher) was moved by Yearsley's narrative to offer to collect subscriptions for *Poems, on Various Subjects.* With fifty pounds from her father and four hundred new subscribers, she helped Yearsley establish a reputation independently of More. *Poems on Various Subjects* contains thirty individual works. Along with poems to benefactors, the volume includes sensual lyrics celebrating physical love and the ecstasy of poetic inspiration, polemics, elegies, Augustan imitations, an ode, a Biblical critique, and an indignant poem entitled "To Those Who Accuse the Author of Ingratitude," which describes such individuals as "low, groveling, and confin'd" of sense. Though she sees herself as Chatterton's successor, she distances herself somewhat from the persona of a humble, uneducated milkwoman. In poems such as "On Jephthah's Vow, Taken in a Literal Sense," she condemns patriarchal modes of thought and behavior, testing the limits of what readers would tolerate from a woman of her social standing. She speaks authoritatively about poetic inspiration, celebrating imagination, emotion, and the intuitive.

Andrew Becket, writing for the *Monthly Review,* praised "the same originality of thought and expression [as in the earlier volume], the same boldness and grandeur in the imagery." The *Critical Review* also applauded the poems, observing, "In regard to modulation of numbers, particularly in blank verse, we know few authors superior to the Bristol milk woman. Her sentiments are often equally just and original, her diction strong and animated, and her pauses judiciously varied." For the most part, reviewers took Yearsley's side in her dispute with More. The *Critical Review* observed, "Miss More, in a prefatory letter, speaks highly of Ann Yearsley's moral character. On their disagreement we are told she has charged her 'with every vice that can disgrace the sex.' Either the encomium, or accusation, must be unjust; and Miss More cannot escape the imputation of improper partiality, or unjust censure. A few months could not have caused so strange an alteration in this poor woman's character."[9]

---

8. "Ann Yearsley and the Clifton Records," in *The Age of Johnson: A Scholarly Annual,* ed. Paul J. Korshin (New York, 1990), 301–29.

9. *Monthly Review* 77 (1786): 485–86; *Critical Review* 64 (1786): 435.

Yearsley's poems now began to appear regularly in the *Universal Magazine*, the *Annual Register*, the *European Magazine*, and in Bristol's *Felix Farley's Journal*. In February 1788 Yearsley brought out *A Poem on the Inhumanity of the Slave-trade*, taking on some of the most powerful and affluent people not only in Bristol but in all of Britain. In the abolitionist tradition, she reproaches so-called Christians who trade in human lives, calling them "slave[s] of avarice," "Hypocrites," "a vile race of Christians," and "thieves." Vivid and moving images portray the effect of slavery on the family. The book was not widely reviewed, but Yearsley was now a self-assured poet, exercising tighter narrative control over her material and wearing her lack of formal education as an emblem of pride. Her next major work, *Earl Goodwin, an Historical Play,* a five-act tragedy in blank verse based on the eleventh-century reign of Edward the Confessor, endorses violence as a means to achieve justice and individual rights. One of her most explicitly feminist works, it portrays independent women characters and critiques patriarchal institutions. Produced in 1789 at the Theatre-Royal, Bristol, and at Bath, it received praise from the *Gentleman's Magazine* but a mixed review from the *European Magazine*. When it was published in 1791, the *Analytical Review* damned it and the *Monthly Review* gave it qualified approval.[10]

During the hay harvest of 1789, two of Yearsley's small sons were whipped by a footman for trespassing on the property of Levi Eames, one of Bristol's most powerful businessmen. That incident, along with a related altercation the following year that caused Yearsley to miscarry, inspired *Stanzas of Woe* (1790) and *The Dispute: Letter to the Public. From the Milkwoman* (1791). These works speak out against the injustice of the monied class and advocate the rights of children long before that concept was generally accepted. *Stanzas of Woe* received favorable notices in the *New Annual Register*, the *Monthly Review*, the *General Magazine*, and the *English Review*. The *Analytical Review*, however, was not impressed.[11]

At about this time Yearsley moved to Bristol Hotwells, a resort community, and began operating a lending library. But almost immediately after she learned of Louis XVI's execution in 1793, she penned *Reflections on the Death of Louis XVI* and *Sequel to Reflections on the Death of Louis XVI*, privately printed and sold locally. These elegies oppose capital punishment and emphasize the humanity of royal figures. *An Elegy on Marie Antoinette,* which followed soon after, mourns the death of the person and the mother rather

10. *Analytical Review* 11 (1791): 427–28; *Monthly Review*, n.s., 6 (1791): 347–48.

11. *New Annual Register* 11 (1790): [249]; *Monthly Review*, n.s., 5 (1791): 222–23; *General Magazine* 5 (1971): 266; *English Review* 17 (1791): 361–63; *Analytical Review* 9 (1791): 447–48.

than the destruction of the monarchy. For these three elegies, along with another, *Poem on the Last Interview between the King of Poland and Loraski,* the poet abandoned her laboring-class epithet and signed herself simply "Ann Yearsley," as she would sign all her works from this time forward.

In 1795 George Robinson brought out in four volumes Yearsley's novel *The Royal Captives: A Fragment of Secret History. Copied from an Old Manuscript.* Partaking of the gothic romance tradition and the tradition of the "discovered" manuscript, the novel retells from a female perspective the legend of the "man in the iron mask" and critiques abuses of power during the reign of Louis XIV. Including a pre-Byronic anti-hero, the novel is a dreamlike exploration of psychological identity, full of suspense, sensationalism, coincidence, and intricate subplots. In this feminist critique of contemporary England, the laboring-class secondary characters interact with the aristocracy in a manner that challenges the very nature of class distinction itself. Joseph Johnson's *Analytical Review* gave the book a five-page notice, hailing it as "the production of a genius above the common level"; the *European Magazine and London Review* praised the author's "considerable skill and felicity"; and the *English Review* applauded Yearsley's style and concluded that the "poetry in these volumes is simple and beautiful." Not surprisingly, Robinson's *New Annual Register* puffed it. The *Critical Review* and the *Monthly Review* were less enthusiastic but recommended the book to readers.[12] Despite this generally positive critical reception as well as pirated editions in Ireland and America and an unauthorized periodical abridgement,[13] sales were not encouraging and Yearsley never published another novel.

Her next book, *The Rural Lyre; a Volume of Poems* (1796), included sonnets, lyrics, elegies, epistles, and a fragment of an epic. It contains some of Yearsley's most pointed feminist commentary, idealizes female nurturing, and emphasizes the domestic roots of justice and order. This book was not acknowledged by most of the major national reviews and seems to have ended Yearsley's literary career. The poet, now widowed, retreated from public view and later lived in seclusion in Merksham, Wiltshire. She died in 1806, having achieved financial security as a poet, novelist, and historical dramatist. Her valorizing of inspiration and natural genius, her experiments with form, her championing of the dispossessed and marginalized, and her explorations of the human psyche anticipated the poetic practice and ideology that later would come to be defined as romanticism. But she never escaped the label "peasant poet" during her lifetime or afterward.

12. *Analytical Review* 21 (1795): 291; *European Magazine and London Review* 27 (1795): 94; *English Review* 24 (1794): 472.

13. In the *Weekly Entertainer* from 23 March to 29 June 1795.

MAJOR WORKS: *Poems, on Several Occasions,* ed. Hannah More (London, 1785); *Poems on Various Subjects,* ed. Hannah More (London, 1787); *A Poem on the Inhumanity of the Slave-trade* (London, [1788?]); *Stanzas of Woe, Addressed from the Heart on a Bed of Illness, to Levi Eames, Esq. Late Mayor of the City of Bristol* (London, 1790); *Earl Goodwin, an Historical Play . . . Performed with General Applause at the Theatre-Royal, Bristol* (London, 1791); *Reflections on the Death of Louis XVI* (Bristol, 1793); *Sequel to Reflections on the Death of Louis XVI* (Bristol, 1793); *The Royal Captives: a Fragment of Secret History,* 4 vols. (London, 1795); *An Elegy on Marie Antoinette of Austria, Ci-devant Queen of France: With a Poem on the Last Interview between the King of Poland and Loraski* (Bath, [1795?]); *The Rural Lyre; a Volume of Poems* (London, 1796).

TEXTS USED: Texts of "Anarchy" and "Peace" from *The Royal Captives.* Texts of "The Captive Linnet" and "Soliloquy" from *The Rural Lyre; a Volume of Poems.*

Anarchy

"Furies! Why sleep amid the carnage?—rise!
  "Bring up my wolves of war, my pointed spears.
"Daggers yet reeking, banners filled with sighs,
  "And paint your cheeks with gore, and lave your locks in tears.

"On yon white bosom see that happy child!
  "Seize it, deface its infant charms! And say,
"Anarchy view'd its mangled limbs and smil'd.
  "Strike the young mother to the earth!—Away!

"This is my æra! O'er the dead I go!
  "From my hot nostrils minute murders fall!   10
"Behind my burning car lurks feeble Woe!
  "Fill'd with my dragon's ire, my slaves for kingdoms call!

"Hear them not, Father of the ensanguin'd race!—
"World! Give my monsters way!—Death! keep thy steady chace!"*
                                                              (1795)

* The end quotation mark is missing from the original.

Peace

"What howlings wake me!—my fair olives die!
 "Storms shake my bow'r, and drive me to the plain.—
"Ah! direful Anarchy, thy chariots fly
 "O'er worlds of weeping babes, o'er worlds of hero's slain!

"Order! Bright angel down yon rainbow glide!
 "From the mild bosom of my God appear!
"O'er Gallia spread thy snowy pinions wide—
 "O! cool the fever'd mind! and whisper to Despair.

"Envenomn'd and unwelcome war! will man,
10 "Long nurse thy furies or prolong thy stay?
"Will not his fine, reflective spirit scan
"Those desolations that have mark'd thy way?

"Yes!—He shall wearied leave thy crimes, and prove,
"All that is worthy MAN, is found with ME and LOVE."

            (1795)

The Captive Linnet

Mycias, behold this bird! see how she tires—
Breaks her soft plumes, and springs against the wires!
A clown more rude than gracious brought her here
To pine in silence, and to die in snare.
Her haunt she well remembers: ev'ry morn
Her sweet note warbled from the blowing thorn
That hangs o'er yon cool wave; responses clear
Her sisters gave, and sprang through upper air.
E'en now (by habit gentler made), at eve,
10 A time when men their green dominions leave,
They sit, and call her near her fav'rite spray,
Meet no reply, and pensive wing their way.
This wound in friendship dear affections heal,

Their young require them: to their nests they steal;
Nurse them with warmth, with hope, with true delight,
And teach the danger of an early flight. —
Delicious toil! raptures that never cloy!
A mother only can define her joy.

Perhaps, dear Mycias, this poor mourner's breast
Was yesternight on her weak offspring prest! —   20
The down scarce breaking on their tender skin,
Their eyes yet clos'd, their bodies cold and thin;
Waiting when she would kindly warmth impart,
And take them trembling to her gen'rous heart.
Where are they now, sweet captive? Who'll befriend
Thy mourning children, as the storms descend?
The winds are bleak, thy mossy cradle's torn —
Hark! they lament thee, hungry and forlorn!
Each shiv'ring brother round his sister creeps,
Deep in the nest thy little daughter sleeps.   30
Again the blast, that tears the oak, comes on:
Thy rocking house, thy family are gone!
One to an hungry weasel falls a prey;
Another chirps, but not to hail the day:
Too weak to live, he seeks no casual aid,
And dies, rememb'ring thee, beneath the shade.
Where could thy daughter go? More weak and shrill
Her voice was heard. The ants forsake their hill. —
Through that republic Addison display'd,
When he unsated hunger virtue made,   40
And gave, unwisely, ant-like souls to man —
The barb'rous rumour of misfortune ran.
Alike pourtray'd in hist'ry and in verse,
For prey industrious, obdurate and fierce:
Voracious columns move! The victim's voice
Invites her foes, who sting her, and rejoice.
Keenly their riots on her frame begin:
She tries to shake them from her downy skin;

39 Through that republic Addison display'd] Joseph Addison (1672–1719), British essayist,
poet, and dramatist, published his theories about natural law, self-intent, and mercantilism in
The Free-Holder, or Political Essays, published from 23 December 1715 to 29 June 1716.

Their organs touch her springs of being—Strife
50   She holds not with her fate—she trembles out of life.

O Mycias! What hath yon barbarian gain'd,
Who with malicious joy this linnet chain'd?
Could she at morn salute his untun'd ear?
When dull with vice could she the gaoler cheer;
Hail him with strains of liberty; proclaim,
With harmony he hates, her maker's name:
Or peck from him the crumb withheld so long,
That her heart sicken'd e'en at freedom's song?
No: see, she droops, rejects his aid—confin'd—
60   Her dreary cage she scorns, and dies resign'd.

Mycias! thus spreads unseen more ling'ring woe,
Than e'en thy sympathising soul must know:
Wisely ordain'd! He mocks the proffer'd cure,
Who bids his friend one fruitless pang endure:
Since pity turns to anguish, when denied,
And troubles swell, which must in death subside.
Ah! fly the scene; secure that guilt can find
In brutal force no fetter for the mind!
True! Violated thus, it feels the chain,
70   Rises with languor, and lies down with pain;
Yet bless'd in trembling to one mighty WHOLE,
DEATH is the field of VICTORY for the SOUL.

                                             (1796)

Soliloquy

*Begun from the circumstance of the moment, and prolonged as the images
of memory arose in the mind of the author, February 27, 1795*

Author to her son.	Go you to bed, my boy.
Son.	Do you write to-night?
Author.	I do.
Son (laying his watch on the table).	See, how late!
Author.	No matter—You can sleep.

How patiently toils on this little watch!
My veins beat to its motion. Ye who sing
Of atoms, rest, and motion, say, why Time
Sets in this toy a larum to my heart.
O sacred Time! thy moment goes not down   10
But I go with it! Sixty coming hours
Are with us poor expectants of more price
Than sixty years sunk to oblivion. Rise,
Dear Memory, silent fascinating pow'r,
Hated by many: I will be thy slave,
Thy willing slave. Then lead thy shadows round,
Forever sacred to my pensive mind.

  Instructive Spirit, hail! For thee I call
Mild Contemplation, from the barren rock
Where mourns the ship-wreck'd mariner, to trim   20
My midnight lamp. Hail, much rever'd in death!
Thou knew'st to chart the moral world, and bend
The springs of thought to wisdom: thou wert wont

---

8 Of atoms, rest, and motion] Mechanical philosophy is that which undertakes to account
for the phenomena of nature from the principles of mechanics, taking in the consideration of
motion, rest, figure, size, &c. This is also called the corpuscular philosophy. *Yearsley.* [Atomism, a doctrine maintaining that the universe is composed of simple and unchangeable minute
particles called *atoms,* was propounded by Greek philosophers in the fifth century B.C. In the
sixteenth and seventeenth centuries certain scientists called "atomists" blended Democritean
and Aristotelian approaches into a general corpuscular theory, which held that secondary physical qualities, such as color, odor, and taste, were caused by the arrangement, shape, and motion
of invisible particles. *Ed.*]

In life to smile, when wilder than the bard
On Cambria's height I struck the lyre: my sigh,
Made harsh and inharmonious by despair,
Thou taught'st to break with melody. This hour,
Led on by Contemplation, I behold
Thine eyes that beam'd benevolence, thy heart
30   Once rich with fine regard. Ah me! that heart
'Mid this inhospitable scene was mine!

    Couldst thou declare how long the storms of fate
Shall beat around me, when I may repose,
Or be as thou art! I have read the code
Of statutes form'd by man for future worlds;
And found his plan, so pompously display'd,
One lot of heterogeneous fragment. Man
Adores in fancy, violates in fact,
Laws serving his frail being. Yon pale moon
40   Forsakes the mountain top, to bring us round
Her renovated splendour; nature works
Obedient and unseen forever: we
May meet in spheres remote—If not, farewel!
I feel and know, those wishes can arise
But from affections growing with my life,
Mingling with hope, oppress'd by fear. The change
Fulfill'd in thee may chill me; ev'ry thought
Oblit'rate; vision, fancy forms, be doom'd
To sink, like beaming glory in the west;
50   Whilst space contracts on my weak eye, and heav'ns,
By human artists coloured, fade away,
As life goes gently from my beating heart.

    Grant this could be—the import were no more
Than as an atom 'mid the vast profound
Impell'd, not swerving from the whole. Suppose,
This frame dissolving, to the busy winds
My ashes fled dividing: shall I know
To mourn?—How like my brethren I display

25 On Cambria's height] Cambria is an ancient name for Wales. "Cambria's height" refers
to the Cambrian Mountains, located in central Wales.

Conjecture without end!—Impatient pow'r
Of thought! where wouldst thou fly? Return, return!   60
Nor lose thy strength in phrensy, nor resign
The form I love.—This watch is down! Ye points,
Attun'd to motion by the art of man,
As tell-tales of his doings, can ye mark
Eternity by measur'd remnants? No.—
Fallacious in your working, ye would say,
With us, the life of man is but a day.

(1796)

Mary Julia Young

(fl. 1789–1808)

Sometimes confused today with Mary Young Sewell, Mary Julia Young was related to the poet Edward Young. One of seven children, she was educated by her mother, lived in London, and appears to have supported herself by writing poems, novels, and translations.

Young also seems to have been deeply involved in theater. Her first publication, a farce entitled *The Family Party; a Comic Piece, in Two Acts,* appeared anonymously in 1789. She wrote a survey of the London stage, *Genius and Fancy; or, Dramatic Sketches* (1791, republished in 1795 as *Genius and Fancy; or, Dramatic Sketches: With other Poems on Various Subjects*), and brought out a memoir of the actress Anna Maria Crouch, accompanied by another theater history, in 1806. She published a long narrative poem with Revolutionary France as a backdrop, *Adelaide and Antonine: or, The Emigrants: A Tale,* in 1793. The *Gentleman's Magazine* called it "an affecting tale, not unpolitically told"; and the *Monthly Review* observed, "Thought it cannot boast high poetical decorations, and is not wholly free from grammatical negligences, it may be read with general approbation."[1] A volume called *Poems* followed (1798, reprinted in 1801 in part 1 of *The Metrical Museum*).

Young published several novels. *The East Indian, or Clifford Priory,* published in 1799 and reprinted the next year in Dublin, is a gothic novel with a focus on the theater; it includes a depiction of a Jewish moneylender with a heart of gold—an early departure from the anti-Semitic stereotype then in vogue. *Right and Wrong; or, The Kinsmen of Naples. A Romantic Story,* published in four volumes in 1803, was her favorite work, set in Italy and Wales. *Donalda; or, The Witches of Glenshiel* (1805) contains ghosts, corpses, and other gothic trappings. *Moss Cliff Abbey; or, The Sepulchral Harmonist* (1803) is another gothic tale. Young had a financial crisis in 1808, when her publisher went bankrupt;

1. *Gentleman's Magazine* 64 (March 1794): 247; *Monthly Review,* n.s. 15 (1794): 106.

she applied to the Royal Literary Fund for help until she could complete her next work.

MAJOR WORKS: *The Family Party; A Comic Piece, in Two Acts* (London, 1789); *Adelaide and Antonine; or, the Emigrants: A Tale* (London, 1793); *Genius and Fancy; or, Dramatic Sketches: With Other Poems on Various Subjects* (London, 1795); *Poems* (London, 1798), reprinted in *The Metrical Museum. Part I. Containing, Agnes; or, the Wanderer, a Story Founded on the French Revolution. The Flood, an Irish Tale. Adelaide and Antonine; or, The Emigrants. With Other Original Poems* (London, [1801]); *The East Indian, or Clifford Priory*, 4 vols. (London, 1799; reprint, Dublin, 1800); *Moss Cliff Abbey; or, The Sepulchral Harmonist, a Mysterious Tale*, 4 vols. (London, 1803); *Right and Wrong; or, The Kinsmen of Naples, A Romantic Story*, 4 vols. (London, 1803); *Donalda; or, The Witches of Glenshiel*, 2 vols. (London, 1805); *Memoirs of Mrs. Crouch; Including a Retrospect of the Stage during the Years she Performed*, 2 vols. (London, 1806); *Rose Mount Castle, or False Reports*, 3 vols. (London, bef. 1810); *A Summer at Brighton, or The Resort of Fashion*, 3 vols. (London, bef. 1810); *A Summer at Weymouth, or the Star of Fashion*, 3 vols. (London, bef. 1810); *The Heir of Drumcondra; or, Family Pride*, 3 vols. (London, 1810).

TRANSLATIONS: *The Mother and Daughter, a Pathetic Tale,* from the French of Berthier, 3 vols. (London, 1804); Francois Maria Arouet de Voltaire, *Voltariana*, 4 vols. (London, 1805); *Lindorf and Caroline,* from the German of Prof. Cramer, 3 vols. (n.p., n.d.).

TEXTS USED: Texts of "An Ode to Fancy," "Sonnet to Dreams," and "To Miss ———— on Her Spending Too Much Time at Her Looking Glass" from *Genius and Fancy; or, Dramatic Sketches: with Other Poems on Various Subjects* (1795). Text of "To a Friend, on His Desiring Me to Publish" from *Poems.*

An Ode to Fancy

Tell me, blyth Fancy, shall I chuse
A tragic subject for my muse?
  Her flowing tresses shall the willow bind,
   While fading roses at her feet expire,
  Shall she to love-lorn sonnets be confin'd,
   Or tune to elegiac strains her lyre?
Then, as sweetly responsive sad Philomel sings,
Thrilling cadences float on calm night's dewy wings,
While the stars to her sorrow-dim'd eyes faint appear,
10 And the pallid moon trembling, is drown'd in a tear.

  Or in melancholy's cell,
  Shall I make the songstress dwell,
  To weave a tragic scene of woe,
  Such as Horror's children know?
   There, Jealousy with raging soul,
   Mixes poison in the bowl,
  Swift to the mad'ning brain it flies,
  The victim raves, burns, freezes, dies.
  There, pierc'd by anguish hopeless love expires,
20 There wild ambition fans destructive fires:
   She sees the steelly dagger gleam,
    She hears the murd'rers' hollow tread!
   Hears the birds of omen scream,
    Wheeling o'er his guilty head!
While, wrapt in terror's shadowy veil,
Gliding spectres grace the tale,

  Or, when tremendous thunders roll,
  Light'nings flash, and tempests howl,
   Shall she climb the pendant rock,
30   Its rude base trembling at the shock,

---

7 Philomel] According to Greek legend, Philomela was raped by her brother-in-law, who then cut out her tongue so that she could not reveal the identity of her assailant. Philomela wove her story into a peplos, which she sent to her sister. In the Latin version of the legend the gods changed Philomela into a nightingale.

And from the cloud-capt summit view
The scatter'd fleet, the death-devoted crew!
 Some on foaming billows rise,
 And whirl amidst inclement skies,
Then, rushing down the wat'ry steep,
Beneath the *stormy* ocean *sleep!*
 Others, with rudder broke, and shatter'd mast,
 Emerging from the deep,
Reel before the northern blast;
 While she sails, in shivers torn,   40
Useless o'er the surges sweep:
 On the tempest's rapid wing,
Swift to the fatal rock the wrecks are borne,
 The rock! where never smil'd the verdant spring!
 On its flinty side they dash,
 Bulging with a fearful crash!
 Happier those the sea entomb'd,
 Than these to lingering misery doom'd!
Whom famine seizes for his prey,
And slowly drags the struggling life away.   50

 Or shall she toil o'er barren lands,
 Deserts drear, and burning sands?
 Where the Volcano's flaming head,
 Fills the awe-struck soul with dread!
  When it vomits liquid fire,
  Spreading conflagration dire,
Who can tread the scorching ground?
The air blows scalding steam around.
  Turn,———and on the ocean gaze,
  The flames reflected in its bosom blaze,   60
While o'er the earth, the air, the main,
Fire, usurping seems to reign.

 Or shall she bend her lonely way,
Thro' woods impervious to the beams of day,
  Where wolves howl, and lions roar,
  Thirsting after human gore,

40 shivers] Fragments, chips.

Where the fierce banditti hide,
Cavern'd in the mountain's side,
Disgrace and terror of mankind,
70   With human form, and savage mind!
Who, ere their bleeding victim dies,
Rapacious share their lawless prize.

Or shall she mount Bellona's car,
And drive amidst the din of war,
Fearless of the whizzing ball,
Tho' dying heros round her fall.
And, when the approach of sable night
Stops the still-uncertain sight,
By the pale moon's languid ray,
80   O'er the field of horror stray.
And wading through the ensanguin'd plain,
View the pride of manhood slain?
Exposed, neglected, the brave warrior lies,
Life's purple current stains his livid breast:
With pious hand, say, shall she close his eyes,
And wrap him decent in his martial vest?
Shall she from the sacred ground,
Chace the vultures hov'ring round,
Then, on each corse, grief's pearly sorrows shed,
90   And sing a requiem o'er the silent dead!

Or to the cold, dark, charnel house repair,
And breathe its clammy, its infectious air?
While she opes the grating door,
Death's last mansion to explore,
The rushing wind terrific groans,
And aweful shakes the mould'ring bones.
Shall she dauntless there remain,
While a deep chilling silence reigns around,
And chaunting forth a solemn strain,
100   From the dank walls hear Echo's dreary sound?

67 banditti] Italian for *bandits*.
73 Bellona's] Roman goddess of war; either the sister or the wife of Mars.
91 charnel house] Vault for the bones of the dead.

No Fancy, no, she loves to sport,
 In gay Thalia's comic court,
 There her airy numbers sings,
 While she lightly sweeps the strings.
Jocund, easy, unconfin'd,
Leaving haggard Care behind.
 To a loftier muse belong,
 The graces of the tragic song.
Mine from the cradle to the tomb,
Strives to dissipate the gloom: 110
 Tho' nor skilful, nor sublime,
 She can smooth the brow of Time,
 Charm his sombrous frowns away,
 And with the tedious minutes play.
Then tell me Fancy, *can* I chuse,
A tragic theme for such a muse?

        (1795)

Sonnet to Dreams

Hail gentle spirits! who with magic wing,
 Chace the dark clouds of sullen night away,
And from her murky cave my freed soul bring,
 To revel in the radiant beams of day.

What are you, say? or earthly or divine,
 Who thus can chear the pause of dull repose;
With chymic art the dross of sleep refine,
 And beauteous scenes to *curtain'd eyes* disclose?

What are you! who subduing time and space,
 To bless these moments can a friend restore?   10

 102 Thalia's comic court] Thalia is the Muse of idyllic poetry and comedy. One of the three graces, she is the patroness of festive gatherings.
 113 sombrous] Somber, gloomy, dark.

 7 chymic] Alchemic. Young refers to the process of changing base metals into gold.

I hear that voice—behold that form—that face,
 And grateful own your pow'r can give no more!

Hail gentle spirits! to whose guardian care,
I owe such bliss—yet, know not what you are!

                                                (1795)

To Miss _____ on Her Spending
Too Much Time at Her Looking Glass

While at the mirror, lovely maid
    You trifle time away,
Reflect how soon your bloom will fade,
    How soon your charms decay.

By nature form'd to please the eye,
    All studied airs disdain,
From art, from affectation fly,
    And fashions light and vain.

Turn from the glass and view your mind,
10   On that bestow your care,
Improve, correct it, till you find
    No imperfections there.

Make it the seat of every grace,
    Of charms that will encrease;
And give bright lustre to the face,
    When youth and beauty cease.

Charms, that will gain a worthy heart,
    And lasting love inspire,
That will thro' life true bliss impart,
20   Nor yet, with life expire.

                                                (1795)

To a Friend, on His Desiring Me to Publish

With artless Muse, and humble name,
Shall I solicit public fame?
Shall I, who sing the pensive strain,
To soothe a mind oppressed with pain,
Or in the maze of fancy stray,
To pass a cheerless hour away,
Boldly to meet Apollo rise,
And flutter in his native skies?
Presumptuous, giddy, proud, elate,
Forgetting Icarus' sad fate,   10
High on my treacherous plumage soar,
And fall, like him, to rise no more?
Or, to assume a strain more common,
Shall I, an unknown, untaught woman,
Expose myself to dread Reviews, —
To paragraphs in daily news?
To gall-dipp'd pens, that write one down, —
To Envy's hiss, and Critic's frown?
To printers, editors, and devils,
With a thousand other evils,   20
That change the high-rais'd expectation
To disappointment and vexation,
And chase, abash'd, from public fame,
The artless Muse, the humble name?

(1798)

10 Forgetting Icarus' sad fate] In the Greek legend, Icarus, the son of Daedalus, constructed wings to allow him to fly. Ignoring his father's advice, Icarus flew so near the sun that the wax in his wings melted, and he fell into the sea and drowned. Icarus became a symbol for intellectual or artistic overreaching.

19 devils] Boys belonging to the printers, who are call'd so from their black appearance. *Young.*

Sources for Headnotes

Includes only sources not cited in notes to headnotes. General sources may only be cited once in notes.

Maria Abdy

Arthur H. Beavan, *James and Horace Smith. A Family Narrative Based Upon Hitherto Unpublished Private Diaries, Letters and Other Documents* (London, 1899); Boyle, *Index; Feminist Companion.*

Lucy Aikin

Humphrey Carpenter and Mari Prichard, *The Oxford Companion to Children's Literature* (New York, 1984); Anne Crawford et al., eds., *The Europa Biographical Dictionary of British Women: Over 1,000 Notable Women from Britain's Past* (Detroit, 1983); *DNB; Encyclopaedia Britannica,* 9th ed. (1891); *Feminist Companion;* Barbara Brandon Schnorrenberg, "Lucy Aikin," *New Dictionary of National Biography* (Oxford, forthcoming); William S. Ward, *Literary Reviews in British Periodicals, 1798–1820: A Bibliography with a Supplementary List of General (Non-Review) Articles on Literary Subjects,* 2 vols. (New York, 1972).

Jane Austen

David Cecil, *A Portrait of Jane Austen* (New York, 1979); Margaret Crum, *English and American Autographs in the Bodmeriana,* Bibliotheca Bodmeriana, Catalogues, 4 (Cologny-Genève, 1977), 17, 104; *DNB; Feminist Companion;* David Gilson, *A Bibliography of Jane Austen* (Oxford, 1982), 370–71; idem, "Jane Austen's Verses," *Book Collector* 33, no. 1 (1984): 25–37; J. David Grey, ed., *The Jane Austen Handbook* (London, 1986), 392; *Times Literary Supplement,* 14 January 1926, 27; Janet Todd, ed., *British Women Writers: A Critical Reference Guide* (New York, 1989).

Joanna Baillie

Margaret S. Carhart, *The Life and Work of Joanna Baillie* (New Haven, 1923); Sarah Tytler [Henrietta Keddie] and J. L. Watson, *The Songstresses of Scotland,* 2 vols. (London, 1871).

Anna Letitia Barbauld

Lucy Aikin, "Memoir," in *The Works of Anna Lætitia Barbauld, with a Memoir,* ed. Lucy Aikin, 2 vols. (London, 1825); *DNB; DLB* 109; Lonsdale, *Eighteenth-Century*

Women Poets; Henry Crabb Robinson, *On Books and Their Writers,* ed. Edith J. Morley, 3 vols. (London, 1938); Betsy Rodgers, *Georgian Chronicle: Mrs. Barbauld and Her Family* (London, 1958); Todd, *Dictionary.*

Mrs. E.-G. Bayfield

Feminist Companion; Literary Journal 3 (16 February 1804): 164; *National Union Catalogue;* William S. Ward, *Literary Reviews in British Periodicals, 1789–1797: A Bibliography with a Supplementary List of General (Non-Review) Articles on Literary Subjects* (New York, 1979).

Elizabeth Bentley

Allibone, *Critical Dictionary; Critical Review,* n.s., 3 (1791): 94–95; *Feminist Companion;* Landry, *Muses of Resistance,* 209–16; *Gentleman's Magazine* 92 (February 1822): 153; John MacKay Shaw, *Childhood in Poetry; A Catalogue, with Biographical and Critical Annotations, of the Books of English and American Poets Comprising the Shaw Childhood in Poetry Collection in the Library of the Florida State University,* 5 vols. (Detroit, 1967–68); [John Watkins and Frederic Shoberl], eds., *A Biographical Dictionary of Living Authors of Great Britain and Ireland; comprising Literary Memoirs and Anecdotes of their Lives; and a Chronological Register of their Publications, etc.* (London, 1816).

Matilda Betham

Ernest Betham, ed., *A House of Letters. Being Excerpts from the Correspondence of Miss Charlotte Jerningham . . . and Others, with Matilda Betham, etc.* (London, 1905); M. Betham-Edwards, *Six Life Studies of Famous Women* (London, 1880), 231–303; *Feminist Companion;* Todd, *Dictionary.*

Susanna Blamire

Chambers' Edinburgh Journal 11 (1843): 238–39; Henry Lonsdale, *The Worthies of Cumberland* (London, 1873); Lonsdale, *Eighteenth-Century Women Poets;* Frederic Rowton, ed., *The Female Poets of Great Britain: Chronologically Arranged* (London, 1853; facs. reprint with critical introduction and bibliographical appendixes by Marilyn L. Williamson, Detroit, 1981); Walter Scott, *The Letters of Sir Walter Scott,* ed. Herbert J. C. Grierson, 12 vols. (London, 1932–37); Todd, *Dictionary;* Sarah Tytler [Henrietta Keddie] and J. L. Watson, *The Songstresses of Scotland,* 2 vols. (London, 1871).

Countess of Blessington

The Literary Life and Correspondence of the Countess of Blessington, ed. R. R. Madden, 2 vols. (New York, 1855); Boyle, *Index; DNB;* J. Fitzgerald Molloy, *The Most Gorgeous Lady Blessington,* Beaux and Belles of England (New York, n.d.); Alfred Morrison, *The Collection of Autograph Letters and Historical Documents formed by Alfred Morrison . . . The Blessington Papers* (n.p., 1895); Michael Sadleir, *Blessington-D'Orsay: A Masquerade* (London, 1933).

Mary Ann Browne

Allibone, *Critical Dictionary;* Boyle, *Index; Feminist Companion;* Mitford, *Recollections,* 222–27; *Nineteenth Century Short Title Catalogue, 1816–1870,* 2nd ser., vol. 6 (Newcastle-upon-Tyne, 1986); Jane Williams, *The Literary Women of England* (London, 1861), 547–50.

Lady Byron (née Anne Isabella Milbanke)

Malcolm Elwin, *Lord Byron's Wife* (New York, 1962); Harriet Martineau, "Lady Byron," *Atlantic Monthly* 7 (February 1861): 185–95; Ethel Colburn Mayne, *The Life and Letters of Anne Isabella Lady Noel Byron, from Unpublished Papers in the Possession of the Late Ralph, Earl of Lovelace* (New York, 1929); Joan Pierson, *The Real Lady Byron* (London, 1992); James Soderholm, "Annabella Milbanke's 'Thyrza to Lord Byron,'" *Byron Journal* 21 (1993): 30–42.

Dorothea Primrose Campbell

Feminist Companion; Sarah J. Hale, *Woman's Record; or, Sketches of all Distinguished Women, from the Creation to A.D. 1868. Arranged in Four Eras. With Selections from Authoresses of Each Era,* 3rd ed., rev. (New York, 1870).

Ann Candler

Gwenn Davis and Beverly A. Joyce, comps., *Poetry by Women to 1900: A Bibliography of American and British Writers* (Toronto, 1991); *DNB;* Landry, *Muses of Resistance,* 273–74, 278–80; "Memoirs of the Life of Ann Candler," including Candler's own long autobiographical letter of 13 April 1801, in *Poetical Attempts, by Ann Candler, a Suffolk Cottager, with a Short Narrative of her Life,* ed. [Elizabeth Cobbold] (Ipswich, 1803), 1–17; Todd, *Dictionary.*

Elizabeth Cobbold (née Eliza Knipe)

Elizabeth Cobbold, *Poems by Mrs. Elizabeth Cobbold with a Memoir of the Author,* [ed. Laetitia Jermyn] (Ipswich, 1825); *European Magazine* 10 (1786): 290; Todd, *Dictionary.*

Sara Coleridge

Sara Coleridge, *Memoir and Letters of Sara Coleridge,* ed. [Edith Coleridge], 2 vols. (London, 1873); Earl Leslie Griggs, *Coleridge, Fille: A Biography of Sara Coleridge* (London, 1940); Bradford Keyes Mudge, *Sara Coleridge, A Victorian Daughter: Her Life and Essays* (New Haven, 1989); review of *Memoir and Letters of Sara Coleridge* in *Edinburgh Review* 139 (January 1874): 44–68; Eleanor A. Towle, *A Poet's Children: Hartley and Sara Coleridge* (London, 1912); Mona Wilson, "A Neglected Fairy Tale," in *These Were Muses* (1924; reprint, Port Washington, N.Y., 1970).

Hannah Cowley

DLB 89; *DNB; European Magazine* 39 (April 1801): 176–77; *Feminist Companion; Monthly Review* 35 (June 1801): 175–79; Paul Schlueter and June Schlueter, eds., *An Encyclopedia of British Women Writers* (New York, 1988); Todd, *Dictionary.*

Ann Batten Cristall

Critical Review, n.s., 13 (1795): 286–92; *DNB; Feminist Companion,* 248; Basil Taylor, *Joshua Cristall* (London, 1975); *Collected Letters of Mary Wollstonecraft,* ed. Ralph M. Wardle (Ithaca, 1979), 172, 187–89, 194, 196, 379, 421–22.

Catherine Ann Dorset

British Critic 37 (January 1811): 67–68; *DNB; European Magazine* 56 (October 1809): 290; *Gentleman's Magazine* 77 (September 1807): 846–48; Stanley J. Kunitz and Howard Jay Craf, *British Authors before 1800* (New York, 1952); *Literary Panorama* 3 (February 1808): 965–66; *Monthly Magazine* 24 (30 January 1808): 629; *Poetical Register* 7 (1809): 596.

Maria Edgeworth

Marilyn Butler, *Maria Edgeworth: A Literary Biography* (Oxford, 1982); *DLB* 116; *DNB;* James Patrick Muirhead, *The Life of James Watt,* 2nd ed., rev. (London, 1859), 521; Todd, *Dictionary.*

Susan Evance

James Robert de Jager Jackson, *Romantic Poetry by Women: A Bibliography, 1770–1835* (Oxford, 1993).

Catherine Maria Fanshawe

Mary Berry, *Extracts of the Journals and Correspondence of Miss Berry, from the Year 1783 to 1852,* ed. Lady Theresa Lewis, 3 vols. (London, 1865); *DNB;* John Gibson Lockhart, *Life of Sir Walter Scott,* 5 vols. (Boston, 1901), 4:124–26; Mitford, *Recollections,* 157–68.

Anne Grant (Mrs. Grant of Laggan)

Mrs. Anne Katherine Elwood, *Memoirs of the Literary Ladies of England, from the Commencement of the Last Century,* 2 vols. (London, 1843), 2:66–97; George Eyre-Todd, ed., *Scottish Poetry of the Eighteenth Century,* 2 vols. (London, 1896), 2:141; *Memoir and Correspondence of Mrs. Grant of Laggan,* ed. J. P. Grant, 3 vols. (London, 1844); Emily Morse Symonds [George Paston, pseud.], *Little Memoirs of the Eighteenth Century* (London and New York, 1901), 237–96; Walter Scott, *The Journal of Walter Scott,* ed. W. E. K. Anderson (Oxford, 1972); idem, *The Letters of Sir Walter Scott, 1808–1811,* ed. Herbert John Clifford Grierson (London, 1932); George Ticknor, *Life, Letters, and Journals,* 2 vols.,

6th ed. (Boston, 1877), 1:274, 278–79; Jane Williams, *The Literary Women of England* (London, 1861), 519–43; James Grant Wilson, *The Poets and Poetry of Scotland; from the Earliest to the Present Time,* 2 vols. (London, 1876), 1:338–40.

Elizabeth Hands

Feminist Companion; Landry, *Muses of Resistance;* Todd, *Dictionary.*

Mary Hays

Analytical Review 25 (1797): 174–78; Olive Banks, ed., *The Biographical Dictionary of British Feminists,* 2 vols. (New York, 1985), 1:215–17; *British Critic* 9 (1797): 314–15; *Critical Review,* n.s., 19 (1797): 109–11; *Feminist Companion;* Gina M. Luria, "Mary Hays's Letters and Manuscripts," *Signs* 3, no. 21 (1977): 524–30; idem, introduction to *Memoirs of Emma Courtney* (New York, 1974); Burton R. Pollin, "Mary Hays on Women's Rights in *The Monthly Magazine,*" *Etudes anglaises* 24, no. 3 (1971): 271–82; Todd, *Dictionary.*

Felicia Hemans

Henry Fothergill Chorley, *Memorials of Mrs. Hemans, with Illustrations of her Literary Character from her Private Correspondence,* 2 vols. (London, 1836); *DLB; DNB; Feminist Companion; The Works of Mrs. Hemans; with a Memoir of her Life by her Sister,* ed. [Harriett Hughes], 7 vols. (Edinburgh and London, 1839); Peter W. Trinder, *Mrs. Hemans* (Cardiff, 1984).

Mary Howitt

DLB; DNB; Mary Howitt, An Autobiography, ed. Margaret Howitt, 2 vols. (London, 1889); Amice Lee, *Laurels and Rosemary: The Life of William and Mary Howitt* (London, 1955); Emily Morse Symonds [George Paston, pseud.], *Little Memoirs of the Nineteenth Century* (n.p., 1902); Carl Ray Woodring, *Victorian Samplers: William and Mary Howitt* (Lawrence, Kans., 1952).

Anna Maria Jones

Andrew Ashfield, ed., *Romantic Women Poets, 1770–1838: An Anthology* (Manchester, 1995); Mrs. G. H. Bell, ed., *The Hanwood Papers of the Ladies of Langollen & Caroline Hamilton* (London, 1930); *DNB;* Sir William Jones, *The Letters of Sir William Jones,* ed. G. H. Cannon, 2 vols. (Oxford, 1970); *Memoirs of the Life, Writings, and Correspondence of Sir William Jones,* ed. Lord Teignmouth, 2 vols. (London, 1835).

Lady Caroline Lamb

DLB 116; *DNB;* Leslie A. Marchand, *Byron: A Biography,* 3 vols. (New York, 1957); Lady Morgan, *Lady Morgan's Memoirs: Autobiography, Diaries and Correspondence,* 2nd ed., rev., 2 vols. (London, 1863); Samuel Smiles, *A Publisher and his Friends: Memoir and Correspondence of the Late John Murray*, 2 vols. (London and New York, 1891).

Letitia Elizabeth Landon

DNB; Laman Blanchard, *Life and Literary Remains of L.E.L.,* 2 vols. (London, 1841); Anne K. Mellor, *Romanticism and Gender* (New York, 1993); Brenda Hart Renalds, "Letitia Elizabeth Landon: A Literary Life" (Ph.D. diss., University of South Carolina, 1985).

Mary Leadbeater

DNB; Feminist Companion; Clara I. Gandy, "The Condition and Character of the Irish Peasantry as Seen in the Annals and Cottage Dialogues of Mary Leadbeater," *Women and Literature* 3, no. 1 (1975): 28–37.

Helen Leigh

Feminist Companion; Miscellaneous Poems (Manchester, 1788).

Isabella Lickbarrow

Feminist Companion; preface and list of subscribers in Lickbarrow's *Poetical Effusions* (Kendal, 1814).

Lady Ann Lindsay

Auld Robin Gray; A Ballad by the Right Honourable Lady Anne Barnard, Born Lady Anne Lindsay of Balcarras, ed. Walter Scott (Edinburgh, 1825); Robert Chambers, *A Biographical Dictionary of Eminent Scotsmen,* rev. Thomas Thomson (New York, 1971); idem, *Chambers' Cyclopaedia of English Literature,* 3 vols. (Philadelphia, 1902–4); *DNB;* Alexander Dyce, ed., *Specimens of British Poetesses* (London, 1827); Leigh Hunt, "Specimens of British Poetesses," *Men, Women and Books: A Selection of Sketches, Essays, and Critical Memoirs from his Uncollected Prose,* new edition (London, 1891), 282–84; George Eyre-Todd, ed., *Scottish Poetry of the Eighteenth Century,* vol. 2 (London, 1896); Jessie P. Findlay, *The Spindle-Side of Scottish Song* (London, 1902); Lord Lindsay, *Lives of the Lindsays; or a Memoir of the Houses of Crawford and Balcarres . . . together with personal narratives by his brothers . . . and his sister, Lady Anne Barnard,* 3 vols. (London, 1849); Lonsdale, *Eighteenth-Century Women Poets;* Eunice G. Murray, *A Gallery of Scottish Women* (London, 1935); Walter Scott, *The Private Letter-Books of Sir Walter Scott,* ed. Wilfred Partington (London, 1930); Todd, *Dictionary;* Sarah Tytler [Henrietta Keddie] and J. L. Watson, *The Songstresses of Scotland,* 2 vols. (London, 1871); James Grant Wilson, *The Poets and Poetry of Scotland; from the Earliest to the Present Time,* 2 vols. (London, 1876), vol. 1, pt. 2.

Janet Little

Feminist Companion; Moira Ferguson, "Janet Little and Robert Burns: The Politics of the Heart," in *Romantic Women Writers: Voices and Countervoices,* ed. Paula R. Feldman and Theresa M. Kelley (Hanover, N.H., 1995), 207–19; Landry, *Muses of Resistance;* [James Paterson], *The Contemporaries of Burns, and the More Recent Poets of Ayrshire, with Selections from their Writings* (Edinburgh and London, 1840); William Wallace, ed., *Robert Burns and Mrs. Dunlop,* 2 vols. (New York, 1898).

Maria Logan

Lonsdale, *Eighteenth-Century Women Poets;* Todd, *Dictionary;* Robert Watt, *Biblioteca Britannica; or, A General Index to British and Foreign Literature* (Edinburgh, 1824).

Christian Milne

Feminist Companion; preface to Christian Milne's *Simple Poems on Simple Subjects* (Aberdeen, 1805); Elizabeth Isabella Spence, *Letters from the North Highlands, during the Summer of 1816* (London, 1817).

Mary Russell Mitford

DLB; DNB; A. G. K. L'Estrange, ed., *The Friendships of Mary Russell Mitford,* 2 vols. (London, 1882); *Feminist Companion;* James T. Fields, *Yesterdays with Authors* (Boston, 1872), 263–352; *The Life of Mary Russell Mitford, Told by Herself in Letters to her Friends,* ed. A. G. K. L'Estrange, 2 vols. (New York, 1870), 2:82–84, 86.

Elizabeth Moody

Lonsdale, *Eighteenth-Century Women Poets; Monthly Review* 27 (1798): 442–47, 73 (1785): 432–35, 81 (1789): 455–57, and n.s., 3 (1790): 400–402; *Monthly Visitor* 6 (September 1799): 37.

Hannah More

DLB 109; *Feminist Companion;* M. G. Jones, *Hannah More* (New York, 1968); Clare Midgley, *Women against Slavery: The British Campaigns, 1780–1870* (London, 1992), 29, 32–33, 48, 58; Janet Mullane and Laurie Sherman, ed. *Nineteenth-Century Literature Criticism,* vol. 27 (Detroit, 1990), 323–60.

Countess of Morley

Allibone, *Critical Dictionary; The British Library General Catalogue of Printed Books to 1975* (London, 1984); J. B. Burke, *A Genealogical and Heraldic Dictionary of the Peerage and Baronetage of the British Empire* (London, 1865); *DNB;* Sarah J. Hale, *Woman's Record; or, Sketches of all Distinguished Women, from the Creation to A.D. 1868. Arranged in Four Eras. With Selections from Authoresses of Each Era.* 3rd ed., rev. (New York, 1870), 848; Michael

Sadleir, *XIX Century Fiction: A Bibliographical Record Based on His Own Collection*, 2 vols. (London, 1951), 1: item 1441; Robert Lee Wolff, comp., *Nineteenth Century Fiction: A Bibliographical Catalogue Based on the Collection Formed by Robert Lee Wolff*, 5 vols. (New York, 1981–84), 3:44, item 4155.

Carolina, Baroness Nairne

Rev. George Henderson, *Lady Nairne and Her Songs*, new and enl. ed. (Paisley, [1905]); Kington Oliphant, *Jacobite Lairds of Gask*, 2nd ed., enl. (London, 1869); Charles Rogers, ed., *Life and Songs of the Baroness Nairne: With a Memoir and Poems of Caroline Oliphant the Younger* (London, 1869); [Margaret Stewart Simpson], *The Scottish Songstress: Caroline Baroness Nairne* (Edinburgh, 1894).

Caroline Norton

Alice Acland, *Caroline Norton* (London, 1948); *DLB* 21; *DNB; Feminist Companion;* Percy Fitzgerald, *The Lives of the Sheridans*, 2 vols. (London, 1886); Lee Holcombe, *Wives and Property* (Oxford, 1983); *The Letters of Caroline Norton to Lord Melbourne*, ed. James O. Hoge and Clarke Olney (Columbus, Ohio, 1974); Jane Gray Perkins, *The Life of the Honourable Mrs. Norton* (New York, 1909).

Henrietta O'Neill

Anthologia Hibernica 2 (1793): 319–20, 384–85; J. B. Burke, *A Genealogical and Heraldic Dictionary of the Peerage and Baronetage of the British Empire* (London, 1865); *DNB; Gentleman's Magazine* 103, pt. 2 (August 1833): 130–32; Roger Manvell, *Sarah Siddons: Portrait of an Actress* (London, 1970), 20, 21, 92; David James O'Donoghue, *The Poets of Ireland: A Biographical and Bibliographical Dictionary of Irish Writers of English Verse* (Dublin, 1912; reprint, Detroit, 1968), 365; Sarah Kemble Siddons, *The Reminiscences of Sarah Kemble Siddons, 1778-1785*, ed. William Van Lennep (Cambridge, 1942), 2–4.

Amelia Opie

Annual Review 1 (1802), 7 (1808): 522–24; Cecilia Lucy Brightwell, *Memoir of Amelia Opie* (London, 1855); idem, *Memorials of the Life of Amelia Opie, Selected and Arranged from her Letters, Diaries, and Other Manuscripts* (Norwich, 1854); *British Critic* 20 (November 1802), 34 (August 1809): 183–84; *DNB; Eclectic Review* 5 (March 1809): 274–77; *European Magazine* 42 (1802): 43–44; *Feminist Companion;* Margaret E. MacGregor, *Amelia Alderson Opie: Worlding and Friend*, Smith College Studies in Modern Languages 14, no. 1–2 (1933); *Monthly Magazine* 14 (January 1803); *Monthly Review* 39 (1802): 434–35, 57 (December 1808): 436–38; *New Annual Register* 23 (1802); *Poetical Register* 2 (1802), 6 (1807); Donald H. Reiman, introduction to Amelia Opie's *Poems* (1802), reprinted (New York, 1978); Lady Anne Isabella Thackeray Richie, *A Book of Sibyls* (London, 1883), 149–96; Jacobine Menzies Wilson and Helen Lloyd, *Amelia, the Tale of a Plain Friend* (London, 1937).

Isabel Pagan

George Eyre-Todd, *Scottish Poetry of the Eighteenth Century,* vol. 2 (London, 1896), 36–39; *Feminist Companion;* [James Paterson], *The Contemporaries of Burns, and the More Recent Poets of Ayrshire, with Selections from their Writings* (Edinburgh, 1840), 113–23; Alex Whitelaw, *The Book of Scottish Song; Collected and Illustrated with Historical and Critical Notices* (Glasgow, 1845), 466–67.

Ann Radcliffe

DNB; Edinburgh Annual Register, (1823), 331–32; *Feminist Companion;* Robert Miles, *Ann Radcliffe: The Great Enchantress* (Manchester, 1995); E. B. Murray, *Ann Radcliffe* (New York, 1972); Todd, *Dictionary.*

Emma Roberts

Allibone, *Critical Dictionary;* Boyle, *Index; DNB; Feminist Companion; Gentleman's Magazine* 15 (May 1841): 544; John Cam Hobhouse, *Recollections of a Long Life,* ed. Lady Dorchester (London, 1910), 2:291–92.

Mary Robinson

Robert D. Bass, *The Green Dragoon: The Lives of Banastre Tarleton and Mary Robinson* (New York, 1957); *DNB; Feminist Companion;* Philip H. Highfill Jr., Kalman A. Burnim, and Edward A. Langhans, *A Biographical Dictionary of Actors, Actresses, Musicians, Dancers, Managers and Other Stage Personnel in London, 1660–1800,* vol. 13 (Carbondale, 1991), 30–47; John Ingamells, *Mrs. Robinson and her Portraits,* Wallace Collection Monographs, 1 (London, 1978); Lonsdale, *Eighteenth-Century Women Poets; Morning Post,* 5 July–1 August 1800; *Memoirs of the Late Mrs. Robinson, Written by Herself, With Some Posthumous Pieces,* ed. [Maria Elizabeth Robinson], 4 vols. (London, 1801), republished as *Memoirs of the Late Mrs. Robinson, Written by Herself. A New Edition* (London, 1930); Paul Schlueter and June Schlueter, eds., *An Encyclopedia of British Women Writers* (New York, 1988); Todd, *Dictionary.*

Anna Seward

Margaret Ashmun, *The Singing Swan: An Account of Anna Seward and Her Acquaintance with Dr. Johnson, Boswell and Others of Their Time* (New Haven, 1931); James L. Clifford, "The Authenticity of Anna Seward's Published Correspondence," *Modern Philology* 39 (1941): 113–22; *DNB;* Gretchen M. Foster, *Pope versus Dryden: A Controversy in the Gentleman's Magazine, 1789–91* (Victoria, B.C., 1989); E. V. Lucas, *A Swan and her Friends* (London, 1907); "Miss Seward," *Ladies' Monthly Museum* 2 (March 1799): 169–76.

Mary Wollstonecraft Shelley

Mary Shelley, *The Journals of Mary Shelley,* ed. Paula R. Feldman and Diana Scott-Kilvert, 2 vols. (Oxford, 1987); William St. Clair, *The Godwins and the Shelleys* (London, 1990); Emily W. Sunstein, *Mary Shelley: Romance and Reality* (Boston, 1989).

Charlotte Smith

Catherine Anne Dorset, "Charlotte Smith," in Sir Walter Scott, *Biographical Memoirs of Eminent Novelists, and Other Distinguished Persons,* vol. 4 (Edinburgh, 1853), 20–70; Florence May Anna Hilbish, *Charlotte Smith, Poet and Novelist (1749–1806)* (Philadelphia, 1941); Bishop C. Hunt Jr., "Wordsworth and Charlotte Smith," *Wordsworth Circle* 1 (1970): 85–103; *DLB* 39; Burton R. Pollin, "Keats, Charlotte Smith, and the Nightingale," *N&Q* 211 (May 1966): 180–81; Charlotte Smith, *The Poems of Charlotte Smith,* ed. Stuart Curran (New York, 1993); Judith Phillips Stanton, "Charlotte Smith's 'Literary Business': Income, Patronage, and Indigence," in *The Age of Johnson: A Scholarly Annual,* ed. Paul J. Korshin (New York, 1990); Rufus Paul Turner, "Charlotte Smith (1749–1806): New Light on her Life and Literary Career" (Ph.D. diss., University of Southern California, 1966); George W. Whiting, "Charlotte Smith, Keats, and the Nightingale," *Keats-Shelley Journal* 12 (1963): 4–8.

Agnes Strickland

DNB; Feminist Companion; A. J. Green-Armytage, *Maids of Honour: Twelve Descriptive Sketches of Single Women Who Have Distinguished Themselves in Philanthropy, Travel, Nursing, Science, Poetry, Prose* (Edinburgh, 1906); Una Pope-Hennessy, *Agnes Strickland: Biographer of the Queens of England, 1796–1874* (London, 1940).

Ann Taylor and Jane Taylor

Doris Mary Armitage, *The Taylors of Ongar* (Cambridge, 1939); G. Edward Harris, *Contributions towards a Bibliography of the Taylors of Ongar and Stanford Rivers* (London, 1965); Mrs. Helen Cross Knight, *Jane Taylor: Her Life and Letters* (London, 1880); Grace A. Oliver, ed., *Tales, Essays and Poems by Jane and Ann Taylor with a Memoir by Grace A. Oliver* (Boston, 1884); R. Ellis Roberts, "Another Jane," *New Statesman* (1 May 1926), 79–81; Christina Duff Stewart, *The Taylors of Ongar: An Analytical Bio-Bibliography,* 2 vols. (New York, 1975); Lucy Bethia Walford, *Four Biographies from "Blackwood": Jane Taylor, Elizabeth Fry, Hannah More, Mary Somerville* (Edinburgh, 1888); Virginia Woolf, "The Lives of the Obscure—I: Taylors and Edgeworths," in *The Common Reader* (London, 1925), 154–67.

Mary Tighe

E. R. Mc. C. Dix, "The First Edition of Mrs. Tighe's Psyche," *Irish Book Lover* 3 (April 1912): 141, 606–9; C. W. Gillam, "Keats, Mary Tighe, and Others," *N&Q* 199 (February 1954); Patrick Henchy, *The Works of Mary Tighe, Published and Unpublished,* Bibliographical Society of Ireland Publications 6, no. 6 (Dublin, 1957).

Charlotte Elizabeth Tonna

Monica Correa Fryckstedt, "Charlotte Elizabeth Tonna: A Forgotten Evangelical Writer," *Studia Neophilologica* 52, no. 1 (1980): 79–102; *Gentleman's Magazine* 26 (October 1846): 433–34; Charlotte Elizabeth Tonna, *Personal Recollections* (New York, 1843); idem, *The Works of Charlotte Elizabeth,* with an introduction by Mrs. Harriet Beecher Stowe, 3 vols. (New York, 1845); L. H. J. Tonna, *A Memoir of Charlotte Elizabeth, Embracing the Period from the Close of her Personal Recollections to her Death* (New York, 1847).

Elizabeth Trefusis

Cabinet 4 (December 1808): 396; *Feminist Companion; Monthly Review* 57 (1808): 206–9; Hester Lynch Thrale Piozzi, *The Intimate Letters of Hester Piozzi and Penelope Pennington,* ed. O. G. Knapp, 3 vols. (London, 1914), 3:317n.

Jane West

Allibone, *Critical Dictionary;* Paula Backscheider, Felicity Nussbaum, and Philip B. Anderson, eds., *An Annotated Bibliography of Twentieth-Century Critical Studies of Women and Literature, 1660–1800* (New York, 1977); *British Critic* 18 (November 1801): 524–29; Gwenn Davis and Beverly A. Joyce, comps., *Poetry by Women to 1900: A Bibliography of American and British Writers* (Toronto, 1991); *DNB; Feminist Companion;* Gina Luria, introduction to Garland edition of Jane West, *Letters to a Young Lady in Which the Duties and Character of Women are Considered* (1806; reprint, New York, 1974); Hazel Mews, *Frail Vessels: Women's Role in Women's Novels from Fanny Burney to George Eliot* (London, 1969), 28; John Nichols, *Illustrations of the Literary History of the Eighteenth Century,* 8 vols. (London, 1817–58), 8:329–31; Paul Schlueter and June Schlueter, eds., *An Encyclopedia of British Women Writers* (New York, 1988); John MacKay Shaw, *Childhood in Poetry; A Catalogue with Biographical and Critical Annotations of the Books of English and American Poets Comprising the Shaw Childhood in Poetry Collection in the Library of the Florida State University,* 5 vols. (Detroit, 1967–68); Todd, *Dictionary;* William S. Ward, *Literary Reviews in British Periodicals, 1789–1797: A Bibliography with a Supplementary List of General (Non-Review) Articles on Literary Subjects* (New York, 1979).

Helen Maria Williams

DNB; Feminist Companion; Gary Kelly, *Women, Writing, and Revolution, 1790–1827* (Oxford, 1993); Todd, *Dictionary.*

Dorothy Wordsworth

Feminist Companion; Robert Gittings and Jo Manton, *Dorothy Wordsworth* (Oxford, 1985); Susan Levin, *Dorothy Wordsworth and Romanticism* (New Brunswick, N.J., 1987); Todd, *Dictionary;* Dorothy Wordsworth, *The Poetry of Dorothy Wordsworth,* ed. from the Journals by Hyman Eigerman (New York, 1940).

Ann Yearsley

Ralph Edward Ball, "The Literary Production of Ann Yearsley: A Case Study of Class, Gender, and Authorship in the Late Eighteenth Century" (Ph.D. diss., University of South Carolina, 1995); Landry, *Muses of Resistance;* Mary Waldron, "Ann Yearsley and the Clifton Records," in *The Age of Johnson: A Scholarly Annual,* ed. Paul J. Korshin (New York, 1990), 301–29.

Mary Julia Young

Allibone, *Critical Dictionary; Critical Review* 68 (1789): 245; *Feminist Companion; Gentleman's Magazine* 64 (May 1794): 457, (June 1794): 558, (August 1794): 749; *Monthly Review* 81 (September 1789): 285 and n.s. 15 (1794): 105–6; Todd, *Dictionary; Town and Country Magazine* 21 (October 1789): 468.

Select Bibliography

Allibone, Samuel Austin. *A Critical Dictionary of English Literature and British and American Authors Living and Deceased from the Earliest Accounts to the Latter Half of the Nineteenth Century.* 3 vols. Philadelphia, 1870–71.

Alston, R. C. *A Checklist of Women Writers, 1801–1900: Fiction, Verse, Drama.* Boston, 1991.

Ashfield, Andrew, ed. *Romantic Women Poets, 1770–1838: An Anthology.* Manchester, 1995.

Backscheider, Paula, Felicity Nussbaum, and Philip B. Anderson, eds. *An Annotated Bibliography of Twentieth-Century Critical Studies of Women and Literature, 1660–1800.* New York, 1977.

Banks, Olive, ed. *The Biographical Dictionary of British Feminists.* 2 vols. New York, 1985.

Baylen, Joseph O., and Norbert J. Gossman, eds. *Biographical Dictionary of Modern British Radicals.* Vol. 1, *1770–1830;* vol. 2, *1830–1870.* Brighton, 1979–84.

Bax, Clifford, and Meum Stewart, comps. *The Distaff Muse: An Anthology of Poetry Written by Women.* London, 1949.

Behrendt, Stephen, and Harriet Linkin. *Approaches to Teaching the Women Romantic Poets.* New York, forthcoming.

Bell, Peter. *Regency Women: An Index to Biographies and Memoirs.* Edinburgh, 1991.

Betham, Matilda. *A Biographical Dictionary of the Celebrated Women of Every Age and Country.* London, 1804.

Bethune, George W., ed. *The British Female Poets: with Biographical and Critical Notices, by Geo. W. Bethune.* Philadelphia, 1848.

Blain, Virginia, Patricia Clements, and Isobel Grundy, eds. *The Feminist Companion to Literature in English: Women Writers from the Middle Ages to the Present.* New Haven, 1990.

Boos, Florence, with Lynn Miller. *Bibliography of Women and Literature: Articles and Books By and About Women from 600 to 1975.* 2 vols. New York, 1989.

Boyle, Andrew. *An Index to the Annuals.* Vol. 1, *The Authors (1820–1850).* Worcester, 1967.

Boyle, George, ed. *Boyle's Fashionable Court and Country Guide, and Town Visiting Directory.* London, January 1835, January 1839.

Breen, Jennifer, ed. *Women Romantic Poets, 1785–1832: An Anthology.* London, 1992.

British Museum. *General Catalogue of Printed Books. Photolithographic Edition to 1955.* 263 vols. London, 1965–66.

Burke, J. B., ed. *A Genealogical and Heraldic Dictionary of the Peerage and Baronetage of the British Empire.* London, [various dates].

———. *A Genealogical and Heraldic History of the Landed Gentry.* London, [various dates].

———. *History of the Commoners of Great Britain and Ireland.* London, [various dates].

Carpenter, Humphrey, and Mari Prichard. *The Oxford Companion to Children's Literature.* New York, 1984.

Chambers, Robert. *A Biographical Dictionary of Eminent Scotsmen.* Glasgow, 1835. Revised by Thomas Thomson. New York, 1971.

Coleridge, Henry Nelson. "Modern English Poetesses." *Quarterly Review* 66 (September 1840): 374–418.

Crawford, Anne, et al., eds. *The Europa Biographical Dictionary of British Women: Over 1,000 Notable Women from Britain's Past.* Detroit, 1983.

Davis, Gwenn, and Beverly A. Joyce, comps. *Poetry by Women to 1900: A Bibliography of American and British Writers.* Toronto, 1991.

Dyce, Alexander, ed. *Specimens of British Poetesses.* London, 1827.

———, ed. *Recollections of the Table-Talk of Samuel Rogers.* 3rd ed. London, 1856.

Elwood, Mrs. Anne Katherine. *Memoirs of the Literary Ladies of England, from the Commencement of the Last Century.* 2 vols. London, 1843.

Eyre-Todd, George, ed. *Scottish Poetry of the Eighteenth Century.* 2 vols. London, 1896.

Faxon, Frederick W. *Literary Annuals and Gift Books: A Bibliography, 1823–1903.* Boston, 1912. Reprint. Pinner, Middlesex, 1973.

Feldman, Paula R., and Theresa M. Kelley, eds. *Romantic Women Writers: Voices and Countervoices.* Hanover, N.H., 1995.

Findlay, Jessie P. *The Spindle-Side of Scottish Song.* London, 1902.

Gilpin, Sidney. *The Songs and Ballads of Cumberland and the Lake Country: with Biographical Sketches, Notes, and Glossary.* 2nd ed. London, 1874.

Green-Armytage, A. J. *Maids of Honour: Twelve Descriptive Sketches of Single Women Who Have Distinguished Themselves in Philanthropy, Travel, Nursing, Science, Poetry, Prose.* Edinburgh, 1906.

Haefner, Joel, and Carol Shiner Wilson, eds. *Re-visioning Romanticism: British Women Writers, 1776–1837.* Philadelphia, 1994.

Hale, Sarah J. *Woman's Record; or, Sketches of all Distinguished Women, from the Creation to A.D. 1868. Arranged in Four Eras. With Selections from Authoresses of Each Era.* 3rd ed., rev. New York, 1870.

Hall, S. C. *Retrospect of a Long Life: from 1815 to 1883.* New York, 1883.

Hamilton, Catherine J. *Women Writers: Their Works and Ways.* 1st ser., London, 1892; 2nd ser., London, 1893.

Hickok, Kathleen. *Representations of Women: Nineteenth-Century British Women's Poetry.* Westport, Conn., 1984.

Highfill, Philip H., Jr., Kalman A. Burnim, and Edward A. Langhans. *A Biographical Dictionary of Actors, Actresses, Musicians, Dancers, Managers and Other Stage Personnel in London, 1660–1800.* 16 vols. Carbondale, 1973–93.

Horne, Richard Hengist, ed. *A New Spirit of the Age.* London, 1907.

Jackson, James Robert de Jager. *Annals of English Verse, 1770–1835: A Preliminary Survey of the Volumes Published.* New York, 1985.

———. *Romantic Poetry by Women: A Bibliography, 1770–1835.* Oxford, 1993.

Johnson, C. R. *Provincial Poetry, 1789–1839. British Verse Printed in the Provinces: The Romantic Background.* London, 1992.

Kavanagh, Julia. *English Women of Letters: Biographical Sketches.* 2 vols. London, 1863.

Kreissman, Bernard. *Minor British Poets: Part One, The Romantic Period, 1789–1839.* Davis, Calif., 1983.

Kunitz, Stanley J. *British Authors of the Nineteenth Century.* New York, 1936.

Kunitz, Stanley J., and Howard Jay Craf. *British Authors before 1800: A Biographical Dictionary.* New York, 1952.

Lamb, Charles, and Mary Anne Lamb. *The Letters of Charles and Mary Anne Lamb.* Edited by Edwin W. Marrs, Jr. 3 vols. Ithaca, 1975–78.

Landry, Donna. *The Muses of Resistance: Laboring-Class Women's Poetry in Britain, 1739–1796.* Cambridge, 1990.

Lonsdale, Henry. *The Worthies of Cumberland.* London, 1873.

Lonsdale, Roger, ed. *Eighteenth-Century Women Poets: An Oxford Anthology.* Oxford, 1989.

———. *New Oxford Book of Eighteenth Century Verse.* Oxford, 1984.

McGann, Jerome, ed. *The New Oxford Book of Romantic Period Verse.* Oxford, 1993.

Miles, Alfred H., ed. *The Poets and Poetry of the Century.* 8 vols. London, 1891–97.

Mitford, Mary Russell. *Recollections of a Literary Life; or, Books, Places, and People.* New York, 1852.

Moir, David Macbeth. *Sketches of the Poetical Literature of the Past Half-Century.* Edinburgh, 1851.

Moultin, Charles Wells, ed. *The Library of Literary Criticism of English and American Authors.* Vol. 4, 1785–1824. Gloucester, Mass., 1959.

Murray, Eunice G. *A Gallery of Scottish Women.* London, 1935.

Nangle, Benjamin. *The Gentleman's Magazine. Biographical and Obituary Notices, 1781–1819: An Index.* New York, 1980.

National Union Catalogue, Pre-1956 Imprint. London, 1968–.

Nineteenth Century Short Title Catalogue, 1816–1870. Newcastle-upon-Tyne 1983–.

O'Donoghue, David James. *The Poets of Ireland: A Biographical and Bibliographical Dictionary of Irish Writers of English Verse.* Dublin, 1912. Reprint. Detroit, 1968.

Oliphant, Mrs. Margaret. *The Literary History of England in the End of the Eighteenth and Beginning of the Nineteenth Century.* 3 vols. London, 1882.

[Paterson, James]. *The Contemporaries of Burns, and the More Recent Poets of Ayrshire, with Selections from their Writings.* Edinburgh and London, 1840.

Poetical Register, and Repository of Fugitive Poetry for 1802. London, 1803.

Rafroidi, Patrick. *Irish Literature in English: The Romantic Period.* Vol. 2, pt. 4. Gerrards Cross, Buckinghamshire, 1980.

Reynolds, John Hamilton. *Selected Prose of John Hamilton Reynolds.* Edited by Leonidas M. Jones. Cambridge, Mass., 1966.

Riga, Frank P., and Claude A. Prance. *Index to the London Magazine.* New York, 1978.

Robertson, Eric S. *English Poetesses: A Series of Critical Biographies, with Illustrative Extracts.* London, 1883.

Rogers, Charles. *The Modern Scottish Minstrel; or, The Songs of Scotland of the Past Half Century.* 6 vols. Edinburgh, 1855–57.

———. *The Scottish Minstrel: The Songs of Scotland Subsequent to Burns, with Memoirs of the Poets.* 2nd ed. Edinburgh, 1885.

Ross, Janet. *Three Generations of Englishwomen.* London, 1893.

Rowton, Frederic, ed. *The Female Poets of Great Britain. Chronologically Arranged.* London, 1853. Facs. reprint with critical introduction and bibliographical appendixes by Marilyn L. Williamson. Detroit, 1981.

Sadleir, Michael. *XIX Century Fiction: A Bibliographical Record Based on His Own Collection.* 2 vols. London, 1951.

Spender, Dale. *Mothers of the Novel: 100 Good Women Writers before Jane Austen.* London, 1986.

Stephen, Leslie, and Sidney Lee, eds. *Dictionary of National Biography.* 22 vols. London, 1921–22.

Sutton, David C., ed. *Location Register of English Literary Manuscripts and Letters: Eighteenth and Nineteenth Centuries.* 2 vols. London, 1995.

Symonds, Emily Morse [George Paston, pseud]. *Little Memoirs of the Nineteenth Century.* Freeport, N.Y., 1902.

Thorne, J. O., and T. C. Collocott, eds. *Chambers Biographical Dictionary.* Rev. ed. Edinburgh, 1974.

Todd, Janet, ed. *British Women Writers: A Critical Reference Guide.* New York, 1989.

———. *A Dictionary of British and American Women Writers, 1660–1800.* Totowa, N.J., 1987.

Ward, William S. *Literary Reviews in British Periodicals, 1789–1797: A Bibliography with a Supplementary List of General (Non-Review) Articles on Literary Subjects.* New York, 1979.

———. *Literary Reviews in British Periodicals, 1798–1820: A Bibliography with a Supplementary List of General (Non-Review) Articles on Literary Subjects.* 2 vols. New York, 1972.

———. *Literary Reviews in British Periodicals, 1821–1826: A Bibliography with a Supplementary List of General (Non-Review) Articles on Literary Subjects.* 2 vols. New York, 1977.

[Watkins, John, and Frederic Shoberl], eds. *A Biographical Dictionary of the Living Authors of Great Britain and Ireland; comprising Literary Memoirs and Anecdotes of their Lives; and a Chronological Register of their Publications, etc.* London, 1816.

Whitelaw, Alex. *The Book of Scottish Song; Collected and Illustrated with Historical and Critical Notices.* Glasgow, 1845.

Williams, Jane. *The Literary Women of England.* London, 1861.

Wilson, James Grant. *The Poets and Poetry of Scotland; from the Earliest to the Present Time.* 2 vols. London, 1876.

Wolff, Robert Lee, comp. *Nineteenth Century Fiction: A Bibliographical Catalogue Based on the Collection Formed by Robert Lee Wolff.* 5 vols. New York, 1981–84.

Wu, Duncan, ed. *Romanticism: An Anthology.* Oxford, 1994.

Index of First Lines

Author-Title Index

Library of Congress Cataloging-in-Publication Data

British women poets of the romantic era : an anthology / edited by
Paula R. Feldman.
p.   cm.
Includes bibliographical references and indexes.
ISBN 0-8018-5430-X (alk. paper)
1. English poetry—Women authors.   2. Women—Great Britain—
Poetry.   3. English poetry—19th century.   4. English poetry—18th
century.   5. Romanticism—Great Britain.   I. Feldman, Paula R.
PR1177.B76   1997
821'.70809287—dc21   96-47417
CIP